THE AKRON OFFERING

CRITICAL EDITIONS IN EARLY AMERICAN LITERATURE

 • First Edition 2013 • Manufactured in the United States of America All inquiries and permission requests should be addressed to the Publisher, The University of Akron Press, Akron, Ohio 44325-1703.

17 16 15 14 13 5 4 3 2 1

ISBN: 978-1-935603-53-5 (paper)

LIBRARY OF CONGRESS CATALOGING-IN-PUBLICATION DATA
The Akron offering : a ladies' literary magazine, 1849–1850 : a critical edition, complete and annotated / edited by Jon Miller. — First edition.
pages cm. — (Critical editions in early American literature)
Includes index.
ISBN 978-1-935603-53-5 (pbk. : alk. paper)
1. American literature—1783-1850. I. Miller, Jon (Jon S.) II. Akron offering.
PS501.A435 2013
810.9'003—dc23

2013014441

The paper used in this publication meets the minimum requirements of ANSI NISO Z39.48–1992 (Permanence of Paper). ∞

Cover image: Sketch of the "South side East Market Street, from Howard to Main, the 'Old Stone Block,' Ohio Exchange, etc., 1845," by Samuel Alanson Lane. From his book, *Fifty years and over of Akron and Summit County*. Cover design by Amy Freels.

The illustration on page 208 is courtesy of The Graphics Fairy, http://graphicsfairy.blogspot.fi

The Akron Offering was designed and typeset in Bembo by Amy Freels, with assistance from Lauren McAndrews, and printed on 60-pound natural and bound by BookMasters of Ashland, Ohio.

THE AKRON OFFERING

A Ladies' Literary Magazine, 1849–1850
A Critical Edition, Complete and Annotated

Edited by Jon Miller

The University of Akron Press
Akron, Ohio

THE

AKRON OFFERING.

JUNE, 1849.

NORMAN AND CORNELIA CAMPBELL, OR "TRUTH STRANGER THAN FICTION."

BY C. CUMINGS.

CHAPTER II.

CORNELIA CAMPBELL's paternal grandfather was a native of Scotland—his parents were among the noblest of the land, and possessed of much wealth until he was seventeen years of age—then, reverses, not necessary here to detail, came upon them, and they were obliged to retire to comparative poverty and obscurity.—George, the son above mentioned, was their eldest, and had been raised amid all the appliances of luxury, and knew nothing of the necessity of attending to business; but, notwithstanding all this, he had an ardent, enterprising disposition, that needed but the stimulus that poverty gives, to enable him to show himself a man of sound sense, and practical business talent. He had heard of the success of some of his countrymen in the American colonies, which then belonged to England, and he longed to try his skill among those who depended on themselves for fortune and for fame. His parents were unwilling to part with him, but his energies were roused and he must have a wider field of action than there presented itself.

"Mother," he said, "of what use is the noble blood that you say courses through my veins? It does not make me really noble, and,

Each number of The Akron Offering *appeared with the same masthead*

Contents

June 1849

July 1849

August 1849

September 1849

October 1849

November 1849

December 1849

January 1850

February 1850

March 1850

Preface

Preparation of this edition began in a graduate seminar in scholarly editing that I taught in the fall of 2009 for the Department of English at The University of Akron. Melissa Cigoi, Elizabeth Corrao, Shane Fliger, Kim Hackett, Arnissa Hopkins, Bobbie Hopkins, Jacob Lauritzen, Jeremy Sayers, Jennifer St. Clair, and Nichole Sterpka all worked on individual numbers. At first I considered editing only a selection of the works—in the style of the old Norton edition of *The Lowell Offering*—but after a closer look it became clear that it would be best to do the entire thing.[1] In the seminar we read and discussed the scholarship on American periodicals, making editions, scholarly editing, and textual criticism. Each student prepared a text of one number, making and applying their own decisions about editorial policy, and each student wrote a paper about an article from their number. After the course ended, Elizabeth Corrao and Jeremy Sayers volunteered significant time and effort to the project of paragraphing the dialogue in "Which is the Fortunate Man?" By email we worked out the differences in our interpretations and came to a consensus about which character was saying which words in the more stubborn passages. I am grateful for the contributions of these students. My understanding of my responsibilities as an editor—to both the modern reader and the original authors—was greatly enriched by the conversations we had in that class.

At the start of 2010 I collated the student texts, transcribed the neglected numbers, and started over. For the next two and a half years, I painstak-

1. Benita Eisler, ed. *The Lowell Offering: Writing by New England Mill Women (1840–1845)*. New York: Norton, 1977.

ingly edited this rough, variously-edited transcription into an exact replica of the original. After much thought about editorial practice and a few false starts, I then emended this copy into the text of this edition, documenting and explaining each necessary correction in a spreadsheet. I then researched and wrote all of the footnotes. In many cases this research discovered information that called for additional changes to the text. My ability to gloss passages in the text—quotations, references to current events, biographies of obscure people, etc.—improved steadily over these years. In the end I was astonished by the extent to which *The Akron Offering* can be explained through such attention to its literary allusions and cultural references.

In the notes, readers will discover a great many citations to primary materials now archived and freely accessible through Google Books. In the final revision wherever possible I cited Google Books as it is the most open, accessible, and comprehensive of the current digital archives. In the end I understood this project as an illustration of the profound extent to which such digital archives can be used to curate old literary periodicals. The supporting research provides an unprecedented opportunity for a modern reader to achieve a full comprehension of such content on a first reading. I also recommend that readers interested in antebellum American literature take the time to collect, examine, and perhaps even read the cited PDF facsimile editions. They are now freely available through the Google Books service. As someone who spent hundreds of hours reading microfilm and daydreaming about interlibrary loan in the 1990s, I am so thankful for Google Books and the research libraries that agreed to digitize their content. I am especially grateful for such access to the rare books of Harvard University, the New York Public Library, University of Michigan, and Oxford University. I know that we still have only an inkling of how these digital archives will change our understanding of early American literature and our practice of literary scholarship. I would like to thank the University of Akron Press for encouraging this project and I am grateful for helpful conversations with David Fahey, George Miller, Michael Schuldiner, and William Proctor Williams. Finally, I would also like to thank Miriam Bennett and my children, Maya and Rowan, for sustaining me with all their love and support.

Introduction

On April 5, 1849, a prospectus appeared in an Akron, Ohio weekly newspaper announcing plans for a new "Magazine for Ladies!" to be edited by Akron's own Calista Cumings, an unmarried educator in her thirties or forties. The prospectus staked a claim on high ground. An "intellectual, literary bouquet," *The Akron Offering* would gather articles to unite the rich and the poor in the appreciation of creative literature and "remarks on various subjects connected with the welfare of mankind in general." "The heart will be addressed in tones of sacred truth," Cumings promised, "and the mind, we will hope, will dwell with pleasure on the mental creations portrayed on its pages." The well-to-do women—the "Ladies of Akron"—were specifically addressed as likely patrons and subscribers. But the periodical was not proposed as an exclusive luxury, and Cumings made clear that she would not raise funds by leveraging the social influence of her patrons. "No list of contributors' names," she wrote, will be "proclaimed as an assurance of merit in its contents." To those whose homes were (she wrote in verse) "but varied beauty, / A vision fair and bright," this "little work" would "bind in true humility / To Him who rules on high." And as it humbled readers who might suffer from an excess of material blessings, it would also "help" those who were "struggling" with "daily life." Sold "at so low price as to be within the reach of all," the "lowly Offering" would be made with a "humble hope" to minister to the mental and spiritual needs of readers without the use of "Engravings or Fashion Plates" (see "Prospectus" on p. 25).

From May 1849 to April 1850, *The Akron Offering* appeared in monthly, 32-page numbers filled with original and selected tales, essays, sermons, poems, and editorials. Throughout the *Offering*, contributors tempered their longing for literary fame with modesty and a down-to-earth seriousness of purpose. As the author of "American Literature," an essay in the February 1850 number, writes: "No sensible person will believe that the most able authors are generally those who rise up and claim their place beside wide known names, and lay their volumes proudly upon the dusty old tomes they have scurrilously imitated, but on the other hand, we see the most valuable minds the most reserved and isolated, so that in the present scrambling of the multitude, we miss them" (369). In its day *The Akron Offering* went unnoticed by the majority of antebellum American readers outside Northeastern Ohio, and since then it has been missed by readers and scholars of American literature as well. As this edition demonstrates, however, the magazine rewards study. Many items are of high literary quality. And a patient examination of even the more amateur productions can yield valuable information for readers interested in better understanding the history and literary history of Ohio and the early American west.

Akron's location on the Ohio and Erie canal makes *The Akron Offering* a good example of the "decentralization of literary life" that Ronald J. Zboray describes as the result of the transportation revolution, which so altered book and magazine distribution in the 1840s and 1850s. The fact that *The Akron Offering* was published in the west was probably not a significant disadvantage as it cultivated a local audience. The west was full of recent migrants from the eastern United States, and western readers did continue to read the eastern publications. And many eastern magazines pushed, through advertisements and general attention to western themes, for a greater audience in the west. But *The Akron Offering* was the product of a brief period in which western readers were unusually interested in promoting and nurturing the growth of western authors. There was pride in local writings and some anticipation of a day when a western state like Ohio would be equal, in literary output, to any of the eastern states. It was not yet clear or certain that continuing improvements in printing and transportation technologies would lead inevitably to a national literary marketplace dominated by the publications of just one or two cities. And as the notes glossing the magazine's many literary allusions suggest, the broad literary knowledge of the magazine's contributors suggest that western readers were not compelled to choose between western magazines and eastern magazines. There was both the time and the desire to read all the magazines.[1]

Two qualities about *The Akron Offering* distinguish it strikingly from the eastern magazines that are better known today. First, it emulated the shrinking violet: again and again, truth, beauty, and the life worth living are portrayed as incompatible with vanity and earthly self-promotion (see pp. 429 and 442). Cumings only advertised the *Offering* as a "humble" magazine. Humility is one of its most consistent themes and humility, of course, is not the easiest path to immortality. *The Akron Offering* was also characterized by the lower production values of provincial printing offices. Lacking the crisp machine-set type, engravings, and fashion plates of the prosperous big-city journals, *The Akron Offering* was not as physically appealing to those who regarded books and magazines as elegant furnishings. The inclusion of engravings may have contributed to the greater longevity of Cleveland's contemporaneous literary magazine, *I Have Come* (later *Moore's Western Lady's Book*; see p. 453). The humble appearance of the magazine probably did not do much to encourage its preservation in the families that once subscribed to it. It is also not likely that the magazine had a large circulation: very few copies of *The Akron Offering* have survived to the present day. Patricia Okker mentions the magazine in *Our Sister Editors*, her important study of Sarah J. Hale and American women editors, but since there are no copies in the private and public collections that formed the core of our current microfilm and digital collections, not many scholars have access to its contents.[2] This edition recovers this important, rare, and valuable periodical.

Highlights of *The Akron Offering* include a serialized novel, *Norman and Cornelia Campbell, or "Truth Stranger Than Fiction,"* in which a remarkably strong woman endures the considerable suffering inflicted by evil men who are driven by their jealousy of her attentions and her family's wealth (see p. 30). The novel spans many decades and is set within the story of New Englanders moving west of the Mississippi to serve as Christian missionaries in American Indian communities. Lily Lute of Seville, in Medina

1. Ronald J. Zboray, *A Fictive People: Antebellum Economic Development and the American Reading Public* (New York: Oxford University Press, 1993), 55–68. For an account of western interest in western authors in the antebellum decades, see William D. Andrews, "William T. Coggeshall: 'Booster' of Western Literature." *Ohio History* 81 (1972): 210–20.

2. Patricia Okker, *Our Sister Editors* (Athens: The University of Georgia Press, 1995), 183. For more on American women editors, see Sharon M. Harris and Ellen Gruber Garvey, eds., *Blue Pencils & Hidden Hands: Women Editing Periodicals, 1830–1910* (Boston: Northeastern University Press, 2004).

County, arguably the magazine's star contributor, wrote numerous poems and a series of "Letters to the Offering" that include love stories, feminist opinion pieces, and a description of her adventures as she travelled by herself to that "far-famed city," Akron, to meet Calista Cumings (e.g., pp. 217, 252, 307, and 386). The magazine also includes the notable manifesto on "American Literature" mentioned earlier in this introduction (see p. 366).

Given Akron's place in the movement of women on behalf of their rights—Akron hosted the Ohio Woman's Rights Convention of May 1851, at which Sojourner Truth gave her most famous speech—it is not surprising that concerns about the status of women receive especially vigorous expression in this "magazine for ladies" (for example, see pp. 97–99, 148–51, 228–31, and 349–51). All the claims to modesty and moderate positions should not mask the fact that Cumings, as a woman who created, edited, and published her own magazine, boldly did what women, traditionally, did not do, as Patricia Okker has explained. The magazine not only provided a forum for women to circulate thoughts about woman and her rights, it also—to echo Truth's speech—"*was* a woman's rights." It is probable that Cumings did not enjoy a unanimous support from her neighbors. "Perhaps I might," Cumings writes in her December 1849 editorial, "from some, hear tones of criticism that savored not of good wishes for this enterprise . . . perhaps there may be now and then one who cannot tolerate any work that is not the very essence of bigotry, superstition and intolerance" (314).

A number of other women writers, most anonymous or pseudonymous, contributed literary works that comment on current events and common debates connected with the related movements for temperance, education, the end of slavery, peace, and philanthropy. One remarkably original story set in Ohio, "The Little Coal-Heaver," touches on all of these themes as it describes how an African American Methodist preacher and a philanthropic "widow with a moderate fortune" save and reform an alcoholic "dwarf" (189). Such works participated in what Kathleen Endres describes as the "humanization" of Akron in *Akron's Better Half.* Two works in *The Akron Offering* reflect the conversations that culminated in the 1854 formation of the Summit County Female Labor Association, a labor organization devoted to improving the lives of Akron's many seamstresses. This was, as Endres describes, "a true partnership between the affluent and the working-class women" of Akron. Both "Grinding the Face of the Poor" (360) and

"Havn't the Change" (447) educate readers about the painfully impoverished lives of this large group of Akron's working women, and both urge affluent women to do something to alleviate this suffering.[3]

A good percentage of the items in *The Akron Offering* feature religious subjects. This proportion of religious material is typical of the time. The antebellum decades were the most evangelical years in American history. Historians estimate that about one-third of all Americans were actively involved with a church in 1850, and a large majority of these churches were conspicuously evangelical.[4] By the standard of the day, *The Akron Offering* is appropriately religious but not a magazine devoted to religion.

Readers of *The Akron Offering* will also see that Cumings selected a range of material, from a variety of authors, anthologies, and periodicals, to fill the pages with the balance and diversity of material she desired. This was a standard practice at the time. In the 1830s, 1840s, and 1850s, American editors openly and eagerly republished or "selected" works from one another's magazines. Copyright as we know it did not exist, and popular works spread with a speed and, in some cases, textual corruption that was far beyond the control of individual authors or their original publishers.[5] Magazines prided themselves on their original content, but readers also expected a magazine editor to reprint many choice items.

Akron in 1849

In the summer of 1849, Akron was "a beautiful and flourishing town," as one Philadelphia reference work described it, with a population of several thousand that was increasing rapidly. The capital of Summit County, Akron stood at the highest point of the Ohio and Erie canal, which connected Lake Erie with the Ohio River. Given the need for locks to hoist and lower canal boats through the area, the town, first planned in 1825, grew as quickly as expected with the booming success of the nation's canal network. In the 1840s the Pennsylvania and Ohio also connected Akron to Beaver, Penn-

3. Kathleen L. Endres, *Akron's 'Better Half': Women's Clubs and the Humanization of the City, 1825–1925* (Akron: The University of Akron Press, 2006), 25–30

4. See Daniel Walker Howe, *What Hath God Wrought?: The Transformation of America, 1818–1848* (New York: Oxford University Press, 2007), ch. 5, and Mark A. Noll, *America's God: From Jonathan Edwards to Abraham Lincoln* (Oxford: Oxford University Press, 2002), esp. 163–70.

5. See Meredith L. McGill, *American Literature and the Culture of Reprinting, 1834–1853* (Philadelphia: University of Pennsylvania Press, 2003), and two classic studies, William Charvat, *Literary Publishing in America, 1790–1850* (Philadelphia: University of Pennsylvania Press, 1959) and Frank Luther Mott, *A History of American Magazines, 1741–1930* (Cambridge: Belknap Press of Harvard University Press, 1958).

sylvania, making Akron an important hub for western canal traffic. These canals and the nearby Cuyahoga river provided water that powered mills and manufactories whose products were cheaply shipped by canal boats. Summit County farmers brought their wheat to Akron by wagon, where it was milled and purchased for delivery to distant markets. Corn, oats, dairy products, pork, and beef also came to Akron for sale, and three or four mills produced wool cloth from the many large flocks of sheep in Summit County. In 1848 Alex E. Glenn, the editor of *The Ark, and Odd Fellows' Western Monthly Magazine*, praised the city: "For business, real driving go-ahead business, Akron is equal to any, especially for its population."[6] In the 1840s one of Akron's prominent wool manufacturers, Simon Perkins, employed and partnered with John Brown, the abolitionist who later seized the federal arsenal at Harper's Ferry in October 1859.[7] Other natural resources fueled Akron's growth at mid-century: Summit County had quantities of coal and minerals that were useful as ingredients in paint, which Akron businesses manufactured and exported. The busy town was full of "sabbath breakers"—the canal traffic exempted Akron from Ohio's laws prohibiting work or disorder on Sunday—but the town had evolved from its relatively wild and lawless early years and now had churches, schools, and active benevolent and mutual self-improvement organizations such as the Sons and Daughters of Temperance and the International Order of Odd Fellows.[8]

6. Thomas Baldwin and J. Thomas, *A New and Complete Gazetteer of the United States* (Philadelphia: Lippincott, Grambo, 1854), 23–24, Google Books, http://books.google.com/books?id=_5s6AAAAcAAJ; Alex E. Glenn, "Our Tour North." *The Ark, and Odd Fellows' Western Monthly Magazine* 5, no. 8 (August 1848): 222, Google Books, http://books.google.com/books?id=K5geAQAAMAAJ; N.W. Goodhue, "Statistical Report of the Summit County Agricultural Society," *Sixth Annual Report of the Board of Agriculture of the State of Ohio* (Columbus: S. Medary, 1852), 461–64, Google Books, http://books.google.com/books?id=cPsSAAAAYAAJ.

7. For many decades, the citizens of Akron regarded John Brown as one of the city's favorite sons. For example, see Samuel Lane, *Fifty Years and Over of Akron and Summit County* (Akron: Beacon Job Department, 1892), 584, Google Books, http://books.google.com/books?id=nyAWAAAAYAAJ, and Scott Dix Kenfield, *Akron and Summit County Ohio: 1825–1928* (Chicago: S.J. Clarke, 1928), 1:56.

8. These new benevolent organizations figure in the *Offering*. For example, see pp. 156–57. For more on the history of Akron and Ohio in general, see Oscar Eugene Olin, *Akron and Environs: Historical, Biographical, Genealogical* (1917; rpt. La Crosse, Wisconsin: Brookhaven Press, 2001); George W. Knepper, *Akron: City at the Summit*, 3rd ed. (Virginia Beach, Virginia: Donning, 1994); Shirla Robinson McClain, *The Contributions of Blacks in Akron, 1825–1975*, ed. Akron Gallery of Black History Curriculum Committee (1975; Akron: The University of Akron, 1996); Frances McGovern, *Written on the Hills: The Making of the Akron Landscape* (Akron: The University of Akron Press, 1996); Andrew R. L. Cayton, *Ohio: The History of a People* (Columbus: The Ohio State University Press, 2002), and Geoffrey Parker, Richard Sisson, and William Russell Coil, eds. *Ohio & The World: 1753–2053: Essays Toward a New History of Ohio* (Columbus: The Ohio State University Press, 2005).

Much of the bustle of Akron was concentrated in what remains the downtown area along Main Street and one block west, along Howard Street, which once followed the eastern side of the canal. In this business district the town's main and most enduring newspaper, *The Summit Beacon* (later *The Akron Beacon Journal),* was published on Wednesdays by John Teesdale. Many volumes of the early Akron newspapers no longer exist, but the 1849 and 1850 *Summit Beacons* have survived. In them we find attention to local, national, and international news and politics, as well as an abundance of local and national advertisements. Two big stories of 1849 were the cholera—what places had it, what places did not have it, and how it might be treated—and the sudden migration of Americans to California in search of gold. *The Summit Beacon* relentlessly indulges in optimistic fantasies about easy wealth in the far west. For example, in October an editorial declared California as "by far the greatest source of interesting domestic news." "Gold! gold! gold!" it continues, "The most obstinate infidel has 'bid all doubt be gone' as to the reality of the El Dorado, and the romance of real life beyond the mountains, where the rocks remain the color of the setting sun-beams, has thrown all fiction into the shades of Egyptian mid-night." Clapstore's store "at the Sign of the *big red hat*, on Howard Street" announces "thirty five dozen California hats," the shoe stores advertise "California boots," and Bennett & Smith, "at the sign of the HORSE HEAD" offer "Harness, Trunks, Valices, Carpet Bags, Collars, Whips, Bridles, Halters, &c., &c." for those preparing to leave town in search of "California Gold."[9] As Samuel Lane reports in *Fifty Years and Over of Akron and Summit County*, a large number of men left Akron in 1849 and 1850. They had many adventures and some success but they were mainly disappointed in their plans to return with riches. Lane, for example, was forced to shift for himself as a sign painter in San Francisco.[10]

For more on the early literary history of Ohio, see William Henry Venable, *Beginnings of Literary Culture in the Ohio Valley* (Cincinnati: Robert Clarke, 1891) Google Books, http://books.google.com/books?id=57eEAAAAIAAJ; Thomas H. Smith, ed., *An Ohio Reader: 1750 to the Civil War* (Grand Rapids, Michigan: William B. Eerdmans, 1975); David R. Anderson and Gladys Haddad, eds., *Anthology of Western Reserve Literature* (Kent: Kent State University Press, 1992); and Emily Foster, ed., *The Ohio Frontier: An Anthology of Early Writings* (Lexington: University Press of Kentucky, 1996).

9. "California." *The Summit Beacon* 11, no. 27 (October 24, 1849): 3; "Hurrah for California." *The Summit Beacon* 11, no. 26 (October 17, 1849): 3; "California Gold Wanted." *The Summit Beacon* 11, no. 26 (October 17, 1849): 3. All citations to *The Summit Beacon* for 1849 and 1850 are to the 1974 microfilm edition prepared in Columbus by the Ohio Historical Society.

10. See Samuel Lane, *Fifty Years and Over of Akron*, 1106–40, and Lane, *Gold Rush: The Overland Diary of Samuel A. Lane, 1850* (Akron: Summit County Historical Society, 1984).

The gold rush contextualizes a vein of writing in *The Akron Offering*, which includes a number of pieces from the point of view of the women left behind. "Abbey Viola," for example, writes "hie thee home to me dearest, / Nor longer absent be" in her poem "To My Absent Husband" (272). Lily Lute describes a lonely maiden, with moonlit curls of "raven hair" and "clear, blue eyes," who pines at home with her sick mother because

> Her aged sire and lover brave,
> Had sailed, time gone, far o'er the wave,
> And now beneath the far-off skies,
> Where California's treasure lies,—
> They're searching for the precious ore,
> That miners love to lay in store.—

In a startling twist of tone, the poem then thunders

> O! idiotic crazy men!
> Of home treasures ye little ken,
> If but to fill a scanty purse,
> With what will be our nation's curse,
> Ye have left home and that fair maid,
> Her feeble mother's only aid,
> To close that mother's eyes alone,—
> Can gold for her deep grief atone? (44)

Not far from "the sign of the *big red hat*" was the store of Beebe & Elkins, sellers of "Books and Stationery, Drugs and Medicines, Paints, Oils and Dye Stuffs." Here was some of the literary history of Akron. In 1849 Beebe & Elkins advertise their "splendid assortment of Poems and Prose writings, illustrated, suitable for presents, got up in the best style." The titles they saw fit to highlight in a September 19, 1849 advertisement were *Scenes in the Lives of the Apostles, Scenes in the Lives of the Patriarchs, Scenes in the Life of Our Savior, American Female Poets, Lady of the Lake, Pilgrim's Progress, Poets of England and America, Women of the Scripture*, as well as books of "Whittier, Byron, Longfellow, Bryant, and Burns."[11] The Elkins half of Beebe & Elkins was Richard S. Elkins, who came to Akron to publish *The Summit County Beacon* with Laurin Dewey before they sold the paper to John Teesdale in 1848. Dewey & Elkins published a book by Calista Cumings in 1847: her *Rules of Arithmetic in Verse*, which had the follow-

11. "Just Received by Beebe & Elkins." *The Summit Beacon* 11, no. 22 (September 19, 1849): 2.

ing lengthy but descriptive subtitle, *Designed for Children in Any Place, But of Special Importance in Schools, Where They Should Be Recited in Concert.*[12]

Biography of Calista Cumings

This Akron publication of Cumings' arithmetic textbook is significant because it illustrates some of the relatively few facts known about her life. Evidently a schoolteacher in Akron, Cumings was the daughter of Asa and Bathsheba Cumings, who were both born in 1784, in Windsor, Vermont. In 1829, Asa Cumings, also a schoolteacher, endorsed a math textbook in an advertisement signed from "Windsor, Vt."[13] Asa and Bathsheba had three daughters (Calista, Emily, and Lucia) and two sons (George and Edward) who lived to adulthood. Lucia met and married Nahum Fay, a schoolteacher from Reading, Vermont, in 1837. Nahum, Lucia, and the rest of the Cumings family then moved to Zanesville or Akron before the end of 1840. Nahum taught in the Akron schools before working various jobs for the city and county; Emily Cumings never married, taught school for most of her life, and lived with her parents, who depended on her care for many years before their deaths in 1866 and 1867.[14]

Calista Cumings never appears in United States Federal Census, which is notoriously unreliable in its documentation of unmarried women, non-heads of households, and residents of rapidly-growing western cities in the middle of the nineteenth century.[15] It is likely that Calista lived in the home

12. Calista Cumings, *Rules of Arithmetic in Verse: Designed for Children in Any Place, But of Special Importance in Schools, Where They Should Be Recited in Concert* (Akron: Dewey & Elkins, 1847). The book is listed in James M. Greenwood, "Notes on the History of American Text-books on Arithmetic," *Report of the Commissioner of Education for the Year 1897–98* (Washington: Government Printing Office, 1899), 850, Google Books, http://books.google.com/books?id=3TUZAAAAYAAJ. OCLC's WorldCat database of resources held in libraries around the world—which includes more than 240 million records of more than 1.7 billion items in OCLC member libraries—shows no extant copies of Cumings' arithmetic book.

13. "New Arithmetick." *The Craftsman* 1, no. 1 (February 10, 1829): 8, Google Books, http://books.google.com/books?id=KQIjAQAAMAAJ.

14. Nahum Fay's biography appears in Lane, *Fifty Years and Over of Akron*, 111–12.

15. Underenumeration is a known problem with the census in the nineteenth-century. Careful studies produce varying conclusions about the extent of the undercounting, but the scholarship supports a general estimate of at least eight to ten percent for a city such as Akron. See David H. Parkerson, "Comments on the Underenumeration of the U.S. Census, 1850–1880," *Social Science History* 15, no, 4 (Winter 1991): 510–15, JSTOR, http://www.jstor.org/stable/1171465; John W. Adams and Alice Bee Kasakoff, "Estimates of Census Underenumeration Based on Genealogies, " *Social Science History* 15, no, 4 (Winter 1991): 527–43, JSTOR, http://www.jstor.org/stable/1171467; Donald A. Debats,

of her brother George, her father Asa, or her brother-in-law Nahum. (Lily Lute's describes Cumings' home as full of relatives on p. 309.) The 1840 census only records the heads of households, with tick marks that indicate the sex and age range of other residents. Such evidence suggests that Cumings was in her 30s or 40s when she edited *The Akron Offering.* For example, her father Asa Cumings appears in the 1840 census for Akron as heading a household with one male and one female, aged 50 to 59. These must be Asa and his wife, Bathsheba. The home also included one male, aged 15 to 19 (likely Edward), and one female, aged 30 to 39 (perhaps Calista). Brother George, however, appears as the head of a household in the 1840 census for Zanesville. This home included one male, aged 20 to 29 (George); two females, age 20 to 29, one female, aged 60 to 69, and one male, under 5. Calista may be one of the women here aged 20 to 29, or perhaps the three women are George's spouse and two of her female relatives. George died before 1850, and it is not clear what became of his 1840 household. (See Cumings' poem on the death of her brother on p. 198.) Nahum Fay appears in the 1840 census for Akron. He heads a household of one male aged 20 to 29 (Nahum) and three females aged 20 to 29 (Lucia his wife, and perhaps Emily and Calista, or other relatives of Nahum). Calista, in other words, could be living with any of these three men in 1840. The 1850 census, the first to record the names of all inhabitants of a household, lists Asa, Bathsheba, Nahum, Lucia, and two children as two families in one household. Calista's 26-year-old brother Edward appears in the 1850 census for El Dorado, California.[16] Emily and Calista do not appear in the census, but they were likely living in Akron. The census was taken in the summer of 1850, not long after the publication of *The Akron Offering* ceased. In the 1860 census only Emily is named as living with her parents, who were both in their middle seventies. Calista Cumings is nowhere to

"The Historian and Nineteenth-Century Social Accounting, *Social Science History* 15, no, 4 (Winter 1991): 545–63, JSTOR, http://www.jstor.org/stable/1171468. It is also worth noting that many antebellum Americans resisted the project because they thought the collection of such information to be improper and "prying." See Dan Halacy, *Census: 190 Years of Counting America* (New York: Elsevier/Nelson Books, 1980).

16. Lane mentions Edward as one of the men who made the trip to California. Note that in the census, the newspaper, and Lane's history of Akron, Cumings is spelled variously: Cummins, Cummings, Cumings, Commins, etc. See *Fifty Years and Over of Akron*, 1110. Edward later lived in Iowa; in 1873 he was a lawyer and he executed his sister Emily's will in Akron. Both then used the spelling "Cummings." It is too confusing for the modern reader to have the family name spelled differently for different individuals, so I have standardized the spelling of the family name in this introduction.

be found in the 1860 census. This census was not precise, however, and so her omission does not prove that she lived elsewhere.

That said, she may have died not long after the end of *The Akron Offering*. She repeatedly mentions her health over the course of her magazine. In the July 1849 number she cryptically promises that she is "not discouraged." At the end of the August 1849 number she writes: "We are still alive, kind Reader, and still laboring to make the *Offering* acceptable and profitable to you. Sometimes we are weary but never discouraged" (137, 172). This "discouragement" may allude to the criticism she likely experienced for being a woman who edits a magazine for women in a time and a place where some did not consider this proper. Or it may allude to a grave state of health. The January 1850 editorial comments on preparing for death (351), but this is not unusual for the period, when so many Americans regarded life as a preparation for the afterlife. The February 1850 editorial refers somberly to a "sickness" that prevents her from working as much as she would like on the magazine (384). And at the end of the volume, Cumings retires *The Akron Offering* with the news that she has not been able to find a suitable replacement for the editorial chair (451).

Emily Cumings owned a plot at Akron's now-historic Glendale Cemetery. Here records indicate that Asa, Bathsheba, Emily, and the Fay family are buried in neighboring plots. The Glendale records are not complete, especially for the period before the Civil War, so perhaps Calista is buried there as well. Today only three tombstones are present in Emily's plot, and they have been made unreadable by the acidic rain of the last century. The 1867 obituary for Calista Cumings' mother, Bathsheba, remembers Calista "as Editress of the 'Akron Offering'" and, with her brother George, as one who "entered the house appointed for all living" before her parents. This fixes the date of Cumings' death as sometime before 1866, when her father died. The obituary also confirms that she died as "Miss Calista Cumings"—pretty clear evidence that she did not marry after she ceased publication of the *Offering*. Finally, Bathsheba's obituary also describes her as a longtime member of Akron's Baptist Church. While this is not certain evidence that Calista Cumings attended the same church, it does accord with the strict Protestant sensibility that characterizes Cumings' writings as well as her taste in literary selections.[17]

17. Obituary of Bathsheba Cumings, *Summit County Beacon* 31, no. 14 (September 26, 1867): 2. Her father's obituary can be found in *Summit County Beacon* 29, no. 41 (March 15, 1866): 2.

The Production of *The Akron Offering*

Cumings' final comments allude to the considerable work that went into the publication of *The Akron Offering*:

> Our own views of the propriety, necessity and practicability of such a work are not the least changed; but we have found that there must be more business done to meet its heavy expenses and make a fair profit, than one woman can accomplish and as we have not yet found a Lady who is at liberty to devote her time and strength as she pleases, that feels herself qualified to assist in the double task of editing, travelling to obtain subscribers, delivering books, collecting subscriptions, keeping accounts, &c. &c., or is willing to take upon herself so much toil and care and risk of pecuniary loss, we are compelled for the present to give it up. (451)

The careful reading, study, transcription, and editing of *The Akron Offering* has yielded some information about how Cumings produced it. At the start, Cumings had no intention of soliciting publications from eastern writers. "There may be a very few, we know there are not many," she writes, "who would stand aloof from such an enterprise, because the celebrated writers for the Magazines of the Eastern Cities are not to give us the benefit of their experience" (27). She imagined the magazine as the work of "friends and acquaintances and persons residing within a few miles of each other" (64) and expected to publish many "first efforts" (28). She may have hoped to find someone to assist her with editing, as she speaks of "those who may arrange and conduct this magazine" as if the editorial board would grow to more than one (27). Both these expectations were not met: *The Akron Offering* would publish contributions from distant places and Cumings never gained a partner editor.

She welcomed the publication of materials anonymously or under pseudonyms. If she herself thought this necessary, perhaps she would not have signed her own name to the magazine. So it could be that she merely respected the inclinations of women who felt that it was improper or unwise to use their real names (see p. 172). That said, she did endorse the use of anonymity and pseudonymity as a means to achieving a free, equal, and fair exchange of ideas. "We are willing you should all judge for yourselves" of the magazine's merit, she writes, "without the possibility of being prejudiced, either for or against, by a knowledge of the real names of the writers of many of the articles" (451; see also 97). Still her editorial comments suggest that she would not publish articles without knowing the real name of the author (see pp. 208, 242, and 279).[18]

The printer is not named in the extant copies I examined, which are bound copies with the original wrappers or covers—if they existed—removed. Given that Cumings had recently published a math textbook with Dewey & Elkins, it seems likely that *The Akron Offering* was also printed by whoever prepared *The Summit Beacon*. In the top left corner of each 1849 paper is an advertisement for "Job Printing of every description." Cumings likely delivered a bundle of handwritten manuscripts and clipped "selections" to this print shop. Either the process, speed, or expense of printing forbade the use of proofs, or the reader for this print shop habitually did a poor job of correcting the compositor's mistakes. *The Akron Offering* was plagued with typographical and other errors in printing, especially in the early numbers. At the end of the second number, Cumings notes that "the present No. we think is not sullied by as *many* 'unsightly spots' as was the first, and we expect ere long, to be able to feel that it is all that could *reasonably* be expected" (100). At the end of the third number, she addresses her critics by emphasizing first, that the magazine "goes as a messenger of peace"; second, that "no one writing for this, pretends to infallibility"; third, that "we believe that the articles that have appeared in the Offering, that were sent us by others," (here she modestly excludes her own writings) "will compare favorably with articles found in other works of the same size and price"; and fourth, that "faults there *have been* and *they have been or will be* corrected" (136).

Evidently one of the causes of "unsightly spots" were the handwritten manuscripts that contributors submitted to Cumings. Editors, compositors, and print-shop readers often had trouble making sense of the handwriting of antebellum authors. A passage from Joseph T. Buckingham's *Specimens of Newspaper Literature* was reprinted in numerous periodicals in 1850, and it well explains the situation:

> Many, who condescend to illuminate the dark world with the fire of their genius . . . little think of the lot of the printer, who, almost suffocated by the smoke of the lamp, sits up till midnight to correct [their] false gram-

---

18. These attitudes towards authorship, anonymity, and literary celebrity may anticipate those described by Robert J. Scholnick in his study of Emily Dickinson and the literary magazine *Round Table* in the 1860s. See Scholnick, "'Don't Tell! They'd Advertise': Emily Dickinson in the *Round Table*." In Kenneth M. Price and Susan Belasco Smith, eds., *Periodical Literature in Nineteenth-Century America* (Charlottesville: University Press of Virginia, 1995), 166–82.

> mar, bad orthography, and worse punctuation. I have seen the arguments of lawyers, in high repute as scholars, sent to the printer in their own handwriting, many words—and especially technical and foreign terms—abbreviated, words misspelled, and few or no points, and those few, if there are any, entirely out of place. I have seen the sermons of eminent Divines, sent to the press, without points or capitals to designate the division of the sentences—sermons which, if published with the imperfections of the manuscript, would disgrace the printer's devil if he were the author. Suppose they had been so printed. The printer would have been treated with scorn and contempt as an illiterate blockhead—as a fellow better fitted to be a wood sawyer than a printer. Nobody would have believed that such gross and palpable faults were owing to the ignorance or carelessness of the author. And no one but the practical printer knows how many hours a compositor, and after him the proof reader, is compelled to spend in reducing to a readable condition, manuscripts that the writers themselves would be puzzled to read.[19]

In the closing remarks for February 1850, Cumings notes that "several other articles" that came in time for inclusion "needed to be re-written," and she expresses the hope that she will soon be well enough "to do all necessary copying and not be obliged to select so many articles already printed" (384). The original materials were more often marred by printing errors than the selected materials, since only the selected materials were given to the printer in a neat, printed form. The use of handwritten materials also troubled the printers in that they sometimes failed to accurately count words and mark off the page breaks. On more than one occasion, the printers were forced to tighten the leading or vertical spacing of the lines and maybe reduce the point size so as to fit all the text. (See figure 1 opposite.)

In preparing this critical edition of the entire run of *The Akron Offering*, great care was made to record all emendations, as well as all the possible and declined opportunities to emend the text. As there were not a few textual problems, this table ran to over 1,300 entries.[20] The goal was a

19. The original is in Joseph T. Buckingham, *Specimens of Newspaper Literature, with Personal Memoirs, Anecdotes, and Reminiscences.* 2 vols. Boston: C.C. Little and Brown, 1850. The source for this quotation is an excerpt presented as "Printers and Printing," *The Green Mountain Gem* 7 (1849), 295. American Periodicals (125967261).

20. The table of emendations, too large to include in this volume, is available at my website, http://jonmiller.org.

258 EXTRACT.

tinges the whole stream; and where he yields to the love of the beautiful, it is equally apparent. There are those who would cut off the young from all acquaintance with his works, because they are sometimes degraded by unworthy ideas or too truly reflect some of the dark epochs of his life. But it is to be feared that the mind that cannot discriminate between the genuine poetry and the folly and the vice of those writings, will be unsafe amid the moral exposure of all life and literature. Indeed, there can scarcely be conceived a book at once more melancholy and more moral than Moore's Life of Byron. It delineates the vain endeavors of a gifted spirit to find in pleasure what virtue alone can give. It portrays a man of great sensibility, generous impulses and large endowments, attempting to live without settled principle, and be happy without exalted hopes. There is no more touching spectacle in human life. Genius is always attractive; but when allied to great errors it gives a lesson to the world beyond the preacher's skill. What awful hints lurk in the affected badinage of Byron's journal and letters! What an idea do they convey of mental strugglesj After reading one of his poems, how significant a moral is his own confession; "I have written this to wring myself from reality." And when he was expostulated with for the misanthropic coloring of his longest and best poems, who can fail to look "more in pity than in anger," upon the bard when he declares "I feel you are right, but I also feel that I am sincere."

The apparent drift of Byron's versified logic is skepticism. He continually preaches hopelessness; but the actual effect of his poetry seems to me directly the reverse, No bard more emphatically illustrates the absolute need we all have of love and truth. His very wailing is more significant than the rejoicing of tamer minstrels. No one can intelligently commune with his musings and escape the conviction that their dark hues spring from the vain endeavor to reconcile error and the soul. Byron's egotism, his identity with his characters, his cynicism, his want of universality, his perverted creed and fevered impulses have been elaborately unfolded by a host of critics. The indirect, but perhaps not less effective lessons he tanght, are seldcm recognised. The cant of criticism has blinded many to the noble fervor of his lays devoted to nature and freedom. All his utterance is not sneering and sarcastic; and it argues a most uncatholic taste to stamp with a single epithet

Figure 1: Page 258 from The Akron Offering

well-prepared edition and not a careless one.[21] Many accepted practices in mid-century American publication, would be considered incorrect today. An example is the use of the comma in a "simple sentence" between what mid-century Americans called a "lengthened nominative" and the verb—as exemplified by the comma in the previous sentence.[22] The goal of this edition of *The Akron Offering* was to correct the obvious and obfuscating errors, while honoring the common practices of the day. An explanation of this method requires a summary of what has changed in a reader's expectations for printed materials since 1850.

First of all, it is worth noting that the "ideal of correctness" that regarded less than perfect spelling, grammar, and punctuation as unacceptable dates only to the 1870s. In the above quote, Buckingham describes the heroic effort that might be required from a printer to produce a "correct" publication. The 1850 idea of "correct," however, is not so punctilious. As Albert Kitzhaber has explained, a widespread emphasis on achieving an exacting superficial correctness only appeared in American schools in 1873, after Harvard College began to emphasize the demonstration of this (in an application essay) as a prerequisite for admission.[23] When antebellum Americans complained about poor punctuation, it was not because such practice violated a precise and universally-known standard, but because poor punctuation garbles sense and, in rare cases, because poor punctuation reduces expressive force. "That punctuation is important all agree; but how few comprehend the extent of its importance!" wrote Edgar Allan Poe. "The writer who neglects punctuation, or mis-punctuates, is liable to be misunderstood—this, according to the popular idea, is the sum of the evils arising from heedlessness or ignorance. It does not seem to be known that,

21. The approach to textual editing described in this introduction is indebted to the study of work by many scholars,—but especially Fredson Bowers, "Textual Criticism," in James Thorpe, ed., *The Aims and Methods of Scholarship in Modern Languages and Literatures*, 2nd ed. (New York: Modern Language Association of America, 1970), 29–84; G. Thomas Tanselle, *Textual Criticism and Scholarly Editing* (Charlottesville: The University Press of Virginia, 1990); Joel Myerson, "Colonial and Nineteenth-Century American Literature," in D. C. Greetham, ed., *Scholarly Editing: A Guide to Research* (New York: Modern Language Association of America, 1995), 351–64; John Bryant, *The Fluid Text: A Theory of Revision and Editing for Book and Screen* (Ann Arbor: The University of Michigan Press, 2002); Modern Language Association, "Guidelines for Editors of Scholarly Editions." Revision of 29 June 2011. http://mla.org/cseguidelines; Erick Kelemen, *Textual Editing and Criticism: An Introduction* (New York: W. W. Norton, 2009); and William Proctor Williams and Craig S. Abbott, *An Introduction to Bibliographical and Textual Studies* (New York: Modern Language Association of America, 2009).

22. For example, see John Wilson, *A Treatise on Grammatical Punctuation* (Manchester: By the author, 1844), 17, Google Books, http://books.google.com/books?id=c78AAAAAYAAJ.

23. Albert R. Kitzhaber, *Rhetoric in American Colleges, 1850–1900* (Dallas: Southern Methodist University Press, 1990), 199–204.

even where the sense is perfectly clear, a sentence may be deprived of half its force—its spirit—its point—by improper punctuation." Poe noted that "there is no treatise on the topic—and there is no topic on which a treatise is more needed" before suggesting that he might soon write an essay titled, "The Philosophy of the Point." (In the 1840s punctuation marks were known as "points," or punctuation points.)[24] Despite Poe's notion that there was "no treatise on the topic," there were in fact grammars published at that time in England and America. First popularized by and for compositors who struggled with the unpointed scrawl of lawyers and eminent Divines, such books were quickly adopted and revised for use as textbooks in the ever-expanding public school systems. By the 1850s, they were legion and by 1860 there was a clearer consensus on the best ways to punctuate a sentence. Nevertheless, in preparing this edition I developed a tolerance and even an appreciation of the period's more relaxed approach to such things, and I only corrected punctuation that was clearly confusing. I made these corrections as lightly as possible. For example, where two sentences are combined in the original with a comma—what we now call a "comma splice"—the comma was changed, if necessary, to a semi-colon, to retain the sense that these sentences are joined.

Another feature of antebellum American literature that is reproduced here as it appears in the original is the irregular or inconsistent use of capitalization. At this time it was still acceptable—in print and especially in manuscript—to capitalize whatever nouns the author wanted to capitalize. The Result can be jarring. Readers familiar with the mid-nineteenth-century manuscripts of Emily Dickinson, who capitalized some of her nouns, will recognize the practice. Throughout Cumings' serialized novel, for example, names of family members—"Brother," "Sister," "Father"—appear capitalized or uncapitalized. And there is no clear and consistent rationale for when she writes "Sister" and when she writes "brother." It seems likely that Cumings' compositor set her manuscript in type just as it appeared in her handwriting, and it seems likely that Cumings, with some nouns, wrote whatever version of the letter came most comfortably from the hand. In her editorial comments she expressed an awareness of "unsightly blots," and she noted that she was making careful copies of poorly handwritten manuscripts. And still the practice continued, even

24. Edgar Allan Poe, *Marginalia—Eureka*. Vol. 16 of *The Complete Works of Edgar Allan Poe*, edited by James A. Harrison (New York: Thomas Y. Crowell & Company, 1902), 130, Google Books, http://books.google.com/books?id=VW1KAAAAYAAJ.

after the error rate decreased in the later numbers. If this was not a conscious artistic decision, then it was a casual, accepted practice, and I found no good reason to regularize or modernize it. The capitalization of some words that we always or never capitalize today also varied from article to article and, in some cases, within articles. Again this was tolerated in this edition because it was tolerated at the time. Thus readers will find the "christian" alongside the "Christian" throughout this edition. Finally, question marks and exclamation points did not necessarily end a sentence in 1849 and 1850. Readers will often find words beginning with lowercase letters after these marks. As this was a common practice, it was not emended except for the reasons already described.

As there was a much weaker consensual ideal of correct punctuation and capitalization, so was there more tolerance in 1849 and 1850 for variant spellings of common words. In most cases, where variant spellings were not misleading or obviously in error, words are reproduced here as they originally appeared. Again, words can be spelled differently from article to article, and words can be spelled differently within the same article. There was no attempt in this edition to regularize or modernize spelling, just as there was no attempt to regularize or modernize punctuation. In many cases I searched databases of antebellum primary texts to determine if a variant spelling was common or very unusual and thus, likely an error. Spellings that I learned to tolerate and which the reader will find in this edition include "appals," "canvass," "chrystal," "complexion," "connexion," "moralise," "paralise," "rain-bow," "recognise," "sympathise," "vallies," and "waggons." As Walt Whitman will "loafe" in 1855, so will things "develope" in *The Akron Offering.* That said, as editor I do not pretend to infallibility, and so it is possible that a very careful reader will discover an inconsistency in my application in this or another editing principle. Again, it was not the goal to create a rigidly idealized text, but rather to create a well-prepared text and not a careless one.

The em-dash was a versatile mark in this period when punctuation was more rhetorical than strictly determined by regular and proscribed rules. Dashes could stand alone and dashes could be used in combination with other marks. With the dash, there are more choices. A sentence can end with a period or with a period-dash. There is the comma, and there is the comma-dash; there is the semi-colon and there is the semi-colon-dash. The difference is slight but can be—or seem—meaningful. Such use of the em-dash can be found throughout antebellum literature and was more common, even in classic, published works such as *Uncle Tom's Cabin*, than many readers today might expect.[25] One need only look for it to find it most everywhere in the publications of the 1840s and 1850s, and it does not take much study to see that antebellum writers often did something with the difference between a period and a period-em-dash.—For example one common mid-century use of the period-em-dash, which I attempt to illustrate here, is to separate a final sentence from the rest of the preceding paragraph so as to deliver a conclusion, an afterthought, or some other comment worth this distinction.

This brings us to paragraphing. This was not an exact science in 1850. In his history of the English paragraph, Edwin Herbert Lewis explains that until 1866, writers on composition paid "no serious attention" to the paragraph "as a structural unit" though writers were practicing its use in well-developed ways. The "theory of the teachers was so many years behind the practice of the writers."[26] Perhaps the greatest and most urgent textual problems of *The Akron Offering* lay in the paragraphing of dialogue and, to a lesser extent, the punctuation of dialogue. For example, Jenny's story, "The Little Coal-Heaver," weaves in and out and different methods of presenting dialogue. In parts the dialogue is presented in a manner that modern readers might associate with scriptwriting, though in these cases it is my guess that the author was imitating dialogue that she found in some of the popular tracts of the 1830s and 1840s.[27] In some articles dialogue is paragraphed as we expect it to be today: each time a different character speaks, there is a paragraph break and a new set of quotation marks. In other articles the dialogue was not paragraphed, and characters speak to one another in the course of one long, continuous paragraph, with or without the appropriate punctuation marks. And in some cases the dialogue appears with a mixture of paragraphing and punctuating practices. (See figure 2 on the following page.)

---

25. For example, see Harriet Beecher Stowe, *Uncle Tom's Cabin* (Boston: John P. Jewett, 1852), Google Books, http://books.google.com?id=8m4RAAAAYAAJ.

26. Edwin Herbert Lewis, *The History of the English Paragraph* (Chicago: The University of Chicago Press, 1894), 20, Google Books, http://books.google.com/books?id=4DwjAAAAMAAJ.

27. Dialogue is thus variously formatted, for example, in "Parley the Porter" by English writer Hannah More (1745-1833). For a typical American printing of this massively reprinted tale, see *Elegant Narratives* (New York: American Tract Society, n.d.), 6-9, Google Books, http://books.google.com/books?id=eogOAAAAIAAJ.

THE LITTLE COAL-HEAVER. 213

do despise a *mean* drunkard yet. I looked over the company—there was not a sober one among the lot. I felt thankful that my children had no such example. The colored preacher had gone away or I should have tried to have him fall on some plan for me to get away before my family was ruined. I thought I would try and step out of Brown's without any one seein me. "Stop here Eph," says Brown, "and drink somethin before you go." "I won't do it," says I. "You won't hey? why,you aint half as much a man as your Sam. Betsey, tell Sam. Higgins to come in and show his daddy how to drink whiskey." "You'd better wait till he's able to stand," says Bill Jones—"he's had too much already, and it made him sick; why, he's been a vomitin till he's pale as ashes." "I made a pitch for the door, and hunted round for my poor boy. I found him in the fence corner, he was the sickest child I ever saw. I called my gal." Polly," says I, who made Sam drunk?" "Nobody," says Polly,—Betsey Brown gave him the whiskey, but he made himself drunk; she give me some too, and she sends some to Mother every day, so she does," "I tell you I was 'stonished, I could now see how it was, and what made Polly and Sam take up so with Brown's children, and what made Becky (that's Mrs. Higgins,) act so queer—sometimes laughin, sometimes cryin—and sleep—why she'd sleep for a whole day together—when she'd wake up, she scolded so unmercifully that it drove me into the coal bank to get out of hearin. Here was sickness, poverty, and drunkenness, before me. Well, to cut the matter short, I went into town next day and came home drunk for the first time in my life, and if I go home sober to-night, it will be the first time in three years."

Mrs. B. I never in my life listened to such a tale of wo. You are more to be pitied than I had any idea of, and really if there could be a case of jnstifiable abandonment, it would be such as yours. I observed in the first part of your narative that you spoke of the goodness of the Lord in directing your course, &c., &c.—Suppose that the Lord were to raise you up friends as good as your old friend Smith, the preacher, and that by their attention, you would find in a few weeks an improvement in the condition of your affairs, could you be induced to try to become a sober man ? There is, Mr. Higgins, such a thing as disinterested kindness to be found

Figure 2: Page 213 from The Akron Offering

WHICH IS THE FORTUNATE MAN?

BY MISS ANNIE MIDDLETON.

"So Robert Hunt has taken himself off?" said Lewis Maynard, joining a group of students assembled on the college-grounds at S——. "I do'nt wonder; what a deuced pretty rage he got into in the class this morning." "Why, I did not notice it—what did he do?" exclaimed a youth who had lately entered. "Do!" echoed the first speaker—"that's the beauty of it, he never does anything. If he would hurl a book at the tutor's head, or knock somebody down in his wrath, it would be finishing the thing in a fine manly way. Instead of that, he turns red, then pale, trembles, clenches his hand, and is completely topsy-turvy for the rest of the day." "What was he angry at this morning?" returned the boy, who had before addressed him. "Why, he's been trying for the valedictory ever since he entered college, and that great bully, George Addington, (is he anywhere near?) has been determined that he shall not succeed; and as he is too lazy and too stupid to oppose him studying, is purposed to do it by teasing; so ridicules, mocks and sneers at Robert, till he is just fit for the lunatic asylum. I'd fight him if I was beat to a jelly for it, or else be cool and indifferent, and take no notice of his batteries, for he'd stop soon enough if he saw it did not tease. But Robert Hunt is too cowardly for the first, and too much of a baby for the last. I wonder, for my part, why his mother did not keep him at home in pin-a-fores. But where has he gone?" "Down to the bridge with Gerald Morton," answered one of his companions. "Yes," continued Lewis Maynard, who had worked himself up into something of a rage: "I suppose Gerald is giving him a sugar-plumb, as usual, and that he'll walk him back again quite cooled down. I cannot imagine how Gerald can take such an interest in the puppy, unless Bob has a rich father, uncle, or something else, and he expects in one way or another to get paid for it." "Robert's father has not as many dollars as Gerald's has thousands," interrupted one of those quiet, yet commanding voices, which make themselves heard—"and Robert Hunt is no coward, as you, and you, and you," and he pointed to one and another of the group, and then paused, with an emphatic *you*, at Lewis Maynard, "can testify, who saw him, at the risk of his own life, last winter pull little Dan Allan out of the river. Robert is no coward, but he considers it vulgar and ungentlemanly to fight, and is unhappily too sensitive to adopt the other alternative, and endure with stoicism the rough-and-tumble of this 'work-a-day world.' But I do not wonder that *you*, Lewis Maynard," and he pointed again at the youth who had been chief orator, "cannot understand *this*, any more than you can imagine how Gerald Morton can have no other motive than self-interest for his kindness to him." The boys, with one involuntary movement, turned and looked at the individual addressed; one near him whispered, "Will you stand that, Lewis?" and after a pause of five minutes, "Coward—coward," was uttered by different voices in the group. Lewis Maynard's face had changed from red to pale, and pale to red, several times during the brief interval, but at the opprobrious term his eye flashed, and glancing around at his companions, he exclaimed, in a firm tone—"I am no coward, and I'll fight the one who dares call me so; but I did wrong, I acknowledge, in accusing Gerald Morton of anything mean, and selfish, and interested. I did very wrong," he repeated, "and I desire all, who heard me make the accusation, hear me retract it. Gerald is as noble a fellow as ever lived, and I only wonder how he can endure that little, snivelling Robert Hunt. Richard Graham," he continued, walking up to the youth who had corrected him, "your reproof was deserved; but I beg that you'll take back what you said, as to my not un-

Figure 3: Page 48 from The Democratic Review

In the course of preparing this edition, I was startled to discover that distinguished precedents can be found for long stretches of unparagraphed dialogue. The best example is Annie Middleton's story, "Which is the Fortunate Man?" Cumings selected this story from an 1846 number of the *United States Magazine, and Democratic Review*, a well-made and prestigious magazine that published many of the best-known and most illustrious authors of the period. In *The Akron Offering*, the tale—which has quite a lot of dialogue—appears with hardly any paragraph breaks. There are sections where it requires much concentration to determine which character is represented as speaking which parts of the conversation. Thinking that it would be easy to emend this tale by examining the original, I discovered that *The Akron Offering* printed the tale almost exactly as it had originally appeared in the *Democratic Review*. (See figure 3.) Why either magazine would publish the story without paragraphing the dialogue—the practice was already common if not standard by 1846—is hard to say. Nevertheless, out of all of the tales that were published in the *Democratic Review*, Cumings only chose this one to republish in her *Akron Offering*. So the inadequate paragraphing of dialogue was clearly not an obstacle to her comprehension and appreciation of the story. It is hard to imagine how the story could be read and admired best of all with such punctuation, but the facts of the case suggest it was. Since I could only make sense of important sections of the story after carefully dividing the speech into paragraphs, "Which is the Fortunate Man?" appears in this edition with paragraphed dialogue. Likewise, since it was considered too distracting to read conversations with inconsistently paragraphed and punctuated dialogue, in most cases these practices were regularized and thus modernized in this edition.

The abbreviation of character names was another practice, fairly common for mid-century American periodical literature, that was emended when necessary for sense. In Cumings' novel, for example, there are places where "C." and "B." are unnecessarily obfuscating, especially in the early chapters as the reader is just beginning to fix their understanding of the characters. In such cases "Campbell" and "Benton" are substituted. In other cases, the abbreviations were allowed to stand because their referents should be clear enough in the reader's mind. And in other articles, some characters are never fully named. Thus it is no one other than "Mr. T." and "Mrs. T." who "grind the face of the poor" in the February 1850 number.

LETTERS TO THE OFFERING. 327

Morgan's mind was above little things; he despised all kinds of deception, and for this reason would not hold a secret correspondence with Annette, and only staid in the city long enough to hear from her lips that she would be true to him, till he should return with wealth sufficient to secure her father's consent. Where he went none knew, and we did not hear from him until the next winter, when I received a letter dated at Mobile, in which he stated that he was in good business and if fortune favored him as it had since he left us, he should return in two years. I read the letter to Annette, and was pleased to see her look happy again, as she had not in many months. Not long after, I left the city and joyfully turned my face towards my northern home, which I had not seen for eighteen months. It was a sunny morning in March, and as our boat left the landing and swept proudly up the broad river and we began to near the country, *I* looked back at the smoky city, fast fading from my sight, and wondered how *I* had ever lived so long in a pent up town, while the country was so beautiful and the people there so friendly and unselfish, in comparison with the residents of a city; and fathers were not so cruel, but would let their children marry whom they loved.

From these reflections *I* was startled by a voice that sounded so familiar, *I* was certain *I* had heard it before, and leaning over the guard, *I* tried to get a view of the persons on the lower deck, for the sound seemed to come from there; but *I* saw only a couple of boatmen and was about turning away, when one of them looked up, and beneath the slouched hat, *I* discovered the face of my old friend Morgan: the recognition was mutual and in another moment, with the old hat in hand he stood beside me; and what cared *I* for the sidelong glances of the upper ten, that were simpering about? *I* never was ashamed of honest worth in whatever guise it appeared.

He excused his appearance by saying he had a chance of doing much better in Pittsburgh than Mobile, and to save money was now working his passage, there and receiving the wages of a deck hand. *I* commended him for his economy and assured him success would crown his efforts if he kept on in the way he had begun. " *I* feel sure of that," said he, "and shall not consider any honest labor degrading or difficult, so long as Annette is the prize."

I left the boat at Steubenville, and the last *I* saw of Morgan he

Figure 4: Page 327 from The Akron Offering

Other emendations were applied to what were more clearly printer errors, or, if not errors, unnecessarily distracting printer decisions. At one point in the magazine, for example, the printers evidently ran out of the capital roman "I" and began substituting capital italic "*I*"s. The result is unreadable; the excessive use of the italic *I* undermines the seriousness of the tale, and even begins to look like a cruel joke played on the editor who would not be discouraged. (See figure 4 opposite.) Many numbers have errors that appear to be of the "foul case" variety. Here it appears that similar-looking pieces of type were chosen by accident: a "u" for an "n" makes "miud," a "b" for an "h" makes "Excbange." These were easy and obvious emendations to make. And there are places where the printers, through negligence or perhaps even malice, appear to comment on the quality of an article through particularly atrocious work. Stretches of Cumings' novel exhibit viciously mangled punctuation, perhaps to protest her handwriting or to sabotage her enterprise; the guest editorial by "Porcia" at the end of the March 1850 number is printed with errors that are especially degrading given that the editorial rants, most undemocratically, against the vulgar speech of those that "never were and never will be—Ladies or Gentlemen" (417).

Porcia's snobbery brings us to a final, concluding observation: the modern reader can easily discover more "bigotry, superstition, and intolerance" than the contributors appear to have recognized within themselves. Writings on religion and the American Indian are especially capable of exposing the period's ignorance and mean spirit. That said, Cumings' editorial practice—as well as her writings—illustrate a recognizably midwestern literary culture of industry, humility, graciousness, and a profound respect for reason, truth, and a spiritual interpretation of beauty. The diversity of viewpoints in *The Akron Offering* also testifies to the region's open-mindedness and Cumings' commitment to nurturing a forum where western Americans could freely exchange ideas and debate their values. While there is much to question here, there is more to admire. And close study of this critical edition also suggests that we have much, much more to learn.

April 1849
Prospectus

Magazine for Ladies!

The Subscriber, believing that the Ladies of Akron will look favorably on an effort made by one of their own sex, in their own town, to arrange for them and others an intellectual, literary bouquet, unexceptionable to the most refined taste and most exalted sense of virtue, and at so low price as to be within the reach of all, lays before them the proposed plan of a small *Magazine* to be called

THE AKRON OFFERING,

and printed once every month on good paper and with good type.

The Offering will contain Original and Selected Tales, Poetry, Essays, &c., &c., besides remarks on various subjects connected with the welfare of mankind in general, whether they have not received the attention due from intelligent, accountable beings.

There will be no list of contributors' names proclaimed as an assurance of merit in its contents, there will be no Engravings or Fashion Plates, but the heart will be addressed in tones of sacred truth, and the mind, we will hope, will dwell with pleasure on the mental creations portrayed on its pages.

Is thy home but varied beauty?
A vision fair and bright;
And dost thou love thy duty,
And walk in heavenly light?
This little work will seem to thee,
A new and added tie,

To bind in true humility,
    To Him who rules on high.

Is daily life thy portion?
    In pleasures or in woes;
Hast thou on life's broad ocean,
    No haven of repose?
This Offering will help thee,
    Though struggling to be blest,
And point thee to Eternity,
    For everlasting rest.

Is thy heritage, the anguish
    The wounded spirit feels?
In sickness dost thou languish?
    Crushed by life's ills;
These pages shall awaken
    The thoughts that give the power
To meet earth's strife unshaken,
    And fit for death's dark hour.

To all, this lowly Offering
    In humble hope is made,
That, while our efforts proffering,
    Its pages light will shed,
That mutual good securing,
    Will gild each darkened path,
And be a light enduring,
    When we shall sleep in death.

Terms.—$1.00, to be paid on the delivery of the first number, which, if sufficient encouragement be given, will be issued in the month of May.

No subscription received for less than one year.

Calista Cummings.[1]
Akron, March 28, 1849.

1. This prospectus appears in *Summit Beacon* 10, no. 50 (April 4, 1849): 2. Cumings' name is spelled variously in documents that name her. In the *Offering*, however, it almost always appears as "Cumings." See n. 16, p. 10.

THE AKRON OFFERING.

May, 1849.

To Readers of The Offering.

Subscribers for the Offering, with deep humility and a lively sense of gratitude, we would speak a few words to you, that may be deemed necessary for a full understanding of the plan and purpose of those who may arrange and conduct this Magazine. The Prospectus shows you something of this and also what is to be expected from its patrons. You all feel that this part of our country is as yet, deficient in many things and that one thing, very necessary and appropriate, is a well conducted medium of intelligence among ourselves, through which, each person capable of instructing, may speak to the rest of its readers and each in turn, receive a benefit, making this work a mutual effort for the good of all designed to elicit the writing talent that in many instances would, were no home work established, forever remain a latent principle, doing but little good to its possessor and reflecting no blessing on the community around. There may be a very few, we know there are not many, who would stand aloof from such an enterprise, because the celebrated writers for the Magazines of the Eastern Cities are not to give us the benefit of their experience. We would honor the cultivated mind wherever it may be, but in this work we depend on ourselves; yes, we all believe that Ohio has as sound minds, as pure hearts and as ready pens as other places can claim and that by cultivating the talents we possess, and becoming experienced in writing for the public eye, we may justly hope to produce in time a work worthy the patronage of the most highly gifted minds in our happy land.

Among the subscribers for the Offering are persons from almost every calling in life, pursued in this part of our country, and of almost all kinds of religious faith; such too, will be the writers for this work, some having natural capacity for and practical skill in persuasive argument, in handling every subject with the cool touch of reason and showing us every link in the bright chain connecting cause and effect, some fitted to shine by the power of quick perception, the flash of genius or the strength of refined and elevated feelings that respond to everything pure and good, and some first efforts there may be, from those who, perhaps, have long felt that not to write, was to do violence to the spirit that stirred their heart's deep fountains, but that shrinking delicacy that ever exists with a refined, poetical temperament, has kept their effusions from the vulgar gaze. We hope to receive many articles, written when no fetters were on the heart, no fear of criticism was cramping the spirit's power, and truth, mighty in its purity, was warming the soul to a high and holy energy. Would that all writers for this Magazine, would make truth their basis, let their subjects be what they may; even those who write tales, would do well to remember that "truth is stranger than fiction" and that to the judgement worthy an effort to please, fiction has not even the semblance of a charm when it exceeds the bounds of probability. Every one has seen or heard or known enough in this strange world, to form a better ground-work for a tale of thrilling interest than any person's imagination could afford; and although you may not always have a right to connect all the events in any person's life, and publish them, you can at least, when you portray characters, make them true to life. Thus much will be expected in this department.

We hope every person, capable of writing on any subject calculated to enlighten the mind or make better the heart, will condescend to help sustain this humble effort.

Each practical christian, we hope will freely tell us of the blessedness there is to be found in a faithful discharge of duty, of the high hopes that animate and cheer him as he travels the narrow path, and the happiness that awaits him when freed from trials and temptations here; he shall join the company of the redeemed in a clime where sorrow comes not, where no one needs to be forgiven, and all is peace and joy forever and forever. He whose calling is the holy one of winning souls to Christ, whatever may be his particular creed, we would hope and believe, will find time to write much that shall be for the general good, much that will teach us how to trust in God, how to hold sacred communion with our Heavenly Father and to "look at Jesus as the Author and Finisher of our faith."[1]—Most of the subscribers are Ladies and they are expected to do all in their power to benefit their own sex in particular. It is presumed that no one among us makes any pretensions to ability to enlighten the other sex as to their obligations to society or their duties to themselves, and we will fondly hope, that there is no one among us who has any desire to leave our own, appropriate sphere. Let us seek to make our own sex what they should be and we may feel certain, that man will be an equal sharer in the benefit, and we need not, necessarily, feel, that, as a class, our minds are inferior or, by men worthy of the name, are considered thus; we have only a different mission in the world and men of sense believe and know that a woman may have a sound, clear judgement and a highly cultivated mind and still be possessed of a gentle, affectionate heart, a proper regard for every domestic duty and a trembling sense of her dependence for protection on himself. Such men have helped and will continue to assist us in our efforts to establish and sustain a work at home and to make it such as will do us all good. Then let us be grateful for respect, for protection and assistance and make ourselves worthy the confidence of all.

The subscribers for the Offering, as far as making it a blessing to the community is considered, are as members of one household, bound in a certain sense, to set aside selfish feelings and interests and consult the general good. As readers they may reasonably expect to find something that will suit their own taste, or assimilate with their own views, but, they ought not to hope or even wish, that all should be brought to the test of his or her individual judgement.

We must welcome any article, suitably written, that bears the stamp of honesty, a proper respect for all and a desire to know the truth, and I would that all might be able to do this in the true spirit of heavenly charity that causes its possessor to feel that, notwithstanding certain doctrines are to him, as sacred truths, his judgement is not infallible, and another may have just as decided convictions, diametrically opposite. I may be wrong and my Brother right.

We will consider all the influences that may have been thrown around a person in his career through life, and simple justice will compel us to say, that under like circumstances, we might have been worse than he.

---

1. Hebrews 2:12.

As writers for this Magazine, let us each study our own strength and, whatever amount of cultivation our minds may have received, be true to nature, to truth and the God to whom we must render an account for the manner in which we improve His gifts.

In conclusion, may I not say, that we are bound together by ties lasting and endearing. In many instances we have seen you, have looked into your countenances for an expression of feeling in accordance with that, that has urged us to seek you, and have seen the kindling of the sparkling eye that told how the chords of sympathy with every high and holy impulse, were vibrating in responses full and clear, in each true, hoping heart. And shall we falter in a work that we must sincerely feel right in the sight of Heaven?—We trust never!

C. Cumings.

Norman and Cornelia Campbell,
OR
"Truth Stranger Than Fiction."

By C. Cumings.

Chapter I.

On a beautiful afternoon in the summer of 18—, two travellers from New England's rocky shores arrived at an Indian Village, far west of the mighty Mississippi.[2]

They had heard from several tribes, much that excited their curiosity respecting the inhabitants of this particular region, but they were not prepared for what they now saw.

The lands were enclosed and cultivated; comfortable houses, evidently the work of white men, appeared on every hand, while on a beautiful rise somewhat removed from the dwellings, stood a building that seemed like a school house from their own loved home, transplanted by some magic power; and as they gazed they saw what appeared to be, a funeral train slowly and sadly bearing its burden to its last resting place. Wonder made

2. The editor's copy of the *Akron Offering* includes several marginal comments in what look like a nineteenth-century hand. Above the start of this article is written in dip or fountain pen: "This is fine." "Far west": at this time, perhaps Iowa. For more about American Indians and antebellum Ohio, see n. 53, p. 63.

them silent and almost motionless, until the procession returned to the village.—Many of them were Indians, yet there were several white men and their families; but that which most excited the feelings of the elder stranger, was the appearance of the chief mourner in that strange collection of human beings. She was a Lady apparently between thirty and forty years of age and clad in the deepest weeds of mourning; he caught but an imperfect glance of her features as she passed, but that, with the sight of the noble boy she held by the hand, made him almost unable to restrain his impatience to know the truth until a proper time for enquiry. With deep conflicting feelings he turned away to commune with himself until he could find some person at liberty to converse with him. When at last he found a white man who, he judged, would not deem it disrespectful to enquire the meaning of all he had seen, he was told that ten years before that time, a Missionary with his wife and several families had settled among the tribe that inhabited this beautiful part of our country.

He had done all he could while his life and health continued, which was only a few years; "but, the guide, the friend of all, has been the Lady whom you saw to-day," said the man whom he addressed, "she has a heart to feel, a mind to contrive, a hand to perform and a fortune at her command. All love her and all obey; all you see, was done through her influence; she taught the Indian Women to keep the dwellings she caused to be built for them, in proper order; she paid the white men for teaching the Indians to work in an effectual manner. Her money built that school house yonder, and day after day she has there labored to instruct the Indian children or adults or any who can attend, and some are now able to assist in teaching the rest. On Sunday they are all instructed from the Bible. She reads to them, and explains what she reads, prays with them and they are also taught to sing. While the Missionary lived, he preached to them and for a few months past there has been another Missionary here, who would indeed have helped along this labor of love, but death had set his seal upon him before he came here; we buried him to-day, sir, and I never saw Miss Campbell so sad before."

"Miss Campbell? did you say Miss Campbell?" asked the traveller.

"I did sir, such is the Lady's name."

"And may I ask," said he, "the name of him she so deeply mourns?"

"His name is Elton; he came here with one child, the boy you saw to-day; just before he died he gave him to her and she will provide for him better than he could have done, unless he secured his happiness by making her his wife. Some among us imagine that they knew, and loved each other long years ago, and our first minister's wife, it is said, knows all their history, but be this as it may, they would have been a noble couple."

The stranger could not reply, but he hastily wrote his name on a slip of paper and when he could command his voice, asked the man to give it to Miss Campbell.

"Poor, bereaved Cornelia," said he, as soon as he was left alone; "thou art then, still alive, to sacrifice thy fondest hopes, this time, stricken by the hand of thy Heavenly Father. Hush my heart thy tumultuous throbbings and help me oh! God that she may not read what I have suffered, that I may be her friend in this hour of anguish!"

The man soon returned and requested him to go with him to the house where Miss C. lived. It was one she had built for the Missionary who first preached to the benighted minds of the Indians there abiding; his widow was now her friend and companion, although entirely dependent on her bounty and sadly unable, without her influence, to bear her solitary lot. As he entered this dwelling he noticed an old man almost helpless whom he imagined he had seen before, but he passed along. Cornelia Campbell stood before him and for a moment she was overcome by memory's bitter power, but soon the control over her feelings that had helped her to bear so much and accomplish so much, was manifested in the calm dignity of her appearance; her sobs were hushed, her tears were dried, and, although her face was pale as monumental marble, every selfish feeling was banished and she welcomed her old friend and neighbor with gladness in her tones that told of the power of sympathy to lift a weight of sorrow from the suffering heart. He had been her friend in childhood, her Brother's friend and the friend of him whom she had that day looked upon for the last time.

He was familiar with the history of her family, from the time when her Grandfather first resolved to come to America, until the time when she was left alone, to struggle on through life or weakly yield to adverse powers and sink beneath the waves of death.

He had loved her with the true friendship of a noble heart, but she knew it not, for well did he know that her heart could never be his; but her esteem, her friendship he possessed and with that he was content.

She was far away from the scenes where he had been associated with her when the last link that bound her to life seemed to be broken, and feeling that only in a change of scene, amid active usefulness could she bear to live, or hope for strength to be a christian, she resolved to go with some Missionaries and seek to be happy in doing good to the children of another race.

She suffered no one to become acquainted with her expected destination or in any way to have any idea of her intentions, except those with whom she went, and they knew but little of these.—This friend of her earlier years then lost all trace of her and after many fruitless efforts came to the conclusion that she was numbered with the dead. He had been for some time, previous to roaming o'er his Country's broad domains, engaged in writing the history of her Brother and herself and he could never bear to finish, for he believed that, to respect truth, he must present them to the reader, for the last time, in the habiliments of the grave. Now, he beheld her alive and his heart rejoiced.

She noticed not his deep agitation, but enquired with much feeling after all her old friends by the way.

Said he, "A son of one of your old neighbors came with me and is lingering, waiting for a summons from me."

"I will send for him," said Cornelia and immediately she did so.

She remembered him, a little boy and welcomed him with courteous hospitality. She enquired of the elder Gent. Mr. W. if he remembered old Francis who was once the servant of her Mother's Brother and for a long time attached to his son in the house of her Uncle C. who was Guardian to her Brother and herself?

"I do," said he.

"He is here," said she. "And although he was so long in silent league with the enemies of my Brother and myself you are aware that he at last abandoned our wretched cousin Wm. Benton and did his best to assist us to recover our fortune, going back in his testimony, given to the time when the first injustice was done to my Father and Uncle by Wm. B.'s maternal Grandfather and his confederate in crime, the wretched Friedland who was so long known as the hermit of the glen."

"Yes, I remember him well," said he. "He died as he deserved, but I will not pain you. I never liked Old Francis for any thing but that one act of justice; for that I would like to see him, and I believe I did see him, as I came in."

"Doubtless," said she, "for he moves about but little, except when carried, and generally sits near the door, gazing with a vacant look on every thing that passes." Here she paused—up to this time she had not mentioned

Charles Elton or told him any thing of herself. She now felt that it must all appear strange to him, and briefly told him something of what the man of whom he had first enquired, had informed him, concealing, as much as possible however, her own good deeds—and again she faltered and he felt that he must come to her relief in some way, but how could he tell her he knew it all and not wound her feelings?

At last he said, "Suffer me Cornelia to tell you that I am aware that my friend and yours, Charles Elton, is lost to us forever. I did not know he was here or that his wife was dead or that he was doing what was always his duty, and had not seen him since he left our circle."

He had tried to avoid any reference to what had been Elton's real course for a few years after he had been taught to distrust her love for himself, but she knew that he had known how truly they had loved and yet how deeply they had both been wronged and now he knew that he was gone.

Her tears flowed again, but she soon arose and left the room, returning again in a few minutes, leading the same noble boy he had seen with her as she came from the grave of his friend. "This is his son," said Cornelia. "He gave him to me and oh! may I be able to fulfil his wishes concerning him."

Mr. W. gazed sadly on the intelligent countenance of the young being before him; he felt that as he now appeared, so did his Father look at his age, and he feared that the same impulsive nature would impel him to error, strew thorns in his pathway and make him unfit to cope successfully with the trials of life, but he spake kindly to him and wondered not that Miss C. looked upon him with such devoted love; if any thing could prepare him for a life of usefulness and happiness it was her influence.

He and his young traveling companion stayed some weeks at this self-sustained Missionary establishment, looking at the improvements going on and wondering at the power that had transformed so many savages into, at least partially, civilized men, apparently eager for improvement and quick to comprehend instruction, whether it must tax their physical strength or their mental powers. Strife was with them a thing of the past and as Mr. W. wandered over their grounds he felt that the spirit of peace was brooding over the scene and imbuing every heart with its soothing power. He gazed over the far-stretching prairie, until his whole soul expanded into a rapturous glow of admiration; he culled the beautiful flowers, most rare and exquisite in form, in color and in fragrance; he wandered through the groves and up and down the streams, feasting every sense of the beautiful, in contemplation of objects seen or heard, or in that silent communion that comes to the heart as whisperings of some gentle spirit presiding amid the sacred haunts of solitude, alone in its simple and yet sublime grandeur.

He wondered no more, that Miss C. loved the scenes so calculated to inspire the heart with peace nor that she was listened to and her precepts revered. "I too could stay forever here," said he to himself, "bound by chains that will not break, but I must away. Honor, duty, every thing demands it and I will go."

He had several times visited Charles Elton's grave in Company with Miss C. and also alone, and the next day after he decided to leave this paradise in the wilderness, he asked her to go with him once again to that sacred spot. When they were there he told her he should start on the next day, for the scenes of their childhood.

"You know," said he to her, "that I have always been your friend, that I loved your Brother as if he were my own. I have been writing a history, Cornelia, weaving the incidents of your lives into a tale that, with your permission, I will give to the world. Chide me not," said he, as he saw her look of sorrowful regret. "No person's feelings can be wounded by this course except those who have so basely wronged yourself and your Brother, hurrying him to an untimely grave." And he paused. He could not speak to her of her own blighted hopes, but with deep feeling he said, "Suffer me to be the instrument inspired I trust by Heaven, to avenge your Brother's wrongs, not by seeking revenge, save by the burning words of truth, that as arrows from the quiver of the Almighty, shall pierce their coward hearts. Say you will consent and will give me what letters you have in your possession that would throw any light on their transactions."

She did consent. She gave him the letters and much information, and from her inmost soul she was grateful for his zeal in defending her Brother's memory, but her own sorrows she would lock in her own heart, as far as possible.

"Speak not of me," said she, "more than is strictly necessary. Blame not my Guardian too much: he was my dear Father's Brother and although he was a victim to his own weakness, he had much to bear. And one thing more," said she, "I must ask of you, be generous to the memory of him who sleeps beneath this sod."

He looked at her as the tears streamed down her cheeks and could scarce refrain from expressing his admiration and his fervent love; by the strongest effort of his powerful mind, he controlled the strife of his heart and after a few moments' silence, replied, "I will do right, Cornelia; God will help me, and you, I hope, are willing to trust me thus much."

She looked at him in surprise and for a moment he feared his secret was discovered, but, she merely said, "I will trust you my friend. I shall visit the world once again, if I live long, although my stay in it, will be short. My Brother's son is very dear to me and although he has a Mother and other friends, and I may not have him with me, I feel that I must see him once again, must once more stand by my Brother's grave and teach his son to imitate his Father's virtues and cherish his memory and then, I hope to spend the remainder of my days here. And here," pointing to the side of the grave near which she was seated, "do I hope to rest when done with earth!"

The setting sun shed its last lingering rays around her as she said this and to her listener she seemed a being from some celestial clime. A pang shot through his noble soul; he felt that he was an Idolator—a moment passed, and he was a man of sense, pledged to duty and hoping only for happiness in its sacred paths.

Slowly they proceeded to the village. Reader it is not necessary to describe him as he is only the looker-on and portrayer of events in a tale commenced before he left New England and which he now felt that he could complete, if not with pleasure, at least, with some degree of satisfaction. The Lady introduced to you we will for the present leave. She will receive justice at the hands of Mr. W. Again we shall hear from her and in the picture presented to our mental vision, see many things to remind us of her untiring patience in perfecting and carrying out her plans for the improvement of the hearts and minds of the Indians, whose dark brows shaded darker hearts. The sweetest vision of her youth, had been such a scene and such an effort, but she did not dream that she must thus, alone, nerve every faculty of her mind, and feeling of her sensitive spirit, to suffer and endure and falter not in the sacrifice—no—an arm that should have been stronger, a heart that should have been firmer, a nature that ought not so soon, to have shrunk from peril in the path of duty, was then her expected support, but she had seen every Idol of clay removed and had now learned to lean on the arm of her "Father in Heaven" and great was her reward. Before we again visit her we must listen to a condensed account of her Grandfather and Father and Mother, as necessary to an understanding of her own and her Brother's eventful life; then shall we see her as she was, a little girl and a youthful maiden, her Brother too from the cradle to the grave, their friends, their foes,—all will be given of their lives necessarily connected, and the end of all will be portrayed in colors extracted from the fair principles of truth.

To be Continued.

The Bitter Hour.

I die! I die! said the beautiful child
  As she lay at noon of night,
Strange agony seized her little frame,
  Gave to her eye unwonted light.

Good bye! Good bye! she screamed* again
  In the hollow tones of death,
More pallid grew the beauteous cheek
  And fainter still the breath.

Fathom if thou canst the mother's grief,
  The sister's breaking heart,
As in that bitter hour they stood
  So loth with her to part.

She's gone! She's gone! it sounds again,
  The jewel, oh! 'tis fled—
The friends, they wept for O! their hearts,
  Their hearts were with the dead.

The grave received the faded dust,
  Embraced the casket fair;
All silent is her resting place—
  Foul worms will riot there.

The soul's beyond this vale of tears,
  It shines in lustre now,
And gems the radiant coronet
  That decks the Saviour's brow.

I'll call it not a bitter hour
    Nor of my anguish tell,
God gave the child! God took her home;
    God "doeth all things well."

"Anna."

* This word "screamed," will sound strange to those unacquainted with the circumstances of the death of the child referred to, but truth makes it appropriate; she breathed her last "screaming" very loudly "I die I die," "Good bye Good bye." EDITOR.

The Soul's Search After Happiness.

'Twas evening; a beautiful summer evening—The glorious sun was just sinking to rest, behind the fairy summits of the Catskill mountains, as our vessel laden with life, proceeded on her way up the silvery Hudson. Nothing could surpass the beauty of the moving picture, glowing as it was, in the last rays of the setting sun, which seemed desirous to linger near a scene of so much loveliness, lest it should vanish ere he again should finish his daily course; and as if to atone for his absence, he threw a flood of golden light, o'er mountain, river, and wood, so far surpassing in beauty all that I had ever seen in nature, that I almost feared, it was one of those bright visions, we are sometimes permitted to look upon in the magic land of dreams, which fade from the sight, leaving their image engraven on the heart; as if to remind us that there is another and a better world, where sin hath never marred its beauty.

I gazed upon the beautiful landscape, until envious night shrouded it in her dark mantle, and then another picture was revealed, less dazzling, but none the less lovely, and I was alone with nature, for all had sought amusement elsewhere. No sound was heard save, the soft ripple of the waters, which seemed to murmur at our intrusion, and I listened to the "voices of the night"[3] as they spoke their awful mysteries to my heart, and I wished for power, to scan the wonders of that mind, who spake the countless worlds

3. In "Footsteps of Angels," a poem that was well known and often quoted around 1849, American poet Henry Wadsworth Longfellow (1807–82) begins: "When the hours of day are numbered, / And the voices of the Night / Wake the better soul, that slumbered, / To a holy, calm delight." See, for example, Longfellow, *Voices of the Night* (Boston: Redding & Co., 1845), 10, Google Books, http://books.google.com/books?id=UR4CAAAAYAAJ.

"that deck the sky of even,"[4] forth "from dreary nothing."[5] Scarce was I conscious of that wish, when a voice soft, as the tones that float upon the breezes of Heaven, arrested my attention; and turning I beheld a female form of surpassing loveliness; and yet there was a sternness on her brow that told her mission was not always, one of joy; and thus she spake:—

"Mortal, thou art presumptuous in thine aspirations, and yet thou wouldst know the truth, and thy presumption is forgiven thee; my name is Memory; and I have now come to conduct you into the great Past: that you may there read the fate, of those who like thee, have aspired too high. They like thee sought the boon of Happiness; read their fate as it is now revealed to thee, and when thou hast well considered upon it, choose ye the path in which ye will walk, and know thou shalt surely meet the reward, ever attached to such a course. Speak not but follow me."

With the rapidity of thought, we passed from the "sphere of earthliness"[6] and stood in the vast temple of Memory, thronged with the great and illustrious of all ages. And as I looked upon them I was surprised, to see the seal of discontent, every where visible.

A stern military form was near me, and I addressed him. He stood apart from that vast throng as though he disdained to mingle with the common herd, lest he should become as one of them. His aspirations had been for military glory, and universal sway; and after drenching Europe, in human gore, and swaying myriads of minds at will, he terminated his days upon "a lone barren isle," with no friend near to cheer his pathway, to the "silent land" whither he had sent so many, to gratify his unsatiable ambition;[7] and

4. Skies are often "decked"—decked with the sun, the moon, the stars, with gems, or decked with glory, etc., in English and American poetry before 1850. Yet this particular phrase appears to be too obscure or too freely translated for discovery in searchable databases of antebellum books and periodicals. Other short quotes in this essay of an equally generic poetical nature include "beyond the veil" and "aching void."

5. Here "dreary nothing" might echo the well-known poem, "Summer," in the "Seasons" series of eighteenth-century English poet James Thomson (1700–48). "Has any seen / The mighty Chain of Beings, lessening down from Infinite Perfection to the brink / Of dreary nothing, desolate abyss!" A recent American edition was Thomson, *The Seasons . . . For the Use of Schools and Academies* (Improved ed. Portland: Sanborn & Carter, 1846), 48, Google Books, http://books.google.com/books?id=J4w9AAAAYAAJ.

6. The long poem "Queen Mab" by English poet Percy Bysshe Shelley (1792–1822) describes a beautiful evening scene "Where musing solitude might love to lift / Her soul above this sphere of earthliness." A contemporaneous American printing of this well-known passage can be found in *The Poetical Works of Percy Bysshe Shelley*, ed. Mary Wollstonecraft Shelley (Philadelphia: Crissy & Markey, 1847), 23, Google Books, http://books.google.com/books?id=jjJHAAAAYAAJ. See also n. 9, p. 105.

7. Shields alludes to a song by American vocalist Lyman Heath (1804–70), "The Grave of Bonaparte," which begins: "On a lone barren isle, where the wild roaring billows / Assail the stern rock, and the

O how bitter was the thought in that stern hour, that those who had loved him best had also been his victims; and that she who was "his destiny"[8] had suffered most. I hastened to change the scene and approached a female form, surrounded by a group of admirers, who seemed to exist only in her smiles; surely thought I she must have been happy, yet I was mistaken. Gifted above others of her sex in beauty, and intellect, she was unhappy. While others were entranced with the sweet numbers, that fell from her lyre, she sighed in vain for that sympathy, so essential to the happiness of woman, and as thousands knelt in homage at her feet, and worshipped the high intellect given her by Heaven, how few thought of the wealth of affection that ever accompanies great minds. Deep and sensitive feelings are ever associated with genius; if it were not so, how could they so beautifully describe the scenes, which common minds have gazed upon, without exciting one thought of admiration. Yes they look through the bright medium of their own glad spirits; and every thing wears a beauty that is not of earth; and joy, and gladness wells up from the deep fountains of their hearts, uncalled for; and with a resistless power, they cannot comprehend, they are induced to breathe forth their own glad feelings, and seek to awaken a response, in the minds of others.

Yet do they rarely meet with the affection they so much prize, and in bitterness of soul, do they turn from the praises of those who admire their genius, and sigh in vain for one heart to sympathize with them. And bitter indeed is the cup, to one who has not learned to look "beyond the veil,"

---

loud tempests rave, / The hero lies still." The song was known to Americans as part of the repertoire of the very popular (and antislavery) Hutchinson Family Singers. See Asa Hutchinson, *The Granite Songster: Comprising the Songs of the Hutchinson Family, Without the Music* (Boston: A. B. Hutchinson, 1847), Google Books, http://books.google.com/books?id=LO2jtxsIa9AC. Any survey of 1840s American popular culture should include some attention to the Hutchinson Family Singers. For more on their significance, see Scott Gac, *Singing for Freedom: The Hutchinson Family Singers and the Nineteenth-Century Culture of Reform* (New Haven: Yale University Press, 2007).

8. The notion that two are "destined" for one another is commonly romantic and poetical, but one who popularized this choice of words was English poet George Gordon Noel Byron (1788–1824), who wrote, for example, of "her who was his destiny" in his 1816 poem "The Dream." See Byron, *The Poetical Works of Lord Byron* (New York: Appleton, 1847), 486, Google Books, http://books.google.com/books?id=AG1AAAAAYAAJ. Another popular source for descriptions of the "destiny" inherent in "true love" is the 1830 novel *Clarence; Or, A Tale of Our Times* by American novelist Catharine Maria Sedgwick (1789–1867). This narrates the mysterious courting of Gertrude Clarence and Gerald Roscoe, two lovers who are often described as destined for one another. *Clarence* was also republished in 1849, the year of this publication. For an example of such destiny, see *Clarence; Or, A Tale of Our Times*. Author's Revised Edition (New York: George P. Putnam, 1849), 222, Google Books, http://books.google.com/books?id=b1RXAAAAYAAJ. The novel by Cumings that is serialized in *The Akron Offering*, *Norman and Cornelia Campbell, Or, Truth Stranger than Fiction*, resembles Sedgwick's *Clarence* in many ways.

to that upper, and better world, where all will be love, and sympathy, and where all will be known and appreciated as they can never be here. Again I sought one who had not yielded to disappointment; and promised myself better success, for there was so much calmness, in the deportment of the one I now approached that I felt confident he was happy. But no, on a nearer approach, I saw it was the calmness of despair that had deceived me; and that he was of all others the most miserable. He had drank deeply of the cup of pleasure, and dashed it aside in disgust, when he perceived its inability to bestow happiness; learning too had yielded her treasures to enrich his mind, and they too had failed. Honor, Wealth, and Fame, had thrown around him their magic influence, and yet the object was not attained; there was "still an aching void," a restless desire for something not yet possessed, that nothing, save the one thing needful could ever satiate. But pride forbade his seeking the "pearl of great price,"[9] and he wrapped himself in a mantle of despair, and calmy awaited, the termination of an existence, that might have caused myriads of hearts to have rejoiced, as well as filling his own soul with joy, and peace. Sick at heart, I besought my guide to hasten with me from a scene so splendidly miserable, and as we passed on, another picture which in beauty can never be surpassed, arose before my wondering mind; 'twas of a noble youth, whose lofty brow bespoke a giant mind, and upon its clear expanse, I read the unmistakable traces of happiness. Peace beamed from his mild eye, and joy trembled on his lips as he welcomed my guide, for she was indeed pleasant to him. Yet had the cup of anguish been pressed to his lips; and although in the first draught, there was a bitterness from which his spirit turned in pride, yet was he led, to see the hand that presented it, and his spirit bowed before the throne of him who doeth all things well—for he knew that "these light afflictions which are but for a moment, shall work out for us a far more exceeding and eternal weight of glory."[10]

9. Jesus tells the parable of the pearl in Matthew 13:45–46: "The kingdom of heaven is like unto a merchant seeking goodly pearls: Who, when he had found one pearl of great price, went and sold all that he had, and bought it." The text is from Clarke (see next note).

10. Shields quotes Adam Clarke's note to 2 Corinthians 4.18: "But we must remark the that [*sic*] light afflictions work out this far more exceeding and eternal weight of glory, *only to those who do not look at the things which are seen*." See *The New Testament of our Lord and Saviour Jesus Christ* . . . Ed. Adam Clarke (Philadelphia: Thomas, Cowperthwait, 1844), 174, Google Books, http://books.google.com/books?id=RCwNAAAAYAAJ. An English Methodist theologian, Adam Clarke (1760–1832) published a text of the bible with extensive commentary in the early 1830s. It went through many editions in America, where the commentary provided great assistance to Methodist preachers. That Shields appears to have owned and known this bible supports the theory that this author is Ann E. Shields, professor at the Oakland Female Seminary, where students could attend services at either a Methodist or a Presbyterian church. See n. 14, p. 43.

In early youth he had been the idol of an admiring circle of friends, and bright were the hopes that were cherished for him; but the time came when the smiles of friendship, and the endearments of love, ceased to bestow happiness. He saw himself sinful, and polluted, with no hope of salvation save in the blood of Christ; and he brought his wealth of learning, and intellect, and laid them at the feet of him, "who was meek and lowly in heart" and he was made to drink of the "water of salvation which henceforth became to him a well of water springing into everlasting life" and he left the friends of childhood, and severed every tie that bound him to earth and went forth to declare "the unsearchable riches of Christ,"[11] to the dark and benighted heathen; and through toil, and privation he pursued an unwavering course, ever laboring diligently in the great work, to which he was called. But he labored not as one without hope, for he saw thousands of those for whom he sacrificed all, rejoicing in the love of God, that passeth all understanding; and he knew the influence he had labored to exert, would go on widening and widening throughout succeeding ages, and joy filled his heart that he had not lived in vain. At last he died alone; no not alone, for God was with him; and the right arm of Heaven's righteousness was around him, and Christ walked through the dark valley and shadow of death with him; and the souls of those who had gone before, for whose salvation he had labored, stood on the other side of the river of death, to welcome him to the regions of bliss; and as he emerged from the cold stream, Heaven's high arches rang, with the glad songs of the redeemed, joyful that one who had served his Lord so well, was called at last "to lay his armor off and rest in Heaven," and his freed spirit was borne upward, to the throne of God, and he was permitted to join that "innumerable company" who "have come up out of great tribulation and have washed their robes, and made them white in the blood of the Lamb."[12]

Long would I have lingered on a spot so sacred, but my conductress hurried me away. "You have now seen," she said, "how foolish, how worse than foolish, it is to expect happiness from worldly objects. If you seek it in Honor, Wealth, or Fame, you will be disappointed; Love too is fleeting and Friendship is rarely found. 'Seek first then the kingdom of Heaven and all

11. Matthew 12:29; John 4:14; Ephesians 3:8.

12. In his poem, "Death of a Missionary," American poet Nathaniel Parker Willis (1806–67) writes, "How beautiful it is for a man to die / Upon the walls of Zion! to be call'd, / Like a watch-worn and weary sentinel, / To put his armor off, and rest—in heaven!" See Willis, *The Poems: Sacred, Passionate, and Humorous, of Nathaniel Parker Willis* (New York: Clark, Austin, 1849), 78–79. An early (and perhaps first) printing is Willis, "Death of a Missionary." *The New Mirror* 2, no. 3 (October 21, 1843): 44, American Periodicals (136930314). The rest of the sentence quotes from Hebrews 12:22 and Revelation 7:14.

these things shall be added unto you,' and bear in mind, that, they who most faithfully serve their God, are happiest here: and hereafter, they shall be permitted to dwell in the presence of the 'High and Lofty One, who inhabiteth Eternity.'"[13] She ceased speaking, and when I turned to address her she was gone. Consciousness slowly returned, and I was still leaning over the side of the vessel. It appears there had been a lapse, in my recollection and imagination, had seized the moments, to weave a fabric of her own.

A. E. Shields.[14]

13. Luke 12:31; Isaiah 57:15.

14. Searches of the United States Federal Census records through Ancestry.com, the OCLC's WorldCat catalog of North American research libraries, and many other databases of digitized nineteenth-century publications reveal no likely match to anyone known to have resided in northeast Ohio. However, this could be "Miss A. E. Shields," professor of the "Primary Department and Mental Philosophy" at Oakland Female Seminary, a important early American woman's college in Hillsboro of southwestern Ohio. It seems likely that the educated women of Hillsboro would want to support Cumings' new women's magazine in Akron. In the 1840s, Hillsboro was a prosperous, highly-educated town that was well connected to the larger world through two railroad lines. Shields is named in two prominent editorials praising the college: *The Ladies' Repository, and Gatherings of the West* 1 (1841), 96, 320, Google Books, http://books.google.com/books?id=aSvZAAAAMAAJ. Published by the Methodist Book Concern in Cincinnati, *The Ladies' Repository*—described by William Henry Venable in 1891 as "by far the longest lived, most extensive, and most expensive literary periodical ever published west of the Allegheny mountains"—was likely a model that Cumings knew and emulated, in some respects, with her *Akron Offering*. See Venable, *Beginnings of Literary Culture in the Ohio Valley* (Cincinnati: Robert Clarke & Co., 1891), 97–107, Google Books, http://books.google.com/books?id=57eEAAAAIAAJ. On December 18, 1849, Shields married James A. Trimble. See "Married," *Scioto Gazette* 17 (December 20, 1849): col. A, Infotrac's 19th Century U.S. Newspaper Archive (GT3009183567). Captain James A. Trimble, a Revolutionary patriot hero, Indian-fighting Ohio pioneer, and father of former Ohio Governor Allen Trimble, is not recorded in the 1850 census for Highland County, where he is known to have lived. Ann E. Shields Trimble is not recorded in the 1850 census, either. Perhaps they were travelling in the summer after their marriage, or perhaps the census-taker failed to count them. In the 1860 census, Trimble is recorded as 72 years old and living without a spouse. Since "Miss" indicates married status (in 1849) more than it indicates age, "Miss Shields" could have been 60 years old when employed as Professor of the Primary Department and Mental Philosophy at Oakland Female Seminary. Hillsboro was full of illustrious children and grandchildren that Trimble had by a previous marriage. For example, a daughter of former Governor Trimble—and stepgranddaughter of Miss Ann E. Shields—was Eliza Jane Trimble Thompson. Later known simply as "Mother Thompson," she began the famous "Woman's Crusade" of 1873 by praying for an end to the liquor traffic in a Hillsboro tavern. This winter of activism sparked the rapid rise of the Woman's Christian Temperance Union in American politics. For more on the Hillsboro Trimbles, see J. W. Klise, *The County of Highland* (Madison: Northwestern Historical Association, 1902), Google Books, http://books.google.com/books?id=3DsVAAAAYAAJ. For more on Ohio and the birth of WCTU, see Jack S. Blocker, *'Give to the Wind Thy Tears': The Women's Temperance Crusade, 1873–1874* (Westport: Greenwood, 1985). For more on mid-nineteenth-century female academies in general and Oakland in particular, see Jean Ferguson Carr, "Nineteenth-Century Girls and Literacy," in Jean Greer, ed., *Girls and Literacy in America: Historical Perspectives to the Present* (Santa Barbara: ABC-CLIO, 2003), 51–78, OhioLINK Scholarly & Reference E-books, http://rave.ohiolink.edu/ebooks/ebc/GLITE.

The May Moon.

By Lily Lute.[15]

The May Moon through the open door,
Spread its beams on the cottage floor,
Kiss'd the brow of a maiden fair,
Lit the curls of her raven hair,—
Now in her dark and clear, blue eyes,
Mirror'd, it for a moment lies;—
But heeds she not the lovely night,
Nor young May Moon with beams of light;
Her thoughts are o'er the deep blue sea,
With loved ones there they wander free;—
Her aged sire and lover brave,
Had sailed, time gone, far o'er the wave,
And now beneath the far-off skies,
Where California's treasure lies,—
They're searching for the precious ore,
That miners love to lay in store.—
O! idiotic crazy men!
Of home treasures ye little ken,
If but to fill a scanty purse,
With what will be our nation's curse,
Ye have left home and that fair maid,
Her feeble mother's only aid,
To close that mother's eyes alone,—
Can gold for her deep grief atone?
No—with loved ones she'd rather be
A begger of cold charity,—
Than own the richest golden mine,
If left in solitude to pine.
The next May Moon we'll change the scene;
The grass on many graves is green,
Tears in the maiden's eyes are seen,

15. A frequent contributor, "Lily Lute" wrote (and visited) from Seville township in southern Medina County. There are no "Lutes" in the 1850 or 1860 United States Federal Census for Medina County. The name is likely a pen name. For more about Lute, Seville, and her relationship with Cumings, see pp. 3, 307–12, and 453–57.

The color from her cheek has fled,—
Alas! she mourns her mother dead!
And sire and lover where are they?
Bones are bleaching at Monterey,—
Shrouds are weaving—gold is heaping—
Friends are leaving—friends are weeping—
Sighs are heaving,—Death is keeping
Revels in California,
And o'er all shines the moon of May.

For the Offering.

We, whose merits and grievances are herein outlined, feeling ourselves to be a most worthy, but long neglected, class, take the perhaps unwarrantable liberty to address the lady Editress on our own behalf. We are informed that the Offering seeks to develop the now latent talent of the scribbling genus hereabouts. And as we possess a modicum of courage for goosequill warfare, we are more than half inclined to enter the lists, not precisely for "immortality," but for the arousal of that genius, of the possession of which we entertain no doubt. Let it not ill beseem the modesty of your ladyship's humble servants, to intimate, that, at diverse dates, they have strongly suspected themselves of possessing some undiscovered reserves of mental power; but the humiliating conviction will steal across their consciousness ever and anon, that, unless some marvelously felicitous 'calling out' shall soon occur, the world will never owe any wide illumination to their intellectual evolutions. We have made full many a sturdy endeavor, and have called with voices stentorian; but, alas, hitherto the responses have come from distant echo. Never a whit disheartened, we are resolved to

"Try, try again."[16]

The first number of your periodical, we conclude, is to be a capacious tureen, which your friends (and Editresses always have an afflicting number of friends) are to fill with literary succotash, spiced with dribblets of French and Latin quoted from the grammar and spelling-book. And poetry,—

16. The chorus of a popular lesson for children with many variants. For example: " 'Tis a lesson you should heed— / Try, try again; / If at first you don't succeed, / Try, try again!" S. G. Goodrich, *Third School Reader* (Louisville: Morton and Griswold, 1846), 23–24, Google Books, http://books.google.com/books?id=AIISAAAAIAAJ.

what do you say to an occasional donation of unfledged poetry? Rhyme will flow in copious effusions, of course. And then we must write of

> "Glad, warm hearts, and glorious flowers,"[17]

and go into a spasm of raptures about breezes freighted with

> "One drop of fragrance from thousands of roses."

And birds, and fountains, and wavy meadows, and emerald groves, the blush of Aurora, and the holy hush of twilight, when the worshippers of the Father,

> "Ere yet the dark hours be,
> Lift the heart, and bend the knee."[18]

And then the stars,

> "Yon bright and glorious blazonry of God."[19]

charm the eye, inspire the heart, and move the pen. Reminiscences of childhood's fairy dance on beds of roses, incidents of travels, abstracts of history, theses in science, chapters on morals and manners, sketches of Scripture characters, the beauties of truth, the loveliness of piety, pictures of the fancy, and effusions of the heart,—do you say to them all, "come and welcome?" Here, then, is variety presented to our choice, and the door of invitation is so liberally ajar, that each may choose with what offering to enter.

His is a sluggard's soul, that never knows the bliss of a valuable self-originated thought; and his is a sluggard's hand that will not write. What if at first we ill adjust the pattern to the last—the language to the thought; should one claim the elegance of experience without the energy of effort?

But, to wax sympathetic, what award does the lady Editress expect for zeal, and care, and fear, and toil, and weariness, and disheveled hair, and disordered attire, and all the necessary and conventional appurtenances of

---

17. This line is not discovered by search engines of antebellum American books and periodicals. It could be obscure, misremembered, or original verse. The literature of this time abounded with flowers, glory, warm hearts and gladness, so of course this could also be a parody or even a sarcasm, depending on how we interpret the meaning of "Beta."

18. These lines are from "The Hour of Prayer," an often-republished poem by British poet Felicia Dorothea Hemans (1793–1835). For an 1849 version, see Hemans, *The Poetical Works* (Boston: Phillips, Sampson, & Company, 1849), 180, http://books.google.com/books?id=4hM1AAAAMAAJ.

19. From the conclusion of "The Closing Year" by American poet and editor George Prentice (1802–70). The poem often appeared in American school books. For example, see William Holmes McGuffey, *McGuffey's Rhetorical Guide, or Fifth Reader* (Cincinnati: Winthrop, Smith, 1844), 472–74, Google Books, http://books.google.com/books?id=dnoSAAAAIAAJ.

a literary career? Perhaps a whole hail-storm of thanks from an inconveniently grateful generation of hypercritical contemporaries,—a profusion of downy, complimentary flakes, followed by a blinding sheet of "buts," and "ifs," and "ahems," sufficient to pelt one's very shadow out of patience. All this you should joyfully endure for the good of the 'rising' generation.

As our articles will be the very best that can be written on the subjects, without the resurrection of the masters of English prose and poetry of years agone, we shall feel sorely soured at your audacity, if you presume to place them in any but the most conspicuous position. And then, if you please, be so kind as to put a *bell* on them, for the benefit of stupid readers, who might otherwise overlook such priceless excogitations of minds profound. We have been told, that articles which are worthy to be perused, need no puffing. We hope you may show the absurdity of this false philosophy, by bestowing our condescending efforts to enlighten society, the most favorable notice.

On behalf of the Fraternity,

"Beta."

Misfortune, like a creditor severe,
But rises in demand for her delay;
She makes a scourge of past prosperity,
To sting thee more, and double thy distress. —Young.[20]

For the Offering.

Parental Influence.

Parental Influence!—back, far as thought can go
In all the varied acts of man, I trace it—
Is he a villain, (circumscribed by poverty,
Or raised to opulence, by fraud or artifice,
Or claiming for inheritance, with seeming justice,
Kingdoms, thrones, and power unlimited by man,
Betraying still in each degree of degradation,

20. The lines are from "Night 1" of *The Complaint, or, Night-Thoughts on Life, Death, and Immortality* (1742–46), a long religious poem by English poet Edward Young (1683–1765) that saw many English and American editions. For an American printing from the 1840s, see Young, *The Complaint and Consolation; or, Night Thoughts on Life, Death, and Immortality* (Boston: Lewis & Sampson, 1842), 13, Google Books, http://books.google.com/books?id=x1xDAAAAYAAJ.

As intellect and wealth and power are granted him,
The principles that nature's gifts, pervert,
And fit man to become sin's willing victim,
In mean and servile homage bowing low
Beneath the weight of dark, despotic vice,
That he may quench each latent spark of virtue,
And better thence, his coward task fulfil,)
His history tells the fatal cause,—his parents' sin!
Yes, sin!—their sad, their deep neglect of duty!
And is he subject lawful, (weak in nature's gifts
And limited his sphere of action, yet, virtuous still,
Disgracing not the little light his God hath given,
Or is he rich in talent, cultivated high,
His soul expanding, mental stores receiving still,
And all of Science's, Wisdom's charms, that can adorn
The immortal mind, and fit for life's eventful scenes,
Yielding unto his mental strength, his searching power,
Its certain, sweet reward, the rich possession,
And does the praise to merit due, the power, the fame,
Frail nature loves so well, corrupt him never,
But, does he live an honored being, trusted, loved,
Obeying or obeyed, yet daring to fulfil
His every duty, to himself, his fellows round,
His Country and his God, and though his simple robe
May tell of poverty, with malicious art,
His soul's proud freedom, seeks to fetter and debase,
Or does he wear a splendid garb of wealth or royalty,
Possessing still the same firm principles of virtue,
Obeying still the dictates of an honest, feeling heart,
Conferring happiness on all his power can bless;
Prepared for life, for death, for Heaven's enduring state,)
His parent's influence thus shaped his glorious course!
Doubt ye, your power who here are placed as guardians
Of youth? then seek in History's every page, the cause
Of acts portrayed, scan every Nation's destiny,
Their leading minds search out, and dare to bring to light
Their guides,—& doubt ye still? then look where ye, yourselves
Have roamed—the struggling scenes of real life as seen

By you, in other's paths will tell enough to prove
That nature's strongest inclinations bend before
A parent's power, nor cease ye then, but call to mind
Thine own first treasured thoughts, thy heart's deep yearning love
For those whom thou didst fondly call my Father, Mother,
As more than adoration chain'd thine earnest gaze,
And on thy young mind's faint aspiring, their power
Its first, its lasting impress made—think how each word,
Each look, was dwelt upon by thee and treasured as
A guide infallible!—then let thy reason ask
Can nature teach a child to hate, or doth it e'er
A power impart that could not be by love controll'd,
That with fair common sense combin'd, could not its little
Bark keep safe in truth's pure channel?—ask—grant it—never,
'Twould sink, below the beast, the only being here
In its Creator's image made.
Know thou wast formed with powers to love, instinctively,
And has thy heart's first, pure affection like the stream
That onward, gently flows, increasing still in deep and
Far extended power, as near its destined home it comes,
Kept onward still its happy course, as time hath seen
Thy parent's strength impaired and thine own greatness rise
To fill their place in life's career, it was their love,
Their wisdom, gained from Heaven that thus thy spirit
Swayed and firmly, gently led thee on to happiness.
Ah! thou dost owe them much and thou wilt reverence them,
And thine own offspring too, will catch the sacred flame
Of filial love and the rich offering God will bless—
And when thou seest the suffering child of woe,
The lost, fallen victim of degrading passions,
The weak, wretched outcast from fair virtue's circle,
And dost know a tender parent's guiding influence
Might have saved them from this state, a deeper glow
Of gratitude will warm thy swelling heart for all
That thou hast known of mercy from thy Maker's hand—
And though thou mayest each deed of darkness, justly,
Proudly scorn, yet will humanity assert its claim,
Their precious souls thou canst not love, a kindred tie

Thou canst not, wouldst not sever, will bid thee ever seek
Salvation for the lost, and in the ennobling task
Of guiding them to the fair path that leadeth unto life,
Find happiness, the haughty and cold hearted may not know.
——But hast thou learned to look with cold indifference
On those who called thee child, to disregard their judgment
And to admit the awful thought that their own errors
Thus have chilled thy spirit's tenderness, and deeply
On thy life entailed there withering wretchedness,[21]
Well mayest thou dread a contact with the heartless,
Trifling multitude,—thy mind undisciplined,
Trained not, with fortitude to meet the trials that
Fall thick on all the paths of life—taught not, to know
Thyself, unfit for aught that seems like peace or for
The right discharge of even one deep-binding duty—
Yes, well may shuddering seize thy frame and the dense
Darkness that obscures thy mental vision, assume,
If yet it may, a darker shade and all the works
Of fair Creation, seem but the sad reflection
Of thine own, distorted and degraded mind—
Yet, suffer not sweet hope to die, if God hath given thee
Grace to know thy weakness and to discern its cause,
Though deep must be thy spirit's struggle and though, through
Life, this power will be the snare spread for thy soul,
Yet may thy slumbering energies awake to duty,
And in its sweet performance, seem to gain
Full, sacred freedom from unholy influence.
Thus far thou mayest in truth be free, that thy weak heart
Alone may be the sad receptacle of all this strife.—
Responsible to Heaven thou art, thy delegated power
Was given that thou might'st train immortal spirits
For all of happiness that Earth can give and for
Eternal Rest in Heaven, and may no trust betrayed,
At Justice's solemn bar, exclude thee from thy God!
——Thus stands Parental Influence——
Such is its mighty power when from the Father's,

21. Here "entail" means to cut, to carve, to engrave; the physical damage of aging, malnutrition, oppression, etc., was often "entailed" on a character's face in antebellum American literature.

Mother's eye, is caught the same deep inspiration—
But might I trace another scene, it should be a Mother's
Power alone, to counteract all other strength of mind,
Though good or bad and round herself and on the mind
Of infant innocence, to breathe a spell that naught
But death can break, a charm that even a Father's
Well tried skill can ne'er dissolve—such surely must appear
The strength of mind that may be theirs to guide aright,
Though he, who should her wisdom be, her strength and next
To God her all, treads fast the course that leads to ruin's
Darkening brink and for her trust and deep devotion,
Gives, with each revolving hour, an added pang
To crush her too-confiding heart, yes, even then, it may be thus,
But ah! how dark the view when in the Mother, we can see
No traces of these sacred charms, when all her mind
Is bent to thwart the influence that should be obeyed,
But cannot, though a Father strive with all a Father's love,
To save from wretchedness, the minds entrusted to his care.
And does such power rest then with those whose very names
Bespeak what in their breasts should ever glow, that deep
Humility and fervent love that ever graces woman's life,
That sacred charm that truth can give, with all that elevates
Her mind to its own proper sphere, and does the absence
Of these pleasing traits, make her the wretch we've partly
Shadowed forth, then how should Mothers deeply feel
The debt they owe, how much should all reflect, each pause
And with intense anxiety, desire to do their
Maker's will!

"Alma."

"In the struggle of contending interests, though peace is sometimes lost, intellectual energy is roused; and while the strife of emulation, and the restlessness of ambition disturb the quiet of society, they produce in their collision the genius that adorns it."[22]

22. The quotation comes from the "preliminary dissertation" of the 1796 satiric novel, *Translation of the Letters of a Hindoo Rajah* by British writer Elizabeth ("Eliza") Hamilton (1756?–1816). See Hamilton, *Translation* . . . (London: G. G. and J. Robinson, 1796), 1:xxxv, Google Books, http://books.google.com/books?id=jAMwAAAAMAAJ. It was reprinted without attribution in *The Carcanet: A*

Random Thoughts.

Gentle Reader, do you love the soft moonlight, and the sweet breath of flowers, and the rich tones that are ever rising from the great "organ of nature?"[23] If so, I extend to you my hand from this my pleasant little room, and ask you to sit down with me near this open window, through which, is wafted the soft breath of spring; and as we inhale the fragrance of the sleeping flowers, let us spend an hour in conversing, as friends converse who have long been separated, and although we may not be permitted to look into each other's eyes and read the thoughts that slumber there, may not the mind commune with the mind though distance intervenes? And will it not be right pleasant to thee, to learn, that others have looked upon the same landscape, with thoughts similar to thine own? and as we wile away the hour our topics will resemble life: some times we shall be in the merry mood, and then we'll "laugh with those that laugh;"[24] and again sadness may be upon the soul, and will it not encourage thee to bear the ills of life less murmuringly, to learn that others "suffered and were strong?" But whether in joy, or sadness, gentle reader let us have thy sympathy.

Literary Album Containing Select Passages From the Most Distinguished English Writers (London: William Pickering, 1828), 28, Google Books, http://books.google.com/books?id=6RDQAAAAMAAJ. See n. 2, p. 76, for "Man is not an isolated creature." These quotes were arranged so as to fill the page and start the next item at the top of the next page. The fact that Cumings submitted two quotes for such use from the same book suggests that she may have owned the book. That said, this quote was also published without attribution in Park Benjamin's literary magazine *The New World*; see 5, no. 1 (July 2, 1842): 16, American Periodicals (137150849).

23. Here, "organ" means an instrument or means of communication (i.e., "nature is the organ of God"). For an essay on the "organ of nature," which might be the subject of this allusion, see J. G. Blair, "Voices of Nature." *The Ladies' Repository, and Gatherings of the West* 3 (June 1843), 176–77, Google Books, http://books.google.com/books?id=xxkAAAAAYAAJ. For more on *The Ladies' Repository*, see n. 14, above. "Rev. J. G. Blair, A. B. of the Wesleyan University," was Vice Principal and Teacher of Ancient and Modern Languages and Literature at the Blendon Young Men's Seminary near Worthington and Westerville, northeast of Columbus, Ohio. See "Blendon Seminary," *Ladies' Repository, and Gatherings of the West* 2, no. 7 (July 1842), 224, Google Books, http://books.google.com/books?id=qxkAAAAAYAAJ. The Methodist Episcopal Church sold Blendon to the Church of the United Brethren in Christ in 1846, and the buildings re-opened as Otterbein University in 1847. See James G. Burns, *The Educational History of Ohio* (Columbus: Historical Publishing, 1905), 345, Google Books, http://books.google.com/books?id=Ncy7AAAAIAAJ. For more on the antebellum history of Ohio's independent colleges and universities, see John William Oliver Jr. et al, eds., *Cradles of Conscience* (Kent: Kent State University Press, 2003).

24. "Laugh with those that laugh, and weep with those that weep" is an old proverb and translation of Romans 12:15.

Speaking of this word sympathy reminds me, that perhaps I have touched upon one of those subjects that will cause many to start back in alarm lest I should go off into one of those romantic strains, so much feared by the "sober minded," who have gone to the other extreme, and in seeking to avoid sickly sentimentality, they have

> "Laid a cold hand, upon the heart's
> Warm pulse, and crushed the feelings back,
> Which, uttered, form links in the chain of love,"[25]

and as much as they may say to the contrary, in the secret depths of the heart, they crave the sympathy they so much scorn to seek, and bitterly do they mourn its absence when no eye looks in upon their silence; "speak freely thy pure thought then, and kindred souls to thine shall answer;"[26] and perhaps thou wilt find that sympathy, is after all one of Heaven's richest gifts to man. Now do not suppose we mean that silly, romantic affection, that would lead us to weep over the imaginary ills of some love-sick damsel.—For we would not dignify this folly by the name of sympathy. We mean that high, and noble feeling that makes us feel another's wrongs, as though they were our own, in what ever station of life they may be situated, not confined to the sphere in which we move, but reaching its warm hand forth it grasps that of the sufferer wherever he may be found, that is ready not only to weep with those that mourn but will open his purse to relieve their necessities and if needs be they will sit by the sick pillow, and minister to the dying, cheering

25. Lines 2–4 of a sonnet, "Be Earnest!," by American abolitionist, temperance advocate, and editor William Henry Burleigh (1812–71). A printing of this poem, which did not appear in Burleigh's 1841 collection of abolitionist poetry, is Burleigh, "Sonnet." *Ladies' Wreath: A Magazine Devoted to Literature, Industry, and Religion* 1, no. 11 (March 1, 1847): 359, American Periodicals (90502873). The curious can find Burleigh's 1841 book as Burleigh, *Poems* (Philadelphia: J. Miller McKim, 1841), Google Books, http://books.google.com/books?id=NMg0AAAAMAAJ. Google Books and OCLC's WorldCat suggest the poem was most widely disseminated as an exercise in the oration of "word painting" in a very popular 1840s elocution textbook by Cotesworth Pinckney Bronson (1800–66), a New England-born friend of Edgar Allan Poe. Rev. Bronson led Norwalk Academy and ministered to St. Paul's Church in Norwalk, Ohio in the late 1820s; in the 1830s he was dismissed from the church for embezzling funds and worked for a year as an editor of the *Mount Vernon Gazette* (formerly the *Western Aurora*) of Mount Vernon, Ohio, a town about 40 miles northeast of Columbus and 70 miles southwest of Akron. After 1835 Bronson made his living giving lectures and publishing books on elocution, perhaps because he himself overcame some kind of speech impediment. For Burleigh's sonnet as a common school-book exercise in "word painting," see Bronson, *Elocution: Or, Mental and Vocal Philosophy: Involving the Principles of Reading and Speaking . . .* (Louisville: Morton and Griswold, 1845), 139, Google Books, http://books.google.com/books?id=9EiOUgPYlJoC. For more on Bronson, see Edgar Allan Poe Society of Baltimore, "Rev. Cotesworth P. Bronson," August 22, 2009, Edgar Allan Poe Society of Baltimore website, http://www.eapoe.org/people/bronsocp.htm.

26. Lines 12–13 of the same poem. See previous note.

their pathway to the tomb, by speaking to them words of hope and love, bidding the doubting one, to trust in a Saviour, whose sympathy extends to all. Yea, he took upon himself the form of man, entered the world and went about dispensing words of peace, and consolation, to all who sought his presence. Nor stopped he here. He healed the sick and afflicted everywhere, and even wept over the destruction of a city, who had scorned and rejected him and last of all, he laid down his life for his enemies, praying for them even as he expired and shall we blush, to follow in the footsteps of one so infinitely worthy? rather let us rejoice that we are counted worthy to possess the same feeling, and we do rejoice—You my reader and I too, because in the stillness of my chamber, I can feel thy heart beating in unison with mine, as I write to thee of the deep power of sympathy.

Power is something every heart craves, some in one thing and some in another. I recollect how strongly I felt its movings once: and I thought no greater happiness could be mine, than the power to sway the beechen sceptre, over the unruly members of my school. Well I was duly installed and with a due sense of my importance, I entered my dominions. But alas for my dignity, my future subjects were assembled, and mirthfulness had attained the empire and all my efforts to restore quiet were for the time being unavailing. It was my misfortune at that time, to be so diminutive, that even my pupils looked upon me as one of them. My frowns and threats, were alike unsuccessful for they all declared with one voice they would not obey one no older than myself. At last, I succeeded in obtaining order, by promising them a story, and a story I told them that so wrought upon their wills, that henceforth they were as gentle as I could wish, and often in after years I profited by that day's lesson, never to appear superior, where I wished to rule, as those fetters are the strongest which are least felt. But was not that a happy summer? how pleasant the memory of its hours even now, when time that trieth all things has spread over it a shadow that ever resteth there, yet there is much to remember with joy.

But the shadow, would you like to hear of that "and you shall." Alice was one of my pupils, that summer, and a "right goodlie"[27] one, she was a

27. "goodlie": beautiful, comely. The phrase "right goodlie" appears in old commentaries on Shakespeare but was probably been better known to American readers as a playful bit of fake old English popularized by a *Salmagundi* letter. Written by American authors Washington Irving (1783–1859), his brother William (1766–1821), and James Kirke Paulding (1778–1860), the satiric *Salmagundi* papers first appeared in 1807. To read more about high-society New York dandy "warriors" equipped "for the assault" with "silken hose of the gorgeous colour of the salmon" and "right goodlie morocco pumps decorated with clasps or buckles of a most cunning and secret contrivance" in an American edition more likely to be available to 1840s readers, see *Salmagundi: Or, the Whim-Whams and Opinions*

few months older than myself, she appeared more like a companion than otherwise and many were the pleasant walks we had as we wandered in search of "earth's fugitive poetry,"[28] as some author has so felicitously termed the flowers, and as we sometimes ventured into the deep recesses, of the woods and penetrated swamps, and even waded streams, in our enthusiastic love of the beautiful many a fearful tale of danger passed, could our torn dresses, and soiled shoes, have told, but they are silent, and tell no tale of our wild exploits, when no eye could see us save our own. "O those indeed were merry days, the merry days of old."[29] But the summer wore on, and a wandering artist came to our pleasant village; and many were the pretty sketches he presented to the wondering eyes, of the simple villagers, who could not comprehend how such beautiful objects could be thrown on paper with such truthfulness.

Alice saw him and she yielded her heart rich in its affection to his say, and he was in every way calculated to call forth the tender emotion and no wonder, that one so susceptible as Alice, should see the beauties that shone forth from his mind, enriched as it was by study, and travel, and she was worthy of his love and pleasant was it, to think of the bright future that lay before them and many were the hours we spent in talking of the time, when we should be separated. But those dreams were destined never to be realized. Arthur was called to the bedside of a dying parent, and as he bid adieu to Alice it seemed as if the "coming events cast their shadows before,"[30] for it seemed to us who saw them part that it was indeed the last parting. He left and the next news that was wafted to our ears spoke of

---

of Launcelot Langstaff, Esq. and Others (New York: Harper and Brothers, 1835), 2:179, Google Books, http://books.google.com/books?id=o9cgAAAAMAAJ.

28. "Fugitive" means escaping, fleeting, wandering; fugitive poems were short verses, perhaps written for an event, in haste, or in rare moments stolen from a sustained period of serious work. Antebellum poets could claim (of affect) humility by describing their verses as "fugitive." This suggested they were not so idle, fanciful, or vain as to consider themselves full-time poets writing verses for eternal fame. Even poets with no pretense to industry might present a short poem or "fragment" as "fugitive" to suggest that it was quickly composed during a fleeting paroxysm of Romantic inspiration—sure evidence of the poet's elevated sensibilities. In one of the poetical ramblings that make up Longfellow's 1839 romance, *Hyperion*, the narrator remarks, "I wish I knew the man, who called flowers 'the fugitive poetry of Nature,' " before imagining himself "stretching forth his hand" to shake this man's hand. See Longfellow, *Hyperion* (New York: Samuel Colman, 1839), 2:118, Google Books, http://books.google.com/books?id=PP1LAAAAcAAJ.

29. Chorus of a popular song, "The Merry Days of Old." For one text of the lyrics (here titled "The Happy Days of Old") see *The British Minstrel; A Choice Collection of Modern Songs* (London: T. Allman, 1848), 77–78, Google Books, http://books.google.com/books?id=jUEEAAAAQAAJ. Sheet music can be found as "The Merry Days of Old." Levy Sheet Music Collection, JScholarship, Johns Hopkins Libraries, https://jscholarship.library.jhu.edu/handle/1774.2/19993.

30. Popular proverb.

the death of Arthur. Yes he had died in the full bloom of manhood, when life looked most lovely to him; just as he was about to realize his fondest dreams, he was overtaken by the fell destroyer, and with him perished the hopes of one who loved too well. And from that hour she wasted away as the *snow-wreath* wastes before the April sun, and when the early flowers bloomed, we laid her in the narrow house and her pure spirit sought its kindred, in the realms above, and this is the shadow that rests upon that otherwise happy summer. Thus it ever is in life the sunshine and the shadow rests on every landscape, and wise are they who learn not to trust too much to earthly subjects for happiness.

But sadness is upon my soul, and I can write no more; let us hope that another time we will have a merrier mood, not that I despise the sober thought but it is not always well to look "mournfully upon the past."[31]

Lizzie.

Lines for the Ladies' Offering.

All my life my brightest pleasures
I have found in things unreal;
Loving dreams and ever mingling
Truth with shadowy ideal.

Dreaming still, as rapt as ever—
Wandering thought will oft-times find
One sweet memory naught can sever
From its hold upon my mind.

Often at the hour of twilight,
As I've sat and mused alone,
Has that memory round my spirit,
Spells of olden feeling thrown.

31. The injunction to "look not mournfully upon the past" was also popularized by Longfellow in *Hyperion*. See n. 28, above. *Hyperion* 2:111, Google Books, http://books.google.com/books?id=PP1LAAAAcAAJ.

Cherished thought and dream-like pleasure,
Shadowed by a vague regret,
At that hour o'er me stealing,
Twine around that memory yet.

'Tis of a dream of early childhood,
Cherished by my young heart, when
Of all light things 'twas proved the lightest,
Years have passed away since then.

And slowly, gently with them faded
Light that gilded life's young stream,
Till much of thought and sorrow shaded
The last ray from that early dream.

Though 'twas a dream that never perished,
But only fled when others came,
Though others were as wildly cherished
Yet never were they loved the same.

Still I derive my brightest pleasures
As of old from things unreal,
Still in dreams I love to wander
In a world that's half ideal.

Yet my dreams have lost their brightness,
Which they knew in earlier years,
And my heart has lost its lightness,
From the weight of unshed tears.

Maria.

"One Sunny Spot"[32]

The remark is often made "how cold this world,"[33] how uncongenial the heart, how chilling every breath that o'er us blows! Ah! my friend lay aside that sombre face, for I have found "one sunny spot," one spot where "righteousness and peace have kissed each other;"[34] one spot upon which angels gaze with delight. Come, I will show it to you. Start not should I lead you to a poor man's cot, for the poor are God's favorites, and "with the lowly is wisdom."[35] In humility's vale is its site, and you must tread softly for it's "holy ground." As we approach, see nature's beauties smiling all around; the blossoms rich and rare seem to point the inmates of the cot to a land of never-fading flowers. The exterior tells so strongly of happiness we will enter. In a neatly furnished room sits the family. The father and husband left his family in the morning beneath "the shadow of the Almighty's wing."[36] He knew that the name of the Lord was a strong tower and within its walls he safely trusted his wife and children. 'Tis night now; and he is reading to his family from a book so rich in wisdom that the profoundest mind can never fathom it, and yet so simple "that the way-faring man,

32. The use of "gratuitous quotation marks" may indicate an inexperienced author or compositor, or they may serve to make the title an allusion. All quotes were searched, and most were quotations or paraphrases of bible verses. So quotes within this essay that are not glossed—such as "make all her bed for her"—may be allusions to bible verses that are too inaccurately quoted to identify with confidence. The "sunny spot" was a cliché of antebellum American magazine writing, nurtured by a common love of botany, gardening, and farming metaphors. One early popularizer of the cliché is the poem, "Life's Sunny Spots," which was often republished in American literary magazines. An early version, in which the poem is presented as original work, is "Lara," "Sunny Spots." *The New-York Mirror, and Ladies' Literary Gazette* 4, no. 33 (March 10, 1827): 264, American Periodicals (136136860). By the end of the next year the poem was circulating as the work of American journalist William Leggett (1801–39). See William Leggett, "Life's Sunny Spots." *The Critic: A Weekly Review of Literature, Fine Arts, and the Drama* 1, no. 7 (December 13, 1828): 105, American Periodicals (124909954). Leggett was a literary critic for the *Mirror* in 1827; it is not clear why the editors wished to conceal his authorship of "Life's Sunny Spots." Perhaps it was mistakenly attributed to "Lara," whose other poems appear on the same page, or perhaps "Lara" was a fiction designed to conceal the amount of content contributed by the male editors for that Ladies' magazine.

33. The search engines suggest the exact phrase, "how cold this world," was not as clichéd as the author suggests. One example which illustrates the common sentiment is the anonymous poem, "Lines," which include: "I would not live! / My too proud heart / Hath felt how cold this world could be— / Unloose, oh God! the silver chord! / I come! I come! oh grave to thee!" See *Southern Literary Journal* 4, no. 6 (December 1838): 429. American Periodicals (126337007).

34. Psalms 85:10. The first of many quotations from the Bible in this essay. There was no definitive text of the Testaments in antebellum America, there being a great number of common editions. In this essay, many quotations may be approximate, or drawn from an imperfect memory. For more on the variety of Bibles in the 1840s see Paul J. Gutjahr, *An American Bible: A History of the Good Book in the United States* (Stanford: Stanford University Press, 1999).

35. Proverbs 11:2.

36. Psalm 91:1–4.

though a fool can not err therein."[37] The book, my friends is the Bible. He loves to "search the Scriptures, for in them he thinks he has eternal life."[38] He is poor, but still he is happy for the "Lord directeth all his steps."[39]

By his side sits his wife, the partner of his joys or his sorrows, "his heart doth safely trust in her for he hath found the virtuous woman, and her price is far above rubies."[40] The gloom which gathers upon his brow through the day is quickly dispelled by the brightness of her smile. His eyes are the only ones, she ever wished to charm, and upon him she pours the wealth of woman's trusting heart. She clothes herself not with the "outward adorning of gold and costly apparel,"[41] but with the ornament of a meek and quiet spirit. She feels that home is woman's province and she can make any sacrifice, to lighten her husband's cares, and strew his pathway with flowers. "Her children rise up, and call her blessed, for she eateth not the bread of idleness and in her tongue is the law of kindness."[42] Three or four daughters and a son complete the little circle; some of them have approached blushing womanhood; their mother has trained them in the "way they should go;"[43] they are discreet, chaste, sober, and keepers at home. They are fair as the lily and bright as the rose, but the mother taught them that "beauty was vain" and they have adorned the "inner man" with pearls of wisdom.[44] Love is a plant they cultivate, sympathy a flower they cherish, smiles they wear on their lip, kindness dwelleth on the tongue, affection beameth in the eye, and peace sitteth on the brow. When they see the daughters of the rich floating in wealth or rolling in splendor they murmur not, they remember the being who was infinitely better than they are and had not where to "lay his head;" they have learned to be content with such things as they have. How pure the fountain of feeling which gushes in their hearts; is one sorrowful, O how the others hasten to drive away the gloom; is one sick, O how each hastens to soothe the sufferer; with a gentle step they approach the sister's bed, with a soft hand they smooth the sister's pillow; should the illness be protracted, their spirits never tire; and although the flesh may faint, they never think of rest while a sister moans. O how they'll watch and pray. The mother bends o'er her daughter in anguish of spirit, and prays God to "make all her bed

37. Isaiah 35:8.

38. John 5:39.

39. Proverbs 16:9.

40. Proverbs 31:10–11.

41. 1 Peter 3:3.

42. Proverbs 31:26–28.

43. Proverbs 22:6.

44. Proverbs 31:30; Ephesians 3:16.

for her." She is sorrowful, yet rejoicing for an omnipotent hand hath done it. And should the monarch of the grave, take from their hand the youngest, the sweetest, and the fairest sister and daughter, they still are happy, for "faith smiles through affection's tears"[45] and sweetly whispers meet again. Although the heart groans, and affection bleeds, they smile and say

"'Tis God that lifts our comforts high
And sinks them to the grave,
He gave and blessed be his name
He took but what he gave."[46]

Think you, my friend, the world is cold, when spots like this bloom on every side? I fancy you smile, and wonder where, the happiness is, I'll tell you. "It hath its seat and centre in the breast."[47] The wealth of their feelings lies fathoms below the surface. I told you, love they cultivated, and that is a feeling so gentle, so soft and so still, that it bringeth pure enjoyment. If you complain of a cold world, I shall think the icy heart is within thine own breast. Are you a father and husband and still seek a sunny spot? Go to your unhappy home (if such it be) rear the altar of prayer sway the sceptre of love o'er your household and see what affection will do. Are you a mother and wife and complain of coldness? Lady! does God lead you by the right hand? Have you sought first the kingdom of Heaven? What if the "partner of thy life" is unkind, "be thou, kindly affectionate" towards him, let your "love be without dissimulation," "love worketh no ill" and if thou art gentle and kind, his heart will melt before thy goodness, and then thy peace will "be like the river," with joy thou wilt say the "sunny spot," I've found—But I hear the sister and daughter say, where shall I find rest.[48] I'll tell thee. "Trust in the Lord with all thine heart," "in all thy ways acknowledge him and he shall direct thy steps." Be of a "meek and contrite spirit,"

45. Another quote that appears not to be a specific allusion but perhaps an original paraphrase of an antebellum cliché. One example, "Natural affection claims its tears, but faith will smile through them all, and pour its cheering light into the darkness of the grave," can be found in A. J. Prime, "Eunice Marston." *The Columbian Magazine* (July 1848): 297, Google Books, http://books.google.com/books?id=11RMAAAAMAAJ.

46. Lines from a hymn by Isaac Watts (1674–1748) printed as useful for encouraging "Submission to Afflictive Providence." See, for example, Samuel M. Worcester, *Psalms, Hymns, and Spiritual Songs of the Rev. Isaac Watts* (Boston: Crocker & Brewster, 1840), 293–94, Google Books, http://books.google.com/books?id=XuweAAAAYAAJ.

47. Paraphrase of "If happiness hae not her seat / And centre in the breast, / We may be wise, or rich, or great, / But never can be blest," from "Epistle to Davie, a Brother Poet" by Scottish poet Robert Burns (1759–96). See Burns, *The Complete Poetical Works*, ed. James Currie (New York: Appleton and Company, 1844), 167, Google Books, http://books.google.com/books?id=nZkoAAAAMAAJ.

48. Romans 12:10; Romans 12:9; Romans 13:10; Isaiah 46:12.

learn humility, love wisdom and in all thy "gettings get understanding."[49] Cheer your home by your smiles and your kindness; smooth your mother's pathway to the grave. How tenderly she watched you in your infancy, in your childhood; how carefully she guarded you and kept you from evil. Your father, perhaps his locks are already bleached for the winding sheet and his brow furrowed for the grave, have you no words of kindness to cheer his fainting heart? I beg of you to bring sunshine into your own heart and your parents' by your acts of love. Have you no little sister or brother to teach the way to heaven? she may be never so fair, health may bloom on her cheek, intelligence sparkle in her eye; yet death says

"Can I have naught that is fair,
Naught but the bearded grain?"[50]

and the grave says, must I make friends with the old and withered? no, your blooming sister I'll have. Love her then while you may. Do good to all, have the love of God in your heart, seek his smile, and the wilderness would be a paradise and the desert bloom like the garden of the Lord.

"Anna."

For the Offering.

To Mr. and Mrs. N. H. Barker.[51]

On the death of their Daughter—
an interesting child of six summers.

By Mrs. Philomel S. Weed.[52]

A wail of grief has reached mine ear, of bitter helpless woe,
Poured from a crushed and bleeding heart, with agonizing throe,

49. Proverbs 3:5; Proverbs 3:6; 1 Peter 3:4; Proverbs 4:7.

50. Lines from Longfellow, "The Reaper and the Flowers." See *Voices of the Night* (Boston: Redding & Co., 1845), 9, Google Books, http://books.google.com/books?id=UR4CAAAAYAAJ.

51. A search of the 1840 and 1850 United States Federal Census for Ohio through Ancestry.com reveals no obvious or even good match for an "N. H. Barker" and wife. There were "Bakers" in Stark County but no "N. Baker" and wife. The early censuses are not always accurate and reliable, but with all the migration into and out of Ohio in the 1840s, it is also to be expected that many Ohio residents did not stay long enough to be recorded in a decennial census.

52. Philomelia Sophia Scobey Weed (1827–97). The 1850 United States Federal Census records her in Canaan, Wayne County, Ohio as "Philemale" Weed, a twenty-three-year-old from New Hampshire

A bud torn from the parent stem—transplanted to a sphere
Where never enter mortal pain, nor sin, nor grief, nor tear;
The gracious Shepherd came and took into his saving fold,
To deck fore'er with shining gems, of value all untold,
The parents' idol. From their hearts He tore the idol down,
He would not have the place usurped, sworn to himself
and crown;
Two lovely children had they seen smote by the spoiler's power,
Again Death came and took the third, far from the
household bower,
The household band is riven indeed. It is the Mother's wail
Which pierces to my listening ear from every passing gale;
The absent Father little knows what desolation deep
Has swept across his happy hearth, within one little week;
He little thinks his cherished one, is sleeping 'neath the sod,
And her pure spirit winged its way unto the throne of God;
His heart is pining for his home, its bright and cheering scenes,
And he pictures a bright future, fair as the "land of dreams;"
He thinks him of the welcome, that is waiting his return,
Will not his very heart-strings break,—will not his spirit mourn
When he hears the tidings sad, yet true, that his Dove
has left its nest

---

with an unemployed husband, Phineas, and two-year-old daughter, Florence. United States of America, Bureau of the Census, *Seventh Census of the United States, 1850*. NARA microfilm publication M432. (Washington, D.C.: National Archives and Records Administration, n.d.), roll M432_740, page 386B, Ancestry.com. The 1860 United States Federal Census records her as Philomel S. Weed, residing about eight miles south of Canaan in Wooster, Ohio. This part of Wayne County is about twenty-five miles southwest of Akron. In 1860 the Weeds operated a livery stable worth $12,300, a large sum for this time and place. The Weed household included several children, two Scobey family relatives, a servant, and a hired hand. United States of America, Bureau of the Census, *Eighth Census of the United States, 1860*. NARA microfilm publication M653. (Washington, D.C.: National Archives and Records Administration, n.d.), roll M653_1050, page 132, Ancestry.com. In 1847, Weed contributed several items to *The Amaranth: A Semi-Monthly Publication, Devoted to Polite Literature, Science, Poetry and Amusement*, a magazine published in Ashland, Ohio. See "Rena di Albuli—A Tale," *Amaranth* 1, no. 3 (March 20, 1847): 10–11, American Periodicals (124838869) and two poems, each signed from "Jackson, Ohio": "The Heart-Broken," *Amaranth* 1, no. 4 (April 3, 1847): 13, American Periodicals (124845134) and "A Welcome to the Amaranth," *Amaranth* 1, no. 5 (April 17, 1847): 18, American Periodicals (124843367). The Weeds later followed Philomel's father, Dr. John Scobey, to Iowa, where she died. Florence Ida Weed grew up to be the mother of Lou Henry Hoover (1874–1944), First Lady of the United States from 1929 to 1933. For more on Lou Henry and her Iowa childhood with grandmother Philomel, see Anne Beiser Allen, *An Independent Woman: The Life of Lou Henry Hoover* (Westport, CT: Greenwood, 2000).

To seek a more congenial one, in the regions of the blest?
The Mother bears her grief alone—her heart is desolate—
And she sits from morning until night, and ponders o'er her fate,
Reft of her child, her darling one, the present seems a void
Of loneliness and heaviness—her hopes are all destroyed.
Yet is there balm in Gilead. Ye stricken ones, look up!
For He, the high and holy One, who makes you drink this cup,
Can heal the wounds his hand inflicts on those he loves so well,
And bring you peace, and hope, and joy, such as no tongue
can tell,
Then let your trust remain in Him—your faith be ever sure,
He will through Time's short range, and through
Eternity, endure.

Jackson, May 5, 1849.[53]

Reader, the Offering is now before you—you understood what was intended to be accomplished, and you can now see as much of the result of the efforts made, as perhaps could reasonably be expected in the first number, arranged, as many of you are aware, in a short space of time and under circumstances that some would urge as an excuse to satisfy any one who was not pleased, but we have no excuse to make, we have done the best we could and thus we shall ever do.

The different articles in this number were written especially for this work, and their being original, in our estimation, is worthy of consideration, even though in some instances, selections might have been made, that would have evinced greater power of thought and more talent in pre-

53. Many places in Ohio were named to celebrate Andrew Jackson (1767–1845), military hero and seventh president of the United States. Daniel Haskel and J. Calvin Smith's *Complete Descriptive and Statistical Gazetteer of the United States of America* (New York: Sherman and Smith, 1848), Google Books, http://books.google.com/books?id=UOstAAAAYAAJ, lists twenty-eight towns in Ohio named "Jackson." Thomas Baldwin and J. Thomas's *Gazetteer of the United States* (Philadelphia: Lippincott, Grambo, 1854), Google Books, http://books.google.com/books?id=_5s6AAAAcAAJ, lists thirty-seven. Jackson was popular in Ohio in part for his Indian Removal policies, which forcibly relocated Native Americans to areas west of the Mississippi River. For more on Native Americans relocated from Ohio, see Randall L. Buchman, *A Sorrowful Journey* (Defiance, OH: Defiance College Press, 2007). Philomel and Phin met and married in Stark County, so this could be the Jackson in Stark County, then a town of about 1,500, fifteen miles south of Akron. More likely it is the Jackson of adjacent Wayne County. In the 1840s this was a village of a few hundred people north of Wooster, on the road to Cleveland (now Ohio State Road 3), not far from Canaan (see the preceding note). See Baldwin and Thomas, 534, 858.

senting ideas to the dissecting knife of public criticism, but we are not to cull from other works more than is necessary. We feel grateful to every one who has felt interest enough in this undertaking to devote a little time to prepare something for these pages.

Lizzie has told us something about the power of sympathy and we can not conceive how any person uninterested in a work made up of articles written by friends and acquaintances and persons residing within a few miles of each other—perhaps we have wrong ideas, but this magazine seems to us, like a strong bond of friendly trust, a sympathetic chain, binding the hearts of all, for the reason that it is just the simple thing it is, a medium of communication among ourselves, a sort of repository of thoughts and feelings to be cherished as a gift of affection and gazed upon in future years as a memento of the past. Each article will speak for itself and we hope all who have written for this number, will continue to send us something; and that many who have not yet written, will, for the future numbers.

The article by "Beta," you will all perceive deserves the particular notice of both readers and writers of this work.[54] Sure we are that you will all feel grateful for his effort in your "behalf," and as many of you as have a share of the "courage" he speaks of, and a similar sense of "undiscovered reserves of mental power," we hope, will, like him, be able duly to appreciate the "marvelously felicitous calling out" the Offering presents, and, quickened by the inspiration thus breathed upon you, be indeed resolved to "Try, try again." Surely you will now "enter the lists" like soldiers, having on all your armor, the fire of your "genius so fully aroused" that you will feel strong to bear a knap-sack loaded with good things to be added to the general stock as rations for those on duty. "Beta" supposes that we are all to be fed from a "capacious tureen," and the comparison may be correct, only it is not so very "capacious" after all, but it will be full, and the succotash—is it not delightful? What, if some of its ingredients are insipid and to us seem not calculated to nourish our peculiarly delicate natures? What if we can not muster benevolence enough to tolerate them? We'll appeal to justice—if we have a proper regard for our own rights we shall learn to respect the rights of others, and while they are selecting their own peculiar morsel, we shall quietly eat ours, and be thankful.

---

54. The quotes in Cumings' closing comments engage the editorial by the unknown "member of the fraternity," "Beta." See p. 45.

Seriously now, we hope we shall all profit by his remarks on subjects to be written and the manner of treating them, &c.[55] It is only a just rebuke of a silly style of writing far too common in our little world. We'll not forget the deep ridicule and cutting sarcasm that speaks in all he says of sentimental mockery shown in the "spasms" that never yet were indicative of genuine feeling, but yet we could find pleasure in being destroyed, even, with such highly polished weapons as he uses, and we may perhaps, sometimes offend, from the very love of their gleaming brightness, and we shall be vain enough no doubt, to dignify our hearts' exquisite ecstacy with the sweet title of "love of the beautiful," and when we are annihilated we shall be called martyrs for the good of natures more obtuse—but we must not linger now.

Our friend wishes to know "what award" we expect for many things, some of them inseparable from our position, and some we think, not necessarily attendant. On this subject, we would fain[56] be silent, but will briefly say we neither expect nor desire "thanks or compliments," but we simply wish that our efforts may be met in the spirit in which they are made—we certainly do, in some sense wish the confidence of all, and we shall seek to deserve it, but without strength derived from a higher source than our own weakness or the confiding sympathy of friends, we should not have even a faint hope of being able to please any one. What "Beta" has said regarding the feelings of writers as to the disposition of their articles in the Offering, needs no comment, all will understand and profit by it. We are believers in the "false philosophy" he speaks of, and yet we have somewhat departed from its precepts in noticing his remarks; but, setting aside all trifling, we are grateful for the effort he has made to impart instruction to us and to all, and hope he will continue to consider it not beneath his dignity to be a constant contributor to these humble pages, and if he is by any misunderstood or not fully appreciated, he can have a share of the same consolation he supposes will be our portion, viz.: the thought that self is sacrificed for the good of the "rising generation."

C. Cumings.

55. "&c.": et cetera; Latin for "and so forth." The ampersand symbol (&) combines the letters "e" and "t." "Et" is Latin for "and." "c." is an abbreviation for the Latin "cetera."

56. Fain: gladly.

THE AKRON OFFERING.
June, 1849.

Norman and Cornelia Campbell,
OR
"Truth Stranger Than Fiction."

By C. Cumings.

Chapter II.

Cornelia Campbell's paternal grandfather was a native of Scotland—his parents were among the noblest of the land, and possessed of much wealth until he was seventeen years of age—then, reverses, not necessary here to detail, came upon them, and they were obliged to retire to comparative poverty and obscurity.—George, the son above mentioned, was their eldest, and had been raised amid all the appliances of luxury, and knew nothing of the necessity of attending to business; but, notwithstanding all this, he had an ardent, enterprising disposition, that needed but the stimulus that poverty gives, to enable him to show himself a man of sound sense, and practical business talent. He had heard of the success of some of his countrymen in the American colonies, which then belonged to England, and he longed to try his skill among those who depended on themselves for fortune and for fame. His parents were unwilling to part with him, but his energies were roused and he must have a wider field of action than there presented itself.

"Mother," he said, "of what use is the noble blood that you say courses through my veins? It does not make me really noble, and, under the influence of the feelings entertained, in the circle in which you move, the powers given me by nature, will be paralized by indolence, and I shall be but a cipher in the world, a poor miserable simpleton, striving to believe that because I can trace my lineage to some royal villain, I should be content, nor dare to think, or act, lest the sacred drops should lose their virtue, and I should be brought to a level with the despised Plebeian. Common sense bids me disregard all these unworthy distinctions; and the time will come, Mother, when merit will find its proper position—look at America—a vision seems passing before me that tells of strange events; the consequences of which, will be glorious indeed!"

Wearied at last, by his importunities, his parents consented to his wishes—his mother had a small fortune in her own right, and from this he was furnished with every thing necessary for his voyage. His passage to New York was secured in a vessel owned by a friend of his Father, who was coming out himself, and would be a friend to him when he arrived at his destined port. His Mother wished to bestow upon him a few hundred pounds, all that could be spared from the *imagined* necessities of the family; but he would not take it.

"No! Mother, no!" said he, "I have enough to carry me across the ocean, and then I shall have my liberty, and my spirit is already disenthralled—I shall be successful and I hope to meet you again."

Here they parted; he had a safe passage to America, and through the influence of his Father's friend, obtained a situation as clerk to one of New York's most prosperous and honorable Merchants—he applied himself to his business with such zeal and determination, that he soon understood it thoroughly; and his employer felt that his services were almost invaluable—he had been with Mr. W. about five years, when he was admitted as partner in his business; and soon after, he received the hand of his only daughter in marriage. When the Revolutionary war commenced, they had been several years, living in the greatest harmony, and George Campbell felt that to leave his happy family would be a trial indeed; but, his sense of justice would not let him slumber on a post of ease and see right trampled upon, and Liberty forever crushed—he knew that his parents would have favored Royalty and all its prerogatives; but, they were now in their graves—an epidemic had swept away all his Father's family—he felt that his country was now emphatically his home; and buckling on his armor, he went forth with his aged Father-in-Law, in whose soul the fire of patriotism burned with a generous, steady glow, to do battle for its wrongs. Posts of honor and trust were assigned to both, and both were distinguished as officers of great bravery and humanity. A volume might be written of their sayings and doings, and of the events that befel them during the war; but we are only slightly sketching them for the pleasure of those who might be curious as to the ancestry of the particular personages in this history; suffice it then, to say that they discharged every duty. A few months before the close of the war old Mr. W. was mortally wounded—he sent for his Son-in-Law, bestowed upon him his fortune and his blessing; breathed a prayer for his suffering Country, commended his own soul to the God who gave it, and calmly passed into the "Spirit Land."

Of what occurred to Col. Campbell, (as George was called after the war,) we will take no note; but pass along in imagination, until the commencement of the last year of the eighteenth Century, when we will again introduce him to the reader—now an old man—a widower—possessed of a princely fortune, and blessed with the care and affection of two sons, George and Albert. The Mercantile business was still carried on, under the firm of "Campbell & Benton." George Campbell, Jr., was at this time thirty years of age, and had been nine years a partner with his Father and Henry Benton. When he was twenty-two years of age, he was married to a lovely girl, on whom he lavished the most devoted affection for one short year, and then he saw her laid in her last, sad resting place. This was a cutting blow to one possessed of his strong feelings; but he soon rallied from despondency, and in the pressure of business, so far forgot his sorrow as to be able to appear composed—he had an enterprising disposition, aided by a constitution capable of great endurance—he was possessed of quick discernment and practical capacity for the business his Father had found so profitable; yet was there one weak point in his character; he loved the excitement of the wine cup; the usages of the times sanctioned it, and his social qualities rendered him peculiarly liable to be led to excess, but no one dreamed of danger for the generous, high-minded fellow, who was a pattern of prompt exactness and diligence in all matters of business, and of zeal in every joyous or generous enterprise; yet, was this weakness slowly, but surely, gaining strength for his final destruction.

Albert Campbell was two years younger than his brother, and like him, had a firm constitution; but his taste was more refined; his intellectual gifts of a higher order; his moral perceptions giving him clearer views of man's relative duties, and every feeling of his noble nature, fitting him to fill the most exalted station with becoming dignity and usefulness. He seemed formed to control, (not by any assumption of authority) but by the power of sympathy, that all felt who approached him, the influence of a mighty mind, seen in every look, and heard in every tone, calculated to gain the willing reverence of all—all prophesied for him a glorious career of honor and happiness. He and his brother had had every advantage they wished, to assist them to gain a thorough education. George could not patiently pore over the classic page; could not brook the confinement necessary to carry him through the course required for a finished scholar; but Albert could discipline himself to any course he chose, and was prepared at an early age to select his profession, and enter on its prescribed course of study. At twenty-three, he was admitted to practice Law at the Bar of his native State; and every one noted the young Attorney for his manly beauty and commanding eloquence. Col. C. was proud of both his children. George had pleased him by his qualifications for the mercantile business; and as he looked on the shining path, apparently marked out for his youngest son, he felt that he was indeed blessed. Albert had early loved the beautiful and good Elizabeth Benton, Sister of his Father's and Brother's partner. For several years she had been an orphan, and had resided with her brother, who was so much her senior, that he seemed like a Father; and faithfully did he discharge his duty to his darling Sister. Albert Campbell did not sue in vain, when he asked him to consent to their union. They were married amid the congratulations of all who looked on their striking beauty, and knew their exalted worth. Neither his Father or Brother would consent to his living in a separate establishment, and they took up their abode with them. At the period mentioned as the last year of the eighteenth Century, Albert had been five or six years married, and was blessed with two children, Norman, four years of age, and Cornelia, two years. That these children should be lovely can well be imagined; but we will not attempt to describe the deep fervor of the love that filled their parents' hearts for them, the precious gifts of Heaven. They were happy, too happy! Alas, for the hopes of man! a dark, dark cloud was resting o'er their heads, and waited but a little farther concentration of its fury, to burst with terrible destruction on the unconscious victims of its wrath.

Henry Benton came from England with his parents when he was a child—they were in easy circumstances, although not independent; and he was, when very young, in the employ of Col. C.'s Father in-law, and subsequently, the Col.'s only partner, until his son, George, was of sufficient age to join them. He was ten years George's senior—he had been faithful as a clerk, and honest as a partner; but he was so utterly wretched in his domestic relations, that he had gradually become gloomy, and by some, was considered negligent in his business—his health was failing; and it was whispered by some who had known his lineage, that there was in him a predisposition to insanity, and that he would be its victim, unless the painful excitement that had so long oppressed him was removed; and what was the cause of all this? When he was thirty years of age, he married a young lady of whom he knew but little, except that she was beautiful—he deemed her good and gentle; but he found that her temper would forever mar his peace, and her extravagant folly, must eventually reduce them to beggary. He was too honorable to expose her faults, or reproach her for her heartless selfishness and cruelty; and matters had been made worse, by his receiving her Father into his house, whom he soon found was an unprincipled villain in every sense of the word; but he was poor and crippled for life—he could not turn him away. In every possible way he strove to counteract his influence over the mind of his son, William, at this time seven years of age; but all his efforts were vain—he met only contempt and disrespect; and as he looked at the past, the present and the future, his hopes of happiness were crushed forever; his reason tottered on its throne, and it needed only a few more shocks to prostrate it forever. George Campbell pitied Benton for his evident wretchedness, but, he had no idea of its real cause; he deemed it produced by ill health and an inherent melancholy; but he felt that it was incapacitating him for business, and that their affairs must be arranged with a view of dissolving partnership.

About this time, one of their vessels that had been out to sea but a few days, returned, reporting that the money and cargo entrusted to their care, had been taken from them by pirates, who overpowered them by numbers; but as soon as every thing worth having was secured, left them unharmed—this was a loss they felt, and yet, could bear, but it rendered a settlement still more necessary.

Col. C. had, several years before this time, presented each of his sons with a deed of a large tract of wild land, lying on the Connecticut River, in what was at the time, known as the "New Hampshire grants." With a prudence, characteristic of himself, he advised them never to sell this, or in any way invest its value in their business—"keep it as a reserve in case of adversity," said he, "and then you can have a home even if all else is gone." The same principle governed him when he taught them and Benton also, to lay aside something from all their gains that should not be risked, an equal amount, in proportion to ownership, that was their own, individually. He was no niggard, neither were they; they gave liberally to the needy; but, this was for their own hour of adversity, should *it come*. Benton's money thus saved, had all been spent by his wife and her profligate Father.

About three months after the robbery of the vessel before mentioned, Mrs. Benton's Father received a visit from a person calling himself Friedland, who, he said, was an old acquaintance from England who brought letters and a large package from a rich relative lately deceased, the letters purporting to have been written while he was on his death bed, and gave to him, in trust for Wm. Benton, a large amount of money which he had entrusted to their mutual friend, the bearer, desiring him to invest this money in wild land where he, (Wm.'s Grandfather,) should think it promised to become of great value. The old man read this in Mr. Benton's presence, but apparently, took no notice of the strange look of suspicion that for a moment, appeared in his countenance, nor of the almost savage determination that the next instant lighted it, giving place to a look of the keenest suffering, the deepest despair—yet he fully noted it all and swore a yet deeper revenge. Benton's mind was weakened by sickness and suffering, or he would have followed up an investigation of the circumstances connected with the fortune so strangely willed to his child. He believed the whole story false; but he had not the power to act energetically, and thus, time passed on. The old man, in company with Friedland, left the city on horseback, to explore the country, which was then, much of it a wilderness—they proceeded until they found a place which their sagacity told them would eventually be a mine of wealth; and then the old man took the necessary steps to secure five hundred acres to his Grandson, Wm. Benton. When this was accomplished, he said to Friedland:

"Would you like another job, for pay as good as you have received for the last?"

"Yes," said he, "but what are you up to now? The Campbells and your darling Son-in-law are not about to send out another vessel loaded with money, are they? I should think they would be a little short just now."

"They are," said his companion; "but not enough to destroy them; they are expecting a vessel to return in a few weeks, that has been long out, and will, it is supposed, be a rich prize. That must be attended to when it comes near; but what I want of you now, is, to abstract a couple of bags of gold from a chest in the cellar of their store; the money their cunning old Father has taught them to keep so nicely—I'll find a way to humble their pride and thwart their plans; say, will you go and leave me here?"

They were then at a deserted cabin.

"Yes, I'll go sometime, but why in such a hurry?"

But, meeting the frowning brow of one whom he had long been accustomed to obey, he said:

"I will go."

"Well then," the old man said, "here are three keys; one to unlock the outside door, another the door to the cellar, and the last, to open the chest. One of the bags of gold you are to place in Henry Benton's desk, in his private chamber, and cover it up as if for concealment, and lock the desk again; the other bag is yours—now start and be expeditious, and I will stay here until you return—I have every thing necessary to live on until you get back; and so near that I can reach it, is a good spring of water."

It was night when Friedland left—he reached the city and accomplished his task in the allotted time; but all his proceedings in Mr. Benton's room were observed by Francis Lisbon, a fellow whom Mr. B. had rescued from the deepest poverty, and prompted by his benevolence, had *tried* to instruct him how to take care of himself. Francis loved his master, but still he was idle and ignorant. On the night in which Friedland visited his master's room, he had just entered it, to ascertain if he had returned, as he felt anxious about his failing health and strange appearance—hearing a stealthy step on the stair, he stepped into a closet, saw all and comprehended all, but, so much did he fear, that he suffered the villain to depart and said nothing of it all; selfish cowardice governed him and he resolved to let things take their course. Not long after this robbery and while it was undiscovered, they received intelligence of the loss of the vessel they had for some time expected, and also of the failure of a mercantile house largely indebted to them. To Benton's disordered mind, this seemed the last link in the chain of destiny, forged for his final destruction; and even Mr. Campbell, for a moment, quailed, but reflection roused all his energy. His Father was aged and very feeble, languishing on a bed of sickness, from which he had no hope he would ever rise—Benton was worse than sick, and his Brother's time was so fully occupied in the duties of his profession, that he would not, (had not his interest been also involved) have been willing to call on him for assistance in investigating and settling their affairs; but Albert dismissed every other subject, and bent all his energies to obtain a full understanding of their real situation; he soon ascertained that all their possessions must pass away from them, except their Father's gift in land, and what they had saved by his advice, for the dark hour that had so strangely come upon them. For themselves, they mourned not; but they feared the effect of such intelligence on their almost dying Parent, and resolved to be silent on the subject, in his presence.—They tried to encourage Benton.

"Every thing we have owned together," said George C. to him, "must be sold; then our debts will all be paid, and in honor we will be able to commence business again." Benton groaned aloud, and George proceeded in his plans. "The money we have saved, will, in pecuniary matters, be our salvation."

"Mine is gone! all gone!" said Benton, "and not one farthing will be left for me!"

Here the wild gleaming of his eyes admonished them to be careful. George knew not by what means he had lost his money, but Albert comprehended it all, and sought to soothe his excited feelings; speaking to his Brother, he said:

"Perhaps by examination, we shall find that we have enough to allow us to lend Mr. Benton a part, until he can reinstate himself in business." George went, himself, to the box which they supposed contained their treasure, and returned pale and excited—

"It is all gone!" said he, "and we shall all be beggars together!"

"Hush!" said Albert, as he saw Benton sink insensible to the floor.

George ceased, and they both exerted themselves to arouse him from the dreadful lethargy that seemed most fearfully like death; having partially succeeded, they obtained a carriage, ordered a physician, and supported him in their arms to his own house; there he was carried to his private chamber, and every thing done that skill and tenderness could suggest; and although his suspended faculties, in some measure, regained their strength, his incoherent mutterings told of a mind wrecked by a long continued struggle with wearying care and distracting trials. Soon he seemed in a raving delirium; and yet he only gave utterance to feelings that had for years oppressed him; he talked of the being he had so tenderly loved, becoming a viper in his path; her Father, he called a monster—a robber—a wretch sent to torment his weary heart; and for his son, he mourned in all the bitterness of helpless anguish. His wife called his strange expressions "the ravings of a maniac"; and maniac he was; and still he uttered nothing but truth—he had lost the power to be silent. Mrs. Benton pretended to be so much affected by his sufferings, as to be unable to stay in the room; but his sister watched over him as no one else could.

Francis Lisbon knew by Mr. Benton's words, that he was aware of the robbery of the gold from Mr. C.'s cellar, and also felt that he was suspected of being the perpetrator; he felt sorry that his master was thus wronged, but was too selfish to run any risk of being suspected himself, by stating all he knew of the matter. He not only possessed the villain's selfishness, but his miserable cowardice, to such a degree that he resolved to be silent still.

Another week went slowly by—Mr. B. remained much as when first aroused; but Col. Campbell had been laid by the side of the wife whom he had tenderly loved, and early lost. He died in ignorance of the trials prepared for his children—died blessing them and trusting in the mercy of Heaven. His sons felt all the sorrow that the most devoted affection could inspire; but it was at a time when they were obliged to be active, and nerve their hearts to cope with many difficulties. George Campbell was suspicious of Benton's honesty, and his countenance had expressed this feeling when he first saw him after the discovery of their loss. Albert knew his thoughts, but he looked farther, and, suspecting the real criminals, was preparing to arrest them when they both returned. The old man told what he had done to secure a fortune to his Grandson; "and," said he, "he must have some property in the city, and the wild land must be cultivated, and towns must be built, but what is the matter?" said he, addressing George Campbell, having stopped at their store as he came into town. Mr. C. could scarcely endure his vulgar, insulting tones; but he told him of his Father's death, of their recent losses, and the sad state to which Mr. Benton was reduced. The old man said but little, and soon after, in company with Friedland, went to Mr. Benton's house—he was asleep, and they repaired to their own room, to consult on the best means to bring about their plans. About an hour after they returned, Mr. B. awoke to consciousness and reason; he recognized his sister and the physician who were watching by his side; he listened to her words of affectionate endearment, with evident delight; he seemed to have forgotten all his sorrows, and all his business, and thought only of the time when he was a child, caressed by a fond Mother.

"Elizabeth," he faintly said, "will you bring me our dear Mother's Miniature?"

She knew where and how to find it, and hastened to unlock his desk; but to get at the drawer where he kept it, she must move a bag she found in the desk, that with much difficulty she accomplished. In doing this, the string broke and the gold was fully exposed to her astonished gaze. Her Brother heard her exclamation of surprise, and raising himself, saw the gold, and for one brief moment, remembered the past, and comprehended why that bag of gold was there, and who put it there. The dreadful reflection was more than his weakened frame could bear—that one effort of reason was the last he ever made. A long and piercing shriek reverberated through the house, bringing all the family to the room. Mrs. B.'s Father and Friedland saw the gold which Mrs. C. in her alarm had left exposed, and the old man said to his companion, "step into Mr. C.'s and tell them how much worse Mr. B. is," looking at him as he lay writhing in strong convulsions; but, inwardly congratulating himself on what had happened. George and Albert Campbell were in the room in a few moments and both saw what was intended for their eyes, the bag of gold in Benton's desk. George C. felt that this was proof enough, but he quietly closed the desk and locked it, that others might not see it. Mr. B.'s physician was in immediate attendance, he bled him freely, and they felt relieved when his struggles ceased, and he lay apparently free from pain, although still utterly unconscious of every thing.[1]

Mrs. C. and her husband were nearly exhausted from their long continued watching at his bed-side, and the physician urged them to retire—"he will probably remain much as you now see him," said he, "until toward morning—he will not know who ministers unto him, and Francis Lisbon will be faithful in following my directions." He promised to rouse them (their houses were only a few feet apart,) as soon as any change was apparent in Mr. B., and thus they all retired to rest, unconscious that that cloud of dreadful import that had so long been suspended over their heads, was about to break in fearful and overwhelming destruction—and they, its victims—have they no sense of coming wo? None can tell. At midnight the moon was shining sweetly on their dwellings as they stood in calm majestic beauty—the morning sun revealed them, each a burning, crumbling, blackened ruin—and their inmates, where are they?

(Continued.)

1. Bleeding remained a common medical practice for the treatment of disease; it was not until later in the nineteenth century that medical opinion turned against it. See Gilbert R. Seigworth, "Bloodletting Over the Centuries." *New York State Journal of Medicine* 80, no. 13 (December 1980): 2022–28.

"Man is not an isolated creature: he is a link of one great and mighty chain, and each, necessarily has a dependance upon the other. In society he is like the flower blown in its native bed; in solitude like the blasted shrub of the desert—neither giving nor receiving support, the energies of his nature fail him, and he droops, degenerates, and dies."[2]

The Spectre Haunted.

Ah! what is that shadow so stealthily stealing
  Across the bright path of a fair, young girl,
Whose heart is replete with every pure feeling,
  And joy seems dancing on each golden curl?
She is hastening along with impulsive emotion,
  To ask, for a beggar, a gift that will bless—
Her Mother's proud heart knows no generous devotion,
  She sends no sweet message to suff'ring distress.

'Twas thus as the heart of this gentle young creature
  Was shrinking and trembling in bitter regret,
She first saw that shadow, though veiled every feature,
  And only a threat'ning gesture she met.
And thus was it ever each hour, more revealing
  The power that should thwart every hope of her soul,
In childhood, in youth, in maturer years feeling
  A spell that would fain, every action control.

If she wandered alone by the banks of some streamlet,
  Or cull'd the fair flowers, or heard the birds sing,
Or found food for thought in Autumn's pale leaflet,
  Or gave to rich fancy, full scope for its wing,
Around her would fall that same deep'ning shadow,
  In outlines most fearfully semblant of life;

2. "Man is not an isolated creature": This quotation appears, unsourced, in *The Carcanet: A Literary Album Containing Select Passages From the Most Distinguished English Writers* (London: William Pickering, 1828), 229, Google Books, http://books.google.com/books?id=6RDQAAAAMAAJ. See n. 22, p. 51 for "In the struggle of contending interests." Cumings probably sourced both quotations from this same volume. The original appears to be from Robert Huish, *Memoirs of the Late Royal Highness Charlotte Augusta, Princess of Wales* (London: Thomas Kelly, 1818), 54, Google Books, http://books.google.com/books?id=6RDQAAAAMAAJ.

And her heart, as if pierced by some deep poison'd arrow,
Would quail for a moment and writhe in its strife.

Did she wear the rich garb of Poesy's weaving,
Or breathe glowing thoughts by its spirit inspir'd,
Her heart, to the world, its rich treasures giving,
In wealth of true genius and feeling attir'd,
That dark phantom came with its cold laugh, so mocking,
That rang on her ear like the death-knell of hope,
While, secure in his might, in majesty stalking,
He knew that *never*, with his power she could cope.

Did she sit at a shrine where science's pure treasures
Were given its votaries with no stinted hand;
Did she seek for the wisdom that daringly measures
The works of Creation, of matter, of mind,
That spectre would follow, and plant itself by her,
And bid her remember life's *physical* wants,
And by her benevolence, even, defy her
To seek her soul's peace 'mid knowledge's fair haunts.

He hiss'd in her ear his soul-crushing title—
"I'm Poverty's spirit, my fetters are strong,
Thy feelings refin'd, will help thee but little,
Thy knowledge will not thine existence prolong.
Thou hast toiled dost thou say? thy heart was not giving
The heed to its duties, that lengthens life's span,
Thou wast soaring on high, or below thou wast diving,
To gather up something thou never could'st scan!

I've followed thee long, I've haunted thee ever,
In vain are thy struggles, I'll leave thee no more,
My toils are all round thee, no link canst thou sever,
Or hope to escape my full measure of power."
Thus tortured and wronged and in fetters upbraided,
The sweet prayer of faith to her pure heart was given!
God took her to scenes by no sorrow e'er shaded,
And gave her a home in the mansions of Heaven.

"Alma."

Nature's Loveliness

More touchingly lovely
Than all art can boast,
Is the sweet drooping Lily
Or Violet, lost
In its lowliness
Save to the eye
That can in such meekness,
Rich beauty descry.

More glorious fair
Is the bright blushing rose,
Than aught that man's care
On his path ever throws—
Each plant and each flower,
All, in nature's fair state,
Shows how weak is man's power,
His Maker, how great!

"Alma."

Thoughts Suggested While Reading the 15th Verse of the One Hundred and Sixth Psalm.[3]

"And he gave them their request but sent leanness into their soul."

Are there not many who, like the ancient Israelites, forget the works of the God who redeemed them when under bonds stronger than any that Pharaoh ever imposed? who think not of his power manifested in "rebuking the dark waves of despair," that but for his mercy must have engulfed them, and cease

3. Psalm 106 describes the ungrateful Israelites in the wilderness, lusting after flesh, provoking God. Early quotes in this piece of bible commentary allude to the events described in the psalm, such as God "rebuking" the Red Sea. As Adam Clarke glosses verse 15, the Israelites "despised the manna; and called it *light*, that is, *innutritive bread*. God gave *flesh*, as they desired: but gave no blessing with it; and in consequence they did not fatten, but grew *lean* upon it. Their souls also suffered want." See Adam Clarke, *The Holy Bible, Containing the Old and New Testaments . . . with a Commentary and Critical Notes* (Baltimore: John J. Harrod, 1836), 2:333, Google Books, http://books.google.com/books?id=FFAXAAAAYAAJ.

to remember his love, seen in the victory he gives them over their enemies, the sins of their own corrupt natures, more necessary to be feared than were the hosts that perished with Egypt's wretched king? Ah! how many in their journeyings through this wilderness towards the heavenly "Canaan,"[4] forget the pledged word of the Almighty, wait not for his counsel, and trust not in his wisdom and power; but place between themselves and "the perfect law of the Lord," some unworthy object, some idol of *breathing* clay or senseless dust; and seek to believe that this will never cast a darkening shadow on their souls; but find at last, that the pure rays of "the sun of righteousness," are not within the compass of their moral vision, while looking for them through so gross and distorted a medium![5] "God has given them their request, but sent leanness into their souls."—And may we not then, love the precious gifts of Heaven and hope for a blessing in prosecuting the secular affairs of life? yes, we cannot love them too much, if more than all, we love our God!—nor can we be too diligent in business, if all is done with an eye to His glory; but alas! on every hand are those who have forgotten to do this, those who have been spiritually slain, and now mourning their hard fate, and seeking to excuse themselves for all their wretchedness, by imagining that they have been *peculiarly* tried and tempted; and for this, will be pardoned all neglect of duty, or that no duty devolves upon them—but allow me to urge you to look at the inconsistency of your course—ah, ask yourselves where have been your hearts? to what purpose have you applied your mental energies and how have you heeded the teachings of God's holy spirit?—be assured you have desired something forbidden,—have murmured at your lot, or envied your fellow-traveler through this probationary scene, some fancied bliss or real happiness and have perhaps, at last, obtained what you have so much and so strongly coveted, and then have the darkness and miserable "leanness" of the erring soul been most acutely felt; and you have wandered along in the dread labyrinth of distracting doubt or senseless folly, or degrading vice, until completely lost in its mazes you know not which way to look for the original point of your destination—you feel that you are no longer a pilgrim to the heavenly City, but reckless of consequences, rush upon your own certain destruction.

Perhaps your first wrong request was not for any thing you could imagine would harm any one, nothing by human judgment, usually condemned—you asked not for liberty to sin with a high hand in the ranks of the vicious, of any class; but you were *weary*, you wished for "inglorious rest," and would

4. Figuratively, heaven; literally, Palestine, or the Holy Land, an area including Jerusalem that was taken by the Romans from the Jews in the first century CE.

5. Psalm 19:7; Malachi 4:2.

"be carried to the skies on flowery beds of ease"[6]—you felt that it was too much, that you should be required to follow the Captain of your salvation against the enemies marshalled on every side, to oppose his progress—you have cast off your armor and refused to resist his foes, until you have lost the power to contend successfully—you have neglected to sing the songs of Zion, until your tongue is paralized, and you have grieved the "holy spirit," until your heart scarcely feels its strivings—a mind that cannot "comprehend the things that concern its peace,"[7] a heart that throbs not with a quickened pulse under a sense of God's mercy,—every faculty of the soul benumbed and unconscious of every thing but misery, is your wretched portion, and you need not *dream* of an excuse for this! Ah! let us ask God to enable us to repent and turn to Him in sincerity and truth—He will restore unto us the joys of His salvation; will warm our frozen hearts; enlighten our darkened understandings, and loose our stammering tongues! Ah! that we might be clothed with the righteousness of Christ, and be willing to suffer and toil; and, if need be, die, remembering always, that in duty's path we shall not meet any trial that is not for our good—If we trust in God, his Almighty arm will protect and save us, whatever may be our *seeming* peril, and we shall feel that he is with us, and that his Will will be done, and that no power can prevail against Him. For this sweet consciousness, who would not be willing to make any sacrifice required by our merciful Father? who would not wish to be a Christian, that the might be happy here, and hope for bliss beyond

6. In antebellum American religious literature, the Christian missionary often disdains "inglorious rest" and volunteers for what must be "glorious" labor. That idea that it would be unfortunate to be "carried to the skies on flowery beds of ease" is expressed by a hymn by Isaac Watts that contains these lines:

Am I a soldier of the cross,
    A follower of the Lamb?
And shall I fear to own his cause,
    Or blush to speak his name?
Must I be carried to the skies
    On flowery beds of ease,
While others fought to win the prize,
    And sail'd through bloody seas?

See James B. Winchell, *An Arrangement of the Psalms, Hymns, and Spiritual Songs of the Rev. Isaac Watts, D. D., To Which Is Added, A Supplement . . .* (Boston: Lincoln & Edmands, 1821), 112, Google Books, http://books.google.com/books?id=eKoJTRcQQSoC.

7. The exact allusion of this quote is unclear, but it reads like an explication of Matthew 13:15. See, for example, Albert Barnes, *Notes, Explanatory and Practical, on The Gospels: Designed for Sunday School Teachers and Bible Classes* (New York: Harper & Brothers, 1847), 1:158, Google Books, http://books.google.com/books?id=NCkZAAAAYAAJ.

the grave? Oh! that we might so live, that we can never feel that "God has given us our request but sent leanness into our soul!"

Innovator.

A Fool's Soliloquy.

Oh! I wish I did know something,
Could think one blessed thought
That had not its beginning
In other's craniums sought.

Some how, I've learn'd our letters,
Our words—their meaning too,—
'Twas an invention of my betters—
No such thing, could *I* do.

I've read of science's treasures;
Of Mind's Phylosophy;
Of skill, that all things, measures—
And friendship's sympathy.

But science's votaries seem to me,
A proud, conceited set,
That, in their self-complacency,
But little knowledge, get.

And those who study mind, I think
But little of it know—
And who, of friendship's waters, drink,
Will find them bitter grow.

And love, of such undying power
In each old Poet's song,
In modern times, seems but a flower
Form'd not to flourish long.

I've heard of beauty widely spread
    Through nature's every part,
And of the sweet communion shed
    On every feeling heart.

But when I've seen some *seem* to *writhe*
    In ecstacy exquisite,
I've said, for this I'll pay no tithe—
    There's nothing real in it.

I've heard Theologians portray
    Frail man's futurity,
And after all, have turned away
    In dark uncertainty.

'Tis hard to have no heart or mind
    And look so coldly on,
Where others, truth and pleasure find,
    And deem a triumph won.

Once more I'd wish the bliss to taste,
    That thought and feeling give;
But, ah! 'twould be an idle waste,
    And I'll contented live!

Idiota.

For the Offering.

The Graveyard.

There was a grave-yard—its wall was built of massive stone, closely cemented, and so high that none could scale it. There was but one entrance, and that was through a gate upon the east side.

The gate was of solid iron, and so securely fastened that none could open, and should they have succeeded in drawing the bolt, the united forces of earth and the darkened regions could not have turned on its hinges, this immense and massive gate. The graveyard was not a city of the *dead*, alone, but a city of the dying. It was inhabited by human beings; beings who had transgressed the laws of their Judge, and were doomed to wander among the tombs, and to "die without hope, and without God."[8] At the gate stood Justice; unyielding sternness was written upon his brow; and he gazed with cold contempt upon the gasping, dying mortals. At length Mercy, the lovely daughter of Deity, saw, pitied, and with tears in her angelic eyes ran to their relief.

"There are the sick," said she to Justice, "pining and groaning with none to pity, none to console. May I not enter and apply the healing balm?"

"No!" said stern Justice, "they have willfully broken my commands, and now I will give them the reward of their hands."

Again did Mercy plead, but Justice was unyielding. The sight was more than Mercy could endure, for within the gate were thousands of human beings groping among the tombs, and the yawning graves. Their faces were pale and emaciated; no friendly shade wooed them to its embrace; no cooling fount invited them to its waters; no board was spread, and no kind hand wiped away the mourner's tears. The rose faded from beauty's cheek, the light went out from beauty's eye, and one after another drooped and sunk into the grave.

Mercy threw herself at Justice's feet, and sued with all the eloquence of an angel's tongue; still he was inflexible.

While the fair being was still repeating her request, a sound like the music of many harps floated on the breeze, and a noise like the rush of many waters, came rolling through the heavens.

They both raised their eyes, and lo! wide open were Heaven's doors, and forth from the throne proceeded the son of God, attended by legions of angels. Every golden lyre was tuned, and they hasted on rapid wing to carry the fruits of love to some foreign clime. As they drew near, they observed that Mercy was one of their number; they wondered that she should be so far from home alone, and unattended; they paused, and the Son inquired:

"Daughter, what do you here?"

Mercy veiled her face, and replied:

"See you not these perishing millions? I came to relieve; but Justice has barred the gate and I cannot enter."

"Justice," continued the Son, "will you not let Mercy go in?"

"I cannot," said Justice, "for they have broken my laws, they have incurred a fearful penalty, and there is none to pay the debt."

---

8. This phrase appears in many, varied Christian writings of the antebellum period.

A shade of sorrow for a moment, dimmed the radiance of that brow; he drew back, veiled his face, and seemed wrapped in intense agony. At length the cloud passed, and a smile bright as heaven sat on his brow. A glory brighter than ten thousand suns shone around his head, as he replied: "*I'll pay the debt! I'll pay the debt!* Let Mercy enter, and upon me rest the curse."

"But how will you do it," said Justice, "or where?"

"I will shed my blood, four thousand years hence on the hill of Calvary."[9]

"That will do," said Justice, "but I must have a bond, that pay will be sure."

The Son wrote the deed and sealed it with the seal of Heaven.

'Tis done—Mercy enters, spreads Joy and Peace throughout the land, and away flew the Heavenly host, in amazement, wondering why the God of glory would die for sinful man. Years passed, and at length in an obscure town, a child was born. His parents were poor, and *his* head "lay low with the beasts of the stall;" yet the birth of no prince or potentate was ever attended with so grand a pagentry as his.[10] "The theme, the joy, seemed to be more than heaven could hold;" and angels again hasted through the "vast expanse" to publish the news, and to minister to the child, and every harp in heaven struck a higher note.[11]

The child grew, and waxed strong in the spirit; he lived a lowly life; he was hated of men; he was cursed, but he blessed; his spirit was pure and peaceable; he was long-suffering, full of forgiving tenderness. Still he was despised and rejected, and at last doomed to die. The furious mob led him away to a hill called Calvary; nailed his hands and his feet to the accursed tree, and pressed to his blessed brow a crown of thorns. Just before he breathed out his life, Justice appeared ascending the hill. As he approached

---

9. The place where Jesus was crucified. See e.g. Matthew 27:33.

10. Probably a reference to a popular hymn by British bishop Reginald Heber (1783–1826), "Brightest and Best of the Sons of the Morning." It includes the lines, "Cold on his cradle the dewdrops are shining, / Low lies his bed with the beasts of the stall." For a publication of this hymn that is contemporary with the *Akron Offering*, see Rufus Wilmot Griswold, ed., *The Sacred Poets of England and America, for Three Centuries* (New York: D. Appleton, 1849), 404, Google Books, http://books.google.com/books?id=5b5YAAAAMAAJ.

11. Paraphrase of a stanza in "Mortals, awake, with angels join," an evangelical hymn by English Baptist minister Samuel Medley (1738–99). This was a popular song for many antebellum American denominations. It describes a "rapturous song" begun "in heaven": "Swift, through the vast expanse, it flew, / And loud the echo rolled; / The theme, the song, the joy was new, / 'Twas more than heaven could hold." For a later 1840s printing, see *Church Psalmist: Or, Psalms and Hymns designed for the Public, Social, and Private Use of Evangelical Christians* (Philadelphia: Presbyterian Publication Committee, 1847), 289, Google Books, http://books.google.com/books?id=W1AXAAAAYAAJ.

the cross, his stern brow seemed to relent; his iron heart melted, and tears silently wandered down his rugged cheek. He came to the gasping being, and cried, "thou hast paid the debt! the world is free!" Justice read the deed, then tore it up, and scattered to the winds of Heaven.

The Son cried with a loud voice, "it is finished!" and gave up the ghost.

Anna.

The author of the following lines, is a native of this State, and now a resident of Lafayette, in an adjoining Co.[12] She was but nine years old when this was composed, and is but nine years and a few months old at this time.

For the Offering.

Faith, Hope, and Charity.

When sorrow rages in the breast,
And gives the anxious heart no rest;
Amidst this cheerless world of gloom,
Faith lights the pathway to the tomb.

She watches man's last, fleeting breath,
She aids him to the brink of death;
Hope intercedes with Charity,
Sweet sisters in this trinity.

Hope guides the soul through death's domain,
Hope lights its path and makes it plain;
Hope bears us onward in her mission,
And brings us to the blest fruition.

And now the last, best sister comes,
To guide our spirits to their homes;
The greatest and the best is she,
Sublime—transcendent Charity.

12. About twenty-two miles west of Akron, in 1849 Lafayette was a Medina County township of about 900 people with mills, tanneries, and a distillery. See J. R. McCulloch and Daniel Haskel, *McCulloch's Universal Gazetteer: A Dictionary, Geographical, Statistical, and Historical . . .* (New York: Harper & Brothers, 1855), 2:138, Google Books, http://books.google.com/books?id=Y4Q6AQAAIAAJ.

Her office-work shall ne'er be done,
Though years dissolve with rolling sun;
But upwards to her blest abode,
She bears us to the throne of God.

For the Offering.

MISS CUMINGS:—As you may be aware, I am sometimes seized with ————what, in the name of the dictionary, is that Latin phrase, which means scribbling madness?[13] At such times it is the most convenient thing in all the catalogue of conveniences, to have a kind heart connected with the clear head in the chair editorial. In default of this toward circumstance, the chances are decidedly against any of my crude and bantling articles finding their way to the 'generous public.' As one is safe in presuming upon your condescending forbearance, I may as well begin the taxation of your patience, by giving a running sketch of two or three days' travel in Pennsylvania.

Have you ever been from Brookville to Ridgeway and Smethport?[14] Well, I have. Now you must be told, that, after leaving the borders of civilization a little northeast of Brookville, for a distance of many miles but few human beings have as yet invaded the inalienably lawful province of wild beasts, by settling in the country. A strange conceit crossed the threshold of somebody's noddle, a few years ago, to construct a turnpike through the wilderness; which means, as near as one can get at it, a common road turned the other side up. It was along this pike that I pursued the even tenor of my way, with no fear but that of being obliged to keep in it. Out of sheer compassion for the faithful beast that bore me, and a mere sprinkle of apprehension that I might be impolitely unhorsed at some broken bridge or dilapidated corduroy, I secured my pants in the tops of my boots, and made my way full many a mile by virtue of the force of my own understanding.

Aside from occasional soliloquies as to the best method of getting over difficult places, but little occurred to break the thread of my most agreeable reflections. At one time the muses were just beginning to fan me with

13. The reached-for Latin is "*cacoethes scribendi.*" Catharine Maria Sedgwick used the phrase as the title of a short story about a village of superior women with writing ability and, in some cases, literary ambition. See *Tales and Sketches* (Philadelphia: Carey, Lea, and Blanchard, 1835), 165–81, Google Books, http://books.google.com/books?id=EalIAAAAMAAJ.

14. About sixty miles separates these county seats of consecutive, mountainous counties in northern, west-central Pennsylvania.

their wings, and I was falling into a convulsion of ecstacies on the beauties of nature, when my ear was suddenly attracted by an industrious scratching and crackling in the undergrowth by the road-side. Turning my organ of seeitiveness noiseward,[15] what should I behold but a formidable appearance of organized matter in the shape of a huge hedge-hog, clambering upon a large log near at hand. The prickly pugnaciousness of the creature, to be Phrenologically precise, acted excitaciously on my combativeness;[16] and, laying hold of a stone near by, had it not been for a fortunate want of precision in my aim, I should have sent the audacious animal very unopportunely into ———— I was about to say, *eternity*; but, with all due deference to the able advocates of animal immortality, I am so unfortunate as to have a shade or two of unbelief as to the future existence of such quadrupeds. Be that as the arbitrament of the future shall decide, let it here be stated, that I repented unfeignedly of the rash and inhuman intention: for, setting aside the title to live, which all sentient beings possess in inferiority to human rights, a creature that has grown gray in the undisturbed retreats of these vast forests, has earned a right to spend the remainder of its days in freedom from fear of being violently deprived of life. I think it but a poor atonement for so unpardonable a purpose against nature, to make my humble confession to all Hedgehogdom, "through the medium of your valuable periodical," and promise never again to trench on the life or liberty, privileges or immunities, of its inhabitants.[17]

The afternoon of the second day brought me to the door of a rudely comfortable school-house, erected by lumbermen living at various points on a neighboring mill-stream, and intended to subserve the real purpose of a school-room for the children, and a house of worship for the parents. The location was picturesque in the extreme. Tall pines waved above the

15. Turning my eyes toward the noise. Antebellum scientific writing identified a wide variety of body parts as "organs" of some ability. Thus the lungs were "organs of respiration," the tongue "the organ of speech," the muscles "the organs of motion," etc. Of course this is a parody of such scientific language.

16. Phrenology, the science of psychological evaluation through the fondling of the head, was popular at this time. Faculties of the mind were thought to reside, literally, in specific areas of the brain, with the higher faculties located in more forward and upward areas. (This reflects and reinforces the prejudice in favor of large, high, or ample foreheads in the creative literature. For example, see pp. 110 and 139.) Faculties divined by the Phrenologist might include Firmness, Benevolence, Veneration, Deference, Devotion, Comparison, Appetite, Bibativeness (thirst), Acquisitiveness, Conscientiousness. A good source of first-hand information about Phrenology can be found in the *American Phrenological Journal* (1838–69). In 1849, the journal was in its eleventh volume. See *The American Phrenological Journal*. Vol. 11. (New York: Fowler and Wells, 1849), Google Books, http://books.google.com/books?id=soggAQAAMAAJ.

17. A standard, perhaps clichéd phrase for correspondence to an editor.

unpretending structure, a spring of pure water gushed from a bank rich in the hues and fragrance of wild flowers, and the subdued roar of a waterfall came up from a deep gulf an hundred yards away. As I approached the spot, the voice of singing men and women issued from the open door. It was not the Sabbath, but worshippers were there. It was not a temple with gilded spire, but the pure in heart had come to pray and praise. Soon ceased the voice of sacred song, and a man of middle age and noble presence arose in that small assembly, and read with an elegant accent and manly diction: "It doth not yet appear what we shall be: but we know that, when he shall appear, we shall be like him; for we shall see him as he is. And every man that hath this hope in him, purifieth himself, even as he is pure."[18]

I gazed on that meek countenance, that expansive brow, and felt that such a man came on no sordid mission. As the messenger of Jesus kindled with his theme, his face beamed with the light of thought, and his eye flashed with the radiance of sanctified genius, the almost pulseless audience seemed to feel that his was a message of God to them. Truthful tears filled the eyes of the hardy woodsmen. A smile of deep angelic joy lighted their countenances.—And my heart whispered, 'like the pines of their own forests, they bow to nought but the breath of God.'[19]

And he who charmed and awed me thus, had stood high in the walks of literature. But his life was hid with Christ in God: and the thirst of his noble soul for the weal of man, brought him to seek these neglected sheep in the wilderness.

Alpha.

For the Offering.

Random Thoughts.

Another month is gone, bearing to the bosom of the past its deeds, its sorrows, and its hopes; and June is here. The "*moneth* June," with its leaves,

18. 1 John 3:2–3.

19. This looks like an original thought inspired by lines from "Hymn of the Vaudois Mountaineers in Times of Persecution" by British poet Felicia Dorothea Hemans (1793–1835). Hemans was still very popular with American readers in the late 1840s. In her poem, some mountain Christians thank God "For the strong pines of the forest, / That by thy breath are stirr'd." For an American edition of the poem that is contemporary with *The Akron Offering*, see Hemans, *The Poetical Works* (Boston: Phillips, Sampson, and Company, 1849):197, Google Books, http://books.google.com/books?id=4FEZAAAAYAAJ.

and flowers, and sweetly singing birds, is again smiling upon us, giving us glowing promises of a fruitful autumn.[20] And I also, am with thee, "reader mine," at the same window of which I spake to thee "whilom," penning another sheet of Random Thoughts, for thine especial benefit; and I doubt not thou hast right anxiously been awaiting their appearance; and I confess I do desire to have thine optics hitherward directed. And now what shall be the theme, upon which we are to display the vast resources of our mind? Shall it be the "leafy month of June?"[21] O, no—an abler and more pleasing pen hath portrayed its beauties in far more vivid colors, than we have ever dared to use; and Dr. Johnson, has advised us never to touch upon a subject, unless we hope to improve it.[22] Now even the large stock of egotism we possess, does not lead us to suppose ourselves capable of throwing additional lustre, upon so lovely a picture, and however much we may admire the rich genius of fancy, he has scattered with such a lavish hand throughout his description, we must be allowed to differ with him.

Of the spring months, May is *my* favorite—there is something so winning in her smile, as she throws aside the coquetry of April, and assumes a character peculiar to herself, and yet, so strictly feminine is she, that the most fastidious cannot quarrel with her firmness. But above all others, do I love the autumn months, with their many colored robes whose very beauty,

20. "Moneth" is an archaic spelling of "month." Here the quoted phrase invokes an "Ollapodiana" paper of American author Willis Gaylord Clark (1808–41). The humorous Ollapodiana papers ran in New York's *Knickerbocker* magazine, which Clark edited with his twin brother, Lewis Gaylord Clark (1808–73). They were also reprinted in an 1844 memorial edition of Willis's collected writings. "Lizzie" begins this installment of "Random Thoughts" in self-conscious emulation of Clark's papers. Compare its beginning to the first few sentences of the third Ollapodiana paper, published in June 1835: "Another month has gone by, and bless us, reader, here am I again, at the same casement of which I whilome made mention, brewing you another chapter of various topics, 'written as they shoulde comen into my mynde.' 'The moneth June!' A right pleasant month it is—leafy, sunny, and sweet." Lizzie's use of "whilom" and even her spelling of "lustre" may be further homage to this paper. "Reader mine" was a common phrase with which antebellum literary editors playfully addressed their readers. See Willis Gaylord Clark, *The Literary Remains of the Late Willis Gaylord Clark.* Ed. Lewis Gaylord Clark (New York: Burgess, Stringer, and Company, 1844), 37, Google Books, http://books.google.com/books?id=LXEoAAAAYAAJ.

21. Search engines for databases such as American Periodicals and Google Books readily display the astonishing popularity of this antebellum literary cliché—"the leafy month of June." By 1849 the phrase may have lost all reference to anything but itself, but the rage for the cliché probably started with an allusion to "The Rime of the Ancient Mariner" (1798) by English poet Samuel Taylor Coleridge (1722–1834), in which the phrase appears. See Coleridge, *The Poems* (London: William Pickering, 1848), 235, http://books.google.com/books?id=qSOnmVITuZkC.

22. The "abler and more pleasing pen" was that of Clark; see n. 20, above. Many various thoughts on composition—some apocryphal—were attributed to English writer and lexicographer Samuel Johnson (1709–84).

speaketh of decay—and then the soft low breathing of the winds, as they seem to mourn the absence of the flowers, with which they sported in the long summer day. And then at night I love to go out into the "cathedral vast" and commune with those who passed away like flowers of the spring time

"Whose memory like rare odor, fills the heart,
Nor fades, but—richer grows, and is of it a part."[23]

And then I muse on one who was called away in the "dew of his youth,"[24] ere yet the high and noble aspirations, that had filled his soul, had made themselves a form—and I have sometimes murmured, that one so promising was not permitted to register his name among the great ones of the earth. But—God called him home, and, we must not repine.

How much evil has this same spirit of repining brought upon the human family! Where, indeed, do we not see its effects! I am acquainted with a certain person, who seems to delight in making himself, and every one around him, perfectly miserable.—And, it is really strange, to see the various means he uses. If he meet with any unexpected good fortune, he will tell you, that some evil will follow; and, when evil does come, he feels that Heaven is most unjust in afflicting one, who never deserved any thing but good.—Congratulate him upon being in possession of all that would seem necessary to render one happy, and he tells you of some one who exceeds him in wealth, and, consequently, happiness is beyond his reach, so long as one surpasses him.

---

23. Lizzie quotes "An Autumn Reverie," an obscure poem by the American poet William Falconer (1820–c.1885?). The original lines are "In this cathedral vast, by tall elms reared, / While through yon leafy oriel streams the sun / On those old boughs, by many an Autumn seared / I'd dream of friends who life's rude race have run— / Whose memory, like rare odor, fills my heart, / Nor fades, but richer grows, and is of it a part." See William Falconer, "An Autumn Reverie." *Graham's Magazine* 21, no. 4 (October 1842): 209, American Periodicals (135687938). Edna B. Triplett reports biographical information about Falconer after suggesting another of his poems inspired details in "The Raven." See "A Note on Poe's 'The Raven,'" *American Literature* 10, no. 3 (November 1938): 339–41, JSTOR, http://www.jstor.org/stable/2920543. American Periodicals shows that William Falconer wrote dozens of poems for *The New-Yorker* in the mid- to late 1830s. Around 1840 he was signing poems from Paris, and later in the 1840s he contributed poetry to the *Southern Literary Messenger* and *The Ladies' Companion*. Triplett describes these poems as the work of the William Falconer of Snowdoun, Montgomery County, Alabama—the author of *Bloom and Brier; or, As I Saw It, Long Ago: A Southern Romance* (Philadelphia: Claxton, Remsen & Haffelfinger, 1870), Google Books, http://books.google.com/books?id=CAYtAAAAYAAJ. This evidence suggests that Falconer was educated in the North, visited the continent when twenty years old, and then returned to Alabama. He appears in the 1860 census as a married forty-year-old "farmer" with four children and considerable property; the slave schedule records dozens of slaves on his property. United States of America, Bureau of the Census. *Eighth Census of the United States, 1860*. NARA microfilm publication M653. (Washington, D.C.: National Archives and Records Administration, n.d.), roll M653_19, page 44, Ancestry.com.

24. Psalm 110:3.

He has entirely abandoned literary pursuits, because there are so many who know more than he possibly can,—that, he can never excel. We doubt not that, if all the obstacles were removed, and the whole world was possessed by him, he would murmur because there was no more of it.

There are others who repine, because they cannot make so fine an appearance as some one of their acquaintance. I shall have to confess myself of these. I have often mourned because others possessed greater advantages for obtaining information, and not because I had not better improved those which were within my grasp. And, now, if we have done wrong in time past, let us not add to our sin by vainly regretting the past: But,

"Let us, be up and doing,
Heart prepared for any fate;
Still achieving, still pursuing,
Learn to labor and to wait."[25]

Reader, I am cut short in this, my first sermon, by circumstances beyond my control; and the space, I hope, will be occupied—and trust by abler thoughts than can possibly be wrung from the cranium of one whose brain is as barren of thoughts as is the desert of Sahara. So thou are freed from farther lucubrations of mine for the present.

Nothing more, save

Ever thine, Lizzie.

My Own Heart.

'Tis but a wreck's and blighted thing,
That throbs within my breast;
That pierc'd by sorrow's withering sting
Seeks not on earth its rest—
And yet, it can its burden bear,
It asks no trust or love,
But casts its bitter cankering care
On him who reigns above.

25. An improvisation on the conclusion of Longfellow's "Psalm of Life": "Let us, then, be up and doing, / With a heart for any fate; / Still achieving, still pursuing, / Learn to labor and to wait." See Longfellow, *Voices of the Night* (Boston: Redding & Co., 1845), 9, Google Books, http://books.google.com/books?id=UR4CAAAAYAAJ.

E'en friends have called me proudly cold,
 And deem'd I scorn'd the weak;
But *still* my thoughts will be controlled,
 For tears they'd vainly seek,
Save when alone, then could they find
 A triumph *meanly* great,
And every *pitying, envious* mind
 Its *wondrous love* could sate.

And am I proud and coldly stern?
 No, not to genuine truth;
But from the heartless throng I turn,
 And memory wanders forth
To scenes unsullied by a tear,
 To friend and hopes long gone;
But soon the present, dark and drear
 O'er all the past, is drawn.

And let it be—I can endure
 All that my lot can be;
My heart can its own bliss secure,
 Or writhe in *silent* agony—
And if its dread recoiling power
 Should in destruction come,
'Twill throb with torturing strength no more,
 But rest in peace, at Home.

Misanthrope.[26]

A Sketch from Life.

Once I was a sojourner, for several months, on a broad and beautiful prairie, many long, weary miles from "Mississippi's rolling flood"—beautiful, *surpassingly* beautiful, but poorly defines the loveliness of the scenery there exhibited![27] Do you ask "*what* was lovely?" I could answer, *every*

26. A "misanthrope" hates all people.

27. The author describes a visit to what might be Minnesota, Iowa, or Missouri, as these prairie states extend hundreds of miles west of the Mississippi River and were then filling with settlers. In the 1840s there was attention to the material and spiritual poverty of some Americans in the "far west."

thing, but will particularize somewhat. First, imagine yourself gazing on a meadow that looks in the distance, like a far-spreading sea, that, gently stirred by the passing breeze, seems inviting you to a sail on its mimick waves, while here and there appears a little grove that looks like some fertile island blooming on the bosom of the deep. And what a horizon is there! in some instances bounded only by the weakness of human vision; in others, beautifully relieved by rolling bluffs covered with the hardy hickory and the majestic oak and all their inferior attendants, while at their feet flow the deep-banked creeks that are bearing their tribute to the exacting stream that requires so much to fill its broad, deep channel. Let us take a nearer view—the illusive sea has disappeared, but beauty lingers still. Here are flowers that would shame any collection whether ambitious man or gentle woman had been their presiding genius, and while we are admiring and wondering and feeling our own insignificance, our ears are greeted with notes of almost heavenly harmony—'tis a concert given by the wild birds of prairie and forest, and we listen to their music with real delight. One sweet songstress is the "Phebe," pleasant anywhere, but mark the difference, *here* it only sings "Phebe," *there* it sings "very, pretty, little Phebe" just as distinctly. Those loud, far-reaching notes are from a bird that, from ignorance of its real name, we will call the bold beggar; he sings from the tops of the tallest trees, "Jew, Jew, give me a little," and it sounds almost as if meant for a reproach, but surely every person would gladly grant any reasonable donation to his majesty.[28] Soon you will see troops of little Quails watched by their anxious mother, while she utters a peculiar cry that strongly appeals to the human heart for sympathy and protection, and in the distance we hear the voice of their more cautious and less loving sire, calling "Robert White, Robert White"—anon, the drumming of the "whirring Pheasant" is borne

---

The short stories of Michigan writer Caroline Matilda Kirkland (1801–64), for example, describe such things. In "The Bee-Tree," part of her 1846 collection *Western Clearings*, Kirkland explains that "among the various settlers of the wide West, there is no class which exhibits more striking peculiarities than that which, in spite of hard work, honesty, and sobriety, still continues hopeless poor." See Kirkland, *Western Clearings* (New York: Wiley and Putnam, 1846), 66, Google Books, http://books.google.com/books?id=f6YRAAAAYAAJ. "Home Missionary Societies" were established by eastern Americans to send missionaries and financial aid to the west of America. For a sample of home missionary literature, see *The Home Missionary* 22, no. 2 (June 1849): 25–60, Google Books, http://books.google.com/books?id=gJ4PAAAAIAAJ, which includes this comment about northeast Ohio: "though this region has been so long under missionary culture, it has not made a proportional moral advancement . . . . Many of the churches are destitute of preaching, and a still larger number of townships contain no religious organization of the denomination [Congregational] acting through this Society; and none of much efficiency of any denomination" (38).

28. The Phoebe bird is a common medium-sized tyrant flycatcher. The noisy begging bird might have been some kind of jay.

on the breeze in sounds of the deepest fullness while the strange language of the prairie chicken and the melancholy notes of the "Mourning Dove" mingle with all the rest and no jarring or discordant sound is heard.[29] Do you now desire some exhibition of *sublime grandeur*? then look in the dim distance—see a cloud of smoke, anon, a lurid flame, rising, and spreading, and advancing, with the fury of ten thousand demons, encircling all things, and seeming so terrible emblematical of the last, great conflagration! Is not every sense of the beautiful now gratified? no!—with all your enthusiastic love of nature, you are utilitarian enough to wish to analyze the soil, and ascertain its capacity for producing an abundant harvest of edibles; thinking there would be beauty in extensive fields of wheat and corn, and the endless variety of good things, *intended* as a blessing, but many times, *converted* into a bitter curse—Well then look at it—it is all you can wish; and the fields are ready for the plough—no trees to cut down; no stumps or stones in the way; and then such a range of pasturage! You can keep thousands of "bleating sheep," and "lowing cattle,"[30] and there is plenty of timber to be converted into the right form for building purposes; and there is clay and sand suitable for making brick—and can there be any draw-back to happiness in such a place as this? Alas! yes. Truth compels me to present the other side of the picture, dark and sorrowful though its coloring must be!

Those beautiful flowers can not be approached, without danger of feeling the Rattle Snake's fangs, bringing almost certain death for your audacity; and after you have listened all day to the melodious songs of the happy birds, your ears are at night saluted with the fearful notes of the "boding owl," and the hideous screaming of the "prairie Wolf."[31]

Those Creeks have not the clear water, and the pebbly bottoms, that characterize New England's pleasant streams. Ague—that horrid fiend of darkness, is stretched along their banks in sullen pride, and o'er all this fair scene, he stalks in conscious power.[32]

29. "See! from the brake the whirring pheasant springs / And mounts exulting on triumphant wings" are lines from a poem, "Windsor Forest," by English poet Alexander Pope (1688–1744). See Pope, *Complete Poetical Works* (New York: George A. Leavitt, 1848), 304, Google Books, http://books.google.com/books?id=LFkZAAAAYAAJ.

30. In poetry, sheep often bleat and cows often low (bellow). These phrases are in quotation marks because they are clichés.

31. The "boding" (portending, foreshadowing, generally being an evil omen) owl is another cliché of nineteenth-century literature. Thus the quotes. Likewise much was written about the intelligent "prairie wolf." Today we call this a coyote.

32. An "ague" was an episode of chilliness or shivering, or a sickness characterized by alternating

Again we see the prairies on fire; but *now* we think only the threatening danger, and are aware that unless human ingenuity interposes some hindrance, all the beauty we have so loved to look upon, will, in a few moments be swept away; and if the neighborhood boasts any inhabitants, they are in danger of losing their little all. Many times this is the case. And now let me tell you the dwellers in this far-off region. They have generous hearts, and open hands, and are bound together by true fraternal feeling—but they suffer many hardships, and endure many privations, that many know nothing of, and could not have the courage to meet—almost all went there, with but little more than enough to carry them there—in a few weeks they were prostrated with the ague; their energies deadened, their provisions and money gone—they could not return to their former homes, and had not strength or means to make themselves new ones. Perhaps all the settlers for several miles around could not, a few years ago, have mustered a team sufficient to turn the prairie sod, as it should be, but by all their united exertion they may have succeeded in raising, or in some way obtaining just enough to save them from actual starvation—some families have lived there for months on but little more than hulled corn and a little honey, and they did the best that could be done under the circumstances, at the time; and, if you think you could do better *now*, just imagine yourself there, with no money in your pocket, and no articles of trade—you take up a claim and undertake to break and fence a part of it;—you have no money to pay for making rails or for ploughing, and would be very unlikely to find an opportunity of getting it done for an exchange of labor; you feel yourself bound to render an equivalent for your board while you are building your own cabin, &c., and when you have accomplished that, you find that your land remains "as it was," and not even a fence mars its native beauty. Thus you would become discouraged, and at last somewhat indifferent—content to live in a cabin, to wear *any thing* for clothing, and *live* on any thing you can get, shaking half the time with the ague, and believing you can do nothing better than "wear it out," as the saying is. Many a one has been brought to this, and worse than this. I have seen women—who had been delicately reared, obliged to be seen with bare feet, and apparel that once they would have rejected altogether. Some have told me that they had always had enough to eat of *something*, but it had been the same kind, and that the coarsest, from week to week, and month

---

bouts of ague and fever. The ague was common in the far west. For a literary illustration of the western ague, see "The Bee-Tree" of n. 27, above.

to month, until they so utterly loathed it, that they could scarcely swallow enough to keep them alive. I have seen *one*, so overcome, by receiving, from a more fortunate neighbor, a change of food, that even while she ate it, the tears of gratitude flowed down her cheeks. This destitution is not caused by neglect on the part of the husbands and fathers. They love their families as well as you; but they are fettered by poverty. There are a few happy exceptions to the general privation, but what a difference between the most fortunate *there* and those of many other places! The parents there, are, many of them, intelligent but they *cannot* have time to educate their children; and in many places they can have no schools and there is no gathering to church on the sabbath, and no one to "dispense unto them the word of life."[33] And what would bring about a better state of things in any of those lovely regions that were so recently the red man's home? Alas! the humiliating truth makes itself understood. *Money,* in energetic hands, can accomplish all that you, in imagination brought about when you first looked on the scene; and this alone, aided by time, can do it. It is no place for a *poor* man, unless a *rich* one is his friend. Many among *us* have wealth that does them no *real* good; *there* they might make many hearts happy, and at the same time increase their own possessions. Let them go there and become familiar with their wants and then return to some of the heartless displays of extravagant folly in our cities or large towns, and they will *feel* on this subject. Well do I remember my feelings while witnessing the expense and display of a large party in one of our southern towns, soon after my return from the West. When asked why I did not join the revelers, I answered, "such things were *never* right for me, but *now,* they would bring a double curse." I remembered what I had seen of suffering and privation, and it appeared to me that indulgence in such unnecessary luxuries, was nothing better than robbery, and so it seems to me still. If any one does not like the picture I have presented, let him or her adopt measures to erase the sad colors from the landscape from which I drew; and then, I will efface the darkness from my picture, and all shall be retouched with the pencil of hope, and the coloring shall be joy and peace, and we will rejoice together in the good accomplished.

Alma.

33. Another cliché of the time, this means "to preach Christianity." The essay ends with a indirect plea to fund home missionary societies. See n. 27, above.

Hap-Hazzard Ideas.

In the first number of the "OFFERING," "Lizzie" ventured to address its readers under the title of "Random Thoughts," and she *may* talk to us in the second number, but even if she does, perhaps she will not take up the same subjects that are floating through *my* mind. I will think she will not, at any rate; and, as I think it my duty to add my mite of *intelligence* to our general repository, and as I cannot think on any subject over five minutes, I am obliged to write something after her fashion, *perhaps*. I have a great curiosity to know who the writers in the Offering are, but I know I can not, so that question is settled. I shall not even ask. I am not going to tell you any of my own *exploits*, although I *could*; but I am going to take different subjects, and look at them, and *inflict* on you, gentle reader, *my opinion*—you will be *grateful*, I think, and so I begin.

We are mostly Ladies, I suppose, and therefore I will commence with talking a little about "Our Rights;" (don't be frightened until you know what I mean,) much is said about "woman's sphere;" and is there really a particular sphere allotted and prepared for her, and if so, what does it imply? That she is differently constituted from the other sex, is a fact no one can deny; even those who would impose upon her, duties equal to those accomplished by the sternest manhood, cannot be ignorant that she is *physically* incapable of competing with man, at least in *our* country. But the Ladies are not so much afraid of being considered *physically* weak, as they are of being *intellectually* undervalued; and some, to prove themselves equal to man, have almost entirely "unsexed" themselves; proving, by every act she does, that there *is* a *particular* "province for woman," and that *they* have stepped out of it. I think I hear some "Abbey Kelleyite" contemptuously ask me what I mean.[34] I will tell you what I mean; or, rather, first, I will tell you what I do *not* mean. I do not mean that woman is *inferior* to man, or *need* to be incapable of understanding any subject, as well as himself. I do not think she should be *hindered* from acquiring knowledge in any department, if, by spending her time for this purpose, she is not neglecting any *higher* duty. I do not think

34. An abolitionist and feminist, Abby Kelley Foster (1811–87) was often attacked by antebellum conservatives for both her political opinions and her controversial decision to tour as a public speaker after the birth of her daughter in 1847. In Northeast Ohio, she was associated with the abolitionism of Oberlin College. See Jane H. Pease and William H. Pease, "Foster, Abby Kelley," *American National Biography Online* (Feb. 2000), American National Biography Online, http://www.anb.org/articles/15/15-00236.html, and J. Brent Morris, "'All the truly wise or pious have one and the same end in view': Oberlin, the West, and Abolitionist Schism." *Civil War History* 57, no. 3 (September 2011): 234–67.

she should be a *drudge* to lordly, lazy men; nor that she should shrink from attending to business of responsibility, if circumstances make it necessary. But, I do think that she is *different* from man, and cannot, *as well*, combat with the difficulties to be met in life's uneven path. I would see her able, if left alone, to do every duty necessary to success in business—but, I would see her a *woman* still. Let her be educated; she cannot know too much. But, while her *mind* is receiving strength, let her be taught that her *heart's* affections are a sacred trust; that these, rightly cultivated, give her more enduring power and happiness, than would a *giant* intellect, unattended by the influence of holy sympathy. I have seen women that *were capable* of attending to a vast deal of complicated business—enough to perplex and weary *any* man; and, they performed it with untiring perseverance. But was this their happiness? No. It was their duty.—For *this*, they did it; and they had pride, and strength of nerve to bear—and to *seem* not to feel; and they were sustained because it was *right*.—But, for happiness, they retired within the circle of tried friendship, and enduring affection, and they found it. Or, if denied *this,* they know not the *deepest* happiness the heart can receive. They may have all the strength of purpose to perform every duty in life—they may be Christians indeed; but furrows, not planted by age, or the cares of business, will be seen to mar their visage; grey hairs, not caused by time, will cover their heads—and the fretted thread of their existence will *often*, be early and suddenly severed. I scarcely know how far I have got in this subject, but I must leave it—perhaps I have said enough to stimulate some sounder judgment and abler pen; if so, I shall be truly thankful.

There are some other subjects trying to get a hearing in my mind, but I will only look at one more *now*, and that shall be politeness; but I will not weary you with many *ideas*, I promise you.

I have seen some people who appeared to think, that to be polite, one needed only to learn a certain set of *forms*, and heartless *words,* and they were equipped for every emergency. Oh! how disgusting is such an exhibition! and how *poor* and *mean*, would the performer feel, if he or she, could know that just as plainly as any sentiment was ever expressed on their countenance, their deception is stamped there. Have you not seen a vain, soft looking creature, arrayed in all the finery she can manage to get, simpering out some unintelligible *jargon*, which she called politeness? and have you not seen an empty-headed *simpleton*, calling himself a *man*, in the same predicament, but too lazy to work, shining only in borrowed plumes, that *never* will be paid for? Many such live, or *pretend* to live on this round world—they are in every community—the children of honest-hearted, hard-working parents, sometimes join their ranks, and appear to think it disgraceful for them to work—while their old Father and Mother toil from day to day—Miss must thrum a piano, while her Mother works in the kitchen, or the son must be lounging about, spending time and money for worse than nothing, while his Father *digs* for their daily bread. And they will meet you, as if by their parade of soft *nothings*, you would be *blind* to their want of common sense, or the possession of the first principle of politeness, truth, in heart and act. I suppose that I might have said that a naturally refined and feeling heart, combined with common sense and a love of truth, is the real essence of politeness; and that one possessed of these, will very rarely offend; and that is the substance of it all; and yet, much more might be said, but I forbear.

Porcia.

Our Readers.

Reader, another month has passed away. Again we send you the Offering, filled, if not with the very best the world affords, at least with the best we could gather from the articles written for its pages, and we hope that every one can find something to interest or in some way gratify.

We have not heard from all who wrote for the first No.; they probably did not know that this No. would be issued so soon—we shall hope to hear from them in time for the third No.

We are happy in being able to say that we have some new correspondents, and we are grateful to all who have given us the assistance of their pens, and hope they will feel that this implies, not only a feeling sense of their kindness, but also a just appreciation of their merit as writers; but we are none of us, angling for praise—a higher and better motive governs us. We are as sisters and brothers having one aim and object, and certain of mutual trust and sympathy; we speak to each other in confidence, and to those who are looking on, in humble hope that a blessing may be reflected on them.

Gentle reader we are with you in spirit and in truth and we confidently expect to be able to please and interest many, in the articles presented in the Offering.

The present No. we think is not sullied by as *many* "unsightly spots" as was the first, and we expect ere long, to be able to feel that it is all that could *reasonably* be expected. We are content to let time prove the worth of such a work; humble though it be.[35]

Friends, we cannot be cold-hearted and indifferent while journeying along together,—we would not be, and may we be better and happier for having spoken to each other; for having *tried* to do each other good, and may the God of mercy keep you all in perfect peace.

C. Cumings

35. *The Offering* was noted in Akron's main newspaper, *The Summit Beacon*, in early July:

> THE AKRON OFFERING, for June, has been on our table some time. It is an improvement upon its predecessor of May. Miss Cummins continues to labor assiduously; the best indication of which is the large amount of original matter. Success to her.

See "Our Book Table," *Summit Beacon* 11, no. 11 (July 4, 1849): 3.

THE

AKRON OFFERING.

July, 1849.

For the Offering.

The Eloquence of Truth.

Truth is always eloquent: It is divine, and claiming such an origin, it comes needing no recommendation and seeking not the applause of men. It belongs on high, yet breathes through all the Creator's works the influences of Heaven, encouraging the humble and moving to good deeds this world's willful. It is no heartless show—no vain exhibition of barren imagery—no semblance glittering to please and alluring to deceive; but the persuasive voice of Heaven in bold and stirring strains; or with an angel's mildness and in melting tones of love.

There is a dignity in the eloquence of truth that we nowhere else behold. It has a richness and beauty that render it attractive—a clearness and force that always brings conviction.

There is no language like the language of truth. Who lives and has not felt its influence? Let the beating heart answer. Its soft whispering voice finds its way to the soul and steals attention. We behold and we admire, and as we listen we are charmed and moved by its power.

The calm impressive tone inspires our confidence, the tone of truth that comes from a peaceful heart and a soul conscious of rectitude.

No manner so impressive and fascinating as that from the genuine feelings of the heart and prompted by a soul sincere.[1]

---

1. A reader of my copy of *The Offering* marked passages in this copy with pencil, as though preparing a part of the text for elocution. In the sentence beginning "No manner so impressive," the reader

No arguments like the arguments of truth to convince and move the mind to action; their power is well nigh irresistible. What avail sophistry and the glare of rhetoric? How tame and contemptible, even they become when truth stares them in the face and life's duty comes. What gives to that orator his touching eloquence, his power to move the thinking multitude? It is the truth that shines in every sentence.

He aims in every word to unfold the truth in all its harmonious proportions. Truth beaming from the countenance, speaking from the eye and giving expression to the whole man, tells upon the listener as nothing else can tell. We can hang upon his lips in breathless attention.

What power in the exhibition of real feeling! We mingle with the cheerful and we are cheerful. We see the suffering and bereaved; we sympathize and weep. The burst of feeling from the heart moves us to and fro as winds the forest.

The Muse, true to nature and in the language of passion, sings of duty and of love and records the imaginings of a soul alive to every beauty. She culls the choicest flowers and sets them in happy order before us. We behold the bright collection and our own souls glow with kindred emotions.

The living lines abound in rich beauty true to nature and in true sentiment. They excite our admiration and enkindle the noblest feelings.

So too does life become eloquent as the character bears upon it the impress of truth. He is an example of living eloquence known and read of all men, whose face beams with truth and whose every act is marked with uprightness. Unavailing is the most learned display in comparison with the influence of that meek man, whose life is consistent with truth and whom none behold but to recognize the image of the divinity he loves.

Our Saviour's life was a perfect model of living, eloquent truth. Every word and act told upon the destiny of the world. The heart lingers around such a character and turns again and again to view its excellence if it copies not the example.

Witness that social circle assembled at noon and eventide.—Hear that father whose head is silvering with years and care while he reads from that old volume the words of brightening truth to the listening group around him. Hear their sacred song and the fervent petition of that humble, hop-

---

underlined "that." In the next paragraph the final word, "sentence," receives emphasis. In the paragraph after, emphasis is placed on "tells," "can tell," "are" (in "we are cheerful"), and "heart" and "us" in "heart moves us." "So too" and "life" at the start of a following paragraph are underlined, and the sentence that begins "Unavailing is the most" is marked with an "X" beside its first letter.

ing man. Witness this scene and feel not if you can, the sacredness of that consecrated place.—What is it but the sweet influence of truth that moves us now and will make us look back with reverence to those hallowed scenes and witness with grateful emotions that old Bible and that old arm chair.

The inspired volume, a monument of the past, still points on to the future. No eloquence has ever reached us like the eloquence of that sacred book. Its friends and foes unite in this. The willing mind reads again and again with increased delight. Its silent eloquence fixes the attention and assimilates the votaries of its excellence to its own most lovely character.

But why so powerful to the heart of man?

"Because of its momentous truth. It speaks to him in his real character and condition, addresses his deepest wants, his highest hopes and brings life and immortality to light."[2] Earth would be a dark and cold abode indeed had it not such a light and lifegiving visitant.

Could we combine in one man, arguments of truth fitly arranged in truthful words, truthful manner and truthful tone inspired with feelings appropriate to the truth, we should behold the profound, the finished orator. Give him the Bible and we shall have a Paul who reasoned of righteousness, convincing thousands, putting to silence the gainsayer and contending successfully against an unbelieving world.[3]

A Luther arises in the midst of darkness when men began to have dreams that were not all dreams.[4] With what admiration do we think of the Prince of the Reformation. Truth beamed from his countenance and his burning words overawed and confounded his haughty and powerful adversaries.

Such eloquence alone moved on that glorious reformation and its tones still sound with deeper interest to us as we peruse the glowing pages of its latest history. Lands rejoice in the freedom it has wrought and the proud church of Rome trembles before the increasing light. A Whitefield speaks to thousands eager to catch his thrilling words.[5] What gives him such power but the simple eloquence of truth?

---

2. Search engines such as American Periodicals and Google Books show that "momentous truth," "real character and condition," "deepest wants," and "highest hopes" were all common phrases or even clichés in American religious writing of the 1840s, but they do not make obvious a source for this quotation.

3. St. Paul, the apostle of Christianity and author of epistles in the New Testament, lived and died in the first century CE.

4. Martin Luther (1483–1546) was the German religious leader of the Protestant Reformation.

5. An English Methodist leader who repeatedly toured America, George Whitefield (1714–70) sparked "awakenings" and did much to nurture the growth of Methodism in America.

The prospect widens. The fire that was first enkindled in the hearts of men by such eloquence, now warns the hearts of other, distant men. And crowds ere long will enlist in this holy war far greater than were ever moved by that eloquent and zealous hermit. The voice of truth shall ring from land to land and a thousand years shall witness its peaceful reign.

Philalethes.[6]

For the Offering.

To an Invalid.

Ah! Mary thou wast beautiful
When no cloud of sorrow dim'd thy sky,
The rose then bloom'd upon thy cheek
And brilliant was thine eye;
But now deep pain and weariness
Have mark'd that mild and thoughtful brow,
Life's evening shades thus early press
And gather round thy path-way now,—
Nor distant seems that solemn hour
When my heart must break—for thou wilt die;
Thy spirit then, with us no more,
Will mingle with the lov'd on high.
Thou wilt be gone,—Thy kindred dear
Will drop the tear of grief for thee,
And methinks with many here,
Thou wilt live in memory.

D. L.

For the Offering.

Random Thoughts.

Another chat with you reader, if you please, for I should die of ennui, if I had no means of throwing off the superabundant information, accumulated since last we met, and this random method, or rather want of method pleas-

6. This ambiguous signature could refer to a number of ancient Greeks, most notably Demosthenes Philalethes, a physician who lived around 1 A.D., or his tutor Alexander Philalethes. This choice of pen names might suggest the author was a doctor.

eth me well, and as I am not ambitious, I seek only to please for the present moment, leaving the glory of posthumous fame, to the thousand *little* celebrities of the day, who are wasting all the energies of life, in toiling for the good of the "rising generation."[7] I feel perfectly willing to let Posterity take care of itself, and I have no doubt, I shall receive as much gratitude from the young scapegrace, as those who sacrifice so much for him. If I succeed in beguiling one sorrowing heart from its cares, even for a few moments, I shall count myself far happier than those, whose names are recorded upon the register of fame. But if any one *should* have penetration enough to see the coruscations of genius, that play around these emanations from my cranium, his applause will be gratefully received, as justly due, though wholly unexpected; it is so seldom that genius meets with the reception it so richly merits.[8]

By the way, how I hate geniuses,—who appear to be elevated from this "sphere of earthliness" by their own egotism alone, and looking down upon others who possess more sense, but less self-esteem, as though they were little elevated above the "cattle upon a thousand hills."[9] I happen to be acquainted with one of these "Byronian" characters, whose melancholy egotism, is displeasing to all except himself—but he really seems to take so much pleasure in supposing his common-placeisms above the comprehension of other minds, that it would really be cruel to unscale his eyes, and yet reader, I must confess, I have been so malicious as to insinuate, (mildly of course,) that his loftiest flights of fancy, had reached the level, where my imagination ceased to act, having sought a higher place, than could be reached by one so weak of wing as his "dear muse."—Ever prateth he, of "strength of feeling," "love of the beautiful," "unappreciated genius," and "posthumous fame," with such a lackadaisical air, that it is impossible to subdue one's risible faculties, while listening to his plaintive tale.[10] I know not when he first began to feel the movings of the mighty spirit of Poesy; it must have been when quite young, for at fourteen we find him penning lines to his "ladye love," and as this love must of course, be a hopeless one, he has ever since sent forth the "deep wailings," of a wounded heart, to

7. Lizzie responds to pp. 45 and 63.

8. A "coruscation" is a flash, a sudden burst of light, as produced by the combustion of inflammable gas.

9. Another use of this quote from Shelley's *Queen Mab*; see n. 6, p. 39. For Byron, see n. 8, p. 40. In 1849, "cattle upon a thousand hills" was a common American cliché, taken from Psalm 50:10. As the tone of this essay suggests, the remaining phrases are also clichés of antebellum American romantic literature. With some, search engines such as those for American Periodicals and Google Books reveal a comical degree of popularity.

10. "Risible": able to laugh, laughable; "faculties": powers of the mind.

entrance the wondering world. Poor fellow, how I pity him—may he meet the oblivious fate he so much merits, with a resignation becoming one, who sought, but found not immortality in *romance.*

That last word suggests to me, one of the pleasantest books ever produced; it is a novel, but I shall not tell *what* novel, lest some should condemn my taste, and perhaps many have done so already,—and now suppose I give you a disquisition upon novels. Almost every paper and book of morality, speaks of the vast amount of evil produced by reading fictitious works, and we must confess that much that has been adduced is true, and yet we think it will appear that these evils arise more from an immoderate use, than from the works themselves—do not misunderstand me, we do not mean those ephemeral productions, with which the land is literally flooded; these are many of them too insipid to excite any thing but disgust, and I rejoice that it is so; it is a sure indication that the *evils* attendant upon their multiplicity will soon pass away.[11] Writers have been multiplied, as were the frogs upon the coast of Egypt,[12] and imagination has been drained to furnish thrilling scenes, to cause the youthful blood to chill, and it would be strange indeed, if there were no bad novels; the greater wonder would be if there were none; and yet their very multiplicity gives us the surest indication of the cessation of their production; every walk in life has lent its quota to the novelists' pen, and there is nothing new under the sun upon which they can exert their fancy, and those who now write, only pass over the same ground occupied by their "illustrious predecessors," and there is so much sameness to the later productions, that they cease to please, and that is the main object with such works. In a novel life is spread out before us like a map, and we may there learn without the bitterness of experience how to avoid the many errors of life. Youth ever looks upon the bright side of the picture—friends smile and they confide—hope whispers to them of the bright future, and they listen with pleasure

11. In her book, *Revolution and the Word: The Rise of the Novel in America* (New York: Oxford University Press, 1986), Cathy N. Davidson describes the prejudice against novels in America from the Revolution to the early nineteenth-century. At mid-century, fiction remained a target for some preachers and editors. For example, American bishop Leonidas Lent Hamline (1789–1865) attacked fiction while editor of the important (especially in the West) literary magazine *The Ladies' Repository*. This was published in Cincinnati for the Methodist Church's Western Book Concern. In one editorial Hamline writes that "nothing can be more killing to devotion than the perusal of a book of fiction," and he specifically excoriates a minister rumored to have recommended, to the young daughter of his friend, *The Scottish Chiefs*, an 1827 historical romance about William Wallace and Robert Bruce by Scottish novelist Jane Porter (1776–1850). See "Editor's Table," *The Ladies' Repository, and Gatherings of the West* 3, no. 1 (January 1843): 32, Google Books, http://books.google.com/books?id=e8gRAAAAYAAJ. Note also that *The Akron Offering* was criticized for publishing too much "light reading" by a rival editor, A. Moore. See p. 241.

12. Exodus 8:5–7.

to the syren voice, and after experience had taught them the falsity of these views, the heart retires within itself, and they resolve no longer to trust what has so often deceived them—they fancy themselves alone, in this heroical misanthropy, and yet there is not one who has arrived at maturity, that has not experienced the same. There is a spice of romance in every heart—then why scorn we those, who have but written, what is all too true, in pleasing colors, leading us to trust even when deceived, and portraying the nobleness of suffering innocence, and vice again is ever represented as bringing upon itself sooner or later, the fearful fate that always pursues the guilty one.

But I hear some one ask "why not find this in real life?"—We do—yet biographers are so fearful of being romantic that all these are left for the novelists' pen, and the only reason that can be given for the partiality evinced for novels, is their truthfulness. It speaketh to the heart as though it was its other heart, and they learn there how much may be suffered in silence, and they too are willing to do so. There are some minds that never would grasp an idea if it came to them in the solemn garb of an historical axiom; yet as it is given in novels they appreciate it as it deserves and profit therefrom. They require something more stimulating and after they have reveled in a world of romance long enough, the mind will of its own accord, seek higher good than mere present enjoyment; at least such was my case. I was not permitted to peruse one, and there was nothing in the world of letters presented to me in real history that answered to my own wild imaginings.—When about eight years old, I chanced to meet with the "Scottish Chiefs," and from that time until I was sixteen I lived in a world of romance; stealthily of course.[13] I cannot tell you the rapidity with which books were literally devoured by me; no one dreamed of it save the lady whose library furnished me, and she could not imagine how I could dispose of so much reading. Every thing received a hearing from me, and I can never describe the rapture I experienced when I first read "Paradise Lost," and the almost adoration I felt for Satan as there portrayed.[14] "Pollok's Course of Time," followed next, then—but no, I will not tell you all; suffice it that I was happy, and no one knew of it for I feared to speak lest I should betray myself, and be denied my pleasures.[15] I grew up

13. See n. 11, above. Lizzie appears to agree with the minister attacked by Hamline, as here she explains how Porter's novel characterized an immoderate reading practice that led to more serious and devotional texts.

14. Epic Christian poem, popular in antebellum America, by English poet John Milton (1608–74).

15. Scottish poet Robert Pollok (1798–1827) published *Course of Time*, an epic poem on the future of mankind, in 1827. Written in blank verse and divided into ten books, Pollok's epic was often compared to *Paradise Lost*. To read an American edition of the poem, see Pollok's *Course of Time*, 4th American ed. (Amherst: J. S. and C. Adams, 1828), Google Books, http://books.google.com /books?id=j6xUAAAAYAAJ.

a timid child, because I felt this necessity for concealment, and here let me say, that every parent ought to look after the amusements of their children, and see how they spend their leisure hours; seek their confidence and make them feel that you are their best friend, by denying them nothing that is not really injurious; let them read novels, even when children, and do not fear that their minds will be polluted by any thing there found—their own purity will guard against this, and by thus permitting them to select their own reading, you lay the foundation for a sounder structure—better read them when young than after you have become older.

I would say to all, read—and if you do not read anything else, read novels; boys too—it is better you should be at home, even reading novels than frequenting the various haunts of vice, every where found; and after you have reveled long enough in an imaginary world, you will seek something more substantial in the real, and you can then call out the lessons of morality there learned, and practice them.

Lizzie

For the Offering.

A Freak of Morpheus.[16]

By Lily Lute.[17]

On a sultry afternoon in August, when every plant and shrub seemed withering under the scorching of the summer sun, and the only air in the dusty town was like the breath of a furnace, I wandered forth towards the wood in search of some shady thicket where I might be fanned by a cooler breeze. I sought a path leading along the banks of a beautiful stream, that wound among the hills, and along the vallies like a silver thread, until its meanderings were lost in the distant wood. I wandered on, through meadows and over hills, stopping sometimes to watch the graceful swing of the mowers, to listen to the ring of their scythes, the song of the reapers, or to catch the faint hum of the village I had left, till the sounds at length died away in

16. A "freak" is a sudden change of place; a whim, a daydream. Morpheus, in Roman mythology, is the god of sleep and dreams.

17. Antebellum American women often combined familiar names with romantic or amusing surnames to create pen names such as Fanny Forester, Ruth Rover, Dolly Dindle, Grace Gayfeather, and Fanny Fern. For more on Lute, see n. 15, p. 44.

the distance, and, wearied and faint, I began to look about for a shady seat. At the foot of a hill I espied a small grove, whose thick shade promised a cool retreat from the burning sun. I entered, and having a book with me, seated myself on a fallen tree, and was soon buried so deeply in the mysteries of the Sketch Book, that night drew on ere I was conscious of the time.[18] I arose and looked for the setting sun, but it had disappeared, and I could only see its bright, golden track in the western sky; and, as the shades of twilight were fast deepening into night, I was hastening to leave the grove, when a light in the east promised soon to show me Cynthia's pale face,[19] and I returned to my seat to enjoy another view of the lovely landscape, which was soon brightening under the rays of a full moon that shone with almost mid-day splendor, while the stars peeped gaily out, contributing their little light to add, if possible, new beauties to the scene—a scene that in rural beauty could not be surpassed; it was one of nature's loveliest. There were fields whose golden grain, ready for the sickle and wet with the tears of night, drooped heavily; and pastures, in white clover clad, where the gentle kine,[20] eased of their luscious burdens, rested lazily, while orchards bending beneath the burden of their ripening fruit, cast broad shadows over the waving grass. Meadows in luxuriant garb arrayed, sent forth balmy odors on the night-breeze, which springing up, had moderated the air and rendered it delightful; and now it played with the long streamers of the green corn sending them out dancing to the sound of their own music, and then sweeping gently through the lofty trees, lifting their dewy leaves with a pleasant, rustling sound. The lowing ox and tired horse, freed from the labor of the field, came to refresh themselves in the stream, while a few songsters in the grove warbled lowly as the moon shone brightly into their nests, and the night-hawk wheeled and sported in the blue ether above. I had been sitting, I know not how long, gazing at the glittering, cloudless sky, reflected in the bright water at my feet, when I was startled by the sound of approaching footsteps, and a moment after a couple entered the grove and seated themselves near me. I soon found by their conversation that they were lovers; and as they sat with uncovered heads, where the moonbeams fell full upon their faces, I saw that they were very beautiful.

18. Washington Irving (1783–1859) published essays and short fiction as *The Sketch Book of Geoffrey Crayon, Gent.* (1819–20). *The Akron Offering* contains many examples of the antebellum genre, the "sketch," which was not quite the same thing as a "short story." For more on the sketch as a distinct genre, see Kristie Hamilton, *America's Sketchbook: The Cultural Life of a Nineteenth-Century Literary Genre* (Athens: Ohio University Press, 1998).

19. "Cynthia" is another name for Artemis, the Greek goddess of the moon.

20. Cows.

The lady was very young, not over sixteen I judged, and fair as the dawn. A brow that vied with the lily in whiteness, was shaded by a profusion of jetty curls, which encircled a head of such classic beauty as might have served a model for Powers' Eve;[21] her full black eyes, wore an expression of softness seldom ever seen in black eyes, and their lustre was heightened by the glow of her cheeks, whose deep rose-tints seemed deepening still with excitement; her beautifully curved lips were such as an artist loves to paint, and when they opened, disclosed a set of pearly teeth that an Houri would have been proud of.[22] Her companion was also quite young, his age could scarce have exceeded twenty years, and his form was so slight and boyish, as to give an idea of extreme delicacy of constitution; his eyes were of that clear blue so rarely found, except in early days of childhood; his ample forehead bore the stamp of intellect, and his light hair curled as gracefully about it as though a mother's hand had just threaded its silken mazes.[23] They had at first conversed in low murmurs, but now their conversation became audible, and I gathered from it that this was a stolen interview.

"Yes, Jessie," said the young man, "it would be much better to part now—now while our hearts are young in love—our love free from passion. If I go now, you are so young, you will soon forget me and love again some one more favored by fortune than I am, or can ever expect to be."

"Indeed, indeed, Frank," said she, while tears almost choked her utterance. "You wrong me—you do not know my heart, or you would not wound it thus. Forget you! you, whose image is enshrined in my heart, and worshipped with the purest devotion ever mortal felt. O, I would lay down my life for you—and can you for a moment believe I could ever forget you?"

"No, my sweet Jessie, I believe I was wrong; I believe you do love me to some extent; I can read it in those soul-beaming eyes; can feel it in the convulsive clasp of that delicate hand—but what can I—what must I do? Your father has forbidden me his presence, and commanded me never to enter his house again; then, how can I hope he will ever consent to our union?"

"While you are poor and friendless, he never will. Alas! that it should be so in our own free and enlightened America, where talent and worth

21. Ohio sculptor Hiram Powers (1805–73) was an antebellum sensation with his life-size statues of women, *Eve* (1842) and *The Greek Slave* (1845). The full nudity of these statues, which were also regarded as representations of ideal womanly virtue, made for lively museum debates. For a nuanced reading of the meaning of these statues and their press coverage, see Joy S. Kasson, "Narratives of the Female Body: The Greek Slave." In *The Culture of Sentiment: Race, Gender, and Sentimentality in Nineteenth-Century America*, ed. Shirley Samuels (New York: Oxford University Press, 1992), 172–90.

22. In Islam, a "houri" is a nymph of paradise.

23. See n. 16, p. 87.

should be passports to the first circles, and fathers should be proud and happy to bestow their daughters on men of genius and worth; if he were not my father, I should say many bitter things of him, but he is, and as such, I love him, and dare not disobey him."

"Nor will I ask you to, and were I certain by toiling a few years I could win you, most willing would I tax this frail body with the most incessant toil; but what can I hope, when by the greatest exertions I can only support myself? How, then, can I amass a fortune that would satisfy your father?"

"Be more hopeful, dear Frank, you are yet young, and already you are a skillful artist, while your pen contributes to the best periodicals of the day. Every production of your pen and pencil, if executed with skill, will inspire you to do better, until ere long you will rank among the first of our country's poets and painters; and then, when you are known to fame, your works will command money as well as adulation; and if, in your transit from obscurity to renown, you have not learned to forget your loving Jessie, my father will readily sign her over to the distinguished Frank Fleetwood. Ha! ha! how happy I shall be then, Franky."

"O, you are a lovely prophetess, and I should be quite happy now, were I as sanguine as you are."

"And you *are* happy now, I know it; I can see it in your dancing eyes. O, I knew I could chase the blues away from you—how I wish you would be as happy as I am—why, I never have the blues, and father says he will send me to a convent if I don't laugh less and reform my hoidenish ways, and Mr. Bodeen says I am a perfect daughter of Momus."[24]

"Mr. Bodeen! and pray, Jessie, who is Mr. Bodeen?"

"He is a bewhiskered dandy with rotten brains, whom my father wishes me to marry, because he thinks he is rich, but I know he is not, and there's the fun of it. I'll make pap think I am quite willing, and have him prepare for a splendid wedding, and then manage to let him know how hard the whiskerando's purse is crying for *quarters*.[25] Will not that be rare sport?"

And she clapped her hands with childish glee, while her silvery laugh rung out on the clear night like a peal of musical bells.—Frank caught the infection, and laughed too, right merrily. At this moment my attention was attracted from the lovers, by the sudden agitation of a cluster of bushes that grew just back of them, and I discovered that the bushes contained a mass of something in the shape of a human form, and as it slowly emerged from

24. Momus was the Greek god of satire.

25. "Cry for quarter": ask for mercy.

them into the light, I came to the conclusion that it must be the dandy of whom Jessie had spoken; for he had a very wicked face to which was attached a monstrous pair of whiskers, resembling in color a faded brick-bat,[26] and his clumsy person was foppishly dressed and bedecked with a profusion of Jewelry. I watched him as he stealthily approached the couple, wondering all the while what he was going to do; but when I saw him raise a heavy club I was no longer at a loss how to interpret his movements and tried to scream, but the sound stuck in my throat and with all my exertions, I could not utter a sound loud enough to be heard. However, Frank discovered him in time to spring aside, just as the club came down with a force that sent the dandy into the stream. I saw in a moment, that he could not swim and that without help must surely drown. Frank saw it too and with a noble impulse hastened to his assistance, and as he was an expert swimmer, soon brought the dandy to the shore—but they had scarce gained a footing, when the villain clutched his preserver and throwing him back into the water, tried to hold his head under. Frank struggled manfully but his strength began to fail, when a missile from an unseen hand, came in contact with the head of the villainous dandy and sent him back into the stream—the water closed over him and he sunk down—down—O, pshaw! I am awake now and that was all a dream.

For the Offering.

Lines for Jane L. Sims of Litchfield, Ohio.[27]

True thoughts, and pure ones,
    Upstart in thy breast,
Images beautiful,
    Break on thy rest,
Thy heart's gushing tenderness
    Beams from thine eyes,

26. A "brickbat" is a piece of a brick.

27. A toddler, Jane Sims appears in the 1850 census with her father, John W. Sims, in Sharon township of Medina county. United States of America, Bureau of the Census. *Seventh Census of the United States, 1850*. NARA microfilm publication M432. (Washington, D.C.: National Archives and Records Administration, n.d.), roll M432_709, page 319B, Ancestry.com. Larger than Litchfield, which had about 800 residents, Sharon had a population around 1300. Both towns were west of Akron: Litchfield, about thirty miles west and Sharon, about twelve miles west. See Daniel Haskel and J. Calvin Smith, *A Complete Descriptive and Statistical Gazetteer of the United States of America* (New York: Sherman & Smith, 1848), 349, 608, Google Books, http://books.google.com/books?id=UOstAAAAYAAJ. John W. Sims was a wagon maker and Philomel Weed's family operated a livery stable, so perhaps the twenty-one-year-old writer met the three-year-old girl as her father called on business.

And the demon of passion,
    In stern fetters lies.

Oh! be it thus ever
    Through Life's winding way;
May nought from thee sever
    Pure Virtue's mild ray;
May beautiful visions
    E'er burst on thy sight,
Their brightness dispelling
    The blackness of night.
True, fond hearts are beating
    In union with thine;
And responses are leaping
    From each pulse of mine;
And in days of the future,
    Where'er you may dwell,
Remember the Friendship
    Of your Philomel.[28]

Jackson.

For the Offering.

Vine Cottage.[29]

By Mrs. Philomel S. Weed.[30]

It was on a delightful afternoon in the month of July, while making the tour of the Eastern States, I chanced to stop at a small Inn, near the pleasant town of Bloomingrove, situated in the southern part of New Hampshire.[31]

28. For Philomel S. Weed, see n. 52, p. 61.

29. In my copy of *The Akron Offering*, a reader wrote "Good," in what looks like a nineteenth-century hand, in the margin above the title of this story. The hand and the ink appear to be the same as those of the critic of the volume's opening story. See n. 2, p. 30.

30. See n. 52, p. 61.

31. A fictional place; there was neither a "Bloomingrove" nor a "Blooming Grove" in New Hampshire. Ohio, on the other hand, had numerous "Bloomfields," a "Bloomingburg," a "Bloomingdale," a "Blooming Grove" (in Mansfield County), a "Bloomington," and a "Bloomville." "Blooming" names were popular in the midwest. See Thomas Baldwin and J. Thomas, *A New and Complete Gazetteer of the United States* (Philadelphia: Lippincott, Grambo, 1854), 115–17, Google Books, http://books.google.com/books?id=_5s6AAAAcAAJ. See also Daniel Haskel and J. Calvin Smith, *A Complete*

Being somewhat fatigued with travelling, I concluded to remain a few days, to recruit[32] myself and horse. It was a most beautiful and romantic spot. The village stood upon a plain at the foot of a high hill, and was bounded at the southern extremity by a small, but beautiful and mirror-like lake. It contained about twenty-four houses, of modern structure, very neatly built. In my casual walks through the place, I had frequently observed a small, neat looking cottage, nearly concealed from view by vines and shrubbery. The evergreen and myrtle had been trained by a well directed hand and taste, as was evident from the luxurious festoons which graced the windows and door-way. While taking my usual walk one evening, I noticed a young girl seated in an arbor covered with honeysuckles, at the end of the Cottage.—On my return I inquired of "mine host,"[33] Mr. Waters, "who inhabited the sweet-looking Cottage of which I have spoken?"

"What! Vine Cottage? Oh! the widow Ashbel and her daughter, live there. Mr. Ashbel died about a year ago, and it made Clara almost crazy, but I guess she's got most over it now, for she's coming to the ball to-morrow night with George Morrison. They say he's courting her, but I don't believe it, for she never liked him, though her father did, and tried to make her promise to marry him because he's rich, and old Ashbel wanted Clara to marry a rich man; but I don't believe she'll have him, any how; for her mother lets her do just as she's a mind to."

I felt quite interested in Mr. Waters' relation, and upon intimating a desire to obtain an introduction, he said he could easily procure me a ticket to the ball, as it was to be held at his house, and his son was one of the managers, and there I would have a good opportunity of being introduced.

The evening came, and with it the company. It was to be a social dance, and no strangers were there except myself, and of course I attracted much attention. I had been introduced to, and danced, laughed, and chatted with half the ladies in the room, but no one by the name of Miss Ashbel, and nearly out of patience that she was not there, I was inquiring of Mr. Waters the reason—"there she is," exclaimed he, and looking around, I saw a lady and gentleman entering the room.

At a glance I knew it was the same lady I had seen at Vine Cottage. But how shall I describe Clara Ashbel as she appeared to me that evening?

Descriptive and Statistical Gazetteer of the United States of America (New York: Sherman & Smith, 1848), 68–69, Google Books, http://books.google.com/books?id=UOstAAAAYAAJ.

32. To repair with fresh supplies.

33. My innkeeper.

Her person was below the ordinary size, but faultless and sylph-like[34] in its proportions,—her head and face were of a delicate size and shape—her eyes were of a blue color, Yes! they were beautifully, mildly blue—and then such hands and feet! you would have thought they belonged to a fairy.

The gentleman who accompanied her would have been good looking, but for a certain jealous expression about his eyes,—he appeared to regard Clara as his own property, while in her, I thought I could discover marked manifestations of aversion towards him.

"Mr. Morrison," said Mr. Waters, Jr., "let me introduce you to Mr. Lawrence. He is a stranger in our place, and we must do our best to entertain him while he stays."

Mr. Morrison extended his hand, and after a short conversation, during which I discovered that he possessed a well-informed mind, we separated to seek partners for the next cotillion. I danced with Miss Ashbel, while Mr. Morrison selected Miss King for a partner.

"Clara do not bestow so many smiles on Mr. Lawrence. George's gooseberry orbs are looking at you as jealous as you please; do see him," said one of the ladies nearest Clara, to her in a low voice.

"Fie! Annett, ain't you ashamed to talk so? Mr. Lawrence will hear you;" and on looking at me, her brow flushed as she discovered that I had heard them. I cast a look at George, and he seemed the very personification of jealousy; for Clara and I were carrying on an agreeable conversation, in the most agreeable manner. I was surprised at the expression of his countenance, but said nothing.

Meantime I had fallen in love with Clara, myself; for besides being remarkably beautiful, she had been well educated, and her ready flow of wit and spirits made her a pleasing companion.—When the company parted for the night, I slipped my card into Miss Ashbel's hand, and asked permission to call upon her in the morning. She granted it, and bidding Mr. Morrison 'good evening,' I sought my chamber. My dreams that night were of a pleasant kind, and in them Clara often appeared to soothe my sleeping visions.

The next morning after paying particular attention to my toilet,[35] I wended my way toward the dwelling of Mrs. Ashbel. The Cottage stood

---

34. Airy; light; like a sylph, an imaginary being that lives in the air.

35. A toilet is a piece or set of furniture used for dressing—a chest of drawers or a table, for example, perhaps with a mirror and washing-bowl. The word was also used to indicate a dressing-room with such furnishings, the act or ritual of getting dressed, or the final outfit, that sum of whatever toiletries, clothing, and accessories. As daily bathing became a more important part of such preparation in the United States, "bath-room" and "toilet" became more interchangeable terms.

some distance from the road, and in front of it was a well-cultivated garden. The exterior of the house presented a most inviting appearance; the windows were shaded by a curtain of vines, as also was the whole front of the house, from foundation to roof.

At the end of the Cottage was the arbor of which I have spoken, and seated in it was Clara, who left it and entered the house as she saw me approaching. I knocked and she came to the door and invited me into the parlor.[36]

Mrs. Ashbel soon came in, to whom Clara introduced me as Mr. Lawrence who was spending a few days in their village, and with whom she formed an acquaintance the evening previous. Mrs. Ashbel's greeting was courteous and friendly, and during my stay, her conversation upon the various topics that were introduced, shew an extensive acquaintance with the manners and customs of the world. Clara said but little, but that little was worth a good deal from others. I left them with an invitation to call as often as inclination prompted.

For a week I visited there regularly, during which time I had discovered that I loved Clara, with my whole heart. Her unaffected manners and conversation, so unlike that of the city belles with whom I had associated, her sweet disposition, and the engaging graces of her person, had won upon me, until I found that without her, life would be a desert without a single Oasis to rest my heart upon. But I,—a stranger,—how could I hope she had any interest in me more than common Friendship. From day to day did I defer leaving the place; 'tis true my business was not urgent—but why stay so long without any apparent object?

I had met George Morrison but once at Vine Cottage, and he manifested the same symptoms of jealousy he had on the night of the ball. I knew he loved Clara and "wooed her for his wife"[37] and I thought I knew she disliked him.

One evening upon calling at Vine Cottage I found Mrs. Ashbel absent from home, and Clara training the vines through the trellis-work of the arbor. She invited me to enter the house but I took a seat in the arbor,

36. The parlor was an informal sitting room for the use of family and perhaps close friends. In most American homes, the parlor was also the dining room. In larger antebellum homes, these would be separate rooms, and parlors might be found on the upper floors among the bedrooms. A more formal room dedicated for the reception of company would be known as a "drawing-room" or a "withdrawing-room."

37. After a line spoken by Petruchio to Katherina in *The Taming of the Shrew* by William Shakespeare (1564–1616). See *Dramatic Works of William Shakespeare* (Boston: Phillips, Sampson, and Company, 1850), 2:484, Google Books, http://books.google.com/books?id=DSEAAAAAQAAJ.

telling her I proposed sitting there, it was so cool and pleasant. My mind was in such suspense that I was determined to bring matters to a crisis. I begged her to take a seat beside me, which she did, blushing as though she divined my object.

"Clara," said I, "have you not thought what detained me in this place so long? Oh! Clara, I do love you with my whole soul.—Say, dearest, must I continue hereafter to live without hope?" I received no answer and by her violent agitation I knew she was weeping. "Oh! Clara, for my sake, for your own sake, answer me."

"Oh! leave me now, I beseech you, leave me, and come to-morrow, and then"—she said no more but bursting into tears, rushed from the arbor.

I returned to my own room with feelings little to be envied. I could not account for her strange conduct and agitation. It was an enigma to me, and how to solve it I knew not. I spent that night and the next day in a state of mind bordering upon insanity; and towards evening went to Vine Cottage to hear the decision upon which depended the happiness or misery of my future life.—Clara looked pale—very pale—and after I was seated she looked anxiously and nervously towards her mother as if wishing her to begin the conversation.

"Mr. Lawrence," Mrs. Ashbel at length said, "Clara has related to me your conversation of last night." She paused as if expecting me to speak.

"Mrs. Ashbel," said I, "from my early childhood to speak with candor has been my first object. If you will favor me by listening, I will give you some insight into my past life." She bowed her head in token of assent, and I proceeded. "My parentage is wealthy and respectable. I was born in the city of Baltimore and have always resided there. My father is a merchant, and I was educated for the same profession, but my health being precarious, the business proved too confining for me and I was advised to travel. For the last two years I have travelled nearly all the time. I have visited the principal towns and seaports in the United States, and my health is much improved; but until I stopped in your sweet village, I have found nothing to detain me long in one place. I have now given you a slight sketch of my uneventful life—but I am not yet done. From the first moment in which I beheld your daughter, I have loved her with an intensity of passion of which I have hitherto deemed myself incapable. I know not that I have excited in her bosom one responsive feeling—one chord that will vibrate, to my own heart-strings."

"I know nothing of the state of Clara's feelings upon the subject," replied Mrs. Ashbel, "she must speak for herself. Clara, be candid with Mr. Lawrence, for his happiness and your own is involved in your answer."

Clara was opening her lips to speak, when glancing towards the window, she uttered a loud shriek and rushing forward, fell senseless in my arms, exclaiming "George Morrison." Mrs. Ashbel sprang towards her, and at that instant the quick, sharp report of a pistol was heard from the direction of the window, and Mrs. Ashbel, with a groan, sank to the floor. The report was heard by the neighbors, who immediately came in, and we soon succeeded in restoring Clara, who had only fainted, while a surgeon was being summoned to attend upon her mother. A few minutes brought him, and he assured us she was not dangerously hurt, her only injury being a flesh wound in the arm, which a few weeks would heal.

The first confusion incident to such a scene being over, all were anxiety to know the meaning of it. One of the neighbors affirmed that as she was running with all speed toward the house, she had seen a man whom she took to be George Morrison, looking in at the window. But, Clara, the only one who knew with certainty who it was, refused to converse on the subject before so many, but whispered me, "I have great deal to say to you another time," and added, "it is no more than I expected." I left them in the care of attendants, and returned home in what I may call a happy state of mind, for since the attempt upon my life, there had been something in her demeanor towards me, which spoke of hope and requited love.

And what could have been George Morrison's motive for wishing to take my life? I had never injured him—but jealousy, that foul fiend of darkness, I knew was at the foundation, and I depended upon Clara to unravel the whole mystery for me.

The next morning I went early to Vine Cottage, and found Mrs. Ashbel very comfortable, and Clara quite recovered from the effects of her fright although weak and excited. After remaining a short time in the room with her mother, she invited me into another apartment. When we were seated, Clara said, "Mr. Lawrence, I do not doubt but your motives for visiting here are pure and honorable, and as you have been so frank and candid with us, you shall be met in the same spirit. I will tell you of my acquaintance with that bold, wicked man, who would have murdered you. We had removed to this place from our dear Southern home in Savannah,[38]

38. Savannah, Georgia, was then a prosperous port city and railroad hub of about 16,000 people, including perhaps six or seven thousand slaves. See Thomas Baldwin and J. Thomas, *A New and*

on account of the delicate state of my health, and had spent some three or four months in entire seclusion with the exception of the acquaintance of Mr. Morrison's family, who had visited us on our first coming hither, and with whom we have ever since been intimate.

"At our first meeting, George was very polite and attentive, and after a very short acquaintance, asked my permission to visit here in the character of my lover, and if not repugnant to my feelings, my future husband. I told him it was impossible for me to receive visits of such a nature from him,—that I had no attachment for him or any one else, stronger than friendship would sanction,—but he urged his passion with so much ardor, that, at my father's urgent desire, I consented to receive his visits. For a year he was very constant in his attentions, which I endured with an ill grace, as I had never given him any encouragement, and had frequently told him I could never marry him. His rage and jealousy at such times were unbounded,—he used the most violent language—and threatened fearful vengeance against every gentleman who dare presume to address me," she added, while a blush suffused itself over her sweet face.

"I know it! I know it!" I replied. "Oh, give me the right to protect you, sweet one, and if mortal arm can sweep the sorrows from your life's pathway, mine shall be that arm."

She frankly extended her hand—that so-much coveted treasure, and softly murmured—"my heart is already yours. My hand *shall* be, when you see fit to claim it."

Words are inadequate to express the ecstacy of that moment, and I hasten to conclude my tale.

On inquiry, George Morrison was found to be absent from home, and his friends strongly affirmed that he had embarked for Europe on the morning previous to the dark transactions of that night, on important commercial business. Did not his absence tell the tale?

Six months from that period the vows were pronounced which made me the happy husband of sweet Clara Ashbel. Years have passed since then—dear little forms are clustering around our hearth—sweet musical voices are lisping our names—time has wrought its various changes—yet have I never for one moment regretted my first acquaintance with the dear inhabitants of Vine Cottage.

Complete Gazetteer of the United States (Philadelphia: Lippincott, Grambo, 1854), 1053–55, Google Books, http://books.google.com/books?id=_5s6AAAAcAAJ.

About twelve years after our marriage, as we were quietly drinking tea one sunny afternoon, a carriage drove rapidly to the door, and a gentleman alighted and handed out a lady and two children. As they advanced to the door, I noticed, Clara start and turn pale as death. I looked into the gentleman's face, and saw the features of my once deadly enemy, George Morrison.

"Oh! give me not another such look;" he cried, as he met my horrified gaze; "I cannot endure it, after the years of anguish I have already suffered." He then told us of the terrible remorse that had followed him year after year,—and after amassing a large fortune, his determination to return to his native land and seek out the beings he had so wronged, obtain their forgiveness if possible, and be no longer lashed by the stings of an unbraiding conscience. He had in the mean time loved and married an interesting and lovely European lady, and we now rank Mr. and Mrs. Morrison among our warmest friends—and many a happy evening is spent with them in talking over past scenes, and enjoying the present at Vine Cottage.

Old Hickory, Wayne Co., Ohio.[39]

The Poet.

From Lamartine—By J. S. Du Solle.[40]

Thou dark-eyed, pensive, passionate child of song!
Enthusiast! dreamer! worshipper of things
By the world's crowd unnoticed, 'mid the throng
Of beautiful creations, Nature flings
The sunlight of existence o'er!
The wings of the rude tempest are not half so strong
As thy proud hopes—thy wild imaginings:
Stop! ere their bold and sacrilegious flight
Reach a too-dazzling height,
Venturing sunward, till the flashing eye
Of reason, grown delirious bright,
Kindle to madness, and to idiocy;

39. The name of a post office in Wayne County. See nn. 52 and 53 on pp. 61 and 63.

40. This poem appeared (as the work of "J. S. D. S.") in the July 1837 number of the New York City literary periodical, *The Knickerbocker*. See J. S. D. S., "The Poet." *The Knickerbocker* 10, no. 1 (July 1837): 33, American Periodicals (137195484). The version of *The Knickerbocker* includes a ten-line epigraph in French that is omitted here. Alphonse de Lamartine (1790–1869) was a French poet and politician.

And, from excessive light,
To hideous blindness fall, and tenfold night!
Stop! melancholy youth!
Though bright and sparkling be the tide of song,
And many a sunbeam o'er its waters dance
Meandering along—
Though it be heaven to quaff of—yet, in truth,
A deadlier venom taints its gay expanse,
More deep, more strong,
Than to the subtlest poison doth belong!
A very demon haunts its fœted air,
Infatuating with its serpent glance
The wanderer there;
And, with a sad but most bewitching smile,
Luring the credulous one to its desire:
Stirring new feelings, passions, hopes awhile.
And burning thoughts, whose mad, unholy fire,
With its own strength illumes its own funeral pyre!
Stop, if thou'dst live!—or hath life left for thee
No charms, that thou its last terrific scene
Should'st with such passion worship? Can it be,
That the world nothing hath thou'dst care to win?
No gem, no flower, no loveliness, unseen?
No wonder unexplored, no mysteries
Still undeveloped to the eagle eye
Of Genius, or of Poesy?
Where are the depths of the dark, billowy sea?
Its peopling millions—its gigantic chain
Of gorgeous, glittering waters—wild as free,
Where the big orbed sun—the blue veiled sky?
And its magnificent, diamond-glittering mine
Of ever-burning stars? Oh! can it be,
(Thou fond idolater at every shrine
Where beauty lingers,) can it be that thou
Hast treasured up earth's glorious things, till now
Thou deem'st it uselessness to turn,
Some unfamiliar object to discern,

  And so
Her loveliest features unregarded go?
Away vain thought! Such phrenzy ne'er were thine!
Since, in the humblest, homeliest flower that grows—
Thy very life breath, as it comes and goes—
There are a thousand things, whose origin,
Whose secret springs, and impulses divine,
No human art nor wisdom can disclose!

Stop, then sad youth! for life is not *all* care,
But, hath its hour of rosy-lipped delight;
While the cold grave hath little save despair,
The weary, world-worn spirit to invite.
Stop! I conjure thee! bid the muse away!
Her fatal gifts relinquish or resign;
Her haughty mandates heed not nor obey:
E'en *now* thy brow hath sorrow's pallid sign—
Thine eye, though bright, is like the flickering ray
Of a 'stray sunbeam, o'er some ruin'd shrine,'
Lighting up vestiges almost divine,
In sad, yet, dimly-beautiful decay!
Thy cheek is sunken, and the fickle play
Of the faint smile that curls thy parted lip
Hath something fearful in it, though so gay!
A something treacherously calm, and deep,
Such as on sunny waters seems to sleep,
When hid beneath some passing shadows gray,
The subtle storm fiend watches for his prey.

Stop! ere thine hour of dalliance be over;
Ere Health abandon thee, and quench her light
In the dark stream of death (the faithless rover!)
  Ere Hope herself take flight
Down to the depths of that dark-flowing river,
Whose somber shores are clothed in endless night;
Ere thou be wrested from us—and for ever!
Blotted, like some loved planet, from our sight!

And, save the ties
That not e'en Destiny itself can sever,
A feeble reminiscence or a name
Be all thou leav'st us of thee 'neath the skies—
Or some rude stone, perchance, to greet our eyes,
And, with its speechless eloquence proclaim:
'Here lies
Another victim to thy love, O Fame!'

Knickerbocker.[41]

"Faint praise is disparagement"[42]—and no proverb more true than this. Ask a man his opinion upon any subject, and if he says "O, I like it very well—tolerably well" and then qualifies it with a few "buts" and "ifs," you may be assured that he has some *particular dislike* for it, or from some *selfish* motive, is unwilling to give his honest opinion.

"Two things are indicative of a weak mind," says Saadi, the Persian Sage, "to be silent when it is proper to speak, and to speak when it is proper to be silent."[43]

41. *The Knickerbocker, or New-York Monthly Magazine* (1833–65) was an important antebellum magazine that was brought into prominence by twin brothers Lewis Gaylord Clark and Willis Gaylord Clark (see n. 20, p. 89). It paid much attention to the West; Caroline Kirkland (see n. 27, p. 92), for example, was a regular contributor. Frank Luther Mott describes the magazine as being "plainly deteriorated" by 1850. See Mott, *A History of American Magazines, 1741–1850* (Cambridge: Belknap Press, 1958), 1:606–11. Edward L. Widmer describes the political context of New York's 1840s magazines in his *Young America: The Flowering of Democracy in New York City* (New York: Oxford University Press, 1999). "The *Knickerbocker,*" he writes, "was not 'Democratic' in any sense" (151)

42. Old proverb. This and other American proverbs of the time can be found in *The Treasury of Knowledge, and Library of Reference* (New York: Collins, Keese, and Co., 1839), 445–48, Google Books, http://books.google.com/books?id=o2RTAAAAYAAJ.

43. This quote attributed to Saadi, classical Persian poet of thirteenth-century Iran, could have been sourced from a number of places. The proverb appears in French ambassador Joseph Michel Tancoigne's *A Narrative of a Journey into Persia, and Residence at Teheran* (London: William Wright, 1820), 265, Google Books, http://books.google.com/books?id=LxD3tYJ6pTAC, but in a different form (ending "and speaking when silence should be kept"). The quotation appears in this form in *Destiny: Or, The Chief's Daughter*, an 1831 novel by English writer Susan Edmondstone Ferrier (1782–1854). See *Destiny* (Philadelphia: Carey and Lea, 1831), 1:34, Google Books, http://books.google.com/books?id=v2soAAAAMAAJ. A passage from *Destiny* including this Saadi quote appears without attribution in a column of "Prose Excerpts" published in *The New-York Mirror* 14, no. 2 (July 9, 1836), 14, Google Books, http://books.google.com/books?id=_nxNAAAAYAAJ.

Norman and Cornelia Campbell,
OR
"Truth Stranger Than Fiction."

By C. Cumings.

Chapter III.

We draw near to a collection of human beings a little distance from the raging fire and behold the bloated and disfigured remains of the old man who had been the worker of wo to so many hearts. By his side is one whom the flames and smoke have not injured, whose distorted features even in death, show that this is a mad-man's corpse—'Tis Henry Benton, who has evidently passed away in strong convulsive agony—a little farther on is George Campbell for a moment exhausted, resting his head on the unconscious body of his Brother whom he had just brought from their burning house and by him, a friend has just laid his wife in whom life was forever extinct. George found them both, crushed by a ponderous beam near the principal entrance to their house.

There was Mrs. Benton unharmed and also her son, and Francis Lisbon too, was looking on the scene in safety—George C. soon recovered consciousness and roused himself to action. "My Brother is not dead," said he, and following the suggestion of a friend took measures to remove him and all the rest to his house. There they found Norman and Cornelia with their nurse who had been the first to escape from the fire.

Oh! what a group are now collected in that house—that young Mother is sleeping quietly, her little girl and boy are standing by her and she heeds them not and they though so young, receive such an impression of her features, such an idea of her goodness while living, and her happiness even though dead, that they never forget that solemn hour; but in all future time remembered that they *once* had a Mother worthy of being loved—and it strengthened them in virtue and nerved them in trial.

Their Father was alive but as yet unconscious even of his own situation. Mrs. B. infringes no rule of propriety in her deportment, but oh, how callous and selfish is her heart—she talks of the duty of resignation, while with a tearless eye she looks on the ruin that her own wickedness has wrought.

Francis Lisbon told George C. that on the night of the fire, about midnight, Mr. B. seemed restless and, thinking some change was about to occur, he opened the door to go to Mrs. C., having promised to call her if such should be the case; that that moment Mr. B. sprang from his bed with the fury of a demon; that he only succeeded in getting a few steps from the door when he received a blow that made him senseless until the cry of fire aroused him.

All now believed that Mr. B. in his frenzy, brushed the bed curtains into the blaze of the burning candle as he jumped to the floor; but this could not account for the fact that every building in the city owned by Campbell or Campbell & Benton, were that night destroyed. Francis remembered that Friedland was not in the house that night, and yet he recollected that one of the first objects he saw after he was roused, was his form passing stealthily along, through the crowd then assembling round the fire, while under a cloak intended for concealment, he saw that same bag that he once saw him put in his Master's desk—but all this he kept to himself.

The dead were buried, and still Mr. C. had not strength to realize what had happened, and when at last, reason returned, memory carried him back to the night of the fire and he implored his brother to tell him all. George felt that he must tell him the truth, and although he did it with kind care and consideration, his words almost destroyed the heart-broken man.

"Oh! my Brother!" said he, "how inscrutable are the ways of Providence![44] my heart rebels at its decrees. My life was very dear to me, but my career is almost ended; and my children will be left without Father or Mother. Oh! Brother, leave me alone a little while; I would seek to be reconciled to my Father's will—I would think of my children and make every arrangement in my power to secure their happiness."

George left the house in almost unbearable wretchedness—he was met by a messenger saying that their vessel, supposed to have been lost, was in the harbor richly loaded. Among the rest of the wealth shown him were the identical bags of gold that were taken from their Cellar. The Captain took them from a piratical-looking craft that had attacked them when only a few days from New York. George hastened to tell his Brother of their good fortune, hoping that he might live to share their brightening prospects; but Albert quickly destroyed every hope.

44. Providence, a common theme in antebellum American literature, was understood as "the care and superintendence which God exercises over his creatures." See Noah Webster, *An American Dictionary of the English Language* (New York: Harper & Brothers, 1846), 651, http://books.google.com/books?id=XKERAAAAIAAJ. See also pp. 151 and 280.

"I am glad," said he, "for your sake and my dear children; but my days are numbered, and now while I have strength, let me tell you all my thoughts and wishes concerning my children."

George listened attentively, and his Brother continued:

"I give them to you and in trust for them all that may be left for them. I wish you could find it in your heart to leave the city and live awhile amid scenes pure and holy in their influence. I have been told that our land on the Connecticut is worth attention—can you consent to superintend the converting of the wilderness into towns, and villages, and fruitful gardens, and cultivated fields?"

"Yes, Brother, I could scarcely endure living here—all I love will be lost to me, but your precious children—I will go, and for their sake, try to bear all my lot."

Albert warmly thanked him, and proceeded to say that he wished him, from what was due him in his professional business, to purchase a Library, in every respect such as his children would need to enable them, although in a new country, to become finished scholars. "Also," said he, "a Library of Law Books for Norman, who is to be early taught that it is my desire that he should study law with my friend Mr. S., of this city, if he is alive when he shall be of suitable age and acquirements—keep their nurse with them George—she was once a rich man's wife, was well educated and will be able and willing to instruct them until suitable persons can be found, and I wish them to feel that it is their duty ever to provide for her. One thing more—give them the miniatures of my wife and myself which you will find in the shop of Mr. P.; tell them whose they are and bid them keep them; and now let me rest."

From this time he seemed rapidly hastening to the grave, but lingered until the last day of the year 1799, that year that had opened to him and to all his family with such seeming promise of happiness and prosperity, and had brought so much of sorrow, disappointment and death.

The setting sun shone on his features as they were stiffening in death. He had kissed his children, prayed for them, and bidden then remember their dying Father, but still love and obey their Uncle. He had commended them all to Heaven, and in the triumphs of humble faith and hope, was passing through the dark valley that leads to that blest inheritance beyond Jordan's swelling waves.[45]

45. The passage echoes a sermon by English Primitive Methodist preacher John Nelson, "On the Dominion and Power and Death," in which man looks forward to the afterlife and "the rich

The struggle was short—a moment passed and all was still—his soul was in "the spirit land," and the lookers-on gazed with awe on the lifeless clay before them.

Again did Norman and Cornelia look on the form of a parent arrayed for the grave; again did the same hallowed impressions fall upon their spirits, and thought and feeling, as a mantle from the departed, settled upon them with pure and ennobling influence. Their nurse wept as an enlightened Christian weeps, while she felt a strange sense that the happiness of the dear objects of her charge would depend much on herself. A shadow was on her spirit—it was not all sadness, but hope shed one feeble ray and she turned to her Father in Heaven for strength and happiness.

Even Mrs. Benton was moved to thought in some slight degree, and Francis Lisbon could not entirely forget that he might have saved them all, much of the trouble that had fallen upon them; but he resolved to turn all he knew to his own advantage.

Albert Campbell was buried by the side of his Elizabeth, and as his Brother stood by his grave, he felt that he was left in almost utter loneliness, and yet, he felt that the little things left to him, needed consolation, and after the burial he took Cornelia in his arms while Norman was seated near his side, and tried to cheer them; but he understood not the language of Heaven; alas! he had a sceptic's soul; and they turned for comfort to their kind and intelligent nurse.

George Campbell, or (as he is now alone) Mr. Campbell gave Mrs. B. her share of the wealth brought in their vessel, and arranged his affairs for an absence from the city.

He had begun to feel that Mrs. Benton had been wronged, and gave her the first assurance of her influence over him by requesting her to consent to live with and care for Norman and Cornelia in his absence. The spell was already upon him that was to enslave his naturally noble spirit. She had appointed him Guardian to her son, and in this capacity he was to visit his possessions in New York, as he was on his way to his own, on the Connecticut River. She rightly calculated her power, and with nicely weighed

inheritance which lays beyond Jordan's swelling waves." See Nelson, *A Series of Sermons & Lectures On Important Subjects* (Hull: For the author, 1830), 85, Google Books, http://books.google.com/books?id=LKnoOS2qRTAC. Death's "dark valley" and "Jordan's swelling wave" also figure in "The Dying Mother's Prayer," a poem by American poet Lydia Sigourney (1791–1865). See *Poems* (Philadelphia: Key & Biddle, 1830), 264, http://books.google.com/books?id=LxJnG40zGYAC. That said, like "the spirit land," such phrases were part of a common religious language. The "valley of the shadow of death" appears in Psalm 23:4. In the bible the Jordan River—now the eastern border of Israel—is often a site of swelling, crossing, and baptizing. E.g. see Jeremiah 12:5.

hesitancy, consented to his proposition; and then did Mrs. F., their nurse, feel that the dark shadow was assuming a definite form; but she hoped, and prayed, and trusted in God.

Mr. C. found Wm. Benton's possessions to be capable of yielding a vast income and set in motion every thing necessary to produce this effect.

His own and his Brother's children's possessions were enough to satisfy any reasonable expectation and he arranged every thing for a removal there, the following spring. Then he hastened back and, urged on by the blind spirit that possessed him, offered his heart and hand to Mrs. Benton who received it just before they started for those *then* distant wilds.

Suppose now that we see them not again for fifteen years, but merely say in that time Mrs. C. has made her power felt most sensibly, by all and at last in a fit of passion had suddenly died. We shall not find her when we again look on this family, but we can trace her influence and the effect of her deeds in all.

We will now enter a beautiful village on the banks of the Connecticut,[46] with stores, taverns, churches, school-houses, elegant dwelling houses and all the appurtenances that betoken business and prosperity.

As we enter this sweet place we pass a farm that at once fixes attention. You enquire for the owner and are directed to visit a mansion near at hand that combines all the "etceteras!" that make the whole of comfort, convenience and elegance. The hand of taste is visible in the disposition of every thing you see, but why that start as I introduce to you a man whom I call Mr. Campbell? You look for familiar features, but his eyes are red, his face and form are bloated, and every look betrays a nervous irritation that makes it almost impossible to recognize the once handsome George Campbell; but in his bland and courteous tones there is something like himself, something that tells that the spoiler has not entirely triumphed and might, by the efforts of a decided will, be thwarted in his purpose of destruction. He is in some sense a business man yet, and you hope he may be saved from a drunkard's death.

You find that his wife has been a year or two dead, and your first anxiety is for those lovely orphans that have been so long under her care. Surely, that little, loving girl, must exhibit the baleful effects of such an example, and as you look on Wm. Benton, his appearance strengthens every despair-

46. Running north to south in New England, the Connecticut River forms the border between New Hampshire and Vermont before bisecting Massachusetts and Connecticut.

ing thought of those once lovely children; but, remember that every one who looked on Wm. Benton's face in boyhood, predicted for him just such a manhood as he now exhibits. For him you need hope no good, but leave him to fulfill his destiny, and remember that Norman Campbell was one who, every person believed, could not be contaminated by bad example; they called him the image of his highly gifted Father, and wove for him the brightest web of happiness and glory; but we will now introduce to you a young Lady of eighteen summers, of such an appearance as surprises you, not into an exclamation of silly admiration, but of affectionate respect.

You know her at once; it is your sweet, little pet, Cornelia Campbell transformed into an intelligent, high-minded woman.—You find no effect of her strange companionship, except in a thoughtful, melancholy air not natural in one so young and possessing by nature, so joyous a disposition. During Mrs. C.'s life, Cornelia was the cementing bond of the family, the only one having power to stay the reproaches of the weak-minded woman, whom she tried to reverence as a mother, or soothe the irritated feelings of him whom she wished to love as a Father.

She is now preparing for a walk with Wm. Benton and we will take the liberty to follow and listen to their conversation.

He assumes all the gentleness in his power and thus addresses her: "I am here, Cornelia, to tell you that I love you and ask you to become my wife as soon as I am of age."

The first look she gives him is of surprise; the next scorn, deep, bitter scorn; then it seemed a look of pity and at last, a feeling of restraint as if bound by a sense of duty; but she answered him calmly.

"William, when we were children I tried to love you as a Brother, yet I have learned to be thankful that you are *not* my Brother. I tell you plainly I would rather die than be your wife and I command you never to address me on this subject again."

Thus saying she abruptly leaves him, and could she see the malignant glare of his eyes, or hear his muttered threats of deep and deadly revenge, she would tremble for her future happiness; but when next they meet, he greets her as cheerfully as usual and she believes him indifferent to her decision.

You are anxious to see her Brother, he has been for some time at a distant school, but is hourly expected at home, indeed, he has just arrived, accompanied by a friend who lingers a little, while Norman hastens to embrace his friends. With deep, reverential love he clasps his uncle's extended hand, shows every desire for confidence as he approaches William, greets old Francis with the kind tones of affection, and the glad cry that escapes him as he folds his sister, who has just entered the room, in his arms, mingles with her heartfelt words of endearment and tells of holy confidence and love.

Continued.

Selected for the Offering.

"Never Give Up"[47]

"Never give up." 'Tis the secret of glory,
    Nothing so wise can Philosophy preach,
Think on the names that are famous in story,
    "Never give up," is the lesson they teach.
How have men compassed mortal achievements?
    How have they moulded the world to their will?
'Tis that 'midst dangers, and woes and bereavements,
    "Never give up," was their principle still.

47. An imitation of "Never Give Up" by English poet Martin Farquhar Tupper (1810–89). First published in Tupper's *A Thousand Lines*—(London: Hatchard & Son, 1845), 20, Google Books, http://books.google.com/books?id=YQ4EAAAAQAAJ—the poem was widely copied in American periodicals. For example, see *Liberator* 15, no. 17 (April 25, 1845): 68, American Periodicals (91237610). Tupper's poem is very different, however; this imitation borrows his message, his form, and his chorus, with mostly new words. Following the *Liberator* publication, Tupper's first stanza reads:

Never give up! it is wiser and better
    Always to hope than once to despair;
Fling off the load of Doubt's cankering fetter,
    And break the dark spell of tyrannical care;
Never give up! or the burden may sink you,—
    Providence has kindly mingled the cup,
And, in all trials or troubles, bethink you,
    The watchword of life must be, *Never give up!*

The Akron Offering's version of "Never Give Up"—or parts of it—was also often republished in the nineteenth century and never, so far as I can discover, attributed. Like Tupper's poem, it appears to have been introduced to the United States from Britain. Later in the nineteenth century, lines or stanzas from both poems are mingled and attributed to later, impossible authors. For a full version of the poem contemporary with *The Akron Offering*, see "Never Give Up," *Hogg's Instructor* 3, New Series (March 1849): 88, Google Books, http://books.google.com/books?id=BUIFAAAAQAAJ. There is one notable difference between this publication of the poem and the poem in *The Akron Offering*: in the *Hogg's Instructor* version, men have "compass'd immortal achievements." Perhaps thinking this presumptuous, this version deems it sufficient to boast that men have "compass'd mortal achievements."

"Never give up",—though o'erladen with sorrow,
Shake not the yoke, 'twill more bitterly gall;
"Never give up," for there cometh a morrow
Fraught with delights to compensate for all.
"Never give up,"—bear your fate with serenity!
Crouch not ignobly like slaves, in the dust;
Life's a rough passage to realms of amenity,
Dark is the journey, but travel we must.

"Never give up,"—It can last but a season.
Will you—because a cloud bursts on your way—
Basely surrender your manhood and reason,
Weeping for griefs that must end in a day?
What though the tempest around you be raving?
Soon you'll have emptied life's rancorous cup,
Soundly you'll sleep where the willows are waxing;
Thunder won't wake you—"Never give up."

"Never give up." It were impious to dream of it,
Keen though your anguish be, never forget
That there are fortunes, (O, raptures to dream of it!)
Bright and immortal in store for you yet.
Ere the night fall—if by virtue a meriter
May you not, mourner in Paradise sup,
Compeer of angel's and Heaven's inheritor?
Think of your destiny—"Never give up."

Extract from a letter written by a Lady in Western New York to a friend in Lucas County, who has kindly sent to us for insertion in the Offering.

Since the reception of yours, I have tarried week after week, in the hope that something new and not sad, would transpire, that my letter might be more than a record of the doings of the "Great Reaper."[48]

There is such a combination of every thing horrible, pouring in upon us every day, that there is great risk of becoming, either callous or despairing. Fires, murders, floods, wrecks, explosions, Cholera, small-pox, crowd one

48. The "grim reaper"; death.

upon another in confusion dire, each striving to outdo his fellow, and all outdone by that worst curse, War. "Great Fire in St Louis,"[49] "Cholera in Cincinnati,"[50] "Mob in New York,"[51] "Crevasse in New Orleans,"[52] "Riot in Montreal,"[53] "Famine in Ireland,"[54] "Revolution in Italy,"[55] "War in Hungary," "Massacre in India,"[56] "Revolt in Spain," "Conspiracy in France,"

49. On May 17, 1849, St. Louis nearly suffered complete destruction by fire. For more, see *History of the St. Louis Fire Department: With a Review of Great Fires . . .* (St. Louis: Central Publishing Company, 1914), 27–28, Google Books, http://books.google.com/books?id=HxUPAQAAMAAJ, and Laura Wilson, *The Great Fire of St. Louis in 1849* (St. Louis: Jefferson National Expansion Memorial, 1938). This disaster was the subject of a lithograph by American artist Nathaniel Currier (1813–88).

50. Reports of the progress of cholera were regular summer items in 1840s American newspapers, including Akron's own *Summit Beacon*. See p. 7. Towns and cities developed population densities that required, for the sake of public health, heavy and unpopular investments in public infrastructure. Inadequate or nonexistent water and sewage systems bred cholera outbreaks, small and large, every summer, throughout the country. Cincinnati suffered horribly from cholera in 1849. See *Charles E. Rosenberg: The Cholera Years: The United States in 1832, 1849, and 1866* (1962; Chicago: University of Chicago Press, 1987).

51. There was a large riot at the Astor Place Opera House on May 10, 1849, which ended with many deaths and injuries. The riot was sparked by long-running jealousies between English actor William Charles Macready (1793–1873) and American actor Edwin Forrest (1806–72). The two objected to each other's treatment and performance of Shakespeare. Macready's May 10 performance of *Macbeth*, part of his farewell tour of America, was met with intensely different feelings by the working-class, anti-aristocratic fans of Forrest and the well-to-do, elitist supporters of Macready. A militia was summoned to protect the Opera House and its patrons from injury, but paving stones were thrown and a massive riot followed. For a contemporary account with various documents related to the Macready-Forrest rivalry, see *Account of the Terrific and Fatal Riot at the New-York Astor Place Opera House, on the Night of May 10th, 1849* (New York: H. M. Ranney, 1849), Google Books, http://books.google.com/books?id=s9m_TmbOyToC. For more on the history and meaning of the riot, see David Grimsted, *Melodrama Unveiled: American Theater and Culture, 1800–1850* (1968; Berkeley: University of California Press, 1987) and Bruce A. McConachie, *Melodramatic Formations: American Theatre and Society, 1820–1870* (Iowa City: University of Iowa Press, 1992).

52. A "crevasse" is a break in a levee. On May 3, 1849, a hundred-foot-wide levee break flooded a large section of New Orleans; this was the worst flooding in New Orleans' history before Hurricane Katrina in 2005. See Richard Campanella, *Bienville's Dilemma: A Historical Geography of New Orleans* (Lafayette: Center for Louisiana Studies, 2008), 205.

53. 1849 was a "year of riots" for Montreal and other Canadian cities. The Montreal riots were unusually violent and included the burning of the parliament building. These riots did much to prompt the creation of urban police forces and anti-riot military forces. See Elinor Kyle Senior, "The Influence of the British Garrison on the Development of the Montreal Police, 1832 to 1853." *Military Affairs* 43, no. 2 (April 1979): 63–68, JSTOR, http://www.jstor.org/stable/1986660.

54. From 1845 to 1852, Ireland experienced an intense famine that resulted in much death, disease, and immigration to America. There is an extensive literature on this. To start, see Colm Tólbín, *The Irish Famine: A Documentary* (New York: St. Martin's Press, 2002), and Arthur Gribben, ed. *The Great Famine and the Irish Diaspora in America* (Amherst: University of Massachusetts Press, 1999).

55. American periodical readers were startled and gripped by the steady news of political revolutions throughout Europe in 1848 and 1849. For an introduction, see Michael Rapport, *1848: Year of Revolution* (London: Little, Brown, 2008).

56. In early 1849, the British-Indian army fought the final battles of the Second Sikh War (1848–49). This ended with British annexation of the Punjab, an area that is now divided between India and Pakistan. The choice of the word "massacre" suggests a bias toward one side or the other in this con-

"Wreck on the Hudson."[57] One would think that with such highly seasoned dishes served every morning for breakfast, the human system would become so deranged, that life would cease to contend with its arch enemy; yet, strange as it may appear—it does seem that the *individual* is just as much troubled about the weather and enraged at the loss or lateness of a meal, and as unhappy in the delay of a promised gratification; as interested in the cut of a sleeve or the shape of a hat, as though the mass were not struggling for freedom, or against disease with an energy almost superhuman!—

"The triflers will be triflers still,
In each event of good or ill,"[58]

so there is no use in complaining.

Happy are they in the hard strife which men call life, who feel that above the smoke and dust of the conflict, their Father watches still; who hear amid all the din, a still small voice that speaks of peace. Oh! if people would only realize that virtue is Heaven, that vice is Hell, and forget this constant looking for reward, this constant dread of punishment!

Don't you think that, if our Divines (that is the generality of them,) for some are right on the subject, (would condescend to come down from Theological technicalities and teach that the little fault of the present moment, the

---

flict. It is not possible to determine what news story made such an impression on the author of this piece, but it is likely that the author, reading American and perhaps British periodicals, would have read about the many and various barbarisms attributed to the Punjabi people, who were portrayed in English-language descriptions of the conflict as unusually savage and bloodthirsty. For example, there was a report that the British Colonels seized areas characterized by the widespread practice of "female infanticide," resulting in "truly appalling" proportions of males to females. See "The Calcutta Review," *Biblical Repertory and Princeton Review* 21, no. 3 (July 1849): 419–21, Google Books, http://books.google.com/books?id=-k8AAAAAYAAJ. For context, see T. Khosla, "The Plight of Female Infants in India," *Journal of Epidemiology and Community Health* 34 (1980): 143–46, JSTOR, http://www.jstor.org/stable/25566171; Michael H. Fisher, "Indian Political Representations in Britain during the Transition to Colonialism," *Modern Asian Studies* 38, no. 3 (July 2004): 649–75, JSTOR, http://www.jstor.org/stable/3876685; and Miles Taylor, "The 1848 Revolutions and the British Empire," *Past and Present* 166 (February 2000): 146–80, JSTOR, http://www.jstor.org/stable/651297.

57. On the night of May 17, 1849 the steamer Empire, carrying hundreds of ladies and gentlemen in elegant rooms, collided with the schooner Noah Brown and sank in the Hudson River. At first it was thought that hundreds had perished, and for several weeks there was intense interest in the swift trial of potentially criminal parties as well as in the discovery of survivors, bodies, debris. There was also much interest taken in the wreck itself, which was towed to the foot of Rutgers Street, on the East River, and visited daily by crowds of New Yorkers drawn to "the melancholy spectacle." Reports of *The New York Herald* were widely copied. For just one specimen of the coverage of this wreck, see "The Steamer Empire—Another Body Found." *The Cleveland Herald* 139 (June 15, 1849): 3, Nineteenth Century U.S. Newspapers (GT3004922921).

58. Searches of the antebellum book and periodical databases cited elsewhere, as well as a search of Chadwyck-Healey's many American & English Literature collections, suggest this is a piece of original verse.

angry word, the transient unkindness are leaving stains on the soul which will endure age after age) their teaching would be more effectual?

The Heaven of a man, "saved as it were by the skin of his teeth,"[59] will be a very inferior sort of Heaven.

How can they expect Religion to take root when they appeal continually, to the selfish part of man's nature? "Good Master what shall we do to be saved?"[60] they expound as though it meant only a desire to escape punishment. It is to be saved from sin and not the penalty that man should strive and pray.

The generous, the bold, the noble though erring spirit finds nothing attractive in the spiritual teachings of the sniveller who would frighten him with hob-goblins and descriptions of future torment; or persuade him to Heaven because it is the better berth. He hands Religion over to the miser, the narrow-minded, trembling, cowardly one who will serve Satan to the last minute and then seek to sneak out of his partnership.

If Christianity were preached as exhibited in the life of its founder, the world would not resound with complaints of the hard-heartedness of man and the depravity of all, save the especially exempt, whose exemption by the way, is often like many a title to good things, a thing of parchment.

Selected

Reasons for Risibility.

By E. M. Fitzgerald.[61]

"Why do you laugh so much?"—*Query in a ball-room.*

Sweet coz![62] I'm happy when I can,
    I'm merry while I may,

59. Job 19:20.

60. Luke 18:18.

61. Edward M. FitzGerald (1809–83) is best known today for his *Rubáiyát of Omar Khayyám* (1859), which recommends drinking and merry-making. After appearing in a London annual, this poem was often copied in American periodicals. For example, see *The New-York Mirror* 16, no. 30 (January 19, 1839): 238, American Periodicals (136133038). Here an editor of the *Mirror* praised FitzGerald: "A more graceful, sprightly and fascinating poet than Fitzgerald is not to be found in the circle of modern English writers." FitzGerald did not collect the verses that he wrote (as "E. M. Fitzgerald") for English annuals in the 1830s. See David J. O'Donoghue, *The Poets of Ireland: A Biographical Dictionary* (London: David J. O'Donoghue, 1892–93), 74, Google Books, http://books.google.com/books?id=wUQLAAAAYAAJ.

62. Cousin.

For life's at most a narrow span,
    At best a winter's day.
If care could make the sunbeam wear
    A brighter, warmer hue,
The evening star shine out more fair,
    The blue sky look *more* blue,
Then I should grow a graver man;
    But since 'tis not the way,
Sweet coz! I'm happy when I can,
    And merry while I may!

If sighs could make us sin the less,
    Perchance I were not glad;
If mourning were the sage's dress,
    My garb should still be sad;
But since the angels' wings are white,
    And even the young saints smile—
Some virtue wears a brow of light,
    And vice a robe of guile—
Since laughter is not under ban,
    Nor goodness clad in grey,
Sweet coz! I'm happy when I can,
    And merry while I may!

I've seen a bishop dance a reel,
    And a sinner fast and pray;
A knave at top of fortune's wheel,
    And a good man cast away,
Wine have I seen your grave ones quaff
    Might set our fleet afloat;
But I never heard a *hearty* laugh
    From out a villain's throat;
And I never knew a mirthful man
    Make sad a young maid's day;—
So coz! I'm happy when I can,
    And merry while I may!

Selected.

A Little Word.[63]

A little word in kindness spoken,
    A motion or a tear,
Has often healed the heart that's broken,
    And made a friend sincere.

A word—a look—has crushed to earth
    Full many a budding flower,
Which, had a smile but owned its birth,
    Would bless life's darkest hour.

Then deem it not an idle thing
    A pleasant word to speak;
The face you wear—the thoughts you bring—
    The heart may heal or break.

To Our Readers.

We might fill a long table with views of different subjects, but will simply send you our friendly greeting and talk with you a little about what particularly concerns the Offering.

The third number is now ready to go forth to the little world where it circulates. It goes as a messenger of peace, and we would return many thanks to all who have assisted us to make it in any degree, worthy the patronage of the public. No one writing for this, pretends to infallibility; but we will give our opinion of them in as few words as possible—briefly then, we believe that the articles that have appeared in the Offering, that were sent us by others, will compare favorably with articles found in other works of the same size and price—faults there *have been* and they *have been or will be* corrected—Criticism we expect—anything based on truth will be regarded.

63. An extraordinarily popular and often-reprinted poem, this first appeared without a signature in *The Portland Tribune*, a small literary paper, around 1841. It was the work of paper's editor, Daniel Clement Colesworthy (1810–93). See "Portland Poets," *Christian Reflector* 5, no. 34 (August 24, 1842): 4, American Periodicals (135930202). Colesworthy included the poem near the front of his 1865 collection, *A Group of Children and Other Poems* (Boston: Antique Book Store, 1865), 22, Google Books, http://books.google.com/books?id=JaBXHUIizhAC.

The story-readers owe Mrs. Weed of Jackson and Lily Lute of Seville, many thanks.

"The Eloquence of Truth" will please all who have taste and love the sacred principle there portrayed.

The "extract of a letter" sent us by a Lady in Lucas Co. suggests many thoughts worth remembering and we are allowed to expect something from her pen soon. Lizzie gives us her ideas in her usual "random" manner and it is pleasant to trace her thoughts; we hope we shall not be forgotten by her or any one who *has* written for the Offering, or by those whose *could* write in a suitable manner.

It gives us pleasure to be able to say to you that we are not discouraged and may hope shed its purest ray for you all.

C. Cumings.

THE
AKRON OFFERING.
August, 1849.

Norman and Cornelia Campbell,
OR
"Truth Stranger Than Fiction."

By C. Cumings.

Chapter IV.

Gentle Reader, Norman Campbell is before you. His early promise of beauty and nobleness is more than realised. You mark his commanding form and figure, the noble contour of his head that tells of intellectual strength, of moral greatness and passions all subservient. The kindling glance of his dark eyes that beam with thought, with hope and happiness, combined with his gentle suavity of manners, completes the fascination of his appearance, and it is acknowledged that there are some natures that can not be corrupted. But he now introduces the companion of his journey, who had entered the house at the same moment that Cornelia met her Brother. He was a moment unnoticed, and in that short space of time, a passing glance at each of the unguarded group, revealed the true feeling of their hearts. His own throbbed with an almost uncontrollable impulse of sympathy as he looked upon the sister of his friend, as he is presented to her, while the tears of glad emotion are still lingering on her cheek, as she turns to welcome her Brother's friend, and all unconsciously to themselves, their hearts are receiving a mutual impression of regard that can never, no never, be erased.

And who is he that she should love him? his name is Charles Elton; he is the son of a poor, but eloquent and pious Clergyman, and is entirely dependant on himself. Of so much her Brother had informed her in one of his letters. He is small in stature and his golden hair floats over a forehead of such dimensions as a Phrenologist would now love to look upon;[1] but it is the eye and mouth that fascinate—each tells of brilliant wit and easily excited feelings, and yet over all, there is an expression of stern determination that can not fail to mark him as one who will yield no point of his own code of honor.

Such is the being who is to be for several weeks, an almost daily visitor at the house of Mr. Campbell.

Cornelia, from consideration for William Benton, had not told her Uncle or Brother of his proposition to her, believing it of no consequence; but his eye is on her as she gazes on the handsome stranger, and he reads a tale of mutual love; but, he repeats to himself as he leaves the house, "I will mar her peace!—let her love him, but hide, oh! my soul, the exquisite revenge I will have on *her*, on *him*, and on her proud *Brother*, who looks as if descended from a long line of Kings, and born to rule even those who have wealth that *can*, that *shall* crush him!!"

"Hark ye," says old Francis, "talk not so loudly, or others may hear your soliloquies, and become aware of the uncertain tenure by which you hold your boasted possessions. By the by, sir, I am getting old, my foolish love for my old Master's son has kept me silent, but as your riches are now at your own disposal, you are to secure me an annuity to please my own ideas of living, or I shall take the right course to obtain it."

"Yes, yes old man you shall have all you ask; so now be quiet and leave me," said Mr. Benton as he turned angrily away to brood over the fiendish feelings that were searing and scathing the last feeble remains of good that had ever tried to find a place in his heart. As soon as he could command himself sufficiently he sought out Henry Herbert, a young man, who with his Uncle, Julius Herbert, had been a resident of their little village about one year.

Julius Herbert was a widower of forty-five years of age—his nephew was his partner in the mercantile business and ostensibly, heir to his reputed immense wealth.

Henry Herbert was twenty-five years of age and as far as features and complexion were concerned was handsome; but to Cornelia Campbell, whom he admired, he was peculiarly disagreeable.

---

1. See n. 16, p. 87.

Benton had a game of his own to play, and chose Henry Herbert as an instrument to accomplish his own purposes. He accosted him in a friendly manner and informed him that Miss Campbell's Brother was at home; and, "by the by," said he, "there is a young man with him who seems well calculated to gain the affection of just such a girl as Cornelia Campbell. You must be active sir, or your hopes in that quarter will be vain, but you must not be too precipitate either. You know her love for her Uncle and her Brother. She dreams not that her Uncle is involved in debt or that he has in any sense injured *them* in pecuniary matters. In this secret lies all your power; but you must not by any means let her or her Brother know, at present, anything about the real state of their affairs, for *he* could now arrange them with but little trouble. Wait a little and you will be able to control them all."

Henry Herbert listened, well pleased with the villainy of Benton and resolved to profit by the hints he had given him. He was a wily villain, and although he did not understand all Benton's projects, he comprehended his own interests enough, to determine to remain quiet while Norman Campbell and Charles Elton remained in town.

Young Elton had several distant connections in the town where he now found himself, but he spent most of his time in the society of his friend and his sister. The time was fast approaching when Cornelia must bid them adieu and they must wend their way back to their mental toil. Charles could not go without asking Cornelia to grant him her love. This he did with all the ingenuousness of his impetuous nature, and as truly and fervently was it returned; but she deemed him hasty in his decisions and feared to confess her heart's affection—but she could not conceal it all; he was satisfied with what he saw and with her promise to correspond with him and soon after bade her farewell.

Norman was well pleased that his sister should love Elton and he fondly hoped that her future years would be unclouded. He understood in some measure, how keenly she had suffered in her feelings in the trying position in which she had been placed, and as he looked on her Uncle, he felt that she yet had much to bear and when he was gone, had to bear it alone—true her Uncle loved her, but he was not always himself, and he feared he was growing worse instead of better. Their old nurse, Mrs. F. had been to them a Mother and had taught them their duty faithfully, and faithfully had they fulfilled their Father's dying request in providing for and obeying her. She was now almost helpless but happy in the love lavished upon her, in her old age, by the dear children whom from infancy she had tenderly loved. Norman felt as he bade her farewell, that she must soon leave them, and it was with a saddened heart that he left his home to pursue yet a little longer, the studies necessary for success in the profession his Father had wished him to engage in.

Charles Elton went with him, and they journeyed on in silence for some time, each too busy with thought to heed the lapse of time. At length Charles spoke, first, of his love for Cornelia, as being a new incentive to keep him in the path of honor and at last he said, "Norman you may call me superstitious if you will, but with all my happiness there is a weight on my spirit that has oppressed me since first I saw your cousin, William Benton. In one of my rambles with your sister, I mentioned this impression and she seemed strangely confused and I felt that she had the same undefined dread, although she expressed no fears and soon changed the subject."

Norman immediately cast away the look of abstraction he had worn since they started on their journey, and answered his friend. "You are a strange fellow," said he—"what if I should tell you that she thought you were afraid her affection would be given to him in your absence?" But, seeing a troubled look in his countenance he quickly added, "I was but jesting Charles, and from the same feeling that prompted Cornelia to keep her real views of William's character from you, viz.[2] a sense of shame mingled perhaps, with a sense of duty, to hide as far as possible, the failings of one whom we have tried to love as a brother. William is not what he should be and you know not the proud, yet generous nature of my sister—lover though you are, you do not fully appreciate her character. But with all her knowledge of him she, I think, has no fear of him, nor need you have. She is not like you Charles and yet in some respects, you are as one. Shall I sketch you both?"

"Yes, do," said Charles.

And Norman continued—"She, like you, has the quick feeling and fervid imagination that make her deeply sensitive to the trials incident to human life; but she has reflection and strength of purpose to combat with difficulties that far surpass your own. Cross *you* in love and you will have no forgiveness for the offender, but, wrapt up in your own injured dignity, will vent your feelings in the burning words of Poesy; your duties will be neglected and you will be in danger of being irretrievably lost in a vortex of dissipation. Make *her* the victim of disappointment and she will feel it as acutely as yourself, but whatever duties may devolve upon her, will be faithfully performed and

2. Abbreviation of the Latin ("videlicet") for "namely" or "that is."

she will be ever ready to sacrifice her own feelings to advance the happiness of others. Her grief will be shut up in her own heart; there you will see her pride and real nobleness and strength of character and in all she does will be manifested principles, purposes, and power, such as but few men can claim."

"Well Norman," said Charles, "you alone are worthy of such a sister. You have poetry enough in your soul, but you are shielded by such a calm, discriminating judgment that there is no danger of your ever being the victim to *any* passion. But you will be tried in affliction; you are included in the number of those whose destinies are in some way, to be influenced for evil, by that same Benton."

"Well," said Norman, "I shall submit with as good a grace as possible; but I shall try to hold him guiltless until his crimes are proved, and now let us talk a little common sense."

We will not quote their conversation farther, but will simply say that they arrived in safety at the place of their destination and re-commenced the studies that were to fit them, one for the profession of the Law and the other for the Ministry. We will now leave them and go back to the village they left, the home of Cornelia C. and Wm. B. and some others having a conspicuous part to act in the scenes I am transcribing for you.

Continued.

"In Adversity, the mind grows strong by buffeting the tempest."[3]

For the Offering.

The Elm by My Cottage.

I love its tall, majestic height,
Its branches wide and free,
Its *old bent limb*, and gnarled root,
They *all* have *charms* for me.

3. Popular quote from *Tamerlane* (1701), a play by English writer Nicolas Rowe (1674–1718). In the original the mind grows "tough" by buffeting the tempest. For an American edition of this time, see *The British Drama: A Collection of the Most Esteemed Tragedies, Comedies, Operas, and Farces* (Philadelphia: Thomas, Cowperthwait, 1838), 2:82, Google Books, http://books.google.com/books?id=S7BUAAAAYAAJ.

I love the murmur of its leaves,
    When morn springs o'er the lea.
So gladly welcomes it the breeze,
    Oh! it has charms for me.

I love its solemn stillness too,
    Ere clouds in tempest break,
Its silence does the heart subdue
    Nor bid one murmur wake.

I love its cool refreshing shade,
    Its presence seems to be,
For pleasant contemplation made,
    And this has charms for me.

In days of yore the brooklet ran,
    Beneath this old elm tree
As pure 'tis now as it 'twas then
    And *still* has *charms* for me.

How quiet is my little cot,
    Beneath this old elm tree—
I ask on earth no dearer spot,
    This, has such charms for me.

'Twas here I spent my childhood's dawn,
    In mirthful joy, and glee,
With airy bounds I traced the lawn,
    Then rested 'neath this tree.

Oh! who would give this quiet home,
    For fashion's tapestry,
Not pleasure's hall nor princely dome,
    Have half such charms for me.

'Twas here I learned my evening prayer,
    And still I bend the knee

Oh with one faithful *heart* to share,
What bliss, these charms would be.

Sybil.

For the Offering.

Travels Through New York &c.

Wish some of the numerous readers of the Offering, would inform me why Ohio is called the "Buckeye State."

They may all speak at once. I may be the only one ignorant of the reason. I know that there is an unpalatable nut growing there, denominated buckeye, but whether that took its name from the State, or the State from that, I am unable to determine from any observable connexion between them.

The cognoman is not classical, sounding not as great as "Yankee Land," "Land of steady habits," "granite," or "Empire State";[4] yet, there may be something noble connected with it, of which every buckeye may be proud. Ignorance is often inexcusable. Why did I not inquire of some interesting citizen while travelling through that delightful land of bright-eyed children, intelligent young Ladies and Gentlemen, happy parents, and venerable age?

Not long since it was my good fortune to visit some of the western States. Journeyed through the "Empire State" on board one of the fine packets that sail the Erie Canal[5] I thought by the mirthfulness and hilarity that reigned on board, that the little girl's mistake, in calling the packet a racket, was quite appropriate. However I do not concur with the opinion of some travellers in saying there is nothing agreeable in such a scene. There is much to amuse and not a little to instruct. Would time allow, something might be said in relation to it.

I am aware that circumstances and humor contribute much to render anything pleasing or otherwise. Where *one* would see nothing but sunshine,

4. "Yankee Land" was a nickname for New England or the northeastern states, collectively. The other nicknames are for the states of Connecticut, New Hampshire, and New York.

5. A "packet-boat" or "packet" was a canal boat that carried passengers from point to point on a regular schedule. Passengers could stand on deck or rest below deck in a long and narrow parlor, which might convert into two rows of narrow bunk beds (for overnight trips) with a curtain dividing the women from the men. Meals were often served. More expensive packet boats might offer better meals, more space, more privacy, or entertainment such as live music. The poorest travellers might travel by "line-boat." Line-boats had no amenities; mainly they hauled goods such as flour or lumber. For a rich narrative description of packets, line-boats, and travelling by canal in the 1840s see Jacob Abbott, *Marco Paul's Travels and Adventures in the Pursuit of Knowledge: On the Erie Canal* (Boston: T. Harrington Carter, 1843), Google Books, http://books.google.com/books?id=ousXAAAAYAAJ.

another's ken might reach below the horizon and discover a cloud soon to arise. *One* might be amused by a concert of half a dozen infant voices breaking forth at "noon of night;"[6] *another*, with more of the nervous in his composition, would go into spasms. What might please *me* might appear very insipid to a more profound *personage*—I therefore forbear.

We arrived at Buffalo at 6 o'clock P.M. Would it were against all law to have over fifty runners attack at one boat at a time.[7] Baggage must be watched with an Eagle's gaze or it is gone forever from your possession. Indeed, one must have a good bump of individuality or he will lose *himself* amid the discordant vociferations falling heavily upon the auditory nerve.[8]

Quite a company having become acquainted within a few days, (and by the way, one forms friendships rapidly when travelling by the same conveyance,) we proceeded together to "Huff's Hotel."—"Mine Host" always has a table in waiting.[9] Solids and fluids disappeared rapidly before us. I wonder not we are called a nation of gourmands and that the mouth is said to be the most prominent feature on the face of American society.[10] After supper we repaired to the different sitting rooms to discuss the various topics of the times.

---

6. Midnight; "'Twas noon of night" begins one of the "Odes of Anacreon" by Irish poet Thomas Moore (1779–1852). See, for example, *The Poetical Works of Thomas Moore* (Philadelphia: Crissy & Markley, 1847), 252, Google Books, http://books.google.com/books?id=ym8_AAAAYAAJ.

7. "Runners" were men hired to recruit passengers for train, boat, or stagecoach agencies. They were competitive and aggressive; they hounded travelers, at times ingeniously, anywhere near inns, hotels, depots, and landings. For example, see Abbott, 28–31.

8. Another phrenology joke; see n. 16, p. 87.

9. "Huff's Hotel" was a large hotel near the canal at the corner of Main and Scott Streets in Buffalo. Founded by William Huff, in 1849 the proprietor ("mine host") was Peter Young. Next door to "Bennet's New Temperance House," Huff's Hotel prospered in part from the business of its barroom. See Sylvester J. Mathews, *Memories of Early Days of Buffalo* (Buffalo, 1913), 197–98, Internet Archive, http://www.archive.org/details/memoriesofearlydoomathrich. See also *The Commercial Advertiser Directory for the City of Buffalo* (Buffalo: Jewett, Thomas, 1849), 210, Google Books, http://books.google.com/books?id=T-o_AAAAYAAJ.

10. In the 1830s *Domestic Manners of the Americans* (1832) by English travel writer Frances Trollope (1779–1863) called attention to the abundance of food in America. "The ordinary manner of living is abundant, but not delicate," she notes; "they consume an extraordinary quantity of bacon." See *Domestic Manners of the Americans* (London: Whitaker, Treacher, 1832), 2:129–30, Google Books, http://books.google.com/books?id=mo4IAAAAQAAJ. The book was a sensation in Britain and America, in part for its attention to American table manners and American food. When reviewing the book, for example, *Blackwood's Edinburgh Magazine* lustfully quotes Trollope's description of American duck. See 31, no. 5 (May 1832): 846, Google Books, http://books.google.com/books?id=Jz2W1NcIETsC. Trollope had stayed in Cincinnati. An unsigned 1833 essay published by James Hall (1793–1868) in his Cincinnati *Western Monthly Magazine and Literary Journal* comments on Trollope's emphasis on the "voracity" of American appetite. "To a stranger," it notes, "inquiring what is the important feature upon the broad face of American society, it is not mischievous wit alone

Soon the king of day retired behind the occidental hills on a bed of magnificent clouds and I retired to my finely furnished apartment with a feeling of satisfaction, anticipating a fine sail on Lake Erie's beautiful mirror. Morpheus soon paid me a visit.[11] We had not so cordially met for some time. He did not leave till the tintabulum of the breakfast bell. Breakfast over, a number of our company repaired to the harbor to select our boat and what splendid aquatic castles America can boast of. I am proud to be called an American citizen.

At ten o'clock "all hands on board" and our present dwelling began to move like a thing of life.

The worthy captain, the pleasant company of passengers, the jovial and communicative sailors, the cheerful rays of the sun as he rose high in the cloudless sky, the mild zephyr that wove into beautiful ripples the surrounding waters—all betokened a grand excursion; but alas all things around us are deceitful and typical of the events of human life, ever changing!

Toward evening the wind increased, the low muttering of the distant thunder (although there is music in it) was not welcomed with a smile, and the zig zag lightning began to play sublimely, yet frightfully among the dense clouds. All things seemed ominous of an approaching storm—darkness came suddenly upon us and with it a deluge of rain, rendering the hour gloomy and *terrific*.[12] Truly it was a scene of distress, a solemn subject of meditation. The passengers did not retire to rest as usual, but collected themselves in groups reeling to and from like persons who had paid their devotions at the shrine of Bacchus.[13]

I threw my cloak about me and reclined my weary body on a sofa; but not to sleep. Near me lay a helpless female, apparently in the agonies of death—she had been taken on deck where the raging storm would not permit her stay. She was brought back to her friends in a state of insensibility, among nearly helpless beings groaning and moaning in agony.

In one direction stood a group, a motley collection who seemed deaf to the cries and blind to the distress around; unmindful of the awful threat-

---

that responds, *the mouth*. In every class, in every circle, it is literally the *absorbing* topic." Speaking of the fourth of July, the article continues: "Disguise it as we may, freedom's anniversary is nothing more than a reeking hecatomb to the glory of cooks; and if there be one day of the year whereon oblivion shrouds revolutionary virtue, it is this, when all our better faculties are shrouded in the gloomy wish to drink and devour." See "Patriotic Reflections of a Gourmand," *Western Monthly Magazine and Literary Journal* 1, no. 3 (March 1833): 125–33, Google Books, http://books.google.com/books?id=HVkUAAAAYAAJ.

11. See n. 16, p. 108.

12. Dreadful; causing great terror. This word did not mean "excellent" or exciting in a good way until after the Civil War.

13. The god of wine, in Roman mythology.

enings of God in the storm above them or the billows beneath. From one direction we could hear the screaking of a violin and the untimely notes of a flute and some, we were told, were shuffling cards.

Beneath us the firemen were endeavoring to raise the steam, while the vessel seemed to wage a continual warfare with the tempestuous waves.

Such was our condition, tossing on the raging billows of Erie several miles from land in the midst of darkness and terror!

I thought, should the vessel give way and we should flood the gates of Eternity, while some would rejoice in a happy deliverance and some would stand aghast before a heart-searching and rein-trying God! However about three o'clock the wind lowered, the storm ceased and we were enabled to make our destined port, happy to set our feet once more on "terra firma."[14]

Lida.

Every time you spend one dollar and twenty-five cents, you throw away an acre of the best land in the world. Let the *penurious* or *benevolent* mind reckon this to suit themselves, and they cannot fail to see what this fact suggests.[15]

For the Offering.

"Here Hope That Smiling Angel Stands."

When beauty fades, and youthful bloom,
Looks forward to the shrouded tomb,
O what can lift the spirits wing,
To leave its fragile covering—
To burst the bonds so strongly dear,
And pierce *alone*, a shade so drear?

'Tis *Hope*—that ever radiant star,
Which beams from Calvary's hill afar,[16]

14. Latin: "solid earth."

15. $1.25 per acre was "the regular Government price" (the price set by Congress) for unsold public lands in the West. Indiana and Illinois still had many acres for sale at this price. Acres that had already been cultivated or farmed were worth more. See *Steele's Western Guide Book, and Emigrants Directory* (Buffalo: Oliver G. Steele, 1849), 27, 35, Google Books, http://books.google.com/books?id=U25NAAAAYAAJ.

16. In the New Testament, Calvary is where Jesus was crucified. See e.g. Mark 15:22.

Which guides the Pilgrim on his way,
Brightens the spirit's parting ray;
It bids the trembling sinner come,
And leads the joyful Christian home.

I've seen a Mother fondly cling,
To this frail world of suffering,
Where pain had every nerve unstrung,
And sickness grasped her little *one*—
This *Star* illumed her troubled breast,
And changed her fears to heavenly rest.

When friends in gentle accents told,
Her lovely babe in *death* was cold,
No tear suffused her fading cheek,
She looked around most sweetly meek,
"My darling babe I soon shall see,"
In yonder blest eternity.—

She spoke,—her eyes more brightly gleam
Till closed as in a pleasing dream,—
I saw in *one dark coffin* laid
That *Mother*, and her *darling babe*;
Those clay-cold cheeks in *death* were *fair*—
Hope's rainbow—promise lingered there.

C.

Hap-Hazard Ideas.

Continued.

In the second number of the Offering I told you *some* of my ideas of woman's rights and I will now continue my remarks somewhat.[17]

Some women feel that the reason why they are not allowed to help make the laws &c. &c., is because they are considered as possessing inferior *minds*, with those bestowed on the men. And what if such were the fact? What kind

17. See p. 97.

of woman is it that could not value such an opinion for just as much as it is worth, and not consent to make herself ridiculous in endeavoring to *prove* that *her* mind is equal to *man's*? can not such a one see that she is betraying her own *individual* weakness and casting suspicion on all her sex?

If such would sit down and read and calmly reflect, they would *know*, that since woman was first created, her influence has been *greater* than man's; her power for good or evil far exceeds his and every *sensible* man *knows* it, and why need we be irritated at the sneers of any poor simpleton that has not brains enough to enable him to feel his own necessities?

It is true there are some things that are *not* right, but: Sisters in this world of change, there are many ways to undertake to correct evils that are worse than *vain*, for instance the laws of our land are perhaps, not just as they should be; but is there any one among you that would be willing to go to our State or National Legislatures as members in either department standing among Legislators or Senators battling in degrading warfare as do the *hatted* heads when they assemble? no—no—not one among you having sound sense and proper feeling would do that—such understand a *better* policy than that—they will use their influence at home!—and let me tell you that if you would use it rightly, every *wrong law* would be *repealed*.

And is not such power enough to satisfy any woman's ambition? must some, possessing more impudence than sense, be continually lecturing to woman about her *trampled rights* and be allowed to cast a mist before her true path, leading her to pursue one that must end in darkness?

Such persons tell you that you have a *right* to help make all laws, a *right* to hold any office, to be Lawyers or Ministers, and they pick out what they consider most desirable as bringing most *ease* &c., &c. and hold up to you, to incite you to be dissatisfied with your lot; but *I* tell you that if you partake of *these* things you are in duty bound to go through every department in life and relieve *all*, of their burden. For instance, in war be a soldier—strap your knapsack on your back and away to the battle-field—you'll have a *right* not only to kill your fellow-creatures but you can use great swelling *words* and big round *oaths* can come out of your mouths and you can be valiant against the enemies of your country and your husbands if you have any, can stay at home like good men and take care of the children and pray that your *precious* lives may be preserved. Be sailors too, and away o'er the briny deep, sing your songs of mirth and glee—you can learn to suffer, to swear and to forget as well as they—and what, if at last, you perish? you will die *proving* what *woman could do* and your example may help some other poor creature to cast off the *unnatural* shackles that bind society.

You can go into the unbroken forest and fell the trees, or take a team of six or eight pairs of Oxen and break the prairie sod—you can maul rails from one week's end to another or go into the blacksmith's shop and be a regular son of vulcan[18]—no use in being fastidious—be a surgeon—go into the dissecting room—see the remnants of frail humanity scattered all around you—is it not delightful to cut off their limbs?—they have no power to resist and their *friends* do not *know* what you are about—ah! it is so *noble* and has so much *honor* in it—surely you will not shrink from it, you will learn to be indifferent to any little *feeling* you *once possessed*, and because you are a *woman* on such a *high mission*, you can perhaps, learn to think it could make no difference even if life was *not quite* gone—oh! horror!—we'll talk about something else, but we can not leave *woman, gentle woman* in such a scene as this, we will look at her as she really is—man's equal in mental power, his *superior* in moral perception and that spirit of generous forgetfulness of self that so eminently fit her to be what she is, his *help-mate* in this probationary scene—the star that leads him from evil and influences him to do good, the daughter, sister, wife—mother of heroes, statesmen, and Divines.

Can any one calculate the power, the influence of woman? no!—'tis as wide as creation, as broad as the habitable world. What man has ever lived whose mind was not in some *peculiar* sense made to be what it *was* or *is*, by his mother's influence? *high* in the lists of fame or *low* in the depths of iniquity, that *man had* a *Mother* that shaped his course in life, and can woman complain of want of power? rather should she tremble at the thought of her fearful responsibility and in the right discharge of her high and ennobling duties, learn to know that the reform of evils can alone be brought about.

Commence at your own fireside. Have you daughters, teach them to be something *more* than senseless clods of clay, decorated to attract the attention of some brainless fop. Teach then to *know themselves* and rightly

18. To "maul rails" is to pound or drive fence-posts; a "regular son of vulcan" would be a blacksmith (after Vulcan, the god of fire and blacksmiths in Roman mythology). Sojourner Truth rejected the argument that women are not strong enough to do "men's work" in her famous speech at the Akron, Ohio Woman's Rights Convention in the Stone Church on High Street on May 28, 1851. "May I say a few words?" Truth was reported to have said. "I am a woman's rights. I have as much muscle as any man, and can do as much work as any man. I have plowed and reaped and husked and chopped and mowed, and can any man do more than that? I have heard much about the sexes being equal; I can carry as much as any man, and can eat as much too, if I can get it. I am as strong as any man that is now." See Nell Irvin Painter, *Sojourner Truth: A Life, A Symbol* (New York: W. W. Norton, 1996), 125.

to value that precious jewel, the immortal mind, and the holy power that emanates from a heart alive to every sentiment of truth and sacred affection. Have you sons, prepare them for *life* as it is, let their minds receive the highest possible cultivation but neglect not their hearts; prepare them for adversity, while you teach them how to gain prosperity. Give them right views of man's relative duties, teach them how to value woman, by the respect you, yourself command, not by exacting words, but by deserving it—and be assured that what ye deserve ye will have.

Let *man* stand in the *public arena*—it is his place, but let him not forget that *woman* fitted him for his station, and let *woman* remember that *this* is *her honor* and a nobler crown than she could ever receive by standing there herself!

Porcia.

Good nature is one of the sweetest gifts of Providence. Like the pure sunshine, it gladdens, enlivens, cheers. In the midst of hate, revenge, sorrow and despair how glorious are its effects.[19]

For the Offering.

Musings.

Beyond, beyond this Sea of life
What can we know? how end the strife?
How satisfy the soul's desire,
Kindled by an immortal fire?
How stretch the thought, and search the plan
That Deity has formed for man?
How scan eternity's decree

19. The earliest printing of this maxim that I can find is Robert Bailey Thomas, *The Farmer's Almanack . . .* for 1841 (Boston: Jenks & Palmer, 1840), 40, Google Books, http://books.google.com/books?id=p28TAAAAYAAJ. It was then republished (as here) as page-filling material. A possible source for Cumings is *The Ladies' Garland and Family Wreath* 3 (1849), 74, American Periodicals (136977704). Cumings often selected from *The Ladies' Garland*. See n. 101, p. 415; n. 37, p. 417; and n. 38, p. 440. Frank Luther Mott describes *The Ladies' Garland* as "an example of the cheap periodical for women—a type which flourished in the forties." See Mott, *A History of American Magazines, 1850–1865* (Cambridge: Belknap Press of University of Harvard Press, 1938), 672. Another possible source for Cumings is *The Ark, and Odd Fellows' Western Monthly Magazine*, which published the maxim twice within one year. See 5, no. 9 (September 1848): 266, and 6, no. 8 (August 1849): 236, Google Books, http://books.google.com/books?id=K5geAQAAMAAJ. For more on the Odd Fellows and *The Akron Offering*, see n. 24, below.

Filled with its *own immensity*?—
Ah me!—can creatures of an hour
Expect omniscience to explore
And lift the veil where hidden lies
Eternity's dread mysteries?
Impossible!—'tis not for man,
The wisdom of a God to scan;
'Tis not for *man* to penetrate
The darkness of unfathomed *Fate*.—
The future,—"where is it?" 'tis where,
The mind of man must e'en despair,
Of knowing *how its* boundaries lay,
So long as he inhabits clay.

For the Offering.

"Peace, Be Still"[20]

A Story From The Bible.

By Vesper.

A little band of fishermen and sailors launched their bark at "dewy eve" upon the glassy surface of smooth and tranquil waters.

The sun had finished his course through the "pathless heaven" and laid aside his fiery robe and retired.

Pale Diana[21] came slowly forth from the "chambers of the east" looking so melancholy and sad that she seemed to mourn the absence of the glorious King. The lesser stars reverently retired and hid their faces before the

20. This story is based on Matthew 8:23–27 as well as "Christ in the Tempest" by James Greenleaf Whittier (1807–92), a poem written about 1830 when Whittier was publishing in the *New England Weekly Review*. For an early printing, see *American Masonic Record and Albany Literary Review* 4, no. 30 (August 21, 1830): 240, Google Books, http://books.google.com/books?id=EGwgAQAAMAAJ. "Christ in the Tempest" was republished frequently and anthologized. Vesper returns in March, 1850, in much the same style. See p. 408. Many of the quotes in the story come from the Whittier poem. Other quotes are from the bible: "chambers of the east" (Ezekiel 40:10), "Master carest thou not that we perish" (Matthew 8:25), "man in his own image" (Genesis 1:27), "spirit of heaviness" (Isaiah 61:3), "furnace of affliction" (Isaiah 48:10), and "seven times more than it was wont to be" (Daniel 3:19). Others are sufficiently clichéd to have no clear source (e.g., "soft and fair"). Others are too brief or obscure to be sourced with the various search engines cited elsewhere in these notes. "Dewy eve" comes from John Milton's *Paradise Lost* (1:743).

21. In Roman mythology, the goddess of the moon.

moon's mild beauty; the more brilliant ones modestly bestowed their little light, respectfully advancing, "attendant graces of the Queen of night;"[22] while far out upon heaven's azure floated a few snow-white, fleecy clouds, whose folds were "soft and fair."

The sweet tranquility of nature gave to these sailor's hearts a heavenly rest and while they sat eagerly quaffing rich draughts from nature's loveliness, their Master stole away, laid his weary head upon a pillow, and gave for a few moments, his worn body to the quiet arms of sleep:—Meanwhile the fantastic vapors which had been borne on the slightest breath of heaven, became as one: dark and ominous. It spread—grew still larger, larger and dark—o'ershadowing the earth by its black and fiend-like wings, and grasping the heavens with its Herculean arms—yes, 'twas midnight on the waters;—the mighty winds had come forth to engage in nature's battle;—cloud on cloud rolled thick and threatening like frowns on Deity's brow. The great waters groaned in heart, and sent from depths profound, the tall billows, that laughed as they lashed the rocking bark. The vast sky "stopped with murmuring thunder" and the clouds immense

"Reeled heavily in the darkness, like a shower
Shook by some warning spirit from the high
And terrible wall of heaven"—

while ever and anon the lightning's lurid glare would blaze athwart the sky, so fierce and terrible, that for "aye" it seemed a "fiendish torch" lit, blazing, and red from Satan's altar and sent to "lighten some doomed spirit to its burning home." The little ship seemed almost lost and swallowed up; its feeble power well nigh exhausted; it could but little longer combat with the huge waves that rose and fell, like the bold upheavings of a mighty giant, struggling to release itself from a premature grave.

In wild despair were the sailors and loud above the storm were heard these words—

"Master carest thou not that we perish?—"

He came upon deck, he bared his brow to tempest, calm and serene as a God he stood; he trembled not as he beheld the warring elements, and while the maniac winds ruthlessly played with his floating locks, a smile of ineffable benignity and love lingered upon his countenance. He stepped

22. In Greek mythology, the three Graces were goddesses—of charm, beauty, etc.—that only attended; they never ruled. In 1849, "the Queen of Night" was a common poetical name for the moon. Here the "attendant graces" might be stars and perhaps Venus or some other heavenly body.

forth, raised one arm, possessed of power which no man can boast, and said in sweet, silvery tones: "*Peace be still.*"

Those soft and thrilling accents pierced the waves and they went moaning into silence; the winds retired to their caverns and the clouds, where "shone the lightning and slept the latent thunder" went muttering away into oblivion, and in a moment all was beautiful and gay, and "no trace of tempest lurked behind."

And is it thus? Is there a power so great? a being so beautifully mighty, that the "uprisen storm" will bow at his presence, and the mountainous waves do sacred homage?

Yes, there is a "Ruler of earth and sea," and this Being so infinitely great and glorious made "man in his own image," and the form of frail dust claims His infinite regard.

Then when storms and tempests shake our souls we have but to trust in our Master as did the sailors and the gentle words, "*Peace, be still,*" will drive all storms away.

How sweet these words to the sinner's soul, when he has been long bound down by the weight of his own guilt, when he has mourned in sackcloth and ashes and been oppressed with the "spirit of heaviness," then the soft words, "*Peace, be still,*" giveth him beauty and joy and the garment of praise.

When sore temptations surround us on every side and there seems to be no *way* of escape, God Himself points out the path and whispers to our tossed and wavering souls, "*Peace, be still.*"

When we walk through the "furnace of affliction," apparently heated "seven times more than it was wont to be;" when poverty oppresses, when friends forsake, and when

—"Death enters where
The household group was young and fair
And turns the scene to weeping,"

oh! with what triumph do we then greet the heavenly words borne by some celestial dove; how soon our stricken souls revive, our bitter tears are dried, and our hearts which were as the burning desert, in which fall showers of sand, bloom like the rose beneath its influence for we know 'tis the "dread Ruler of the tempest," that designs to smile upon us and sweetly whisper to *our souls, "Peace, be still."*

The Stranger's Burial.

Saw ye the train in such solemn, sad array,
Slow bearing to the grave, a cold form of clay?
And marked ye the members that as mourners there,
Shed, in anguish of spirit, affection's tear?
And asked ye the station, the home, or the name
Of one who in death, such deep respect could claim?
'Twas no kindred tie, 'twas no Father or Mother,—
'Twas a stranger's burial—the "Odd Fellow's" Brother.

His home was far off, and no kindred could come,
To hear his last message and soften his doom;
But his Brethren were there each wish to obey,
To point him to Heaven, and with him to pray;
To watch o'er him e'en to his last, fleeting breath,
And to wipe from his brow, the cold damps of death;
Then lay his remains where they'll ne'er be forgot—
In that green, resting place, the "Odd Fellow's lot."

And thus do they ever, thus "Masons" and "Sons"
To their wandering Brothers, the friendless ones
Who can claim no kindred, no soothing power
To minister to them in death's trying hour;
And widows and orphans of such may find,
Protection and friendship, and honor combined
In each true Mason's soul, and no "Son" will depart
From the principles bound on each Odd Fellow's heart.

Ah! who that has friends, though much wealth theirs may be,
Would have them 'mong strangers, no sympathy see?
And receive no care but the cold, measured form
That is purchased with gold, and no heart can warm?
And who, if in poverty friends must forth go,
Would feel that they *may* not e'en *one* blessing know;
But in deepest privation, their last breath *may* yield
And their bodies be laid in some lone "Potter's field?"[23]

23. A "potter's field" is a cemetery where the bodies of unknown people or the very poor are buried. The name comes from Matthew 27:7.

Ah ye wives, or daughters, or sisters, or Mothers,
Reproach not your husbands, Fathers or Brothers
For wearing the badges these orders impose;
But let your pure influence, wherever it goes,
Help the railing or doubting, the wealthy and poor
Enlist under banners that thus will secure
Sweet peace to the weary—oh! teach each loved one
To be "Mason," "Odd Fellow," and "Temperance's Son."[24]

Then if they leave you, on life's tide to be tossed,
Though the strength of humanity's bond be lost,
They'll meet on each shore, those who like them will bear
The talisman true, that shall save them from care—
And if they must *die*, their *graves* ye can *find*,
And gratitude's evergreen, richly entwined
With memory's rose, in sweet verdure shall bloom—
Their Order's memento, the lone stranger's tomb.

Oh! then hasten young men your names to enroll,
And leave them unstained on benevolence's scroll;
Be Masons, "Odd Fellows" and generous "Sons,"
And be *more*, be ye holy and guileless ones
Whose souls in their fullness, Creation embrace,
And seek richest blessings for all our lost race!
Oh! deign, pure Religion's rich precepts to heed
And be, in nobleness "*Odd Fellow*s indeed!"

C. Cumings.

---

24. The Freemasons, The International Order of Odd Fellows, and The Sons of Temperance ("Masons," "Odd Fellows," and "Sons") were active fraternal organizations comprised primarily of white, middle-class Protestant men. Focused on mutual self-improvement, these societies offered insurance benefits and other social advantages. The Sons of Temperance were explicitly in favor of temperance, which in 1849 necessitated total abstinence from alcoholic beverages. As the poem suggests, membership in one of these organizations could be especially beneficial for men who travelled much on business as most urban centers would have a lodge or group or representative prepared to offer assistance and hospitality. Membership in these fraternal societies brought many other social and financial benefits. In Akron all three societies were active in 1849. Women were meeting as the Daughters of Temperance, a sister organization of the Sons of Temperance. By 1859, the Sons of Temperance were no longer organized in Akron but the city had two busy halls, one for the Masons and one for the Odd Fellows, on either side of Howard Street between Market and Mill. See *Williams' Akron, Wooster, and Cuyahoga Falls Directory, City Guide, and Business Mirror* (Akron: W. G. Robinson, 1859), 15, Akron Public Library, http://www.akronlibrary.org/internetresources/sc/CityDirectories/akroncitydir1859.pdf.

For the Offering.

Time.

Believe not life is marked by time,
Or hearts by long acquaintance warmed,
For there are hours that compass years,
And love, time never scathed or formed.

This essence of congenial souls,
No barrier finds in space or clime,
From land or wave disdains control,
And triumphs o'er the power of time.

A——.

For the Offering.

"How Blessings Brighten as They Take Their Flight."[25]

A thought was suggested while contemplating the last scene, of the beautiful Diorama, which has been exhibited here, for the past week.[26] In the back ground Babylon is seen soaring up with its lofty palaces, and turrets

25. By 1849 this was a common proverb, often repeated and almost never attributed to its source, the long religious poem *The Complaint, or, Night-Thoughts on Life, Death, and Immortality* (1742–46) by English poet Edward Young (1683–1765).

26. An enormous painting of Biblical events by Ohio portrait and panorama painter John Insco Williams (1813–73) was in Akron as part of an statewide tour. As *The Summit Beacon* notes:

> Panorama of the Bible.—Mr. J. I. Williams, of Cincinnati, an artist who has with him the highest recommendations from many men of taste and science, and has called forth the warmest testimonials from the press at the several points of the State he has visited, has made arrangements to exhibit his beautiful Panorama of the Sacred Scriptures, in this place, at the Universalist Church, for a few days, commencing THIS EVENING. The Painting is one mile and five furlongs in length.—Mr. Vaughn of the Cleveland True Democrat writes us that he has known Mr. Williams for years, that he is an artist of great merit, and that the effect produced by the exhibition is highly favorable upon the mind. Those who are familiar with Bible History, can readily imagine that the Painter would find in the events recorded much to call forth his highest efforts. Such an exhibition all may attend with profit and pleasure.
> Admittance 25 cents, children, under 12 years of age, 15 cents.

"Panorama of the Bible," *The Summit Beacon* 11, no. 14 (July 25, 1849): 3. See also Silas H. Chase and John Insco Williams, *A Short History of J. Insco Williams' Panorama of the Bible* (Cincinnati: Office of the Daily Times, 1849). The record in OCLC's WorldCat database notes this thirty-six-page book describes the panorama: "the length of the entire painting is 8,640 feet, and near ten feet in breadth." Williams had been a mentor of Lilly Martin Spencer in Cincinnati. See n. 15, p. 256.

which seem almost lost amid the clouds. In the fore ground we have the Euphrates gently rolling by, one of the cold streams of Babylon; the banks of which are adorned with numerous willows. Under the gracefully drooping branches, is seen a group of Jewish maidens, bewailing their exile from their native land; while their harps hang unstrung on the adjacent willows. Their captors demanded of them the song, but they replied "How can we sing the songs of Zion, in a strange land." Although surrounded by the gorgeous splendors of Babylon, its gardens, its fountains, its scenery, had no charms for them; they thought only of their far distant homes, the scenes of their youth. The harp had no song for the stranger; each heroically resolved

> "That ne'er shall its soft notes be blended
> With the voice of the spoiler by me."[27]

The whole scene is a masterly production, and delineated with an accuracy, that leaves a permanent impression on the mind of the spectator. This short sketch is introduced only, as a prelude to the suggestions of a few thoughts. "How blessings brighten as they take their flight." Man might be happy. Everything around him admonishes that he should be so. Nature in every department is eminently calculated to administer to his supreme felicity.

The heavens above us, obedient to fixed and immutable laws, move on in magnificent splendor, and unbroken harmony. The earth around us presents a Panorama of everything beautiful, grand and sublime; so varied its scenery, so lyric its poetry, that the eye is always relieved by its variety, and the ear never wearied by monotony. Through nature God speaks to man. He is heard in the rolling thunder, and seen in the vivid lightning. Every breeze that floats o'er our heads, every flower that blooms beneath our feet, every stream that glides by its flower-decked banks, the birds that pour forth their choral songs, to hail the first rays of the rising sun, the dew drop, and the rainbow, the lily of the valley, and the snow on the mountain's top, all bespeak his presence. The roar of the ocean, the mighty cataract, the glitter of the noon-day sun, the sublimity of the night, all proclaim this grandeur. "His Presence gives them existence; his Will their law and force; his Wisdom their order; his Goodness their beauty."[28]

---

27. Final lines of "By the Rivers of Babylon We Sat Down and Wept," a popular poem by English poet George Gordon Noel Byron.

28. Line from "The Relation of Nature to God," a chapter published from lectures given in Boston by Unitarian clergyman Theodore Parker (1810–60). See *A Discourse of Matters Pertaining to Religion* (London: Chapman Brothers, 1846), 171, Google Books, http://books.google.com/books?id=d_IRAAAAYAAJ.

Yet from all these external means of happiness, man learns no lessons of wisdom or profit. He has within him the elements of happiness, when they are permitted to develope themselves, in their natural and legitimate channels. There is an adaption of all things to his wants, and convenience; made a little lower than the angels, he is justly styled the "lord of creation." The brute acknowledges his dominion; for him the earth yields its choicest fruits, and rarest flowers; the very elements are subject to the power of his mighty intellect; he laughs at the ocean's wave, and the electric fires are obedient to his behests.

He too was formed for society. The intelligent principle can only be developed, but by social intercourse. Mind acts upon mind; its manifestations in a great degree are similar. Yet observation and experience teaches us, that society is a mass of discontent materials, moving in contrary directions, perverting its natural relations; each administers to his own unhappiness, and spurns Heaven's choicest gifts, scattered so profusely around him.

Man, proud, restless, and ambitious, ever searching after the ideal, enjoys not the actual; always indulging in golden dreams of future happiness, enjoys not the present. He has not yet learned that the great secret of happiness is present contentment, that to realize life, is to possess a calm and quiet spirit. Thus he pursues phantoms and shadows, ekes out a miserable existence, and when the silvery locks of old age admonish him, that he can no longer, if he would enjoy life, with its numberless sources of pleasure, he despairingly exclaims "How blessings brighten as they take their flight."

Turn over History's instructive page, read the fate of nations and kingdoms, now no more; once rose proudly the regal palace, and the temple of the Gods; peace dwelt within, and tranquility without their walls; the arts and commerce flourished, the chief sources of a nation's wealth; propitious were the omens of future stability and greatness; but not content with the present, visions of military glory, ambitious projects of universal conquest, and splendid triumphs hastened on and completed their downfall; their name is now known only in history's page, or in the records of song. A race of degraded slaves mournfully points out to you the magnificent ruins, and exclaims, "how blessings brighten that long since have taken their flight."

We as a nation occupy a more elevated position in the world's history, than any which has preceded us. Nobility rears no palaces on our soil, nor dares it breathe the air consecrated to freedom.—Yet we are not wholly secure; although peace has thrown her mantle over our shoulders, and the constitution stands as a fortress to protect our rights, yet international differences may demolish, even this bulwark, and while "destiny" is madly kindling wars of conquest *we may* witness the mighty crash of a falling Republic, and appreciate our blessings only as they take their flight.

Learn then to be content with the present, enjoy life as it rapidly hurries along; though the waves of adversity may roll high, bear steadily onward, let the "soul spring immortal o'er sorrow,"[29] and then shall life shower around us innumerable blessings that shall never take their flight.

R.

For the Offering.

To A Friend.

It is good to live in some employ,
We may soothe grief and create joy,
Perhaps before that life shall end,
We too, may want a cheerful friend.

How oft in youth life's path we view,
All strewed with flowers enriched with dew,
But alas! before life's eve comes on,
We find our roses mixed with thorns.

Then as our days glide swiftly on,
We'll heed our ways and shun the storm,
Then when our days on earth shall end,
In Heaven we'll find a faithful friend.

Cora.[30]

Description of the Buckeye.

Lida's wish to be informed why Ohio is called the Buckeye State, suggests the idea that, perhaps, there *may* be many who would be interested

29. Phrase from "Come, Tell Me Thy Sorrow," a poem by English poet Charles Swain (1801–74) that was reprinted several times in American periodicals in the mid-1840s. One American printing is *The Eclectic Magazine of Foreign Literature, Science, and Art* 7, no. 2 (February 1846): 283, Google Books, http://books.google.com/books?id=N4yYXoyScKUC.

30. For another work by this unknown author, see p. 207.

in a description of the Buckeye and the origin of the term as applied to the people of Ohio.[31]

For the benefit of those who may not have the work in which is found the best description of it I have ever seen, I will give the address by Doctor Drake, delivered at the celebration of the 45th anniversary of the first settlement of Cincinnati on the 26th Dec 1833.—EDITOR.[32]

MR. PRESIDENT AND YOUNG GENTLEMEN:

"Being born in the East, I am not *quite* a native of the valley of the Ohio, and, therefore, am not a Buckeye by birth. Still I might claim to be a greater Buckeye than most of you, who were born in the city, for my Buckeyeism belongs to the country, a better soil for rearing Buckeyes than the town.

"My first remembrances are of a Buckeye cabin, in the depths of a cane brake, on one of the tributary brooks of Licking river; for whose waters, as they flow into the Ohio, opposite our city, I feel some degree of affection. At the date of these recollections, the spot where we are now assembled, was a Beech and Buckeye grove; no doubt altogether unconscious of its approaching fate. Thus I am a Buckeye by engrafting or rather by inoculation, being only in the bud, when I began to draw my nourishment from the depths of a Buckeye bowl.

"But why are the natives of our valley called Buckeyes? and to whom are they indebted for the epithet? Mr. President—the memory that can

---

31. See p. 144.

32. Daniel Drake (1785–1852) was a Cincinnati physician, educator, and naturalist. The event referenced here was the "Buckeye Dinner" of December 26, 1833. The young Ohio-born gentlemen of Cincinnati got up this dinner, whose plans grew to include older guests of honor (including Drake) and an elaborate series of songs, speeches, and toasts. A total of about 160 men gathered around tables set up in the Cincinnati Commercial Exchange on the riverbank. The feast was comprised almost entirely of "the productions of Ohio soil" and included, "in honor of the old Pioneers, a pair of uncommonly fat and delicious raccoons." Between the tables were placed "four capacious Buckeye Bowls, manufactured from the tree" and from these "flowed plentiful streams of rich *Sangaree*," a wine made by Nicholas Longworth from grapes grown near the city. The original and full record of this dinner, including the text of the address copied here, is *Celebration of the Forty-Fifth Anniversary of the First Settlement of Cincinnati and the Miami country on the 26th day of December, 1833, by Natives of Ohio* (Cincinnati: Shreve & Gallagher, 1834), Sabin Americana 1500–1926 (CY3806060509). The description of the meal is on pages 3–4; Drake's speech can be found on pages 32–37. Another guest of honor was General William Henry Harrison (1773–1841), future ninth President of the United States. He attended the dinner "in the garb of a farmer." See "The Buckeye Dinner," *The Western Monthly Magazine* 3, no. 15 (March 1834) 145–57, Google Books, http://books.google.com/books?id=psocAQAAMAAJ. This coverage of the dinner also includes a text of Drake's speech. The version reprinted in *The Akron Offering* includes an additional full paragraph (beginning "But why are the natives of our valley called Buckeyes?") as well as three additional, scattered sentences. These additions indicate that Cumings must have selected a later, revised version of the speech, which was undoubtedly reprinted very often in Ohio newspapers and magazines.

travel a few years into the last century, and it only, can supply the answer. As the Buckeye has a soft wood, and is peculiar to the valley of the Ohio, latter emigrants to both banks of the river, thought it a fit emblem for the native children, whom they found untaught, and awkward, amusing themselves in the shade of its luxuriant foliage! or admiring the beautiful dyes of its ripening nuts, and Buckeye was, therefore, at first, a nickname—a term of derision. Those very children, have, however, raised it into a title of honor! They have no higher eulogy.

"The tree which you have toasted, Mr. President, has the distinction of being one of a family of plants, but a few species of which exists on the earth. They constitute the genus *Æsculus* of the botanist, which belongs to the class *Heptandria*. Now the latter, a Greek phrase, signifies *seven men*; and there happens to be exactly seven species of the genus—thus they constitute the seven wise men of the woods; in proof of which I may mention, that there is not another family on the whole earth, that possess these talismanic attributes of wisdom. But this is not all. Of the seven species, our emblem-tree was discovered *last*—it is the youngest of the family—*the seventh son*! and who does not know the manifold virtues of a seventh son![33]

"Neither Europe nor Africa has a single *native* species of *Æsculus*, and Asia but one. This is the *Æsculus Hippocastinum* or Horsechesnut. Nearly three hundred years since, a minister from one of the courts of Western Europe to that of Russia, found this tree growing in Moscow, whither it had been brought from Siberia. He was struck with its beauty, and naturalized it in his own country. It spread with astonishing rapidity over that part of the continent, and crossing the channel, became one of the favorite shade trees of our English ancestors. But the oppressions and persecutions recounted in the address of your young orator,[34] compelled them to cross the ocean and become exiled from the tree, whose beautiful branches overhung their cottage doors.

"When they reached this continent did they find their favorite shade tree, or any other species of the family to supply its place in their affections? They did not—they could not; as from Jamestown to Plymouth, the soil is too barren to nourish this epicurean plant. Doubtless, their first impulse

33. Various medical powers, such as the ability to heal scrofula with a touch of the hand, were ascribed to seventh sons by popular superstition. A quack doctor might claim to be a seventh son. Drake—a medical professor—is having fun with his subject.

34. The "young orator" was Joseph Longworth. He kicked off the after-dinner festivities with a fervent address on the virtues of Ohio's Revolutionary War-era ancestors. See *Celebration of the Forty-Fifth Anniversary*, 4–12.

was to seek it in the interior; but there the Indian still had his home, and they were compelled to languish on the sands of the sea board. The revolution came and passed away: it was a political event, and men still hovered on the coast; but the revolving year at length unfolded the map of the mighty West, and our fathers began to direct their steps thitherward. They took breath on the eastern base of the Allegheny mountains, without having found the object of their pursuits; then scaled its lofty summits—threaded its deep and narrow defiles—descended its western slopes—but still sought in vain. The hand of destiny, however, seemed to be upon them; and boldly penetrating the unbroken forests of the Ohio, amidst savages and beasts of prey, they finally built their 'half-faced camps' beneath the Buckeye tree.[35]—All their hereditary and traditional feelings were now gratified. They had not, to be sure, found the Horsechesnut, which embellished the paths of their forefathers; but a tree of the same family, of greater size and equal beauty, and, like themselves, a native of the new world. Who of this young assembly, has a heart so cold, as not to sympathize in the joyous emotions which this discovery must have raised? It acted on them like a charm,—their flagging pulses were quickened, and their imaginations warmed. They thought not of returning, but sent back pleasant messages, and invited their friends to follow. Crowds from every state in the Union soon pressed forward, and, in a single age, the native land of the Buckeye, became the home of millions.[36] Enterprise was animated; new ideas came into men's minds; bold schemes were planned and executed: new communities organized; political states established; and the wilderness transformed, as if by enchantment.

"Such was the power of the Buckeye wand; and its influence has not been limited to the west. We may fearlessly assert that it has been felt over the whole of our common country. Till the time when the Buckeye tree was discovered, slow indeed had been the progress of society in the new world. With the exception of the revolution, but little had been achieved, and but little was in prospect. Since that era, society has been progressive, higher destinies have been unfolded, and a reactive Buckeye influence,

---

35. "Half-faced camps" were temporary shelters with an open side. A primitive version is illustrated in Rudolph Barnes Marcy, *The Prairie Traveler: A Hand-book for Overland Expeditions* (New York: Harper & Brothers, 1859), 133–34, Google Books, http://books.google.com/books?id=cWkoAAAAYAAJ. A more deluxe version is shown in Robert Judson Aley and Max Aley, *Indiana and Its People* (Chicago: O. P. Barnes, 1912), 135–36, Google Books, http://books.google.com/books?id=jwFwAAAAMAAJ.

36. In 1849 the population of the state of Ohio was just under two million; in 1833 it was just over one million.

perceptible to all acute observers, must continue to assist in elevating our beloved country among the nations of the earth.

"Every native of the valley of the Ohio, should feel proud of the appellation, which, from the infancy of our settlements, has been conferred upon him; for the Buckeye has many qualities which may be regarded as typical of a noble character.

"It is not merely a native of the West, but peculiar to it; has received from the Botanists the specific name of *Ohioensis*, from its abundance in our beautiful valley; and is the only tree of our whole forest, that does not grow elsewhere. What other tree could be so fit an emblem of our native population?

"From the very beginning of emigration, it has been a friend to the 'new comers.' Delighting in the richest soils, they soon learned to take counsel from it, in the selection of their lands; and it never yet proved faithless to any one who confided in it.

"When the first 'log cabin' was to be hastily put up, the softness and lightness of its wood, made it precious; for in those times laborers were few, and axes once broken in harder timber, could not be repaired. It was, moreover of all the trees of the forest that which best arrested the rifle bullets of the Indian.

"When the infant Buckeyes came forth, to render these solitary cabins vocal and make them instinct with life, cradles were necessary, and they could not be so easily dug out of any other tree.—Thousands of men and women, who are now active and respectable performers on the great theatre of western society, were once rocked in Buckeye troughs.

"In those early days, when a boundless and lofty wilderness overshadowed every habitation, to destroy the trees and make way for the growth of corn, was the great object,—*hic labor, hoc opus erat.*[37] Now, the lands where the Buckeye abounded, were from the special softness of its woods, the easiest of all others to 'clear,' and in this way it offered valuable, though negative assistance to the 'first settlers.'

"Foreign sugar was then unknown in these regions, and our reliance for this article as for many others, was on the abounding woods. In reference to this sweet and indispensable acquisition, the Buckeye lent us positive aid; for it was not only the best wood of the forest for troughs, but everywhere grew side by side with the graceful and delicious sugar maple.

"We are now assembled on a spot, which is surrounded by vast warehouses, filled to overflowing with the earthen and iron, domestic uten-

37. Latin: This effort, this was the work.

sils of China, Birmingham, Sheffield, and I should add the great western manufacturing town, at the head of our noble river. The poorest and the obscurest family in the land, may be, and are, in fact, adequately supplied. How different was the condition of the early emigrants! A journey of a thousand miles, over the wild and rugged mountains, permitted the adventurous pioneer to bring with him a little more than the Indian or the Arab carries from place to place—*his wife and children*. Elegances were unknown, even articles of pressing necessity were few in number, and when lost or broken could not be replaced. In that period of trying deprivation, to what quarter did the 'first settlers' turn their inquiring and anxious eyes? The Buckeye—yes, gentlemen, to the Buckeye tree; and it proved a friend indeed, because, in simple and expressive language of those early times, it was 'a friend in need.' Hats were manufactured of its fibres—the tray for the delicious 'pone' and 'johnny-cake'—the venison trencher—the noggin—the spoon, and the huge, white family bowl for mush and milk, were carved from its willing trunk; and the finest 'boughten' vessel could not have imparted a more delicious flavor, or left an impression so enduring.[38] He who has ever been concerned in the petty brawls, the frolic and the fun of a family of the young *Buckeyes* around the great wooden bowl, overflowing with the 'milk of human kindness,'[39] will carry the sweet remembrance to his grave.

"Thus, beyond all the trees of the land, the Buckeye was associated with the family circle,—penetrating its privacy, facilitating its operations, and augmenting its enjoyments. Unlike many of its loftier associates, it did not bow its head and wave its arms at a haughty distance; but might be said to have held out the *right hand of fellowship*; for, of all the trees of our forest, it is the only one with *five* leaflets arranged on one stem,—an expressive symbol of the human hand.

"MR. PRESIDENT AND YOUNG GENTLEMEN, I beg you to pardon the enthusiasm which betrays me into continued trespasses on your patience.

38. "Pone" and "johnny-cake" were varieties of corn bread very commonly eaten by early pioneers. "Johnny cake" was cooked by spreading the batter (corn meal, salt, lard, and water) about a quarter-inch thick on a "johnny-cake" board about three to four inches wide and fifteen to twenty inches long. This board—often a piece of what we might call "clapboard" today (a "shingle" in antebellum American)—was then set near the fire to bake. "Pone" was much the same thing, baked in thicker loaves and only after the batter was left to rise for half a day. For old-time pioneer recipes, see "Housewife's Department," *Monthly Journal of Agriculture* 2, no. 1 (July 1846): 46, Google Books, http://books.google.com/books?id=zVzOAAAAMAAJ. Trenchers are pieces of wood used as plates and cutting boards. Noggins are small wooden cups. "Boughten" means "store-bought" (as opposed to homemade).

39. Popular saying; originally from Shakespeare's *Macbeth* (1.4.17).

As an old friend of the Buckeye tree, I feel, that to be faithful, I must dwell still longer on its virtues.

"The original 'ditty' which has just been sung with so much animation, sets forth in homely but hearty phrases, some of its figurative characters.[40] Let me in humble prose, recount a few of them with others not yet 'said or sung.'

"In all our woods, there is not a tree so hard to kill as the Buckeye. The deepest 'girdling' does not 'deaden' it, and even after it is cut down and worked up into the side of a cabin, it will send out young branches, denoting to all the world, that BUCKEYES are not easily conquered, and could with difficulty be destroyed.[41]

"The Buckeye has generally been condemned as unfit for fuel, but its very incombustibility has been found an advantage, for no tree of the forest is equally valuable for 'backlogs,' which are the *sine qua non*[42] of every good cabin fire. Thus treated, it may be finally though slowly, burnt—when another of its virtues immediately appears, as no other tree of our woods affords so great a quantity of alkali; thus there is piquancy in its very ashes!

"The bark of our emblem-plant has some striking properties.—Under a proper method of preparation and use, it is said to be efficacious in the cure of ague and fever, but unskillfully employed, it proves a violent emetic; which may indicate, that he who tampers with a BUCKEYE, will not do it with impunity.[43]

"The fruit of the Buckeye offers much to interest us. The capsule or covering of the nut, is beset with sharp prickles, which, incautiously grasped, will soon compel the aggressor to let go his hold. The nut is undeniably the most beautiful of all which our teeming woods bring forth; and in many parts of the country is made subservient to the military education of our sons; who, assembling in the 'muster field,' (where their fathers and elder brothers are learning to be militia-men) divide themselves into armies, and pelt each other with Buckeye balls; a military exercise at least as instructive as that which their seniors perform with buckeye sticks. The inner covering of the nut is highly astringent. Its substance, when grated

40. Drake refers here to a song "written for the occasion" and sung "with great glee by all the company to the tune of Yankee Doodle." It began: "Buckeyes! tune up, / And let us sing, / A ditty, or sich matter, / To that ar tree, / Which all agree, / That we was christened arter." For the full lyrics, see *Celebration of the Forty-Fifth Anniversary*, 19–20.

41. To "girdle" a tree is to cut the bark in a ring or belt all the way around its trunk, so as to kill it.

42. Latin: An essential thing.

43. For ague, see n. 32, p. 94. An "emetic" is a medicine that provokes vomiting.

down, is soapy, and has been used to cleanse fine fabrics in the absence of good soap. When the powder is washed, a large quantity of starch is obtained, which might if times of scarcity *could* arise, in a land so fertile as the native soil of this tree, be used for food. The water employed for this purpose, holds in solution an active medicinal agent, which unwarily swallowed, proves a poison; thus again admonishing those who would attempt to 'use up' a Buckeye, that they may repent of their rashness.

"Who has not looked with admiration on the fine foliage of the Buckeye in early spring, while the more sluggish tenants of the forest, remain torpid in their winter quarter; and what tree in all our wild woods, bears a flower which can be compared with that of our favorite? We may fearlessly challenge for it the closest comparison. Its early putting forth, and the beauty of its leaves and blossoms, are appropriate types of our native population, whose rapid and beautiful development, will not be denied by those whom I now address, nor disproved by a reference to their character; while the remarkable fact, that almost every attempt to transplant it into our streets has been a failure, shows that it will die in captivity, a guaranty that those who bear its name can never be enslaved.

"Finally, the Buckeye derives its name from resemblance of its nut to the eye of the buck, the finest organ of our noblest wild animal; while the name itself, is compounded of a Welsh and a Saxon word, belonging therefore to the oldest portions of our vernacular tongue, and connecting us with the primitive stocks, of which our fathers were but scions planted in the new world.

"But, Mr. President and Gentlemen, I must dismiss this fascinating topic. My object has been to show the peculiar fitness of the Buckeye to be made the symbol-tree of our native population. This arises from its many excellent qualities. Other trees have greater magnitude, and stronger trunks. They are Hercules of the forest; and like him of old, who was distinguished only for physical power, they are remarkable chiefly for their mechanical strength. Far different is it with the Buckeye, which does not depend on brute force to effect its objects; but exercises, as it were, a moral power, and admonishes all who adopt its name, to rely upon intellectual cultivation, instead of bodily prowess."

From the Episcopal Recorder.[44]

Prayer.

Come let us pray? 'tis sweet to feel
 That God himself is near;
That while we at his footstool kneel,
 His mercy deigns to hear.
Though sorrows crowd our dreary way,
This is our solace—let us pray!

Come let us pray! the burning brow—
 The heart oppressed with care—
And all the woes that throng us now,
 Will be relieved by prayer.
Jesus will smile our griefs away—
O glorious thought—come, let us pray!

Come, let us pray! The sin-sick soul
 Her weight of guilt must feel—
But hark! the glorious tidings roll,
 Whilst here we humbly kneel—
Jesus will wipe that guilt away,
And pardon grant—then let us pray!

Come, let us pray! the mercy seat
 Is now prepared and free,
And Jesus ready stands to greet
 Sinners like you and me—
O, loiter not, nor longer stay
From him who loves us—let us pray!

44. This was a six-column, four-page newspaper published weekly by William Suddards, rector of Grace Church in Philadelphia. This poem is attributed to "Iota" and signed "Philadelphia, April 1844" in *Episcopal Recorder* 22, no. 7 (May 14, 1844): 28, American Periodicals (89902625).

For the Offering.

That Dear Old Bench in the Cottage Porch.[45]

By Lily Lute.[46]

That time-worn bench in the cottage porch,
O, spare it, stranger, spare
That dear old seat of the olden time,
My grandsire placed it there;—
And there "lang syne"[47] he used to sit,
And puff—the smoke would curl
From the old clay pipe I filled for him
When I was a little girl.

He has long been gone, that dear old man,
Death closed his weary eyes,
But still I cherish that senseless thing,
As 'twere a sacred prize;
E'en every notch on its old grey side,
I value as a gem,
For I've been told of the gay boy whose
Busy fingers made them.

'Twas my sire, my honored, loving sire,
Mischievous then and wild,
With his little knife those notches cut,
When but a little child.
And then when he had older grown,
'Twas here with joyous pride,
He brought a young and loving girl,
Whom he had his bride.

45. With his important 1850 book, *The Architecture of Country Houses,* American landscape and domestic architect Andrew Jackson Downing (1815–52) did much to promote what we now recognize as ideals of American suburban living. For Downing, a homeowner with a porch like this has "a real appreciation of the beautiful and truthful in cottage life." See *The Architecture of Country Houses* (New York: D. Appleton, 1852), 84, Google Books, http://books.google.com/books?id=KAtMAAAAYAAJ. For more on the history of this distinctly American architectural feature, see Michael Dolan, *The American Porch: An Informal History of an Informal Place* (Guilford, Connecticut: Lyons Press, 2002).

46. For more on Lute, start with n. 15, p. 44.

47. Long ago.

And on this bench they used to sit,
When daylight's work was done,
While still the bride her knitting plied,
Tho' twilight hid the sun:
As years passed on, at eve sometimes,
The wife came here to knit,
While by her side her loving lord,
Would sometimes come and sit.

But many cares engrossed them now,
When daylight's work was o'er,
For two boys and a baby-girl
Were added to their store.
More years passed on, the baby-girl,
Now grown unto a maid,
Has one by her lov'd ones seen
Within the grave-yard laid.

No Father now to care for her,
No Mother for a guide,
No Brother's love, alas! no home—
O! better she had died—
She'll feel it so when her old home
Has faded from her gaze,
For she must leave, forever leave,
Those scenes of happy days.

"Ignorance is vain, it hates reform, and not being able to conceive the need of it, thwarts it, ridicules it, or rejects it."

For the Offering.

Canzonet.[48]

In a summer's night
When the stars are bright,

48. A light song, perhaps to sing while dancing a jig.

And the winds in soft murmurs die;
From the mountain's height
I take my flight,
Where the fair maids sleep and sigh.

From their blushing cheeks
I sip nectar sweet,
While they dream of Lovers afar,
When I get my fill
Then I wipe my bill,
And fly to the streamlets near.

When Sol doth appear
All nature to cheer,
I fly to my downy nest,
And there I remain
Refreshment to gain,
'Till she sinks in the reddening West.

When the night bird sings
Then I clap my wings,
And trill my merry, merry song,
My bugle I blow
And away I go,
Among the crowded throng.

The first one I meet
I give kisses sweet,
'Till he slaps his face with a stare;
I quit my gripe
As he drops his pipe,
And I laugh to hear him *swear.*

Musquito.

To Readers and Correspondents.

We are still alive, kind Reader, and still laboring to make the *Offering* acceptable and profitable to you. Sometimes we are weary but never discouraged.

This Number contains articles from several new Contributors.— "Sybil" formerly lived in Ohio; now lives in Kentucky. The Elm by her Cottage we hope will bloom in rich verdure as long as she lives.

The article by "Vesper" is beautiful, but much of it sounds quite familiar. If we are mistaken we would humbly ask pardon.

The piece signed "C." was written by a Lady (who lived in Medina County,) about one week before she died, and without having any reference to herself, seemed prophetic of her doom.

The "Musquito's song" and "Musings," were written by a Lady who does not live in Summit County, but she will not allow you to know more. Both pieces are good—hope she will favor us again and give her name.

"Cora" is a new Contributor—hope to hear again. "Lida's" journey is interesting. Her question concerning Ohio, &c., she will find answered in an Address by Dr. Drake. Hope it may prove interesting to many.

The article by "R." is beautiful, and will be read with much pleasure by all. Please let us hear again from you, Sir.

"Lily Lute" gives us a piece of poetry that will draw tears from your eyes, or you are stronger than we. Please, dear Lily, do not forget us.

We scarcely know what to think of "Lizzie."[49] Suppose we ought to believe that she is not in the land of the living, for were she, she would certainly do as she agrees.

Where are "Philalethes," "Beta," and "Alpha?"[50] The readers of the Offering are asking after you with much anxiety. Be kind enough to speak to them again, will you, and let the fifth Number be enriched by many beautiful gems of thought and feeling.

To all who have so kindly assisted us we return many thanks. Many are making untiring efforts to make the Offering *all* it should be, and, our mutual labors *will* be blessed. Time will prove all things, and steady perseverance can accomplish much.

C. Cumings.

---

49. See pp. 52, 88, and 104. "Lizzie" does not provide another column of "Random Thoughts."

50. See pp. 45, 86, and 101. No additional works were signed by these pseudonyms.

THE AKRON OFFERING.
September, 1849.

From the Democratic Review.[1]

Which is the Fortunate Man?[2]

By Miss Annie Middleton.[3]

"So Robert Hunt has taken himself off?" said Lewis Maynard, joining a group of students assembled on the College grounds at S——. "I don't wonder; what a deuced pretty rage he got into in the class this morning."

1. The literary organ of New York City's "Young America" movement, the *United States Magazine, and Democratic Review* was edited by John L. O'Sullivan (1813–95) and published the works of many antebellum writers who are well known today. As William Charvat summarizes the movement, "they were for labor unions, universal education, literary nationalism, cheap books, and literature for the people; they were against the banking interests, monopoly, and aristocratic British cultural influence" (74). There is much scholarship concerning "Young America" and *The Democratic Review*; for a start, see Robert D. Sampson, *John L. O'Sullivan and His Times* (Kent: Kent State University Press, 2003); Edward L. Widmer, *Young America: The Flowering of Democracy in New York City* (New York: Oxford University Press, 1999); and John Stafford, *The Literary Criticism of "Young America"* (Berkeley: University of California Press, 1952). Charvat's summary comes from his review of Stafford in *Modern Language Notes* 69, no. 1 (January 1954): 74, JSTOR, http://www.jstor.org/stable/3039729.

2. The source for this selection is *The United States Magazine, and Democratic Review* 19, no. 97 (July 1846): 46–55. The story was printed originally—in *The Democratic Review* and in *The Akron Offering* and—with only a few paragraph breaks. See illustration on p. 21. In this text I have inserted paragraph breaks, especially to separate lines of dialogue. It is otherwise too difficult for a modern reader to make sense of the story. See preface, p. xv.

3. Not much is known about "Miss Annie Middleton." Census records suggest this was a common name. Annie Dewolf Middleton of the prominent Charleston family was married and thus not a "Miss" in the 1840s, and her daughter Annie was not born until 1847. This Annie Middleton published a number of short stories in the 1840s, mainly in *The Democratic Review* and *The Columbian Lady's and Gentleman's Magazine*, an elegant New York City production. Another tale for the *Democratic Review,* "Scenes from the Life of Diderot," also features unparagraphed dialogue. See *United*

"Why, I did not notice it—what did he do?" exclaimed a youth who had lately entered.

"Do!" echoed the first speaker—"that's the beauty of it, he never does anything. If he would hurl a book at the tutor's head, or knock somebody down in his wrath, it would be finishing the thing in a fine manly way. Instead of that he turns red, then pale, trembles, clenches his hand, and is completely topsy-turvy for the rest of the day."

"What was he angry at this morning?" returned the boy, who had before addressed him.

"Why he's been trying for the valedictory ever since he entered college, and that great bully, George Addington, (is he anywhere near?) has been determined that he shall not succeed; and as he is too lazy and too stupid to oppose him by studying, is purposed to do it by teasing; so ridicules, mocks, and sneers at Robert, till he is just fit for the lunatic asylum. I'd fight him if I was beat to a jelly for it, or else be cool and indifferent, and take no notice of his batteries, for he'd stop soon enough if he saw it did not tease. But Robert Hunt is too cowardly for the first, and too much a

---

States Magazine, and Democratic Review 20, no. 105 (March 1847): 227–31, Google Books, http://books.google.com/books?id=A4VUAAAAYAAJ. Evidently many editors and readers of the 1840s were not troubled by paragraphs that include dialogue from more than one character. A close reader of American literary periodicals of the 1830s and 1840s will find many such examples; the practice was more common than we might expect today, perhaps because antebellum writers and readers of fiction had more experience reading fiction in handwritten manuscript. Paragraph breaks were often abandoned in manuscript to save space on what might be expensive paper. Middleton's published fiction has paragraphed dialogue in some places and unparagraphed dialogue in others. For example, two Middleton stories for *The Columbian*, "Much Ado About Nothing" and "Gossiping; or, The New Cashier," have paragraphed dialogue. See *The Columbian Lady's and Gentleman's Magazine* 5, no. 2 (February 1846): 91–93, Google Books, http://books.google.com/books?id=IExMAAAAMAAJ and *The Columbian Lady's and Gentleman's Magazine* 5, no. 5 (May 1846): 205–10, Google Books, http://books.google.com/books?id=IExMAAAAMAAJ. Not all of her *Columbian* stories were paragraphed regularly, however: "Wooing, Wedding, and Repenting," like her *Democratic Review* stories, has plenty of dialogue and very few paragraph breaks. See *The Columbian Lady's and Gentleman's Magazine* 6, no. 3 (September 1846): 97–100, Google Books, http://books.google.com/books?id=IExMAAAAMAAJ. Like all authors, Middleton would have delivered her stories in handwritten manuscript. Perhaps her manuscripts lacked paragraph breaks and her editors (or their compositors) puzzled out where to insert them or not as they pleased. Or perhaps Middleton only experimented with the one paragraph, one speaker rule that gradually emerged over the nineteenth century. Finally, it does not appear that Middleton's stories suffered with readers for wanting such paragraph breaks. In 1847, Caroline Kirkland included Middleton in a list of authors that she especially encouraged to write for her new magazine. Kirkland's wish list also included Lydia Maria Child, Lydia Sigourney, Catharine Maria Sedgwick, William Cullen Bryant, Henry Wadsworth Longfellow, T. S. Arthur, and Edgar Allan Poe. See prospectus printed inside the front and back covers, *Union Magazine of Literature and Art* 1, no. 2 (August 1847), American Periodicals (126417111). All the databases searched for this edition indicate that Middleton did not publish again (under this name, at least) after 1847.

baby for the last. I wonder, for my part, why his mother did not keep him in pin-afores. But where has he gone?"

"Down to the bridge with Gerald Morton," answered one of his companions.

"Yes," continues Lewis Maynard, who had worked himself up into something of a rage: "I suppose Gerald is giving him a sugar plum, as usual, and that he'll walk him back again quite cooled down. I cannot imagine how Gerald can take such an interest in the puppy, unless Bob has a rich father, uncle, or something else, and he expects in one way or another to get paid for it."

"Robert's father has not as many dollars as Gerald's has thousands," interrupted one of those quiet, yet commanding voices, which make themselves heard—"and Robert Hunt is no coward, as you, and you, and you," and he pointed to one and another of the group, and then paused, with an emphatic *you,* at Lewis Maynard, "can testify, who saw him at the risk of his own life, last winter pull little Dan Allen out of the river. Robert is no coward, but he considers it vulgar and ungentlemanly to fight, and is unhappily too sensitive to adopt the other alternative, and endure with stoicism the rough-and-tumble of this 'work-a-day world.' But I do not wonder that *you,* Lewis Maynard," and he pointed again to the youth who had been chief orator, "cannot understand *this,* any more than you can imagine how Gerald Morton can have no other motive than self-interest for his kindness to him."

The boys, with one involuntary movement, turned and looked at the individual addressed; one near him whispered, "Will you stand that, Lewis?"—and after a pause of five minutes, "Coward—coward," was uttered by different voices in the group.

Lewis Maynard's face had changed from red to pale, and pale to red, several times during the brief interval, but at the opprobrious term his eye flashed, and glancing around at his companions, he exclaimed, in a firm tone—"I am no coward, and I'll fight the one who dares call me so; but I did wrong, I acknowledge, in accusing Gerald Morton of anything mean, and selfish, and interested. I did very wrong," he repeated, "and I desire all, who heard me make the accusation, hear me retract it. Gerald is as noble a fellow as ever lived, and I only wonder how he can endure that little snivelling Robert Hunt. Richard Graham," he continued, walking up to the youth who had corrected him, "reproof was deserved; but I beg that you'll take back what you said, as to my not understanding anything noble and generous, however deficient I may be in these qualities myself. I certainly have the capacity and heart to admire them."

"I do take it back," answered the individual addressed, warmly grasping the proffered hand, "I fully and entirely take it back; for much as I may have doubted your nobility and generosity before, you have eloquently proved yourself possessed of both, this morning."

"And now, boys," cried Lewis Maynard, after a moment's silence, throwing himself into a pugilistic attitude—"Who's for a fight?" Nobody accepted the challenge; and the bell ringing soon after, each individual hurriedly obeyed the summons, having gained, perhaps, some new ideas as to what true courage, nobility, and generosity were, in the brief interval.

Love was the motive of Gerald Morton's kindness to Robert Hunt—disinterested, ardent affection, which fills young hearts, aye, old hearts too, (to the exclusion of every mean and unworthy feeling,) oftener than some people in this world will allow—Love, in spite of his weaknesses, or rather the more for them, for the deepest pity added strength to his affection. He had, as the boys said, led Robert away, but for some time he did not speak, leaving the soft, sweet air and thousand sights of rural summer beauty beneath their eyes, to exert their tranquilizing influence, before he addressed his companion. At length they reached the bridge which spanned the river, where Robert, unable any longer to endure the violence of his suppressed emotions, flung off the affectionate clasp on his shoulders, and resting his head on the railing of the bridge, burst into an uncontrollable fit of tears.

"Yes, despise me as you will," he exclaimed, "you cannot despise me more than I do myself; and as I have given way to the most unmanly anger, I may as well yield to these unmanly tears."

"Despise you, Robert?" repeated his companion, in a sorrowful tone, "how little you know what is in my heart."

The boy, perhaps, was struck by the sincerity and emotion in the speaker's voice, for he raised his head, and gazed long and inquiringly in the other's face.

"Gerald," he exclaimed, at length, "Gerald Morton, I believe you, with my whole heart and soul I believe you; love and pity you feel for me, but not contempt. You are all that is fair, and frank, and noble,—but I—what am I?" and the boy with a gesture of despair, buried his face again in his hands.

"Your greatest fault is this undervaluing of yourself, dear Robert," said his companion, kindly. "You exaggerate your faults or rather infirmities, to a most frightful extent, and then start in horror from the phantom you yourself have raised."

"No! there is no exaggerating them," returned Robert, sadly. "Have I not again and again vowed to myself, and vowed to you, that I would not let that fool, idiot, that puppy of a fellow," he muttered between his compressed teeth—"George Addington, by his contemptible tricks rouse me to anger, and yet do I not daily yield to the temptation? But oh, Gerald—if you knew the bitter pride that poverty makes, and if you knew the hell upon earth I endure with this suspicious, sensitive temper of mine, you would indeed give me your deepest pity and sympathy."

"You have them now—you have them now," said his companion, in a choked and agitated voice.

"A child's glance will at times almost madden me," Robert continued, scarcely regarding the interruption; "every feeling that I have in the world seems to be a curse to me. I never look at my sisters' grace and beauty, but I gnash my teeth at the thought, that they will be sacrificed to some uncouth booby who has money, or waste their lives in the dreary, desolating struggle with poverty, which killed my poor mother. My father's gloom and misanthropy check the tenderness which should fill to the fount a child's nature; but I think how different he might have been, had fortune been kinder; and I have the picture of an old age like his before me, sternness and harshness, a distress to himself, and a terror to everybody else. I shall be just like him, only worse."

"Stop, Robert, stop!" exclaimed Gerald Morton—"do not talk any more such wild and desperate, nay, they are wicked words. We have each our destiny in our own hands, to make or mar, as we will. No man, unless he desires, need be the victim of circumstances.—We must control fortune, not be governed by it—shape our own way, not follow in gloom and despair that which the veriest trifles have made for us; and, my dear, dear Robert, your father's errors, inasmuch as you feel the germs of them in your own bosom, should be viewed with the greatest leniency and tenderness; at the same time that you resolve with all your strength and might, and power, not to yield the eightieth part of an inch to these baleful, morbid tendencies."

"Yes," said Robert, looking with a despairing admiration at his companion, "you can talk like an angel—and what is more—you can act like one. Ah, Gerald, why must you have everything? wealth, love, genius, and a temper that would make life with a crust of bread happy."

"Not quite," answered Gerald Morton, laughingly; "but as you have set me the example in flattery, I'll turn the tables on you. Let lady Fortune go for once, we'll see what Nature has given you, a handsome face, a graceful and goodly outside—you can't deny *that* Bob; a very wise head for such a young pair of shoulders. President Mason asserts it, the whole college acknowledges it; and a heart full of strong affections, and warm admiration for everything that is lovely and of good repute. The only shadow on the picture you've thrown yourself; for never tell me that a man endowed so liberally, cannot fight the foul fiends, melancholy and despair, even unto the death. I tell you, Robert Hunt, you make your own troubles."

"And poverty?" asked his companion, reassured and strengthened by his words.

"Poverty!" echoed Gerald Morton, almost scornfully, "what man with a head and hand in this country need fear poverty; a competency is within the reach of all who have ordinary talent and prudence, and what do you want more?"

Little did Gerald reck[4] the need he'd soon have of the fortitude and resolution he was so commending. On the afternoon of that same day, as he was alone in his room, he received a message from the President, requesting his immediate presence.

"My dear young friend, I have bad news for you," exclaimed the kind hearted old man, when Gerald appeared (breathless and glowing with haste) before him.

"My father has failed, then?" asked Gerald Morton. "Well, sir, I've thought such a thing very possible; a merchant's is the most precarious life under the sun; but that is not such very bad news, for in my philosophy, sir, poverty is no evil."

"Your father has failed," answered the President, hesitatingly—"but, my dear Gerald, it is not that alone, can you bear something worse?"

A dim dreadful apprehension slowly seized Gerald Morton; he trembled violently, his face grew deadly pale. "Oh! sir, do not say, do not say he's dead"—he wildly exclaimed; "do not cut off all hope. Tell me that he has but the feeblest breath of life in him, that I'll once again hear him call 'Gerald,' and I'll bless you;" and he awaited in breathless agony the one little word from his companion; but it was not spoken. "No! no!" shrieked Gerald Morton, throwing his arms frantically over his head—"he's dead! he's dead!" and fell senseless on the floor.

4. To care for, to regard.

When Gerald revived, a number of his companions were around him, and Robert Hunt was kneeling on the floor by his side, bathing his face with some strong perfume.[5] He gazed at first from one to the other in amazement, but catching a glance at the President's face, the whole melancholy truth flashed across him. He covered his face with his hands.—"How did it happen, sir?" said he at length, in a choked, subdued tone.

The President made a sign, and the collegians left the room, all save Robert Hunt, who, with the keenest love and sympathy on his face, still retained his kneeling position by the side of his friend.

"Can you bear to hear it yet, Gerald?" asked the President.

"Yes, sir," answered the youth. But oh! in how different a tone from the clear, hopeful one of the morning—such a subdued, quiet despair in the voice.

"I think you had better wait till to-morrow, my son," persisted the kind old man.

"Oh! no, sir, tell me now," said Gerald, with a beseeching look.

"Your first supposition was correct," began the President,—"the firm of Morton, Atkinson, & Co. are bankrupt, owing to the embezzlements and villainy of one of the junior partners, who fled as soon as it was discovered. Mr. Atkinson went immediately down to your father's house to consult with him and take the necessary steps about the matter. They sat up till late that night, talking; indeed it was two o'clock before Mr. Atkinson left him, and the servants found him in the morning in the same position, in an arm-chair, before a table covered with papers; but he was dead, quite dead. A disease of the heart—so the physicians say—which he has had for years, and this sudden shock killed him. The last words he said, as he pressed Mr. Atkinson's hand in parting, were, "I can bear this very well; but my poor boy—"

"I think I'd better go to my room," said Gerald faintly. He had overrated his own strength; each word was a dagger to his heart.

"And now leave me for a short time, Robert," he exclaimed, as his faithful friend assisted him to a seat; "a little time alone, and then I'll see you." And Robert went out and left him with his grief.

"Oh! I have had such wicked thoughts," said Gerald Morton, holding out his hand to his friend some two hours after, "such wild, wicked thoughts. To think that that man's villainy killed my father; to think he was murdered, absolutely murdered—Robert, it drives me mad. He might have been in prosperity and comparative health now, but for that scoundrel. Ah!

5. Some perfumes were used and regarded as stimulants; perfumes were sold in drug stores. This could be an aromatic of peppermint, camphor, ginger or any other invigorating essence.

Robert, you need not tell me this is wrong—I know it—it is all as it should be; this man was but the instrument that doeth all things well." And in spite of his firm, manly heart, Gerald Morton burst into an agony of tears. "We loved each other so dearly," he continued; "I was but a baby, three years old, when my mother died, and he was father, mother, all to me. Ah! what more than feminine gentleness and patience he lavished upon me. He never gave me but a look, Robert—it was sufficient to subdue all my childish petulance, and I kept not my highest thought from him. Father! father!" and with that wild cry Gerald rose up strong and firm; his face was pale, but his voice was once more clear and calm.

"I need not ask you, President Mason," he said, going to that gentleman's apartment some hours after, "whether you'll trust me for the payment of my last year's expenses here; I know you will, sir; and now, with many, many thanks for all your kindness, good-bye."

The President pressed his hand, but was too much overcome to reply; and when he raised his head, Gerald was gone.

With the money in his possession, he paid all his little debts; the only one remaining of any consequence, was for keeping a horse which had died a fortnight before. He described his position briefly to Mr. Jenkins, and said, on going out, that he would send the money as soon as possible.

"Aye, aye," muttered the man, "fair words cost but little—what business had a beggar's brute to be keeping a horse?"

Gerald's blood boiled; his first impulse was to fell the man to the earth. "He's poor, however," was his next thought; "he's goaded to harshness by poverty." And then a vision of this poverty, dark and cheerless, rose before him—abusive words, cold looks, neglect and suffering, with not a ray of love or tenderness to gleam across his path; and it recalled his one master-grief—his father! What were all, if he had but his father! Gerald paused; a comforting, blessed thought rose within his heart. Could his father have endured poverty, with age and sickness, and increasing infirmities in its train? Could he relinquish the luxuries which habit had rendered necessary; emerge from the intellectual, melancholy seclusion in which for years he had buried himself, and without youth or hope, and their thousand bright words of encouragement, wrestle once more with the world? He could not—he was therefore removed in mercy; and on that wretched night, from his misery and destitution, Gerald thanked God that he had taken away his father. His heart was light that he alone was to suffer. He wept, but it was with happiness, and a strong, bold, resolute spirit of yore, possessed him. He could do all, he could endure all. His father had born the pang but for an evening; it was lightened to him therefore, for a life-time.

It was several days after the funeral, a gay, sunny day,

"When flowers and trees, and birds and bees,
Most beautiful things,"[6]

were doing their utmost to make earth glad. Human hearts nature, alas! has in her keeping. Gerald's head rested on the garden gate. He had taken his farewell of his home. The next day there was to be an auction, and the place itself, and every vestige and remnant of the old familiar things, were to pass into the hands of strangers. All that sweet childish reminiscences had endeared; all that made *home,* were to vanish. A houseless, forlorn wanderer on the face of the earth—Poor Gerald!—nay, rich Gerald—rich in fortitude and resolution—rich in pure heart—rich in a high intellect—rich in everything that is noble, good, and exalted!—many a millionaire might have envied the penniless Gerald Morton.

To be Continued.

From the Shooting Star.[7]

The Vale My Childhood Loved.

By Mark Mingleton.

I came to the place where I was born, and said, "The companions of my youth, are they all gone?"
And echo answered, "all gone!"

I

Forests, streams, and mountain peaks!
Once more my tear-dimmed vision seeks

6. Paraphrase of lines from "The Frost" by New England poet Hannah Flagg Gould (1789–1865). The poem was reprinted repeatedly in the 1840s. For example see *The Female Poets of America*, ed. Rufus Wilmot Griswold (Philadelphia: Carey and Hart, 1849), 48, Google Books, http://books.google.com/books?id=DnQFAAAAQAAJ.

7. *The Shooting Star* was a literary magazine published by Horace Minor in Cincinnati. OCLC's WorldCat catalog records no extant copies. See William Henry Venable, *Beginnings of Literary Culture in the*

The scene that once ye bore,
Where, O where, hath beauty fled!
Your charm of other days is dead,
And why? my childhood's o'er.

II

Changeless, yet all-changing time
Thou foe of every scene and clime,
Why mask my native vale?[8]
Why smite the trees that gave me shade,
Why hide the paths where I have strayed,
Why smother mem'ry's tale?

III

Yet my vision is not blind,
A thousand things are left behind,
Dear ruins of that day:
Streamlets from the mountain's brow
Did bubble then the same as now,
One mellow, living lay.[9]

IV

Riv̂'let of my childhood's vale,
Though changed, thy waters may not fail,
They glide as erst away;
Gently in the mead they sleep
Where silent willows bend to weep,
And ducklings stop to play.

V

Purling through the wood they glide
And ripple by the cornfield's side,

Ohio Valley (Cincinnati: Robert C. Clarke, 1891), 127, Google Books, http://books.google.com/books?id=57eEAAAAIAAJ. American Periodicals, Google Books, and WorldCat reveal no further publications for "Mark Mingleton," which may very well be a pseudonym. Cumings thanks this author for numerous submissions and describes him as from Cincinnati in the editorial closing this number. See p. 208.

8. "Vale" is a poetic word for valley.

9. "Lay": song.

And wash the bridged highway.
Dashing by the rocky steep,
And flashing there, they foam and leap
With thunder mist and spray.

VI

Since I left thee, gentle stream,
My course hath been like thine, 'twould seem,
A varied, crooked way,
Rushing wild and gliding still,
By gloomy shade, and frowning hill,
In darkness and in day.

VII

But I come again to look
Upon thy bosom, little brook,
And hear thy lulling song:
I'll trace again as I have done
The course thy merry windings run
And wander with thee long.

VIII

I'll strive again to be a child
Artless, griefless, straying wild,
Drinking nought buy joy and thee,
Joining in thy tuneful glee
Plucking lillies from thy side,
Dancing in thy pearly tide,
Stooping to thy kissing wave,
Fruit stained face and hands to lave:
I will seek the crowded wood,
Where a thousand trees have stood,
Mocking time with blooming bough
From my birthday until now;—
There beside some well-known tree
I'll pause and sit, old brook by thee:
Weave again bright hopes of bliss,

Dream of fairer worlds than this,
Join in converse sweet—with whom?
Childhood's friends?—they're in the tomb,
Or scattered where I may not see:—
Perish! vain, fond reverie!
Vanish streamlet in thy glen!
Youth will not come back again,
Youth's love'd friends will not reply
To my bursting, heart-born sigh!
Brook! I would thou wert forgot,
And the thoughts thy view hath brought:—
Fly, associated scenes!
To the grave my yearning leans:—
Childhood's hopes and childhood's friends
Alike are fled and pleasure ends,
Ends in grief too deep to tell—
Native valley, fare thee well.

IX

Forests, streams, and mountain peaks,
A weak farewell my crushed heart speaks,
  I gaze on you no more:
Where, O where, hath beauty fled,
Your charm of other days is dead,
  And why?—my childhood's o'er.

For the Offering.

Decision of Character.

Much has often been said about the importance of decision of character, and something more may, perhaps, be said advantageously.

"What is decision?" says some one of our readers; "is it in your estimation, that sulky stubbornness that will never change an opinion although convinced that it is a wrong one?" Such a sentiment is somewhat decided certainly, but it is not what is meant when we are taught that it is good for us to be decided; and yet a person possessing only a *proper* degree of firmness is not apt to change an opinion, for the reason, that he does not form one, without sufficient proof, and *change* is no part of such a person's nature.

We will look at some characters destitute of this principle, and when we have traced their feelings and actions we will contrast them with what we believe to be reasonable and correct characters and their views and doings in the world, and any one may judge between them.

To dwell a moment in the region of love and romance, who has not known young Ladies, and Gentlemen too, who have always existed in a dull, foggy atmosphere, of sickly sentimentality, always fancying they were in love with some one, yet ever ready to change—pleased most with the last pretty face they saw? It is enough to say of such persons that as they are in this, so are they in every thing else—poor weak ciphers in creation. We will let them pass. Place them beside that man or woman of firm principles, whose love or friendship is not easily gained, and when once given *is not* and *can not* be recalled, even though it may be placed on an unworthy object. There let them stand and perhaps foolishness may have a little light reflected on *it*.

Look at politicians a little while, if you can keep track of them. To-day some of them may be denouncing men and measures that tomorrow they may be hugging to their bosoms in love and confidence—oh! honest decision; thou dost not dwell much in the political world—self, that dreadful tyrant, sits enthroned even there.—Look at that sneaking apology for manhood that will go to the polls and vote with the *multitude,* let them go as they will, and then compare him with the man (*there are some such)* who would study to know the truth and what would do the greatest good, and then he would use all his influence to promote the same, even though in so doing, he should stand alone or should lose his life!

This is what I call decision, right feeling, proper principle, or true moral courage. And who possesses this? How many of the young men of Akron or any other place possess enough of this to enable *them* to stand alone on *any* subject, to be what is right, should they be in defiance of all obstacles and regardless of all relative consequences?

In fifty years, how many of your names will be remembered for great or glorious deeds, for high mental and moral attainments, for *any thing* done for the benefit of our race or for *your own* good even? Perhaps not many—and why? they lean upon each other until the last prop is gone and tottering to the very verge of their existence, each will fall into an unhonored grave. *Some* may battle nobly with adversity and write their names high on their country's tablets, or deep in the hearts of their fellow-beings, or broadly on the destinies of the world and proudly in all the Archives of the future. Such have decision of character and will exercise (if the term pleases you) an imperious will.

Look at the heroes of olden times—they perchance were not superior to many others in understanding, or did not more desire the accomplishment of many things; but they dared to say I *will* do it, and a new inspiration was breathed upon them; and all who came in contact with them felt its influence and yielded to the controlling power that moved them. Many were mild and good, and honorable; but such could not lead the van when the car of reform began to move—they would have been trampled by the multitude; but in every emergency, a courageous soul was ready, one who in almost all instances had helped to bring about the events that gave him the power he coveted. And thus it will ever be. The decided will control the wavering. Decision connected with goodness and great mental capacity gives a human being greater power than many crowned heads possess, and makes him a blessing to the world—connected with intellectual strength and deficient morality, it gives the accomplished, powerful villain, the world's curse, a tyrant on a grand scale, and all the petty tyrants only lack the discernment that fits them for a wide theatre of display—they are content to figure in the private circle, to possess and exercise the power of an ignoramus.

Surely proper decision is of vast importance! Without it man is nothing but a weak, pitiful slave to his own ignorance or indolence, or another's caprice. How many times does such a one stand with folded hands and let an opportunity pass that, seized upon by a powerful, energetic mind and will, might by its mighty consequences, have electrified the world! And alas! how often this will be repeated—man's judgment will sleep—his doom will be sealed and he will wear the chains he himself has forged.

And is there any thing beautiful in a character that can not see, or seeing will not act? one in short, who has no proper decision?

Such persons many times, possess many good qualities; they may have wit, and genius, and love of goodness, and, considered rightly, these *are* valuable, but when we know that their possessor has not steadiness of purpose enough to accomplish *any* thing, it is not admiration we feel for such a person, but that sentiment so galling to the proud heart—pity—confidence we *can not* have.

In whom have we confidence? in those whom *nothing* can turn aside from the path of duty—The allurement of a tempting world or the sneers or ridicule of the multitude—all alike unsuccessful. Be such, oh! ye men and women and a world would rally under the banner you should raise and honor the character that had confidence in itself.

Alma.[10]

Selected for the Offering.

We Might Have Been.

By L. E. Landon.[11]

We might have been! These are but common words,
And yet they make the sum of life's bewailing;
They are the echo of those finer chords,
Whose music life deplores when unavailing;
We *might* have been!

"We might have been so happy!" says the child,
Pent in the weary school-room during the summer,
When the green rushes, 'mid the marshes wild,
And radiant fruits attend the radiant comer,
We *might* have been!

It is a thought that darkens o'er our youth,
When first experience, sad experience, teaches
What fallacies we have believed for truth,
And what few truths endeavor ever teaches,
We *might* have been!

Alas! how different from what we are!
Had we but known the better path before us—
But feelings, hopes, and fancies, left afar,
What, in the wide, bleak world, can e'er restore us?
We *might* have been!

10. The unknown "Alma" also contributed items that begin on pp. 47, 76, 78, 92, and 440.

11. By English poet Letitia Elizabeth Landon (1802–38), who became famous as "L. E. L." This poem is part of a series, "Three Extracts from the Diary of a Week." Literary magazines selected it many times in the late 1830s and 1840s. See Laman Blanchard, *Life and Literary Remains of L. E. L.* (London: Henry Colburn, 1841), 2:248–50, Google Books, http://books.google.com/books?id=Cl7RAAAAMAAJ.

It is the motto of all human things,
    The end of all that waits upon mortal seeking,
The weary weight upon hope's flagging wings,
    It is the cry of the lone heart while breaking;
        We *might* have been!

And when, warm with the heaven which gave it birth,
    Dawns on our world-worn way love's hour Elysian,
The last fair angel lingering on our earth
    The shadow of that thought obscures the vision;
        We *might* have been!

A cold fatality attends on love;
    Too soon, or else too late, the heart-beat quickens;
The star which is our fate springs up above,
    And we but say, while round the vapor thickens,
        We *might* have been!

Life knoweth no other misery. The rest
    Are single sorrows; but in this are blended
All sweet emotions that disturb the breast;
    The light that was the loveliest ended;
        We *might* have been!

Henceforth, how much of the full heart must be
    A sealed book, at whose contents we tremble;
A still voice murmurs 'mid our misery,
    The worst to bear, because we must dissemble;
        We *might* have been!

Life is made up of miserable hours;
    And all of which we craved a brief possessing,
For which we wasted wishes, hopes, and powers,
    Comes with some fatal drawback on the blessing;
        We *might* have been!

The future never renders to the past
    The young beliefs entrusted to its keeping;

Inscribe one sentence—life's first truth and last—
On the pale marble where our dust is sleeping;
We *might* have been!

For the Offering.

The Little Coal-Heaver.

By Jenny.[12]

"Now what's a poor fellow to do in a case of this kind I'd like to know? Here's the *thirty-second* day of December in the year of our Lord one thousand *eighteen hundred* and forty-five—cold as *blazes*—snow *ancle-deep* and comin down like all wrath!—and here's me what's got a load of coal to sell—putty spectable load for the size on't and all I ax is fifty-six cents."

"Do'nt want any *to day* hey? now that's a likely story—but I say they *do* want it—*so* they do. Well, well, I'll just stand here a little while longer, somebody may come along after a while, and give me the dimes for it."

"I 'spose the reason they don't want it, is because I look so smutty[13] and ragged like—and the old hoss, *poor old soul.* The boys need'nt laugh—their hip bones would stick up too, if they have to live on post hay and sleep out in the open air—and the rope tackling—*they* don't look quite so slick as that ere chap's new harness just across the street. There now! if he ain't putten out another load at that house! That makes three he has sold since I came to town—and they *did'nt want* any more."

"Oh! if I was a rich man, or only well to do in the world I know how I'd do, I'd always buy of the poorest looking critter that come along, 'specially if his wife had the 'flammatory rheumatiz[14] and had'nt no blankets to keep her warm—nor no clothes nor nothing to eat, hardly—That would be like the man we read of in the Bible—"Do unto other folks as other folks would'nt—I cant say the rest, but it means charity. Them's my sentiments."

12. "Jenny" is known only as "a lady from Zanesville." See p. 208. Additional contributions signed "Jenny" are on pp. 237, 265, 312, and 313. The 1850 census records a few "ladies" who may have used this nickname in Zanesville in November of 1850: sixty-six-year-old Jennette Allison from Scotland, who lived with her seventy-five-year-old retired husband, Andrew, and sixty-five-year-old Jennette Summers from Virginia, who lived with her retired husband, Jacob. (Eighteen-year-old Jenette Haas, who was born in Germany, appears to be boarding as a servant in the valuable home of John Rehl, merchant.) Our nineteenth-century hand deems this "Good." See n. 2, p. 30.

13. Soiled with soot or coal dust.

14. Rheumatoid arthritis.

"I aint as drunk today as I was yesterday—not by a jug full—and I know what's what, as well as the fattest on 'em!"

And here the little man (for he was a mere dwarf) drew from his pocket a flask, the contents of which he turned down his throat.

"Well," said he, resuming his soliloquy, "I know what I can do—can't stand here much longer; but I did'nt want to put this load in at Jake Rigg's; but I reckon I must. I own him for three quarts already, and he'll be glad to get his pay; I'll take the rest *out with him,* and I'll be out of *his* debt. 'Honor bright,'[15] say I, I believe in paying debts when I can't help it—them's my sentiments agin."

During his long *confab*[16] with himself the little coal-heaver was standing with his back to the houses, not dreaming that he was heard or even noticed by any one. But in that he was mistaken. There was one attentive listener, a *woman* whom the very wretchedness of his appearance attracted to the spot. Not a syllable was lost upon her and she now imagines herself pretty well "posted up" in this history of one of the visitors of "Jake Rigg's,"[17] between whom and herself there existed not the most friendly relations.

Mrs. Bates was a widow with a moderate fortune sufficient however for the support of herself and two children, one a son of about seventeen and a daughter some two years younger. She was endowed with an unusual share of sympathy; her whole aim seemed to be devoted to the advancement of every person's happiness except her own; blessed with an iron constitution, she was capable of enduring almost any amount of fatigue and exposure, without endangering her health.

To have expected to find Mrs. Bates at her own house on a stormy day was a thing entirely out of the question. There were a great many destitute families in the village, from various causes and a great deal of sickness, particularly among children, and our widow had ample space for the exercise of her favorite pursuits this winter; her own means were too limited to enable her to meet the demands that were daily pressing upon her. The greater portion of her life had been spent in the same town, and as she knew every person, she was at no loss for resources, but became a

---

15. "A protestation of honor among the vulgar," according to John Bartlett. See *A Dictionary of Americanisms: A Glossary of Words and Phrases, Usually Regarded as Peculiar to the United States* (New York: Bartlett and Welford, 1848), 179, Google Books, http://books.google.com/books?id=NhVAAAAAYAAJ.

16. Short for "confabulation": an easy, friendly conversation.

17. Presumably Jake Rigg's place—a tavern or a grocery, perhaps—sells alcohol by the flask. The 1850 Census for Akron and for Zanesville suggests that "Jake Rigg" is a fictitious person.

most successful beggar of old clothes, bed clothing, any thing and every thing that could be used for the comfort of the suffering.

That Mrs. B. should become deeply interested in the case before her is not to be wondered at, nor should we be at all surprised if a two-fold plan for relieving the sick wife and converting the drunken husband had been going on in her mind long before she ventured to speak to him.

As the draining of the flask seemed to be doing its work she saw there was not a moment to lose, and stepping forward she thus accosted him.

"How do you sell your coal sir?"

"Only fifty-six cents madam."

"Very cheap sir, I'll take it, *just* drive into the alley there and turn in at the gate on the right hand, I'll send a boy to open the gate and show you where to deposit the coal." The boy was instructed to bring him into the kitchen just as soon as possible and he did so.

"Take a seat, Mr.—what shall I call you!" said Mrs. B.

"Ephraim Higgins, madam."

"Not quite so near the stove Mr. Higgins, it will make you sick after being out in the cold so long," & before he had time to thank her, Mrs. B. assisted by Sally, the kitchen maid, brought forward a little table, on which was placed hot coffee, bread and butter and a slice of ham, and set it before him. "Help yourself Mr. Higgins," said Mrs. B., "it will do you good."

"Thank you, thank you madam," said he, "you are very kind; yes, I am quite cold and shiverin-like. My old cotton clothes haint got much heat in 'em, and my feet's been wet all day."

We very seldom find a family who all think alike or see eye to eye on any one subject; but such was really the case in Mrs. B.'s family; even the servants seemed to vie with each other in little acts of kindness to the poor who frequented the house.

While Ephraim was entertained in the kitchen, the "old hoss" was receiving his modicum of attention in the back yard, and after the boy had fed, watered and rubbed him down effectually, Sally, determined not to be outdone, handed out a couple of old blankets and threw them over him to prevent him, as she said, from catching cold.

Continued.

Norman and Cornelia Campbell,
OR
"Truth Stranger Than Fiction."

By C. Cumings.

Chapter V.

Soon after Norman's and Charles' departure, a cousin of Mrs. Campbell's came to make Mr. Campbell's family a long visit. Her name was Laura Brainard. She was thirty-five years of age, and still retained much of that striking beauty that in early life had made her a heartless coquette. She was the cool, calculating being that could immolate everything holy at the shrine of self. Conquest had been her glory, but now she feared a forsaken old age, and when she was introduced to Julius Herbert, believing him to be possessed of great wealth, she resolved to become his wife. From Mr. Benton she learned the state of Mr. C.'s affairs, and also the feelings and intentions existing between Cornelia Campbell and Charles Elton. Benton also told her of Henry Herbert's regard for Cornelia, and by promising to use his influence with Julius Herbert in Miss Brainard's favor, engaged her co-operation in an attempt to separate Cornelia and Charles, and ultimately to cause her to consent to marry young Herbert.

"You can tell her," said Benton to Miss B., "any tale you please of Elton's dishonor or falsehood, but it will have no effect on her; but you can send him a line as from a disinterested friend, hinting at her forgetfulness of him and looking favorably upon Herbert, and it will produce an impression that, if we rightly follow it up, will bring him here. We must so manage it all, that Norman Campbell shall see nothing alarming, or he will be here also, and then nothing could be accomplished; but let Elton come alone, and I will make his own words and acts prove himself unworthy her regard—she will scorn to unite herself to meanness—they will be separated, and I shall gain sweet *revenge!*"

Miss B. was well qualified for the task imposed upon her, and so well did she know how to wound a trusting heart, that only a few weeks elapsed before Charles Elton made his appearance among them. He came alone—he would not breathe in Norman's ear the tales that had come to him, but he said to himself, "I will be just to one who, if there is truth in woman, is pure and noble." He made no inquiries, but framed some pretext to gain leave of absence for a short time, and presented himself at Mr. C.'s door with strange and contending emotions.

Cornelia was surprised to see him, but she met him with a beaming smile of sacred trust and affection. The gloom left his brow, but still there was a restraint upon him not usual, and Cornelia said, "Are you ill, Charles?"

"I am not," he said, "but I have recently received intelligence that has, I doubt not, affected my whole demeanor. It is this," he said, handing her a letter he had received from an unknown hand. Cornelia read it, and the paleness that overspread her countenance was construed by him into something like evidence of guilt. She, however, soon recovered her self-possession, and replied—"It grieves me, Charles, to think that this should have disturbed your peace, or caused you to doubt my truth—you will surely believe my assertion, that this tale is utterly false—no doubt it had its origin from the same source as the tales that have been circulated here, and repeated to me, telling of everything evil in connection with you; but I did not doubt your honor, Charles, or your love for me, nor do I mean this as a reproach."

"Forgive me, Cornelia," said Charles, "I was wrong, but henceforth I can meet the machinations of our enemies with a firm and happy spirit, for doubt of thee can ne'er intrude."[18] She did forgive him, but while he retired happy in his renewed trust and confidence, her heart was ill at ease.

He had doubted her *once*—that bond that bound them was not perfect. She had given him the first affection of a heart that could not change, but she could not help doubting the enduring nature of his regard for herself; still she hoped and trusted and prayed for wisdom and for peace; and the next day she was able to meet him with calm composure.

They conversed long on various subjects. She talked of her brother, of his high hopes and noble determinations—they wandered along by the banks of the beautiful river that formed the eastern boundary to their thriving village. Their hearts were tuned to sympathy with nature in all its works—they loved each expanding flower, each scene of bold or fair, each note in its rich and varied music—all that God had made to bless the creature, man. They looked at the burning stars as they appeared, and talked of the different theories concerning them, together with the faith of ancient astrologers, and the idea that some one in the ascendant at a person's birth was emblematical of their destiny, continually shadowing forth, their fate—then came the idea of the communion of mind with mind, independent of physical presence—hearts

18. A common or clichéd phrase in antebellum American poetry, "ne'er intrude" (as the "thee") here suggests that Charles has literary habits, if not affectations.

that had loved, loving on, and still, though widely separated, vibrating to each other's joy or sorrow; and lastly, they spoke of that holy trust in Heaven that supports and cheers under all circumstances; and Charles alluded to what he considered his duty as soon as he felt himself qualified. "My home must be among the poor Indians," said he. "Can you go with me there, Cornelia? I am selfish to ask it, but tell me freely your views of such a course."

She struggled a few moments with her feelings, and then she answered, "Charles, I would rather go with you on such a mission than to be mistress of a palace, and both live at ease. Yes, to help you in such a glorious cause would be happiness indeed." He looked on her animated countenance, and felt that he was not worthy of her love. Little did either think that this evening would never be forgotten by them; but that memory, through every day of a long life, would present to each the peculiar sensations of happiness that then thrilled their souls, and bring such an image of the other as to make it impossible to cast aside the love that would thus, under the circumstances in which they would be placed, become real torture. They lingered long, but at last they bade each other good night, and each retired to rest—no, not rest, for that dark shadow that had so oppressed Charles months before, now seemed to plant itself between him and happiness, and in tones of bitter mockery bid him hope for nought but misery. Cornelia, too, was sad, and sleep visited not her pillow; but she arose in the morning calm and tranquil.

While she was attending to the duties that devolved upon her, ministering to her uncle's wants, and taking care of her old nurse, &c., Charles wandered forth alone, along the path they had pursued the night before, and farther on and on he went until he reached a kind of natural arbor, and, wearied by his long walk, he entered it, and reclining himself to rest was soon almost unconscious of everything; but approaching footsteps and voices partially roused him, and hearing his own name mentioned, he moved from his recumbent position, and the speaker's next words determined him to remain quiet.

"I say, old man," said the voice of Benton, addressing an aged, decrepit semblance of a man, whom Charles had before seen and recollected to have heard called "the Hermit of the Glen," and who was now approaching from an opposite direction. "I know that this is your handwriting," (holding up a letter,) "it is directed to Charles Elton, and contains information of the true character of a certain lady."

"I had deemed this knowledge confined to myself."

"How dare you, sir, while professing so much friendship for myself, and living on my bounty, thus offend me, and bring disgrace on the daughter of one who, were he living, you would not dare to meet? No excuses—I see how it is, you love this young Elton better than Cornelia Campbell or myself, and could not bear to see him wed a false-hearted girl. But you have failed in your intention—your missive is in my power, and you need give yourself no uneasiness about this engagement. I myself heard her promise Henry Herbert that she would marry *him* in a few months; but I do not think it necessary to proclaim this to Elton, he will know it soon enough—he leaves to-morrow, and before he returns she will be the bride of another, and he will escape the *honorable* alliance; but I shall find a suitable way to reward you for your kind motives toward myself, so now be off, or I will punish you on the spot."

The old man again attempted to apologize, but was sternly rebuked, and immediately turned and was soon lost sight of in the dense forest.

Benton tore the letter in a thousand pieces, and muttering—"let people mind their own business, I say,"—left the spot, and soon after met his confederate, to congratulate each other on their undoubted success.

Charles could scarcely breathe or bear to live; so sudden, so apparently indisputably true, was the horrid tale, that his own reason reeled on her throne;—he moved not for nearly an hour, and at last he started as if from the grasp of some deadly foe.—"Had they but told this to *me,*" he said, "instead of *each other,* I should have believed it utterly false;—but it is true! Oh! God, it is true!—I have loved her as I can never love again!—but no—perish the degrading thought!—I will be a fool no longer, but account myself happy in being saved from wretchedness. I will not even see her again." This he more than once repeated, and again he sunk exhausted by the anguish of his feelings.

At length reflection came, and he was able to be calm.—"I will not steal away like a thief," he said, "I will see her, and she may account for our separation as she pleases." He then arose and went to take leave of his friends in the village, as all knew he was to leave in the morning. Some noticed his unusual paleness, but for the time he was his own master, and went steadily through his allotted task. Toward evening he went to Mr. Campbell's house & found Cornelia alone in the parlor. She immediately noticed his strange appearance; he scarcely spoke for some minutes; at length he said, "when I parted with you last evening, I little thought my mind toward you could ever change; but it has, and I *can not, will not,* tell you why; but I am here to tell you that it is for the best that we should separate forever." He stopped, almost unknown to himself he was cherishing the hope that she would make enquiries that would lead to an explanation, and she be able to prove all he had heard, false.

She answered not at first, but a start as if an arrow had pierced her heart, told him he was heard and understood. She clearly comprehended that this was the work of an enemy, and that by explanations and assurances, she could convince him of her innocence. "But," she said to herself, "I have done it once—I will not do it now." She saw her dearest hopes passing away, and felt that the world to her would henceforth be a desert. She could scarcely command her voice, and a tear gathered in her eye, but the pride aroused in her soul, consumed it, and with apparent calmness she said—"I agree with you, Charles, it *is* best for us to part forever." Charles was bewildered, but Cornelia, with perfect composure said, "you are so soon to leave town, Mr. Elton, that I cannot allow myself to detain you—farewell." He could only murmur: "Farewell" in reply, and found himself alone. He immediately left the house, and after spending a sleepless night, left the village.

Instead of going back to school, he went to his Father's house in an adjoining county, and for several weeks was scarcely conscious of any thing. Prostrated on a bed of sickness we must leave him for the present.

Cornelia's calm demeanor did not deceive Benton—he knew that she was wretched—he knew that he had made her thus, and he could scarcely suppress his fiendish exultation. "But this is not enough," said he to himself, "she must consent to marry Herbert." Miss B. was constantly telling her any thing she deemed calculated to bring this about, and at last she was informed that her uncle had given Herbert a deed of the last dollar's worth of property that had ever belonged to himself, and that her own and Norman's was his, several months before. This was in part true. When intoxicated he knew not the value of property, and remembered not what he said or did. Benton took advantage of this—taught Herbert how to proceed, so as, ostensibly, to gain the property for himself; while, in reality, he purchased it for Benton.—To this information was added, what was by her called the generous offer of Herbert to give it all back if Cornelia would become his wife. This offer he had made to his uncle, and it was now presented to her.

She had just seen her old nurse slumbering in perfect helplessness, and had looked upon her uncle in a heavy, death-like sleep of intoxication, when Miss B. gave her a note with the foregoing information. She was utterly wretched before, but this was too much to bear. She tried to look at it calmly—to reason for the good of others. "My dear old nurse will have no shelter in her dying hour.—My uncle will accuse me of cruelty and ingratitude to himself; and I must see my brother, my dear brother, toil for a bare support,—and I—I would die to save him from—oh God, help me! and if it may be right in thy sight, take me home!"

In the morning her uncle was told that this was a proper time to present this subject to Cornelia.

Degraded as he was, he could scarcely bear to look at one whom he had so wronged. He saw that she was very pale and strangely changed within a few months;—but he could pass all this by, and ask of her the sacrifice of every cherished hope. "I will marry him," said she, very faintly, and she could not even attempt to speak another word.

In a few days Miss B. and Julius Herbert were married, and immediately left for a distant western city. Time passed on. Cornelia had written to her brother the result of her engagement with Elton; but she could not tell him of the state of their affairs or the measures resorted to, to save them all from absolute penury. She knew he would not permit her to sacrifice herself for him, nor for any consideration whatever. She suffered Herbert to call once and make arrangements for the time the wedding was to take place, &c. Her uncle showed her the deeds ready to be signed by H. conveying the property back to the original owners, and she tried to be resigned to the course she had promised.

A few days before the marriage was to take place the old Hermit before alluded to, brought her a letter informing her that Henry Herbert was a married man and a villain—that he had disposed of all their property to Mr. Benton—that Herbert was gone, but Benton was ready to marry her, and would bestow the property as Herbert had agreed to, in case she consented to be his wife.—The letter was signed by Benton.

This roused all the slumbering energies of Cornelia's nature.—She saw all that had been done, and who had done it, and all the consequences likely to result from it; but she merely said to the old man, "you may tell Mr. Benton that he had my answer long ago," and immediately left the room.

She sought her Uncle, read to him Benton's letter and, her heart melted with pity as she gazed on his horror-stricken countenance and heard his words of bitter agony and reproach toward Benton. "I am now a beggar," he said, "and so are you, and so is Norman—and Benton! that villain Benton has got it all! and I—how have I fulfilled the trust reposed in me by a dying brother! leave me, Cornelia, leave me to my well-deserved torture!"

Cornelia dared not leave him—she knew that his mind was enfeebled by strong drink, and that his passions were powerful. She tried to calm his excited feelings, but in vain, until at last, he seemed exhausted, and slept—she left the room a few moments, and when she returned he was in strong convulsions. She immediately sent for a Physician, and every thing was done that could be done, but she was informed that he could live but a few days.

A friend immediately volunteered to go after Norman. Benton called, and even by the side of the dying man whom he had so basely wronged, he reproached Cornelia with being the cause of the suffering they witnessed. Mr. Campbell was insensible of his presence, and she bade him *be gone,* in such a manner that he was obliged to obey.

Mr. Campbell had no interval of perfect reason; but passed from one fit into another until the third day from his attack, and when he ceased to breathe. Norman did not arrive until the next day; what a cup of sorrow was prepared for him to drink! We will not attempt to describe his feelings as he gazed on the remains of his Uncle, or looked on the pale face of his suffering sister, and heard from her, an account of all that had transpired. They buried their Uncle, and were sitting in sorrow by the side of their old Nurse, when a note from Benton was handed to Norman, saying that if Cornelia would become his wife, he would allow all that had once been theirs, to be transferred back to them; but if she still refused, they must leave the premises immediately.

"Infamous wretch!" said Norman, "tell him I would sooner see my sister starve than be the wife of such a mean, cowardly villain! We both utterly despise him and all that he *says* or *does* or *can do,* and God will *curse* him!—this is my answer—take it back to him," said he to the messenger. Again they are alone. They *can* not, *will* not stay there. Night gathers around them, the last night they will ever find shelter in their childhood's home.

Continued.

Lines Written at My Brother's Grave.[19]

By C. Cumings.

My Brother, my Brother, thou hast rested here alone
While weeks, months and years, long, weary years have flown—

19. For more on this brother and Cumings' family, see introduction, pp. 9–11.

And again I'm permitted to stand by thy side,
While memory comes with its o'erpowering tide
To torture a heart that with cold sorrow oppressed,
Would fain by thy side find its last final rest.—
I think of the time when in childhood we strayed
By the far-off streams in the Green Mountain's shade;
When a Father, a Mother, and Sisters were there,
And we culled the bright flowers and dreamed not of care.
I see thy bright smile when a brother was given,
As thy heart welcomed warmly, this rich gift of Heaven.
Again on a Grandmother's face do we gaze,
As she tells us the tales of her own young days;
And a Grandfather's tears are flowing like rain
As he fights for his children, his battles again;
And our school-mates dear—all as children we loved,
From the dark, dreamy past, in one circle seem moved.
I see thy young manhood when thought stirred thy soul
And thou scorned in thy nobleness, passion's control,
But bowed thy young heart low at knowledge's fair shrine,
And quaffed the rich draughts that the spirit refine.
I see thee alone leave our dear native hills,
Unaided 'mong strangers to combat life's ills.
I mark how unflinching thy dark, kindling eye
As clouds gather round thee, obscuring thy sky,
For truth was thy strength, pure honor thy shield,
And Justice thy champion, and hope's azure field
Opening fair to thy view, bade thee ne'er be dismayed,
For envy's dark form at thy feet should be laid.
And not yet, oh! not yet is the circle complete,
For thee honor and friendship and happiness meet;
Love twines its bright wreath and a fair bride has come
In pure, holy trust, to thine own happy home.
And time in its transit, for thee, again hath won
A sweet precious gift. I hear a darling son
Lisp sweetly "My Father," and I know that 'tis well
With the heart of my brother, and must this sweet spell

Be broken by sorrow? Why will not death take
The heart that no joy for another can make?
I see thee again where the bright flow'rets bloom
In luxuriance wild round each sweet prairie home,
I list to thine accents, the rich words that well
From a heart that communion with nature doth feel;
I see thy rich smile through many a long day,
As we journeyed homeward through beauty's highway.
Ah, how vivid the thought of the glance of thine eye,
Of thy parting hand and thy last "good bye!"
How little we thought that the last look was given!
That we met not again "till we meet in high Heaven!"
The scene is now closing—a sick bed I see,
Watched by the young Brother whose sweet infancy
Thou hailed with delight—and thy loved wife is there,
But grim death heedeth not her stricken heart's prayer.
Thy orphan boy asks for his Father to come,
And thy Parents weep on, in thy once happy home,
While thy Sister's wrung heart only God can see,
As it bitterly throbs in its deep agony.
The sweet spell is broken—the strong man is gone,
Another proud triumph the Destroyer hath won,
Its dread knell is sounding—low lies the loved form
That has battled so nobly with tempest and storm;
Thy heart that throbbed warmly with rich love and trust
Must be rendered back to its own native dust!
They brought thee home—and thy cold clay we gave
To the dark embrace of the sad, silent grave,
And again God hath given me strength to be here,
To shed o'er thy ashes affection's pure tear.
I came to thy home and 'twas desolate all,
I saw not thy loved ones, I heard not thy call;
I traced all the paths that thy feet used to tread
And I heard but the echo that tells of the dead;
I met with thy friends, and their warm love for thee,
Soothed and yet deepened my sad heart's misery;
I gazed on thy portrait—thy deep speaking eyes

Seemed telling the tale of earth's severed ties,
Of affection forgotten, devotion grown cold
Or transferred to a glittering circlet of gold;
And they asked for the son, that dear, noble boy
That once was a source of rich pride and joy;—
And he's far, far away, and I see him not—
But thou wilt not be long, by thy child forgot;
A power shall be given to thought, yet to gain
All the links of the past, all the truth to obtain,
And he'll gaze on thy features with rapt, earnest love
While memory's power on his young heart shall move;
And he'll visit thy grave as a pure, holy shrine
While he asks of his God, His protection Divine;
And thy spirit we'll hope, may come to him then,
His guardian angel from sorrow and sin.
Oh! my Brother, my Brother, thy grave seems a home
Where rest can be given—earth's trials ne'er come;
The world seems far off with its dim, distant din
Of strife and commotion, of sorrow and sin,
And thy pure spirit seems, from the bright realm above,
To come to thy sister—and accents of love
Breathed low to her sorrowing, trembling heart,
Seem strengthening to bear in life's drama its part.
It whispers of peace when release shall be given,
And we part nevermore in the mansions of Heaven.

And yet I must wander from this sacred spot,
But these moments by me will ne'er be forgot.
A little while yet, I must look on earth's strife,
Then I'll share with thee, Brother, "Eternal Life."
Through Grace, rich Grace unto thee will I come,
And we'll know no sorrow in our sweet, happy home.

Zanesville,[20] August, 1849.

---

20. The poem suggests that Cumings' brother George lived in Zanesville, where he worked as a lawyer. In 1849 Zanesville was a prosperous and rapidly expanding town that was well connected, by railroad and canal, to the larger world. Between 1840 and 1850 its population grew from about 4,700 to nearly 8,000. About eighty miles south of Akron, it was noted for its schools, its athenaeum

For the Offering.

Letter from Aunt Betty.

Dear Niece:—Did I not know that you have almost unbounded patience I would not intrude upon your notice these rambling thoughts of mine. But being alone I must think and so I'll tell you what I'm thinking. I'm thinking of the strange *consistency* of whom shall I say? If I say all, it will include dear-self, well of people in general. If we should see a man, wishing for a good crop of wheat, sowing thistleseed with now and then a grain of wheat we should at once pronounce him very inconsistent; but, if in reply to our expostulations he should say he would continue to sow the seed, and trust to the Giver of all good for a blessing upon it, knowing that He is able to raise the best of grain from ever so poor seed, what should we think of Him. Should we not think it just, that, notwithstanding all his trust in providence, when harvest comes he finds his fond hopes blighted, and learns that what he sows he also reaps? Should he then blame the divine Dispenser of food for not causing the fruit to be such as he desired? Should we not think it awful blasphemy? Yet we daily see (if not practice) inconsistencies as glaring. Look at the manner in which children are trained, and see what beautiful consistency is there. We say they must not tell lies. Looking out we see a lady whom we dislike coming in, and say in hearing of the child, "I wish that lady would call somewhere else, I do not wish for her company;" but she comes in, and we must make ourselves agreeable, so we commence telling her how glad we are she called here, and really hope she will call again; and so on. What is the lesson given to the child? Why that he may tell a *little lie* rather than be thought *impolite*; for in these days of reform it is necessary to *appear* what we ought to *be*, kind to all; so if we have no respect for a person, we must make up in *words* what we lack in *substance*. If, when we find our child has a habit of fibbing, we would reflect, we might easily trace the effect back to the cause. But no, we will *chastise* the child for following our example, and murmur at what we are pleased to call the will of the Lord. And thus far it *is* his will, that we shall reap what we *sow*. In like manner we sow the seeds of envy, selfishness, and various other evils, and when they grow up and exhibit their fruits at home, at least we grieve, and seek, but do not see the cause; but rest upon the *happy* conclusion, that it *was* to be! Why are we so blind? Can we not see at a glance that what we

with a reading room, and its library of nine thousand volumes. See Daniel Haskel and J. Calvin Smith, *A Complete Descriptive and Statistical Gazetteer of the United States of America* (New York: Sherman and Smith, 1848), 746–47, Google Books, http://books.google.com/books?id=UOstAAAAYAAJ. Cumings' trip to Zanesville may have improved connections between *The Akron Offering* and the literary people of that town. See pp. 189, 231, 278, and 286.

sowed we are reaping? But, we say, we gave them a deal of good instruction, we told them it was wrong to do so, *yes*, with our *lips* we told them this, with our *conduct* we told them it was right. Whose fault is it that they show what we have taught them? Have we not sowed the thistle seed, and trusted to Providence! O may we open our eyes to see our awful neglect of duty towards our children, and teach them from their infancy by our precept and example to do right, and from right motives, and when they bring forth the fruit of veneration to God, obedience to parents, respect for age, and love for all, we may thank the bountiful Giver of good, that through his blessing we have been enabled to sow good seed in their young minds, and to reap the happy fruit. Then shall we not have reason to rejoice with exceeding great joy that what we sow we shall surely reap? But really I shall try your patience beyond endurance if I continue; so wishing you much wisdom and goodness,

I am, yours in love,
Aunt Betty.
Akron, August 1, 1849.

To My Sister on the Death of Her Child.[21]

Sister, thou but little knoweth
 Of the love I've felt for thee,—
Still within my heart it gloweth
 As in thy sweet infancy:

And I loved that gentle creature
 That so filled thy heart with joy,
Oft, in fancy, traced each feature
 Of thy beauteous, lovely boy.

Saw his sweet, mild eye imploring
 Kindness that all freely gave,
And each day, new charms adorning
 This rich blossom for the grave.

And I mark'd thy deep devotion,
 As thou watch'd his opening mind,

21. For more on Cumings' sisters, see introduction, pp. 9–11.

Promising the richest portion
The maternal heart can find.

Ah, how winning was each action,
Prompted by his guileless heart,
Banishing each sad reflection,
Bidding all but hope depart!

He was all thou could'st have asked,
Yet his race was quickly run;
But a few short months he basked
In affection's genial sun.

And how chang'd thine image seemeth
Since that solemn, parting hour!
Fancy no rich colors lendeth;
All seems touch'd by sorrow's power!

Every scene where he was present
Wants its purest, brightest charm;
Night and morn his place is vacant,
Thou canst clasp no more, his form.

Never more he'll spring to greet thee
Or his Father fondly kiss;
But, mementos daily meet thee,
Telling of thy former bliss.

Often too, I see thee weeping
Where his lov'd remains now rest,
But, his spirit is not sleeping,
'Tis triumphant with the blest!

This thou knowest—still doth nature
Deeply mourn its sever'd ties;
Memory shows thee every feature,
Anguish wrings unconscious sighs.

Sister, thou wert all too happy,
'Twas thy maker dealt the blow;
Would that thou couldst meet it meekly;
And sweet resignation know!

Had thy little Oscar tarried
He'd perhaps have learn'd to sin
And his Parents' bosoms wearied
With a never ceasing pain.

Now he's happy—think, then, sister
E're thou murmur'st at thy lot,
Let not grief so deeply fester,
That thy blessings are forgot.

Think of him who mourneth with thee,
But suppresseth oft the sigh,
That his love may fondly soothe thee
And thy tears of sorrow, dry.

Then as long as love is beaming
Fervent in thy husband's eye,
Think that fate is kindly dealing,
O, forget to weep and sigh.

Though thy heart is deeply bleeding.
For thy lov'd, thy precious one,
Mercy still, is strongly pleading
That repining thoughts be gone.

Look around thee—desolation
Deeper, marks full many a one!
Cast thy thoughts o'er broad creation,
See what spoils grim death hath own!

Many a heart hath nought to bind it
To a home made cheerless all;

Child, companion, each denied it,
    By stern death's relentless call.

And how often degradation
    Worketh changes worse than this,
Blasteth Hope's fond expectation,
    Banishes domestic peace!

Thou'rt not thus—thy home is pleasant,
    Happiness hath crowned thy choice:
Though thou'st lost thy smiling Infant
    Still thou hearest affection's voice.

Prosperous gales now waft thee forward
    To, we trust, a good old age,
Hope lights all thy journey onward
    To life's solemn, closing page.
Then be grateful and be happy,
    And forget not as ye go,
To bestow the balm of pity
    On each suffering child of wo.

May rich grace sustain and aid thee,
    Quelling all thy spirit's strife;
And the hand that's ever led thee,
    Guide thee to Eternal Life.

Then thou'lt meet thy child in Heaven,
    And its joys will be thine own,
There nought needs to be forgiven,
    Care and pain are never known.

Dear loved sister, mourn no longer—
    Though 'tis dark to human sight,
Let thy trust in God be stronger,
    Know He doeth all things right.

C. Cumings.
Windsor, Vt.[22], 1839.

---

22. The capital of Windsor County, Vermont, had a population of about 2700 in 1839. See Daniel

For the Offering.

Time.

A beautiful temple reared its snowy columns in a spot where nature needed not art to attract and fascinate the eye. It glittered in the rays of the morning sun, and was adorned with statues fresh from the hand of masters whose names were pronounced with reverence in many lands—statues almost breathing with the life they so closely resembled. And roses, shrubs, and most beautiful plants of every kind sprang up and twined around its graceful colonnades. And the young and fair dwelt within it. Their fresh, pure loveliness, as they glided through and around it, or seated themselves under the ancient trees that shaded this Elysian retreat, while their voices echoed from tree to tree in tones of sweetest music, made the scene seem more of heaven than earth. Among those fair ones was a beautiful girl, seated beneath the shade of a shrub or tree, the foliage of which presented a most grand and sublime aspect. She appeared to be musing over a large book of poems. Her eyes were of a dark brown, and dark auburn hair hung in graceful ringlets about her snowy neck. Her cheeks were of that rosy hue which indicates health and beauty. In short, nature had done all she was competent of doing in the short space of sixteen summers. My heart fluttered with joyous emotion as I looked upon those beautiful ones. But ere sixteen summers more passed by, I saw that time had dimmed those sparkling eyes, and changed those rosy cheeks to a pale, sunken, and death-like appearance. I also discovered one, an old man with silver locks, and step so soft and noiseless it awoke not the faintest echo. But he was tall and strong, & went on his way with a slow, firm tread. He paused not, and there was that in his look that paled the cheek of every one, yet they dared not move, for his eye had the power of the basilisk, and none could flee. The roses paled on their cheeks, and the elastic grace with which they moved was gone. Their forms were bent; and they tottered along feeble, faint, and slow, yet nought of pity or remorse could stay the course of the old man. His breath fell on the flowers, and they too faded, their leaves fell on the ground and withered away. Yet still he passed on, and entered that temple where clustered the brightest gems of art, and lo! those living, breathing images, fresh from the sculptor's chisel, and bearing almost the impress of

---

Haskel and J. Calvin Smith, *A Complete Descriptive and Statistical Gazetteer of the United States of America* (New York: Sherman and Smith, 1843), 734. Google Books.

divinity, slowly crumbled into atoms, and fell one by one from their places to the earth. The graceful columns that supported that glorious fane, fell mouldered, blanched, and broken, from the place where they stood—I could gaze no longer; for the old man was approaching, yet ere I closed my eyes I saw written upon his stern and wrinkled brow one word—Time.

Cora.[23]

☞ This number of the Offering contains the commencement of a story written expressly for it, by a lady in Zanesville. It is made up of facts, and exhibits life as it too often appears. Most sincerely do we hope it may do much good, and it appears to us well calculated to show each poor, degraded being, his folly, and to encourage the benevolent heart to persevere in endeavoring to save that which was lost.

The first story, "Which is the better man?" forcibly illustrates the folly, (aye worse then folly) of submitting to be governed by one's own uncontrolled temper, and it gives us, in beautiful contrast, the disposition ever subject to reason.

"Aunt Betty" tells us truths that have often been repeated, nevertheless they are truths still.

Several articles were not received in season for this number. None will be printed where the writer's name is not made known to the Editor.

We are much indebted for articles written by "Mark Mingleton," of Cincinnati, and several others. One piece appears in this No., the others will, in due time.

We think that all understand that any communication suitable for such a work, will be thankfully received. Are there not some scientific characters that will condescend to talk through the Offering, to many, who perchance, have not had their opportunity for gaining knowledge? Please let us hear from such, that your names may be remembered for your benevolent efforts to enlighten the minds of your fellow beings.

C. Cumings.
September 1849

---

23. For more by this unknown author, see p. 160.

THE
AKRON OFFERING.
October, 1849.

For the Offering.

Bible Influence.

The stability of all civil and moral institutions, depends upon the intellectual and moral improvement and elevation of the mind.—This position has become an admitted axiom, and needs no argumentation to sustain its truthfulness. But how to attain this and by what means, has been and still is a subject, which elicits much speculation; and the different theories which have been proposed, by which to arrive at this desirable end, are almost legion. Amidst the speculations of the age, the one great, important means for securing this end has been almost entirely overlooked, and indeed its adaptation to improve the mind and give stability to our republican institutions, has been seriously questioned, by many of the self styled Philosophers and Political and Moral *reformers* of the times; viz: the influence of Bible truth. It will be admitted, that the mind may expand intellectually, so far as the mere acquisition of science is concerned, without direct Bible influence. But man being constituted a moral as well as an intellectual being, will be left, by such training, without any moral balance, exhibiting a monstrous, one-sided development of the mind; and appearing on the stage of real life, presents the spectacle, like a ship in a storm without ballast or rudder, at the mercy of every wave, incapable of steering the ocean of life, and in safety reaching the haven of repose, the high and heavenly destination of man as an intellectual and moral being.

If such then are the phenomena of mind, when under the influence of science, refinement and cultivated society, what must be expected from the mass of uncultivated mind, unrestrained and unsanctified by Bible influence? In the language of Franklin to the infidel Paine: "If men are so wicked with religion what would they be *without* it?[1] The true answer to this question is presented to us, in the history of the infidels' native country, during the period when France abjured God, rejected the Bible and the institutions of religion—deified reason—voted God and the Sabbath out of existence and enthroned the Goddess of reason in their place. The consequences were, bloodshed, rapine, wars, intemperance, and lewdness together with every other corruption that could debase and degrade a nation.[2] What was then witnessed in a single nation, would be seen and felt again throughout the world, under the same circumstances. In truth, the world would present one vast theatre of crime and debauch. Facts as they even now present themselves to the observing mind, fully warrant this assertion. From whence are all the civil, social and moral evils, with which this nation and the world are afflicted and cursed? We unhesitatingly affirm from those, who are not under Bible influence, whether they be intellectually cultivated or ignorant. Let us specify a few of the immoralities and locate them if we can.

1. We notice sabbath desecration. It is the great effort of infidels and profane men, to beget a disregard for the christian's sabbath in the minds of the people.[3] And why? Because with it goes the Bible and the moral influence

1. "If men are so wicked with religion" is the start of a famous passage from a copied and incomplete letter by Benjamin Franklin (1812–78), commonly assumed to have been addressed to the American deist and political pamphleteer Thomas Paine (1737–1809) on the occasion of reading a draft of his "infidel" writings. See Benjamin Franklin, *The Works of Benjamin Franklin*, ed. Jared Sparks (Cambridge: Folsom, Wells, and Thurston, 1840), 10:281–82, Google Books, http://books.google.com /books?id=GFcCAAAAQAAJ.

2. Critics of the French Revolution often interpreted its excesses and failures as the work of atheism and deism. For an example of such reasoning in another Western literary magazine for women in the 1840s, see Edward C. Merrick, "Philosophy of Modern Infidelity," *The Ladies' Repository, and Gatherings of the West* 8, no. 12 (or 9, no. 6) (December 1848): 359–61, Google Books, http://books.google .com/books?id=z8YRAAAAYAAJ. A frequent contributor to *The Ladies' Repository*, "Professor Merrick" was one of the seven faculty members at the Ohio Wesleyan University in Delaware, Ohio, about twenty miles north of Columbus in the center of the state. He taught French. See *Catalogue of the Officers and Students at the Ohio Wesleyan University, for the Academical Year, 1846–1847* (Cincinnati, 1847), 7, Google Books, http://books.google.com/books?id=h4vOAAAAMAAJ.

3. "Sabbath breaking" was a point of much political and legal debate in antebellum America. Most states had laws concerning what people could do on a Sunday. In 1831 Ohio enacted legislation penalizing "any person of the age fourteen years and upwards" who "shall be found on the first day of the week, commonly called Sunday, sporting, rioting, quarreling, hunting, fishing, shooting, or at common labor, (works of necessity and charity only excepted)." See Harmon Kingsbury, *The Sabbath: A Brief History of Laws, Petitions, Remonstrances and Reports, with Facts and Arguments, Relating to the Christian Sabbath* (New York: Robert Carter, 1840), 22, Google Books, http://books.google.com

it is now so happily exerting over the minds of thousands. But should they succeed in blotting the sabbath from the remembrance of society, what are the consequences which we might expect to follow? What the moral character of our citizens then would be, may be seen in the character of those who now habitually profane the sabbath and remember not the sabbath day to keep it holy. Again we may learn the true answer to the above question by looking at the moral character of those who secure a livelihood on our thoroughfares.[4] Those thoroughfares have literally become high ways to corruption and hell.[5] And why? There is no sabbath observed among most of those who engage in business along these lines. Their moral character is just what we should expect from habitual sabbath breakers. The God of the Bible is not feared or reverenced. The influence of the Bible is not felt.

2. Profanity and blasphemy are sins of no rare occurrence among us, but where do you find these sins prevalent? Among those who disregard Bible truth. I regret to say that these immoralities are often met with among those, who lay great claims to refinement and intellectual cultivation. This however only proves our position that the influence of the Bible alone can elevate man to this high and noble rank which he is designed by his Creator to occupy in the scale of being.

3. Intemperance with its legion of burning and bitter curses, social, civil and moral, is another of those immoralities, which abounds among those, who disregard the word of God and its heavenly teachings. From these sources flow the great moral evils, which prevail so extensively among us. There are many other vices and immoralities to which we might advert, which all proceed from the same source and unchecked, unrestrained must bring swift destruction upon us. But we have named the most prevalent,

/books?id=xxQNAAAAYAAJ. Such laws were difficult to enforce because antebellum police forces were very small by today's standards; sabbath breakers everywhere were far more likely to receive a scolding or an angry look from a neighbor than they were likely to receive a ticket or some other formal penalty.

4. Work related to the canal was exempt from the 1831 sabbath-breaking law described above. Watermen, tollkeepers, shopkeepers, bartenders—anyone providing a service to travelers could work as usual. Few places in northeast Ohio would have been as bustling on a Sunday as Akron.

5. Nineteenth-century Akron historian Samuel Lane records an anecdote about the naming of the city. The namer of the city, Simon Perkins, considered many classical-sounding names. (Inspired by the Greek word for "high," "Akron" was chosen because the city would stand on the highest point of elevation along the canal from Lake Erie to the Ohio River.) Each name was ridiculed by his friend Calvin Pease. Lane writes that Perkins settled on "Akron" in part because he expected the name would confound Pease's inevitable attempt to "perpetrate a pun" on his choice. "Ah, yes, I see!" Pease responded. "*Ach-e-ron—river in hell, hey?* A very appropriate name indeed!" The canal was commonly regarded by clergymen as a "hellish" river for reasons such as those presented in this essay. See Lane, *Fifty Years and Over of Akron and Summit County* (Akron: Beacon Job Department, 1892), 36, Google Books, http://books.google.com/books?id=nyAWAAAAYAAJ.

and shall attempt to prove, that proper Bible influence alone can reach these evils and effect a radical cure.

1. Past experience and facts prove this position. Whenever the mind has been under the influence of Bible truth, whether cultivated or ignorant, refined or rude, we have seen a character of moral symmetry which at once commanded our admiration and confidence. Innumerable instances might be specified to sustain this remark. Again, all agree, that if mens' minds can be so influenced, as to carry out Bible principles, at all times and under all circumstances, the brightest state of moral elevation would at once be attained.—Intellect would be sanctified, the moral nature of man would predominate and give direction to all his actions and intercourse among men. We should then no longer need legislation to protect individual rights, nor prisons and penal laws to punish the reckless and vicious.

2. One of the wisest Statesmen of the age,[6] holds the following language: "All societies of men must be governed in some way or other. The less they may have of stringent State government, the more they must have of individual self-government. The less they rely on public law or physical force, the more they must rely on private and moral restraint. Men in a word, must necessarily be controlled, either by a power within them, or a power without them; either by the word of God or by the strong arm of man; either by the Bible or the bayonet. It may do for other countries and other governments to talk about the State supporting religion. Here under our free institutions, it is *religion* which must support the State."

The Bible is ample in its legislation of rules and duty, in respect to all classes and relations of society, and needs no emendation or addition. It does not need for its completeness or perfection either the Mormon or Davis' appendix.[7] It teaches rules and subjects, the high and the low, the rich and the poor, parents and children, each and severally, their relative duties with such minuteness and distinctness, that if carried out in actual life, must result invariably, in the highest possible happiness of each and all.

---

6. The author quotes Robert C. Winthrop's "Address Delivered at the Annual Meeting of the Massachusetts Bible Society in Boston, May 28, 1849." A descendant of the governor of the Massachusetts Bay Colony, Winthrop (1809–94) was then a Congressman from Massachusetts and a controversial Speaker of the House. As a conservative Whig, he was opposed by the antislavery "Conscience Whigs." The Whig party was breaking up in 1849 and 1850, and many Conscience Whigs would soon leave to join the Free Soil Party. For the full text of the quoted speech, see Winthrop, *Addresses and Speeches on Various Occasions* (Boston: Little, Brown), 165–73, Google Books, http://books.google.com/books?id=wLY6AQAAIAAJ. The quoted passage is on page 172.

7. A reference to two recent and much-discussed works of religious revelation: the *Book of Mormon* (1830) published by Joseph Smith (1805–44) and *The Principles of Nature, Her Divine Revelations, and a Voice to Mankind* (1847) published by Andrew Jackson Davis (1826–1910).

"Diffuse," says the writer above quoted,[8] "the knowledge of the Bible and the hungry will be fed, and the naked clothed. Diffuse the knowledge of the Bible and the stranger will be sheltered, the prisoner visited, and the sick ministered unto. Diffuse the knowledge of the Bible, and temperance will rest upon a surer basis than the mere private pledge or public statute. Diffuse the knowledge of the Bible, and the peace of the world will be secured by more substantial safeguards than either the mutual fear or the reciprocal interests of princes or of people. Diffuse the knowledge of the Bible, and the day will be hastened, as it can be hastened in no other way, when every yoke shall be loosened, and every band broken, and when there shall be no more leading into captivity."

It is the influence of the Bible, in a word, by which the very fountains of philanthropy must be unsealed, and all the great currents of human charity set in motion. It is here alone, that, we can find the principles, the precepts, the examples, the motives, the rewards, by which man can be effectually moved to supply the wants and relieve the sufferings of their fellow men, and to recognize the whole human race as members of a common family and children of a common parent. The Bible is omnipotent in the motives it furnishes to enforce and constrain obedience. It refers to the dignity of our natures; the destination and immortality of our souls; the internal peace of a good conscience; the favor and blessing of the Almighty; a tranquil death and a blissful immortality. It is awful in its denunciations against the wicked and ungodly. There is more power in Bible influence to restrain men than in legislative enactments and penal laws. Its influence universally felt, alone can elevate a nation intellectually, socially and morally.

I close these observations upon Bible influence by quoting a paragraph from the farewell address of the father of this great nation.[9] He observes: "of all the dispositions and habits which lead to political prosperity, religion and morality are indispensible supports. *In vain would that man claim the tribute of patriotism who would labor to subvert these great pillars of human happiness, these firmest props of the duties of men and citizens.*—The mere politician, equally with the pious man, ought to respect and cherish them. A volume could not trace all their connexion with private and public felicity. Let it be simply asked,

8. Another quote from Winthrop's 1849 Massachusetts Bible Society address. See Winthrop, 166.

9. The quotation comes from the 1796 farewell address of George Washington (1732–99). Often studied and extraordinarily well known in 1849, it was republished frequently in a wide variety of books and magazines. One place to find the full text is *Addresses and Messages of the Presidents of the United States, from 1789 to 1839* (New York: McLean & Taylor, 1839), 54–64, Google Books, http://books.google.com/books?id=NRxVAAAAYAAJ. This passage is on page 60.

where is the security for property, for reputation, for life, if the sense of religious obligation *desert* the oaths, which are the instruments of investigation in courts of Justice? And let us with *caution indulge the supposition* that morality can be maintained without religion. Whatever may be conceded to the influence of refined education on minds of peculiar structure, *reason and experience both forbid us to expect that national morality can prevail in exclusion of religious principles.*"

G——— S———[10]

10. George Schlosser appears in the 1850 United States Federal Census as a neighbor of the Cumings family and a Congregational Clergyman. United States of America, Bureau of the Census, *Seventh Census of the United States, 1850*. NARA microfilm publication M432. (Washington, D.C.: National Archives and Records Administration, n.d.), roll M432_732, page 385A, Ancestry.com. Born about 1812 in Pennsylvania, Schlosser lived in Akron with his wife Mary and their four daughters. A German Reformed minister, Schlosser worked as a Congregational missionary in the late 1840s and early 1850s. This is not surprising because the German Reformed Church was not so well established in Northeast Ohio, which was settled as the Western Reserve of Connecticut; Connecticut Congregationalism dominated the early religious organization of the area. In Henry Harbaugh's *The Fathers of the German Reformed Church in Europe and America* (Reading, Pennsylvania: Daniel Miller, 1881), Schlosser is named as a German Reformed pastor and theological educator for two significant "fathers" of the German Reformed Church, Jesse Hines (1806–79) and Jesse Schlosser (1812–75). Jesse Schlosser remained in Akron, where he was pastor of Grace Reformed Church after the Civil War. See V:181; Google Books, http://books.google.com/books?id=RoQfAAAAYAAJ. George Schlosser also mentored Wilson Dewitt Webb (1823–87) prior to Webb's 1848 ordination as a Congregational minister. See *The Congregational Year-book, 1888* (Boston: Congregational Publishing Company, 1888), 43, Google Books, http://books.google.com/books?id=gCJKAAAAMAAJ. William Henry Perrin, in his 1881 *History of Summit County, with an Outline Sketch of Ohio* (Chicago: Baskin & Battey), describes Schlosser as "a powerful speaker, talented and able in debate" who preached as "a German Reformed minister" in the early 1850s "at and around" Johnson's Corners, an area near present-day Norton and Barberton, about ten miles southwest of Akron. See 592, Google Books, http://books.google.com/books?id=XpM6AQAAIAAJ. Samuel Lane omits any mention of Schlosser but his book focuses on the history of the better-established downtown churches of the 1890s. In the 1840s, the German Reformed community worshipped in various locations and languages; services were held in English and in German. The First German Reformed Church of Akron was not founded until 1855. See Lane, 189–90, 202–03. In W. E. Barton's 1890 article, "Early Ecclesiastical History of the Western Reserve," Schlosser is named as a Missionary for the (Congregationalist) Connecticut Society from 1849 to 1851, and as an agitator in a controversial Congregationalist meeting at Oberlin in June, 1850. See *Papers of the Ohio Church History Society* (1890), 1:40, 50, Google Books, http://books.google.com/books?id=UdjbAAAAMAAJ. Schlosser's 1849–51 departure from the German Reformed church is explained perhaps in the 1852 *Acts and Proceedings of the Synod of the German Reformed Church*, where he figures as a former Clerk of the Synod who owed money to the Church. A committee was formed to track him down and collect. He was excused from repaying one bond to a German Reformed Board of Trustees on the grounds that they were unable to found immediately a Western Theological Seminary,—as promised when soliciting the bond. Schlosser may have hoped to work at this Seminary as a professor; perhaps a need for employment led him to work for the Congregational Church. See *Acts and Proceedings of the Synod of the German Reformed Church* (Columbus: Smith & Cox's Steam Presses, 1853), 50–51, Google Books, http://books.google.com/books?id=bXsQAAAAIAAJ. Finally, Schlosser is named as one of the men who took "an active part in the proceedings" of the Akron convention for Woman's Rights in May, 1851. This is the convention at which Sojourner Truth gave her most famous speech. For mention of Schlosser, see Elizabeth Cady Stanton, Susan B. Anthony, and Matilda Joslyn Gage, eds., *History of Woman Suffrage*

For the Offering.

The Orphan.

By Clarissa Clairmont.[11]

'Twas eve, and twilight's soft and pensive gloom,
Had shrouded nature, in her mild embrace:
And o'er the silvery waters of the lake,
Its simple vesture hung, with modest grace.

A stranger I, weary of traveling far,
Did venture forth, upon that heavenly night,
To visit an old churchyard, not remote,
For in such scenery wild, I took delight.

Oh 'twas a dear sequestered spot, half hid
Beneath the dark'ning shades of shrubbery tall,
Where many a dewy floweret peeped forth,
And ivy clustered round her mossy wall.

I looked around upon the grassy mounds,
Where deep beneath them, lay in calm repose,
Those very beings, which in life once moved,
But now lay prostrate like the blighted rose.

And as I gazed, I saw a lovely child,
Whom ten bright summers scarce could call their own,
Couched amid the tender grass and flowers,
And breathing forth a soft unearthly moan.

And then she raised her tearful eyes to heaven,
And clasped her little hands so meekly there;

(New York: Fowler & Wells, 1881), 1:114, Google Books, http://books.google.com/books?id=bUGHAAAAMAAJ. For a description of the Akron convention, see Nell Irvin Painter (who corrects the heavily embellished account of Stanton, Anthony, and Gage) in *Sojourner Truth: A Life, A Symbol* (New York: Norton, 1996), esp. 120–29.

11. Searches for other publications under this name yield no results. Searches of the 1850 United States Federal Census through Ancestry.com show that while there are some "Clermonts" in or near Summit County, there are no "Clarissas" and none of these Clermonts are in Sharon. The alliteration and literary connotations of the name suggests that it is a pen name of the usual antebellum variety. See n. 17, p. 108.

And softly said, "dear Father do forgive,
A friendless child, and listen to her prayer."

She ceased, and silence, deep, profound, ensued,
As midnight, in the dark and shadowy glen;
And if e'en true loveliness, on earth was found,
'Twas in that calm, sweet face before me then.

Then from her supplication she arose,
And trembling, stood beside a new made grave;
And thought alas, how soon must she alone
The trying conflicts of this cold world brave.

I stole somewhat abruptly to her side,
And whispered soothing words into her ear;
Saying, dear child fear not, I'll be thy friend;
Now tell me the sad cause that brought thee here.

She started at the unexpected sound,
Gazed wildly round her, then in accents mild,
Replied, "I've come to weep, and pray near mother's grave,
For I am now a poor lone orphan child."

" 'Twas yesterday, and ere the brilliant sun,
Had risen to his meridian, on high,
That this cold, damp earth was closed forever o'er
The safe retreat, where her remains now lie."

"Dear father, too, in death is sleeping low,
And winters cold and drear, have intervened,
Since he was laid close here, where mother rests,
And his dark grave is now o'erspread with green."

"He died of grief,"—my mother often said,
"For being banished from his father's door:
An exile in the cold and cheerless world,
To look upon his long loved home no more."

Good heavens! I cried, and is it here I find
That injured brother, whom I long have sought,
Oh, father! father! could you now behold
The deep distress your cruel words have wrought.

And thou sweet child, my brother's cherished one,
Art safely rescued from a life of care:
And mid the pleasures of my mansion home,
Thou'lt be like a rich gem to dazzle there.

I brushed the golden tresses from her brow,
Took her soft hand in mine then we withdrew,
Leaving the lovely willows, drooping there,
While the mild zephyr sighed a kind adieu.

Sharon, 1849.[12]

Letters to the Offering.

Number 1.

By Lily Lute.[13]

My Dear Offering:—You and I have often had a dish of chat together, but I have never addressed a letter exclusively to yourself before, and if I am presumptious in so doing now, you will please pardon me, for I really feel like talking to you this morning.

Just now, as I sat looking out at yonder beautiful grove whose leaves are already beginning to fade as the Autumn winds sigh among them, I began thinking of the many friends that have walked with me under those glorious old Maples, in the gloomy autumn time, when the falling leaves were mingling in one gorgeous mass on the shady slope, and how we danced and played among the withered leaves. I always loved the sound of leaves rustling to the tread of feet;—and how many times we have sat by the dark

12. Ohio had four "Sharons" in 1849. All had populations of one or two thousand. The closest "Sharon township" is about twelve miles to the west of Akron, in the eastern part of Medina county,.

13. For Lute, see n. 15, p. 44.

Chippeway,[14] whose waters I can see now through the clear openings as they dance gaily along, sparkling in the clear morning sun. Yes, how often we have sat there throwing pebbles into the stream, and weaving bright dreams for the future, which were never to be realized. And those friends—where are they now? Dead—or married. And most of them married young, quite too young.—And, by the way, my dear Offering, what do you think of early marriages? I am not in favor of them myself. Just like an old maid, say you. Well, I am not quite an old maid yet, though on the wrong side of twenty; but if I were, hear what an old maid would have to say on the subject; she must certainly have more experience than a young girl, and if she possesses a mind for observation, she has more knowledge of the world than a married woman. Her vision is not circumscribed by the limits of the household; she has not the petty cares to vex her, nor the continued round of laborious *chores*, that keeps the house wife ever on the move from the garret to the cellar, and her brains on the rack in search of the best recipes for pies, puddings, catsups, and a hundred other dishes that make up the salmagundi of edibles which must be prepared for the palate of husband, children, visitors, and the droppers-in for a dinner. Then in addition to these, there is the making of clothes, the ironing, the mending, the taking care of children, the house-cleaning, the dish-washing, the milking, the churning, the bed-making, the sweeping, the dusting and all the other etceteras too numerous to mention. Who will wonder that woman learns so little after she is married, when they take into consideration the multiplicity of her cares and the amount of labor she is required to perform. If by over-work, she can obtain a few moments for reading, her mind is weary and wanders from her book to her family affairs. If she possesses the means of travelling she can seldom leave her family; then her only respite is in making an occasional afternoon visit, where she meets perhaps a half dozen neighboring women, and they discuss the best mode of making apple-sauce, the latest cut of a sleeve, or if they are inclined to "mischief-making," as the old ladies say, they retail the most interesting scandal that they have heard of their absent neighbors. And what other subjects would you expect them to talk of? These are the only subjects they are familiar with, for the reason that their minds were not formed when they took upon themselves the responsibilities of wives and mothers; and who ever saw a husband laboring to instruct his wife, or one that ever pretended to hold conversation with her upon any literary subject? If a man is intelligent and fond of literature, he soon tires of the trifling conversation of his young wife,

14. Chippewa Creek runs south from Chippewa Lake in Medina County, just west of Seville, about nineteen miles southwest of Akron.

and spends his leisure hours in reading, or seeks some more congenial mind to converse with, while the young wife is left to seek such pleasures as she can. She wonders why she is thus neglected, and begins to ask herself what she has done to merit it: she consults her mirror, for she believes he loved her for her personal charms, and most likely he did, and she concludes that her dress or hair is not in a becoming form, and she arranges and re-arranges them, until the glass gives back a finer image, and if she succeeds in eliciting a compliment from him, she is satisfied for the time. But then, he still neglects her for his books or his more learned friends, and she has again recourse to her toilet; her vanity increases with every successful attempt, until her extravagant bills draw from him a severe reproof, and she, despairing of pleasing him, flies to some dear friend for sympathy, or dresses now to please the *world*, as she cannot please her husband. He has told her perchance, as many men do, that he does not love her for her intellect, and she never thinks of dressing her *mind* instead of her *person*, and then her cares increase with her years, and if she wishes to inform herself she has very little opportunity.

Now, had she been older, she would have known, if she had a common share of common sense, that there was something more to be done in life than to shine: that a pretty face, a pretty dress or pretty curls, would not keep her husband's affections long, and therefore would have studied her duty and her books, instead of her dress and her glass.

I once heard an opinion advanced in favor of early marriages, which was, that "young minds were easily moulded, and if a man married a young wife he could mould her to his wishes." Now he does not want such a wife, let him think as he will about it, he wants a wife with a mind as matured as his own, and in proportion as *he* is intellectual, *she* should be, that she may be his companion, not his toy and slave. Man does not know himself, and therefore, does not believe that this process of moulding would mould his wife, into a slave, but so it is almost invariably. I would not have a husband that I could mould to my wishes, for I know that I, like all others that possess power, would abuse it, and when I found I had made him subservient to my will I would *despise* him: Just so it is with man, let him possess complete power over his wife and he will abuse her. There are but few among the intelligent class of females, who have lived to the age of twenty-five or thirty without marrying, that have not employed the most of their time in useful studies, learned to govern themselves and to improve their time; their characters are formed and in short they are fitted to become wives and mothers. My grandmother, who had married at sixteen, a man of thirty-two, used to say to me, "never marry till you are twenty-five, now is your time for improvement," and so it was. I would that young girls would take the advise of those ladies who have married young, then we should not see so many unequal and unhappy mothers. And girls, would you take my advice you would not marry till you were twenty at least, twenty-five is young enough—now is your time for improvement—Study—not to catch a beau or a husband but to improve your minds. Do not spend too much time on dress—a fine exterior never caught a man that was worth having—if a plain dress and studious habits do not attract the attention of the butterfly throng, your cultivated mind and amiable disposition will attach you to some man of worth; and do not fear to defer the first offer, or discard it altogether, if it come not from a worthy person, for take my word for it you will have as many and as good offers after you are twenty as before.

"Every fool can find faults that a great many wise men can not mend."[15]

For the Offering.

Seville.[16]

By Lily Lute.[17]

When first my young eyes beheld thee,
Loved Seville! thou wert wondrous fair,—
Thy laughing streams, thy verdant meads,
And flowers blooming every where.

And still thou art most beautiful,
With thy neat homes, thy fertile vales,

15. An old proverb, often printed in American schoolbooks. For example, see C. P. Bronson, *Elocution: Or, Mental and Vocal Philosophy: Involving the Principles of Reading and Speaking* . . . (Louisville: Morton and Griswold, 1845), 38, Google Books, http://books.google.com/books?id=9EiOUgPYlJoC. Cumings may have owned or taught from this book: see n. 25, p. 53. Also, this barb could be directed at a recent critic of *The Akron Offering*. See Cumings' editorial at the end of this number, p. 241.

16. Small village in Medina County, described in 1848 as having one fulling mill, one furnace, one saw mill, one tannery, two schools, and 249 inhabitants. See Daniel Haskel and J. Calvin Smith, *A Complete Descriptive and Statistical Gazetteer of the United States of America* (New York: Sherman & Smith, 1848), 607, Google Books, http://books.google.com/books?id=UOstAAAAYAAJ.

17. For Lily Lute, see n. 15, p. 44.

Thy gardens and thy golden fields,
    And more, thy health-improving gales.

Thy aged Oaks and branching Elms,
    Whose boughs perchance, o'ershade the tomb
Of some strange race, now turned to dust,
    Who saw them in their infant bloom.

How many suns have seen them stand,
    Towering proudly to the skies?
How many summers clothed them green,
    How many autumns changed their dyes!

O, had they tongues, those green old Trees,
    How many tales could they not tell
Of ancient warriors sleeping here,
    Who in some bloody carnage fell!

Perchance this very spot hath been
    Pressed by a monarch's lordly feet;
Or this sweet shaded stilly nook,
    Was some fond lovers' blest retreat.

And see yon leaning trunk decays,
    Where once in all its leafy pride,
It spread its branches to the breeze,
    And, mayhap, screened an Indian bride.

It may have echoed to the sound,
    That wild war's deadly blasts have rung,
And dying groans have filled the air,
    Where now the songs of peace are sung.

See now those fields of waving corn,
    Where once a mighty forest stood,
The red man roamed in safety then,
    For then it was his own wild home.

But white men came with deadly steel,
And red men fell like forest leaves;
Then rose a christian hamlet here,
Whose sons in a God of Peace believe.

From the Democratic Review

Which is the Fortunate Man?[18]

By Miss Annie Middleton

Concluded.

Robert Hunt followed his friend very soon to town, but had a weary search before he could discover him. He had passed from one gloomy, dirty street to another, till he reached, at length, a long, narrow avenue, lined with tall, dingy-looking, brick houses, with that peculiarly melancholy expression which no houses but those in a city can possibly have. The very sunshine, as it streamed through, brought not a ray of gladness to the soul, but rendered the filth and misery more apparent. Robert's heart sunk as he ascended the steps of one of them. Could Gerald live here? Children's cries met his ear, oaths and imprecations—everything spoke of poverty and distress. The slatternly woman who replied at length to his repeated summons, said that "she did not know whether Mr. Morton was in or not, but his room was in the third story, and he might see for himself." Robert opened the door and entered. Gerald was not there; and he surveyed the premises with a groan. A carpetless room, bare, dirty walls, the windows obscured by smoke and filth, and excepting a miserable cot and rickety chair, the apartment was entirely destitute of furniture.—And Gerald lived here—Gerald Morton, whose life had been like a fairy-tale—victories, success, and happiness. Gerald, so luxuriously nurtured, so tenderly cherished; all that the most unbounded love and wealth could bestow, at his command! None of Robert Hunt's own miseries ever gave him the sense of exquisite pain, which he experienced for the first ten minutes in that wretched room. He covered his face with his hands, and groaned aloud.—When he raised his head, his eyes fell upon the pictures of his friend's father and mother, which rested in magnificent frames against the wall—most

18. See pp. 19–22 and 173–81 for more on this selection.

incongruous-looking objects for such a place—the sole link between Gerald's past and present existence. His mother's had been taken in the prime of life, and love, and happiness; a radiant, joyful, beautiful face, fair and dimpling, with laughing eyes, and careless, unstudied, girlish grace, it stood out from the canvass; the head set so faultlessly, on the snowy, swelling throat, and one hand holding back the luxuriant waves of soft brown hair. It might have been Hope, or Eve in her innocence, or a Peri,[19] or fairy, or creature celestial: not a sorrowing, yearning, care-stricken mortal. She died before a hope had withered. The picture diverted Robert even from his sorrowing thoughts; and as he was regarding it his friend entered. A cry of surprise, a warm embrace, tender, hurried, affectionate words, and Robert raised his head from his friend's shoulder, and looked at him. Gerald was weary; his face had grown thin and pale; his clothes were dusty, and looked old and shabby; yet there was something in his face which checked Robert's condolence and pity. It was neither pride nor reserve, but a collected, cheerful, confident look. His eye was bright and calm. No sickness of the soul was there. Poverty had done its work on the body; the cheek had grown pale and haggard; the manly, athletic figure, (even in that short space,) had wasted, but the heart was strong and firm. How could Robert pity him? He evidently did not pity himself. No! more than in his prosperous, successful days, Robert Hunt envied Gerald Morton. As he stood there leaning carelessly against the rough mantle piece, the very room seemed light, and gay, and bright around him.

"Well, Robert," he answered. With the first it was a question, the last was confirmatory. It *was* well with him.

"What are your prospects?" continued Robert.

"I have none," answered his companion.

"Somebody, then, must have left you a little legacy, I'm sure," said Robert, "for never a man spoke despairing words in that tone."

"No, Robert," answered Gerald, "I have neither prospects nor money, and am in a famous way of trying the experiment of the effect of starvation in brightening the wits."

Robert looked aghast. "Where are all your friends, and your father's friends?"

---

19. The "Peri" often appears in American and English literature of this period. In Persian mythology, a "Peri" is spirit banished from paradise until completing some penance. See *Encyclopaedia Americana: A Popular Dictionary of Arts, Sciences, Literature, History, Politics, and Biography*, ed. Frances Lieber (Philadelphia: Lea and Blanchard, 1849), 10:16, Google Books, http://books.google.com/books?id=348KAQAAIAAJ. For American readers of the 1840s, the Peri was usually beautiful and weeping.

"Why," said Gerald, "if I had any idea of being misanthropical, I might say I had none. The truth is, dear Robert, everybody in this world of ours is very much taken up with his own plans, schemes, and interests, and has, consequently, little time to attend to other people's. I've no doubt I should have the sympathy and assistance of dozens, if they could take breath long enough to understand my position. There are some, I acknowledge, to whom Gerald Morton, dressed *comme il fait*,[20] in his father's handsome carriage, and Gerald Morton, dusty and on foot, are very different objects."

"Is it possible you have found any difference?" asked Robert Hunt, hurriedly.

"Certainly, my dear fellow, I expected it; I've been cut dead by numbers of my fashionable acquaintances. Mothers and daughters, who have hitherto been radiant and profuse in smiles and civilities, walk now, with most imperturbable faces, past me, or dart into shops anywhere to avoid speaking. One expects nothing more from them. They belong to the class, who, while you dress well, live well, talk gaily and lightly, and help them to 'fleet the time carelessly,' are the most delightful acquaintances in the world; but they vanish with the sunshine."

Robert Hunt's face was eloquent with sympathy, anger, and grief.

"Nay," continued Gerald, who saw the effect of his words, "do not look so unhappy for me, dear Robert, for, indeed, I am not at all so; it is a long lane that knows no turning, and in the mean time I'm rich in hopes."

We will pass over, (if you please,) a score or more of years, and bring no longer young Gerald, but getting-old Gerald, (some slight approaches manifest of relentless time,) before you. He was seated in a large arm-chair before a comfortable fire, and children of various sizes and ages around him. A very pretty girl of seventeen stood leaning against his chair, and his face was turned towards her.

"Now, father," she exclaimed, "you have so often promised to tell us everything about yourself—not in snatches, but a nice long story—and you'll never do it; come, tell us to-night. Mr. Merchant said, the other day, that it was as good as a play. Everybody knows all about you but your own children."

"Play! indeed," repeated Gerald Morton:—"Some parts of it rather like a tragedy, were they not, Louise?" he said to Mrs. Gerald Morton, who sat on the other side of the fire-place.

20. "comme il fait" is French for "as he does" or "as it does."

"Well, now, father, this is not telling it," exclaimed Louise the Second; "come, do begin; tell us what you did when grandpa died."

"I was left without a penny in the world, my dear—scarcely a decent suit of clothes; and for a short time there seemed to be a fair prospect of my starving."

"That's contrary to your doctrine, father," exclaimed a roguish, saucy-looking boy; "you say nobody need starve who isn't bed-ridden."

"Nor need they," returned his father. "I *did'nt* starve, but labored under a disadvantage, my child, of which you'll never have to complain. I was the son of a rich father, and people set it down as a paradox, that as I lived daintily, I could never work roughly; and while they were arguing the matter, I came (as I have told you) very near starving. At length your mother's uncle, Mr. Rivers, concluded to make the experiment, giving me a mere pittance at first, then (as he saw I was fit for something) a very handsome salary, and even talked of taking me into the firm."

"Then you fell in love with mother, didn't you!" interrupted Louise.

"Yes," said Mr. Morton, "then mother fell in love with *me*; & when we both went to ask (with the full expectation of obtaining it too) her uncle's blessing, we were received with a torrent of anathemas; and I was favored particularly with the titles of 'beggar,' 'presumptuous,' 'ungrateful,' and nobody knows what, till he cooled down with inquiring 'how the deuce I expected to maintain his niece?' "

"And what *did* you say,—what *did* father say, mother?"

"He looked very proud and superb for a moment or two," answered Mrs. Morton, "hurt and surprised, and a little bit angry. And then, with his irresistible way, (you know he has an irresistible way, when he chooses, Louise—."

"He *always* has an irresistible way," replied his daughter, and she stooped, and kissed with the tenderest love, the clear, calm forehead turned towards her.

"Well, he put on his *most* irresistible way then, and told your uncle, or rather my uncle, that he expected to maintain his wife as he maintained himself, by his own exertions;—that he had no designs on his (Mr. Rivers') fortune, for he expected no more with me than if I was the niece of the poorest man in the land;—that as to being a 'beggar,' 'presumptuous,' and 'ungrateful,' he could not see what possible right he had to any of these remarkable appellations; and to conclude, that he had no idea of the thing meeting with Mr. Rivers' disapprobation, or he never should have offered himself to me, and now of course, he would prosecute the affair no further; and he bid us both good evening."

"What *did* you do, mother?" asked Louise.

"Why, I stood admiring him, and thinking how prince-like and noble he was, and all sorts of fond, foolish things, and yet being very much afraid I should have to go after him and declare I wouldn't be given up; but Mr. Rivers saved me the trouble, for he called out—'Do you know you are very impertinent, sir; and do you know you have a confoundedly cool, proud way of saying impudent things; and do you know I like you all the better for it, you rascal? Take her; I'd rather she'd married you without a penny, than the wealthiest man in the land.' "

"Charming," exclaimed Louise; "now *that* certainly was quite like a play—and you married mother?"

"Yes," replied Gerald Morton, "and we lived with Mr. Rivers, and were very happy there, too; and he intended (the kind old man) to leave her most of his fortune; but died suddenly, without making his will, and she had but a most insignificant part, and was obliged to leave the house where she was born—where all her pleasant, childish days had been spent—."

"Just as you did, Father, before," interrupted little Ben.

"Yes, and then we went into a small, inconvenient house, with the plainest furniture in the world; but we were very happy there too—were we not, Louise?"

"Happy! father," echoed his daughter, "I wonder where you wouldn't be happy? if you had only a crust of bread, you'd be happy."

It was the same speech which Robert Hunt had made so many years before, and recalled his old friend and the scene on the bridge vividly. Poor Robert! his prophecy had worked its own accomplishment. "He should be just like his father, only worse." He had yielded, as it was his destiny, to his morbid tendencies, and was now a miserable, unloved, prematurely-old man. Although singularly successful, without any effort of his own either, in all that is most prized in this world, yet the apparent blessings were changed to curses by the use he made of them. A distant relative died soon after he left college, and left him, by mere chance and caprice, a large fortune. Always generous, his father and sisters were handsomely provided for, and he became very much attached to a lovely girl, and appeared, in a fair way of being happy at last, himself. But he got the idea that her whole family were violently in favor of the match for mercenary motives and doing all in their power to bring affairs to a crisis. This produced a coolness and constraint on his part towards his mistress, and he ceased almost entirely in his attentions: she, imagining that he had merely entertained himself flirting with her; that she was mistaken in ever supposing he had dreamt of any particular interest, married a man who had no such scruples. Her marriage opened Robert Hunt's eyes too late, and nearly killed him. He married, too, a very fine woman, but as he never had any great amount of love for her, their union was not a happy one. Honors fell thick upon him; he had every gift without solicitation that the sovereign people could bestow, but nothing could yield the peace and contentment which must have its source in the heart. And men, tho' they admired his genius, and respected his uprightness of character, feared and disliked him. His very children had a sense of awe and oppression in his presence, and it was like a shadow on the hearth when he entered. He saw it all, and it ate into his soul. He saw that the laugh and jest were hushed when he appeared; he saw that their caresses and love were lavished upon their mother, and they gazed with fear and constraint in his face when he addressed them. And he knew it was all his own work, and he cursed himself for it, too. He did everything but govern himself and change. Did I say nobody loved him? Yes, Gerald Morton loved him yet, for he knew him to his heart of hearts, and loved him with a love passing the love of woman, for the deepest pity still lingered with it; and now he was going out this dark, stormy night from his pleasant home to see him. "Oh, don't go, father," exclaimed Louise, "we thought we should have a pleasant evening."

"And to see that cross Mr. Hunt," said little Jeannie, "I shouldn't think you'd want to go, father; his scowl is enough to frighten the heathen."

"Charles Hunt says he wishes his father was half as pleasant as you, father," said Ben; "he told me the children were always so glad when he went away from home."

Mr. Morton sighed heavily, but went all the more for the children's speeches. Louise's little fingers tied the muffler around his neck, and she kissed him, and begged him the last thing, "to come home very early."

And leaving warmth, and light, and love, he went to face the cold, stormy night. It was a long walk, and his thoughts were of Robert Hunt, from the time he left his own till he reached his friend's house; not on his faults, but the generous, noble traits in his character, his womanly affection and tenderness, at the time of his own great sorrow; his forgetfulness of self when the weal of those he loved was concerned. And Gerald Morton reproached himself that he had ever ceased his warning and encouragements, and let the coolness which seemed to have environed Robert like a crust, ever spring up between him and the friend of his early love. There were lights flashing from every window in Mr. Hunt's house. He rang, but nobody answered; and hearing loud shrieks, he walked in. A group had collected around Mrs. Hunt who was lying on the stairs in violent convulsions. Mr. Hunt had cut his throat in a sudden fit of insanity, when alone in the room with her, and in a vain cry at the top of the stair-case for assistance, she had fallen in her agony to the bottom. Medical assistance was called in, but life was extinct. He died a victim to an uncontrolled, miserable, morbid temper.

The spirit of Reform and Conservatism, considered in a general sense, and also several of the branches of Reform now engaging public attention, examined particularly, the first chapter containing remarks on Woman, her Rights, Duties, &c., and the succeeding numbers to contain, as time and space will allow, an examination of many of the enterprises of the age *intended* to elevate human beings in the scale of morality and intellect.—Editor.

For the Offering.

Reform and Conservatism.

Chapter I.

By Maud Wellington.[21]

Long ago, Reform launched its boat in the tide of human affairs and many and bitter have been its struggles with the spirit of satisfied self-complacency that chained so many hearts on the fatal sand-bars of egotism and indolence. One of these principles was conceived in a spirit of pure benevolence and desire to do good, the other is the essence of selfishness, unconscious though its possessor may sometimes be, of any sentiment worse than veneration for established opinions, and thus have they battled.—One, with all the might of its enterprising, energetic nature, seeking to make it a war

21. A search of the 1850 and 1860 United States Federal Census reveals a number of Wellington families in Northeast Ohio, but none in Akron. A search for names—Matilda and Madeline, for example—for which "Maud" might be a nickname also fails to produce a likely match. Of course "Maud Wellington" could be a pen name, and "Mrs. Maud Wellington" could have died or moved away before the census was taken in the summer of 1850. Google Books, American Periodicals Series Online, and WorldCat discover no further publications signed "Maud Wellington."

of extermination, the other, whose office is stern endurance, firmly withstanding the shocks of every onset and looking with cool contempt on every effort of their young opposer to change feelings and views so time-honored as their's—thus have they both lost sight of truth.—One, though the brain may be dizzy in concocting its wild chimerical schemes, will unhesitatingly swallow any dose administered by anyone who will enlist under its banner and go on a crusade against established usages—the other, although the brain may be paralised and an apathy almost like death, be stealing over the senses, will close its eyes to the light, and shut its ears to every sound indicating innovation, aye, will die, in its stoical firmness, rather than take medicine from the daring, unholy hand of a Reformer.

From these opposing principles has arisen a spirit of investigation willing, aye, anxious to know the truth, and be pleased gentle reader to follow this spirit in its examination of these opposing powers—not far back in the annals of history need we look, but our own times—scenes familiar to all, will furnish material sufficient to give us right views. Reform and Progression are the watch-words of the present age and by calm reflection we may hope to arrive at just conclusions.

The old spirit of resistance to change, said man was made to govern, woman to obey. Man may range creation for happiness and for knowledge; Woman should find *all* her pleasures in the domestic circle, looking not on the political world and caring not for the strife of opposing parties, civil or religious, subservient in all things to her acknowledged head, her sovereign Lord, breathing not even in a whisper, thoughts unsanctioned by his majestic self.

Reform said, Woman is degraded—as an individual she has the same right as man—she should be engaged in some pursuits, help make the Laws, be eligible to the same offices &c. &c. There is no particular sphere for woman and as many allow as such an assertion, consent to be considered inferior to man.

And what does truth say? It draws a line between the two, and while it agrees with the most ultra advocate of "woman's rights" that she is man's equal in *capacity* to understand anything that taxes the intellectual powers, is as well fitted by nature to become versed in all that makes the profound scholar and philosopher and may be morally, scientifically, politically and religiously able to compete with him for wisdom's ever-blooming wreath, and that her heart and mind *should* thus be cultivated, it still says she should never, *unnecessarily* stand in the public arena. If left alone, it becomes her duty to use her faculties to emancipate herself, and many times, many others, from the thralldom of adverse circumstances. Because her Idols are removed she is not, with an Idiot's dread, to shrink from a contact (if need be) even with the heartless multitude, and fall ingloriously in the ranks of hopeless poverty or degrading infamy—no—though thus left to struggle alone, driven as it were from her appropriate sphere, the scenes of her dearest duties, she will still feel that for her there is and must be a choice of pursuits; still, on the new ground she occupies, there is for her a proper place. She would not (if she might,) mingle with those who go to the Polls and vote for this or that measure or man, she would not stand in the halls of Legislation and participate in the fierce debate—nor in the courts of justice learn to make plain common-sense ideas appear past comprehension, as do the Lawyers, many times—nor would she on the Judge's seat expound the Law—nor as a Juror, listen, nor in the sacred desk consent, to minister in holy things.

Do you ask what is left for her? On the supposition that she is educated as she *should* and *may* be, you will many times find her in the school room, laboring to instruct children, or young gentlemen and ladies in such things as they, unfortunately, too often, can not learn at home, from either Father or Mother. With Woman's gentle firmness and patience, she strives to eradicate the impressions of ignorance, left in dark and disfiguring colors, by the careless hands of parents, and how many, in this thankless toil have died! and how many more will swell the ranks of martyrdom e're her labors will be fully appreciated and rewarded! And Woman has her pen and may learn to wield it effectually, and in such a manner that its influence may be felt as long as time shall last! and e're long she will be the only Physician *for her sex—for her sex* it *should be*, and we will fondly hope that every woman who has devoted, or will devote, her time and talents to the study of Medicine, will wish every man to trust himself and his fellow, while *she* administers the healing draught exclusively to *her own sex*.

And do you ask why Woman should not enter the lists[22] with man, a candidate for honors, offices, and preferment, when it is acknowledged she could fill any station with success? The reason is, there is a dearer, a higher, and holier mission, for her—that, in her appropriate sphere of Wife and Mother, she may do more to reform a world than in any other way—then let truth be listened to and each one seek to find that happy medium that always exists between two extremes; let the Mother feel that her children will come on to

22. "To enter the lists" is an idiom meaning to accept a challenge or to enter a competition.

the stage of life prepared to act their part or not, as she has discharged her duty or not, and she will not seek to leave her charge to unholy hands, while she shall strive to please a gaping crowd of simpletons, by lecturing on "Woman's trampled Rights." She will abide where God and Nature have placed her, and man will learn to look on her as possessing power far superior to his own—he will not be content to mate himself with ignorance and silly pride, and thus the world will be reformed, and truth will shed its certain light on all.

Akron, 1849.

[The following question, the author tells us, was suggested to his mind while in a state of suspense as to the fate of an absent and dear friend, whom he had left in New England; and these lines were written on hearing of her death. There is much in them to admire—much that tells of the strength of human affection, and it is right and manly to mourn;—but look upon those who are more bereaved than if their friends were numbered with the dead, mourning those on whom degradation has set its withering seal; yea, look upon the *World* as it *is*—let your sympathy be enlisted for the wretched, and, though you will not *forget*, you will learn to *bear*, and, trusting in the wisdom and mercy of God, will not murmur at His decrees.—Editor]

For the Offering.

Where is Rebecca?

Where is Rebecca?—my heart hath sung
To melancholy, with weeping strain:
Where is Rebecca?—no fond line doth come,
To cheer me with its sweet smile again.
Where is Rebecca?—the lone night doth last,
And linger, still waiting for the dawn;
Where is Rebecca?—the weeping flowers ask
As springing up they glisten in the morn.
Where is Rebecca?—each budding day
Bursts forth with this inquiring song;
Where is Rebecca?—fills the roundelay
Of warbling birds that sail the clouds among;
Where is Rebecca?—'tis the murmuring strain
Of bounding stream and whispering glade;

Where is Rebecca?—I breathe it yet again,
As 'tis caught and sung by tripping maid.
Where is Rebecca?—swells from yonder hill,
While no answering voice brings lov'd reply;
Where is Rebecca?—each trickling rill
Leaps lonely o'er its pebbly shore—to sigh.
Where is Rebecca?—oh, can it truly be
That she hath hushed the welcome tone?
Where is Rebecca?—to chant the melody
That voiced forth for me—for me alone?
Where is Rebecca?—to stay the passing hour,
And clasp the fleeting moments as they fly;
Where is Rebecca?—to pen the happy line,
That so fondly I loved as love-light on high.
Where is Rebecca?—oh, tell me bright star,
Sparkling so brilliantly in yon blue sky.
Where is Rebecca?—oh! sound it afar,
I am longing, longing—deeply longing am I.
Where is Rebecca?—hark! that sound,
The answering echo speeds to my ear;
Where is Rebecca?—'tis hymned around
As breathings from a higher sphere.
Where is Rebecca?—she hath fled away,
Amid the starry paths of Heaven to roam;
Where is Rebecca?—angel voices say
She hath gone—gone to join her home.

D. S. F.[23]
Zanesville, Sept. 1849.[24]

---

23. Another unknown author and another Zanesville production that may have been recruited when Cumings visited in August. See pp. 189, 198, and 208, as well as the notice of the *Offering* found in n. 44, p. 278. An exhaustive search of the 1850 census for Zanesville finds only one resident with the initials D. F.: David Forster, a German-born nineteen-year-old confectioner boarding with his employer. See United States of America, Bureau of the Census, *Seventh Census of the United States, 1850*. NARA microfilm publication M432. (Washington, D.C.: National Archives and Records Administration,n.d.), roll M432_717, page 210B and roll M432_717, page 195B, Ancestry.com. If there was another "D. F." in Zanesville, the Census missed him. Or perhaps he moved further west, as so many Ohio residents did. Maybe he went for the gold in California. See introduction, p. 7.

24. For more on Zanesville in 1849, see n. 20, p. 201.

Norman and Cornelia Campbell,
OR
"Truth Stranger Than Fiction."

By C. Cumings.

Chapter VI.

Cornelia was the first to break a painful silence. "Brother," she said, "allow me to tell you my plan for our future course of action. You feel that you cannot leave me, but you can. I have a firm friend in Mrs. L., who lives near our school house, and I can instruct the children belonging to this school, and take care of our dear old nurse too, for Mrs. L. will give us a room in her house and board us in her own family on reasonable terms, and you can, if you wish, go to our Father's friend, Mr. S., in New York, and you can then have the satisfaction of feeling that you are fulfilling our Father's wishes, and also that you are preparing yourself to be able to find a home for your sister, and *I* shall be happy in the thought that I am doing what I can to prevent my being a burden to you, and the means of deranging the plans you have laid down for the accomplishment of your purpose. Yes, we shall both be happy in the thought that we are doing our duty."

Norman's eyes were full of tears as he looked on his devoted sister, and heard her make arrangements that plainly manifested her insensibility of every selfish principle. "Dear sister," said he, "it would be hard for me to leave you, and I should fear that I should thereby fail in my duty. We will go and see Mrs. L., and for the present, if she consents, both take up our abode with her, and then we will decide what I am to do."

They could not move their Nurse that night, and both sat by her until morning dawned. As soon as he could, Norman went to Mrs. L.'s and asked permission to bring her there. "Yes," said the kind hearted woman, who knew their history, "you will all be welcome, and I shall be the person obliged." Norman could scarcely speak his thanks, but immediately returned with those commissioned by Mrs. L. to assist in the removal. Suffice it to say, that it was accomplished before the brutal Benton arrived, and that when he came he found but the bare walls of a mansion that had sheltered his infancy, youth, and manhood, wicked and ungrateful as he had ever been. Francis Lisbon was with him, and, wretch as he was, he could not but *feel* as he looked around and know that Mr. C. had been led on to intemperance and death, by the villainy of Benton's nearest relatives in the commencement, and by

Benton himself, finally ruined. And he knew too, that this property was not Benton's, even by law; neither did it belong to Herbert, but yet he could hold his peace; for the sake of immense sums of money promised him by Benton, he could see those wronged, whom even he, base as he was, loved for their ennobling virtues; yes, *loved*—but only a *little*—*self* was his God, and he saw this property sold and the avails[25] pocketed by Benton, without even a sigh of regret; for he was going with him to his princely possessions in the State of New York, to revel for the rest of his days, in perfect idleness and luxury—such was Benton's promise, and thus they departed.

Norman's friends at last persuaded him that it was right that he should, for the present, leave his sister in their care, and he also consented that she should be the teacher of their children, and saw her established in her new vocation; then with just enough money to take him to New York, he decided to start immediately; but who shall tell the conflict of his feelings as he thought of all that had been, and gloomy forebodings for the future sought to overshadow his naturally hopeful spirit; or who shall describe the feelings of his sister, when reflection came with its torturing power? Vain would be the effort. Reader, let your imagination present the scene of parting of that Brother and Sister, and we shall hasten along to the time when Norman stands before his Father's friend, now somewhat advanced in life, but still an active member of the Bar, where once stood Albert Campbell, with such high hopes of a glorious life of usefulness and happiness. He was now a widower, having but one child, a daughter, who was justly beloved by all.

Immediately after Norman arrived at New York City, he went to the office of Mr. S. and told him his name and situation; but casting no blame on his Uncle, and forbearing even to reproach the villain Benton.

"You need no introduction," said the aged man of the Law, "I seem to see my early friend as he appeared at your age—give me your hand young man, I want no guarantee of your capacity or character, and you shall ever find in me, a friend. You are to be my student, and you will consent also to become my clerk, and thus you can cancel any fancied obligations you may feel in becoming an inmate of my house, a member of my family;—in short, my home must be your home—no scruples, for I shall be the person receiving a favor."

Norman's heart was too full for utterance, but his eloquent look of gratitude brought tears into the old man's eyes.

---

25. Profits; a New England term word for the proceeds of goods sold, or for rents collected.

"Your father was very dear to me," he said, "and you are almost his express image—you must go with me to the place where we together conned the lessons that were allotted us, and also to your father and mother's graves."

Norman did indeed feel an anxious desire to visit his parents' graves, and his friend, who seemed to understand his wishes, proposed going that afternoon. When they arrived at the sacred place, Norman could scarcely speak—so powerful was memory, that he was entirely overcome, and sat down and wept tears, sacred and purifying in their influence, and arose strengthened to try to fulfill his father's dying request, and do honor to his name and memory.

The old man then took him to his own dwelling. "On this spot," he said, "your grandfather's house stood; here you and your sister were born, and your friends enjoyed much happiness, and," he might have added, "here your mother perished, and your father received his death-blow," but he forbore, and kindly said, "I know you will feel more at home here than any where else. I am almost alone, and the arrangement I have made will be to us, I hope, a mutual blessing."

Norman could not but consent, and was passively led to a chamber appropriated to his use, and was soon after summoned to tea, and introduced to Helen S., the daughter of his friend. She was seventeen, a brunette, and possessed of a kind heart and a head sounder than usually belongs to an only child and heiress to a large fortune. She was accomplished and beloved by all, and Norman was not blind to her attractions; but his mind was busy with the thoughts of the purpose that brought him there, and the Providence that had led him to the home of his fathers; but her mind was unoccupied by engrossing thoughts, and her heart was ready for the impression which, unconsciously to himself, his appearance produced. Norman was usually calm and collected, but his situation was *now* so strange that he felt bewildered. He had been told of the friendship of Mr. S. and his Father, but he was not prepared for so much kindness. He felt that he was, as it were, brought home and surrounded by mementos of the past, for, on every hand, notwithstanding the many changes that had occurred, he recognised objects long since engraved on memory's tablets, almost faded away, but now renewed.

His exciting thoughts kept him awake nearly all night, and he was not alone in his wakefulness. Mr. S. had thoughts he did not deem necessary to communicate to anyone, and over the visions of the fair Helen, we must, from necessity, cast the veil of silence.

Norman immediately commenced his studies, and also the office allotted him by his kind friend, and had not been many days thus engaged, when a young man entered the office whom Mr. S. introduced to him as Virgil Richland, whom he had forgotten to tell him was his student at law, who had been for some time absent.

Norman beheld him, judging from his dress, a man of fashion, with delicate form and complexion, never soiled by exposure, judging from the expression of his countenance; one with some capacity, but too much elated with his own consequence to pay much deference to the opinions of others, and too indolent to apply himself to any business; but he resolved to deserve his respect and give him a cordial greeting as his expected fellow student, to which Richland replied with seeming good will.

Norman subsequently learned that this young man had a fortune at his command, and that he had traveled over a great part of the world, and also that his facilities for gaining information had been abused, and that he possessed an envious, revengeful disposition, which will be manifested as we pass along. He was at this time twenty-five years of age, and Norman twenty-two. Norman lost no time, but soon satisfied his friend that he had not misjudged him in any thing. He commended his industry, and Richland soon perceived that he was a great favorite. This was a rebuke to his pride that he could scarcely brook; he learned also that he was installed as a member of the old man's family, and there also, his vanity suffered, for he had secretly resolved to offer himself to the fair Helen S., but something whispered "it is now too late, this fellow with such a piercing, yet gently melting eye, and such a noble form, and air of winning frankness and grandeur, will captivate her heart, and I, with all my wealth, will be cast into the shade of this child of poverty!"

Thus did envy begin its work—and thus they passed along for two years, when Norman was deemed competent to be admitted to the Bar of his native State, and Richland was also to present himself for admission.

Norman had toiled as only the persevering and earnest-hearted *can* toil, and yet he had found time to love and to gain a heart in return, or rather, this took no extra time, ere they were aware, the work was accomplished. "But," said he to himself, "not until I can release my sister from her arduous toil, and be able to maintain myself and her, will I dream of becoming a husband."

Helen S. had given him her heart, had promised him her hand, and her father approved it all. Norman heard frequently from his sister, and had once been to see her.—Their old nurse still lived, and Cornelia was still attending to the same duties as when he left. Elton they had not seen, and Benton was, it was said, living like a Prince on his estate, and all, introduced in this story, were busy in deeds yet to be brought to light—none forgetting the rest—none idle; and, *consciously* or *unconsciously*, each was helping to weave a web that encircled them all in its tangled meshes.

Would'st thou from sorrow find a sweet relief?
Or is thy heart oppressed with woes untold?
Balm would'st thou gather for corroding grief?
Pour blessings round thee like a shower of gold.
'Tis when the rose is wrapped in many a fold
Close to its heart, the worm is wasting there
Its life and beauty; and when, all unrolled,
Leaf after leaf, its bosom, rich and fair,
Breathes freely its perfumes throughout the ambient air.

C. Wilcox.[26]

For the Offering.

The Little Coal-Heaver.[27]

By Jenny.

Chapter II.

The day was drawing to a close. The wind which had been blowing from the south-east, had shifted round to the north and gave promise of a bitter cold night.

Mrs. Bates sat in her own room, waiting for her *protégé* to finish his supper, hoping that by the time this was accomplished he would be sober enough to converse, intelligibly. She was as yet, ignorant of the distance he lived from town, so she had him called in to receive his pay, when the following dialogue ensued.

Mrs. B. How far do you live from town Mr. Higgins?

26. American poet Carlos Wilcox (1794–1827) served as a Congregationalist minister in Connecticut in the 1820s. Often republished between 1828 and 1849, these lines are a canto in his long poem, "The Religion of Taste." See *Remains of the Rev. Carlos Wilcox* (Hartford: Edward Hopkins, 1828), 206, Google Books, http://books.google.com/books?id=v384AAAAYAAJ.

27. For more of this and Jenny, see n. 12, p. 189.

Hig. About two miles madam, I live at the upper diggins, my cabin stands on the right side of the hill.

Mrs. B. I think I heard you saying something of your wife's illness, has she been a long while sick and what is the nature of her disease?

Hig. Well madam, I should think she *was* sick, she's been 'flicted these four years—she catched a violent cold crossin the mountains comin to this state and she haint seen a well day since.

Mrs. B. I hope your neighbors are kind to her and visit her often. I saw six or seven cabins at the upper banks last summer. You have neighbors have you not?

Hig. Neighbors madam! a plenty on em sich as they are—I don't want to say nothin about nobody; but they are a poor drunken set, cusin, swearin and fighten all the time. I don't want any sich *cattle* to come there to disturb my wife, and teach my children their bad tricks, no,—nobody comes to see her—my biggest gal does all that is done for her Mother, and that aint much for the poor thing haint got anything to do with.

Mrs. B. Does she suffer very acute pain so as to be unable to walk about and attend to her family?

Hig. Lord bless you madam, she can't walk a step, and she's lost the use of her right arm and then the way she screams when we try to turn her in bed, or even when we walk across the floor is terrifyin. It seems strange that hardly anybody cares for poor people, in this country—you're the only Lady that ever spoke a kind word to me since I left "Old Virginny."

Mrs. B. It is now getting late and is high time for you to be at home with your family; I have a few words of advice to give you which I hope you will take kindly as it is meant for your good.

Hig. Certainly madam, for I couldn't take anything unkindly that you should say to me; why you're the best Lady this side of old Virginny that I know.

Mrs. B. You are greatly mistaken sir, there are many Ladies in town, who would have done more for you than I possibly can, had you fallen in with them as you did with me.

Hig. No—no madam, that can't be possible. Who'd have bought my coal? fed my hoss, given me my supper and—

Mrs. B. I insist upon being heard sir—you seem to be a man of sense and intelligence; and it gives me much pleasure to hear you express yourself so feelingly about your family. You seem to despise your neighbors on account of their low vices and will not permit your wife to be annoyed, nor your children contaminated by their coarse and vulgar conversation; why is it then that you indulge so freely in one of the vices that you condemn in others?—This to say the least of it is very inconsistent Mr. Higgins.

Hig. I know it good Lady, I know it.

And here he became so choked with emotion that he could say no more. The whole group stood in perfect silence for some moments—at last the poor fellow wiped his eyes on his ragged sleeve and tried to compose himself to listen to Mrs. B.

Mrs. B. I don't wish to hurt your feelings, by any means, but I *do wonder* that a man, so sensible of his responsibilities, should pursue a course, so eminently calculated to defeat his own purposes. It is as much as a man can do, to support a family in this country by labor, even with the use of all his faculties, mental and physical; and that too, with the assistance of his wife, supposing her to be in perfect health. But, by an indulgence in the use of ardent spirits, you not only deprive yourself of the ability to support, but even protect them from the *encroachments* and injurious influence of the low people by whom you are surrounded.

Higgins. You can't understand it, I know, and it's impossible for you to know anything about it without seein' the inside of a poor coal heaver's cabin, that's fix'd as I am, and if it won't be axin' too much, for you to listen, I'll tell you in ten *minutes* how it happened that I got to be sich a beastly drunkard as I have bin for about three years.

Mrs. B. Go on, sir, I'll listen, for I am really anxious to know.

Hig. Well, when I first come to this town four years ago last spring, I was a stranger, fifty cents was all the money I had, I had hard work to find a shelter for my family that night; for, if there had bin any empty houses, nobody could expect me to pay rent, and jist as I was about to give up to stay in the street, I met a colored man, as *you* call 'em, in *this* country, in old Virginny we call 'em "niggers." He was a mighty decent, well dressed fellow, and so says I, "Mister," says I, "can you tell me where I can git a place to put my family into for a day or two; I'm a stranger, just landed from old Virginny. My woman and two of the children's sick, and I've got no money, and it's most night, and here we are in the street." "Well," says he, "you are in a *bad fix*, sure enough, and it looks mightily like for rain—and, I was a goin' to say, if you'd stay all night with a man of my color, why you'r quite welcome, and it'll be better than to stay in the street, any how."

Mrs. B. And you accepted his hospitality, did you not sir?

Hig. In course I did, madam. I could'nt do nothin' else.—Well, he led the way to his house, and he called his wife and a couple of his gals out, to help get us all into the house, and it was well we got in as soon as we did, for sich thunder and lightnin', and sich hard rain and hail, as we had that night, I never saw in my life. I had one hoss and a little waggon. The same that I have yet—he found a shelter for both, and put me and my family into a room by ourselves. And I declare I was overpowered, and could'nt help cryin', to think that a black man, showin' sich kindness to me a stranger, when nobody else seemed to care, nor hardly took the trouble to answer me when I'd ax 'em about a house. Well, the black critters did all in their power. They made my wife some tea, give us all somethin' to eat, and help't wash the children, and put 'em to bed. After my folks were all asleep but me, I could'nt sleep for thinkin' how good the Lord was, in directin' my course so as to fall in with that black man, for I found out that he was a Methodist preacher, by the name of Smith. You see, I was a Methodist class leader in Virginny. Well, as I was sayin', I was a lyin' wide awake when I heard Smith a readin' a chapter. After that they begun to sing.

The day is past and gone, the evenin' shadows appear,
Oh may we all remember well, the night of death is near.[28]

And sich a prayer as that man made! and the way he did pray for the poor stranger fallen in with him!! Well, I got up by times in the mornin', and the weather was fine, it was in the latter part of May; there was a heap of houses about bein' put up, and Smith told me to go and try to git work, and my folks might stay where they were till I got another place.—When I'd ask if they wanted a hand to carry the hod, or to haul sand, or to clear away rubbish, they all told me I was too small a man to be able to do a big day's work. Some laughed at me, and ax'd me if they wer'nt all *giants* where I come from; and in a little while there was a set of the onmanerliest boys, all around me, whoopin' and hollerin' and called me Goliah, and Jack the Giant Killer,[29] that I was almost disheartened, for I had to put up with everything and there was no help for it.

28. A hymn; for the full lyrics see *The Christian Psalmist, A Collection of Tunes and Hymns* (Louisville, Kentucky: S. W. Leonard, 1854), 275, Google Books, http://books.google.com/books?id=4sgBVwaK8aAC.

29. "Goliah" is an alternate spelling of "Goliath," the giant warrior of the Old Testament. See 1 Samuel 17. "Jack the Giant Killer" is an eighteenth-century English folk tale that was perhaps universally

At noon when I met Smith agin I told him all about it. The poor feller was sorry, shook his head, and says he, I see but one chance for you Mr. Higgins and that is, to dig coal. You get one third of all you dig, and you have a hoss and waggon, and there's a bank above town; and they have put up half a dozen cabins for the families of the diggins; you can bring your coal to town and I'll always buy yours, while I stay here; but I shall be sent away next year, to preach on some other circuit. Well the good feller went out to the banks, with me and saw my family safe landed in one of the cabins. And as long as I live I shall never forgit that black critter and his wife, they were so clever. We were glad to find five or six families was all settled round, within about ten rod of one another, and close as that to my cabin. They seemed mighty civil at fust, but in a few days, I saw by the children what the old ones must be; and I soon found them to be jist what I told you a while ago; a poor drunken set. They *ruined* me madam; they actually ruined me. Well, as I told you, Becky, that Mrs. Higgins, was sick when I went there, but she made out to get round, and keep things snug, and keep the children in, till towards winter, when she got so bad with *pains* in her limbs and swellin' in her joints, that she give up all hopes of bein' anythin' but a poor cripple all her days. She'd lay and cry, and fret to see the children look so dirty and ragged.

Continued.

To Our Readers.

The sixth Number of the Offering is at hand and contains, like its predecessors, "Tales, Essays and Poetry." We are sorry that Mr. Moore is so *dreadfully* shocked at the *light reading* found in this humble work; but hope that a self-complacent glance at his own *wonderful* productions, exhibited in his *matchless* Magazine, will counteract the sad effects he has experienced and that he will be able to remain as *powerful* an advocate of all that is good, as *convincing* a denouncer of all that is bad, and as much a *real gentleman* as he has ever been, and we shall go on our way, rejoicing that we can expect such *condescending courtesy* from so distinguished a personage as the *gallant* Editor of "I Have Come."[30]

known in the 1840s. For a full, scholarly edition of this time, see James Orchard Halliwell, *Popular Rhymes and Nursery Tales* (London: John Russell Smith, 1849), 60–77, Google Books, http://books.google.com/books?id=FoP4O6K5zIAC.

30. For more on Cumings and Moore, see p. 453–57.

We feel under many obligations to the Author of the first piece in this Number, and hope that these humble pages may be honored again by him, and that what he has written will be appreciated as it should be.

We are grateful to Lily Lute that amid all her cares, she does not forget the lowly Offering. Shall hope for a second letter from her in season for the seventh Number.

Clarissa Clairmont also has our thanks, shall hope to hear again.

The second chapter of the "Little Coal-Heaver" is excellent and all that is to come we know will be worthy the perusal of all.

Abby Viola's song to her husband was, by mistake, left out of this No. will appear in the next. J.R. S——y will please let us know the name of the Author of the article sent to us from those initials. P——e. H. also will send us a name, both articles are good.

C. Cumings.

THE
AKRON OFFERING.
November, 1849.

Norman and Cornelia Campbell,
OR
"Truth Stranger Than Fiction."

By C. Cumings.

Chapter VII.

The day of trial for Virgil Richland and Norman Campbell came. The former was rejected, the latter admitted; and then did revenge assume a tangible form, and was admitted to Richland's heart as a precious guest; but he waited the proper time. Years passed on, and his only business was to seek in every possible manner, to sully young Campbell's rising fame. To help him, he gained a willing assistant in a widowed sister-in-law of Mr. S., who had recently come to New York, from one of our southern cities. She was poor, but ambitious and designing, and had one son, a profligate wretch, who had spent the largest part of a fortune left him by his Father, and also nearly all his Mother's fortune. He called himself a gentleman; boasted of his manners—of his success in gaining young Ladies' hearts—of his pure, Aristocratic blood—and seemed to look with the utmost contempt on every person he considered not of as high lineage as himself. Norman Campbell, he particularly despised—"he is a narrow-souled Yankee," said he, "poor as poverty can make him, and he need not think that from the low, filthy class, where he originated, he can emerge to the light of refinement that spreads itself around *my* path! Poor fool that he is! When *his* ancestors were cringing and crawling in the lowest departments of *trade*, to amass wealth, a sixpence at a time,[1] Norman Campbell's were moving among the most highly honored of their native land, allied by blood to 'Scotia's' Kings, and by noble deeds to every soul of pure, unsullied honor.

Trace them farther down. When Algernon Sheldon's Grandfather, by dint of miserly meanness, was able to load a vessel with merchandize, and sail to Virginia, endeavoring to pass himself off as an *Aristocrat* from the mighty city of London, and something altogether better than could be found in the New World, Norman Campbell's Grandfather, beside many honors that clustered thickly around him, was the possessor of wealth that far exceeded his—while Algernon Sheldon's Father was weak and irresolute, spending his time with his hounds and horses, and his drinking, sporting, companions, Norman's Father was decking his brow with the unfading laurels bestowed on votaries of wisdom, science and virtue. Algernon's Father died while sitting by his Goblets of Liquor—his companions round him—the mark of the beast left full on his features.[2] Norman's Father, though young, and dying suddenly, was honored and lamented, and in his features, even when dead, might be seen something that told of truth, of honor, and of sterling integrity. And Algernon Sheldon himself—how had he lived? sunk in the lowest depths of vice—and yet he dared to try and treat Norman Campbell as an inferior.

His Mother and Richland seconded him in every thing he did to injure Norman, or rather, it might be said, his Mother suggested every thing, and he followed as she dictated. She was resolved that he should marry Helen, or in some way become his Uncle's heir. Richland discovered this,

1. A sixpence is half a shilling. The United States switched to Federal money after the Revolution, but the habit of quoting prices in shillings persisted in the 1840s. The value of a shilling varied from region to region. According to Frederick Emerson's *North American Arithmetic* (Boston: Jenks and Palmer, 1842), a "shilling" meant 16 2/3 cents in New England, Virginia, Kentucky, and Tennessee; 13 1/3 cents in Pennsylvania, New Jersey, Delaware, and Maryland; 12 1/2 cents in New York and North Carolina, and 21 3/7 cents in South Carolina and Georgia. See p. 61. Google Books, http://books.google.com/books?id=prk2AAAAMAAJ.

2. Revelation 13:16–17. The biblical sense of the phrase has been interpreted in many ways. Here it appears to be used in a manner, common for the period, that is well illustrated by this passage from Ralph Waldo Emerson's 1841 lecture, "Spiritual Laws": "A man passes for that he is worth. What he is, engraves itself on his face, on his form, on his fortunes, in letters of light which all men may read but himself. Concealment avails him nothing; boasting, nothing. There is confession in the glances of our eyes; in our smiles; in salutations; and the grasp of hands. His sin bedaubs him, mars all his good impression. Men know not why they do not trust him; but they do not trust him. His vice glasses his eye, demeans his cheek, pinches the nose, sets the mark of the beast on the back of the head, and writes O fool! fool! on the forehead of a king." See Emerson, *Essays* (Boston: James Munroe, 1841), 130–31, Google Books, http://books.google.com/books?id=GloJAAAAQAAJ.

and although he would fain[3] have gained Helen for himself, he felt that to see Norman Campbell ruined, he would give up every thing of hope or happiness; but he felt that, farther than to wound his feelings, they had no power—as long as he could be seen and heard, there was a living, breathing truth, about him, that contradicted every thing they could say.

He was trying to arrange some plan to accomplish his purpose, when he met William Benton, and they felt that they were necessary to each other. The object of each was the same, and neither cared by what means brought about. Richland listened to Benton's plans and felt that they would succeed. Every effort to produce any belief of Norman's unworthiness on Helen or her Father, or any but those envious of his brilliant talents and glorious success, had failed; but he now congratulated himself, and could scarcely wait until their plans could be put in operation.

Before the effects of their schemes were visible, Helen's Father died very suddenly, and Mrs. Sheldon, his Brother's widow, insisted that Helen should take up her abode with her, as she was the only female relative she had in the city. Helen felt the propriety of this, and yet, although she did not understand her Aunt's intentions, she disliked her, and could not but despise her cousin Algernon's character, and felt a dread creeping over her as she entered their house; but her Aunt understood human nature, and knew how to make Helen feel that Algernon's faults were of no account against him; they only marked him as the *high-born gentleman*, and thus she succeeded in making her, in some sense, a dupe to her heartlessness; but nothing could shake her faith in Norman Campbell, or change her love for him, and as they did not expect to be united for several years, Mrs. S. contented herself with the hope that they would in some way, be finally separated.

Norman Campbell took lodgings at a tavern, and although he could see Helen but seldom, on account of her Aunt's management to prevent their meeting, he had no doubt of her love or constancy, and though the wealth that it was expected was now hers, would have placed them above every embarrassment, he would not marry until, from his own property, he could secure and maintain an establishment worthy of Helen and his dear Sister, who had all her life suffered so much, and so nobly discharged every trying duty.

About this time he was informed, without any suspicion of design in the information, that a certain tract of land could be purchased on long credit,

3. Fain: gladly.

and on such very low terms that, beyond a doubt, a short time would enable the purchaser to realize a handsome sum in the advanced price for which it might be sold; seeing no *probable* risk, he purchased the land, and not many weeks has passed, before he was told that a gentleman in the city inquiring for the owner of that land with a view to buy it, and soon after, a written offer was brought to him by one who was his friend, and who saw nothing in this but an opportunity for him to realize a large sum by its sale. He agreed if the man brought the specified amount, he would give him a deed of the land and, very soon, a stranger stood before him, who gave him his name, secured a deed of the land, and paid the money for it as he had agreed.

Norman immediately paid for the land—the amount specified when he purchased it—and prepared to visit his sister, intending to persuade her to come to the city with him, as she had informed him of the death of their nurse and he hoped to be able to provide for her as she deserved. He started on his journey for that purpose, and now we will leave him and hasten to Cornelia.

She has just recovered from a long sickness occasioned by over-exertion of mind and body. Mentally and physically she had suffered much more than her brother had ever even dreamed, and now as you look at her, she seems strangely excited. She is reading a letter and near her sits a man whom you recognize as Francis Lisbon; the last you saw of him before, he was with William Benton, his pliant slave; but now he is evidently, a friendly messenger to Cornelia Campbell, and that letter is from her Brother and she grows paler and paler as she reads and comprehends the intelligence it conveys to her.

And what is it that can work on her feelings and rouse her to sudden energy of purpose as she finishes it and so closely questions the old man by her side? Reader, that letter tells her that her brother is confined within the walls of a prison, by the ingrate Benton, on a charge of fraud and false representation in the sale of the land above mentioned—their plan *had* in a measure succeeded, and Benton and Richland now believed that his utter ruin was certain. Mrs. S. and her son were rejoicing that so much was accomplished and deemed it best to keep Helen in ignorance until after his trial. She did not expect to see him for some weeks, perhaps months, as she believed him gone to his sister, and as he was arrested a considerable distance on his journey, and was not in the city, they found it easy to keep this knowledge from her.

Benton, in his joy, forgot to be generous to old Francis, and beside this, the old man's heart was touched. He visited Norman in his prison, and told him all the truth; adding, that he would carry a letter to Cornelia, and if the old hermit of the Glen was still alive, would seek to persuade him to add his testimony, which must be of the greatest importance, as he was no other than the guilty Friedland.

It was not Norman Campbell alone that Benton was determined to destroy; he was preparing to send his own emissaries to the home he had made desolate, to bring Cornelia to himself. All this Francis Lisbon had learned, and he hastened as fast as his age would permit, to warn Cornelia of her danger, and of what was preparing for her Brother, and to assist her to thwart the plans laid by Benton and Richland. Her Brother had, in his letter, instructed her how to proceed, and desired her, if possible, to be present at his trial at such a time, telling her when, adding that he hoped much for her and for himself, and trusted all to her prudence and energy.

She had always been afraid of the old hermit of the Glen; but she felt that she must seek him even in his strange abode, and with no attendant but old Francis, she immediately set out. When they reached the cave where she had been told he lived, a sickening fear, for a moment, took possession of her whole being; but by a strong effort she shook it off and followed old Francis into the rude door which was open, and a horror almost froze her heart as she gazed on the form of Friedland who looked more like a skeleton than a living man, and evidently could not stir from his couch. He glared upon them, but seemed unable to speak; they gave him some cold water that old Francis found in a beautiful spring not far from the door, and he seemed somewhat revived. Cornelia went herself to the village and brought wine and some light nourishment, and after a time, he spoke, indistinctly at first, but at last clearly, and told her all his guilt, all the truth from the commencement of the wrongs done to her friends "and," said he, "in yonder box," (pointing to a small one almost hid in a niche in the rock,) "is proof of all I say—I am about to die—starved in my old age by one who but for me would have had nothing but disgrace—yes, William Benton forsook me, and left me without one cent to save my life. When the little I had saved was exhausted, I laid down here to die, for I could not go to the village, and for weeks I have been thus helpless, and I could not die until I could feel that I had done one act of justice. Hasten for a Magistrate. Let it be witnessed that as I die, I testify to the truth of what the manuscript in that box contains."

Cornelia herself, went for a Magistrate whom she could trust, and there in that abode of horror, did the wretched Friedland testify as he desired, and then did she learn, not only every thing done to injure her Father, her Uncle and her Brother, but also the means that were used to prejudice Elton's mind against herself; but as she looked on the tortured soul before her, her heart melted in pity for his sufferings. A man, almost a hundred years of age, had retained every faculty of mind necessary to the most acute suffering, and there he lay, moaning in unutterable anguish, breathing imprecations against all who had sanctioned his course of life—and thus he died—no light from the spirit world beaming on his path through the dark valley, no convoy of angels hovering near to bear him to a blissful home beyond the swelling waves of Jordan; but, to his distempered vision, was revealed grim, horrid demons, scarce waiting for the quivering breath to leave the shrunk and famished clay, e'er they should claim the writhing, shrinking, shrieking soul—yes, such a death-bed, did such a life as his had been, procure; and whether there was hope beyond the grave or not, *he* knew none, saw none, felt that there was none, and thus passed away.

Cornelia could not look upon him in his last, agonizing moments, but turned away in sad reflection. Had no peril menaced her Brother of herself, she would have been entirely overcome, but prompt action, and that rightly directed, could alone save them, and after Friedland ceased to breathe, she hastened back to the village to prepare disguises suitable for herself and old Francis, while the Magistrate who was present, took it upon himself to see that Friedland was decently interred. He also proffered his services to accompany them on their journey, and promised to protect old Francis from the vengeance of Benton.

The next day every thing was ready, and the three started in the quickest conveyance then to be obtained. Cornelia secured the box given her by Friedland, arranged every thing to ensure their not being recognised, if met by Benton or his agents, and then gave herself up to thought.

Without alarm or accident, they arrived at the town where Norman was confined, and through the kindness of his friends, were admitted to him, without being seen by Benton and without his being apprised of their arrival. Strange and conflicting feelings agitated the hearts of that Brother and Sister—sorrow had bowed them low; but amidst it all, sweet hope shed its cheering beams. They wept in each other's arms, but as soon as their feelings were calmed, Cornelia gave her Brother the box given her by Friedland, and they proceeded to examine its contents, assisted by the man who had accompanied her there. The manuscript furnished abundant proof of what the reader of this story has long been aware, viz. that the land purchased by Wm. Benton's Grandfather was paid for, by money that belonged to the Campbells alone—the robbery of the bags of gold was committed by Friedland, instigated by William's Grandfather also, and that William Benton himself had kept this immense wealth to himself, after having been fully made acquainted with the facts by Friedland and old Francis—also, that the property that their Uncle had, when intoxicated, made over to Henry Herbert, had never been paid for by him or Benton. George Campbell *was* indebted to Henry Herbert in a small sum, and was made to believe that he must give him a deed to all this property to liquidate the debt. William Benton, by previous arrangement with Herbert, substituted his own name, instead of Herbert's, and thus hoped to place them all in his own power. It was Friedland who set the fires that destroyed the property of the Campbell's, and the lives of Albert Campbell and his wife, instigated in this also, by the same wretch, Wm's. Grandfather who forgot his caution, drank to intoxication, and perished in the flames.

"Besides all this," said Norman, "old Francis has brought me a man who will testify that he heard the arrangement made between William Benton, Richland, and the man to whom I sold the land—that Benton gave him the money to pay for it, and was to pay him five hundred dollars to follow his directions and be quiet, and with all this proof of their villainy I am content to meet them; yes, I long for the time to come, when he will be seen as he is, and Richland too, will learn a useful lesson."

It wanted but a few days to the sitting of the court, and all their fear was, that Benton might learn of what old Francis had done, and that they were in possession of proof of the truth; but Norman quietly prepared to defend himself, and also to arrest Benton as soon as the proper moment should arrive.

Continued.

"The Norwegians, proud of their barren summits, inscribe upon their rix dollars—'spirit, loyalty, valor, and whatever is honorable, let the world learn among the rocks of Norway.'"[4]

4. This sentence by British writer Charles Bucke (1781–1846) was republished several times without attribution in American magazines and anecdote collections. The original is in Bucke's *The Philosophy of Nature; or, The Influence of Scenery on The Mind and Heart* (London: John Murray, 1813), 2:138, Google Books, http://books.google.com/books?id=wv4LAAAAMAAJ. Bucke has "rix-dollars" and

For the Offering.

Never Despair.

"None e'er drank a cup of earthly sort,
That might not hold another drop of gall:
The saddest human look,
Has hope in't: faint, indeed, but still 'tis hope."—Pollok.[5]

Though clouds and storms surround thy sky,
And all looks dark and drear,
Though Life's fond hopes all blighted lie,
Crushed by the spoiler here;
And friends who flattered once, have proved
Unkind and false to thee,
And those who once so warmly loved,
Now pass with coldness by;

Yet yield not thou to dark despair,
Think not, no sunny ray
Will e're arise to brightly cheer,
Life's rough and thorny way.
Hast thou one heart that loves thee still,
One, 'mid the desert gloom,
Whose tender chords will kindly thrill
To sweet affection's tone;

To whom with fond, confiding love,
You can each thought reveal,

"whole world." Cumings' text follows other copies. See, for example, John Frost's *The Book of Good Examples; Drawn from Authentic History and Biography; Designed to Illustrate the Beneficial Effects of Virtuous Conduct* (New York: Appleton, 1846), 71, Google Books, http://books.google.com/books?id=ipkMAAAAYAAJ. Here Bucke's sentence is plagiarized as the final paragraph in an essay on "Love of Country."

5. Passage from Book 9 of *The Course of Time* (1827), a popular ten-book epic poem by British poet Robert Pollok (1798–1827). Note the original is "And man ne'er," not "none"; the look "Had hope in't" and it still "'twas hope," not "'tis hope." Also "Adelia" omits more than three lines between "gall" and "the saddest look." Perhaps Adelia intends to improve the original with such changes. Or maybe she is copying from a corrupt copy or reciting from imperfect memory. Or perhaps such alterations arise from the compositor failing to read her handwriting. For example, see *Pollok's Course of Time,* 4th American ed. (Amherst: J. S. and C. Adams, 1828), 276, Google Books, http://books.google.com/books?id=j6xUAAAAYAAJ.

Whose Friendship will more constant prove,
With life's increasing ill;
One lovely flower that brightly blooms,
To deck thy cheerless home,
That richly sheds its sweet perfumes,
And smiles for thee alone;

One gentle star to guide thy way,
O'er life's tumultuous wave,
To still shine on with undimmed ray,
Though tempests wildly rave;
One crystal fountain flowing near,
Amid the dreary waste,
Whose cooling waters—sweet and clear,
Refresh thy longing taste;

One bright oasis 'mid the gloom,
That shrouds all else in night;
That to the wanderer, sad and lone,
Brings joy and fresh delight;
One tranquil voice thy heart to cheer,
With sorrow's weight oppres'd,
To kindly dry the falling tear,
When anguish fills the breast.

Till that sweet flower is faded,
And perished from thy sight,
Till that bright star is shaded,
By clouds of darkest night;
Till that warm heart is rudely crushed,
By cold, relentless tread,
And that lov'd voiced in silence hushed,
And numbered with the dead;

Till that clear, springing fount is dry,
And dark that sunny spot,
Oh, ever pass regardless by
Life's woes, and heed them not.

Above its threat'ning storms and frowns,
 Bright rainbows tints appear,
Sweet Hope, with Angel smile, looks down,
 And whispers, ne'er despair.

Adelia.
Lancaster, Ohio, Oct. 6, 1849.[6]

Letters to the Offering.

Number II.

By Lily Lute.

My Dear Offering:—To-day I have been wandering by meadow and hamlet, over hill-tops and vallies, through orchards, among the heaps of red, green and golden colored apples, and away to the gay old woods; where, with canvass, palette, colors and brushes, I attempted to paint some heavy masses of foliage which yet hang in all their gorgeous beauty; but with all my "mimic skill," I could not "copy the refulgent dye,"[7] to produce the desired effect in a picture. And the cause of my failure was, I did not feel in a mood for painting, there in that deep solitude, amid the relics of the dead summer—that was a place to think! to think of the past, of departed friends; and I did think sadly and tenderly of one with whom I had loved to climb the woodland hill, to sit beneath the shade of some branching tree, and I with my pencil to sketch the far-spreading, lovely landscape, while he would clothe the same subject in the most beautiful words, stopping ever and anon, to help me on with my

6. The prosperous capital of Fairfield County, Ohio, Lancaster lay about one hundred miles southwest of Akron in a "beautiful and fertile valley" on the Hocking River, which drains to the Ohio. In 1850, the Hocking Canal connected Lancaster to the Ohio and Erie Canal and thus to Akron. Lancaster, with about 3500 residents, had more population than Akron. The only "Adelia" of Lancaster in the 1850 United States Federal Census is Adelia A. Embrick, the twenty-four-year-old wife of William Embrick, a fairly prosperous shoemaker. See United States of America, Bureau of the Census, *Seventh Census of the United States, 1850*. NARA microfilm publication M432. (Washington, D.C.: National Archives and Records Administration, n.d.), roll M432_677, page 298A and roll M432_717, page 195B, Ancestry.com. American Periodicals Series Online appears to yield no other publications by this "Adelia," and of course "Adelia" may have been a pseudonym. For more poetry by Adelia, see pp. 292, 325, 411 and 429.

7. The lines "Can the pencil's mimick skill / Copy the refulgent dye?," come from the "Evening" section of "Day: A Pastoral" by Irish poet John Cunningham (1729?–73). See Cunningham, *The Poetical Works* (Edinburgh: The Martins, 1781), 93, Google Books, http://books.google.com/books?id=JgsUAAAAQAAJ. Written when Cunningham was about twelve years old, this poem was often quoted and anthologized in the nineteenth century.

sketch. We were old friends, dear old friends of "lang syne,"[8] when Hope was young and danced gaily along the flowery path before us. Alas! Hope grew faint and was often hid by brambles that began to grow up beside our pathway, and our path grew thorny and finally opened upon a broad, rough road, where we each took our way, and in our after journey have not often met. If I ever saw a Genius, he was one; and possessed more native talent and fine feelings than any person I have ever known. He was a poet of the first class, and a splendid prose writer, besides possessing a remarkable talent for painting. In person he was comely, in conversation witty, intelligent and pleasing; brave in danger but sensitive and shrinking from public opinion, and often in company as timid as a very girl. But he has gone the way of all the earth. He died lately, in the summer of life, while yet the bloom of manhood was fresh on his brow; and I mourned for him as a sister would mourn for a dear brother, for a brother he was in spirit. He was almost the first person that had discovered anything pleasing through my plain exterior, and O! how much I thanked him for it—how I joyed that I had found a kindred soul among mortals—and one too, that could be interested in poor me, who had ever been passed by for those on whom nature had lavished her showy gifts, and often I sighed for that celestial gift that seemed to attract all hearts; for I felt that I had as warm a heart, as good feelings and as bright an intellect, as many a beauty whose lightest smile was received as a great favor by her worshippers; among whom I generally saw men of talent and high attainments; then happy was I to find one of them that could turn aside from the glittering throng, come down from his dignity and acknowledge that women *sometimes* had minds as well as the lords of creation.[9] And he was the only Genius I ever saw that was not captivated by every pretty face he met, or that could find anything agreeable in a plain person. How often I have wondered to see men of mighty minds, united with the most silly, senseless, soulless women;—women whose highest aims were to wear the finest dresses and show the prettiest faces—and if by dint of powdering, painting, puffing and maneuvering, they could win a few compliments from the butterfly beaux, they would feast on them for weeks. Do not suppose, from what I say, that I pretend to despise

8. Long ago.

9. Generally, a reference to the descendents of Adam, to mankind, to the people, according to the common American Christian view of the day, put on the earth to rule over God's creation. By the late 1840s, however, the phrase was often used by women to jeer the collective self-importance of men. It appears this way, for example, in a poem read at the July 1848 convention on Woman's Rights in Seneca Falls, New York. Titled "The Times That Try Men's Souls" and written by Philadelphia's Maria W. Chapman, the poem explains that "So freely" do women "move in their chosen ellipse, / The 'Lords of Creation' do fear an eclipse." This poem was republished in numerous magazines.

beauty, for with the eye of an artist I could not. No—I love, I admire beauty in everything, from the tiny flower to the human face divine. A ruddy sunset, a lovely landscape, a fine picture, and everything beautiful in nature or art I love; but no embellishments of art can beautify the face: paint may cover, furs may shade, plumes may wave, silks may rustle, and jewels may flash, yet through all these, looks out the face more hideous still for the beauty that surrounds it: paint cannot brighten the eye or change the expression; beauty comes from within, and if there is not a beautiful soul shining through, no outside ornament can make it lovely. A face is never beautiful to my eye, where it is only the depth of roses and lilies that bloom on the complexion: there must be a beautiful mind beaming out at the eyes, opening the lips and lighting up the whole face, or there is no beauty. In my sojourns in different places, I have often been astonished to find the whole society of a town, ruled almost exclusively by a belle, in whose milk and water face[10] I could not glean one gleam of intelligence—it was as inexpressionless, as a blank drawing-book—and yet they would declare she was divinely beautiful and accomplished. Accomplished! and what could she do? perhaps she could sing, for nature had given her a voice and it required very little exertion to use it, and perhaps she could dance most gracefully too,—so much for the poetry of sound and motion—both well enough if she could do anything else. Well, perhaps she could stitch away her precious time, in stitching her precious life into a piece of cloth, with various colored worsteds, making awkward looking things she called pictures! O, deliver my eyes from looking on such pictures often. But could she read understandingly? O, she had not need of that to show off with, besides her mother who was her prototype, had told her that it would dim the brilliancy of her beautiful eyes to read much. Could she write and speak her own language correctly? Why, she could write well enough to place her name on a card, in letters that looked as though they had been set in stocks;[11] and as regarded speaking, what little she said, she could roll out with such a pudding accent[12] as was *delightful* to hear; and if she did

10. An insulting expression; "milk and water" suggests a lack of substance, weakness, feebleness, or wishy-washiness. The expression alludes to a common beverage—weak, diluted milk. Pure milk was relatively expensive and rare in the 1840s. Little Rollo of Jacob Abbott's didactic children's fiction orders "milk and water" with his first dinner at a busy inn. See Jacob Abbott, *Rollo's Travels* (Boston: William Crosby, 1840), 35, Google Books, http://books.google.com/books?id=e_AXAAAAYAAJ.

11. "Stocks" are heavy timbers that fit together and lock about the hands or feet to subject a person to public viewing and various torments.

12. A "pudding accent" is a sickly-sweet, overfed mumbling. In Herman Melville's *Redburn* (1849), the first pawnbroker appraises the fowling-piece with an "Indian-pudding accent," a "peculiar" way of talking "as if he had been over-eating himself with Indian-pudding or some other plushy compound." See *Redburn: His First Voyage* (New York: Harper & Brothers, 1850), 32–33, Google Books, http://books.google.com/books?id=7sh2-5vM7mYC.

make little grammatical blunders they were winked at, *"she was so unsophisticated!"* All her studies, which were many while at school, had been dipped into lightly, most especially the common branches; her geographical knowledge was so wonderful, she was sure the Mammoth Cave was in Europe, and Niagara Falls in the city of New York.[13] Thus much for her intellectual acquirements—and what was her kitchen education? Kitchen! she would almost faint at the idea of soiling her delicate fingers with kitchen work—and as to sewing on coarse cloth, making shirts or any thing of the kind, it would be decidedly vulgar. The picture is not overdrawn, it is a lamentable truth; I am acquainted personally with ladies of this same description—and what are they good for? To make wives for the men that are dying for them? Useful wives indeed, they will make, and pretty mothers for a future generation—there are too many such mothers now, and the number is ever increasing. Alas for the fate of our Glorious Republic, if such are to be her mothers—we can almost see the end of it—for it is the mothers that make a nation wise, great and good. Had the men of the revolution such mothers, think you they would ever have achieved their Independence? No—great men ever have great mothers; examples of this we have everywhere. Our greatest men of the present day, are self-made, generally springing from the poor classes, and their histories will invariably tell that they had high minded, energetic mothers. I knew two brothers who were very skillful artists, and remarkably intelligent men—inquiring of one of their neighbors concerning the artists' family, he said "their father died when they were young, but their mother was a very eccentric, clever woman, possessing great energy of character;" and in describing her personal appearance, he said "she was very good looking, but had such a gait," imitating her as he walked across the room!—in a moment I recollected the artists both had the same peculiar gait, which was so very odd that it was a subject of remark wherever they appeared; and I have heard many a derisive laugh from the soap-lock dandies[14] as they passed, and seen

13. The Mammoth Cave is in Kentucky. The Niagara Falls are on the Niagara River, the border between Ontario and New York, between Lake Ontario and Lake Erie.

14. Some men styled their hair with soap in the 1840s. In a popular "soap-lock" style, the hair was cut short in the back and long in the front. The hair in front—long enough to come down to the ears or maybe the collar—was then parted in the middle and soaped to lie smooth and flat. In May 1844 Alexander Duncan, a Democratic Representative to Congress from Cincinnati, gave a speech declaring that "husbands shall be men; not things, but men; not wasp-waisted coxcombs and tight-laced soap-lock dandies." See Richard Hopwood Thornton, *An American Glossary* (Philadelphia: J. B. Lippincott, 1912), 2:826, Google Books, http://books.google.com/books?id=rokVAAAAYAAJ. John Russell Bartlett defines "soap-lock" as "a name given to a low set of fellows who lounge about the markets, engine-houses, and wharves of New York, and are always ready to engage in midnight rows or broils. It is, in fact, but another name for a Rowdy or Loafer. The name comes from their wearing long side locks, which they are said to smear with soap, in order to give them a sleek appearance."

many a pretty lady's pretty finger pointed in derision—poor simpletons! I would give more for one word from the object of their sport, than all their simpering lips could utter. We are all too easily attracted by the glitter of an object, and too careless to examine its purity—and this failing is more prevalent among the opposite sex than our own—the men generally lose their hearts through their eyes, while the women lose theirs through their ears—they listen as well as look. Men, too, are oftener actuated by impulse; they see a lady with a pretty face, graceful carriage and showy appearance, and they are desperately in love, without knowing whether she has a mind or heart—the ornament is so dazzling they cannot see that the jewel is false, that the gilding will in a few years wear off, and leave the sordid brass. The prettiest face must grow old and withered, and then if the possessor has not cultivated intellect, what a miserable companion for a person of sense—the beauty that charmed is gone, and of all the tiresome things in creation, a silly old woman is the most tiresome. Some men seem to fear clever women, and I have heard men of talent remark, that they would not have a talented woman, for such a one never had much heart—do they judge by themselves? If they do they are mistaken. I have always found the most talented women make the most affectionate wives and mothers. The best artist in America is a woman—she has painted this year's prize picture for the Cincinnati Art Union; the beauty of the piece I cannot find words to describe, but she has painted many others as beautiful.[15] I am intimately acquainted with her, and a more devoted wife I never saw. Many a lover of the art have I seen spellbound before the creations of her fancy, and yet they would make remarks on her personal appearance, and say that they would not have such a wife. No—they would never have a Genius, but a charming, helpless creature, in

---

See his *Dictionary of Americanisms: A Glossary of Words and Phrases, Usually Regarded as Peculiar to The United States* (New York: Bartlett and Welford, 1848), 319, Google Books, http://books.google.com/books?id=gWUPAAAAYAAJ.

15. Probably a hyperbolic reference to Cincinnati artist Lilly Martin Spencer (1822–1902), who conquered Cincinnati and had recently moved to New York City to compete with artists there. (Note that Lute writes about living in Cincinnati in the mid-1840s on pp. 387–93.) Spencer's whimsical, domestic style would undoubtedly appeal to Lily Lute. See Robin Bolton-Smith and William H. Truettner, *Lilly Martin Spencer: The Joys of Sentiment* (Washington: Smithsonian Institution Press, 1973). Cincinnati's Western Art Union opened to much fanfare in 1847. Like the American Art Union of New York City, its subscribers received a periodical, a specially-commissioned engraving, and a chance in a lottery to win one of the many individual pieces purchased and displayed by the Art Union. Their mission was not just to display and promote the work of American artists in a museum context but also to distribute their work into the area homes. In 1849 Spencer's "Life's Happy Hour" was reproduced as the engraving to be offered to all subscribers. See "The Western Art-Union," *The Literary World* 120 (May 19, 1849): 440, Google Books, http://books.google.com/books?id=HAYxAQAAMAAJ. Today the location of the original is not known. See April F. Masten, *Women Artists and Democracy in Mid-Nineteenth-Century New York* (Philadelphia: University of Pennsylvania Press, 2008), 263n52.

her innocent simplicity, all lovely and loving—did they but know that what a young girl is innocent simplicity, will in a wife be silly insipidity, perhaps they would pause awhile, and encourage their chosen ones to learn something useful: and as for loving, if a woman of talent and good sense cannot love, who can? What is love? "It consists not in raptures and enthusiasm; it is not to wander in the moonlight, to listen to the song of the nightingale, to kneel before the beloved, to look deep into the eyes of the beautiful maiden, to languish and pine for a kiss! No; *this* is not the art of love; to preserve its fire, its divine treasure; to carry its riches through life as if in pure gold: to spend it for him alone to whom the heart is devoted; to be always ready to sympathise, to smile, to weep, to assist, to counsel, to encourage, to alleviate; in short, to live with the beloved as he lives, and thus, by virtue of an indwelling of heavenly power, to preserve invariably a heavenward direction. And this art is the highest, the tenderest love. He or she who possesses it knows what love is."[16] Can a puny minded woman love thus, a husband whose capacities are far above hers? Can she sympathise, assist, counsel, encourage and alleviate when she cannot understand him? Ah! no—she is not a companion, she is only a toy, an ornament to show off his establishment. And when will this state of things be bettered? Not until men erect a standard of excellence, from which to choose wives, where worth is placed above beauty, then all will strive to reach that mark, and instead of adorning their person to the neglect of their minds, they will spend their time in acquiring useful knowledge.

Selected for the Offering.

A Psalm of Life.[17]

By H. W. Longfellow.

What the heart of the young man said to the Psalmist.

Tell me not in mournful numbers,
    Life is but an empty dream,

16. Quote from Leopold Shefer, *The Artist's Married Life: Being That of Albert Dürer.* Trans. J. R. Stodart (London: John Chapman, 1848), 173–74. Google Books, http://books.google.com/books?id=zKdbAAAAQAAJ. An extract with this passage was also published in *Gazette of the Union, Golden Rule, and Odd Fellows' Family Companion* 9, no. 9 (August 26, 1848): 157. Google Books, http://books.google.com/books?id=qSTnAAAAMAAJ. A few minor alterations have been made. For example, the original capitalizes many nouns and uses dashes. Lute's version also inserts the phrase "to look deep into the eyes of the beautiful maiden." This phrase is lifted from a sentence a few lines above the original quotation.

17. This version varies from the original mainly in punctuation and capitalization; all exclamation

For the soul is dead that slumbers,
    And things are not what they seem.

Life is real, life is earnest,
    And the grave is not its goal:
Dust thou art, to dust returnest,
    Was not spoken of the soul.

Not enjoyment and not sorrow,
    Is our destined end or way;
But to act that each to-morrow,
    Find us farther than to-day.

Art is long, and time is fleeting,
    And our hearts though stout and brave,
Still like muffled drums are beating
    Funeral marches to the grave.

In the world's broad field of battle,
    In the bivouac of life,
Be not like dumb, driven cattle,
    Be a hero in the strife.

Trust no Future, howe'er pleasant,
    Let the dead past bury its dead;
Act, act in the living Present,—
    Heart within, and God o'er head!

Lives of great men should remind us,
    We can make our lives sublime;
And departing, leave behind us
    Footsteps on the sands of time:

Footsteps, that perhaps another,
    Sailing o'er life's solemn main,

---

points, for example, have been replaced with less enthusiastic punctuation marks. Again we cannot know why these slight changes were made. They could be the result of a conscious, artistic re-working, or they could be the result of accident. See Henry Wadsworth Longfellow, *Voices of the Night* (Boston: Redding, 1845), 8–9, Google Books, http://books.google.com/books?id=UR4CAAAAYAAJ.

A forlorn and shipwrecked brother,
 Seeing, shall take heart again.

Let us then be up and doing,
 With a heart for any fate,
Still achieving, still pursuing,
 Learn to labor and to wait.

For the Offering.

Scenes in the Life of an Artist,
OR
The Power of Kindness Upon the Heart of a Child.

"Charles," said the teacher of some dozens of boys and girls, "you may bring me your Reader and I will point out your lesson, as you have been absent a day or two." The boy addressed, had just entered the room, and was now busy in marking a slate.[18]

He raised his eyes with a kind of indifferent stare on hearing his name pronounced, and presently proceeded to search for his book. It was soon found and brought to the Mistress. As she commenced turning the leaves, he recollected the pencilings he had made on almost every page, and quickly hung his head with shame. He had been severely reproved for defacing his books, and now perhaps a heavier punishment awaited him.

"Charles you have some fine drawings here,—did you do them all yourself?" Half raising his eyes, with his countenance plainly saying "Is it possible she will not scold me," he replied that he did.

"Some of your figures are very natural," she added; "there is a horse, did you not have a pattern to take it from?"

"I drew it from one I saw standing in the street," said he, almost ready to weep at this unexpected notice taken of his "scriblings," as they had always been called.

"I am glad that you can draw so correctly, and think your sketches deserve a better place than the blank leaves and edges of a book. Besides I don't think it quite neat, or in good taste, to mark thus what was given you for another purpose. You shall have some sheets of paper for drawing, and I should be much obliged if you would give me one of your pieces."

18. A smooth stone tablet for writing with chalk.

It is scarcely necessary to say that Charles was pleased with this request, and felt willing to do any thing his teacher desired. Though but ten years of age, he was well accustomed to the voice of disapprobation.

Of his father he had no recollection, and being deprived of his mother at the early age of four years, he was left almost penniless, to the cold charity of the world.

An Uncle, pitying his forlorn condition, received him to his family, but he understood not his disposition, or the character of his mind; and attributed his usual silence and timidity, to dullness and want of apprehension.[19] He was much annoyed by his inclination for sketching whatever he saw, and as he yielded to it without reference to time or place, he ascribed it to carelessness and a disposition to mar every thing he touched. Kindness, therefore, and encouragement in his favorite pursuit, were quite subduing.

Scene II.

"Brother, you have come just in time to accompany us," said Julia Hayes, as a youth of seventeen entered the apartment. "O yes," exclaimed Mary, "how glad I should be to have Henry with us," and she hastened to get her bonnet.

"I going too," said little Kate, as she received her brother's kiss. "I have been good to-day, & Julia promised Mary and me a walk."

"I should be pleased to be your gallant," said Henry, to Julia, "but before I promise my services, I will venture to ask, where you intend to take me."

"I want to visit the new Artist's rooms," said Julia, "and thought I would do so, to-day, if you came in season to attend us."

"O, that is a happy thought, I have been waiting for an opportunity to go there. Mr. Becworth says he is superior to any artist in the city. His pieces are all spoken of as very fine, especially his portraits. Is he an American? It is said, he is a native of this state, and that he resided a short time in this city some years ago, but he has since, spent a long time in Italy, and other parts of Europe."

Scene III.

"I understand you are having the portraits of your children painted by the new Artist," said Mrs. Blake after being seated in the parlor of Mrs.

19. Here a "want" is a deficiency or defect in something essential. In 1849 "apprehension," the act or power to perceive or comprehend, also meant originality, the ability of the mind to form new ideas, and more generally intellect, as measured by the ability to objectively contemplate something without passing judgment on it.

Hayes. "My children visited Mr. N.s' rooms several weeks ago, but not to sit for their portraits."

"Well it is very strange, my husband was there three days since and told me he was painting your children, all upon the same canvass, that it was admirably executed, and nearly finished."

"I am really surprised; but the painting is no doubt designed for some other family. Yet I should like to see it, if it bears so much resemblance to my children, and when Mr. Hayes returns I think I will."

Scene IV.

The artist is busily engaged. A gentleman stranger and lady with a little girl, enter his apartment. He exhibits his work. One piece after another is viewed,—some admired, some recognized as acquaintances. "Perhaps you would like to see this," at length said Mr. N., turning aside a curtain that concealed a large picture.

"O ma," exclaimed little Kate clapping her hands, "see! there is brother Henry, and Julia and Mary too! and Oh! this is my kitty! is'nt it mine pa? And who is it holding the kitty? is it me?" said she, looking at herself.

"I see," said Mr. Hayes with some emotion, "that you have painted correct portraits of my children, but for what purpose, I can't conceive."

"It is but just that I should explain myself sir, but first let me ask of your lady, if she recognizes a piece I have in this corner;" and he advanced to an obscure part of the room, and removed a curtain that concealed from view, a lady, evidently the Mistress of a school. Boys and girls were seated on opposite sides of the room. One boy stood before the teacher, looking very much like a culprit. The lady was just turning her eyes from a book to speak to the child. "Do you recognize that scene?" said Mr. N.

Mrs. Hayes looked bewildered, as if trying to recollect something long past. "The lady looks like the portrait you have painted of my daughter, but the place seems familiar to my own mind. Yes it must be, the same old fire-place, the seat in the corner, the desk,—it is, it must be, the school house in W., as it was more than 20 years ago."

"But do you recollect that boy, the careless scribbler standing before you? for you perceive that you are the mistress of this scene."

"Charles Norris?" said Mrs. Hayes, looking at Mr. N.

"Yes," he replied, "and that shame-faced boy has now the honor of standing before you, Charles Norris, the Artist."

"And now," he continued, after the first expressions of surprise and congratulation had passed, "allow me to present you with this representation of your lovely children, as a token of the respect and affection I have ever cherished for you. For what I am, I owe in a great degree to the encouragement you gave me, (the first I ever received,) when standing there before you. The instruction also which you subsequently bestowed, and the correct taste with which you judged of my pieces, and pointed out defects, aided me much."

"But how did you know Mrs. Hayes, to be the same person and how have you painted these portraits without the originals to sit for them," said Mr. Hayes.

"I will tell you," replied the artist. "I traced her history for some years, after she was my teacher, and knew her husband's name. Yet at length I lost sight of her. But after I went to Europe, I painted that scene in the school room from recollection, so deeply was it impressed on my mind. And I keep it to show to my friends, that they may see the point from which I have risen, and also that they may know something of the power a few words can exert over a child, either for good or evil."

"But I promised to tell you how I painted your children. A few weeks ago, when exhibiting my work to various callers, a young lady, accompanied by a youth and two little girls came in. I was at once reminded of my old teacher. I enquired their names; and soon learned they were your children. I then conceived this design; and by the aid of a friend well acquainted in your family, and by visiting the schools where your girls attend, and the office where you son is employed, I managed to see them when I wished."

This explanation given and the present accepted, Mr. and Mrs. Hayes returned to their home, happy in possessing so distinguished a friend, and more than ever impressed with the necessity of studying well the minds of children, that instruction adapted to their wants may be timely bestowed.

M. A. B.

Schoolcraft, Michigan.[20]

---

20. Schoolcraft lies in Kalamazoo County in southwestern Michigan, about 25 miles north of the Indiana line. This is not close to Akron. The quickest route to Schoolcraft may have been 30 miles north to Cleveland by canal, 100 miles by boat across Lake Erie to Detroit, and then about 130 miles by stagecoach over an old trans-territorial road that roughly follows present-day I-94. See J. H. Colton, *Colton's Traveler and Tourist's Guide-Book through the Western States and Territories* (New York: J. H. Colton, 1855), 78, Google Books, http://books.google.com/books?id=VVAVAAAAYAAJ. See also George Newman Fuller, *Economic and Social Beginnings of Michigan* (Lansing, Michigan: Wynkoop

Selected for the Offering.

Passing Away.

By Mrs. Jewsbury.[21]

I asked the stars, in the pomp of night,
Gilding its blackness with crowns of light,
Bright with beauty and girt with power,
Whether eternity were not their dower;
And dirge-like music stole from their spheres,
Bearing this message to mortal ears:—

Hallenbeck Crawford, 1916), lxv, Google Books, http://books.google.com/books?id=DmZ5AAAAMAAJ. In his 1854 *New and Complete Gazetteer* (Philadelphia: Lippincott, Grambo), Thomas Baldwin describes the Schoolcraft area as having fine soil, a village with many stores, and a population of 1101. See p. 1057; Google Books, http://books.google.com/books?id=_5s6AAAAcAAJ. This area had been recently settled by immigrants from the eastern United States who were attracted to its timber and its fertile plains and prairies. It is curious that *The Akron Offering* would receive a contribution from this place. The identity of the author is also intriguing. In the editorial that closes this number, Cumings addresses the author as "Miss B." and suggests that her station in life makes it difficult, unlikely, or perhaps selfish ("inconsistent" with what she owed her another—with her "duties") that she would take the time to write enough to become a published author (see p. 279). Miss B. could have married and changed her name or moved away from Schoolcraft between November of 1849 and August of 1850, when the Federal Census for Schoolcraft was taken. Still an examination of the census discovers interesting people: excluding those under six years of age and those who clearly have their name through marriage, three candidates remain as potential authors of this tale. None appear to have published—under these full names at least—in books or magazines that are readily searchable by the major databases cited elsewhere in these notes. And the Census suggests that all three may have lived under circumstances that imposed "arduous duties" that Cumings describes as perhaps inconsistent with authoring tales about schoolteachers who encourage young men to become artists. Two possible matches for "M. A. B." lived in the home of prosperous farmers David and Mary Burson: seventeen-year-old Minerva and thirteen-year-old Mary. Minerva Burson was the second oldest of nine children ranging in age from 18 to 2. Mary Burson was old enough to have five younger siblings. The third potential "M. A. B." is twenty-one-year-old Mariah Boutwell, the oldest daughter of James and Lucy Boutwell, who kept a large and valuable hotel in Schoolcraft. This "Miss B." most likely had "arduous duties" as well; fictional descriptions of such establishments during this period typically describe the innkeeper's oldest daughter as a valuable maid who attracts male customers and is subjected to what we would now call sexual harassment. For the best-known example of this, see Flora Slade in T. S. Arthur's *Ten Nights in a Bar-Room* (1854). A recent scholarly edition is *Ten Nights in a Bar-Room*, ed. Jon Miller (Acton: Copley Publishing, 2002). Boutwell's Hotel was large and busy: the 1850 census records eighteen people residing there. Guests include a family with three small children, headed by a single woman; two daguerreotypists; a forty-year-old prosperous merchant; and a very prosperous forty-year-old Virginian with no occupation. (A twenty-two-year-old painter named Charles Combs lived next door. Coincidentally, perhaps, "Charles Norris" is the painter in the tale.) Hotels and the bar-rooms they typically included were prime spots for the reading of distant newspapers and magazines. Proprietors subscribed to periodicals for their customers to read, and travellers left reading materials behind for others to enjoy. While it is far from certain that "M. A. B." was one of these farmer's daughters or this twenty-one-year-old hotelkeeper's daughter, both scenarios are plausible and the exercise of identifying such candidates promotes an understanding of how this midwestern literary periodical might gain readers and a contributor from such a distant location.

21. Torn between household duties and literary ambition, and supposedly tortured by a spirituality

"We have no light that hath not been given;
We have no strength but shall soon be riven;
We have no power wherein man may trust;
Like him we are things of time and dust;
And the legend we blazon with beam and ray,
And the song of our silence, is—"Passing away."

"We shall fade in our beauty, the fair and bright,
Like lamps that have served for a festal night;
We shall fall from our spheres, the old and strong,
Like rose-leaves swept by the breeze along;
The worshipped as gods in the olden day,
We shall be like a vain dream—"Passing away."

From the stars of Heaven, and the flowers of earth,
From the pageant of power, and the voice of mirth,
From the mists of morn on the mountain's brow,
From childhood's song and affection's vow,—
From all, save that o'er which soul bears sway,
Breathes but one record—"Passing away."

"Passing away," sing the breeze and rill,
As they sweep in their course by vale and hill;
Through the varying scenes of each earthy clime,
'Tis the lesson of nature, the voice of time;
And man at last, like his father's gray,
Writes in his own dust—"Passing away."

---

that rejected her literariness as worldly, English poet Maria Jane Jewsbury (1800–33) contributed heavily to British annuals in the 1820s. In 1849 older American women readers would have associated her with women writers such as Lydia Sigourney and Felicia Hemans. See Jewsbury, *Lays of Leisure Hours* (London: J. Hatchard and Son, 1829), 33–35, Google Books, http://books.google.com/books?id=OfJLuv3q-gIC. "Passing Away" was often selected and anthologized in the 1830s and 1840s. For example see Sarah Josepha Hale's *The Ladies' Wreath: A Selection from the Female Poetic Writers of England and America*, 2nd ed., (Boston: Marsh, Capen, Lyon, and Webb, 1839), 203–04, Google Books, http://books.google.com/books?id=nQJaAAAAMAAJ. In many details (e.g., the missing epigraph, the frequency of semi-colons, and the use of quotation marks) the *Akron Offering* version more closely follows the Hale version than the original.

For the Offering.

The Little Coal-Heaver.

By Jenny.

Concluded.[22]

Mr. Higgins. One day I was tryin to bake some corn bread in the coal fire—got it half burnt up, when who should come in but Jim Brown. He's the meanest one of the whole lot. "What makes you look so molencholly, Eph?" says he. "I was just a thinkin, says I, how I was brought up, and how my folks live in Virginy, and how bad I should feel if any one on 'em should see how I live."—"Come over to my house," says he, "and I'll give you somethin' as'll raise your spirits." Well I went over and there was the whole batch on 'em, *men, women* and *children*, and such a noisy set, such caperin round—all a talkin at once. "What's the matter," says I, "Jim?" "Nothin mor'n a little jolification," said he—"such as we often have"—"look at them young ones there," (pointing to the children,) "why they are just as merry as crickets, and the women are just as merry and sociable as can be—I have no objection to the women takin a dram, they know when to stop, and if they do happen to take a little too much, and get quarrelsome, I know how to *settle the hash*,[23] I walks right in among 'em, gives my woman a slap side of the face, send her a reelin', the rest take the hint and then, may be there aint a *scatterment*."

Well to see such a house full and not a sober one in it, and to see that great big six footer with hardly half sense when he's sober, and hear him brag that he could *settle* a parcel of drunken women by slappin his wife in the face, I just thought it was as good as any tempeance lecter I ever heard, and as poor and miserable as I was, I thought myself somebody compared with Brown and the rest of the clan, and I always did despise a drunkard, and do despise a *mean* drunkard yet. I looked over the company—there was not a sober one among the lot. I felt thankful that my children had no such example. The colored preacher had gone away or I should have tried to have him fall on some plan for me to get away before my family was ruined. I thought I would try and step out of Brown's without any one seein me. "Stop here Eph," says Brown, "and drink somethin before you go." "I won't do it," says I. "You won't hey? why, you aint half as much a man as your Sam. Betsey,

---

22. Earlier installments are on pp. 189 and 237.

23. Swaggering nineteenth-century American slang for ending a disagreement (a "hash") with a beating.

tell Sam Higgins to come in and show his daddy how to drink whiskey." "You'd better wait till he's able to stand," says Bill Jones—"he's had too much already, and it made him sick; why, he's been a vomitin till he's pale as ashes." I made a pitch for the door, and hunted round for my poor boy. I found him in the fence corner, he was the sickest child I ever saw. I called my gal. "Polly," says I, "who made Sam drunk?" "Nobody," says Polly. "Betsey Brown gave him the whiskey, but he made himself drunk; she give me some too, and she sends some to Mother every day, so she does." I tell you I was 'stonished, I could now see how it was, and what made Polly and Sam take up so with Brown's children, and what made Becky (that's Mrs. Higgins,) act so queer—sometimes laughin, sometimes cryin—and sleep—why she'd sleep for a whole day together—when she'd wake up, she scolded so unmercifully that it drove me into the coal bank to get out of hearin. Here was sickness, poverty, and drunkenness, before me. Well, to cut the matter short, I went into town next day and came home drunk for the first time in my life, and if I go home sober to-night, it will be the first time in three years."

Mrs. B. I never in my life listened to such a tale of wo. You are more to be pitied than I had any idea of, and really if there could be a case of justifiable abandonment, it would be such as yours. I observed in the first part of your narrative that you spoke of the goodness of the Lord in directing your course, &c., &c.—Suppose that the Lord were to raise you up friends as good as your old friend Smith, the preacher, and that by their attention, you would find in a few weeks an improvement in the condition of your affairs, could you be induced to try to become a sober man? There is, Mr. Higgins, such a thing as disinterested kindness to be found in this community. I have myself been sometimes engaged in connection with other ladies in providing necessary food and clothing for the destitute, and if you will promise me your co-operation in this matter, I will report your case this very evening to a few of my particular friends, and will visit your family to-morrow. What say you sir, are you willing to make the sacrifice?

Mr. Higgins. If I didn't I'd be the most ungrateful critter in the world—I'd lay down my life to see my family in a better way than they are; yes, Lord bless you, I'll promise you that from this day I'll try to keep from gettin drunk—if you come out there to-morrow you'll find me sober.

Mrs. Bates has ordered a few articles to be put up in a box and placed in his little waggon, together with a few things that Sally sent from the kitchen, of her own accord. She then gave him the money for his coal, and an old cloak, telling him to wear it home and then it would do to wrap round his wife when she sat up. It was quite dark when he started from town, and he went home sober, with a heart overflowing with gratitude to that good being who had led him to the house of the widow Bates.

"How glad I am Mother," said Eliza Bates, "that you happened to think of sending your old cloak to poor Mrs. Higgins; I wish I had asked leave to send mine to Polly."

"You can do that my dear, in future, if necessary," was her Mother's reply. "We have already attended to their immediate necessities, and I intend to see them to-morrow."

"Only think, mother," said Eliza, "of any one being dressed in ragged cotton clothes at this season of the year—why he had but one sock on, and his shoes were much too large, and were stuffed full of straw, and when the tears ran down his smutty face, he had to wipe his eyes on his sleeve."

It was truly gratifying to her mother that there was no need of pointing out to Eliza these marks of destitution. No pains had been spared to inculcate principles of benevolence in her children, from the first dawning of their observation, nor had it been "seed sown by the way side."[24] Early impressions are said to be hard to erase, and I believe this is true. I remember to have seen Eliza Bates when she was under seven years of age—she had just finished her first sampler; it was framed and hangs in her chamber to this day—her teacher had selected for her this beautiful motto:

Teach me to feel another's wo,
  To hide the fault I see,
The mercy I to others show,
  That mercy show to me.[25]

This little incident, in our opinion, had its weight in connexion with other influences that were brought to bear upon the training of the little girl and her mother always found a *ready* if not a very *powerful* ally in Eliza in all her operations.

---

24. In farming, seed that does not grow; seed that falls to where it is not covered with earth, watered, etc., or is maybe eaten by birds. In the "Parable of the Sower," Mark 4 of the New Testament, Jesus explains that the word of God is like seed: with some it takes root and flourishes, with others it falls by the way side.

25. Passage from an early eighteenth-century poem, "The Universal Prayer," by English poet Alexander Pope (1688–1744). To read this in a late 1840s American edition, see *The Complete Poetical Works of Alexander Pope* (New York: A. Leavitt, 1848), 2:55–56, Google Books, http://books.google.com/books?id=LFkZAAAAYAAJ.

Early next morning, (it was the sabbath) Mrs. B. put on her hood and cloak, and started to visit the poor destitute family, as she had promised. There stood the "cabin on the hill side, close by the poplar," as Ephraim Higgins had described it. She knocked at the door.

"Pull the string whosumever you are," said a feeble voice from within. "I say, pull the string, for I can't git up to let you in."

She lifted the latch, and the door opened, and there, sitting erect on a chair, was a *something* that looked more like what we might conceive of an Egyptian Mummy than BODY, with a soul in it. There could be no mistake. Then wrapped carefully round the figure, was the identical old grey cloak that had been given to Ephraim the evening before, and without further ceremony, she drew a three legged stool close to the fire, and very near the poor woman.

"This is Mrs. Higgins, is it not," said Mrs. B.

"Yes, my name's Becky Higgins;—and what's *your* name? for I never saw *you* before."

"My name is Bates. Is your husband at home?"

"Oh, no, he's gone to meetin'—where he hain't bin for five years. He's a man as drinks mighty hard, but some town body talked to him yesterday about it, and he says he's bound to quit it, and join the church agin, and try to *be somebody*."

"I suppose he alluded to *me*—I had a conversation with him yesterday, and he made me some such promise."

"Oh, are YOU the lady? Why God bless you. Yes, he told me you were comin' out here to-day, but I didn't think you'd take the trouble to come and see sich poor folks; and you sent me this ere cloak, and a good many more things, to eat, and to wear too;—and Ephraim says its the *good man's doins arter all*—that *he* put it into your heart to send us these things, and to talk so kind to him, and that's the reason why he's a goin' to try so hard to quit drinkin."

"I am glad *indeed*, Mrs. Higgins, that your husband takes so correct a view of the subject. Every good, and every perfect gift comes from above, and he need not thank *me* for anything that I *have done*, or may *yet* do for you."

"Oh, yes, but he does thank *you too*,—and he said before he started meetin', that he did'nt think it would be sich hard work to leave off drinkin',—that he'd stick to it,—if it half killed him, he's *bound* to do it."

That Ephraim's wife *was*, in point of intellect, far inferior to himself, was very perceptible—every allowance, however, might be made for her stupidity; she had never been well enough to leave the house for a single day from the time she went there to live,—and her only associates, were the wives of the four or five *worthies*, of whom we had some account, in the preceding chapter;—something has been said too, of the liberality of the two ladies, in supplying Mrs. H. from time to time with a *certain* article of very *questionable utility*, from the use of which, we doubt whether she derived any *great* amount of *benefit*, either *mental* or *physical*. Her language and manners, as well as her absurd notions, were peculiar to the poorer classes of her native state. On being questioned with regard to the cause and progress of her malady, the *first* she attributed to witchcraft—and her not having been cured, she said, was entirely owing to a mistake she made in the *witch doctors* prescription. He was a *seventh son*,[26] and so were his father and grandfather—he had assumed to kill witches at a dollar a head, *payable in advance*;—by killing, he only meant to destroy their power to do harm. His mode of treatment was, to write down on paper *nine words*, or characters, (very *potent* and mysterious, no doubt,) and to roll it up into as many pills, one of which was to be taken every *Friday* morning before sunrise, and *without speaking* a word. She, however, forgot the latter part of the directions, and began to *scold* Ephraim and the children before swallowing the *first*, and that mistake had given the witches full power over her to all future time.

The inside of the cabin did not present so harrowing a spectacle as was anticipated;—but whether it was, that Becky's account of her husband's good resolution "to persevere, though it should half kill him," had given her the earnest[27] of a speedy improvement in their state and condition, we cannot say, but there certainly was a very cheerful fire, and a tolerably *clean* hearth,—and the children, too, were at home, not cutting round with the neighbors' children as had been their wont.[28] Polly and Sam were trying to spell out the hard words of a chapter, while the *little* girl sat in the corner, amusing herself with building a cob house[29] for the kitten. The poor things were miserably clad it is *true*; but that she considered a matter of small import, and could easily be remedied. Mrs. B. examined the swollen and distorted limbs of the patient very tenderly;—talked a great deal

26. See n. 33, p. 162.

27. First fruits; the first of many coming rewards.

28. Habit.

29. A house made with corn cobs, which people saved for different reasons. Children used them as building blocks.

about the sickness, at that time prevailing in town, and of several cases very similar to her own, and of the various remedies that were employed, *successfully*. Encouraged her to hope that something might be done for her relief;—recommended the warm bath, and other external applications, and offered to assist Polly in these little attentions to her mother, as often as practicable, say twice or three times a week.

The gratitude of the poor woman was *unbounded*—she declared that Mrs. Bates was the very best lady in the whole world, and *know'd* more than all the doctors this side of old Virginny. And after talking with Polly about the necessary preparations for bathing her mother, charging her to have plenty of *snow* water heated against[30] she should be out, on the next morning—and promising to bring with her, some books for Sam, that had easier reading in them, than the testament; and showing little siss, a *new* way to build a cob house, Mrs. B. shook hands with them all and left, without waiting for Ephraim, aş she had sundry other calls to make in town. She penciled a note, on the blank leaf of the book that the children had, as there was no other paper to be found, and requested Polly to give it to her father.

> "MR. HIGGINS,
> *My dear Friend*:—I have spent an hour very pleasantly with your family. Am rejoiced that your first step, after the resolve you made yesterday, was to go to the house of the Lord—"Seek first the kingdom of Christ and *His* righteousness, and all things shall be added unto you."[31] I hope my visit may be profitable to myself as well as that of your family. Shall be out to-morrow and bring my family physician.
> Yours, &c.,
> E. BATES."

"Whatsoever thy hand findeth to do, do it with thy might,"[32] used to be a favorite text with Mrs. Bates, but had grown threadbare, and decidedly stale—having been quoted so often, whenever there was any exhibition of *tardiness*, among the junior part of her family—but, as *every thing* is said to come into play once in seven years, so this same old, hackneyed text was called into requisition. Here was a case that admitted of no delay. *True*, a few days, or even weeks, would make but little difference with Becky, who had been so long without attention, but the neglect of a single day might prove *fatal* to Ephraim's newly formed resolves. Every thing seemed to favor

30. Here "against" means "in preparation for" or "in preparation for the fact that."

31. Matthew 6:33.

32. Ecclesiastes 9:10.

a speedy "taking hold," for on returning, Mrs. B. met Doctor ———, on his way to visit a patient a little beyond the diggins, and she requested him to call there, and examine the case, and make report to her that afternoon. He did so; and the following was the report: "That the patient had been suffering from a low typhoid inflamation of the muscular and glandular tissues, with a general atrophy of the cellubur structures, in consequence of unwholesome and innutritious diet. The want of personal cleanliness producing a depraved state of the glands and secretions generally."[33] The mode of treatment was very simple.—The Doctor furnished all the medicines gratis, as well as giving Mrs. B. all the directions, and said he would "look in" at Mrs. Higgins once in a while, to see how she was *getting along.*

Next morning bright and early all hands were busy making preparations for the second visit. John, the boy who fed "the old hoss," was very officious. He was sorry he had no *new* clothes, for *then* he could give Sam Higgins his old ones—but he *could* spare his *linsy hunting* shirt,[34] just as well as not. Sally suggested that among a variety of small matters, a *bar of soap,* and a few old *towels* would be *first rate.* All things being in readiness, Mrs. B. accompanied John, started, each carrying a basket. The latter grunting and muttering, not because of its being too heavy, but because his basket might have held MORE. There was *room enough,* he said, for two or three more loaves of *bread.*

They reached the cabin about eight o'clock. Becky had suffered greatly during the night with pain, and chillyness. Ephraim looked like another being—talked very little, for, as he said, he had no words to express his thankfulness. The countenances of all, beamed with hope and gratitude. One of the baskets contained an entire suit of clothes for Ephraim, nor were the "sock and shoes" wanting, Eliza having taken charge of that part of the preparation herself. Polly was careful to have things ready; and now the warm water and soap was liberally, but carefully administered to the parts affected—after which, the same process, in the use of hot vinegar and salt, and then, a linament of some kind, prepared by the doctor, was applied to the joints and well bathed in, before a hot fire, and the patient soon found herself dressed in good, warm clothes, and *plenty of them,* (thanks to Mrs. B.'s success in begging,) and conveyed to the bed, now made comfortable by the addition of *clean sheets, blanket,* and *coverlet.* The medicine was given her in a draught of hop tea which diffused a glowing sensation, and sent a

33. This is pseudomedical mumbo-jumbo, even by 1849 standards.

34. Linsey-woolsey was a coarse cloth made of blended linen and wool.

moisture to the surface. Next morning she was much better. The bathing was continued, two or three more times a week during the winter, with the happiest results; and against spring, she had so far recovered the use of her limbs, as to be able to walk about the room, and out of doors, when the weather was fine, with the assistance of her daughter, or Sam; and she could do a little mending, which afforded her great satisfaction.

Ephraim was now, emphatically, a sober man, and a consistent member of the church. He also united himself with the Order of the Sons of Temperance.[35] That society, finding that his reformation was a thorough one, took an interest in him, and procured for him other, and more suitable employment than digging coal;—rented a snug little house in town, where his wife could often see her old friend, as well as several other ladies, who had, through Mrs. B., taken a lively interest in her, and where the children could attend the public school.

Five years have nearly completed their circuit, since Ephraim Higgins, SCARCELY sober, formed a resolution to *try* to leave off drinking whiskey, and we are *quite* certain, that he has never tasted any kind of ardent spirits since.

For the Offering.

To My Absent Husband.[36]

Come home my absent husband,
  And sit thee by my side;
And speak as thou wast wont to do
  When first thou called me bride—
I know thy toils do call thee,
  But why so far away,

35. A fraternal temperance society dedicated to mutual support and improvement that was founded in New York in 1842. Earlier temperance societies tended to be groups of elite physicians and their professional relatives or groups of rowdy laborers. The Sons of Temperance distinguished themselves by their embrace of middle-class respectability and their use of Masonic-like rituals, ranks, and passwords. They experienced rapid growth and expansion of their orders, especially in northeastern cities, throughout the 1840s. American men with aspirations to high standing and material wealth enjoyed the advantages of membership, especially as they traveled or migrated. See James D. Ivy, "The Sons of Temperance," *Alcohol and Temperance in Modern History: An Encyclopedia*. Ed. Jack S. Blocker, Jr., Ian Tyrrell, and David Fahey (Santa Barbara, CA: ABC-CLIO, 2003), 2:572–74. For more see n. 25, p. 156.

36. The poem resonates with the much-discussed exodus of husbands to California, expressed elsewhere in the *Offering* as well as in the 1849 Akron newspapers. See p. 7–8.

From her who loves thee as her life
    And weeps thy long delay?

This morn whilst I was wandering
    In fields, midst fragrant flowers,
Striving to forget thy absence
    And wile away sad hours,
I thought if thou wert with me
    How happy should I be—
I heard a footfall, turned to look,
    It was my maid—not thee—

Then hie thee home to me dearest,
    Nor longer absent be,
For my heart is sad and lonely love
    While thou'rt so far from me—
'Tis thine own loved wife that is pleading now
    Then hasten, hasten home;
And promise her that ne'er again
    So far from her thou'lt roam.

Abbey Viola.
Wooster Ohio.[37]

For the Offering.

A Casket of Gems.

Our world is a casket enclosing many bright gems of more or less value that glisten for a time, dazzling the admiring eyes of those who would eagerly

37. The capital of Wayne County, Wooster lies about twenty-five miles southwest of Akron. An 1848 geographical almanac describes it as having about 2000 inhabitants, a court house, a jail, a bank, a United States land office, five churches, twenty-five stores, tanneries, mills, printing offices, and two weekly newspapers. See Daniel Haskel and J. Calvin Smith, *A Complete Descriptive and Statistical Gazetteer of the United States of America* (New York: Sherman and Smith, 1848), 741, Google Books, http://books.google.com/books?id=UOstAAAAYAAJ. "Abbey Viola" may have been a pseudonym but for what it's worth, the 1850 Federal Census for Wooster includes three "Abigails" and no "Violas." "Viola" may have been a middle name. The Abigails of 1850 Wooster include Abigail Cain, the fifty-one-year-old wife of a sixty-six-year-old painter; Abigail Howard, the forty-seven-year-old wife of the sixty-three-year-old owner of the busy "American Hotel;" and sixty-year-old Abigail Stumborigh, who lived alone. See United States of America, Bureau of the Census, *Seventh Census of the United States, 1850*. NARA microfilm publication M432. (Washington, D.C.: National Archives

grasp them. Wealth, beauty or fame, are the prizes that many would win. Their appearance is attractive but oft times deceitful; merely an external show and the pleasures they afford us are merely transitory. Like the morning dew-drops that sparkle for a time and then disappear. But are there not brighter gems than these, of fairer form, of richer hue, of more enduring substance, to adorn the diadem of youth? Humility glitters in the vale: a bright little gem that we fain would possess; with *Piety, Benevolence,* and *Kindness,* clasped with the pearl of *Contentment*, it forms a beautiful wreath, a coronet that well might encircle the brow of the good and the wise. There's the gem of *Truth*, pure and transparent as the guileless heart that possesses it; a pearl of *Friendship*; most gladly would I make it my own.—Brighter, holier far is its radiance than that which gleams from crystal rocks or coral mines. There's a gem for the *poor*; for the *virtuous poor*; a gem for the *afflicted*; it sheds a halo around their pathway, and bids them look upward from the trials of earth; disperses the thick clouds of sorrow and leads them calmly through this vale of affliction. But is there not another? A prize for the student who has labored so incessantly, early and late that he may obtain it? Yes, we have found it, deeply hidden in the casket but 'tis beautiful and bright, and set round with diamonds; well worth the labor expended in searching for it. 'Tis the pearl of *Wisdom*; sought and admired alike by the lowly and humble, and those, who dwell in palaces; one of the brightest in the coronet of kings and queens. But the brightest gem is reserved for the Christian; yes, for him it is the pearl of priceless value. Well has he won it; it is a mark toward which all his exertions are tending; the star of hope that leads through life's weary pilgrimage. For him then alone is the Pearl of Great Price.[38] It will long be his brightest ornament, and deck his diadem of truth when his Master shall make up his jewels.

Celia.[39]

38. See n. 9, p. 41.

39. In the editorial that closes this number, Cumings describes "Celia" as "Miss W." of Trumbull County, Ohio, and possibly suggests a recent meeting between the two. See p. 279. About forty miles northeast of Akron, Trumbull County was crossed by the Pennsylvania and Ohio Canal. The area was suited for dairy farming and produced cheese, butter, wool, and livestock for export. The capital, Warren, had about three thousand residents in 1850. See Daniel Haskel and J. Calvin Smith, *A Complete Descriptive and Statistical Gazetteer of the United States of America* (New York: Sherman and Smith, 1848), 664, Google Books, http://books.google.com/books?id=UOstAAAAYAAJ. The 1850 United States Federal Census records one Celia W. above the age of four in Trumbull County: twelve-year-old Celia Webb of Johnston Township, the oldest of the five children of grocers John and Julia Webb. "Celia" was also a common pen name at this time.

For the Offering.

Reform and Conservatism.

Chapter II.

By Maud Wellington.[40]

"Moral Reform."

Every enterprise, whose principles, carried out, would tend to improve the condition of human beings, may be considered as belonging to the same class, and we will look at the opposing powers manifested in connexion with some of the subjects to be thus considered. Profanity, intemperance, licentiousness, robbery, murder, and every manifestation of error in any form show a deficient moral perception, or contempt of duty, or recklessness of consequences and a need of prompt reform.

Proud, ignorant, conceited, selfish individuals that are so constituted, or placed in such circumstances that they know not what temptation means, looked upon the victims of vice, of whatever character, as entirely beneath their notice. Let oaths still be heard from profane lips, let the drunkard die in the mire, let the filth of sin be gathered thickly round each profligate wretch, said the stern, unfeeling bigot, of every selfish creed. I will not contaminate *myself* by even listening to appeals for mercy in their behalf—it is in vain to try to make *me* believe that under any circumstance, I should have been like *them*, and *they* know better—let them *die* I say, they deserve nothing else.

The large, warm heart of benevolence stopped not to take counsel from selfishness or even from justice, but lifted the bloated disfigured drunkard from the place where he had fallen, watched by him until his death-like stupor had passed away, then reasoned with him as an erring *Brother*, appealed unto him as a *man*, and, by dint of kind persuasion, heard him make the firm resolve to arise, and assert, and maintain the dignity of manhood; and saw him place his name among those who were released from the fearful bondage of intemperance. And for another class of wretched beings was established a place of refuge where holy influences might be about them, and they might be redeemed from sin, nor by it be again ensnared.

And would truth ask benevolence to concede ought of principles like these? No—but instead of treating those who despise, such efforts, as ene-

40. See n. 21, p. 228.

mies, it would bid all look upon them as objects of pity, and fit subjects for Reform to lay its renovating hand upon, not in anger, but in kindness and fraternal love, striving to win them from their miserable coldness and indifference to others wo, to a correct appreciation of the relative duty of human beings and the happiness to be derived from doing good.

The old spirit of conservatism says if a man is in debt and can not pay it, drag him to jail, oppress him and his family all that is possible, teach him better than to be hungry or naked when he has no sordid dust to render as an equivalent for the necessaries of life; if a man is a robber incarcerate him in a dungeon during the remainder of his days and if he is a murderer, *murder him.*

Benevolence or the spirit of Reform says let the man oppressed by poverty have his liberty, let not even the robber be shut out from the sight of the green fields and the bright heavens, *forever*—and the murderer—that poor creature that has slain his fellow traveller to the grave!—*his* death cannot restore the life he has taken; take down the gallows erected for him; let him live, and do not seek to embitter his wretched existence—Yea, it *almost* asks for liberty for the willful destroyer of human life. And does right decision say thus? not quite—it would give liberty to all who would not abuse the precious boon—it would not "take the life it cannot give"[41] but it would protect all alike; justice must not be forgotten, the murderer *deserves* not liberty, *ought* not to have it, *can* not have it, and anything like sound laws remain in force and in the prison to which he must be banished he can have time to think, "mercy can find him out"[42] even there, and he can learn to be grateful that he was not ignominiously hurried from time to eternity.

The unequal distribution of property has been a subject of much thought and as that which it is supposed will make people happier ought surely to make them better, this may stand with the subjects already treated of.

Philanthropy looked upon Monopolists of the gifts of heaven as they hoarded in fast-closed coffers their useless gold and let millions toil and starve, and dared to breath aloud its enlarged benevolence, its schemes for equalizing comfort and happiness and lo! it was caught up by some *far-seeing sages* and is henceforth made a watch-word by which to accomplish selfish individual, or party purposes. The ignorant are told and sometimes, made

41. An ambiguous quote, this may be an adaptation of "Shall sinful men their right affirm, / To take the life they cannot give; / And thus destroy a brother worm, / When heavenly mercy bids him live?" These lines appear in an anonymous poem in Ann Alexander's *Cruelty and Humanity* (London: Nisbet and Gilpin, 1847) 31–32, Google Books, http://books.google.com/books?id=UekDAAAAQAAJ.

42. Perhaps echoing 2 Timothy 1:16–18.

to believe that the entire social system of our country should be overturned and that in the change proposed, every individual would share alike as to wealth and influence and happiness. No assumption of power by any one, however much he may have been accustomed to exact and receive reverence; there should be no isolated households of Aristocratic pretensions, having for its neighbor the hut where sits squalid poverty in hopeless wretchedness, but all should be one *great household* of brethren, a paradise on earth, the hope of the Philanthropists and christian, realized. And who wonders that a *look* merely at the *surface* should deceive! but let truth search it out and while with benevolence it mourns over the sorrows of those who are haunted by the dark spectre on whose haggard lineaments is inscribed that chilling word, poverty, and though it would inspire the possessors of wealth with willingness to share with the needy, the rich gifts of Heaven, it *will not attempt* to cheat the multitude into the belief that a scheme of universal association *can ever* be *established*, or even if it could, that it would produce happiness or equality or *leave them even liberty*; and in all honesty, in preference to this state, it would point the poor man to a life of toil where he can call a few acres his own, even though his wardrobe is scantily filled and his table shows but the coarsest fare; for then he will not form, as it were, a part of a complicated machine, doing the bidding of masters whose power could be *felt* if not *seen*. Yes, let the Government give its land to actual settlers[43] and let this be exempted from all liability to be sold in payment of debt, for this is right, but let it be their *own*, a *home* for themselves & their loved ones where, when they wish, they can be *alone*, whether in sorrow or in joy—where, in short, they could be *free men*, and wear not the shackles so cunningly forged by those who desire the title Philosophers and Philanthropists—Reformers on a grand scale, while they deserve no better name than Disorganizers of society, & Disturbers of the public peace, and all this from the meanest imaginable motive, a desire for the aggrandizement of self.

43. The "monopolist" argument endorsed here (as an exception to the author's contempt for such things) concerns the distribution of western land to American setters. For various reasons, large areas came under the control of speculators (land "monopolists"). The essay sides with the opinion that the Federal government should not distribute this land—directly or indirectly—through such means. For a fuller version of this argument, see "Freedom of the Land the People's Right," *Western Quarterly Review* 1, no. 1 (January 1849): 28–43, Google Books, http://books.google.com/books?id=9n0oAAAAMAAJ. The idea that settlers should not pay for western homesteads explains much of the emphasis on "free" in the emerging Free Soil Party. Their calls for such a land policy would not be answered until 1862, when the Civil War allowed northern legislators to pass a Homestead Act that never would have passed had the southern legislators still been involved in the federal government.

The question of settling National difficulties by arbitration, and also Slavery, might be justly treated of, under the head of Moral Reform; but we will leave these questions, with perhaps, some others, for the next chapter.

Editor's Remarks.

Every month brings us new subscribers and Contributors, and we are happy that by the aid of so many friends we can present the readers of the Offering in every No. what we believe to be (to use the expressive term furnished by Beta) a palatable dish of "Literary Succotash"[44]—by the way, we are sorry he does not still condescend to help season it, and some others too, have assisted only once or twice—but we have no business to complain—each article was an important ingredient and filled its place in the general compound, to the satisfaction of a goodly number, and in many others have faithfully performed a generous part, and every one, we hope, finds at least one morsel suitable for an undepraved taste, and the pleasure and blessing we trust are mutual.

"Lily Lute," has done us good service, commencing with the first No. and continuing her contributions more than one for every No. Many thanks, dear Lily, and if it may be, we hope each future No. will be graced by something from your pen.

"Jenny" deserves the love and gratitude of all, and may her story incite every one to try and save some poor drunkard, or some drunkard's wretched wife and children from their sad, their fearful state.

"M. A. B." gives you scenes that forcibly illustrate the power of kindness on the hearts of children. Would that every teacher, aye, and every parent

---

44. A dish learned from Native Americans, succotash is a boiled mixture of corn and beans.

In the November 22, 1849 number of *The Zanesville Courier, The Akron Offering* was noted in the top left corner of the editorial page:

> The Akron Offering.
>
> The November number of this periodical is before us. As usual its pages are well filled with interesting reading. The prose is chiefly original; and there is a fair proportion of select and original poetry; The Offering is published monthly at Akron Ohio, by Calista Cummings at $1,00 per annum in advance. The fact that the Offering is published in Ohio, by a Lady of Ohio should secure it a liberal patronage in this State. But apart from these considerations its real merits entitle it to a large and increasing support. We are glad to see that it appears to be prospering. We wish it abundant success.

See "The Akron Offering," *Zanesville Courier* 4, no. 101 (November 22, 1849): 2, Access Newspaper Archive, http://access.newspaperarchive.com/zanesville-courier/1849-11-22/page-2. For more on the connections between Cumings and the people of Zanesville, see pp. 198, 208, and 231.

would try kind and truthful words and looks and acts in all their dealings with children, and the world would soon present a brighter picture, and much of its wretchedness would flee away. We are grateful, Miss B., for this favor, and hope if consistent with your arduous duties, you will honor us again.

We give a hearty welcome to our new friend, "Adelia"—we have just received more of her poetry—pieces breathing through beautifully chosen words, the pure feelings, the bright hopes, and humble faith of one who has learned to trust in Heaven.

Miss W. of Trumbull Co., has our thanks for the article signed "Celia." We think this piece very pretty and hope to be favored again by Celia, herself, and also hope, Miss W. and several more in her place will send us something for the Offering.

"Ida's" piece is very good but she forgot to send us a name.

"Rose Reed's" Story will appear in the eighth or ninth No. Every one will remember that every good article will be gratefully received.

C. Cumings.

THE
AKRON OFFERING.
December, 1849.

Selected for the Offering.

God in the Events of the Times.

By Rev. H. Hervey.[1]

There are two grand sources of information from which we may learn our duty, and from which the wise in every age have learned what they ought to do. One is the *word*, and the other the *providence* of God. In the one God speaks; in the other he acts. By studying the word, we learn what he has revealed as the rule of faith and obedience. By observing his provi-

1. Henry Hervey (1798–1872) lived for nearly four decades in Martinsburg, Ohio, where he was the pastor of the Presbyterian Church, the principal (and founder) of Martinsburg Academy and Martinsburg Female Seminary, and perhaps the editor of a religious periodical. See *The Biographical Record of Knox County, Ohio* (Chicago: Lewis Publishing Company, 1902), 375, Google Books, http://books.google.com/books?id=pREVAAAAYAAJ, and Stuart C. Wade, *The Wade Genealogy* (New York: Stuart C. Wade, 1900), 334, Google Books, http://books.google.com/books?id=iANaAAAAMAAJ. About 40 miles northeast of Columbus and 70 miles southwest of Akron, Martinsburg had a population of about 400 in 1850. Many graduates of Hervey's schools went on to be Presbyterian leaders or the wives of Presbyterian leaders. In B. F. Smith's 1851 report on the condition of the Ohio common schools in Knox County, Hervey's academy is named as one of the most distinguished. "Its usefulness and benefits are indicated by the morality and general intelligence of the citizens of that part of our county," he reports, adding, "(not a rum selling or rum manufacturing establishment to be found in its vicinity.)" See *Documents, including Messages and Other Communications Made to the Fiftieth General Assembly of the State of Ohio* 16, no 2 (Columbus: S. Medary, 1852), 91, Google Books, http://books google.com/books?id=kXYUAAAAYAAJ. Hervey's reputation and influence extended beyond Martinsburg. In 1860, for example, he travelled ten miles north to Gambier, Ohio, where he served as the "Class Orator" for the 1860 commencement at Kenyon College. In his "fine voice" he delivered a "masterly" talk on "The Conservative Influence of the Scholar" in Rosse Chapel (now Rosse Hall) to a large, "fashionable and highly intellectual audience." See E. Owen Simpson, "Kenyon College," *The University Quarterly* 2, no. 1 (July 1860): 196–98, Google Books, http://books.google.com/

dence, in its various developments, we see this rule confirmed. By the one we learn what our duty is at all times and under all circumstances; and by the other our duty at particular times and under special circumstances. The two books we should study, not only attentively, but in connexion, that we may be men of understanding concerning the times, and know what we ought to do. The one illustrates the other, and neither can be studied alone to advantage. If you study the word alone, it will appear dark, inexplicable, and without an intelligible end. But studied together, the one sheds light upon the other, and both become more clear.

The Savior charged some of his hearers with hypocrisy, because they could discern the face of the sky, but not the signs of the times. As we look at the face of nature for the purpose of directing our ordinary actions, so the Savior would have us carefully observe the aspect of God's moral government as developed in the progress of events, that we may have understanding of the times. Not knowing the signs of the times, the Jews opposed and persecuted Jesus, and finally put him to death, which they would not have done had they attended to the aspects of divine providence which indicated the fulfillment of prophecy in the person of Christ. Had they known, they would not have crucified the Lord of glory. The ever varying aspect of the times, are so many developments of the great scheme of God's providence, which is hastening to the accomplishment of his grand purposes concerning our world; and each passing event is an additional manifestation of God's character and will; and he acts most wisely, who, as the leaves of the book of providence are being continually turned, carefully studies the lesson of each day so as to learn more of God—of his wisdom, justice, and mercy; or more of himself, his present duty and future destiny. Let us inquire.

1. *What are some of the distinguishing features of the present times?*

Our times are marked with *revolution*.[2] This feature is more apparent in the old world than in the new. Under the old governments of Europe, the mind of the masses of the people seem to have suddenly awakened from the

---

books?id=nuQSAAAAIAAJ. His son, Dwight B. Hervey, delivered a funeral oration published as "A Discourse Commemorative of the Life and Character of the Rev. Henry Hervey, D.D." (Cincinnati: Bosworth, Chase & Hall, 1872). William L. Fisk, in "The Scotch-Irish in Central Ohio," describes Hervey as a leader of the pacifist, antislavery side of a regional Presbyterian schism in the late 1840s. See *Ohio History* 57, no. 2 (April 1948): 121. Ohio History Online, http://ohsweb.ohiohistory.org/.

2. Hervey alludes to the many democratic revolts against European monarchies—especially in Paris, Vienna, and Berlin—of 1848. Reforms, concessions, and promises were made but then withdrawn in most cases after military suppression. One expression of these revolutions was *The Communist Manifesto* (1848) by Karl Marx and Frederic Engels, which presents history as a class struggle between the working class and the ruling class.

slumber of ages. The spirit of overturning established governments has passed from country to country with electric velocity. Before kings have had time to inquire the cause of agitation, they have been hurled from their thrones and their seats of power overturned. Crowned heads, which inherited, without question, their offices, honors and emoluments from remote ancestors, have suddenly been obliged to come down from their high places, and retreat into obscurity for safety. Venerated titles have been torn with ruthless hand from the brow of those who have worn them, and treated as common property. Constitutions of states have been torn and shivered to the winds; and new ones, the offspring of a day, set up in their place. Those who were taught only to command and accustomed to be obeyed, have suddenly been obliged to cast away the scepter and yield to the control of those from whom they were accustomed to receive obedience only. Dynasties, guarded by formidable military strength, have been swept from their strong foundations by the resistless rush of the popular will; and the voice of the masses are now heard from the chairs of state where, a little before, the will of one, or of a few, commanded the obedience of the many. The spirit of revolution is putting forth its power not only against civil establishments, but against ecclesiastical. Even old Rome, proclaimed for ages infallible, and unchangeable as the seven hills on which she sits, has been made to totter to her fall. He who was styled the successor of St. Peter—God's vicegerent on earth—and who for ages had but to speak and the civil and military powers of kingdoms were summoned to his aid, has been obliged to retire from the ancient seat of the popes, and seek safety in an obscure village; and contributions are being taken, both in Europe and America, in the assemblies of the faithful, to pay the board of the head of the church in his exile. In his absence a republican constitution has been adopted in Rome, the most unlikely place on earth for the prevalence of national liberty. For the defense of this they have maintained a deadly conflict with their French neighbors.[3] More revolutions have occurred within the last eighteen months, or are now in progress, in the old governments of Europe than have taken place perhaps in the last five hundred years. And the changes are of wholly a different character from those heretofore effected. Formerly the changes were wrought by one aspiring monarchy assuming power over the territory and subjects of another; but now it is the effect of the will of the people against all monarchies. Liberty, equality, and fraternity are the

3. For most of 1848 Pope Pius IX (1792–1878) ("God's viceregent on earth") ceded control of Rome to a series of unstable radical governments. At the end of the year he fled to Gaeta, in Naples. In 1849 Napoléon III (1808–73), who had been elected President of France at the end of 1848, lent military support to the Pope's reconquest of Rome. Pius IX returned to Rome until April, 1850.

pledges of unity, instead of nobility, royalty, and hereditary right. The pope, the Jesuits, and the inquisition held the minds of men in awe, and the inquisition, the stake, and the flames were the last arguments of popes in the days of their power. But now the onward progress of a revolutionized sentiment demands the exclusion of the Jesuits, the circulation of the Bible, liberty of the press and of conscience.

Again: The present is an age of *ultraism*.[4] Even right principles are carried to such a dangerous excess as to become wrong. Civil and religious liberty, of which most, even of evangelized nations, have heretofore been deprived by long established customs, by usurpation, and by force, are now the objects of the efforts of the masses of men. To secure these, Europe is shaken as with an earthquake. The remote provinces feel the impulse. To secure these, in the southern states, efforts are continually being made to keep the minds of the people in a state of excitement. Legislative halls are kept in angry strife; and the conventions and courts of the churches partake of a similar spirit. There are many most forward in the ranks of those who are marching for this object, and most vociferous in the shout of liberty, who understand not the meaning of the word, nor know the manner to obtain and preserve it. With many it is *lawlessness*. To do as each one pleases, in both church and state, is the idea. In France a party, considerable in numbers and influence, which was engaged in the popular movement which overturned the throne of Louis Philippe; which were most eager for the annihilation of the titles of nobility, and for restricting the power of the priests; this party appears now as little satisfied with a republican form of government as they were before with the kingly. With extravagant notions of liberty, they know not when to stop. With them, government is to provide them the means of living in ease and pleasure on the property of others without industry and economy. To hold them in check, the government has been obliged to keep an armed force watching day and night. It requires more vigilance and more military force to protect their republic against those who would carry it to excess than it did to protect the previous monarchy—more watchfulness to guard the constitution against those who would carry it into anarchy, than it did to prevent royalty from running into despotism. And in regard to their jealousy of church power—in their fear of Romanism,[5] the prevailing religion of the nation, they have embraced infidelity—in evading the abuses of a system of belief which

4. Extremism.

5. Catholicism.

contained some truth, the recognition of one God and Jesus the Messiah, many have adopted the notion of "No God—no Savior."

Such are some of the extremes in the old world. Are we free from sinful ultraism in the new? Civil and religious liberty has been our high privilege for two ages past; but may not a discerner of the progress of things discover ultra tendencies in the minds of men here? Who may not notice the growing disposition in many to do as "seemeth good in their own eyes"[6] in the state and in the church? Do the youth, now coming up into the estate of manhood, have the respect for authority, for legislative action, for the decisions of established tribunals, for age and office, which their grandfathers had? What point in politics, in theology, in state or church government, is not carried to excess? What branch of internal improvement, of trade, of mechanics, of individual enterprise is not carried to some ultra point, so as greatly to lessen or destroy its usefulness? What absurdity in the form of religious opinion has not been adopted, and found zealous followers in this country of toleration? And what wild and fanatical measures have not been pursued to give it currency? What security have we, that those who now hold one set of measures may not, as soon as the next lecturer comes along, or the next mail arrives, give up the old and adopt a new theory of practice? Creeds, professions, and party connexions are often changed with as much apparent ease as to lay aside an outer garment, and with as little sense of responsibility. The authority of long established opinions, and venerated usage, with those who have leaped to some distant—unheard of point for reforming the age, are abandoned as the tales of the nursery.

Ultraism carries with it into its most distant wanderings certain qualities which may be observed. One of these is a firm and unusual confidence that it is right, and others differing are wrong. This confidence begets censoriousness, and a denunciatory spirit towards others who hold back and hesitate to leap to the ground which they occupy. It disposes of arguments by assertions, and of old opinions by calling them "the prejudice of education." Another quality is recklessness of consequences. It cares not what may follow. It sees so clearly, that though society should be rent by its measures, and the constitution of nations torn and scattered to the winds, and church organizations fall, it *must* occupy and push forward its new positions. These

6. A stock phrase in mid-nineteenth century American religious writing, perhaps inspired by various passages in the bible, that was often used to denigrate attitudes of self-determination as too radical when contrasted with attitudes expressing greater deference for what the government, the church, etc., declares to be good.

features are prominent in the times, and in our country, perhaps more than elsewhere. This spirit is illustrated in certain advocates of the rights of a portion of our southern population; and also in certain extreme opposers of those rights. That this population should enjoy the rights and privileges of which they are deprived, most persons admit. But some men differing from others in regard to the means of reaching this desirable point, see the way so clearly, as if by a ray of overpowering light from heaven direct, hesitate not to follow it; and denounce those who see not with them, though all national and church organizations be sacrificed. Ultra views, if not justifiable, are, perhaps, sometimes excusable, on the ground of the magnitude of the evil to which they are opposed. This may be somewhat so in this case; and longer time, and more experience will probably give all concerned wiser counsels, and more judicious measures. The progress of civil liberty is onward, and it will reach the sons of Africa as well as of Europe. May the Lord hasten it every where by the means which he will approve.

From a view of these two features of the times, what duties may the church learn.

1. From the spirit of revolution abroad, she should be encouraged and excited to still more vigorous and persevering efforts to diffuse the light of divine truth, and employ various instrumentalities which the scriptures authorize to secure the stability and happiness of nations, and for the salvation of the souls of men. The spirit of change abroad in the world, is the very opening which providence is making for the entrance of bible-truth and bible institutions. The entrance of these gives understanding to the simple. It is the direct or reflected light of the word of God, which, diffusing itself into the European mind, is moving it to a contest with darkness; and bringing into deadly conflict the heaving elements for a glorious victory. If the Pope is forced to flee from Rome, the mystery is explained when we learn that there are three printing presses in Italy, issuing the Bible, and one of them in Rome itself.

2. The protestants, the friends of civil and religious liberty should be encouraged to more faithful efforts, because, what is now so rapidly occurring, is just what prophecy long ago foretold would take place, and for which the friends of Zion have prayed for ages.

A consideration of the ultraism of the age should lead to a similar result. If men do go to extremes, it is an evidence that they are thinking and acting, and not in a dead repose. It is perhaps easier to restrain the living than to put life into the dead. The difficulty with the ultra spirit is, not that it has no light, but that it has not enough. Not that it does not think at all; but that it does not think enough. Its error is not that it does not act, but that it acts rashly. It sees something good to be accomplished, but it waits not to see it fully in all its relations; and in reaching towards its object it goes beyond it, or in its haste it fails altogether, or does more mischief in one direction than it does good in another. What this spirit wants is more light and more consideration. It needs not excitement, for of this it has already too much for its discretion. The diffusion of bible principles and gospel institutions will correct this evil. Mankind never become over-excited or ultra in their views and measures with the bible for their guide. As the bible drove the pope out of Rome, so, if it had its influence, would it drive socialism and ultra republicanism out of Paris. Louis Philippe the head of the royalists, and Ledru Rollin the leader of the ultra republicans, are now both in exile in England.[7] True principles cut off extremes. The wisdom that comes from God leads in the midst of the paths of judgment. Korah, Dathan, and Abiram, the insurrectionists are no more allowed to be the rulers of Israel than Pharaoh the despot.[8] If the sea overwhelm the one, the earth swallows up the other. What Europe wants, and our own country, to prevent anarchy and despotism is the diffusion of more of scripture principles. Then their moderation will be known unto all men. Israel's duty is to diffuse there.—*Quarto*[9]

7. The King of France, who abdicated in response to the insurrections in early 1848, Louis-Philippe (1773–1850) spent his final years in Surrey county, England. Alexandre-Auguste Ledru-Rollin (1807–74), after a career as a French lawyer defending republicans, served in the radical 1848 government that was formed after the abdication of Louis-Philippe. In June of 1849, he called for the impeachment of Napoléon III, who was claiming and consolidating increasingly autocratic powers. Ledru-Rollin led a demonstration that turned into a failed insurrection, and he fled to England.

8. In the Old Testament, Korah, Dathan, and Abiram lead a rebellion against Moses during their difficult years in the wilderness. God opens a hole in the ground and swallows them up. See Numbers 16.

9. Edited by Simeon Brown (1808–67), the Zanesville, Ohio *Family Quarto* appeared from 1848 to 1850. Brown's previous periodicals included *The Calvinistic Monitor* (1841–?, published at Fredericktown), *The Family Monitor* (Marion), *The Presbyterian of the West* (Springfield, then Cincinnati) and *The Colporteur* (Zanesville). See J. F. Everhart, *History of Muskingum County, Ohio* (Columbus: J. F. Everhart, 1882), 162, Internet Archive, http://archive.org/stream/cu31924028848673. Brown attended Jefferson College in Canonsburg, Pennsylvania with Hervey in the early 1830s, and his father was a Ruling Elder in Hervey's Martinsburg church. Brown later became a Congregational pastor and moved to Ottumwa, Iowa. See his obituary in *Congregational Quarterly* 10, no. 1 (January 1868): 47–48, Google Books, http://books.google.com/books?id=s-nNAAAAMAAJ.

Selected for the Offering.

"Seem Not—Be."—*Tycho Brahe's Motto.*[10]

By W. C. Bennett.

Out on seeming! shall life ever
  Garb itself in hollow shows,
But a stagnant pool, plague-spreading,
  O'er which green but thinly grows—
But a jungle through whose verdure
  Glide all shapes most foul to see?
Off with empty shows of virtue!
  Off with semblance—*seem not—be.*

Out on all this hollow mouthing—
  Timed devotion—fashioned prayer!
Where breath's alone adoring,
  Sleeps the soul, and take no care!
Where, through easeful self-delightment,
  Six times runs the flood of day,
And the seventh's feigned abasement
  Life's great debt is held to pay.

Out on all these masques of goodness
  This our life doth vaunting wear,
Through whose eyes the subtle evil,
  And sloth's sleepy eye balls glare!
Not for forms of breath-devotion—
  For the shows of good ye see,
Was life given, but for true working—
  Scorn thou semblance—*seem not—be.*

---

10. An earlier American printing of this poem by English author William Cox Bennett (1820–95) is *The Child's Friend* 9, no. 1 (October 1847): 47, Google Books, http://books.google.com/books?id=pbk9AAAAYAAJ. Here the poem is attributed to *The London Inquirer.* A Dutch nobleman, Tycho Brahe (1546–1601) was often described in nineteenth-century literature as an important and dedicated astronomer. Brahe wore a prosthetic nose and studied alchemy.

For the Offering.

Thoughts Concerning a Future State.

The following extract is taken from writings of Fitch W. Taylor, Chaplain to the Squadron commanded by the Commodore George C. Read on a Voyage round the world[11] in the time of the opium difficulties between England and China.[12] It was written after visiting the missionaries at Singapore where he says that among the topics of conversation were "the subject of the resurrection of the dead, the immortality of the soul and the renewal of acquaintances of the Christian dead." He says:

Admitting that our spirits shall remain the precise beings that they now are as to *personal identity*, which it would seem must necessarily be true, and

11. Episcopal clergyman Fitch Waterman Taylor (1803–65) recorded his observations of the world while serving in the American navy under George C. Read (1788–1862) in the East India Squadron (1838–40). The squadron consisted of two war ships, the forty-four-gun frigate *Columbia* and its consort, plus the smaller sloop *John Adams*. One of the newer and more intimidating ships in the U.S. Navy, the *Columbia* was sent to African and Asian seas to establish a military presence for the purpose of protecting American commerce. At one point in the squadron's voyage, for example, Read made a detour to punish the inhabitants of the island of Sumatra, where two dozen piratical Malays had recently massacred the crew of an American trading ship, the *Friendship*, to plunder its haul of opium and Spanish dollars. The East India Squadron voyage was documented from a variety of perspectives in multiple books. See Taylor, *The Flag-Ship: Or, a Voyage Around the World in the United States Frigate Columbia*, 2 vols. (New York: D. Appleton & Company, 1840), Google Books, http://books.google.com/books?id=D9oBAAAAYAAJ (vol. 1) and http://books.google.com/books?id=ENoBAAAAYAAJ (vol. 2). (This selection can be found at 2:87–92.) Another account, authored by an anonymous "Officer of the U.S. Navy," is *Around the World: A Narrative of a Voyage in the East India Squadron*, 2 vols. (New York: Charles Francis, 1840), Google Books, http://books.google.com/books?id=yLIBAAAAYAAJ (vol. 1) and http://books.google.com/books?id=orIBAAAAYAAJ (vol. 2). (Different entries in the OCLC's WorldCat database attribute the work to different authors: Joshua Sidney Henshaw (1811–59), John Henshaw Belcher, and Horatio Bridge are variously credited. Google Books catalogs it as the work of Robert Burts.) And "one of the crew," William Meacham Murrell, wrote *Cruise of the Frigate Columbia Around the World* (Boston: Benjamin Mussey, 1840), Google Books, http://books.google.com/books?id=BgI_AAAAYAAJ. A concise history of the squadron is Charles Oscar Paullin, "Early Voyages of American Naval Vessels to the Orient," *United States Naval Institute Proceedings* 36, no. 4 (December 1910): 1073–99, Google Books, http://books.google.com/books?id=QSNLAAAAYAAJ.

12. In the late 1830s the British were determined to import opium to China, where the narcotic was in high demand along the coast. Because of the social and economic consequences of widespread opium use, Chinese authorities were determined not to alter the isolationist trade policies which had long frustrated the eager English trading companies. American periodicals predicted the start of English hostilities against the Chinese in the years before the "Opium Wars" began in earnest. For more reading on the subject see John Ouchterlony, *The Chinese War: An Account of All the Operations of the British Forces from the Commencement to the Treaty of Nanking* (London: Saunders and Otley, 1844), Google Books, http://books.google.com/books?id=pn9CAAAAIAAJ; Arthur Waley, *The Opium War through Chinese Eyes* (1958; London: Routledge, 2005); and Harry Gregor Geiger, *Opium, Soldiers, and Evangelicals: England's 1840–42 War with China and its Aftermath* (New York: Palgrave, 2004).

which we can not conceive of without the preservation of our memory and the other faculties of the mind, it would seem that some definite and probable inferences may be drawn in connection with the future state.

As to our bodies, although there may be some connection between our present and our *spiritual* body, yet we know that "flesh and blood cannot inherit the Kingdom of God."[13] And I can not conceive of a spirit divested of materiality, as possessing figure or weight, any more than I can conceive of a heavy, thick, oblong, triangular or rectangular *thought*. Nor can I conceive of it as occupying space, any more than does a thought; and no one's head was ever so filled with them as to produce any mechanical dismemberment.—Besides, it is said that our bodies are changing their particles every succession of a few years.[14] We know this from our daily observation as to our nails, hair, etc., and therefore the particles of our body to-day are different from what they will be to-morrow. Our bodies are composed of just what we eat, and therefore are the same particles which have composed the bodies of the animals and vegetables we have eaten. And when these particles are analyzed it is found that the muscles of the ox and the man and the vegetable matter which has been eaten, are composed of the same substances. And when these bodies go to decay, the consolidated gases which compose the particles of which our bodies are constituted, resolve themselves back to their simple elementary elements of oxygen, nitrogen, hydrogen, phosphorus, and their few particles of the *earths*; and while the latter mingle with their kindred dust, the gases composing the greater part of the body, decomposed to their simple elements, rise from their deposit of the grave or are dissipated from the funeral pyre to the gale, and in the whirlwind and the storm, may be, are borne from the spice groves and evergreens of the East to another continent in the West, or are soon re-drank by the vegetable creation, which, in their turn, are re-consumed by beast and man, and become the bodies of others in their day and generation. Thus it becomes neither poetry nor comedy, but a philosophical truth, that the bodies of our grandfathers may be gazing upon us, from the tops of the trees that embower us or resting in the cup of the beautiful lotus as it sleeps on the still bosom of the lake, or is just on the point

13. 1 Corinthians 15:50.

14. This is a common consideration in nineteenth-century meditations on identity. Given the choice of words (especially "particles"), this expression of it appears to echo the article on "Resurrection" in the *Encyclopaedia Britannica* of the period. See "Resurrection," *Encyclopaedia Britannica*, 6th ed. (Edinburgh: Archibald Constable and Company, 1823), 17:764–78, Google Books, http://books.google.com/books?id=ZdAnAAAAMAAJ.

of being devoured by a Buffalo in the shape of a potato, in its turn to be eaten by a Rajah, and for a time to become a part of his Malayship;[15] or in the scattered division of the elements, perhaps another particle has been consumed in a glass of claret, and in its combinations in the system has become the iris of the eye of the proudest princess of Christendom. Thus in these perpetual changes of nature, our bodies may be composed of millions of others; and perhaps not one of them, in fact, belong exclusively to ourselves. What then is the result of these developments of science? It is the confirmation of the sentiment of the apostle, that our bodies shall be "spiritual" bodies, and that "flesh and blood can not inherit the kingdom of Heaven."

But of a spiritual body, as I have before hinted, I cannot conceive of weight, thickness, or breadth, and without these I am unable to conceive of *form* any more than I can conceive of a thought as possessing shape. The difficulty here then, which would present itself to most minds, would be, how shall we recognize our friends in another world, unless we can see them? And how can we see them unless they have a form? And how remember them unless this form be a resemblance of their persons as we have seen them on earth?

But in the first place, I would reply, that we can not now see a spirit, and unless matter shall be in existence when all matter shall have passed away, then we shall have certainly no physical eye to look from. But, how would the idea of the objector improve the matter? Would he, remember his friend as he knew him in his infancy or youth, or riper years, or as a gray-headed man? How should the mother re-call to her vision the little cherub of her affection, which went from her bosom almost as soon as born, to the arms of Him who said "suffer little children to come unto me?"[16] How should the child recall the mother who left it in its cradle, as she went from earth to the peace and purity and bliss of heaven? Or how should the resemblance be fixed for the rotundity and health of the young and blushing cheek, or for the thinner visage though not always less interesting lily features of the young consumptive?

15. A "rajah" or "raja" is a term for a Hindu monarch; "his Malayship" references a raja of the Malay Peninsula. Today the Malay Peninsula consists of Western Malaysia and Singapore. For a mid-nineteenth century American reference book describing the geography and peoples of the Malay Peninsula, see J. R. McCullough and Daniel Haskel, *McCullough's Universal Gazetteer* (New York: Harper and Brothers, 1855), 2:283–85, Google Books, http://books.google.com/books?id=Y4Q6AQAAIAAJ.

16. Jesus says this in the New Testament. See Matthew 18:2–5, Mark 10:14–16, and Luke 18:16–17.

But if these difficulties arise on the supposition, agreeably to a prevalent idea that our spiritual bodies are positive resemblances of our temporal, the apparent impossibility of recognition, as it will appear to some minds, without this external resemblance, tends, they think, to destroy that delightful anticipation of a re-union and association with our friends in heaven. But to me this is far from being the necessary alternative, granting, that the difficulties as above stated in a philosophical view, are real. In the first place it is not the bodies of our friends that we love. The person of our dearest friend in comparison with many others may be very ordinary in external appearance. The form too, changes, and though once interesting may cease to be so. But it is the mind—the soul—the spirit that we love, and it is that which lights up this body; and in our present mode of communication gives forth, through the eye and the lip and the countenance, the real expression of that otherwise concealed being of our friend. It is the thing which loves us, that we love, and which lives when the body crumbles to its original elements. It is that part of our friend that weeps, that is happy; that has made us weep, and has made us happy. It is the soul which has given us its thoughts—the light and shades of its character—and felt when we felt, and smiled when we smiled, and was happy when we were happy, and would live and would die for us. It is this to which our own spirits are bound. And give me the power to commune with *this* through eternity, and to love *this*, and to be happy with this though eternal years, and the body and its resemblances may go to their dust, and pass with the material world at the end of time to their original chaos. It is the indestructible part of my friend—the memory, the imaginative, the perceptive, conceptive and reasoning powers and passions of the soul—to which I wish to be united.

And will it be difficult to find such in the world of blessedness, where, on the supposition that the essence of the soul and personal identity remain, we shall still be social and intellectual beings, and as a consequence, commune with each other? A single idea conveyed to or from our friend, would call up all the *memories of another*, and the recognition be of that which we have loved, and ourselves again be united in sentiment and affection with the social, the intellectual, the loving spirit of our friend. *It may be ideas then, rather than resemblances of form, that shall produce our recognition,* as is often the case in this world. How often have the features of our friend so changed in his absence that we trace not on the re-greeting, any resemblance of him to whom we gave the hand for a long separation! But a single word, a single idea causes the heart to leap with the joys of memory, that tell us we are again with the *unchanged and unforgetting spirit* of one we loved and yet love.

And indeed it is a blessed field of enjoyment which opens before the redeemed one as a *social, intellectual* and immortal spirit, retaining the susceptibilities of his spiritual nature, which shall be gratified in the society of heaven. There he shall meet those, from every age, to narrate the incidents of the past, in the providence of God, relating to the history of the world, and with millions of yet unborn spirits; who, again, shall tell of that which shall come after his own passage from the earth.

Trees and flowers, and streams, Are social and benevolent; and he
Who oft communeth in their language pure,
Roaming among them at the cool of day,
Shall find, like him who Eden's garden dressed,
His maker there to teach his listening heart.

Mrs. Sigourney.[17]

For the Offering.

"It is I; Be Not Afraid."[18]

How sweet to the soul with affliction cast down,
How cheering to those who in sorrow do mourn;
The Saviour's kind promise so feelingly made;
"Weep not, for I'm with thee," Oh, "be not afraid."

When the storms of adversity gather in gloom,
And those who once flattered, then pass by in scorn,

17. The final lines of "Solitude" by popular American poet Lydia Sigourney (1791–1865). The poem was often revised and often copied and reprinted in the two decades before its selection in *The Akron Offering*. Cumings quotes an early version of the poem, which won a prize from "the Judges of Original Poetry" of "the Boston Recorder for 1828." See "H.," "Solitude," *The Ladies's Garland*, 4, no. 37 (February 23, 1828): 148, American Periodicals (137148238). The likely source for Cumings' selection, however, is any edition of Sarah Josepha Hale's *Flora's Interpreter*, which had been republished frequently since its 1832 first edition. A late 1840s edition is Hale, *Flora's Interpreter, and Fortuna Flora* (Boston: Sanborn, Carter, Bazin, & Co., 1848), Google Books, http://books.google.com/books?id=AWsuAAAAYAAJ. The selection in the *Offering* closely follows Hale's selection on page 124, where these lines conclude a page devoted to sentiments inspired by the yellow marigold.

18. Matthew 14:27.

Despair not, or murmur, for Jesus has said,
"I'll never forsake thee," Oh, "be not afraid."

Though sickness may wither the heart's fondest joy,
And hopes that were cherished, in sadness destroy;
In woe's darkest hour, oh be not dismayed,
His presence will cheer thee then, "be not afraid."

Though the sorrows of death may encompass thee round
And the snares of temptation thy footsteps surround;
Oh yield not in anguish: his mercy displayed,
Will firmly sustain thee; Oh, "be not afraid."

Though prostrate in death, you behold the fair form,
Of one dearly loved consigned to the tomb,
Look upward; in mercy and kindness arrayed,
The Saviour is near thee, Oh, "be not afraid."

The child that smiled sweetly and slept on thy breast,
May from thy endearments be suddenly wrest:
But think not in anger, his wrath is displayed
'Tis only to prove thee; Oh, "be not afraid."

Though the one of all others most dear to thy heart,
Is torn from thy presence, and forced to depart;
Yet mourn not as hopeless: in bright robes arrayed,
You'll meet him again: Oh, "be not afraid."

Through all this life's changes, in sadness or joy,
With Christ for your portion; none can harm or destroy;
His sure word is pledged: the promise is made,
"I'll ever be with thee;" Oh, "be not afraid."

Lancaster Nov. 1849.
Adelia.[19]

19. See note for "Never Despair," p. 252.

Norman and Cornelia Campbell,

OR

"Truth Stranger Than Fiction."

By C. Cumings.

Chapter VIII.

Let us enter the crowded court-room where Norman Campbell is to be tried for fraud. There as a prisoner he sits, but oh! how unlike a criminal he looks. Every eye rests upon him in admiration, except those who have been prejudiced by Mrs. Sheldon and her Son or by the weak Richland whose wealth was passport to the good opinion of those, who like himself, were deficient in mental and moral perception and felt themselves entitled to the privilege of trampling under their feet, mind, heart, nobleness, all that exalts a human being and making the world give its allegiance to sordid gold, acknowledging an Aristocracy of wealth and upon its altar making the degrading sacrifice required. Even these, his enemies, look upon him now with envy—they *feel* his superiority and in the humbling consciousness, gnash their teeth with rage.

His friends from the city are there, all satisfied of his innocence, but some of them ignorant of his power to prove it, and wondering as they notice his cheerful and confident manner; but some understand it all and see in his clear eye, something that tells of glorious triumph, of deep and holy scorn, and deeper than all, a thrilling sense of gratitude for the power now given him to vindicate the honor of his friends who had perished, and his own, and to give to villainy, its just reward. Several of this brethren of the bar have proffered their services and he courteously thanks them all, "but," said he, "I will speak for myself first—if I fail, support me—if I do not say all that should be said, act your pleasure—speak for me then and God will bless you."

Look at William Benton—his eye can not rest on Norman Campbell, and in spite of all his fancied security, he feels a strange uneasiness, and Richland, too, is awed by the bearing of him who seems so fully in their power. A few know that a guard with a proper officer are stationed at every possible place of egress from the excited throng that have found their way into the house. Norman's eye glances quietly around and he is perfectly assured that his friends who undertook to put his plans in operation, have completed their task, and the kindling glance of his eye tells them "I am ready" and they almost fancy that they hear the word *vengeance* thrilling in its dreadful appeal to the hearts of all assembled—but no—he is calmly looking at the witnesses brought there to sustain Benton in his assertions and, as their examination now commences, we will listen to it also and leave all idea of retribution to him who hath said "Vengeance is mine I will repay."[20]

Witnesses for the Plaintiff make the defendant appear the guilty wretch his enemies desire him to be considered; but behold a witness for the defendant is produced, one whose veracity, even Benton would not dare to undertake to impeach. He says "I accidentally heard William Benton, Virgil Richland, a distinguished Lawyer yonder," pointing to one in the room, "and the man who bought the land of Norman Campbell, arrange plans and make calculations that they supposed entirely unknown to all, but themselves, if I except a servant of Benton's, an old man who was with him. I will tell you *what* they said and if desired, will then tell you *where* they said it and *why* I heard it. I heard Benton agree to pay five hundred dollars to the man to whom Norman Campbell sold his land if he would take of his, (Benton's) money and offer Norman Campbell so much" (naming the amount paid) "and take a deed of the same in his own name. The Lawyer I have mentioned and Richland agreed with Benton to help him to prosecute Norman Campbell for fraud and false representation in the sale of the land as soon as the man with whom they had bargained, presented his deed.—This is the substance of what I know on this subject."

Look now for a moment on the faces of those whom this man has thus exposed, see them shrink into their own nothingness and yet how industriously their council is preparing to make an attempt to save them from the effects of this testimony—he uses every argument in his power, says all he can say and sits down, and Norman Campbell now rises to speak for himself.—After the customary first address[21] he says:

"The testimony you have just heard I am aware *will* be, *must* be believed and may be deemed sufficient without any remarks from me or from any one; but the strange fact that William Benton the Son of my Mother's Brother, should deliberately undertake to ruin me, seems unnatural and all desire to know the cause and some may feel that, in justice, a reason should be given in order that all mystery may be cleared away and every one be fully satisfied,

20. Deuteronomy 32:35. This idea that God will avenge recurs throughout the testaments. See also Exodus 32:34, Psalms 94:1, Romans 12:19, Hebrews 10:30, etc.

21. I.e., "Your Honor," or "If Your Honor will please to hear me," etc.

but to make it all plain I must be allowed to send for more witnesses who are now waiting in a house close at hand and when I have done this I am willing to abide the issue—yea, I ask not for mercy—deal to me only cold, stern *justice* and if it leaves me in the power of the hollow-hearted villainy that placed me here, then will I be content and if it gives *me* power over my enemies, may the God of Heaven teach me how to use it in accordance with his will."

Here an Officer was sent for the witnesses Norman Campbell desired should be summoned, and soon returned, supporting a decrepit old man and followed by a Gentleman, bearing in one hand a small box and supporting with the other, a Lady closely veiled. They were seated in the proper place, the officer stationing himself near them while profound silence for a moment, reigned through the house—this is broken by a sound as of contention near one of the doors and William Benton is brought forward and a guard ordered to prevent his trying a second time to escape. He knows old Francis and beneath all her disguise, recognizes Cornelia Campbell and from that moment, felt that his doom was sealed—his face is pale and he trembles like an Aspen leaf and every one feels that further proof of deliberate villainy in him, is not necessary, nevertheless, they proceed to examine these new witnesses, not to prove what is already certain, but "to make confirmation doubly sure"[22] by giving the motives &c., &c., that led to such conduct. Old Francis was called upon first and stated as well as he was able, what all are aware he knew—first, of the proceedings relative to the land bought of Norman Campbell—then he told his own history—the fate of his first master, Wm. Benton's Father—of Norman Campbell's Father and Mother—of William Benton's Grandfather and lastly he mentioned Friedland—told of his agency in all the plans of William's Grandfather—revealed every thing they did to secure to William Benton the property that belonged at the time, to George and Albert, Campbell and all they did that ended in the destruction of the lives of Albert Campbell and his wife and of much property belonging to them and their Brother. Then he told of his own long continued silence in regard to all these things, and how at last, he had resolved to be silent no longer, and had accordingly visited Norman Campbell in Prison and told him all the truth—then he told how he went to Miss Campbell and with her to the cell of Friedland and there in the presence of the gentleman now seated by Miss Campbell, listened to his dying confession. He now sat down

22. Antebellum cliché and variant of the also-popular "make assurance doubly sure." The source is Macbeth's speech to Macduff in Act IV, Scene 1 of *Macbeth*. For an American edition of this time, see William Shakespeare, *The Dramatic Works* (Hartford: Andrus, Judd, and Franklin, 1837), 1:331, Google Books, http://books.google.com/books?id=gRcrAAAAYAAJ.

and Cornelia Campbell was called to state whether as far as related to herself, Francis Lisbon had told the truth, and also to state all she knew of the case before them. She commenced where old Francis brought her a letter from her Brother, telling of his arrest by Benton &c., &c. She stated distinctly, what old Francis told her and what Friedland in his last moments said and that the box now in the magistrate's hands who accompanied her to the cell and to her Brother, contained a written manuscript detailing all the events related by old Francis as far as concerned her parents and Uncles—this was in Friedland's hand-writing, signed by himself and attested as correct, almost with his dying breath.

Every eye is turned with admiration and deep respect on the countenance of Cornelia Campbell and then they look on her Brother and feel that they are worthy of each other—and there sits Benton, the perfect image of angry despair and Richland has sense enough to see his own position and feel his own insignificance; and the Lawyer, mentioned as in combination with him against Norman Campbell, betrays the bitter shame he feels. And now the last witness rises—the Magistrate, who accompanied Cornelia to Friedland's cell, to her Brother's prison, and to the present exciting scene, states briefly and clearly all he heard Friedland say, and being requested, he now places the box in the hands of the man designated as the proper person to receive and read it. It is read and listened to with an overwhelming sense of the injustice which the Brother and Sister before them have so long suffered. What did not Benton deserve? every thing but death and even that, almost every one in the house was ready to record as justly merited; but his punishment must have legal sanction. He is placed as a prisoner at the Bar, while Norman Campbell is pronounced innocent amidst a universal shout of approbation and heart-felt rejoicing, while he takes his place as accuser and prefers his charges against the guilty, quailing wretch before him.

For a few moments he seems lost in reflection and struggling to subdue some powerful emotion—he rises calm; but it is the quiet of strong feelings controlled by a powerful, mighty will—a giant intellect has grappled with the deep, the sacred feelings of a heart full of holy impulses, carried back by reflection through all the scenes of the past, and tortured by the thought of all the suffering that had been entailed on his family, but his brow is now clear and he speaks in tones that penetrate every heart. "I speak for my sister and myself. We do not forget that once we had a Father and a Mother—we can remember a Mother arrayed for the grave, a Father lingering many days and then in the morning of his life, yielding himself to death; and we have learned that William Benton's Grandfather suggested to Friedland, his confederate in crime, the idea of setting the fire that destroyed or was the means of destroying our parents' lives—we remember that an Uncle, at our Father's dying bed, promised to protect and love as his own, that Father's orphan children, and we recollect a woman, with a wily serpent heart, who had with her heartless Father been the means of destroying the health, the reason, the property, causing the honor to be doubted and at last the life to be lost, of an upright, honorable man, that gained the hand of another noble man that she might be better able to aggrandize herself and Son and as far as possible, place all who were left of our name and race, under her own control. We remember how that honest-hearted, high-minded man failed to fulfill his high destiny and how he passed away amidst bitter reflections, while reproach for the guilty being who had 'shorn him of his strength'[23] crushed from his heart the sweet forgiveness he wished to feel, and remorse sharpened its deeply poisoned arrow to pierce his bleeding heart as it throbbed and struggled in its expiring anguish! We remember too, the bitter taunts that cruel hearted woman heaped upon those orphans—that little boy and girl—that fair haired girl that devoted herself with untiring care to the task of allaying as far as possible the strife of those who should have been a Father and Mother to her—we recollect how that Brother and Sister tried to love as a Brother, that woman's Son, how his bitter hatred was borne in silence until at last there was nothing in his character that could bid them even hope for any thing worthy of love.

"Yes we remember all these things and the anguish their recollection brings it is not necessary here to attempt to describe. Not for crimes committed by William Benton's Mother, or Grandfather, or his confederate have we arrested *him*, nor yet for his own worst crimes, which you have been *obliged* to hear, as detailed in that manuscript written by Friedland, nor in his last act toward me—these are injuries that no law can reach; no appeal to it, could give *us* back the love and guardianship of our parents for our childhood's years—it could not give *him* his Father before ruin had set its withering seal upon him—it could not give *us* our noble, generous-hearted uncle or any of the joys that the possession of these blessings might have ensured to us. All these things are registered in the Archives of heaven—for justice for these wrongs, we appeal to that Tribunal where

23. A reference to the shaving of Samson, whose superhuman strength depended on his long hair, in Judges 16.

sits the Judge of the Universe!—but *here* we come for redress that *can* be made—we ask for our *own*—that property that was our Father's and our Uncle's and to which William Benton *never* had any *real* right, but which knowing all this, he so long kept possession of—yes for this, his *lightest* crime, we ask the interference of Law. In this give *us* the coldest measure of justice and to *him* give all of mercy that will be to himself a blessing."

He sat down—silence deep and portentous had, while he was speaking, chained the assembled throng; tears now flowed from almost every eye—sympathy for the wronged, warmed every heart—contempt for the degraded villain who had been the serpent in the path of innocence, filled every soul, and at last, the excitement broke forth again, and the dearest revenge that noble natures could desire, was at that moment given to the hearts of Norman and Cornelia Campbell, yes the justice of their cause was understood and their own actions and feelings were correctly appreciated. The weak Richland and the member of the Bar who had joined him in his endeavors to ruin one whom they feared, realized that they deserved and received a share of the same deep and bitter scorn that had been audibly uttered against William Benton, by all who had listened to the testimony produced, and had witnessed the generous forbearance of Norman Campbell in not once alluding to themselves or what they had done. In bitter shame they hung their heads and while from some full hearts that delighted to look at the good qualities of human beings, burst forth the admiration for Norman and his sister, that would not be restrained, and from others, who particularly delighted to punish the guilty, came forth curses and execrations for William Benton and his associates—*they* were still—yes—their countenances and Benton's were fit study for a painter that would portray the meanest passions of human nature, in the moment of their signal defeat, after they have been worked up to the highest pitch of malice—but let us turn away from *them*—the tumult subsides—the Judge is about to charge the jury—he does it in clear tones with the most impressive words, and in the shortest possible time, the voices of all the jury, declare William Benton, guilty of the deepest fraud and the most designing villainy and the Judge declares his punishment to be imprisonment in the State Penitentiary for a long term of years. As it was proved that what he had called his own property was *never* his, but had originally belonged to George and Albert Campbell, it was decided that all he had claimed, belonged to Norman and Cornelia Campbell as heirs to their Father's and Uncle's estate and they were forthwith put in possession of all necessary documents to establish and sustain their rights to the same—but there was a chance for William Benton to *put off* what he knew *must* be the *final* decision of all, he knew he could hope for no mitigation of the penalty of his crimes, but by gaining time, he hoped to be able to avoid the imprisonment, by flight. An appeal was granted but no one would be security for his appearance and he is obliged to take up his quarters in jail to await the session of the court to which he has appealed.

Norman and his Sister, amid the congratulations of all immediately started for the city taking old Francis with them. He knew that Mrs. Sheldon and her Son had been in secret intrigue with Richland and a few others; but he feared them not, and after securing a suitable home for his Sister and himself he presented himself at her door and asked to see Miss Sheldon. The servant ushered him into the parlor where Helen S. soon joined him. He told her all that had happened and that the final decision (about which no one could have any doubt) between him and Benton would be made in a few months—asked her to name a day previous to the expiration of that time, for their marriage, adding that he should then in company with his Sister visit the place where most of their possessions were located and also New England, to attend to the sale of the land that George Campbell supposed he had forfeited to Henry Herbert. Helen consented to his arrangement and although she met the most bitter persecution from her Aunt and Cousin, she faltered not, but at the time appointed, placed her happiness in his keeping with perfect trust and well deserved love. In the interval that had elapsed, Benton had made his escape from jail, and when his case was called in Court, there was no defense and they only had to ratify the first decision and very soon, Norman Campbell, his wife and Sister were on their way to take possession of their princely fortune.

Just before Helen's marriage a will was produced said to have been executed by her Father giving one half his property to Norman Campbell if he married his daughter, and the other half to Algernon Sheldon, his Brother's Son, with the condition that they should support Mrs. Sheldon, Algernon's Mother, equally between them. Neither Norman or Helen believed this to be his will or that he ever cherished a wish that Algernon Sheldon or his Mother, should share his property, any other way than, if they were suffering, that they should be relieved as he would any persons in want; but they could not prove their suspicions and they could now be wronged to that amount, and scarcely feel the loss. The will was put into the hands of the executor named in it, and they started on their journey.

We should delight to linger by their side as they journey along, and look on the beautiful scenery and on their speaking countenances—that dark-eyed, light-hearted bride whose impulsive feelings are ever breaking forth in exclamations of pleasure—that commanding form by her side in whose every movement is seen thought, dignity, warm-hearted generosity and devoted affection, and that Sister—happy in the happiness of those so dear, yet unable to hide from the observing eye, that her heart had suffered too keenly to feel perfect peace any further than its joys are gained from a sense of duty done, and the contemplation of peace in others—but we must, as it were, annihilate time and space and say that all they undertook was accomplished and before they were ready to return to the city, she had heard that Charles Elton had become a dissipated, profane forgetter, of all he once loved and honored. The agony of that dreadful moment was known only to the God of heaven—no human being saw her tears or heard her prayers; she met her friends with her usual self-possession and even her Brother, failed to penetrate the veil of pride that concealed her breaking heart—in connection with this first information of Charles Elton, she soon heard of his marriage to a wealthy young widow. She would not condescend to communicate to him the changes that had occurred in their circumstances, for said she to herself I cannot do this without apparently, seeking to change his opinion respecting myself—let him go—the time will come, even in this world, when he will feel that he has wronged me, yes "time *will* prove"[24] the truth of his regard and the strength of his principles and it will also prove the truth of my poor throbbing heart; but God grant he may never know its bitter strife in its efforts to forget himself.

They returned to the City, and Norman Campbell, although perfectly independent, entered upon the duties of his profession with a noble ambition. Every year gained him new laurels and added many to his friends. Richland had left the city and in the few hearts where envy still lingered, there was no power to injure one so universally beloved. With the most disinterested generosity he had entirely supported Mrs. Sheldon and had been untiring in his efforts to reclaim her son from his profligate course; he had established and sustained him in business and was ever ready to advise and assist. And to all, he gave ready sympathy, and encouraging words.

Years passed on; Cornelia remained much as when she first took up her abode with her Brother. No one but him could understand why she so

24. A popular saying that is too ambiguous to be a quotation or an allusion.

steadily refused every offer of marriage; even some of the most highly gifted and respected gentleman of the city had been made to feel that she could not love them, that she cared not for their love and she constantly refused to plight[25] vows that her heart could not sanction. Her Brother, loved her too well to chide; but it pained him to reflect on the cause, for well he knew that one bitter memory must ever be present to such a nature as hers. She found her happiness in doing good, in the love of her Brother and Sister, and in instructing their little son, a noble boy that well repaid her care; she loved almost to Idolatry; but, dear as were they all to her, she had long felt that she was not doing all her duty. She remembered the words of Elton on the night when they had talked of the duty he felt devolving upon him, to spend his days in preaching salvation to the wandering red man; she too then felt that it was a high and holy mission and in her own mind, devoted her future years to their instruction—as his companion and assistant. *His* name was not enrolled among those who could sacrifice worldly considerations for the benefit of benighted human beings, but not the less, was it *her* duty to spend her life and her wealth for this object.[26] She felt that she needed a more extended sphere of action; inclination and duty both led her to ask permission of her brother to accompany him on a long tour through the western States and some of the then, territories.[27] Business of pressing importance,

25. Pledge.

26. For more on American missions to Native Americans and the role of women in this work, see *Competing Kingdoms: Women, Mission, Nation, and the American Protestant Empire, 1811–1960*, ed. Barbara Reeves-Ellington, Kathryn Kish Sklar, and Connie A. Shemo (Durham: Duke University Press, 2010); Dana Lee Robert, *American Women in Mission: A Social History of Their Thought and Practice* (Macon: Mercer University Press, 1996); and Henry Warner Bowden, *American Indians and Christian Missions: Studies in Cultural Conflict* (Chicago: University of Chicago Press, 1981). An antebellum overview of the nature and extent of missions among Native Americans can be found in Harvey Newcomb, *A Cyclopedia of Missions* (New York: Charles Scribner, 1855), 582–626, Google Books, http://books.google.com/books?id=lw-_zuSAFwkC.

27. These "western" states would be the present-day midwestern United States: Ohio, Indiana, Illinois, etc. In 1849 "some of the then, territories" includes Wisconsin and Iowa, which became states in 1849 and 1846. (The states north of Texas and west of Iowa were not yet admitted to the union.) Today scholars might regard Cornelia Campbell's calling to mission work as an expression of the antebellum idea that the feminine practice of sentimentality and domesticity could redeem the damaging aggression of expansion and empire. See Jane R. Hunter, "Woman's Mission in Historical Perspective," *Competing Kingdoms*, 19–43. As Ian Tyrrell argues in "Woman, Missions, and Empire: New Approaches to American Cultural Expansion," however, it is too simplistic to typecast these missionaries as cultural imperialists. *Competing Kingdoms*, 43–66. Missionary work, with its transnational organizations and allegiances, is better understood in a broader context of globalization and modernization. The work could undermine or support empire, and it could promote or frustrate the oppression of colonized peoples. See Ryan Dunch, "Beyond Cultural Imperialism: Cultural Theory, Christian Missions, and Global Theory," *History and Theory* 41, no. 3 (October 2002), 305–25, JSTOR, http://www.jstor.org/stable/3590688, and "Doing Everything: Religion, Race, and Empire in the U.S. Protestant Women's Missionary Enterprise, 1812–1960," *Competing Kingdoms*, 367–89.

and curiosity, each had a share in inducing him to take so long and tedious a journey and leave his dear devoted wife and precious child who was now some five or six years of age. He felt that this journey would give his sister pleasure, for, like, himself, she loved to commune with nature in all its moods and delighted to gaze on its wildest scenery—he had confidence too, that she had judgement and ability to carry out her own intentions, whatever they might be, with perfect propriety.

His consent was readily obtained and we will now suppose their preparations made, their farewells said and that they have been several weeks on their journey, travelling in a private carriage in company with two gentlemen, who were looking for homes in the West and who willingly consented to drive one pair of horses and take charge of their trunks and several articles then necessary on a journey west—among the rest a box containing rifle and shot gun for each, with all proper ammunition carefully secured. To each carriage was attached a pair of the best horses the country produced and when they arrived near the boundaries of civilization, Mr. Campbell purchased two more horses and all the accoutrements necessary for equestrians, in order that each might have the pleasure of diverging from the track the carriage must take, when necessity or curiosity prompted. He also purchased every article necessary for any exigency that might occur.

Thus equipped, they had travelled through forests with the roughest kind of roads, over prairies where there were no roads, save perhaps, sometimes, the waggon track of an emigrant and sometimes the Indian's trails that marked the paths to their villages; they had viewed nature in almost every aspect and, *beautiful* was inscribed on all; they had visited the emigrants in their log cabins and carried with them sweet remembrances of many a noble mind and honest heart, found beneath the rude shelters of the first settlers of those parts—they had visited several Indian villages and Cornelia had selected the place where she intended to spend her days and her wealth. She had made them understand that she would if possible to find one, send some person to them as soon as she returned home and that she would as soon as in her power, go herself to teach them to read and understand how to talk with their white brethren. Her brother had accomplished his business and they were returning another way home, when just before night they reached a settlement on a beautiful prairie. Two or three log houses were clustered together and they were informed by a boy who came to the door that they entertained travelers and that it was ten miles to the next house. They entered the house intending to stay overnight—the horses were taken care of and a comfortable supper for themselves was prepared by the only woman they had seen, who seemed a poor dispirited creature that mechanically performed her duties; but had no heart, no life, no hope. Cornelia felt a strange sorrow as she looked upon her evidently once handsome features.

A little boy now came in and Cornelia started in surprise—the perfect image of Henry Herbert stood before her. She asked his name. "Henry Herbert," said he.

Her brother came to her assistance. "Where is your Father, my lad?" said he.

"He and aunt Laura and uncle William have been gone several days to the village about twenty miles from this, but they will be at home to-night," said the boy.

"Who is aunt Laura and who is Uncle William and what is your Father's name?" said Mr. Campbell.

"My Father's name is Henry Herbert—Aunt Laura is Uncle Julius' wife, (he was drowned in the night, a short time ago) and Uncle William is sometimes called Bill Benton—his name is William Benton, and Mother tells me to call people by their right names."

Both Brother and Sister were now satisfied into whose hands they had fallen and determined to leave the house immediately. They told Mrs. Herbert that they had concluded to go on as far as the next house and they remarked with surprise her look of thankfulness as they announced their determination. They selected several valuable presents that they felt would be of use to her which with a purse containing several dollars, they bestowed upon this evidently wretched woman. Tears ran down her cheeks as she accepted them from Cornelia's hands. When she could speak she asked to know the name of her benefactors. Cornelia told her, her name and her Brother's and she seemed struck dumb with terror as she listened, but at last she said: "Oh make haste and be gone and may God take care of you—Henry Herbert and William Benton will be here before dark!—is not that enough? go go I say!—you will not meet them and I will not tell them you are here; but *others will*—oh, be gone—be gone!—"

Concluded in the next Number.

Selected for the Offering.

Life's Likeness.[28]

Written in imitation of the poetry of the 17th century.

Life is—what?
It is the shooting of a star,
That gleams along the trackless air,
And vanishes, almost ere seen to naught.
And such is man—
He shines and flutters for a span,
And is forgot.

Life is—what?
It is the vermeil[29] of the rose,
That blossoms but till the rude wind blows,
Then all entombed in sweets, doth fade and rot.
And such is man—
He struts in bravery for a span,
And is forgot.

Life is—what?
It is a dew drop of the morn,
That, quivering, hangs upon the thorn,
Till quaffed by sun-beams, 'tis no longer aught.
And such is man—
He's steeped in sorrow for a span.
And melts, forgot.

Life is—what?
A stone, whose fall doth circles make

---

28. Republished without attribution in American magazines, newspapers, and anthologies, this poem could have been selected from a wide range of sources. In the 1989 Clarendon edition of the poems of English poet John Clare (1793–1864), it appears with the title "Life's Likenesses." See Clare, *The Early Poems of John Clare, 1804–1822*, ed. Eric Robinson and David Powell (Oxford: Clarendon Press, 1989), 394–95. Another version, signed "T. W. C." from "Liverpool," is "Life's Likeness," *The Lady's Monthly Museum; or, Polite Repository of Amusement and Instruction* 6 (November 1817): 297–99, Google Books, http://books.google.com/books?id=3ZgwAAAAYAAJ. An 1840s printing is "Life's Likeness," *Christian Reflector* 5, no. 8 (February 23, 1842): 4, American Periodicals (135943689).

29. Vermilion; a bright, beautiful red color.

On the smooth surface of the lake,
Which spread till one and all forsake the spot,
And such is man—
'Midst friends he revels for a span,
And sinks—forgot.

Life is—what?
It is a bubble on the main,
Raised by a little globe of rain,
Whose hair destroys the fabric it has wrought,
And such is man—
Swelled into being for a span,
And broke, forgot.

Life is—what?
A shadow on the mountain's side,
Of rock, that doth on ether ride,
Driven by the northern gale, with tempest fraught.
And such is man—
He hangs on greatness for a span,
And is forgot.

Life is—what?
It is the sound of cannon near,
Which strikes upon the startled ear,
And ceases ere we can distinguish aught.
And such is man—
He frets and blusters for a span,
And is forgot.

Life is—what?
It is the swallow's sojournment,
Who ere the summer's robe is rent,
Flies to some distant bourne,[30] by instinct fraught,
And such is man—
He rents his dwelling for a span,
And flits, forgot.

30. Boundary; limit; also, brook or stream.

And is this—life?
O yes! and, had I time, I'd tell
A hundred shapes more transient still:
But, whilst I speak, fate whets his slaughterous knife,
And such is man—
Whilst reckoning o'er life's little span,
Death ends the strife.

For the Offering.

Letters to the Offering.

Number III.

By Lily Lute.[31]

I had never been to Akron and I had long wished to see that far-famed city,—and more to behold face to face a "*live*" editress; so one bright Friday morning when the beautiful Indian summer had begun to spread her smoky mantle over dying fields and fading woodlands, I started alone, my conveyance a one horse carriage which I drove myself, independent of beaux[32] and all other kind of waiters.[33] I had not gone far before I discovered that the horse I was driving, whose unpoetical name was Tom, had a predominance of the lymphatic temperament,[34] for though fat, sleek and young, it did not care to show off at the expense of his ease; and as my conscience would never let me abuse horse-flesh, my friend Tom jogged on at his own pace, while I congratulated myself on not having some gentlemen I wot of,[35] beside me to apply the whip. O, I have seen them beat the poor brutes till I shuddered, and I always said to myself, beware! for he that abuses the uncomplaining beast will make a cruel husband.

31. For more about Lily Lute, see p. 3; n. 15, p. 44; and p. 453–57.

32. Boyfriends.

33. Helpers; attendants; servants.

34. Someone who was wanting in energy and vivacity might be said to have a "lymphatic temperament." For a non-ironic description of such a constitution, see Caleb Ticknor, *The Philosophy of Living; or, The Way to Enjoy Life and Its Comforts* (New York: Harper & Brothers, 1836), 283, Google Books, http://books.google.com/books?id=RYUAAAAAMAAJ.

35. "Wot of" means "know of."

Well, as I did not travel at rail-road speed,[36] I had sufficient leisure to admire the beautifully picturesque country, well cultivated farms and neat farm houses, which we find in almost all parts of the Western Reserve. I did not stop except to water, till I reached New Portage—New Portage![37] I had heard of it ever since I was a little girl, and expected to see a town as much larger than our Seville as Seville is larger than three log cabins in the wilderness. But there it was—all before me, a store-house and tavern and mayhap, a blacksmith's shop—I have forgotten—but I know it reminded me of Udder Valley, in Miss Bremer's Strife and Peace, which was so large that the horse's head was at one end of the village while the back end of the carriage was at the other.[38] I drove up to the door of the inn and as I alighted from the carriage, told a boy in waiting, to feed my horse. "How many oats shall I give him?" asked he—now that was a poser—for I did not know whether he needed a pint or a peck, and with an ignorant look I said I did not know. "Don't know how many oats you want given your horse?" No, said I, give him as many as you please, and I turned into the house, where the first object that met my eye was a son of Bacchus[39] stretched upon a bench. I hurried through the room as fast as possible, and in the parlor found some very good papers, which I read awhile, then feeling uneasy,

36. In the 1840s, trains generally went from ten to thirty miles an hour, averaging perhaps fifteen miles per hour, including stops. Freight trains were slower than passenger trains, but ten miles an hour was as fast as a horse-drawn boat could go on the canal. "It is an interesting scene," wrote one observer, "to witness from twelve to twenty cars, each of which accommodates fifty persons with seats, moving at the rate of twenty-five miles per hour, and continuously, without any pausing for relays of horses." See "Railroad Scene," *Ladies' Repository and Gatherings of the West* 2, no. 1 (January 1842): 1, Google Books, http://books.google.com/books?id=hlDQAAAAMAAJ.

37. New Portage lay on the Ohio Canal, about six miles southwest of Akron. It was then a village of a few hundred people. At the end of the nineteenth century, it became a part of Barberton after "America's Match King," Ohio Columbus Barber (1841–1920), invented Barberton as the home for his Diamond Match Company. Seville, about thirteen miles west of New Portage, also had a few hundred inhabitants, plus a store, a fulling mill, a furnace, a tannery, a saw mill, and a school. See Daniel Haskel and J. Calvin Smith, *A Complete Descriptive and Statistical Gazetteer of the United States of America* (New York: Sherman and Smith, 1848), 462, 607, Google Books, http://books.google.com/books?id=UOstAAAAYAAJ.

38. English translations of the works of Swedish novelist Frederika Bremer (1801–65) were in great demand in 1840s America. Here Lute alludes to an early scene in her 1843 novel, *Strife and Peace, or Scenes in Norway*, in which Susanna and Harold argue about which is better, Sweden or Norway. The Swede boasts of "Uddewalla," her native town, where all the men are large and strong. The other retorts: "How can anybody be born in Uddewalla? Does any one really live in that place? It is a shame to live in such a place. It is a shame only to pass through it. Why, it is so miserably small, that when the wheels of your carriage are at one end of the town, the horse is putting his head out of the other. Don't talk about Uddewalla." See Bremer, *Tales of Every-Day Life in Sweden* (Boston: James Munroe and Company, 1843), 8, Google Books, http://books.google.com/books?id=_wQrAAAAMAAJ.

39. An intoxicated man; a drunkard.

began to look about the room, and from my observations, sat down quite contented with myself and glad I did not live in New Portage—just then I glanced toward the window and saw a splendid equipage, containing a lady and gentleman, sweeping down from the Akron road. I could see nothing of the lady except a beautiful white bonnet and plume, but I did not doubt that she was beautiful, for the gentleman was, that is, as much as I could see of him through a pair of shining black whiskers, and then he held his head down to listen and talk to her as men only do to pretty women. Heigh-ho! sighed I, they are lovers no doubt, and very happy—I wish I had a pretty face and a beautiful white bonnet and plume and then—"Your horse is ready," said the boy, and I was glad, for I was displeased with myself and I longed to be out under the open sky again, surrounded by the beauties of nature and fanned by a breeze not laden with alcohol. Out on the road, and passed the Cypress Swamp, and the lovely little lake, and the stony hill, and even the sight of Akron away in the blue distance, did not entirely drive from my imagination the white bonnet: it would come, at first lightly floating on the air like summer down, then a snowy plume waving and nodding over a white bonnet, followed by a pair of black whiskers and smiles and bows, and I could almost hear the music of love, the soft sigh, the melting kiss and the finale, the little word *yes*.

It was evening when I reached Akron, and though Luna and the starry host[40] were doing all they could towards lighting up the city, their lights were not quite as brilliant as gas. However the shop windows were gaily lighted and the busy tradesmen bustling about made the streets look lively and pleasant. The next day I saw it by day-light and was very favorably impressed with the place and the people; and highly delighted with my visit at the home of the intelligent editress of the Offering. May Heaven grant her a long life of uninterrupted blessings; and her dear mother and father and interesting sisters, have my warmest wishes for their welfare, and my heartfelt gratitude for their kind attention to a stranger.

Saturday noon I bade adieu to my friends, the gentlemanly host of that excellent house, "Cobb's Exchange,"[41] and the pleasant town, starting as I

---

40. The moon and stars.

41. A hotel and "stage house"—a place of rest and refreshment where a stagecoach (or, in this case, perhaps a canal boat) could drop off and pick up a fresh relay of horses. This may have been Lute's best choice for overnight accommodations, given that listless Tom would require a stable and care. Operated by Charles Cobb, Cobb's Exchange was at the center of Akron, right by the canal, at the southwest corner of Main and Market streets. Every number of the 1849 *Summit Beacon* contains a prominent ad for "Cobb's Exchange."

supposed for home; then how was I vexed to find myself about mid-afternoon at the little village of Copley,[42] almost as far from home as I was at Akron. "Never Despair,"—said I,[43] and on I went, and still on, and misty twilight was passing away before the merry moon and twinkling stars and I had not reached Wadsworth.[44] I began to fear I had lost my way again and seeing a house at a little distance from the road, I drove up to the fence and without hitching the horse left him and ran over to the house. I had just knocked at the door, when away went the horse down the road and I after him, crying out whoa! whoa Tom! but Tom did not whoa, and I tumbled over the fence and had but just picked myself up, when I stepped on my cloak which threw me down again; but I regained my feet in a hurry and on I went after the horse with my whoa Tom! which at length succeeded in stopping him, and I had just caught him by the bit, when I heard some one coming at full speed, and looking back, I saw a boy coming from the house where I had knocked—"What in the world is the matter?"—asked he as soon as he could get breath—O, nothing, said I only I wished to inquire the road to Wadsworth. "Why, you are on the right road now and almost there," said he; I thanked him, rode on, and soon had the satisfaction of seeing the white village looking up from the gray distance. I spent the night there with some old friends, but as they had a house full of visitors beside myself, I thought I should not commit as much sin in driving home in the morning as I should in staying to trouble them.

On my way home I met a strange funeral procession. It consisted of four or five carriages of men and not one of them in mourning. I looked at the coffin and saw it was long as that of a man, and I said to myself, some poor fellow has died, far away from friends and home and there are none but strangers to follow him to his last resting place. But when I reached home I found it was the corpse of a man who had died sometime before in Westfield,[45] and they were now carrying him to a vault. He had been disinterred by some physicians, as was supposed, for he was found in a barrel

42. Copley, about seven miles west of Akron, was a town of about 1,500 people with saw, flouring, and textile mills. Lute has wandered a little too far to the north on her return trip to Seville. See Haskel and Smith, 152.

43. See p. 250.

44. Now back on the direct route from Akron to Seville, Lute is about seven miles from home—maybe two-thirds of the way—when she reaches Wadsworth, a town of the same size as Copley with a tannery and grain and textile mills. Haskel and Smith, 688.

45. A small town, two miles northwest of Seville. At this time, it had about 1,000 inhabitants, a tannery and four saw mills. Haskel and Smith, 715.

beneath a straw stack, designed, doubtless, for Dr. A's. "*slaughter house*," in Cleveland.[46] And is there no other way to obtain a knowledge of the human system? Must the graves be robbed of their dead for the sake of Science? Hear what Lippard[47] says:—"Alas! Alas! not even the grave was a resting place for you, poor Daughter of the Poor! Many times, in want and misery you wished for death, and prayed God for the resting place of the quiet grave. There, after hunger, cold, sin and despair, you would at last be at peace. They buried you only yesterday in Potter's field. They crushed your limbs into the rude coffin, and laid you to rest without a word of prayer, but the music of a rattling spade and a falling clod. But even in the grave, rest is denied you. You died poor—science now demands your corpse. It is necessary for Science and the world, that even the unblest mould of Potters' field[48] be stripped from your unpainted coffin.

46. One of the most prominent doctors in northeast Ohio, Horace A. Ackley (1810–59) settled in Cleveland and co-founded the medical school at Western Reserve College. Ackley's practice as a professor of surgery generated a great deal of legal trouble and public controversy. A gruff and intimidating man, he used profanity in the classroom and threatened violence to his critics. He was notorious for dissecting corpses, a practice that was illegal and generally objectionable, if not reprehensible, to most people in 1849. Ackley was also subjected to legal scrutiny and urban legend for his methods of procuring corpses for dissection. See "Horace A. Ackley," *Dittrick Medical History Center*, Case Western Reserve University, http://www.cwru.edu/artsci/dittrick and Dudley P. Allen, "Pioneer Medicine on the Western Reserve," *Magazine of Western History Illustrated* 5, no. 2 (December 1886): 71–78, Google Books, http://books.google.com/books?id=6lcjAQAAMAAJ. According to one anecdote, Ackley sent medical students to a graveyard to exhume the body of a pauper. After they were caught in the act, he took responsibility and argued, ineffectively, that "the man had no friends . . . he served no good purpose in life and his body was justly forfeited to medical science." See O. J. Hodge, *Reminiscences* (Cleveland: Imperial Press, 1902), 62–65, Google Books, http://books.google.com/books?id=Vo4UAAAAYAAJ.

47. Philadelphia novelist George Lippard (1822–54) wrote sensational Gothic novels with egalitarian social arguments. His fictions were immensely popular in the late 1840s. This letter ends with Lute quoting from Chapter 14 of Lippard's *Memoirs of a Preacher* (1849). Here Dr. Reuben Gatherwood is disturbed at midnight, in his urban, fourth-story "Dissecting Room" in "an alley narrow and dark," by an equally brutal assassin. With a "homely face . . . agitated by an unnatural enthusiasm" and eyes that are "protruding at all times," Gatherwood was seeking evidence of the immortality of the soul through his anatomical experiments. Lippard's description of Gatherwood suggests some of the abuse that may have been thrown at Dr. Horace A. Ackley. Lippard writes that Gatherwood "belonged to that class of Physicians who open the casket from which a diamond has been stolen, and demonstrate from the very structure of the casket, that it never contained a diamond at all . . . . Reuben was an Atheist. With all his knowledge of Science, the veriest Child babbling amid its toys, could have taught him a Science as far above his own, as the canopy of heaven is above the kennel." See Lippard, *The Memoirs of a Preacher, or, The Mysteries of the Pulpit* (1849; Philadelphia: T. B. Peterson & Brothers, 1864), 137, Google Books, http://books.google.com/books?id=SnElAAAAMAAJ. Note that some antebellum editions of Lippard's novels also have an irregular capitalization of nouns ("poor Daughter of the Poor," "Dissecting Room," "the veriest Child," etc.) and thus display the liberties that were sometimes taken with punctuation and typography in the fiction of this period. See Introduction, pp. 17–18.

48. See n. 23, p. 155.

"The rough lid is torn aside, and your form grasped by the hand of wretches, who are forced to earn a dollar in this way; is huddled into a cart, and borne through the populous city to the inner temple of Science—the Dissecting Room. It must be a comfort to you Poor Woman, to think that all this is done in the cause of Science—Science that did so much for you and yours, while life was in your veins."

For the Offering.

Written for a Lady's Album.

By Jenny.[49]

You ask your friend, Eliza, for a token,
And say, a contribution to your Album
Is worthy proof of their esteem and friendship.
I much regret the absence of the muse,
On this occasion. I would that I were able
To inscribe ought worth your notice, or of *you*.
Howe'er, I'll try in *plain dull prose*, or rather
Twixt prose and verse, to express my ardent wish
That you may sail o'er life's tempestuous Ocean,
Unscathed by rocks that lie beneath its surface
'Gainst which, poor erring mortals sometimes split,
And that your little Barque be manned with Patience
And Resignation in the van; and Faith,
And Hope and Perseverance at the helm
To buffet adverse winds, which "ever
And anon" you'll chance to meet.
            The *blighted* hope,
The loss of kindred dear—the faithless lover
The ungrateful friend and the vindictive foe—
All these, nay, more than these,—may be thy lot—
'Twere vain indeed, 'twere worse than vain, to wish
Eliza might escape the ills of Life
For these *refine* and purify the heart,
They wean us from the world—the earthborn cares,

49. For more on "Jenny," a "lady" from Zanesville, see n. 12, p. 189.

The illusive hopes and unsubstantial joys,
(Vain things of time and sense) and from our eyes
They draw the veil that hides reality. May you
My friend, in wisdom's ways, in virtue's paths be found,
And through the Summer season of your life,
Glide smoothly onward, both receiving and
Dispensing blessings rare. And may you not
Regret the near approach of *Autumn* mild,
That philosophic season of the year,
And winter too, should *he* with his *stern brow*
And shivering touch, o'ertake you e'er you reach
Your destined port, shrink not, but hail him
As the harbinger of Peace who ushers in
That spring which is eternal.

For the Offering.

Despair.—A Fragment.

By Jenny.

* * * My heart is sick,
And each succeeding morn, instead of Light,
Brings Darkness, Storms and Tempests to my soul.
Oh! that I were a *dog*, to fawn and cringe
And lick my master's hand—to catch the bone
Thrown by the greasy wench into the *dirt*—
Receive my meed[50] of praise, or *cuffs*, or *kicks*,
Nay, 'twere better still to be reported *mad*—
For in this case, *kicks*, *cuffs*, or bad report
And all that bore connection with my being
Would soon be found "among the things that had been,"
And *I*, *Poor Dog*, be *negatively* happy.
Yet here I live—live on—or seem to live
And move, amid the busy crowd, myself
As busy—loathing life and all that adds

50. Reward.

To what is *call'd* the happiness of man.—
Why am I thus? Oh, tell me you that I know?
Will this dense cloud, than Egypt's darkness thicker
Remain for aye[51]—And this green earth so bright,
So beautiful—will it afford me naught
Save food and raiment, and a beggar's grave?

To Our Readers.

Summer has come and gone dear reader and winter with its chilling breath has·usurped its place, but it brings in its train, the long, pleasant evenings and I imagine I see many of you in your happy homes after the cares or pleasures of the day are past, examining your papers and magazines, and among the rest, some of you reading the Offering, and looking with approbation on the efforts made to ensure its being an instructive and elevating medium of social communication—and perhaps I might, from some, hear tones of criticism that savored not of good wishes for this enterprise, or confidence in any thing that is not "far-fetched:" and perhaps there may be now and then one who cannot tolerate any work that is not the very essence of bigotry, superstition and intolerance—and some must see every Editor go to the other extreme, and run mad on all the Reforms of the day; but, with all this pitiable conceit and ignorance, we have nothing to do, only to present arguments in favor of the exercise of common sense and that heavenly charity that supposes others may be as conscientious as ourselves, notwithstanding their opinions may lead them to cross the orbit in which we perform our revolutions and another path may be to them "the good and the right way."[52]

Hail to you gentle friends and foes (if we have any) for whatever else may be in these pages, there is no *ill will* to any. Heaven's blessings on you all and one of the greatest of temporal blessings just now, (at least to as many as were born and bred in "Yankee land",)[53] would be a glorious snow-storm—then we could imagine we were at home again—the sleigh-bells would jingle, friends would be greeting each other and Christmas would be coming indeed; but *hush* this is all imagination, and all the space

51. Always; forever.

52. 1 Samuel 12:23.

53. New York and the New England states.

allowed me is nearly occupied, therefore, I will simply say, you cannot read this No. without *thinking* both of this world and the next and thought can injure no one.

Several original articles have been received too late for insertion in this No. Maud Wellington's 3d Chapter on Reform and Conservatism was not ready in season, but will appear in the Jan. No.

The article by a Lady in Westfield will appear in the next.

Thanks to all,
Your humble servant,
C. Cumings.

THE
AKRON OFFERING.
January, 1850.

Selected for the Offering.

Extract from Thoughts on the Poets.

By H. T. Tuckerman.[1]

Byron.[2]

Three thousand copies of Byron's poems are sold annually in this country. Such a fact affords a sufficient reason for hazarding some remarks on a theme which may well be deemed exhausted.—"My dear sir," said Dr.

1. Henry Theodore Tuckerman (1813–71) was a prolific and well-regarded American literary critic of the mid-nineteenth century. Born in Boston, Tuckerman moved to New York City in 1845, where he joined the literary salon of Anne Charlotte Lynch Botta (1815–91) after 1855. There Tuckerman had regular interaction with a staggering collection of literary figures of that time and place. This experience did much for him and his national reputation. As biographer Robert L. Gale writes for *American National Biography*, though Tuckerman "and his vast production have been described by many modern commentators as commonplace, diffuse, and superficial," in his own day "he was revered by his grateful contemporaries as cosmopolitan, graceful, and instructive." See Gale, "Tuckerman, Henry Theodore," *American National Biography Online*, http://www.anb.org/articles/20/20-01029.html. Here Cumings extracts an entire chapter, "Byron," from Tuckerman's 1846 book, *Thoughts on the Poets* (New York: C. S. Francis, 1846), 165–74, Google Books, http://books.google.com/books?id=jLdp96LPH-wC.

2. The writings of British poet George Gordon Noel Byron (1788–1824) were popular in England and the United States in the decades after his death. A notable American edition is the eight-volume *Works of Lord Byron* published by Philadelphia's Carey & Hart in 1839. *Burton's Gentleman's Magazine and American Monthly Review*—then edited by Edgar Allan Poe—declared it "undoubtedly, the best edition of Byron and most splendid specimen of book printing that has appeared in the United States." See 7, no. 1 (July 1840): 57, Google Books, http://books.google.com/books?id=dnNMAAAAMAAJ. At the end of 1849, Akron's Beebe & Elkins book store were advertising the sale of editions of Byron

Johnson, "clear your mind of cant."[3] This process is essential to a right appreciation of Byron. No individual, perhaps, ever more completely "wore his heart upon his sleeve"[4] and no heart was ever more thoroughly pecked at by the daws.—The moral aspect of the poet's claims has never been fairly understood. No small class of well-meaning persons avoid his works as if they breathed contagion whereas it would be difficult to find a poet whose good and evil influence are more distinctly marked. The woods, and flowers, the poisonous gums, and "roses steeped in dew,"[5] are not inextricably mingled in the garden of his verse. The same frankness and freedom that marked his life, is evident in his productions. It is unjust to call Byron insidious. The sentiments he unveils, are not to be misunderstood. They appear in bold relief, and he who runs may read. There is, therefore, a vast deal of cant in much that is said of the moral perversion of the poet. Where he is inspired by low views the darkness of the fountain tinges the whole stream; and where he yields to the love of the beautiful, it is equally apparent. There are those who would cut off the young from all acquaintance with his works, because they are sometimes degraded by unworthy ideas or too truly reflect some of the dark epochs of his life. But it is to be feared that the mind that cannot discriminate between the genuine poetry and the folly and the vice of those writings, will be unsafe amid the moral exposure of all life and literature. Indeed, there can scarcely be conceived a book at once more melancholy and more moral than Moore's

---

alongside Caroline May's late 1840s anthology *American Female Poets, Pilgrim's Progress,* "Poets of England and America," "Women of the Scripture," and books by Whittier, Longfellow, Bryant, and Burns. See "Just Received by Beebe & Elkins," *Summit Beacon* (September 19, 1849), 2.

3. Well-known quote by English author Samuel Johnson (1709–84). The expression begins a remarkable scolding of Johnson's biographer and disciple, James Boswell (1740–95): "My dear friend," Johnson says, "clear your *mind* of cant. You may *talk* as other people do: you may say to a man, 'Sir, I am your most humble servant.' You are *not* his most humble servant. You may say, 'These are bad times; it is a melancholy thing to be reserved to such times.' You don't mind the times. You tell a man, 'I am sorry you had such bad weather the last day of your journey, and were so much wet.' You don't care sixpence whether he is wet or dry. You may *talk* in this manner; it is a mode of talking in society: but don't *think* foolishly." See Boswell, *The Life of Samuel Johnson* (London: J. Richardson, 1821), 5:102, Google Books, http://books.google.com/books?id=gYs-AAAAYAAJ.

4. Iago wears his heart "upon his sleeve / For daws to peck at" in Act 1, Scene 1 of Shakespeare's *Othello* (c. 1603). To see this in an amusing 1849 American edition, see Thomas Bowdler, *The Family Shakspeare* (Philadelphia: J. W. Moore, 1849), 881, Google Books, http://books.google.com /books?id=PVsbAQAAMAAJ.

5. Paraphrase of "Yet I must dote upon thee,—call thee sweet, / Sweeter by far than Hybla's honied roses / When steep'd in dew rich to intoxication." from "To ———," a sonnet by English poet John Keats (1795–1821). To read this in an American edition of this time, see John Keats, *The Poetical Works* (New York: Wiley & Putnam, 1846), 2:133–34, Google Books, http://books.google.com /books?id=qYwVAAAAYAAJ.

Life of Byron.[6] It delineates the vain endeavors of a gifted spirit to find in pleasure what virtue alone can give. It portrays a man of great sensibility, generous impulses and large endowments, attempting to live without settled principle, and be happy without exalted hopes. There is no more touching spectacle in human life. Genius is always attractive; but when allied to great errors it gives a lesson to the world beyond the preacher's skill. What awful hints lurk in the affected badinage of Byron's journal and letters! What an idea do they convey of mental struggles! After reading one of his poems, how significant a moral is his own confession: "I have written this to wring myself from reality."[7] And when he was expostulated with for the misanthropic coloring of his longest and best poems, who can fail to look "more in pity than in anger,"[8] upon the bard when he declares "I feel you are right, but I also feel that I am sincere."[9]

The apparent drift of Byron's versified logic is skepticism. He continually preaches hopelessness; but the actual effect of his poetry seems to me directly the reverse. No bard more emphatically illustrates the absolute need we all have of love and truth. His very wailing is more significant than the rejoicing of tamer minstrels. No one can intelligently commune with his musings and escape the conviction that their dark hues spring from the vain endeavor to reconcile error and the soul. Byron's egotism, his identity with his characters, his cynicism, his want of universality, his perverted creed and fevered impulses have been elaborately unfolded by a host of critics. The indirect, but perhaps not less effective lessons he taught, are seldom recognised. The cant of criticism has blinded many to the noble fervor of his lays devoted to nature and freedom. All his utterance is not sneering and

6. Byron's friend, the Irish poet Thomas Moore (1779–1852) published his *Letters and Journals of Lord Byron, With Notices of His Life* in 1830. For the original John Murray edition from London, see Google Books, http://books.google.com/books?id=fKo_AAAAYAAJ. An edition published shortly before Tuckerman's essay is *The Life of Lord Byron, with his Letters and Journals* (London: John Murray, 1844), Google Books, http://books.google.com/books?id=wIhKVUN82NAC. Hereafter *Life of Byron*.

7. Tuckerman, like many writers of this time, is not always careful with quotation marks. Throughout the essay his quotation marks do not necessarily indicate an accurate quotation of another text. Here he "quotes" an 1813 letter in which Keats describes his new poem, "The Bride of Abydos," as "the work of a week." He explains that he has "really ceased to care" about his literary reputation. "I have written this, and published it, for the sake of *employment*,—to wring my thoughts from reality, and take refuge in 'imaginings,' however 'horrible.' " See *Life of Byron*, 197.

8. A common saying or cliché, probably derived from Horatio's "countenance more in sorrow than in anger." See *Hamlet*, 1.2.

9. Tuckerman abridges a portion of a letter in which Byron explains why he lacks the heart to make suggested changes to a poem. A paragraph later he writes "My whole life has been at variance with propriety, not to say decency; my circumstances are become involved; my friends are dead or estranged, and my existence a dreary void." *Life of Byron*, 136.

sarcastic; and it argues a most uncatholic taste to stamp with a single epithet compositions so versatile in spirit. It is curious to trace the caprice which runs through the habits and opinions of Byron. It should ever be borne in mind in contemplating his character, that in many respects he became, or tried to become, the creature which the world made him. He took a kind of wicked pleasure in adapting himself to the strange portraits which gossips had drawn. Still, with all due allowance for this disposition, the views and acts of the poet were marked by the various contradictions which entered so largely into his nature and fortunes. Compare, for instance, such phrases as "Cash is virtue" and "I like a row,"[10] with some of his deliberate sentiments embodied in verse. His letters to Murray alone display a constant series of cross directions. Well did he observe "I am like quicksilver and say nothing positively."[11] His opinions on the subject of his own art cannot be made to coincide with each other or with his own practice. He long preferred "Hints from Horace" to the first two cantos of "Childe Harold," prided himself more upon his translation of Pulci than "the Corsair," and declared "the Prophecy of Dante" the best thing he ever wrote.—He over-estimated Scott and Crabbe, was blind to the true merits of Keats, and very unreasonable in his deference to Gifford. He charges Campbell with underrating the importance of local authenticity in poetry with a view to protect his Gertrude of Wyoming, without remembering that his own defence of Pope was induced by a motive equally selfish.[12] No man reasoned more exclusively from individual consciousness or was oftener biased by personal motives, and yet when the Countess Guiccioli begged him not to continue Don Juan, he complained that it was only because the production threw ridicule upon sentiment, which it was a woman's interest to sustain.[13]

There is a kind of superstition which seems the legitimate result of sentiment. The idea of destiny will generally be found to exercise a powerful sway over persons of strong feeling and vivid fantasy. When the mind is highly excited in pursuit of a particular object, or the heart deeply interested in an individual, a thousand vague notions haunt the thoughts. Omens and pre-

---

10. *Life of Byron*, 549, 547.

11. *Life of Byron*, 106.

12. The authors named here are English poet and novelist Walter Scott (1771–1832), English poet and clergyman George Crabbe (1754–1832), English poet John Keats (1795–1821), English satirist William Gifford (1756–1826), Scottish poet Thomas Campbell (1777–1844), and English poet Alexander Pope (1688–1744).

13. Though friendly with the much older Count Guiccioli, Byron took his young and beautiful wife, the Countess Teresa Guiccioli (1798–1873), as his mistress. This was during the years of controversy that followed the first publication of cantos of *Don Juan* (1819).

sentiments, every shadow which whispers of coming events, every emotion which appears to indicate the future, is eagerly dwelt upon and magnified. Perhaps such developements are the natural offspring of a great sensibility. They are certainly often found in combination with rare powers of intellect and great force of character. Few men more freely acknowledged their influence than Lord Byron. In his case they may have been, in some degree, hereditary. His mother was credulous in the extreme and had the folly to take her son to a fortune-teller. He planted a tree to flourish by at Newstead, and found it after a long absence, neglected and weedy. He stole a bead amulet from an ill-defined faith in its efficacy. The day after writing his fine apostrophe to Parnassus, he saw a flight of eagles, and hailed the incident as a proof that Apollo was pleased. When leaving Venice, after he had put on his cap and taken his cane, having previously embarked his effects, an inauspicious mood overtook him, and he gave orders that if all was not ready before one o'clock, to postpone the journey. He recalled a gift because it betokened ill-luck, and turned back from a visit upon remembering it was Friday. He even sent back a coat which a tailor brought him on that day, and yet, with true poetic inconsistency, sailed for Greece on Friday. He cherished the most melancholy associations in regard to the anniversaries of his birth and marriage, and had many strange views with regard to the fate of an only child. But the most remarkable among Byron's many superstitious ideas, was his strong presentiment of an early death. This feeling weighed upon him so heavily that he delayed his departure from Ravenna week after week, in the hope of dissipating so sad a feeling before engaging in his Grecian expedition; and when stress of weather obliged him to return to port, he spoke of the "bad beginning" as ominous.[14] In short, he acknowledged that he sometimes believed "all things depend upon fortune and nothing upon ourselves."[15] How far this tendency to fatalism influenced his conduct it would be difficult to ascertain. But opinions of this nature, grafted upon a constitutional liability to depression, certainly help to explain many of the anomalies of Byron's character.

The physical infirmities of the poet have never been sufficiently considered. No one can read his account of his own sensations without feeling that he was seldom in health. They are not the only sufferers who labor under specific diseases, the ravages of which are obvious to the eye. There is a vast

14. In the section of *Life of Byron* detailing many of the superstitions summarized in this paragraph, Moore notes that Byron considered the "bad beginning" to be "a favourable omen." *Life of Byron*, 592.

15. *Life of Byron*, 125n1.

amount of pain and uneasiness, even of a corporeal nature, which is not ranked among the legitimate "ills that flesh is heir to."[16] In nervous persons particularly, how numerous are the trials for which science has discovered no remedy. He used to "fatigue himself into spirits;"[17] and always rose in a melancholy humor; and constantly talks of being "hippish" and of his liver being touched and of having an "old feel."[18] He fancied that like Swift he should "die at the top," but unlike the Dean, he professed no dread of insanity, but declared "a quiet stage of madness preferable to reason."[19] The withered trees on the Alps reminded him of his family. Often in the presence of the woman he loved, he longed for the solitude of his study.—His restlessness, his frequent and rash variations of habits; his wild course of diet, on certain anniversaries eating ham and drinking ale, though they never agreed with him, and then for weeks living upon biscuit and soda water; his inclinations for violent exercises and craving for stimulants, indicated what a victim he was to morbid sensations. Could we realize the suffering incident to such a constitution, preyed upon as it was by an irritable mind and desponding temper, how much should we find to forgive in the poet's career! We cannot but agree with one of his biographers, that his excesses "arose from carelessness and pride rather than taste."[20] We must bear in mind that he never lost a friend, or cherished his resentments; and take in view that singular blindness which rendered him skeptical as to all literary influence upon character which prompted him to ask "Who was ever altered by a poem?"[21] His charities were extensive; his philanthropic aims sincere and noble. "Could I have anticipated," he says "the degree of attention which has been accorded me, I would have studied more to deserve it."[22]

---

16. *Hamlet*, 3.1.

17. *Life of Byron*, 235, 253.

18. Hippish: hypochondriacal; depressed. *Life of Byron*, 479.

19. Byron wrote that he did not fear "idiotism or madness." "Some quieter stages of both must be preferable to much of what men think the possession of their senses," he wrote. Moore glosses the comment about Swift "dying at the top" with this anecdote written by Edward Young (1683–1765) about Irish writer and dean Jonathan Swift (1667–1745): "I remember as I and others were taking with Swift an evening walk, about a mile out of Dublin, he stopped short: we passed on; but perceiving he did not follow us, I went back and found him fixed as a statue, and earnestly gazing upwards at a noble elm, which, in its uppermost branches, was much withered and decayed. Pointing at it, he said, 'I shall be like that tree, I shall die at the top.'" *Life of Byron*, 473 and 473n2.

20. *Life of Byron*, 522. The "biographer" here is Byron's friend, English poet Percy Bysshe Shelley (1792–1822).

21. *Life of Byron*, 541.

22. Tuckerman appears to be paraphrasing Byron's disappointed response to unexpected notoriety as described in *Life of Byron*, 250.

When we attempt to group together the trials of Byron, physical and moral, we find an array which claims, not indeed justification, but allowance for his errors. The weakness of her character to whose guidance his childhood was committed, her ungovernable temper, his lameness, the indifference of his guardian, the homeless year which he passed between Cambridge and London, his isolated position upon entering the House of Commons, the ill-accordance of his pecuniary means with his rank, the unjust criticism that his first early efforts elicited, his return after two years' travel to encounter bereavements, which induced him to write—"at three and twenty I am left alone, without a hope, almost without a desire; other men can take refuge in their families, I have no resource but my own reflections;"[23] and, to crown all, his unfortunate marriage and the social persecution he endured; his long siege of bailiffs and domestic spies—make up a catalogue of troubles which might have driven a meeker being into despairing error.—But he was acquainted through the whole of his brief life with a grief which, however the cynic and the sage may sneer, was to him real and wasting sorrow. His affections craved an object which was never granted them. His frequent allusion to his boyish love, his regrets over that dream when "both were young and one was beautiful," capricious amours on the continent, mingled with the ardent longings with which his poetry overflows, prove him to have been a devotee of that "faith whose martyrs are a broken heart." This unsatisfied love was a fountain of tender desire in his bosom which fertilized and softened his effusions, and to which is ascribable their most pathetic touches. It was in seeking an "ocean for the river of his thoughts"[24] that he bears so many hearts along in the rash bewildering emotion.

The poetry of Byron is the result of passion and reflection. He is not so much a creator as a painter, and his pictures are drawn from feeling and thought rather than nicety of observation.

"I can't furbish," says one of his letters. "I am like the tiger, if I miss the first spring, I go grumbling back to my jungle."[25]

He gives us, as it were, the *sensation* of a place or a passion. Take for instance such epithets as "the blue rushing of the arrowy Rhone," and "battle's magnificently-stern array"—how vividly do they make us sensible

23. Tuckerman combines three separate passages to make this quotation. *Life of Byron*, 135, 115, 139.

24. The first quotation is from Byron's 1816 poem "The Dream;" the second comes from stanza 121 of canto 4 of his *Childe Harold's Pilgrimage*; the third comes from the same section of "The Dream." See Byron, *The Poetical Works of Lord Byron* (New York: Appleton, 1847), 485, 65, 485, Google Books, http://books.google.com/books?id=AG1AAAAAYAAJ. Hereafter *Poetical Works of Lord Byron*.

25. *Life of Byron*, 464.

of the scenes described! He says "high mountains are a feeling;" every thing in the universe and in life which appealed to his sympathies was to him a feeling. It was scarcely allegorical for him to call himself "a portion of the tempest," or to exclaim,

"I live not in myself, but I become a portion of that around me."[26]

It seems, therefore, very irrational for the admirers of a more calm and descriptive class of poets to moralise over Byron's feverish style, as if poetry was not subject to the laws of mental developement. He might indeed have refrained from writing or publishing, but the condition upon which alone his mind could gush forth in poetry, was that its fruits should bear the qualities of the man. He was remarkably susceptible to immediate impressions of a melancholic disposition and earnest things; and these traits of character necessarily colored his poetry; indeed it owes to them its distinguished beauties. Through them he was placed in that intimate relation with what he saw that enabled him to give us the fervid and stirring impressions of Childe Harold, to address with the eloquence of profound sympathy Parnassus and Waterloo, Greece and Lake Leman, Rome and the Ocean, the Apollo and Solitude, the Stars and the Dying Gladiator. "I could not," he says, "write upon any thing without some personal experience and foundation."[27]

The career of this impetuous, but in more than one sense, noble being, is traced in his works most clearly. The very poems whose influence is deemed so baneful, have a moral eloquence few homilies can boast. What lesson has human life so impressive as the wanderings of genius reflected in its creation? Turn from the elevated beauty of Byron's effusions written in Switzerland, amid that exalting air and scenery, when Shelley, as he used to say, "dosed him with Wordsworth,"[28] to the flippant and low rhymes, strung together in the intervals of dissipation at Venice; read the outpourings of his soul in the pensive hour of solitary reminiscence and the bitter lines provoked by resentful emotion; contemplate a glowing description caught from deep communion with some scene of historical interest or natural grandeur, and the week impromptu wrung from a day of ennui and self-disgust; and can anything impart so powerful an impression of the transcendent worth of truth? "O the pity of it, the pity of it," we exclaim with the Moor;[29] and just

26. *Childe Harold's Pilgrimage*, canto 3, stanzas 71, 28, 72, 93, and 72. *Poetical Works of Lord Byron*, 46, 41, 46, 48, and 46.

27. *Life of Byron*, 291.

28. The text of this famous letter can be found in Thomas Medwin, *Conversations of Lord Byron* (London: Henry Colburn, 1824), 293–94, Google Books, http://books.google.com/books?id=4lI6AAAAcAAJ.

29. *Othello*, 4.1.

in proportion as we admire the strength of the wing that bears us through the realms of song, do we feel the misery of every unworthy flight. In the same degree that we sympathize with genius do we contemn the darkness which shrouds from view "the unreached paradise of despair."[30] If to some weak minds the errors of high natures are made venial by its gifts, to many of healthier tone they become thrice detestable, because of the brightness they mar. The antidote more frequently accompanies the bane than narrow moralists are willing to admit. It will not do to prescribe the style of poetic development. Its moral characteristics are indeed legitimate subjects of criticism, rebuke and praise but whether a bard's effusions are passionate or calm, descriptive or metaphysical, festive or sad, depends upon the spirit whence they spring. It is the nature of a willow to droop, and an oak to fling out its green branches sturdily to the gale. Byron with his earnest temper, his undisciplined mind, his impassioned heart could not have written with the philosophic quietude of Wordsworth. It is absurd to lament that his verse is impassioned; such was its legitimate form. And is there not an epoch of passion in every human life? Is it not desirable that the poetry of that era should be written? Cannot these men of even pulse and severe temper permit beings of more enthusiastic mood to have their poetic mirror also? Byron represents an actual phase of the soul's life, not its whole nor its highest experience, but still a real and most interesting portion of its developement. He is not the unnatural painter which many critics would fain make him. In many a youthful heart do his truest appeals find an immediate response. Even the misanthropy with which his writings are imbued is not all morbid and undesirable. How much is there of lofty promise in the very discontent he offers! How does it whisper of desires too vast for time, of aspirations which pleasure and fame cannot satisfy! How often does it reveal an infinite necessity for love, an eternal tendency to progress! Misanthropy has its poetry as well as its pleasure; and the eloquent complaints of Byron have brought home to countless hearts a deeper conviction of the absolute need of truth and self respect than any logical argument. If a few shallow imitators are silly enough to turn down their collars and drink gin, there is another class who mentally exclaim as they read Byron—"What infinite longings are these! what sensibility to beauty! what capacities of suffering! how fatal is error to such a being! let me, of kindred clay, look earnestly for a lofty faith, a safe channel for passion, a serene haven for thought!" The

30. *Childe Harold's Pilgrimage*, canto 4, stanza 122. *Poetical Works of Lord Byron*, 65.

poet's torch is not always a meteor, alluring only to betray, but a beacon-light warning the lover of genius from the rocks and quicksands which made him desolate. Besides, enough confidence is not felt in the native sense and just sentiments of readers. Can we not yield our hearts to the thrilling address to Lake Leman without being pledged thereby to adopt the creed of Don Juan? Can we not accept Byron's tribute to the Venus and Dying Gladiator without approving his bacchanal orgies at Newstead? May we not enjoy the wild freedom of the Corsair without emulating the example of the hero "of one virtue and a thousand crimes?"[31]

For the Offering.

The Evening Hour.

How calm and sweet is twilight's pensive hour,
  How o'er the mind its magic influence steals,
Soothing each troubled thought, each rising fear,
  And chasing from the heart the woe it feels.
How sweet to sit, and with one's thoughts commune,
  Fondly recall the scenes of by-gone years;
To think of Friends now sleeping in the tomb,
  And o'er their memory shed affection's tears.

This is the hour I love to steal away
  From all earth's cares, and toils, and busy scenes,
And in the music of the night-bird's lay,
  Forget the tumults of day's troublous dreams;
To sit and gaze upon those starry gems,
  That glow and twinkle with unfading light,
And think of worlds on worlds in distant realms,
  Whose brilliant glories beautify the night;

To read in them that wonder-working power,
  That formed and guides them at his sovereign will,
To feel His presence at this sacred hour,
  With solemn awe immensity doth fill.

31. *The Corsair* (1814), canto 3, stanza 24. *Poetical Works of Lord Byron*, 117.

I love to watch the clouds in grand array,
    Majestic floating piled like mountains high,
Reflecting back with bright and golden rays,
    The sun's departure from the western sky.

And lovelier still the moon's pale, modest beam,
    Meekly ascending from her calm repose;
In beauteous robes, as night's most favored Queen,
    Adorned to reign supreme, at twilight's close:
This is the hour when visions of the past,
    Like meteor trains come rushing wildly on,
Telling of happier days, too bright to last;
    Of joys departed, and of pleasures gone.

Crowding fond memory's page with rapturous scenes,
    Of earlier years, when hope with rainbow hue,
Shone brightly mingling with our childhood's dreams,
    And all earth's Friendships seemed so fond and true.
Alas! how great the change! a few brief years
    Will sadly prove that all are false as fair,
And the bright picture of our life appears
    As short and transient as that meteor's glare.

How unwise then to seek such fleeting joys;
    On such delusive hopes to place our trust;
To pour our heart's best love on trifling toys,
    Or fix on treasures that corrode and rust.
Better, far better look to that unfailing source,
    Whence joys perennial ever ceaseless flow;
And make the grace of God our wiser choice,
    And seek his favor and his love to know.

Then when life's toils and cares with us shall end,
    And we, Eternity's dread scenes are called to prove,
We may in Heaven find a faithful friend.
    And feel the raptures of Redeeming love.
And though on earth we ne'er again may greet

Those friends whose memory dwells deep in the heart,
Yet in that better land we'll joyful meet,
Where no long farewell tells the hour to part.

Adelia.
Lancaster, October 24, 1849.[32]

For the Offering

Time and Knowledge.

Written at School.

By Adelia Dorlesia Rich.

How great should we consider the importance of our time, when we think of the shortness of life, and the little time we have for improvement. The world abounds in knowledge. In every thing around us there is something useful to be learned if we had investigating minds. When we look around upon Nature we see many things that excite our admiration and astonishment, and at first, it would seem impossible ever to comprehend the laws that govern them. But by close application and investigation, we can make that which seemed a wonder as simple to our minds as the first rudiments of our spelling book. But if we would obtain knowledge we must improve each moment as it flies and when we have spent years in the acquisition of knowledge, we shall find that we have just learned that we know nothing. We shall see a wide field open before us, covered with knowledge, and as we pass through life, we should gather industriously from that field, and even then, when death finds us, it will seem that we have but just entered its borders.

When we look at the starry heavens and consider each twinkling star to be a world larger than our own, and to be at such an immense distance from us and each other, and beyond these, other suns and systems of worlds, which revolve around their suns, we are lost in our contemplation, and think that it would take more than a human mind to investigate the works of God. And when we look around upon our world, although it seems a mere speck in creation, yet it abounds in many things, the ablest Philosophers have been unable to account for. But when we look back a few centuries we can see that great improvements have been made in knowledge.

32. See n. 6, p. 252.

In ancient days there were a few learned men and their wisdom was great and we can now read their productions and gain much information. But knowledge was not so universally spread abroad over all ranks of society as it now is. There were a few wise men and the rest were ignorant, not knowing how to read or write. Now it is seldom we see any in ever so humble a station that cannot read.

And if we try we can accomplish almost anything we undertake and if an education be our object, if we improve our time and are studious, we shall obtain it. How necessary it is that we improve each moment for we have but a short time to spend here, a few days and we shall enter upon eternity.

We have thought ourselves a happy band when we have met here from time to time; but another year may bring its changes as the past has. We can remember the happy faces that used to meet us here, that now are far away and some will never meet with us here again. And where are they? Go to yon grave-yard and you will see their last long resting place, and yet a year agone their hopes were as buoyant, their prospects as bright as ours. But now they are gone. Yet how fondly we cling and think not that our life is like a summer rose exposed to every blast. Whether we live a few days or years or even to old age when we come to lie down in death, we shall think our time has been short and we shall deeply regret our misspent hours.

Westfield, Ohio.[33]

For the Offering.

The Lady and the Gipsy Girl.

Written by a Girl in her Thirteenth Year.

Lady. O! the Gipsy Girl, the Gipsy Girl.
As she puts from her brow that raven curl,

33. Westfield is a township in both Medina county (close to Akron) and Morrow county (90 miles southwest of Akron). The 1850 United States Federal Census records no "Adelia Dorlesia Rich" or even a "Rich" family for Morrow County, Ohio. The census for Westfield of Medina county has John F. Rich, a fifty-one-year-old carriage maker from Vermont, heading a family of five. His youngest daughter—the handwriting is not the neatest—appears to be ten-year-old "Amantta" who was born in New York. The 1850 census was taken by calling at each household or if no one was available, by asking for information at a neighbor's home. This could be Adelia Dorlesia Rich; the 1850 census has many omissions and inaccuracies. On the other hand, a good portion of Ohio's residents soon moved on to another state, usually farther west. The 1860 census has no Adelia Rich born around 1840 in New York; young Adelia could very well have died or married (and changed her name) in the intervening decade. Westfield, Medina county is about two miles northwest of Lily Lute's Seville and twenty miles west-southwest of Akron.

There is an expression in her clear black eye
As she reads the stars in their place on high,
Or leans on the tree with her head on her hand
She brings to mind tales of memory's land.
I wish I could see a Gipsy girl,
With a clear black eye and a raven curl.

Gipsy. You wish you could see a Gipsy girl
With clear black eye and raven curl?
To satisfy curiosity.
To tell your fortune, 'tis true I see,
Ah! lady fair with bright golden hair,
On your brow, there is not a wrinkle of care,
Life has been smoothe, as the lake's silvery sheen,
And storms have not clouded one bright youthful scene,
But yet; there are clouds to darken thy sky.
And cover it even from hope's daring eye.

Lady. Oh! Gipsy girl with the raven curl,
Now call to mind bright memory's pearl.

Gipsy. The Gipsy girl is ever free, to rove on land or on the sea,
She has strayed on the plain in the western wild,
Where carelessly played the emigrant's child,
She makes her home near the broad river's shore,
Near the falls down which chrystal waters pour,
She spreads her tent 'neath the oak tree's shade;
Or she lays her bed in the hidden glade:
Oh! the Gipsy girl is free to roam o'er the land or sea.

Lady. Oh! Gipsy girl, with raven curl,
Bring now to mind bright memory's pearl.
And tell me a tale, of wonder, or glee;
If such are the tales you would tell to me.

Gipsy. Nay lady fair, with bright golden hair.
I would not tell thee tales of care.

Lady. Then tell me of the mysteries,
That hide your art, tell even me
Why fortune in you does confide,
And other enquirers deride.
Say? Gipsy girl, with the raven curl,
Only show me your learning's pearl.

Gipsy. Nay lady fair with golden hair,
'Tis not in my power with you to share
My learning deep.

Lady. Then Gipsy girl, O! Gipsy girl,
As you part from your brow that raven curl;
And read in my face, with that piercing eye,
The tale of my future destiny,
Oh! let me look at the now blank book,
Say, Gipsy girl, with the raven's curl,
Let me see now the future's pearl.

Gipsy. Nay, lady fair with golden hair,
Your brow is not yet clouded with care,
I would have you greet the future with smiles,
And contented, meet with fortune's wiles,
There are clouds, and sunshine, in every life,
And let them come with happiness rife.

For the Offering.

Reform and Conservatism.

Chapter III.

By Maud Wellington.[34]

War and peace next claim our attention. Heroes have so long been lauded for the dreadful faculty of slaying their fellow-beings that it sounds like treason to bravery, to talk of settling national difficulties of a serious nature,

34. See n. 21, p. 228.

without resorting to arms. But who that is familiar with the history of mankind from the creation, can fail to see the evils of contention, whether it has existed between individuals or states and nations? Who that has reflected on the consequences of National strife, has counted the slaughtered millions sacrificed at its altar, has gazed on their ghastly wounds and mutilated remains; and looked upon the helpless parents, the widows and orphans of the slain as they gather around the desolate hearth or are cast forth upon the world's cold charity, can with the Roman of olden time say "My voice is still for war?"[35] Alas many! some, even while in contemplation of the battle-field in all its horrors, and in full knowledge of the sorrows entailed on many of the living, in consequence thereof, feel that there is no other proper way to vindicate national honor, and many who mourn over the evils attendant on war, feel that it is utterly *impossible* to adopt any other course, believing that the idea that "might makes right" is so universal; and the desire for conquest so general, that no other appeal would be heeded and, setting aside the many who have passed away from earth, who while they lived hesitated not as far as in their power to immolate every thing that opposed their progress, at the shrine of a selfish, unholy ambition, there are some with whom right and wrong are words that have no meaning or, at least, no weight, who would hesitate not to wage a war of extermination on all who would not willingly submit to their authority.—The spirit of resistance to change is not more widely disseminated on any subject than on that which says to fight an enemy in virtue, honor, glory, and to stoop to make any, but the victor's terms, is cowardice, treason, dishonor and everlasting disgrace. Even children and gentle women have been so strangely inspired that it needed but a blast from War's shrill clarion to transform as it were, their very natures and make them reckless in their thirst for blood.—But in every land there are some who have calmly reflected on these things and have felt that there *could be* a better way—here one and there one has arisen who has made it manifest that "his thoughts were turned on peace."[36] Reform has begun its work,[37] and against obtaining

35. Opening line of a speech by Sempronius in *Cato* (1713), a play by English writer Joseph Addison (1672–1719). The speech was often included in textbooks on oration. For example, C. P. Bronson, *Elocution: Or, Mental and Vocal Philosophy: Involving the Principles of Reading and Speaking* . . . (Louisville: Morton and Griswold, 1845), 276, Google Books, http://books.google.com/books?id=9EiOUgPYlJoC. For more on this textbook, see n. 25, p. 53 and n. 15, p. 220.

36. Opening line of Lucius's response to Sempronius. See above.

37. A "peace movement" had been ongoing at least since the American pacifist William Ladd (1778–1841) toured the United States for more than a decade after founding the American Peace Society in 1828. The European revolutions of 1848 and the unpopular U.S. war with Mexico (1846–48)

its full object, truth has nothing to urge, and it would fain hope that it will abide by its own fundamental principle and not forget itself as do its agents many times on other subjects, and while crying *peace* be found girded with the soldier's armor, *fighting* to accomplish its purpose. Let nations disband their armies, let the warrior lay aside his arms and let them be converted into implements of husbandry—the earth is broad—all may have homes of peace, and if National differences come, let justice be gained by appealing to cool judgement and sound reason of such as may be appointed to decide.

Such will be the case when Statesmen and those in power in the different nations of the earth, desire the good of all, and methinks there will be as much true love of country then as now, as much of a self-sacrificing spirit and more, much more happiness and prosperity. Then, even truth, without departing from its own safe medium, can say to the world, listen to every word that tells of the ceasing of strife—further every effort that tends to establish *universal peace*.

Slavery

The question raised upon Slavery is to be looked at next—Reform and Conservatism draw as distinct lines on this as on any subject that has ever been discussed. Conservatism says that the authority for enslaving the negro race, was gained from God Himself, through Noah, in the curse pronounced by him, upon his son Ham, that they have always been slaves and can be nothing else; that, because of their mental inferiority, they owe to the white man, allegiance and are incapable of taking care of themselves. Some slaveholders carry this idea so far that they consider the negro, not much, if any, above the brute in intellect, and that he owes him nothing more than is due to his beast and perhaps, feels nothing prompting him to feed or shelter either, but self interest. Yet not many such, we believe, are to be found, while there are many who conscientiously discharge every duty they feel binding upon them in respect to their slaves considered as human beings, although

---

encouraged pacifists to redouble their efforts at the end of the 1840s. For more on the nineteenth-century American peace movement, see Christina Phelps, *The Anglo-American Peace Movement in the Mid-Nineteenth Century* (1930; rpt. Freeport: Books for Libraries, 1972) and Valarie Ziegler, *The Advocates of Peace in Antebellum America* (Macon: Mercer University Press, 2001). An important collection of peace essays from this time is *The Book of Peace* (Boston: George C. Beckworth, 1845), Google Books, http://books.google.com/books?id=VIsOAAAAIAAJ. Three recent anthologies of peace writing are Robert Mann, *Wartime Dissent in America* (New York: Palgrave Macmillan, 2010), Charles F. Howitt and Robbie Lieberman, eds., *For the People: A Documentary History of the Struggle for Peace and Justice in the United States* (Charlotte: Information Age, 2008), and Murray Polner and Thomas E. Woods, eds., *We Dared to Say No to War: American Antiwar Writing from 1812 to Now* (New York: Basic Books, 2008).

of an inferior order, believing them unfit for self government and that it is binding upon them by every law, human and divine, to protect them, to ensure their comfort and as far as they are capable of enjoying happiness, to secure it, and some who own many slaves left them by their parents have a realizing sense that slavery is wrong and that upon the escutcheon[38] of a Republic, a land boasting of liberty, it is a foul and disgraceful blot, but they feel that it was entailed upon them, not only by *their* Fathers but so to speak, by *all* the Fathers of our Country, all the framers of its constitution and they cannot release them and leave them to themselves and feel that they are discharging the duty of sensible men or of christians; they are not able to provide for them away from their plantations, and indeed, could scarcely hope to provide for themselves or families, were their negroes sent away. The sympathisers with the slave, forget the necessities of the master and offer not the whole or a part of what the real pecuniary sacrifice must be if he should be left with but his own hands with which to support his family and they do not realize that he cannot, under existing circumstances, release his negroes. Thus in a spirit of Conservatism, of various degrees of intensity, found existing, not only in the minds of slave-holders, but of many in the free states of our Union and in all parts of the world, and, opposed to this, is that sentiment which has grown out of a principle of benevolence and a wish to do right—denominated Reform.

This not only says that slavery is wholly wrong, but that no individual or nation can be justified by any possible combination of circumstances, in allowing any human being or any number of human beings to take upon them or retain the relation of slave to themselves, and in their mad hurry to accomplish a desirable end, they have sometimes been found asserting that if slave-holders will not let their slaves have their liberty, it is the duty of the free white men of our country to take up arms against him or incite his negroes to kill him or in some way *compel* him to obey superior force.

It says that no legislation can destroy any person's natural right to liberty, and when by any means, the negroes *have* their liberty, assuming and asserting that their race is by nature as capable of elevation as any other, that they are not more degraded than would have been the Caucassian Race[39] under the same circumstances, they who adopt the extreme of the Abolitionist's creed, say that they should be treated as equals, as brethren, should be elevated to the privileges of citizenship, should have the right

38. A shield on which is painted a family's coat of arms.

39. For a history of "the Caucassian Race," see Bruce David Baum, *The Rise and Fall of the Caucasian Race: A Political History of Racial Identity* (New York: New York University Press, 2006).

of suffrage, should be eligible to offices and honors and in short, should be associated with them in all things.

And what does true justice and the most comprehensive benevolence say in this momentous question? It agrees with Reform in the abstract truth, that slavery is wrong and *should be abolished*, but it does not teach us that the negro race *is* or ever *was* or ever *can* be equal to the European or White race in intellectual capacity; it does not teach us that the blacks should ever be associated with the whites in a domestic, social or civil compact, it points not to union with them, in any sense, as right, yet it teaches us to shed a bitter tear for the black man's woes while we forget not the slaveholder's wrongs. It holds in its hands the balance of eternal justice and by it are weighed principles and causes and consequences and all must be satisfied with its irrevocable decisions. It surveys all the ground, sees how bitter the curse of slavery, how evil all its influence, how degrading its tendencies and with honest independence it can say "I would not have a slave to till my ground, to carry me, to fan me when I sleep" &c., &c., but it does not with the sometimes, *almost unthinking* Abolitionist, curse him who cannot, though he would, feel a proud consciousness of freedom thrill to his very soul. He found himself an heir to the portion that is his, an Estate and slave to cultivate the "paternal acres" are his and with it are physical weakness and mental inability to free himself from a position that perhaps may seem as wrong to him as it can to any one.

And what is truth to do now. It seeks the cause of the evil to be remedied and having found it, seeks to understand the best method for removing it and if it cannot be removed, the best manner to counteract its effects. Every person knows that slavery has a foot-hold in this country *now*, because our Forefathers allowed it to gain a place in its constitution, or in other words, received States as such, who had slaves and whose State constitutions gave the power to retain them and did not hinder them from engaging in that unholy traffic; and common sense, and common honesty forbid that individuals or states should seek to compel others to abandon a course sanctioned by the laws of the land. Justice, assuming as granted that all slaveholders would rejoice to see slavery abolished, if it could be done without being wronged themselves, and if the blacks could be suitably provided for, appeals to those who are not slaveholders in this country. It asks of them to give of their substance enough to remunerate the slave-holder for releasing his slaves and then enough to carry them back to their native home where sparkle the "sunny fountains of Africa".[40] It would not have them remain here for this is not their place—if released from their bondage and allowed the unrestricted rights of citizenship, methinks that many a white man would grow restive under the laws likely to be voted for by ignorant negroes, or intelligent negroes either, if any can become such—the tools of designing politicians or leaders in making and expounding law. Such a state of things will never do—neither morality or christianity demands this—look at the extremes of Abolitionism, and horror will seem to seize the mind, and deep disgust compel them to forbear, but look in imagination upon a community where such principles are *fully* carried out, meet in the councils of the men, go to the social parties, look around the streets, visit the schools, the churches, and the domestic firesides and then if you desire the negroes to be at liberty and remain here it seems to me that you must be nearly fit for treason to every thing honorable to humanity or acceptable to the God of heaven! Laugh not at the idea of colonizing the negroes, to a certain extent it has been done, and it could be done for all. "Union is strength" let all who are not slave-holders join together in peace, and the slave-holders themselves would not be outdone in generosity and the work would be accomplished and enough would be found ready to go with them and they could be enlightened to the extent of their power to comprehend, they could be taught how to take care of themselves, and it would be better for them and for us in every sense of the word, than for them to remain here.

Justice, benevolence and true policy unite in this view of slavery and this method of abolishing it and until this can be done, it urges upon all who would ever see it accomplished, that "sleepless vigilance"[41] that on one hand will not allow the extension of slavery and on the other will see to it that our goodly heritage, our heavenly "birth-right be not sold to Esau for a mess of Pottage."[42]

One thing farther these sentiments urge upon every human being, viz: that they allow their minds to become so far enlightened upon the real condition of the different nations of the world that their sympathies be not *all*

---

40. The article endorses a scheme known as "colonization" in which slavery is ended in the south but (in this case) slaveholders are reimbursed for their "property" by the Federal Government and the former slaves are removed to Africa. The idea was most popular in the western United States, where people had less first-hand experience with slaves and slavery. For more on the Colonization Movement, see P. J. Staundenraus, *The African Colonization Movement, 1816–1865* (1961; New York: Octagon Books, 1980) and Floyd J. Miller, *The Search for Black Nationality: Black Emigration and Colonization, 1787–1863* (Urbana: University of Illinois Press, 1975).

41. An old cliché, still popular in 1850.

42. Genesis 25:29–34.

spent on the *negro* slave, while so many thousands of different races and complexions, with at least as elevated natures as the Africans, are sunk in the lowest depths of physical, mental and moral slavery; let the head and the heart expand in its love of freedom and let us even dare to covet liberty and happiness for the degraded poor of England and Ireland. They are our brothers. We should ardently wish to break their galling fetters, to breathe upon them the sweet breath of a glorious and soul-renovating liberty, and bestow upon them liberally the bread and water of life. And in many of the southern countries of Europe we could find much of wrong and oppression but we will hasten to the frozen regions of the North, where, the serfs of Russia drag out a miserable existence—no stronger bonds ever shackled a negro than here bind white men and we hear but now and then a note of lamentation over their sad fate.[43] And this is not right, we should have hearts as large as the world, not circumscribed by the petty limits of states or nations, but in their fullness forgetting selfish considerations and overflowing with love to all. A moment too we will linger in imagination, in some of the kingdoms of Asia, in Turkey or China, where Conservatism reigns in chilling sullenness and our own sex are but poor, degraded slaves, while reform finds as yet, no lodging place in those vast Empires of sluggishness. There our hearts may throb with pity and in all we have looked at, we may find many lessons of importance and as we come again to our own fair shores and survey the vast unoccupied public land and the questions arises shall slavery come here? An *emphatic no* will burst from every heart. What *is* free shall remain free and we will seek by every just and honorable means to break the bands of oppression in America and in all the world and the God of justice will lead to glorious triumph.

Selected for the Offering.

"How Old Art Thou."[44]

Count not thy days that have idly flown,
    The years that were vainly spent;

43. The life of Russian serfs was the subject of many English-language articles and books in the 1840s. For example, see Edward P. Thompson's *Life in Russia: Or, The Discipline of Despotism* (London: Smith, Elder, and Company, 1848), Google Books, http://books.google.com/books?id=usUKAAAAIAAJ.

44. In the 1840s this was a standard selection for American schoolbooks. It appears to have been first published in the London periodical, *The Winter's Wreath*, around 1828, where it was signed "L. H. C." Most often in American republications (there are dozens) it is not signed, or it is attributed to "Anon." The title is sometimes keyed to Genesis 47:8. See *The Museum of Foreign Literature and Science* 12, no. 67 (January 1828): 152, American Periodicals (135911617).

Nor speak of the hours thou must blush to own,
When thy spirit stands before the throne,
To account for the talents lent.

But number the hours redeemed from sin,
The moments employed for heaven—
Oh! few and evil thy days have been,
Thy life a toilsome and worthless scene,
For a nobler purpose given.

Will the shade go back on the dial plate?[45]
Will the Sun stand still on his way?
Both hasten on and thy spirit's fate
Rests on the point of life's short date—
Then live while 'tis called to-day.[46]

Life's waning hours, like the sybil's page,[47]
As they lessen, in the value rise:
Oh, rouse thee, and live! nor deem that man's age
Stands in the length of his pilgrimage,
But in days that are truly wise.

45. The "dial plate" is the face of a sundial. The question is, will time ever run backwards.

46. John Epy Lovell's *The Young Speaker* provides very detailed coaching for hand and body movements while reciting this poem. (See illustration, above.) See *The Young Speaker* (New Haven: Durrie & Peck, 1849), 100, Google Books, http://books.google.com/books?id=Kn8XAAAAYAAJ.

47. One school textbook glosses the poem so: "The following piece is almost a paraphrase of a beautiful expression of scripture. The *Sibyl* alluded to in the fourth stanza, was a sort of prophetess, who is said to have offered nine volumes of her prophecies to the king of Rome at a very high price. When he refused to purchase, she burned three volumes, but asked the same price for the remaining six. It being still refused, she burned three more. This strange conduct induced the king to pay the full price for the remaining three." See William B. Fowle, *The Common School Speaker* (New Haven: J. Babcock, 1844), 68, Google Books, http://books.google.com/books?id=Lj8NAAAAYAAJ.

Norman and Cornelia Campbell,
OR
"Truth Stranger Than Fiction."

By C. Cumings.

Concluded.

Mr. Campbell and his sister needed not to be urged to leave the abode of Henry Herbert and William Benton, but they comprehended no danger that would have menaced them had they been strangers, and, although Mrs. Herbert's words seemed somewhat uncalled for, they did not deem it necessary to ask an explanation and soon after they bade her good bye and departed. They had traveled about an hour after sun-down when they saw three men advancing on horseback from a road that intersected that which they were traveling. By the uncertain light, they could not perfectly distinguish form or features, but one of them immediately rode to the horses' heads attached to the carriage in front, in which were seated the two companions of Mr. Campbell, and in a loud voice which he and his sister recognized as Benton's, commanded them all to stop and give up their money, their arms and horses or instant death awaited them. Mr. Campbell gave the reins to his sister, whose power to control her fears and feelings he knew he could depend upon, sprang to the ground and in an instant was by the ruffian's side, grasped his collar and shouted in his ear, "William Benton, dare you cross my path again; begone, for your own sake begone, or it will not be in my power even to save your life—each of my companions is now holding a pistol ready to discharge at you, you do not deserve your life but go now and you shall not be injured." He now relaxed his hold of him, hoping to see him depart but at that instant he felt himself wounded in his side and almost unconsciously stepping aside, he had just time to see the two men who came with Benton, closing upon them with arms presented, when the report of pistols rang on his ears and he saw Benton and one of his companions fall and the next instant, the other man was bound by the men who had sat quietly in their carriage as long as there was any hope that Mr. Campbell could send the robbers away, but the moment that they saw the blow aimed by Benton, and the menacing movements of his accomplices, they both fired and William Benton and Henry Herbert both fell. Mr. Campbell's wound was but slight and he hastened to the side of the fallen men. Herbert was dead and

Benton, after long continued efforts to restore him to life, gave some signs of returning consciousness. Cornelia Campbell had fully realized all the danger that encircled them, she knew that Benton would kill her brother if he could, but Benton was a coward, and before no one would he quail as in the presence of Norman Campbell. She solaced herself with such thoughts and while keenly watching every movement, quietly kept her seat until she saw her brother apparently recovering himself from the force of the blow received from Benton. She could bear no more—in the same instant that Benton fell, she reached her brother's side, she did not faint, or scream, but looking intently in his face, felt assured that he was not seriously injured, and breathing one long relieving breath, she stepped with him in silence to the side of him who had been the dark shadow on all their paths—there he lay pale and unconscious and though he had so deeply injured them and so well deserved his fate they mourned that they could not have saved him from his dreadful doom, but regret was now unavailing and after they had done all that could *there* be done for him and Herbert, Mr. Campbell requested his travelling companions to place them in their carriage together with the man they had secured and when this was done, they all turned their horses' heads toward the house they had so recently left.

It would be in vain to undertake to portray the bitter anguish of Henry Herbert's wife, the dreadful rage of Julius Herbert's widow, or the sad and sorrowful reflections of Mr. Campbell and his Sister. There lay Henry Herbert cold in death and, kneeling by his side was his heart-stricken wife, and yet in all her mourning, perfectly conscious that he had deserved his fate. In another part of the room, William Benton was groaning in helpless agony while near him, stood the being who had been his willing assistant in all his schemes to injure those who now appeared to her as instruments of Justice in the hands of Heaven. Benton opened his eyes, perfectly conscious of all that had happened and gazed upon the different occupants of the room. "I am dying," he said, "and I would have killed *you*, Norman Campbell, and *you*," pointing to his Sister. "It would have been sweet revenge to have destroyed you both. You are indebted to me or my kindred for every pang you have ever felt, but Cornelia, you do not know all you have to thank me for, but you may be assured that Charles Elton not only believes you perfectly vile, but that you have acknowledged it. In spite of his own reasoning he hoped that all he heard me say to the old Hermit of the Glen, was false; but I took care to destroy each lingering thought that brought peace to his soul. He threw you away, and better still, he threw himself away, and became as degraded as you deemed me when you so proudly scorned my love. Yes, I made you both wretched, and I glory in it. I do not know what is in the future, nor do I care"—then seeing Julius Herbert's wife, he said, "cousin Laura, you will have a nice warm place among those who people the Infernal Regions, and perhaps I shall be allowed to fan the flames that will wreathe around you, for you have kept alive all the evil that lurked in my nature and worked upon my passions until the very flames of hell would almost soothe me, and you deserve this service at my hands." Then he seemed almost exhausted, but suddenly roused himself; his eye rested on the form of Mrs. H. Herbert, who had become insensible to her misery, while Cornelia Campbell, though scarcely able to support herself, was trying to bring her to life and to comfort her wretchedness.

Benton beckoned to Mr. Campbell, who had been listening to him in silent horror, to come to him. When seated by him he said, "that woman is perfectly innocent and her portion has always been sorrow and poverty."

"She shall be protected," said Mr. Campbell, "and at least it will comfort *me* to tell you that I freely forgive you all you have done to me, and my sister I know, cannot harbor resentment."

"Bring her here," said the dying wretch.

He led her to his bed-side, and she calmly said, "I forgive you, William, for the blighting of my hopes, the breaking of my heart, and for destroying him whom I loved." And, bowing humbly by his side, as she prayed that God would pardon the many sins of him who was about to enter the untried scenes of another state of existence: All was still as she there supplicated for mercy for the criminal before her. Once it was noticed that he looked upon her, but immediately closed his eyes and when she rose, his spirit had left the tenement of clay.[48]

Mrs. Herbert was restored to consciousness and Mr. Campbell, in the most delicate manner, made known to her the necessity of sending for all the settlers in the neighborhood.

48. The body; the dead body. Though a cliché in antebellum American literature, this usage of "tenement of clay" is true to the source of the phrase. In English poet John Dryden's satire *Absalom and Achitophel* (1681), a great villain—"A name to all succeeding ages curst: / For close designs"—is described as having a "fiery soul" that, in "working out" its evil ways, allowed his "pigmy-body to decay" and thus excessively deformed his "tenement of clay." The suggestion here is that the dead William Benton looks like a man whose body was ruined by his excessive devotion to evil thoughts and plans. For an American edition of Dryden that is contemporary to *The Akron Offering*, see *Works of John Dryden, in Verse and Prose, with a Life*. Ed. John Mitford (New York: Harper & Brothers, 1847), 1:39, Google Books, http://books.google.com/books?id=9AsyAQAAMAAJ.

She comprehended all he could not bear to tell her, and realized that justice to the living, demanded a clear statement of all that had happened, and signified her approbation of such a course, and confidence in his judgment and kindness. When all were assembled, he briefly told them how Benton and Herbert came by their death, and appealed to their prisoner for testimony of the truth.

He was a man whom they all esteemed highly, and they readily believed his assertion that he was compelled by Benton to go with him when he attacked Mr. Campbell and his companions. He confirmed all that had been told them, and all agreed in justifying them in taking the steps that had resulted in the death of two human beings, and Mr. Campbell now learned that Benton and Herbert had long been suspected of robbery and murder, and that they regarded their death as a providential deliverance. All assisted in burying the dead, and when this duty was performed, and Mr. Campbell had ascertained that Mrs. H. Herbert had friends in New England to whom she wished to go, he made every necessary preparation for her and her children to go with them. Neither he nor his Sister could feel that they ought to endure the presence of Julius Herbert's wife, but they gave her money and begged her to forsake sin and make her peace with Heaven.

Once again they started on their homeward journey. Their reflections may be imagined, and the scenes through which they passed can not now be depicted. When they were within a few day's journey of the City, they fell in company with an acquaintance of Mrs. Herbert's, who, with his family, was going to the place where his friends resided. He kindly took her under his protection.—She received a large sum of money from Mr. Campbell and his Sister, with an assurance of friendship and readiness to assist her whenever she should need. Thus they parted; and Mr. Campbell soon after, complained of pain in his wounded side, which he had almost entirely neglected, deeming the injury very slight.—Before he reached home he could scarcely sit up, and as soon as he was in his own house, he went immediately to bed. The best Physicians were in attendance, and all was done that the love of his devoted wife and Sister could imagine would benefit him, but all in vain. He was deranged for several weeks, and when at last he knew his friends, he could scarcely speak, but just before he died, he said, "my dear wife, my darling Sister, you must be willing to let me go; you must forgive William Benton for being the cause of my death. Like my father I perish in the prime of manhood when hope and happiness seemed beckoning me on to a long life of felicity. Take care of my darling child, my noble boy, and God grant that he too, may not be the victim of villainy. Bid him remember his Father; educate him for the profession of the Law, and teach him to trust in Heaven. May God keep you all—I am willing to die." Thus another of his race[49] was sacrificed to the dark demon of undeserved hate. He was mourned by all—to the poor he had been a generous benefactor, and in all places a truly noble man. His wife was inconsolable—his Sister felt that she could not rouse herself from the dreadful weight of anguish that was scathing her very soul; but she had been trained to endurance, and she received strength from on High. Mrs. Sheldon and her son made great pretensions of affection for them all, and after Mr. Campbell's burial, she had so much anxiety for Mrs. Campbell and her child that she could not bear to leave them and, after a long persevering process of maneuvering, she made her feel that her society and advice were necessary to her peace. Miss Campbell understood this woman's true character, but she knew of no power she had to injure those to whom Mrs. Campbell appeared so devoted, and she tried to feel at ease respecting her. Still she could not but feel that some hidden motive actuated her, and all was soon explained in a letter she received from one who was a very dear friend of her Brother. This informed her that a bill in Chancery, in Mrs. Campbell's name, had been filed against her late husband, stating that Mr. Sheldon's will gave half his property to his daughter and her heirs and nothing about Mr. Campbell, but that he (Mr. Campbell) erased *her* name and inserted *his own* and it said farther that much of his property was purchased with money that belonged to Mr. Sheldon that he never gave an account of, and that he had thus kept back a large amount that belonged to Algernon Sheldon by virtue of his Uncle's will, and that he had never paid more than a trifling amount toward Mrs. Sheldon's support. All this was testified to under oath, by Mrs. Sheldon and her son Algernon.

The court that was to decide this case was to commence its session in a few days. Horror almost took away her power to think, but not long could it chain a mind disciplined as hers had been.—She knew that every word of the charge was false as the malice that invented it, and she taxed all her

49. In the standard American dictionary of the 1840s, Noah Webster's *American Dictionary of the English Language*, the main definition for this word is "the lineage of a family." See Rev. ed. (New York: Harper & Brothers, 1846), 666, Google Books, http://books.google.com/books?id=XKERAAAAIAAJ.

powers to find what facts she could bring against their charges. Her brother had told her his suspicions of Mr. Sheldon's will being a forgery, but of this she had no proof. He told her the whole amount of Mr. Sheldon's property, and how much he had advanced to Mrs. Sheldon and her son and she knew that the amount exceeded all he had ever received of Mr. Sheldon's property, but this she could not bring forward as proof, and thick darkness for a few moments cast its pall around her and yet thought continued its train of investigation. At first she said to herself, Helen cannot know of this—I will tell her and she will brand with ignominy those who dare to use her name to injure the memory of one whose soul knew no dishonor, then she thought of Mrs. Sheldon's influence over her and although she believed she had been deceived and did not realize the consequences of what had been done, she would not ask her to recall the charge—She prayed to her God to strengthen her in this hour of bitter trial, and give her wisdom and power to make plain to all the whole truth, and she felt a calm assurance that she should be able to defend her Brother's memory and bring to light the dark deeds of those combined against him. She felt that she could not then meet her sister or Mrs. Sheldon and she prepared herself to walk to the place where slept her parents and her brother.

She had walked but a short distance when she met a little girl, a daughter of a man who for many years lived with Mrs. Campbell's father. She remembered having seen him and having heard her brother speak of him as a shrewd, well educated man who from some unknown cause had been reduced to poverty. This girl handed Miss Campbell a piece of paper on which was written these words, "I am dying, come to my house and you shall know all the truth. For your brother's sake, for the sake of his child, and for your own sake come, and come quickly."

The signature was that of the girl's father, and Miss Campbell hastened with her and stood in the presence of the dying man.—He saw her and thanked her for coming, and turned to a man who sat by him with several sheets of closely written paper in his hand and requested him to give it to her and seeming to gain strength, he said, "In that document Miss Campbell, you will find proof that Mr. Sheldon never made a will, but that the instrument called his will was a base fabrication. I wrote it myself," he continued, "instigated by Mrs. Sheldon and her son. It will also tell you of charges preferred against your brother and it will prove them all false.—They were to have given me an equal share in what was gained, for I was an accomplice in all they have done, but I am going to my reward. You can thwart all their machinations now, and may God help you—"

"—and may He forgive *you*," said she, bursting into tears as overcome with conflicting emotions she sunk into a chair.

When she looked up he had ceased to breathe. The magistrate present who had legalized this man's testimony gave it to Miss Campbell with his own address and an assurance of secresy and that he would be in court at the proper time. He stayed to attend the interment of the dead and she departed with a heart filled with gratitude to God.

The day came when this case was called in court. Mrs. Sheldon and her son were present and renewed their oaths, while a deep shudder passed over all present, for all believed them deeply perjured. Miss Campbell was there and when the defence was called she handed a friend the testimony she had received, and before he had finished it, the Judge ordered an officer to prevent Mrs. Sheldon and her son from leaving the room. Suffice it to say that when the proper moment came, they were made sensible how heartily they were despised by all. They were both sentenced to the Penitentiary and all the property in their possession was declared to belong to Norman Campbell's estate while a large sum, the thousands they had squandered, remained unpaid. Mrs. Sheldon saw herself unmasked, heard the sentence of the Judge, was seen to swallow something from a phial she took from her pocket and soon slept the "sleep that knows no waking."[50] Her son was conveyed to prison and Miss Campbell returned to her brother's house and then told Mrs. Campbell all that had occurred and helped her to understand how much cause she had to rejoice in a decision that rendered justice to the innocent and the guilty. Miss Campbell loved her sister but she mourned the weakness and indecision that made her so unfit to discharge the duties devolving upon her and her heart soon received another blow in the knowledge that she was receiving the addresses of a wealthy southerner and that in a short time her brother's place would be filled by a stranger and her brother's only child be subject to his will. She could not bear to see this, and hastened everything for her long contemplated departure from all the scenes of civilization, to labor for those who were groping in moral and mental darkness. The Missionary family with whom she intended

50. Common variant of "the sleep that knows not breaking," a phrase in a well-known song in English poet Walter Scott's *The Lady of the Lake* (1810). To read this in an early edition, see (Edinburgh: John Ballantyne, 1810), 38, Google Books, http://books.google.com/books?id=MLEWAAAAQAAJ.

travelling, were soon ready. Old Francis chose to go with her, all who were engaged by her, to go, were ready, the stores of clothing, of provisions, of implements of husbandry, the cattle, horses, tools, books & all things, what remained of her wealth was converted into money, and then she went to the graves of her parents and brother and seating herself near them sobbed as if her heart would break—but her Heavenly Father strengthened her and she left the consecrated spot, feeling that she was protected and should be saved in every trial. She bade her sister farewell, took her little nephew in her arms, kissed him and in silence commended him to God who hath said "I will be a father to the fatherless."[51]

Their journey was completed. Again you see Cornelia Campbell as you first saw her as she returned from the grave of Charles Elton just as Mr. W. entered their settlement as detailed in the first chapter. And there she continued to live, dispensing happiness to all around her. Though sometimes oppressed by the memories of the past, yet never in the hours of her bitter struggling, appearing before those whom she wished to influence. They always saw in her a calm, majestic dignity that, blended with the genuine kindness of her heart, gave a peculiar charm to all she did and acted as a spell on the stern natures of the Indians.

When fifteen years had elapsed she returned to the world she had left, taking Charles Elton's son who was then fitted to enter College a year or two in advance, with her: It was a severe trial to give him up for the time it would take to finish his education, but it was for his good, and duty was her watch-word. She placed him in the same College with her brother's son, George Albert Campbell, who would finish his course at the same time with Cornelius Elton. Young Campbell's mother and step-father were both dead. He remembered the countenance of his father's sister and he had never forgotten her parting words of love and encouragement.—He went with her to his father's grave and there she told him all that Father had endured, the manner of his death, his anxiety for his son, what had been charged upon him since his death, and the dreadful fate of those who had deliberately perjured themselves and brought swift destruction upon their own souls. She did not tell him that his mother was betrayed into sanctioning their fearful guilt in any degree. She had done it in weakness, she had repented, she was forgiven, and she would not cause him to blush for his mother. She returned to her home in the wilderness and when these

51. Psalms 68:5.

young men left College they sought this terrestrial Paradise. They had learned to love each other as brothers, and who shall tell the feelings of her who was to them both, as a mother, the only relation either could claim, as she welcomed them with tearful eyes and a heart swelling with gratitude.

George Albert Campbell was soon located in the city nearest the home of his aunt and his brother in affection, Cornelius Elton.—Every year he visited them. He was a lawyer of the very highest order, a generous pleader for the distressed. Upon his noble brow was twined the brightest wreath of honorable fame, and in his heart were the purest principles of virtuous integrity. And Cornelius Elton was carrying out the wishes of her to whom he owed every thing, "His feet were shod with the preparation of the gospel of peace."[52] He was instructing a remnant of some of the lost tribes of the children of Israel,[53] teaching them to love God because he is merciful & serve him, not in a spirit of servile fear, but in living faith and humble hope to trust in the riches of his grace, and be happy here and to hope for a seat near their father's throne in a future world. And Cornelia Campbell was happy and was still the same calm, yet energetic woman you first beheld, looking forward to the time when her Maker should say she had suffered enough and she might find everlasting rest.

Thus were they all when last heard from and what have we learned by this narrative? We have seen the wicked in his glory and have learned that his "sin will surely find him out"[54] and will work its legitimate result—we

52. Ephesians 6:15.

53. Ten of the twelve tribes of Israel were assimilated by the conquering Assyrians in the eighth century BCE. By 1849 there had been many centuries of debate about what happened to these tribes and whether or not they will be found again. The idea that the American Indians might be descended from these lost tribes was seriously considered from the earliest days of North American settlement. Proponents of the theory included Christopher Columbus (1451?–1506) and American Puritans such as Roger Williams (1603?–83) and John Eliot (1604–90). See William G. McLoughlin and Walter H. Conser, Jr., "'The First Man was Red'—Cherokee Responses to the Debate Over Indian Origins, 1760–1860," *American Quarterly* 41, no. 2 (June 1989): 243–64, JSTOR, http://www.jstor.org/stable/2713024. An antebellum review of the idea can be found in John McIntosh, *The Origin of the North American Indians*, new ed. (New York: Nafis and Cornish, 1843), Google Books, http://books.google.com/books?id=qy5WPZcxcbUC. McIntosh notes that "the opinion extensively prevails, that the North American Indians are descendants of the tribes of Israel" (76). A prominent advocate of the theory during the 1840s was American Jewish leader Mordecai Manuel Noah (1785–1851). A long extract from his 1837 speech on the subject is available as Mordecai M. Noah, *Discourse on the Restoration of the Jews*, ed. D. S. Blondheim (Baltimore: Lord Baltimore Press, 1905), Google Books, http://books.google.com/books?id=Y3ZJAAAAYAAJ. For more on the prominence of the theme in Noah's writings, see Michael Schuldiner and Daniel J. Kleinfeld, *The Selected Writings of Mordecai Noah* (Westport: Greenwood Press, 1999).

54. Numbers 32:23.

have beheld the just man in his season of adversity and have seen that his hour of triumph will surely come, yea we have traced the sinner through all his course and seen the

"Horrid shapes and sights unholy
That ever wander round his couch
When death is busy with his heart
Forestalling all his doom."[55]

and we have looked upon the last hours of the righteous and felt that

"The chamber where the good man meets his fate
Is privileged beyond the common walks of life,
Quite in the verge of Heaven."[56]

And may not we learn to reverence the power and wisdom of the Almighty, that will sustain in any dispensation of his providence, and where his laws are violated and we are the sufferers, may we not learn to "be still and see the salvation of God"[57] knowing that "He is His own Avenger."[58]

55. "Horrid shapes and sights unholy" is a cliché in the mid-nineteenth century that began as a quotation from the English poem "L'Allegro" (1645) by John Milton (1608–74). Search engines quoted elsewhere in these notes do not suggest a source for the rest of the quotation. This could be original verse or perhaps a quotation of a poem from another periodical that has not yet been incorporated to the present-day digital collections.

56. Often quoted in mid-century American religious writing, these lines are from *The Complaint, or, Night-Thoughts on Life, Death, and Immortality* (1742–46), a long poem by English poet Edward Young (1683–1765). A recent American edition at this time is *The Complaint: Or, Night Thoughts* (Philadelphia: Griffith and Simon, 1845), Google Books, http://books.google.com/books?id=BrQyAQAAMAAJ.

57. Another phrase so frequently repeated as to be a cliché. The source may be the diary of seventeenth-century Scottish minister John Blackadder, but even if it is, it is doubtful that all the Americans repeating the phrase would know this. See John Blackadder, *Select Passages from the Diary and Letters of the Late John Blackader, Esq.* (Edinburgh: J. Ritchie, 1806), 14, Google Books, http://books.google.com/books?id=bVQwAAAAYAAJ.

58. A play on a phrase popularized by the often-republished essay, "Domestic Life" (1821), by American writer Richard Henry Dana (1787–1879). The passage reads: "The dignity of a woman has its peculiar character. It awes more than that of a man. His is more physical, bearing itself up with an energy of courage which we may brave, or a strength which we may struggle against. He is his own avenger, and we may stand the brunt. A woman's has nothing of this force in it. It is of a higher quality, too delicate for mortal touch. We bow before it, as before some superior spirit appearing in beautiful majesty." See *Idle Man* (New York: Wiley & Halsted, 1821), 22, Google Books, http://books.google.com/books?id=aL4PAAAAQAAJ.

Selected for the Offering

The Light in the Binnacle[59]

By Miss Catherine H. Waterman[60]

Oh! dread not the shadows that compass thee now,
There is always a period to sorrow,
Tho' darkness may hover awhile o'er thy brow,
Bright joy may disperse it to-morrow.

Think, think, as ye gaze o'er the waters of life,
Though the waves be troubled, and chill,
Think, think ye can see 'mid the turmoil and strife,
The light in the binnacle still.

The flowers may fade that we cherish in youth,
And friends may forget that we were ever,
And hearts that we loved for their kindness and truth,
Have been taught every fond link to sever.

But flowers may blossom again from the earth,
And raptures our bosoms may thrill,
If we see 'mid the falsehood, the fading and dearth,
The light in the binnacle still.

---

59. A "binacle" or "binnacle" is the case in which the compass and lights are kept on board a ship. Rufus Wilmot Griswold notes in *The Female Poets of America* that the author was married to a shipmaster. See 2nd ed., (Philadelphia: Henry C. Baird, 1852), 217, Google Books, http://books.google.com/books?id=EtgQAAAAYAAJ. The search engines referenced throughout these notes cannot find another publication of this poem. It could have appeared in a newspaper, magazine, or anthology that is now missing from these various digital archives.

60. Philadelphia poet Catherine Harbison Waterman Esling (1812–97); her collection of poems, which does not include "The Light in the Binnacle," is *The Broken Bracelet, and Other Poems* (Philadelphia: Lindsay and Blakiston, 1850), Google Books, http://books.google.com/books?id=IGwYAAAAYAAJ. The opening "advertisement" for this volume explains why some 1850 readers valued her writings: "These poems have found favour throughout the country, as they have appeared in various periodical publications, not by learning or art displayed in them, not by ministering to the too prevalent love of morbid excitement, but by their sweet melody and true womanly feeling. They are poems of the affections, welling forth from a heart chastened by the discipline of life, sympathizing with all human sorrow, and loving the beautiful in nature and the true in sentiment with unaffected fervour" (v). "Miss Catherine Waterman" also wrote hymns that were very popular. An interesting account of meeting the elderly poet in 1880s Philadelphia is A. P. Putnam, "A Favorite Hymn and Its Author," *The Unitarian* 3, no. 8 (August 1888): 355–56, Google Books, http://books.google.com/books?id=puJAAAAAYAAJ.

Then dread not the clouds, tho' they gather in night,
So long as one sparkle is given,
Peeping forth like a sunbeam of beauty, and light;
From out the bright portal of heaven.

But steer by the glimmer, tho' faint it appear,
It is meant every heart pulse to thrill,
No darkness appals us, while steady and clear,
The light's in the binnacle still.

For the Offering.

Thoughts.

Any enterprise of woman having in view her elevation, either as it may relate to knowledge or character and position, is commendable. It should meet encouragement and approval of man: if not as perfect as could be desired, condemn not, but encourage by suggesting the improvements desired. The "Lowell Offering,"[61] in its first issues gave me much pleasure, though I did not calculate one half its success.

Who better than woman can know her feelings—failings—wants—aspirations. Let not man laugh at her weakness, or remain unmoved by her prayers. How *many* of the so called "lords of creation" debase themselves, to *each* fallen woman?[62] It is my conviction that women are yet to do much

61. A literary magazine by women in and around New England's mills at Lowell, Massachusetts in the 1840s. As this comment suggests, *The Akron Offering* echoed this important title for readers in 1850. But "Offering" was also a fairly common word for periodicals and gift books (anthologies prepared in handsome style for holiday sales) such as *Friendship's Offering, The Odd-Fellows' Offering, The Monthly Offering, The Religious Offering, The Sons of Temperance Offering, The Iris: A Literary and Religious Offering,* and *The Token and Atlantic Souvenir: An Offering for Christmas and the New Year.* There has been much written about *The Lowell Offering.* For example, see Harriet Jane Hanson Robinson, *Loom and Spindle; Or, Life Among the Early Mill Girls* (New York: T. Y. Crowell, 1898), Google Books, http://books.google.com/books?id=RgwCAAAAYAAJ; an edition of selected writings from the periodical, *The Lowell Offering: Writings by New England Mill Women (1840–1845),* ed. Benita Eisler (New York: Norton, 1977); and Sylvia Jenkins Cook, *Working Women, Literary Ladies: The Industrial Revolution and Female Aspiration* (New York: Oxford University Press, 2008).

62. See n. 9, p. 253 for more on the "lords of creation." To those who put much stock in "propriety," a "fallen woman" could be any woman with at least a reputation for vice. But the term was often a euphemism for prostitutes and other women known to have sex outside of marriage. Sexuality and redemption were intimately related ideas in antebellum America. For more, see Barbara Cutter, *Domestic Devils, Battlefield Angels: The Radicalism of American Womanhood, 1830–1865* (DeKalb: Northern Illinois University Press, 2003); Elaine Frantz Parsons, *Manhood Lost: Fallen Drunkards*

for man's redemption. As a Mother, or Wife, or Sister, in each and all these positions, she will exert a powerful influence over man.

We are in the habit of commending ourselves on account of the high position woman occupies in Europe and America, especially in the United States and England, as though it had been man's work. As well boast our civil liberty as England's gift! True, she *is* exalted and ennobled, but how came it? How came she up from Jewish and Gentile barbarism? She, by conquest through contest, has gained all the freedom she enjoys, and retains it by a characteristic firmness. Does man aid her? so did France our fathers; he will continue to do so, to the extent of her success over him. If her success is greater as her position is higher, does it not prove that herein is her very strength? The power gained is used for new acquisitions. Does man ask when or where it will stop? Answer, *at his side*. When equality is acknowledged.

It does not satisfy me to have it said that woman occupies her true place in this *christian* country. I see more clearly than in pagan countries what she may be but not *all* she is to be. Where she performs the same labor in kind and quality ought the pay to be less with her than with man? Is this so? It is said that woman's judgment is unequal to man's! about what? It as often happens to be equal, sometimes better. Her fancy and feelings sometimes predominate, but how many inebriates in the other sex can be found to cancel them. Nor is it enough to offset a vain woman in this way, her case is infinitely less a perversion.

For one I am willing to be placed on a par with the other sex and allow the girls and boys together to study mathematics, the sciences, political economy &c. &c. without any fears she will contend for places with us, such has not been the result thus far, while on the other hand, attempts to exclude have brought her out in competition.

But I mean not to write a dissertation; feeling pleased at witnessing another attempt of woman to make a journal of her own for her own sex a disposition to notice it in this way arose in the mind, having long desired to see woman come up nobly to defend and maintain herself in a high position on her own account and that of man's also. All that is done for woman is done for the good of the race in a double sense: qualities in degree are *inherited*, and the same *expanded* in cultivation.

---

and Redeeming Women in the Nineteenth-Century United States (Baltimore: Johns Hopkins University Press, 2003); and Scott C. Martin, *Devil of the Domestic Sphere: Temperance, Gender, and Middle-Class Ideology, 1800–1860* (DeKalb: Northern Illinois University Press, 2008).

If your "Offering" accepts this trifle for some odd page it will bear with it the prayer that your humble & unpretending magazine, will call out the talents of your sex towards that mission it is the province of women to fulfill.

Zeta.[63]

To Our Readers

Presuming that you have all had proper reflections upon the flight, changes and mutations of time, we shall let the old year go quietly to its rest, nor *inflict* upon any one our own particular thoughts upon the events that have transpired while it was passing, or our ideas of what is probably in store for us in the year upon which we have just entered, but simply say that we wish you all as much of true felicity as can be expected in this world of trial and a full preparation for that "undiscovered country from whose bourne no traveler returns."[64]

Thanks to "Zeta" for giving his thoughts expression through the pages of the offering. Hope he will condescend to honor us again.

"The Lady and Gipsy,"[65] a correspondent says, was written by a girl in her thirteenth year: hope she will be encouraged to write again.

Beauty, by Ida, will appear in the next number hope she will favor us again.

Any article from the pen of "Adelia" will be gratefully received.

Where is dear "Lily Lute"? hope she is not sick, please let us hear from you as soon as consistent.

We are continually receiving articles from new contributors and we are grateful for this manifestation of interest in a work that we believe will continue to increase in every thing desirable, until it shall become a source of pleasure and real benefit to all. Many thanks friends for so many favors generously bestowed, and for the prompt discharge of your part of our compact, and we trust to be able, faithfully to fulfill our duty, and that we shall be able to journey along with renewed strength and confidence.

C. Cumings

63. An anonymous male author. See mention in editorial below.

64. Hamlet Act 3, scene 1. To read this in a contemporary American edition, see William Shakespeare, *The Dramatic Works* (Boston: Phillips & Sampson, 1848), 7:331, Google Books, http://books.google.com/books?id=8vcjAAAAMAAJ.

65. See p. 328.

THE
AKRON OFFERING.
February, 1850.

For the Offering.

The Soul.[1]

In the affairs of this world, men are governed by a wise and safe maxim. It is this—Secure the higher or more important interest first—even, if need be, at the sacrifice of some secondary or minor interest. If this same principle were adopted and applied to man's immortal interests, we should at once see an entire change in the state of society, affecting the pursuits, business and morals of man. We should then see, that insatiate concern manifested for the full and mature development of the mental and moral powers of the Soul, which now characterizes the pursuit of wealth and pleasure.

Is not our spiritual being worthy of infinite more concern, than our physical and perishing nature? And yet how sadly it is neglected. This is partly owing to the deep corruption of the heart; partly to early and matured habits of vice and intemperance; and partly to a want of sound and comprehensive views of the *nature, powers and susceptibilities*[2] of the *Soul.*

1. The primary definition for "soul" at this time is the "spiritual, rational and immortal substance in man, which distinguishes him from brutes; that part of man which enables him to think and reason, and which renders him a subject of moral government." Today we use words such as "the mind" or "consciousness" or "self" or even "identity" to describe what was often called the "soul" in antebellum America. And as this essay reveals, today we also have a much stronger understanding of the physical basis of mental activity. The belief that the soul was immortal thus raised questions for antebellum Americans about what change or transition might start the continuation of thinking after the body has died. See Noah Webster, *An American Dictionary of the English Language* (New York: Harper & Brothers, 1846), 773, http://books.google.com/books?id=XKERAAAAIAAJ. See also pp. 288–92.

2. Capabilities "of admitting any thing additional, or any change, affection or influence." See Webster, 814.

My object in penning these lines is to direct the attention of the reader of the Akron Offering to this subject—a vast, comprehensive and pleasing theme. I do not expect to fathom my subject, nor indeed present it in a satisfactory light to all who may read the subsequent remarks, but I trust they may excite thought and investigation on some of the topics which we shall introduce to the reader's notice.

We remark then, man is unlike every other being in the world, and constitutes a separate and distinct class of existences; underived from any other species. It has been asserted, we know, that he is only the completion of a chain—commencing with the animalcula which is undiscernable by the most powerful microscope, running up through animate creation, until the Ape or Ourang Outang becomes the progenitor of the human race.[3] Such philosophy is doubtless conclusive proof to all those who embrace this view of the subject; but equally as conclusive proof to us, that they have thought upon the subject about as much as their professed progenitors are capable of. But if man is a mere animal, he is a strange one indeed. He only has improved and progressed of all the animal tribe, since the day God called existence into being. Yet enough of speculation upon this foolish and absurd philosophy (falsely so called,) let us then notice in the following order, the *nature, properties, powers* and *susceptibilities* of the soul.

1. *Its Nature.* The soul then is *divine.* We use the term divine not to designate the character of the soul—for character is the result of conduct; but to designate the essence or subsistence of the soul. That the soul is divine in the sense, we infer from the account given us, as to the measure of its communication to man at his creation. Man is represented as having been

---

3. The author has evidently been reading reviews of *Vestiges of the Natural History of Creation* (1844) by English writer Robert Chambers (1802–71) and *Thoughts on Animalcules* (1846), an important early work on microscopy by English geologist Gideon Algernon Mantell (1790–1852). *Vestiges* advanced crude evolutionary theories of the origin of life and man; the ensuing enormous and intense controversy discouraged Charles Darwin (1809–82) from writing about evolution for more than a decade. Mantell's fame as a scientist began with his 1825 discovery of *Iguanodon*—the first "dinosaur." An American edition with Chambers' supplementary material is *Vestiges of the Natural History of Creation, with a Sequel* (New York: William H. Colyer, 1846), Google Books, http://books.google.com/books?id=UkoWAAAAYAAJ. A digital copy of Mantell's book can be found as *Thoughts on Animalcules; or, A Glimpse of the Invisible World Revealed by the Microscope* (London: John Murray, 1846), Google Books, http://books.google.com/books?id=MBQIAQAAIAAJ. A review of this literature that appears to have inspired this part of the essay is Philotus Dean, "Animalcules," *The Oberlin Quarterly Review* 4 (January 1849): 36–58, Google Books, http://books.google.com/books?id=NLkRAAAAYAAJ. To better understand this period in the history of evolution, see Charles Coulston Gillispie, *Genesis and Geology* (New York: Harper, 1951), especially chapter 6, and Christian C. Young and Mark A. Largent, *Evolution and Creationism: A Documentary and Reference Guide* (Westport: Greenwood, 2007).

created from the dust of the earth, as to his physical nature. But God is represented as breathing into his nostrils the breath of *life* and thus he (man) became a *living soul.* Their figurative representation doubtlessly is designed to teach us, that after the completion of the physical organism of man, God communicated to him a *divine* soul. The manner of this communication is conclusive evidence, that it was in essence a subsistence divine. Then too it is called the *breath* of *life,* imparted by the living God, and consequently man became a living soul. Again the soul is *Spiritual.* This proposition needs no further proof. It is a self-evident truth, affirmed by the universal consciousness of man. We think, we reason, we love, we hate, we joy, we sorrow, and we know that these are phenomena of mind or spirit and not of matter. We know that this mind is either in an active or suffering condition. The soul is *immortal.* The immortality of the soul has been disputed, but if the remarks above will bear the test of scrutiny and pass safely through the ordeal, there remains scarcely the shadow of a doubt, that the soul is immortal and necessarily so. That its nature is such that it cannot die nor be destroyed, but must live forever in bliss or woe according as its character has capacitated it in this state of probation for *Heaven* or for *Hell.*

2. The soul has powers—almost infinite. The capacities of the soul may be demonstrated, by surveying man's past history. Suppose, as is commonly believed that man has been in existence about six thousand years. Then look abroad upon the page of history, and read the achievements of the mind, as they stand out in bold relief upon its pages, in the record of its progress in civilization, the arts and sciences, in inventions and improvements. We stand awe stricken at the demonstrations of the power of the mind as here revealed. Remember too, that all this has been accomplished under many difficulties and counteracting influences. Ignorance and prejudice retarded the progress of knowledge—depravity and vice, the moral elevation of man—and yet through all these barriers the soul breaks forth asserting and maintaining her noble powers and her divine origin. Like a mighty giant, conquering her enemies, and like the rising sun dispelling the moral and mental darkness of the world. In her dawning light we compass creation, ranging the boundless fields of space, bringing her countless inhabitants in view, reading their laws and decyphering their movements with the utmost precision and certainty—now in all this is only faintly and imperfectly disclosed the illimitable power of the soul. Then again how short has been the time, in which all this has been effected—six thousand years—This may seem a long

time, but compared with Eternity, the destined home and habitation of the Soul, it is but a moment in our existence, as a drop compared to the ocean. And as Eternity rolls on, our spiritual powers must unfold with increased momentum. The mind reels beneath the thought and the imagination staggers as it seeks to compass and fathom the powers of the Soul, while through Eternity it continues to develope its capabilities.

3. The Soul has Susceptibilities. The susceptibilities of the Soul are no less astonishing than its powers. We have abundant demonstration of this in our own experience. We know that we are susceptible of almost angelic emotions of joy. Indeed there are recorded instances, when the emotions became so powerfully excited either by joy or grief that suddenly almost momentary death was the consequence—the physical frame being unable to sustain the ocean wave of emotion.

While the nature of the Soul remains unchanged such must its susceptibilities continue to be. They too continuing to mature and develope throughout ceaseless Eternity. Thus only can the Soul be fitted to bathe in the ocean of infinite blessedness in the presence of God; the developement of its emotional susceptibilities must keep pace with the developement of its powers and capabilities.—But the Soul is capable of enduring unutterable woe, for the same reason, and yet how many dash her into pieces at the shrine of passion, lust, pleasure or mammon—this immortal Soul, the image of God.

G——. S——.[4]
Akron, Ohio.

From the Knickerbocker for December.

Twenty Years.

For twenty years we've passed, dear Kate!
    Down Time's full tide together,
And proved all changing chance and scene,
    And met all kinds of weather;
Since when—'twas on your birth-day, Kate—
    We vowed eternal truth;
Two laughing girls, with all the mirth
    Of gay and careless youth.

4. See n. 10, p. 214.

And we have kept our promise, Kate,
    In spite of youth's decaying,
While Time with other's fortunes hath
    All sorts of freaks been playing;
Nor has it left *us* changeless, Kate!
    Mine eye hath lost its brightness,
And your once graceful form hath not
    Its former fairy lightness.

For twenty years will make, dear Kate!
    In maiden beauty, changes;
And many a head it layeth low,
    And many a heart estranges:
Full forty years are on your brow,
    And some few more on mine,
Where shining threads of silver gray
    Begin with brown to twine.

And we are spinsters both, dear Kate!
    Yet happy ones, I trow;
There's many a wedded wife I know,
    Who wears a sadder brow:
And blessings on your birth-day, Kate!
    And blessings on your lot;
You're blest indeed with loving friends,
    For oh! who loves you not?

And far be off the day, dear Kate!
    When one of us lies low;
And one of us is left behind to mourn,
    And strive alone with wo.
We've lived in love, while twenty years
    Have flown full swiftly past;
And when the parting summons comes
    May I be not the last.

Anne Rivers
Albany, September 1841.[5]

5. As the signature suggests, the poem appeared in *The Knickerbocker* 18, no. 5 (November 1841): 378,

For the Offering.

Beauty.

Where is beauty? or rather, where is it not? for if we view the heavens above us, we behold myriads of stars sparkling in their place on high, each inhabited like our earth—perhaps with more intelligent, virtuous, and holy beings than dwell in this lower world. Be it so or not, it is indeed a fit place for Angels. Ah! methinks I would be content to inhabit so bright a sphere.

In earth too, there is beauty. Behold the majestic waters as they wind peacefully through some quiet glen, so calmly that they apparently wish to linger there, yet they pass on—at length the more rugged track they meet, and as if a new idea had suggested itself they rush madly forward, wave after wave dashing hard against the rocks, each endeavoring to surmount its neighbor in loftiness, until they again form a complete body; then without a moment's reflection, they plunge headlong into the chasms below, dash swiftly over the rocks a moment, then—as if reflecting upon their past rashness—and half ashamed, that they should allow their passions to be their masters, they pass calmly by to mingle with the Ocean. Is not this beauty? Yes! 'tis indeed romantic beauty.

Who can but admire the beauties of the vegetable kingdom, from the tiny wild-flower, that modestly lifts its head to those that falsely proclaim themselves its superior, to the most gaudy and ostentatious exotic. Ah! he who does not see beauty and admire the flowers, must surely be blind to the grand—the beautiful.

"Thou hast much to learn, that never found
  a fearfulness in flowers,
Thou hast missed of joy, that never basked in
  beauties of the terrible."[6]

Google Books, http://books.google.com/books?id=u3sgoweRN2kC. For more on this periodical, see n. 20, p. 89. Google Books and American Periodicals Series Online discover other writings by Anne Rivers from the 1840s. WorldCat suggests that her works were not collected in book form. The 1850 United States Federal Census, as searched through Ancestry.com, reveals many people with varied spellings of the name but no good matches—especially if the search is narrowed by reading the poem autobiographically and looking for an unmarried woman in her early to middle forties.

6. The first of three quotations come from "On Beauty" by English poet Martin Farquhar Tupper (1810–89). See *Proverbial Philosophy* (New York: John Wiley, 1850), 227–43, Google Books, http://books.google.com/books?id=wvg9AAAAYAAJ.

That there is beauty in the animal kingdom, especially in man, none can deny; he is endowed with reasoning faculties and it is this that raises him above the brute creation.

"There is beauty of the seasons; grandly independent of externals. It looketh from the windows of the house, shining in the man triumphant." Man has oft endeavored to copy from nature, but how has he succeeded? he may manufacture Automatons[7] and give them motion, but it is not in the power of man to produce life in inanimate beings. Where will the beauty of art compare with that of nature?

Who in viewing the rain-bow is not awed with its beauty and grandeur, as it stretches far across the heavens, presenting the most beautiful and brilliant colors. Does not the imagination often picture it as the pathway to the skies? Does not the eye gaze with rapture upon its unparalleled beauty, and the heart give praise to Him who "doeth all things well,"[8] reminding us that it was placed there as a sign and seal that the world should no more be destroyed by a flood. Indeed every thing in nature is beautiful, and while we can, let us enjoy it.

> "For beauty hideth every where, that Reason's child may seek her,
> And having found the gem of price, may set it in God's crown.
> Beauty nestleth in the rose-bud, or walketh the firmament with planets,
> She is heard in the beetle's evening hymn, and shouteth in the matins of the sun;
> She is the Dryad of the woods, the Naiad of the streams;
> Her golden hair hath tapestried the silk-worm's silent chamber,
> And to her measured harmonies the wild wave beats in time;
> With tinkling feet at even tide she danceth in the meadow."

Ida.
Granger, Ohio.[9]

7. A machine designed to independently complete some specific task. In the 1840s perhaps still the most famous automaton was the chess-playing machine that toured successfully and fascinated the skeptical Edgar Allan Poe. To read Poe's famous "solution" to "Maelzel's Chess Player," see *The Southern Literary Messenger* 2, no. 5 (April 1836): 318–26, Google Books, http://books.google.com/books?id=kU4FAAAAQAAJ.

8. Mark 7:37.

9. Daniel Haskel and J. Calvin Smith's *Complete Descriptive and Statistical Gazetteer of the United States of America* (New York: Sherman and Smith, 1848), 244, Google Books, http://books.google.com/books?id=UOstAAAAYAAJ, describes Granger as having nothing but seven schools, 333 scholars, and just under one thousand inhabitants. Relying on the 1850 census, Thomas Baldwin and J. Thomas's

Selected for the Offering.

Morning All Day.[10]

By Dr. W. A. Alcott.[11]

I have been the companion, the victim of grief,
I have lain down at night without hope of relief,
No gleam in the future—not a single bright ray,
No quiet at night, no morning all day.

Heart-sick of the world, I have sometimes retreated
To forests and glens, and my sorrows repeated;
I have shrunk from the sound of my feet by the way;
No slumbers by night, and no morning all day.

I have wished—oh, how vain!—I had wings and could fly,
From the earth and its turmoil, to rest in the sky,
Where glorified spirits, in brightest array,
Rejoice without ceasing, in morning all day.

But a change has come o'er me, I lift up my head;
The world is all joyous—my sorrows are fled;
No fears or forbodings beset my bright way;
I rise ere the lark, and 'tis morning all day.

Gazetteer of the United States (Philadelphia: Lippincott, Grambo, 1854) records a population of just over 1800. See page 438, Google Books, http://books.google.com/books?id=_5s6AAAAcAAJ. An Ancestry.com search of the 1850 United States Federal Census records several thousand Idas in Ohio. The only Ida in Granger was an infant. Of course "Ida" may have been a pseudonym. Nevertheless, the Idas in nearby Sharon Township are fourteen-year-old Ida Ammerman, the fourth of seven daughters to farmers Richard and Phebe Ammerman, and forty-three-year-old Ida Hoagland, a farmer with six children living at home. Ida Ammerman may have ventured into Granger Township to attend school. See United States of America, Bureau of the Census, *Seventh Census of the United States, 1850.* NARA microfilm publication M432. (Washington, D.C.: National Archives and Records Administration, n.d.), roll M432_709, page 315A, and M432_709, page 317B, Ancestry.com.

10. A search of American Periodicals Series Online shows this poem was reprinted a number of times in the late 1830s and early 1840s. A printing in the *Boston Recorder* attributes it to *The Library of Health.* See *Boston Recorder* 23, no. 18 (May 4, 1838): 72, American Periodicals (124114398).

11. William Andrus Alcott (1798–1859) was an American educator and cousin of Louisa May Alcott's father, Bronson. His *Library of Health, and Teacher on the Human Constitution* was an important and strongly pro-temperance periodical of Boston in the 1830s. For a sample volume, see *The Library of Health, and Teacher on the Human Constitution* 3 (1837), Google Books, http://books.google.com/books?id=nvE-AAAAYAAJ.

You ask for the cause. The reply is soon given;
I have learned how to prize the rich favors of heaven,
I breathe the pure air; think, labor and play;
I repose when 'tis night, but have morning all day.

The world is now hopeful, I heed not its dangers;
My friends and companions no more seem like strangers;
The darkness and clouds have long since fled away,
I have peace all the night, and blithe morning all day.

My youth seems renewed; my thoughts on swift pinions
Explore the condition of monarchs and minions;
All scenes and all trials instructions convey;
I dream not by night—I have morning all day.

O ye who but sleep, while all nature rejoices,
Forsake now your slumbers, and join your glad voices
With that of the robin, that sings from the spray—
With that of the lark—and have morning all day.

And then when the lessons of life are all o'er,
And they who now know us shall know us no more,
When the last gleams of twilight have faded away,
We'll soar to a world where 'tis morning all day.

Selected for the Offering.

Grinding the Face of the Poor.[12]

Extract.

In so large a family as that of Mr. T., there was a good deal of sewing to do, and out of charity, the work was taken from a seamstress who had sewed for the family some time, and given to a poor woman with several small children. Ostensibly only was this charity. Really, it was to save a

12. For more on the growing concern among Akron women with the living conditions of the poor, see pp. 4–5. While this story was reprinted more than once, it appears that Cumings selected it from *The Ladies' Garland* 3, no. 8 (February 1840): 184–86, Google Books, http://books.google.com/books?id=msNBAAAAYAAJ.

few pennies. How could this be?—some one will ask. Let me sketch a little scene; premising that this poor woman's husband was just dead, and she left helpless and friendless, with no apparent means of support. Beside this, she was in very feeble health. By accident Mr. T. heard of her distressed situation, and at the suggestion of the individual who named her case to him, told his wife he thought it would be charity to give her some sewing.

"I think it would, indeed," says Mrs. T.

"Our sewing costs us a great deal," responded the careful husband, "and in this thing we may benefit ourselves, as well as do a deed of charity. No doubt this woman is rather an indifferent sewer, in comparison to Miss R., and therefore her work will not of course be worth so much. And she will no doubt think half the price Miss R. gets, a good one."

"No doubt," chimes the frugal partner.

Mrs. ——— was sent for. After she is seated, the following conversation ensues.

"Can you do plain sewing?"

"Yes, ma'am, as well as most persons."

"What is your price for fine shirts?"

"I hav'nt set any price yet: but I'll work as low as any one."

"But you know that to get work you'll have to do it a little lower than ordinary. People don't like to change."

"Well, ma'am, I am in want, and I will work at almost any price for my children."

"I suppose you will make shirts for a quarter?"

"Yes, ma'am!"

"And calico dresses for the same?"

"Yes, ma'am!

"Well, that's reasonable."

"Boys' common shirts you will not charge over eleven pence for?"

"No, ma'am."

"That's reasonable, and I'll do all I can for you. It does me pleasure to help the poor. Come down to-morrow, and I'll have some work for you." The widow departed.

"Well, wife," says Mr. T., bursting in when he saw the widow depart, "at what price will she work?"

"At just half what Miss R. charges."

"Well, that's something like.[13] It gives me pleasure to befriend any one who is willing to work at a reasonable price. Why! this will save us almost a dollar a week the year round."

"Yes, it will so; and if I keep her at it, or some one else, at the same price, for a year, you'll let me have a fifty dollar shawl, won't you?"

"Yes, if you want it."

"Well, I'll do my best. It is shameful what some of these seamstresses do charge."

It is often well to reverse a picture. Suppose we look at the other side of this. Mrs. ——— has always been delicate.

When a girl she would never sew long at a time without getting a pain in her side. She married a hard-working, industrious mechanic, whose trade was not very lucrative, yielding barely enough for a support. Her health after her marriage was but little improved, when with several small children she was left a widow; she yielded in her first keen anguish of bereavement to despair. But a mother cannot long sit in idleness when her babes are about her. She could think of no way of getting a living for them but by her needle, and as she was a neat sewer, she hoped to get work, and earn food and a scant clothing at least. But she could get no work. No person knew her who wanted sewing done. She applied to several, and was still without means of earning a dollar when her last one was spent. Just at this sad moment, the fact of her destitution becoming more known, Mrs. T. sent for her.

As she carried home her work the day after the interview, she was glad at her heart with the thought that now there was a way of escape, at least from starvation. But little more her yearning heart could promise her. Boys' shirts at twelve and a half cents were her first pieces of work. Two of these by hard work she managed to get done in a day. Had they been made plain, she could have finished them early, and had time to give many necessary attentions to her children. But the last words of Mrs. T. had robbed her of that chance. "You can stitch the collars of these, any how; you can afford it, I suppose, and they iron much better when that is done."

The simple and touching "yes, ma'am," but in a sadder tone than usual, was the only response.

Next morning she was up early, though her head ached badly, and she was faint and weak from having sat so steadily through the whole of the proceeding day. Her children were all taken and washed and dressed; her room cleaned, and a scanty meal of mush and milk prepared for the little

13. An idiom, this means "that is good" or "that is not bad."

ones, and a cup of tea for herself; she could not eat of the food of which her children partook with keen appetites, and she could only swallow a few mouthfuls of dry stale bread.

It was nearly ten o'clock when she got fairly down to her work, her head still aching, and almost blinding her. Somehow or other, she could not get on at all fast. It was long past the usual dinner hour before she had finished the first garment, the children were impatient for their dinner, and she had to make great haste in preparing it, as well for their satisfaction as to gain time.

"Mother, we are getting tired of mush and milk," said one of the little ones. "You don't have all the good things you used to. No pies, nor puddings, nor meat."

"Never mind, dear, we'll have some nice corn cakes for supper."

"You'll have supper soon, won't you, mother?" said another little one, coaxingly, her thoughts busy with the corn cakes.

"And shan't we have molasses on them," said another, pushing away her bowl of mush and milk.

"No, dear, not to-night, but to-morrow we'll have some."

"Why not to-night, mother, I want some to-night."

"Mother aint got any money to buy it with to-night, but to-morrow she will have some," said the mother soothingly.

"O, we'll have 'lasses to-morrow for our cakes," cried a little girl who could just speak, clapping her hands in great glee.

After dinner Mrs. ——— worked hard, and in much bodily pain and misery, to finish the other shirt in which the last stitch was taken at nine o'clock at night.

Soon after breakfast next day, she took the four shirts home to Mrs. T., her thoughts mostly occupied with the comfortable food she was to buy her children with the half dollar she had earned. For it was a sad truth that she had laid out her last dollar for the meal with which she was making mush for her little ones.

After examining every seam, every hem, and every line of stitching, Mrs. T. expressed approbation of the work; and handed the poor woman a couple of fine shirts to make for Mr. T., and a calico dress for herself. As she did not offer to pay her for the work she had done, after lingering a few moments, Mrs. ——— ventured to hint that she would like to have a part of what she had earned.

"Oh dear! I never pay my seamstresses until their bill amounts to five dollars. It is so troublesome to keep account of small sums. When you have earned five dollars I will pay you."

Mrs. ——— retired, but with a heart that seemed like lead in her bosom. When shall I earn five dollars?—not for a whole month at this rate, were but the words that formed themselves in her thoughts.

"We shall have the molasses now, mother, shan't we?" said two or three glad little voices as she entered her house.

For a few moments she knew not what answer to make. Then gathering them around her, she explained to them as well as she could make them understand, that the lady for whom she had done the work did not pay her, and she was afraid it would be a good while before she would, and that until she was paid she could not get any thing better than what they had.

The little things stole silently and without a murmur away, and the mother again sat down to her work. A tear would often gather in her eye as she looked up from the bright needle glistening in her fingers, and noticed the sadness and disappointment pictured in their young faces. From this state of gloomy feelings she was roused by a knock at the door, and a pleasant looking old lady, somewhat gaily dressed, came in with a small bundle in her hand.

She introduced herself by saying she had just seen some pretty shirts at Mrs. T.'s, and that she was so well pleased with the work that she had inquired for the maker. "And now having found you," she said, "I want you to fit and make this calico dress for me, if you do such work."

"I shall be glad to do it for you," said she encouraged by the kind and feeling manner of the lady.

"And what will you charge?"

Mrs. ——— hesitated a moment, and then said, "Mrs. T. gives me a quarter of a dollar."

There was a bright spot for a moment on the cheek of the lady.

"Then I will give you three," said she with warmth.

Mrs. ——— burst into tears and she could not help it.

"Are you in need?" inquired the strange lady, hesitatingly, but with an air of feeling that could not be mistaken.

For a moment the widow paused, but the sight of her children conquered the rising emotion of her pride.

"I have nothing but a little corn meal in the house, and have no money."

A tear glistened in the stranger's eye, her breast heaved with strong emotion, then again all was still.

"I will pay you for the dress before-hand, then; and as I want it done very nice, I will pay you a dollar for making it. Can I have it day after to-morrow?"

"Certainly, ma'am, to-morrow evening if you want it."

The dollar was paid down, and the angel of light departed.—More than one heart was made glad that morning.

Selected for the Offering.

The Poet's Time.

By Canore[14]

I

Why doth the poet linger
    Beside the silent lyre,
And listlessly to time resign
    His muse's brightest fire?
        There dwells among
        Those strings unstrung,
The morning of thy muses power,
And canst thou, Poet, leave one hour
        Of life unsung?

II

The poet liveth ages
    Within an hour of time,
His muse drawn car transporteth him
    To many a viewless clime:
        Should such life rest
        All unconfess'd,

14. "Canore" means "singing" in Italian. Searches of Google Books, American Periodicals, and even Google do not discover a source for this poem. It may have been selected from a lost or forgotten western magazine or newspaper. At least one article that was clearly written for the *Offering* (see p. 330) was mistakenly published under the heading "Selected for the Offering."

And the bright visions of his mind,
Be voiceless, and for aye confined
Within his breast?

III

The Poet's time is fleeting,
Age quelleth sprightly song
A harp string will not keep in tune
If it be strained to long:
The Poet's thought
If utter'd not,
When first his soul hath dreamed its chime,
Is discord at another time,
Or all forgot.

Selected for the Offering.

American Literature.[15]

A becalmed sea, and a landscape wanting all that makes pleasing and picturesque, are good similes for the host of American writers. If a dozen are excepted the proscribed list is robbed of its due. Condemnation is nothing more than the result of a writer's efforts, when he writes with that everlasting object in view, mere notoriety. He need not writhe and foam when he perceives no stir, no revolution, the consequence of his inky bubbles. He certainly proclaims his weakness if he cries out against the public who have no eyes for his works, no hearts for his characters. In speaking of the unruffled sea of mere ink which has no particular merit beyond that of being black or blue, (seldom red,) excuse the pun (read,) it becomes a natural speculation for the mind to seek the causes of such insignificant effects. It were almost too much to say seek, for who can possibly blunder around these causes?—If we see a lake all dead and glassy we need little to fix the chilly conviction that it is frozen, and when we behold a land of our latitudes and longitudes, one vast book table of perplexing leaves which if they affect our atmosphere at all, operate only as an opiate;—why—to feel the real truth is impossible of

15. An exhaustive search of the various digital archives referenced in these notes does not discover the original publication of this article. It may be copied from a western periodical such as *The Shooting Star*, which is referenced elsewhere in this magazine and not now available in these digital archives. See n. 7, p. 181.

course, and so 'tis easier to condemn the times, the people, and the gloomy era of financial sway, or as some would term it, *Moneymania*, than to own at once frankly, at the living and the adamantine truth. We as a Nation are called an original people. Of course those who call us so, *mean* that we are not like any other people on the face of the earth. This is true to our glory, in some respects, and with obstinate unwillingness, we declare that in other respects it is not true. The literature of America is the overflow of the old, long standing, oft falling, oft stumbling Nations of the old world. Just as the waves of the Atlantic pour along and strike and lash our pilgrim honored beach, so flows the foam, the brewing of transatlantic minds to us, and more than nine tenths of our own originality, is that some froth, becalmed, stagnant, frozen stiff, or bound up in dirty puddles. We do write as near as we can, like foreign scribblers, whose very fame is our folly. Our prose writers are mimics of the tamest kind, and our poets where are they? few but women, and one quill is enough for the half of them: such indeed are our poets. The fame they have, is only in a relative sense among themselves. None of their kind readers take the least interest in the dull, worse than prosy jargon which is so nicely measured and rhymed out to them. Their poetry consists in sundry stanzas, thrown by the million into a common box. That box is a famous magazine, truly. When it is opened each contributor pulls out a stanza and without loss of time glorifies it. So the concern has all the advantages of a mutual flattering society. Of course all are poets that belong to it. In this way all obtain readers, it being a matter of courtesy to read each other, though where an acquaintance of a little more than common interest is formed, the parties can puff[16] without reading. This is our dead sea of poetry. There are exceptions, a few—ay, few.

Rising up and showing off to murderous disadvantage the quill-armed mob around them, are a few prior established eminent names. Eminent from merit, merit proven on the hearts of the many; merit felt and acknowledged by all except this mob which cannot see merit.

Now the mass of the people are wondering wherefore no more eminent scribblers are to be discovered on the horizon of literature, and they are led to doubt whether it is in these latter days possible for any to arise in our midst worth a moment's notice. All are not willing to see the downward tendency of the present literary mobocracy, and enough are gulled continually to support our rhyme factories and our hangers-on of fashion. The most successful

16. To praise with exaggeration.

author is the most fashionable one, or the one who possesses the most tact in persuading the flat heads of society, that he is the embodied maximum of Fashion, and the transcendentalist of his compeers.—Not much wonder then need be, that the best minds are sickened and smothered from the loathsome arena;—who of a refined and soaring mind would join his efforts to the self-praised throng, that we may share a thousandth part of his due? Who that has a gem will throw it into the pit of a broken glass? Well, if a young writer would be alone in his glory, it is but to enjoy the enmity of the vain ones, for the mob will strive to crush him before he can have time to place himself in the strong hands of that mighty critic, the public. His name is expunged before he is read, and then he is nobody: fame will have nothing to do with quiet merit, or untrumpeted worth.

Amusing beyond description is the popular literature of the present day in America. A great periodical, called a Magazine, requires but the characteristics, and there are in reality but one in effect, and intrinsic worth. *"Our contributors,"* a smooth faced fraternity generally, and only relieved from monotony of strained eyes, and compressed, we might say collapsed ribs, by the more agreeable smirk of now and then a female Eugene Sue, or Boz,[17] are pictured on the first page; a plate of the ghosts of fashion disfigures the fourth page, and to fill the alternate leaves to the back cover, are certain stanzas of the same soft polished nature, which is so lovely and so transcendent, that human mind may hope to find an idea. He can only see "stars," and "flowers," and "bowers," and "skies," and "eyes," and "love," and "streams," and "beams," and "moons," and two or three other nouns. The work closes with nearly a dozen pages of review, which means flattery and envy.—Let no one deny that our literati hold each other up, and pull down such as might get above them. Their flattery reminds us of a drove of calves who after weaning, persist in sucking each other's ears. Their envy is like all other, a proof of fear, and demerit.—Such, is a sober, and probably just, view of the American literati, if eight names are excepted. We are not tenacious of the octagonical crown, let five fall to the next lowest rank. No harm is done by it. True it may have some effect on that stagnant host—the mass, but the consequences are trivial. The host may smother the bold invaders of their *dead sea.* Could any honest, strong-hearted man or woman of the present day, ask companionship with the eyeless fish of this

17. French novelist Eugène Sue (1804–57) and English novelist Charles Dickens (1812–70). Dickens used "Boz" as his pen name.

muddy sea of scaly *inanimation?* and yet 'tis the heighth of ambition. Who would'nt choose a course all his own, an independent pen, an independent organ of firmness?—What though the oily anathemas of these countless opponents flow smoothly and true to the set rule of an eternal fashion, and in their natural zeal seek to drown? Now, it does seem practicable for some even to stem such a lethe tide: *will* only, is the requisite.—If it be true that an originality dwells among us, the time has come when it is devoutly to be wished that something of it might become apparent in the literature of this country, and it is to touch if possible some of these secret springs, that we in this disjoined paper chat are ambitious.

No sensible person will believe that the most able authors are generally those who rise up and claim their place beside wide known names, and lay their volumes proudly upon the dusty old tomes they have scurrilously imitated, but on the other hand, we see the most valuable minds the most reserved and isolated, so that in the present scrambling of the multitude, we miss them. So the appalling announcement goes forth from the captain of the calm ten thousand of the council of Quilldom, that there cannot possibly be any great first Class minds except what *are.* The august climax is finished: ye who are born now, ye who were born only a few years ago, ye who unfortunately are not yet born, and ye who possibly may never be born,—calm yourselves, ye cannot rise above what is:—what has been! weep for the harps that shall never more be strung!

But to say aught unjustly of ourselves, would be a kind of suicidal slander, would it not? don't dread any such crime;—the worst we can say of ourselves, can only come under the head of honest confession so leaving the matter of American literature to rest, a word may not come wrong as a soother, if we speak boldly of other people than ourselves. Two or three great blind writers in the European part of abused creation, have revolutionized the very foundations of their own society. The most *fashionable* life, is *lane* and *alley* life, the truest portrayer of warm blood and equinoctial passion, is one who sits on an ice hill, and sketches from the frost bitten Sweede; caricature is the only real truth, and the more distorted the more perfect. A bundle of exciting salmagundi is pasted to the back of a wanderer, who has no part or lot in the interest of the matter, but who with strange devotion acts as a paper carrier, and uses his name as a rallying cry, having an acquaintance of considerable extent, as we might suppose a man of his years, would have.

But the old man makes a stir: where? Oh, among us: nowhere else; he electrifies in this steam country: who says so? the publishers? Yes. Well, thousands believe it, and 'tis amusing to see a youth buy it, and then show anger, after poring and striving to understand something wonderful, which he supposes is there, but looks for in vain. Another, less honest, purchases, reads as long as he can endure the silly bore, and then with a sort of mysterious vanity tosses his bewildered head and declares it a treat worth "double the money!"

Oh these things make a stir;—cannot some of our imitators do likewise,—if a Frenchman can turn his pen into an electrical eel, is there no magician here to do likewise with his enchantments?—Yes indeed, but perhaps an oft repeated miracle becomes stale: it is wonderful. We must not strike into the idea of originality however: 'twould be a fearful precedent, and if we dare mention that word with emphasis, how many fall back on their elbows and with strained quills in teeth, gaze, and sneer, and put on airs!

For the Offering.

Life.

How transient, yet how wearisome it seems!
In infancy and youth like flowers of spring.
It struggles on as weak, as frail a thing,
With youth, then vanishes these golden dreams
Which have the inmost temple of the heart
Illum'd with joy above the worldly kind,
But ah! too transitory, too refined
Then comes kind age, most prone to guilt and art;
Avarice exulting in his baneful power,
Impelling onward to inglorious ends,
'Till in old age is wept the bitter hour
Of birth; and penitence at last befriends;
Or in despair, when all with ill seems fraught,
Death as a speedy antidote is sought.

Clare.

Selected for the Offering.

The Reclaimed.[18]

"Most Merciful!
Will man's hard heart be never touched with all
Th' o'erflowing of thy love, and yield itself
To the gentle sympathies, till we shall learn
The noble joy of pouring happiness
Upon the heart of sorrow, and how sweet
The pleasure is of shedding bliss!"[19]

"Ugh! ugh!" coughed I, as I buttoned my surtout[20] closer about me, and drew down my chin into its ample fur collar; "God pity those who have no shelter for their heads to-night."

"God pity them, indeed!" answered a voice close to my ear; "for small pity is shown to the houseless man."

I turned my head. A miserable, half clad, shivering wretch stood by my side. His hat was slouched over his eyes, but not sufficiently to hide a face on which the traces of loathsome intemperance and debauchery were distinctly visible. His fragment of a coat was buttoned as closely around him as its scattered buttons would admit, but not closely enough to conceal the want of a vest and shirt beneath. Sad rents in his nether garments told too plainly that their days had not been few nor exempt from evil; and his feet were scarcely protected from the frozen ground by a pair of tattered shoes. Such a picture of extreme loathsomeness and misery I had never seen; and half involuntarily I thrust my hand into my pocket with the intention of contributing a few pence to his immediate relief. "But he is intemperate," said I to myself; and the small change I had grasped was dropped. "He may perish with cold," whispered my better nature; and my fingers clutched the coin. "He'll spend it for grog," interposed my worldly prudence; and I drew down my hand empty from my pocket.

It was a bitter cold night in the middle of December. The mercury in the thermometer stood below zero, and white frost glittering in the clear starlight

18. Another item copied from the same volume of *The Ladies' Garland*. See n. 19, p. 151. 3, no. 9 (March 1840): 201–3, Google Books, http://books.google.com/books?id=msNBAAAAYAAJ.

19. Lines from "Evening Thoughts" by poet and abolitionist Elizabeth Margaret Chandler (1807–34). Four years before her early death, Chandler moved to Michigan from Philadelphia. See Elizabeth Margaret Chandler, *The Poetical Works* (Philadelphia: Lemuel Howell, 1836), 101, Google Books, http://books.google.com/books?id=bRETAAAAIAAJ.

20. Overcoat.

like countless crystals, whose minuteness impaired not their wonderful brilliancy. There was no breath of wind abroad, but the whole atmosphere was filled with infinite small particles of ice, which pierced the skin with their sharp points, like the invisible spears of a troop of fairies. Arrayed as I was from head to foot in flannel and fur and broadcloth, with all the paraphernalia which an old bachelor deems necessary to enable him to resist the cold, I yet felt as if my blood was curdling in my veins, and my whole man becoming a pillar of ice, in the potent presence of "Old King Frost." Business of an imperative nature had called me, late in the afternoon, to the suburbs of the city; and now my task accomplished, picturing to myself the grate and hot toast which awaited my return, I was making all convenient haste for home, when my reverie was interrupted by a fit of coughing and the interruption of the stranger. Now I had always prided myself upon my charities to the poor—the *deserving* poor—and when Widow Johnson's house was consumed with fire, and all her property and her little daughter with it, I headed a subscription paper for her benefit with the exceedingly generous sum of $5 which I paid in the presence of half the town, who had assembled at the bar-room of the village inn, to talk over the catastrophe, after they had stood to see the house consumed, and had laboured with great zeal to quench the burning chimney after the roof and walls had fallen in. When Philip Brown lost his only cow by a stroke of lightning, I contributed fifty cents to assist him in the purchase of another, although in this case I had some qualms of conscience arising from the manner in which he had been bereft of his property. Many a time and oft have I "forked out" a fo'pence ha'penny for the relief of suffering merit, and had in the process of time, come to the comfortable conclusion that I was a particularly charitable man, in which opinion sundry of my neighbours had told me they fully coincided. But here was a new case, evidently differing from any I had ever relieved. I had always felt for the suffering, but it was the suffering of the meritorious. I was ever ready to relieve poverty, but it was the poverty of the virtuous. Here loathsome vice was clearly the parent of misery. "He has bro't it upon himself," ejaculated I; "his suffering is not occasioned by the visitation of God. He has sown the wind let him reap the whirlwind!" The visitation of God! Alas! what more awful visitation there be from Him than to leave the vicious to their vice! This is a judgment more terrible far than earthquake or pestilence.

I turned upon my heel from the wretched object before me.—"Poor fellow," I ejaculated, "he will suffer, but who is to blame?" And thus choking down an accusing conscience, I strode away.—But his voice sounded reproachfully in my ear like a haunting one, and I was but ill satisfied that I had not at least inquired into his necessities. He had not asked for charity, it was true; but did not his miserable apparel plead for him more eloquently than words? He might be too proud to ask, or he might despair receiving, tho't I; at all events, it would have been well enough to have said a word to him about his wicked course, even if it were not right to give him money. I hesitated. I turned round. Standing in the place where I had left him, I saw the miserable man. His hands were clasped, and his face upturned towards Heaven, and I even fancied I could hear the words of prayer on his lips. "Such a wicked man pray!" thought I. Partly from curiosity, and partly from benevolent feelings, I turned back.

"Why do you stand here?" inquired I, as I approached him. "You will be perished with the cold."

"Very likely," was the quiet reply.

"Why don't you go home?" I asked, really touched by the forlornness of his situation.

"I have no home."

"Then go to your friends," I rejoined.

"I have no friends."

"Have you no acquaintances then, who will relieve you?"

"Yes—the dram seller—when I have money."

"Have you no money?"

"Not a farthing."

"You are a miserable vagabond then."

"I know it. Very true."

"Do you know to what these evil courses will lead you?" continued I, putting on a self-righteous air, and looking, as I flattered myself, peculiarly solemn.

"Yes—*to hell!*" was the fearful, emphatic and startling response.

For a moment I was silent. The exclamation had pierced thro' my heart like steel, and a feeling of mingled compunction and compassion thrilled suddenly through my soul. "I pity you," at length I resumed, "God knows how I pity you; and if I did not look upon you as an incorrigible sot, I would do something for your relief."

"Vice is more an object of compassion than mere poverty," was the reply, "and in me both are united."

"I give freely to the virtuous poor," resumed I, in a renewed fit of self righteousness, "but I am principled against bestowing alms upon the vicious."

"I have not asked alms," was the cool response, "nor a sermon."

"True, but you need both, and were you not a drunkard I would bestow them."

"He maketh his sun to rise on the evil and on the good, and sendeth rain on the just and on the unjust,"[21] replied the man, while a glow which might have been of gratitude or devotion, flashed suddenly over his face. There was something in his tone that went to my heart, I felt the reproof—and had he at that moment seen my face, he would have observed the blush that I felt reddening my cheek.

"True," said I, musing, talking to myself rather than to him.

Oh! the difference between the benevolence of God! One is partial in its operations, and exclusive in its character—and the other embraces the universe within its arms! As such thoughts passed rapidly through my mind, my determination was taken.—My heart grew as tender as a child's. The voice of inspiration spoke to my quickened soul, and its language was, "blessed are the merciful for they shall find mercy."[22] God forgive the self righteous spirit in which I indulged but a moment before. "Come with me, and I will be your friend," said I, looking into his bloated face, and actually taking his skinny hand in my own.

Oh! the luxury of doing good! It is the opening of a new world to the spiritual eye! it is the baptism of love to the religious heart! How beautifully true is the sentiment of Holy Writ: "It is more blessed to give than to receive."[23]

The loathsome and degraded man went with me to my home.—I ministered to his necessities—I watched over him in sickness, bearing patiently the self-imposed toil, and leading him step by step from debasement and disease into the pleasant paths of sobriety and health. This was the first time in which the meek spirit of religion had presided over and guided my once ostentatious charity. And great indeed was my reward! A noble spirit was saved from the fearful death, and still more awful doom of a drunkard, and called back by the voice of kindness from the track of sin to that of true wisdom, whose ways are ways of pleasantness, and all whose paths are peace. A

21. Matthew 5:45.

22. Matthew 5:7.

23. Acts 20:35.

new man he went from under my humble roof, and mingled again with the world. But remembering the whirlpool that had drawn him into this vortex, he has shunned it with a tireless care. Resisting the blandishments that would lure him to his ruin, he has walked with a faultless step in the thornless track of virtue, growing strong of heart, and preserving before the world an integrity unspotted and pure. I saw him yesterday with the glow of health upon his cheek, treading with the step of undegraded manhood among his fellow men, surrounded by an atmosphere of love—honored, useful and happy. "And this, said I, is my reward." With a light step and lighter heart, I went to my own quiet home, while a "still small voice" seemed whispering in my ear, "He who converteth the sinner from the error of his way, shall save a soul from death, and shall hide a multitude of sins."[24]

Selected for the Offering.

The Mansion of Rest.[25]

By Charles J. Fox.

I talked to my flattering heart,
    And chid its wild wandering ways;
I charged it from folly to part,
    And to husband the rest of its days:
I bade it no longer admire,
    The meteors which fancy had dress'd,
I whisper'd, 'twas time to retire,
    And seek for a Mansion of Rest.

A charmer was list'ning the while,
    Who caught up the tone of my lay;
"O come then," she cried with a smile,
    "And I'll show you the place and the way:"
I followed the witch to her home,
    And vowed to be always her guest;
"Never more," I exclaimed, "will I roam
    In search of a Mansion of Rest.

24. 1 Kings 19:12, James 5:20.

25. The poem appears in the Cincinnati *Western Christian Advocate*, where it is attributed to British politician Charles James Fox (1749–1806). See 8, no. 51 (April 8, 1842): 4, American Periodicals (126345646).

But the sweetest of moments will fly,
Not long was my fancy beguiled;
For too soon I confess'd with a sigh,
That the syren deceived while she smiled.
Deep, deep, did she stab the repose
Of my trusting and unwary breast,
And the door of each avenue clos'd,
That led to the Mansion of Rest.

Then Friendship enticed me to stray,
Through the long magic wilds of Romance;
But I found that she meant to betray,
And shrunk from the sorcerer's glance,
For experience has taught me to know,
That the soul that reclined on her breast,
Might toss on the billows of woe,
And ne'er find the Mansion of Rest.

Pleasure's path I determined to try,
But Prudence I met in the way—
Conviction flash'd light from her eye,
And appeared to illumine my way;
She cried as she shew'd me a grave,
With nettles and wild flowers dress'd,
O'er which the dark cypress did wave,
"Behold there the Mansion of Rest."

She spoke—and half vanish'd in air,
For she saw mild Religion appear,
With a smile, that could banish despair,
And dry up the penitent tear:
Doubts and fears from my bosom were driven,
And pressing the cross to her breast,
And pointing serenely to Heaven,
She show'd me the Mansion of Rest!

Selected for the Offering.

A Sabbath at Honolulu.[26]

Sunday, the succeeding day but one, and the only Sabbath I spent on shore at Honolulu, may never be forgotten by me. I preached twice in the seaman's chapel to attentive congregations. The foreign residents and the missionaries attend the services of the chapel—the native services being so arranged by the missionaries as to admit of it. But the service the most peculiar, and which will leave the longest impression upon myself, was the meeting I attended in the large church of the natives. The spacious building was filled when I reached the house. I walked through a long range of these Hawaiians, as I ascended from the door, crowded thick upon the mats and filling the whole area, or were arranged upon their seats occupying the more central part of the building. As I entered the pulpit, already occupied by the Rev. Mr. Bingham and the Rev. Mr. Richards,[27] I looked over a congregation of near three thousand of these worshipping islanders. What a scene was this for a Christian to contemplate in a foreign land, where the same people a few years before were a heathen and a savage nation!

And before me, now, were some who had witnessed, and one, at least, who had been the cause of human sacrifices, to propitiate and atone for a broken *tabu,* which human blood alone could satisfy.[28] A hymn was sung; after which I gave the congregation an address, which was interpreted, sentence by sentence, with such facility by Mr. Bingham, that there seemed but a little break in the continuance of the discourse. It was still throughout

26. Another selection from Episcopal clergyman Fitch Waterman Taylor's *The Flag-Ship: Or, a Voyage Around the World in the United States Frigate Columbia.* (New York: D. Appleton & Company, 1840), 2:278–86, Google Books, http://books.google.com/books?id=ENoBAAAAYAAJ. See n. 11, p. 288.

27. Protestant missionaries for the American Board of Commissioners for Foreign Missions; Hiram Bingham (1789–1869) went to Hawaii in 1820 and William Richards (1793–1847) arrived there in 1823. Notable writings include Bingham, *A Residence of Twenty-One Years in the Sandwich Islands*, 2nd ed. (Hartford: Hezekiah Huntington, 1848), Google Books, http://books.google.com/books?id=-cIRAAAAYAAJ and Richards, *Memoir of the Late Keopuolani, Late Queen of the Sandwich Islands* (Boston: Crocker and Brewster, 1825), Google Books, http://books.google.com/books?id=_IQhAAAAMAAJ. Their work was extensively reported in the American religious periodicals of the antebellum decades, and the history of these missions are included in standard histories of the state. For example, see Ruth Tabrah, *Hawaii: A History* (New York: Norton, 1984), esp. chapter 4, "The Reign of Hiram Bingham" and chapter 5, "The Advent of Democracy," and Gary Okihiro, *Island World: A History of Hawai'i and the United States* (Berkeley: University of California Press, 2008).

28. Much has been written about the taboo system of early Hawaii. For a start, see George J. Tanabe, Jr., "*Ponu* and *Kapu*: Righteousness and Taboo in Hawaii," in *Religion and Public Life in the Pacific Region*, eds. Wade Clark Roof and Mark Silk (Walnut Creek: AltaMira Press, 2005), 139–67.

the house. Attention was arrested, and held.—I repeat not here even the substance of the address, but I assured the islanders that it was happiness for a stranger, from a far land, to witness them worshipping the same God he worshipped—the same Redeemer—the same sanctifying Spirit.—"Their friends, the missionaries," I continued, "who were also our friends, had told us much in their letters sent from the islands, but they had not said all that I, that day, beheld before me. In America, they prayed for the Hawaiians. They prayed for the missionaries among them. The missionaries had left their homes, and friends, and many comforts for long years; and we, who in our ships have been absent from our homes, which are in the same land they left, though but for one year and a half, yet feel how dear that home is to us, and therefore can estimate how much these our missionary friends have been willing to leave for the love of Christ, to spend a life-time of labor among you. In America, therefore, we give them our prayers—we give them our Christian love—we give them our confidence—we give them, sometimes, when we think of them so far away, our tears. But we are also happy that they are among you, doing their duty where they think God has directed them to come. Will you not, therefore, more than ever listen to their words? Will you not be more grateful that they have told you of the immortal soul—the thing within us which thinks, and loves, and is happy, or is sad, and wishes to be happy still and for ever, when the body shall have gone back to its dust? Hawaiians, these missionaries have brought you things worth more than gold—more than gems—more than silver dollars—more than pearls—they have told you how to save for ever this immortal pearl within you; and how, millions of years hence, if Christians, ye shall live on and be happy with the undying saints of heaven, where God shall give to them his friendship as he gives it to his angels. Will ye not hear them?

"I am glad that I can talk with you, through my friend, though I do not understand your language. But I must not talk longer with you. Yet would I ask of you, who are professors of religion, will you give me your prayers? Our ships will soon leave you, as we go on our way around the world to our homes. *We* came not to disturb you. We came to approve of your religious worship, and to tell you so. And when I reach America, I shall tell the Christians there that I have met those who love God among the Hawaiians—that I have heard them pray to our God—sing in our own hymns and tunes—and that I have shed my tears while I have beheld the sight, and thanked God for permitting me to behold it. I shall never be with you again. Christian Hawaiians, through this house! here in your temple I shall not meet you again, but hope to meet you in heaven. Farewell! But when I shall have reached America, I will not forget you. I will not forget how I have heard you pray, sing and worship. I will not forget your green valleys—your home in the islands in the seas. I will not forget these missionary friends; but when the sun wakes up over the hills, and when it goes down in the ocean, I will pray for them and for you. Hawaiians, farewell! Hold fast the religion you love. Let a world, if it will, rage. Still hold ye on to the religion of Jesus Christ. The world will soon crumble to nothing. These mountains and this ocean shall soon be burned up, and then you will want the friendship of Christ. *Hold on, then, to the religion of Jesus Christ!* And when heaven and earth pass away, you shall find Him to be to you more than an elder brother—your Redeemer, and your all. Hawaiians, farewell!"

I offer no apology for introducing this brief sketch of part of the address alluded to, in the form I here present it, and in which, amid the circumstances described, it was delivered. It will more naturally paint the scene that was presented before me, than otherwise could be done. When I had ended my address, Mr. Richards spoke briefly and feelingly to the congregation. A hymn was then sung, in a melody that could not but touch the heart of him, with any feeling, who for the first time looked on such a scene as this. And while my own was melting, *I* thought if ever there were a just cause for *indignation,* it was while hearing flippant man, as sometimes he has been heard, decrying the holy and self-denying men and women who have here been laboring for years to produce the astonishing and glorious effects which I now beheld before me. And never did virtue more justly frown on vice, than wakes the voice of benevolence in displeasure when contemplating the vicious defamation with self-interest, jealous traffic, and depravity of heart, at times indulge against such demonstrations of the righteous work of God's children, who advocate the religion of Jesus Christ in its purity and practice.

On attempting to leave the church, at the conclusion of the services, I found it impossible to proceed for a while, as the warm-hearted natives pressed around me to give me their hands; but moving slowly as I accepted the proffered demonstration of their interest on either side of me, as I passed, I finally broke through their gathered numbers. And when I had reached my room, but a short distance from the church, which overlooks the grounds in the neighborhood, I gazed, with a feasted eye and a full heart, on the streams of men, women, and children, flowing from every door of the large building, and directing their way to their homes, in the quiet and orderly walk of the respectful, who give consideration and conscientious observance to the Sabbath day.

All were decently clad, but in such a manner and variety of costume, in coloring and in material, as to interest the beholder, and to declare *the transition state* of the natives, in their passage from their original savage to civilized life. Here was a passing group, one of whom perhaps was clad in a deep orange-colored gown, with a bright yellow wrapper around the waist, knotted behind by the upper corners, so as to form something like an apron, while the dark bushy hair was filleted with a wreath of yellow feathers, constituting a costly ornament for the head or neck of the female native. Another, in the same group, had thrown a large tappa around him, knotted over one of his shoulders after the style of the Roman toga, and discovering a white shirt beneath, with a chaplet of ferns circling his head, while his dark neck and lower limbs are left in the freeness and bareness of a Highland chief's.—Again, a light blue silk shawl covers a white frock, with a small straw bonnet upon the head; or a crimson shawl over a blue calico dress, with a similar hat. Indeed, almost all the females wear a straw bonnet on the Sabbath, which is manufactured upon the islands; and I am not certain but that the chaplet of leaves or flowers to which I have alluded is only a week-day ornament. And here, again, is seen an old man with a long staff in his hand, and with feeble step, clad in a simple white dress of tappa, the native material of the island, made often beautifully from the bark of the mulberry, now wending his way from a Christian temple, in deep thought and musings, unlike those that attended him from the revel and the sacrifice of former days. And there, the light-hearted group of children, in every color of stripe and figure of silk or cotton, or tappa of coarser or richer material, move on, with free and bounding step. And there, the governor, in his blue cloth frock-coat and white pantaloons, and straw hat, is seen attended by a little boy in his dress of frock-coat and white trousers, and shoes and stockings; and a little girl, in black frock and white pantalettes and jockey hat, all undistinguished from a well-dressed group of Europeans, accompanied by a train of indifferently clad attendants. Many others were in European style, among the males and females—the loose gown, and shawl, and bonnet being the common dress for the female natives. And one group more may serve to fill up the picture. It is the principal woman of the islands.[29] She is drawn by four or five natives,

29. Since these events take place in October 1839, this would be Queen Kalama, also known as

in a small hand-vehicle, with two wheels, not unlike a porter's hand-cart, but a convenient carriage on a plain and smooth path for the principal lady of the islands, who is more than six feet high, and weighs—I know not how much. Her dress is European—the expression of her face good-natured—and her signature required to give validity to the acts of the king and his chiefs. Her son is the adopted heir-apparent to the government of the island,[30] and she has in charge the infant child, who holds, as queen, the same position in the government as does his present majesty as king.

But as the eye lingers on this moving crowd, as they are seen retiring from the house of worship to their homes, presenting so great variety in their dress, they are yet all decently clad, and move at their ease in stillness and propriety, and exhibit evidences of great, though as yet a rude contentment and happiness.

How great is the contrast! How unlike the picture the same people exhibited but a few years ago! Another congregation of equal size, at the other end of the town, was dispersing from the house of worship to which they had gathered, in like order, decency, and rude respectability. The wide avenue, extending for a half mile between the two churches, seemed crowded by the meeting throng.

But it would require the Christian community at home to see, as I have seen to-day, the worshipping thousands of the Hawaiians, duly to appreciate the scene. Over the same congregation of these islanders which I had addressed, the eye of the Christian could look, in late months, as they gathered for worship, and see, not as an unfrequent scene, half the congregation in tears, as the preacher declared to them the truths which have been borne to their understandings, through the labors of the devoted missionary, during the few past years. They bowed their heads in sorrow for their sinfulness—with religious sympathies, in view of the affecting story of the plan of salvation—and resolved to be the disciples of Jesus Christ. And to this church, more than four hundred have been added, on profession of religion during the last year; and more than six hundred to the communion in the second church; and more than *ten thousand*, in all, to the churches on the different islands. And the whole number of the communicants in the different churches of the mission amounts to more that sixteen thousand souls. The

---

Hakaleleponi Kapakuhaili (1820–70), the wife of King Kamehameha III (1813–54). Kalama was tall and regarded by some as the prettiest woman on the island. See Gwenfread E. Allen, "Kalama." In *Notable Women of Hawaii*, ed. Barbara Bennett Peterson (Honolulu: University of Hawaii Press, 1984), 184–85.

30. The adopted son is five-year-old Alexander Liholiho (1834–63), who would reign as Kamehameha IV.

mission has thus been blessed, by an outpouring of the Spirit of God upon its churches, and the ingathering of thousands to the communion. At Hile, on a neighboring island five thousand two hundred and forty-four have, this last year, joined the church. And at Waimea, on the island of Hawaii, twenty-three hundred more. Surely, the heart that has any Christian sympathies for the cause of Christ, or the eternal welfare of his fellow-men, must glow in view of this statement; and the lover of the missionary cause may exult in gratitude to the Giver of all good, for this triumphant exhibition of the success of Christ's cause among the heathen. And tell me, Christian reader, while the tear wakes in memory of the goodness of God to your own soul, and in boundless mercies to these once and but lately benighted savages, can you feel otherwise than an abhorrence at the slang of the infidel and the opposer, who are sometimes heard, either from self-interest or hate, decry so worthy a cause and so worthy a band of devoted men and women, who have blessed, by their residence and efforts, at the sacrifice of friends and home, the whole people of these islands? Believe me, this mission is worthy of the confidence of the Christian community at home; and as surely as the smile of God has rested so signally upon it, so surely it *will* receive the confidence and support of the Christians in America. And I trust, as an Episcopalian, my testimony of confidence and commendation and deep-felt interest in behalf of this Congregational and Presbyterian mission to the Sandwich Islands will not be regarded, under such circumstances, the less unbiased and sincere.

Selected for the Offering.

"No God!"[31]

"No God! No God!" The simplest flow'r
That on the wild is found,
Shrinks as it drinks its cup of dew,
And trembles at the sound;
"No God!" astonished Echo cries
From out the cavern hoar,
And every wandering bird that flies,
Reproves the Atheist lore.

31. Poem by American writer Lydia Sigourney (1791–1865). An early appearance is *Pocahontas, and Other Poems* (New York: Harper & Brothers, 1841), 95–96, Google Books, http://books.google.com/books?id=MnsEAAAAYAAJ.

The solemn forest lifts its head,
Th' Almighty to proclaim;
The brooklet on its crystal urn,
Doth leap to 'grave His name.
High swells the deep and vengeful sea
Along his billowy track;
And red Vesuvius opens his mouth,
To hurl the falsehood back.

The palm tree with its princely crest,
The cocoa's leafy shade,
The bread-fruit bending to its lord
In yon far island glade;
The winged seeds, that, borne by winds,
The roving sparrows feed,
The melon on the desert sands,
Confute the scorner's creed.

"No God!" With indignation high,
The fervent sun is stir'd;
And the pale moon turns paler still,
At such an impious word;
And from their burning thrones, the stars
Look down with angry eye,
That such a worm of dust should mock,
Eternal Majesty.

Selected for the Offering.

The Unfading Flower.[32]

By Heber.

By cool Siloam's shady rill,
How sweet the lily grows!

32. A standard, often-republished hymn by Bishop of Calcutta Reginald Heber (1783–1826). See Heber, *Hymns* (London: John Murray, 1827), 29–30, Google Books, http://books.google.com/books?id=oTVWAAAAYAAJ.

How sweet the breath beneath the hill,
    Of Sharon's dewy rose!

Lo, such the child whose early feet
    The paths of peace have trod,
Whose secret heart, with influence sweet,
    Is upward drawn to God.

By cool Siloam's shady rill,
    The lily must decay,
The rose, that blooms beneath the hill,
    Must shortly fade away.

And soon, too soon, the wintry hour
    Of man's maturer age
Will shake the soul with sorrow's power,
    And stormy passion's rage.

O Thou, whose infant feet were found
    Within thy Father's shrine,
Whose years, with changeless virtue crowned,
    Were all alike Divine.

Dependent on thy bounteous breath,
    We seek thy grace alone,
In childhood, manhood, age, and death,
    To keep us still thine own.

To Our Readers.

Lily Lute's letter is received, but too late for insertion in this No.—it will appear in Number Eleven.

Several other articles came too late and some that were in season, that needed to be re-written, sickness has compelled me to lay aside, hoping that for the next Number I shall at least, be able to do all necessary copying and not be obliged to select so many articles already printed.[33]

33. See introduction, pp. 13–14.

We are under many obligations to G. S. and to many others and we shall not forget the claims binding upon us.

In No. Ten, instead of H. T. Tucker as author of Thoughts on the Poets, should have been printed Tuckerman.

Please excuse an almost uncourteous brevity and when health is again my portion, with pleasure will I resume my pen.

C. Cumings.

THE AKRON OFFERING. March, 1850.

For the Offering.

Letters for the Offering.

Number IV.

By Lily Lute.[1]

Now is the cold and dreary winter time, and I have not spoken to you since the autumn; it seems to me a long, long time. But hark! there goes that serenade again, and if I could only make my old quill[2] dance to the music, how beautifully I would write; but I cannot write when I hear music, for somehow it casts such a spell over me that I long to cover my eyes and see the sounds as they come to my veiled vision in the most beautiful forms and colors. I like the story of the Artist who was in Italy with Ole Bull, and when Ole played any thing that pleased him he would say, "play that again, Ole, while I paint it, for it is the most exquisite red I ever saw, and there! that is the finest blue in the world!" and so on of any color the music suggested to his mind.[3] But that serenade! How delightful when the long evening is drawing to a close, and all without, the trees, the yard, the house-tops and as far as the eye can reach, over hill and plain, seems sleeping beneath a mantle of purity,

1. For more on Lily Lute, see pp. 3; n. 15, p. 44; and 453–57.

2. Steel pens gradually replaced quill pens in the nineteenth century.

3. This anecdote is part of "Recollections of Ole Bull" by American abolitionist Lydia Maria Child (1802–80). Ole Bornemann Bull (1810–80) was a Norwegian violinist. See *The Columbian Lady's and Gentleman's Magazine* 5, no. 2 (February 1846): 75, Google Books, http://books.google.com/books?id=PFlFAAAAYAAJ.

that sparkles as if set with diamonds, whenever Rob Horn looks down from his cold place among the clouds.[4] And then all is so cozy and warm within, and every thing appears so dreamlike; the candle is dying away in the socket, the old clock ticks, ticks away on the wall, the cricket chirps away on the hearth, and old Tabby lifts her head from the rug and purrs, as we draw the great arm chair nearer the fire, and sink down amid the cushions watching the red coals mouldering and falling through the grate—then mayhap we drop off into the land of dreams, and

"Ah! mortal tongue can never tell
Those symphonies which seem
Too bright for harp or evening bell;
The music of a dream."[5]

Then from the sweet dream we are awakened by the dulcet tones of viol, guitar or flute, which fill the still air with melody—O, I can think of nothing more heavenly than dreaming where music sounds;—and how much I thank those handsome Troubadours, who of late have made such delicious music beneath my windows.

Speaking of serenades, reminds me of one I had while in Cincinnati, in the winter of 1843. I was boarding on Third street, opposite a Music Store, and so near the Assembly Rooms that I could hear the music made there for dancing, almost nightly, and on a clear night could distinctly hear the Garrison band at Newport;[6] so that either one or the other of these estab-

---

4. The moon. This is an obscure literary allusion. In a story by American writer Caroline Chesebro' (1825–73), a spirit punishes "Rob Horn" for his ambitious duplicity in love by transforming him into "The Man in the Moon." See "The Man in the Moon: A True Story," *Graham's Magazine* 34, no. 2 (February 1849): 91–87, Google Books, http://books.google.com/books?id=INYRAAAAYAAJ. The story is also collected in Chesebro', *Dream-land by Daylight: A Panorama of Romance* (New York: Redfield, 1851), Google Books, http://books.google.com/books?id=ojIgAAAAMAAJ.

5. As noted later in this sketch, these lines are from "The Music of a Dream" by Cincinnati painter and poet Horace S. Minor (1822–c.1849). Minor edited and contributed to *The Shooting Star*, a lost and forgotten Cincinnati literary magazine. In a biographical notice he is described as a "conception of Shelley": "that physical gentleness, combined with intense love of the ideal beautiful, good and free, with its rebellious warfare upon the dwarfing and deforming conventionalities of life, were his; but he committed no breach of those conventionalities, and his morals were irreproachably pure." See William T. Coggeshall, *Poets and Poetry of the West* (Columbus: Follet, Foster, and Company, 1860), 434–35, Google Books, http://books.google.com/books?id=7GEoAAAAYAAJ.

6. A Cincinnati directory for 1839–40 places the Assembly Rooms at the southeast corner of Pearl and Walnut. See Ohio Name Index, American Antiquarian Society, http://www.morganohiolibrary.com/OhioBusiness.html. This area was two short blocks north of the Ohio River. It is now Interstate 71 as it passes the National Underground Railroad Freedom Center just west of the baseball stadium. A "splendid brass band" was attached to the United States military garrison across the river at Newport, Kentucky. See "A Procession by Moonlight" in Cincinnati's *Masonic Review* 4, no. 1 (October

lishments furnished me with sweet sounds nearly all the time. One evening shortly after I commenced boarding there, I had a call from a gentleman of my acquaintance, who was much pleased with my situation on account of the music; and in the course of a conversation on the subject, I remarked there was nothing so delightful as the music of a dream. "So one would think," said he, "after reading Minor's poem under that title, and as I play the guitar I think I shall act the Troubadour some night under your window."

I retired late that night and was so tired and sleepy that I had hardly settled myself in my nightcap, before Somnus caught me and I was wandering away in Dreamland's most beautiful regions, when twang! twang! came up the notes of a guitar, and a manly voice began singing,

> "Thou, thou reign'st in this bosom."[7]

I knew who the singer was, therefore as I was tired, thought I would not get up, and lay half dreaming till the song was finished; then all was still for a few moments, and fearing he would be offended if I did not show myself, commenced dressing and in a moment after heard a shutter open on an adjoining house. My room opened on a piazza and was above the windows where the shutter opened, so I stepping cautiously out and looking down saw, as the moon shone brightly, one of the most charming faces, leaning on one of the prettiest little hands, the arm of which rested on the window sill, and the pretty eyes were looking anxiously down towards my gallant minstrel. I drew back and soon the music struck up again—but this time it was under the window of the strange beauty, and the song was

> "O, who art thou, fair lady, say?"[8]

As it ended I looked out again, just in time to see a snowy handkerchief flutter from the window and fall at the feet of the delighted musician. He caught it up, waved it towards the beauty, then walked slowly away, never deigning a look at me. I sought my pillow again, saying to myself, there is seed sown for a love affair, for I knew the young man, whose name was

---

1848): 58, Google Books, http://books.google.com/books?id=yroaAQAAMAAJ.

7. A glee; for music and lyrics see *The Boston Glee Book* (Boston: Wilkins, Carter, and Palmer, 1839), 167, Google Books, http://books.google.com/books?id=I4g6AAAAMAAJ.

8. The line is too ambiguously common to be identified with certainty. It could be an improvisation on "Oh! Lady Fair"; see *The Boston Glee Book* (Boston: Wilkins, Carter, and Palmer, 1839), 249, Google Books, http://books.google.com/books?id=I4g6AAAAMAAJ. It could also be part of "The Owl." See *Blackwood's Edinburgh Magazine* 30 (July 1831): 792, Google Books, http://books.google.com/books?id=VJNmKqSvjVAC.

Morgan, had a large share of romance in his composition, besides he was always ready to fall in love with every pretty face he met.

The next day I had another call from Mr. Morgan, but not a word said of the serenade; and after talking of the theatre, the Razor Strop man etc.,[9] he expressed a wish to see a picture which I was just finishing, and when I told him I would bring it down to the parlor, he said, "O, no—let me go up to your studio and see the other pictures for it is some time since I saw them." I led the way to my room where he stopped a few moments to examine the paintings, then walked to the window and spoke of the fine view I had from the piazza. I knew he thought to get a view of a fair stranger from there, and I opened the door and walked out with him.—"Delightful! delightful!" he exclaimed, looking down at the windows of the next house, instead of the broad and beautiful Ohio, the Garrison and the woody hills of Kentucky that rose up in the distance—and then leaning over the balustrade, he hummed the air he had sung the night before; soon that shutter was pushed out a little, when the wind caught it, and swung it suddenly open, while two golden curls danced gaily after but were quickly drawn back. Morgan, who had been standing with one hand in his vest, now drew forth a bouquet of rare exotics and threw it into the window; then out peeped that lovely face with those Heavenly eyes, which dropped beneath the fond gaze of my friend, and the face was again hid from our sight, and we saw no more of it that day.

The evening following was cold and stormy and I saw nothing of Morgan, but the next was such a night as, "love-sick swains their lasses woo in,"[10] clear and mild, with a breeze as still and soft as a May morning. The clock on Beecher's Church[11] had told the hour of eleven, and no guitar

9. Henry Smith, "the celebrated Razor Strop Man," was a peddler of pieces of leather (strops) used for sharpening razors. Evidently he was quite the comedian, and a great many jokes and puns are attributed to him in the American newspapers of the 1840s. A "reformed drunkard," Smith was also promoted by pro-temperance editors as a model of sober industry. A full-length temperance biography of Smith, with an appendix of his "original songs, queer speeches, humorous letters, and odd, droll, strange, and whimsical sayings," is *The Life and Adventures of Henry Smith, The Celebrated Razor Strop Man* (Boston: White and Potter, 1848), Google Books, http://books.google.com/books?id=MJo9AAAAYAAJ.

10. A string of clichés alluding to the conventions of the period's romantic ballads.

11. First president and professor of theology at Lane Theological Seminary and father of Harriet Beecher Stowe and Henry Ward Beecher, Lyman Beecher (1775–1863) was pastor of the Second Presbyterian Church of Cincinnati on Fourth Street between Race and Vine, at the present-day location of the McAlpin condominiums. Perhaps the tallest structure in town, the church's clock tower can be seen in the 1848 panorama of the city taken from a Newport rooftop by Charles Fontayne and William S. Porter. See "Cincinnati Panorama of 1848," The Public Library of Cincinnati and Hamilton County, http://1848.cincinnatilibrary.org/.

sounded; I laid down my book and walked out on the piazza, where I stood looking down on the sleeping city, and up at the full round moon, thinking of far away home in the quiet village where I had left so many dear friends, and I wondered if some of them were not then looking at the same bright moon and thinking of me—when my revery was broken by a foot-fall on the pave below, and looking down, I saw Morgan step lightly up the walk and stop beneath that same window, so I drew back into the shadow of a post, while "he gaily touched his guitar,"[12] and sung,

> "Wilt go with me and be my bride?"[13]

When he had done, the shutter slowly unclosed and a fair hand dropped a note, which Morgan caught, pressed it to his lips again and again, then dashed off with all speed.

A day or two after, while I was sitting in the parlor, I received a call and card, from Miss Annetta Ambol, who was no other than Morgan's fair enamorado. She came, she said, to see my pictures—she was very fond of paintings and had heard of mine and wished to see them. Ha! ha! thought I, laughing in my sleeve, my poor pictures are coming into notice. After thanking her for so much condescension, I waited on her to my room, and when she had admired my miserable daubs sufficiently, she sat down and chatted away so pleasantly, I almost fell in love with her myself. We were soon on the most friendly terms, and before she left had planned a dozen excursions to the country the coming spring, for the purpose of sketching; and even thought of going as far as the Miami valley, where there are such fine landscapes.

We parted with a mutual promise of meeting often, for I was really much pleased with her, so frank and witty, and intelligent as well as handsome.

Two days had not passed ere she came again, bringing a basket of fruit and nuts, which she said were selected on purpose to give me a little treat, for a boarding house was not like one's own home, and she feared I did not often get such things there. She had not been there long, when word came that a gentleman wished to see me: thinking it was Morgan, I said send him up, and true to my expectation Morgan came. I introduced him to Annette,

12. "Gaily the Troubadour / Touched his guitar" are the first lines of "Welcome Me Home" by English poet Thomas Haynes Bayly (1797–1839). See *Songs and Ballads, Grave and Gay* (Philadelphia: Carey and Hart, 1844), 58, Google Books, http://books.google.com/books?id=cKo-AAAAIAAJ.

13. Lines from an Irish ballad known as "Eileen Aroon" and other spellings of the name. See "Aileen A-Roon, A Legend of Ireland," *Chambers' Edinburgh Journal* 9 (June 6, 1840): 195–96, Google Books, http://books.google.com/books?id=ImQiAQAAMAAJ.

who in her blushing confusion, dropped her handkerchief—Morgan sprang forward to pick it up, but in is haste, he blundered and his foot caught in the carpet which threw him forward against Annette, who to save herself, caught hold of the easel, but that only made matters worse, for down went easel, picture, paints and brushes, together with Annette and Morgan; and to add to the confusion, Mrs. L., the lady of the house, who was in the next room, heard the crash and came running in, and just as she had crossed the threshold, stepped on a paint tube, which slipped under her foot and down she went,—away went cap and wig, and false teeth rattled over the floor, and she arose from the mass of ruins looking like a grey witch painted. Morgan had risen and lifted Annette from the floor and was trying to restore order, while I stood ready to burst with laughter; and when I found there was no one hurt, I let my risibles have full play, in which exercise all joined me, even the discomfited Mrs. L. who soon took herself out of the room and left us to talk over the matter. The ice being thus comically broken; Annette and Morgan were better acquainted in a few moments than they would have been in weeks, had not the accident happened. The afternoon passed off very pleasantly and when Annette left, with one of her sweetest smiles she said, "now Miss ———, do call often, and Mr. Morgan I should be very happy to see you at our house." That was what Morgan had been wishing for, and now he was almost beside himself with joy; and could not stay three minutes after she had gone. But the next day he was back again, and invited me to call with him on Miss Ambol; I went with him, and without waiting a fashionable length of time, we were ushered into a drawing-room, where we found Annette with her brother, who had just returned from college. After introducing us she said, speaking to me with her lips and to Morgan with her eyes, "I am glad you have come, for brother Archie is getting tired of me, and was going out to make up a party for the theatre to night, but now he will not have to go, for we will just make a nice party—will you not go Miss ———? Archie would like to be your escort I know, for I have been telling him all about you, and he said he would certainly fall in love with my amiable Artist." It was my turn to blush and be confused now, but Archie came to my aid and said all the fine things gents generally say on such occasions; and showed me a collection of paintings he had bought lately, played the piano for me, and in short played the agreeable to the best of his abilities; while Morgan and Annette, *tête-à-tête* on the sofa, seemed all unconscious that the world contained others than themselves. I saw that they were deeply entangled in the meshes of the blind God, and disliked to break the spell that hung over them; but I wished to return, and asked Morgan if he was ready to accompany me, and then he seemed so unwilling to tear himself away that I complied with their solicitations, staid to tea, and went from there to the theatre.

And now all went merry as a marriage bell. Scarce a night passed that we did not attend some place of amusement, or spend the evenings together, either in my room, or at Mr. Ambol's, and when spring came, such delightful rides to the country, such climbing of hills, such walks by moon-light and sails up the Licking,[14] is delightful to think of even now. The lovers were happy as a pair of larks, and Archie and myself, though not in love, were always of their company so that I hardly painted a stroke for weeks. But the sun cannot always shine, and one bright May morning, our sun was darkened by the departure of Archie, who went to take the place of his father in business at New Orleans. Annette expected opposition from her father and therefore was somewhat prepared for what followed when he came; for as soon as he found that Morgan was visiting Annette, he very politely asked him to discontinue his visits at his house.—And why? Why, forsooth he was *poor*! Only a clerk in a drug-store.—Yes, he was *poor*! so it mattered not if he had a giant mind, brilliant talents and a noble soul;—he should not think of mating himself with the daughter of wealth—what though that wealth had been earned by fraud.

Morgan's mind was above little things; he despised all kinds of deception, and for this reason would not hold a secret correspondence with Annette, and only staid in the city long enough to hear from her lips that she would be true to him, till he should return with wealth sufficient to secure her father's consent. Where he went none knew, and we did not hear from him until the next winter, when I received a letter dated at Mobile, in which he stated that he was in good business and if fortune favored him as it had since he left us, he should return in two years. I read the letter to Annette, and was pleased to see her look happy again, as she had not in many months. Not long after, I left the city and joyfully turned my face towards my northern home, which I had not seen for eighteen months. It was a sunny morning in March, and as our boat left the landing and swept proudly up the broad river and we began to near the country, I looked back at the smoky city, fast fading from my sight, and wondered how I had ever lived so long in a pent

14. The Licking River of Kentucky drains into the Ohio at Newport.

up town, while the country was so beautiful and the people there so friendly and unselfish, in comparison with the residents of a city; and fathers were not so cruel, but would let their children marry whom they loved.

From these reflections I was startled by a voice that sounded so familiar, I was certain I had heard it before, and leaning over the guard, I tried to get a view of the persons on the lower deck, for the sound seemed to come from there; but I saw only a couple of boatmen and was about turning away, when one of them looked up, and beneath the slouched hat, I discovered the face of my old friend Morgan: the recognition was mutual and in another moment, with the old hat in hand he stood beside me; and what cared I for the sidelong glances of the upper ten, that were simpering about? I never was ashamed of honest worth in whatever guise it appeared.

He excused his appearance by saying he had a chance of doing much better in Pittsburgh than Mobile, and to save money was now working his passage there and receiving the wages of a deck hand. I commended him for his economy and assured him success would crown his efforts if he kept on in the way he had begun. "I feel sure of that," said he, "and shall not consider any honest labor de-grading or difficult, so long as Annette is the prize."

I left the boat at Steubenville, and the last I saw of Morgan he was busy at his work; and when a year after I returned to Cincinnati, I could hear nothing of him. Annette was in Orleans with her brother, where she was going to spend some months, and I staid in the city but three months, I did not see her. And I heard nothing of either of them again till the next winter, when I went once more to the city; and almost the first person I met when leaving the cars was Morgan. He accompanied me to the hotel, told me of all his future plans and prospects, that he was in business for himself, and with a good capital of his own; that he was addressing Annette now with her father's consent, but should not be married till he could build a house suitable to hold so fair a bride.

I stayed in the city six months, and as Archie was again at home, we renewed out old flirtation, and walked and rode and sailed and visited saloons, concerts, theatres etc., but now, though Annette was always of the company, Morgan was too much engrossed in business to be with us often.

I left them in July, '47, and have not heard from them since, but presume the handsome Annette is now Mrs. and is perchance at this moment rocking the cradle for a second edition of D. L. Morgan.

For the Offering.

The Lambs of Heaven.

"O come Ma'ma 'tis beautiful,
O 'tis a sight to see,
Come to the garden where the rose
Gives honey to the bee."

" 'Tis eve my child, the flow'rets all
Their petals fair have closed;
The honey-bee has sought its rest;
Thy brother needs repose."

"I'll hush him in his cradle-bed
And sing the Chick-a-dee
O take him in your arms and come
He'd so delighted be."

Thus pressed, the mother must comply
And come with free good will
To the white rose-tree blooming there;
The eve was calm and still,

And soft white clouds in many moulds,
At Heaven's portal prest,
Like saintly bands that waiting stood
To enter their sweet rest.

With hands upraised young Emma stood,
As to devotion given,
"O look Ma'ma, the lovely sight,
The sweet young Lambs of Heaven."

'Tis spring again, the white rose-tree
Is blooming fresh and fair;
They deck the brow of the early dead
That's coldly slumbering there.

At evening now that mother mourns
Tho' whispers sweet are given;
"Thou'st given thy little one to be
A sweet young Lamb of Heaven."

Elizabeth.
Schroon, N. Y.[15]

Selected for the Offering.

The Lover's Talisman; Or, The Spirit Bride.

By Mrs. Seba Smith.[16]

"Anna," said a young collegian, "you are a noble girl—no die-away airs, because your lover is so long absent; no making all the rest of your admirers feel, that they are just the last persons in the world that you care any thing about—no, no; you are not so selfish as all that, Anna."

A shadow passed over the face of the fair girl, and the smile died away upon her lips.

"Indeed cousin, this *might* be a cutting reproach; but you do not intend it as such—I know you do not."

"Never," said the youth, passionately; "I meant only to commend my cousin's sweetness of temper—her constancy is——"

Anna raised her finger.

"I have issued my interdict upon that score, cousin; but do you know I have a Talisman that will ensure me the constancy of William—and it is of a kind, too, that is valueless in case of fickleness upon my part!"

"Indeed; initiate me into its mysteries, Anna; there are a pair of blue eyes, that I should like amazingly to fix for me alone; and when you are married, sweet coz,[17] perhaps your Talisman will be transferable."

15. Schroon was a town of about two thousand people on the Schroon River in New York. It would have connected to Akron through the Erie Canal. See Thomas Baldwin and J. Thomas, *A New and Complete Gazetteer of the United States* (Philadelphia: Lippincott, Grambo, 1854), 1060, Google Books, http://books.google.com/books?id=_5s6AAAAcAAJ.

16. In 1850 Elizabeth Oakes Smith (1806–93) was enjoying great attention as the author of a feminist series on "Woman and Her Needs" for Horace Greeley's *New York Tribune*. The first publication of this story appears to have been in an 1839 number of *The Southern Literary Messenger,* but Cumings appears to have copied it from the Philadelphia periodical, *The Ladies' Garland*. See 3, no. 9 (March 1840): 214–19, Google Books, http://books.google.com/books?id=msNBAAAAYAAJ.

17. Cousin; a pet name.

"Aunt can describe its virtues best, cousin George; and if she will tell you the story of Hannah Newton, you will never be at a loss to understand the nature of the Lover's Talisman."

Mrs. B., the aunt, raised her eyes from her needle, and a faint smile played over her placid features. She was an unmarried lady of nearly fifty, dressed with great simplicity, her hair neatly parted over her forehead, which was still smooth and fair. The plain muslin cap, with its fine satin strings, denoted a member of the Society of Friends.[18]

"Thee is very fond of that story, Anna; but thee must not rely too much on the power of the Talisman, as thee calls it; for ours is the constant sex, Anna, and we remember long, it may be, after we are forgotten."

I observed a faint blush stole to her cheek as she uttered this, and for the first time I began to ask myself why Mrs. B. (I use the English term of Mrs. as applied to a certain age, as I think it dignified, and altogether proper,) with all her sweetness of manner, and feminine excellencies, should still have remained, like "the last rose of summer, left blooming alone."[19] But the tone of the voice, the flitting blush, and more than all the sentiment she had expressed, revealed to me at once a record of wasted affections, of lonely watching, and midnight tears—of the bitterness of sorrow, known only to Him, who seeth in secret, and of that "concealment, that prayeth like a worm in the bud"[20] upon the human heart.

Mrs. B., from that time, became with me an advocate for the whole sisterhood of those who are to seek for a kindred spirit amongst the pure essences of the invisible world, instead of the grosser elements of earth. She told the story with a grace and pathos, that I dare not even hope to transfer to my pages—I can only give the details, leaving my readers to imagine the many fine touches of feeling and beauty, which could be imparted only by the lips of Mrs. B.

The Story of Mrs. B.

Hannah Newton, at sixteen, was merely a quiet, sweet-looking girl, with small pretensions to beauty; for she had nothing of that regularity

18. Quakers. For more on the Friends' use of "thee"—seen here in the story—see Ezra Kempton Maxfield, "Quaker 'Thee' and Its History," *American Speech* 1, no. 12 (September 1926): 638–44, JSTOR, http://www.jstor.org/stable/452011.

19. Opening line of a poem by Irish poet Thomas Moore (1779–1852). See *The Poetical Works of Thomas Moore* (Philadelphia: Crissy & Markley, 1847), 334, Google Books, http://books.google.com/books?id=ym8_AAAAYAAJ.

20. Shakespeare, *Twelfth Night* 2.3. See *Dramatic Works of William Shakespeare* (Boston: Phillips, Sampson, and Company, 1850), 1:280, Google Books, http://books.google.com/books?id=DCEAAAAAQAAJ.

of feature, and brilliancy of complexion, that are supposed to be essential to it. She was neither a blond nor a brunette, but a mixture of both—her eyes were neither black nor blue; they were, I believe, hazel, but they owed much of their power to long curved lashes that veiled their extreme tenderness of expression, and made them appear much darker than they really were.—I say this of Hannah in the early part of her life, for at thirty she was called beautiful by those to whom an elevated expression of countenance, combined with softness and grace of manners, constitute beauty.

Her mother was a pale, gentle woman, with large blue eyes, who had always been an invalid, and whose delicacy of look and demeanor contrasted strongly with the rough, harsh manners of her husband. Constant ill health had made her winning and dependent as a child; yet beneath all this softness of exterior, she carried a fixedness of principle, an elevation of mind, and strength of purpose, that had their full share of influence over her stern, imperious companion. Whatever might have been his previous irritation of feeling, no sooner did he enter the presence of his wife, than all traces of it disappeared, even as if his rigid brow had been swept by the wing of his good angel.

Hannah had inherited all the fine womanly qualities of her mother, superadded to an excellent constitution, and a dash of her father's energy of will. It was well for her that it was so, for even from a child the duties of a woman had been exacted from her, and she was at once sister and mother to the little group about the domestic hearth. As she approached maturity, she became the friend and companion of her mother, the nurse of her sick room, and even the utterer of her religious faith and devotion, as physical suffering sometimes dimmed the vividness of exalted truths. At such times the high-minded girl might be seen kneeling by the bed-side, and with clasped hands, pouring forth the simple, fervent prayer of a young heart, deeply responding to the blessed truths of revelation.

The mother pressed her to her bosom with tears and blessings, for her progress to the tomb was made a pleasant pilgrimage, while cheered and supported by such a child.

At this moment an addition was made to the little family, in the person of a youth of rare piety, and such powers of intellect, as to warrant the elders in setting aside their ordinary rules for his benefit. Andrew Horton was an orphan, left pennyless by his young parents, who both died of an epidemic when he was scarcely a year old; bequeathing this, their only earthly gift, to the charity of the church. He became, as it were, the property of the church, and each individual of it claimed a right for the discharge of kindly offices in behalf of the little orphan. As he grew up, he was evidently, not unworthy of their solicitude. He was of rare modesty, deep piety, and such wonderful intellectual endowments, that all eyes turned to him, as one destined to become a leader in Israel, a burning and a shining light in the temple of the Lord. Unusual care was bestowed upon his education, as was meet for one who was hereafter to become the expounder of the Word, and a voice to the people of the Lord.

Friend Newton had now claimed his privilege of entertaining, at least for one year, the favored youth, while he should prosecute his studies, and engage in those acts of devotion and piety, which so engrossed his affections, and were so appropriate for one called to his high and holy vocation.

Mrs. Newton listened to the lofty utterance of prayer from the lips of the pious young man, with a new strength, and felt her faith quickened, and her hopes elevated, while she heard the truths of her religion explained and illustrated in his clear, vigorous manner, with the glowing language of his aspiring imagination and fervency of spirit.

Hannah, always retiring, and occupied with household matters, had but little time for converse with the youth; but in the secrecy of her own heart, she sat even at his footstool, and imbibed not only the stores of wisdom from his lips, but the far more dangerous lessons of youthful love.

Andrew Horton scarcely noticed the quiet, unobtrusive maiden, so occupied was he in his studies and devotions. But when it became necessary for him to accept the hospitality of another of the brethren, he started to perceive how often the image of Hannah mingled in his dreams and obtruded in his meditations. He missed every where her sweet voice and placid smile, and felt that she much henceforth be to him what no other maiden ever could become.

The affliction of the little family, occasioned by the increased illness of Mrs. Newton, seemed to justify his frequent visits, and Andrew Horton, more than once, upon his return from the bed-side of the dying, threw himself upon his knees, and besought forgiveness from the Father of Spirits, that his visits should have been rather the promptings of earthly attachment, than those of a high and holy sense of duty.

All sternness and pride of manhood forsook Friend Newton, as he stood by the side of his dying wife. He threw himself upon his knees, pressed her hands in his own, and the tears streamed from the eyes even of the strong man. Andrew Horton was there, and his rich deep voice breathed the language of prayer. He ceased—the soul of the sufferer had taken its flight upon the wings of his lofty aspirations; the mystery of life had ceased in the cold form before him.

Hannah arose with pale cheek, and approached the bereaved husband.

"Go with me, my father," she said, gentle putting her arm in his, while she pressed her lips to his pale damp brow. The old man arose with the docility of a little child, and she led him forth to an inner room, where none might witness the agony of that moment. When she placed the large arm chair for him, and had adjusted the cushions, he opened his arms to his child, and she fell upon his bosom. It was an unwonted tenderness, for Mr. Newton had never expressed any thing like it for any other being than his wife.—Now that she had left him, he yearned for some heart to which he might reveal the burden of his sorrows.

"Thee has been a dutiful child, Hannah, though I may never have told thee so before. It always grieved me, Hannah, that I expressed so little tenderness for thee; but it wasn't in me—I couldn't do it—but I love thee just as well, child. And I might have made thy mother a great deal happier, but for my stern, hard ways. Oh, Hannah, Hannah, the grave is the revealer of all hearts. What would I not give to hear her say once again that she forgives me!" and the old man bowed his head upon the bosom of his daughter, and wept like a child.

Hannah had wept too, but she felt that she ought not to witness the humiliation of her parent, and she raised her head calmly—

"Thee has ever been a good father to us all, and my mother loved and blessed thee to the last."

"Hannah, Hannah, I was unworthy of thee!" His voice was choked by a gush of tears.

Hannah turned to the Bible, and read a part of the fourteenth chapter of John. "I will not leave you comfortless, I will come unto you," and gradually the anguish of her father became soothed, and he pressed her again to his heart, saying—

"Thy voice is like thy mother's, Hannah, and thee will be to me all that a child can be; I know thee will; and I will subdue my nature for the sake of thee and the little ones."

He kept his word—from that day a gentleness was infused into his manners, and a tenderness of feeling hitherto unknown. If occasionally his former spirit gained the ascendancy, he went alone to the chamber that had witnessed the suffering and death of one so gentle, and when he returned, it was as if her mantel had fallen upon him.

Andrew Horton found himself the pupil, rather than the teacher of the noble girl; and his own zeal and piety were strengthened by his intercourse with her. They had exchanged their pledges of fidelity, and Andrew was about to leave the vicinity to prosecute his mission in a distant field. It would be many years ere he would return. Hannah, in the multiplicity of household avocations, in attendance upon her sick mother, in the exercise of her own religious views, to which the silent worship of their sex afforded ample encouragement, had imbibed a lofty enthusiasm, a shade of spiritual mysticism, little in accordance with the practical faith of her people. She has watched the operations of her own mind, and compared them with circumstances and events, till she saw a mysterious connexion between them, and even at times was led to a something verging upon the spirit of prophecy. She delighted to dwell upon the inter-communication of mind with mind, and the power which she believed it had to influence a congenial spirit, even though separated at ever so great a distance. The mind was unsubjected to the laws of the body; it traversed the fields of space, and lived in the past as well as the present. Even the future, under certain circumstances and states of the mind, she believed might be revealed to it. Why then should not the intense thoughts of the human mind, especially when directed to an object of attachment, go forth like winged messengers, and work their influence upon the distant and beloved! For this reason, she said, she would keep her thoughts and imaginations pure, that no emanation from her own mind should mislead the conceptions of another; that no unhallowed emotions should ever be associated with her in the minds of those she loved.

Andrew Horton listened to these mystical views of the lofty girl, until his own mind shared a portion of her enthusiasm—if it were a weakness or error in judgment, it was at least a harmless one,—one that to them could only purify and exalt, while it never could mislead another. Therefore, he gave himself up to the beautiful illusion, that established a perpetual intercourse between himself and Hannah in the long period of absence.

"I do not ask," said Hannah, "whether I shall be forgotten.—You cannot forget me, unless I cease first to think upon you. For Oh, Andrew, *I* can never forget you; and the emanation of my thoughts will momentarily create an image of myself within your mind. Do you realize, my friend, what it is to love one like me? You can never forget me, even should you desire it; for my thoughts, fixed as they will be upon you, will forever present an intense image of myself to your mind. You may cease to *love*, but you can not cease to think upon me. I hold the talisman, that will ensure me this. But, Oh! Andrew, when you shall *desire* to forget me, think not I can remain ignorant of the fact. No, never. While the attachment is mutual, and the thoughts and memory of each other pleasant to the mind—the emanations of each will conjoin, and there will be produced upon the fancy of each, the most vivid conception of the other—it will be as if a pleasant painting of each should be presented to the eye. But should the affections of either become cold, the image of that one will fade from the vision of the other. He may retain the memory, but that vivid impression that brings up the eloquent eye, the speaking lip, and the very tones, and look of endearment, will grow less and less distinct, till it shall fade altogether away. Now, Andrew, this must be the case with you. My image will be forever distinct to you, for I can never cease to think upon you. But should yours fade from my mind's eye, alas! I shall know too well how to interpret it."

Andrew Horton's brow contracted.

"Hannah, I did not expect this from thee. Have I ever given thee cause for distrust!"

"Never, my friend," she said, laying her hand upon his; "but thee will have many snares to encounter, Andrew. Beautiful faces will look up to thee in thy holy ministrations; timid maidens, who will flatter more the pride of thy heart, than ever Hannah could, will tremble and weep at the fervor of thy eloquence, and come to thee as to a spiritual guide. Would it be surprising then, if vows to one like me should be forgotten?"

The youth trembled under her searching, anxious glance; but he drew the hand to his bosom and kissed the lofty brow of the impassioned girl. Hannah's head fell upon his shoulder, and tears started from her eyes.

"Hannah, thou hast a lofty soul, and thy love is to me dearer than aught on earth. Do not distrust me, Hannah, I shall have thy prayers and thy blessings, and that mystery of inter-communication of thy soul with mine, which of itself will be an amulet to preserve me from danger. All that is noble and pure in life is associated with thee, and thou well knowest it is contemplations like these that I delight."

Two years passed away, and the smile grew faint upon the lip of Hannah. She had taken the child, who was an infant at her mother's death, upon her knee, and its cheek rested upon her bosom.

"Hannah, dear, don't thee humber?" said the child, lifting its eyes to her face.

"Humber, my dear—what does that mean!"

The little one heaved a deep sigh. "There, to do so, sister—that was a humber."

Hannah felt the tears her spring to eyes.

"No, Georgy, I won't do so any more—it is wrong. I must make thee feel quite happy."

The child kissed her cheek many times, and put his arms around her neck, calling her a dear sister.

From that time Hannah went about her daily avocations, with a strong purpose to forget her own sorrows, in ministering to the happiness of others. The child had taught her to feel the selfishness of concealed suffering, and she wrestled in prayer for strength to sustain her under the many trials of her lot. She felt a strong internal conviction, that Andrew Horton had ceased to regard her with his former attachment. Impressed with this belief, she wrote a letter in answer to one of his, from which I shall extract a few sentences.

"Thy letters reach me with the same punctuality as ever, and their language is still tender; but, Andrew, the spirit is wanting. It is as if the sentiments turned to ice under thy pen. There should be no disguise between us. Thee should never attempt it with me, Andrew, for I can divine all. Thy image has almost faded from my sight, and I know that thee *desires* to forget me.—The vows that bind thee to me have become shackles. It would more become thy calling, Andrew, if thee would tell me so at once; for deceit must be painful to thee. I absolve thee from thy vows, my friend; thou art free to do as seemeth to thee good. I will try even to forget thee, that my image be not troublesome, as I know it will be, if I continue to think upon thee. My thoughts, fixed on thee, will perpetually create in thy mind an image of myself, which I would not do, if thy affections are fixed upon another.

"Farewell, my dear friend; I say this for the last time, and thee will forgive the utterance. Do not distress thyself upon my account. I was made for endurance—it is a woman's destiny. I would forgive thee, if I had ought to forgive; but the affections are not to be schooled like wayward children. I cannot even now believe they are transferable. Farewell—and may thee be very, very happy."

In the reply of Andrew Horton, he confessed all. Hannah had indeed divined the truth. He spoke of a sweet, gentle girl, whose witchery had chased the love of Hannah from his heart. But he implored her forgiveness, he deprecated his own fickleness of heart, and conjured Hannah to forgive him, to forget him, and be happy in some new attachment.

Hannah's proud lip curled in scorn, and she laid the letter upon the coals of the hearth. She went about her accustomed duties with a new pride, a womanly spirit of endurance, that, knowing the worst, had nerved itself for the trial.

Then years passed way, and Hannah had become like unto Deborah, in the estimation of her people. Her proud beauty, her fervent piety, and the burning power with which she sometimes expounded the truths of her religion, had raised her up to be a leader amongst her people; little short of a prophetess, indeed, did she seem to many, as she held forth in the congregation.

It was rumored that Andrew Horton would return and explain the scriptures once more in the place of his nativity. Hannah took her seat early, amongst the matrons—for time had abated nothing of the interest with which she once regarded him, although it had become modified by the circumstances in which he was now placed. Ten years had elapsed since the reception of that last letter, yet Hannah Newton felt her limbs tremble as she found herself once more in the presence of Andrew Horton.

She raised her eyes, as a stranger sat down upon the form beside her. It was the bride of Andrew Horton—a fragile, fair girl, whose eyes were fixed upon her husband, through the whole exercises, as if the only divinity she worshiped were vested in the manly form of the preacher. As the rich tones of his voice once more broke upon Hannah's ear, and she encountered those deep, passionate eyes, she closed her own, for a new weight of misery seemed pressed upon her heart. Why had he returned, to do away at a glance, that firmness which it had cost her years to acquire?

Hannah was quite alone when Friend Horton called. She arose with native self-possession, and spoke to him as to a brother.

The preacher struggled for utterance.

"Hannah," he at length said, "I have taken this long journey only upon thy account. I have come to implore thee to forget me. Thee has had much to forgive, Hannah; but thee cannot have suffered as I have done. When I took the hand of my bride at the altar, thy form seemed to come between me and her—and oh, Hannah, I felt then, and have not ceased to feel, that thou art the wife of my spirit."

"Andrew Horton—I must not listen to this. Thee wrongs the fair girl who lives only in thy smiles. Why didst thou return to bring new sorrow to my heart, and to plunge thee deeper in sin?"

"Hannah, I returned not for this, but to implore thee to forget me. Thee cannot have forgotten that intercommunication of spirit with spirit, of which we used to talk. I feel its full power now; for thy image is ever with me, and daily am I taught to feel the constancy of thy attachment."

"Why should'st thou return to tell me this? I think of thee, Andrew, as the husband of another. I pray for thy happiness, thy usefulness, and that thee may be preserved from temptation. Friend Horton, this is unworthy of thee. I forgive thee—but let us part."

"Nay, Hannah, thee must hear all. I come not to speak of aught that might wrong my bride; no, it is for her sake as well as my own, that I implore thee to forget me. When her cheek is pressed to mine, I see only thee, Hannah. When she sleeps upon my bosom, with her fair arms about my neck, it is thy form, and thy arms that seem to entwine me. I shrink from her caresses as from a deadly sin, for I bestow them as unto thee. Mary is as a sister unto me; but thou, Hannah, art the bride of my spirit."

Hannah turned deadly pale, and covered her face with her hands, while low moanings escaped her heaving bosom.

"Andrew, I foresaw all this, when I warned thee of the peril of loving one like me. I knew the nature of thy sex—delighting in the timid, the trembling and dependent—and that should one like this cross thy path, the love of Hannah would be a shackle. It is as I foresaw—but I will not reproach thee, Andrew; it was thy nature."

"And most bitterly have I suffered. My broken vows have rung a perpetual knell in my ears, and barred up the avenues to enjoyment. The loving, the trusting Mary, hath been the victim of my error. And thee, too, Hannah. The blight hath fallen from me upon two spirits, of whom the world is not worthy. Woe, woe is me!" And he pressed his hand to his brow, for the large veins were swollen and rigid with the intensity of his suffering.

Hannah laid her hand gently upon his shoulder.

"Andrew Horton, thou art called not to ease and enjoyment, but to labor and trial. Gird thyself for the contest, and be strong even in the strength of the Most High. I will strive once more to forget thee. But, oh God! have I not striven? Have I not wrestled day and night with tears, and many prayers? Andrew, I will pray yet again, that this bitter cup may pass away from us. But, oh! when I pray to forget, even in the agony of my spirit, do I not still remember thee? I will strive yet again. Andrew, return to thy bride; be all to her thou hast promised to be, that thy conscience upbraid thee not for wrong done to the gentle and timid, whose spirit is ill able to bear suffering of any kind, far less to have it dealt out without measure, as it hath been to me. Farewell." She pressed his hand gently, and left the room.

For many years had Hannah Newton discharged the duties of her sex with a pale cheek and placid brow, sympathising in the sorrows of all, but herself seeking sympathy from none; for with a mind lofty and exalted as hers, human sources of consolation were utterly unavailing. She stood alone in the majesty of grief, seeking consolation only from the Great Comforter. But now the smile lingered about her mouth, and the light returned to her eye—yet her step grew feeble, and her brow assumed a more transparent beauty. The image of Andrew Horton again mingled with her dreams, and visited her mental vision. She felt, she knew, that her love was still dear to him, that he turned to her with the fondness of earlier days. She knew this, but it filled her with doubt and anxiety. Had Andrew Horton, the minister of the Most High, dared to forget his vows to his wife, to her whom he had sworn to love and cherish? Or was the fair bride at rest, gone in her youth and beauty to the bosom of her God?

Again Andrew Horton, with pale cheek and a loftier beauty stood by the side of Hannah. He told how the sweet, child-like Mary, had fallen asleep, like a young flowret blighted upon the stalk.—He dwelt upon her love, her beauty, 'till the tears of Hannah mingled with his own.

"And now, thee wilt be my own wife, Hannah, even as thou has been the bride of my spirit. I shall acquire new strength with a spirit like thine. Thee will caution, advise, and elevate me.—Thy love shall purify and exalt me. Mary was a beautiful child, slumbering upon my bosom; when doubt and suffering came upon me, she would fling her white arms around me, and mingle her tears and sighs. But thou, Hannah, would'st have dispelled my doubts; thou would'st have led me to the true sources of consolation; and thy prayers would have been as the dew of Hermon to my spirit. Thy caresses would have blessed, while they exalted me. Wilt thou not be my own wife, bride of my spirit?" He drew her to his bosom—her cheek rested upon his. She pressed her lips to his, and her arms encircled his neck. A deep sigh escaped her, and her head fell upon his shoulder.

Andrew Horton raised her from his bosom and gazed upon her face. Hannah Newton was to be only the spirit's bride. She was dead!

For the Offering.

When Shall We Meet.

To M. F. T.

When shall we meet? shall it be in spring,
To remind us of youth and op'ning flowers?
When we joy'd in hearing the wild bird sing
Its holiday notes to the passing hours?
    If then we meet,—it will surely tell,
    That 'tis time to wake from the dull repose
    Which keeps us from knowing the blissful spell
    That gilds life's stream as it onward flows.

When shall we meet? shall it be when the sun
Has parch'd the leaf that its rays once cherished?
'Twill remind us that years pass on,
And we'll then mourn the hopes already perish'd.
    If then we meet,—we shall surely learn,
    That the heart's harp breathes a sorrowing strain,
    And we'll grieve to know that no sweet return
    Of the joyous past can be ours again.

When she we meet? shall it be when the leaf
Falls from the branch of the old forest tree?
'Twill remind us then the hours are brief,
And verge on the shore of eternity.
    If then we meet—we shall surely know,
    That meeting then is a meeting only;
    And sigh to feel the pulse throb slow
    In the hearts that hence are drear and lonely.

When shall we meet? shall it be at morn?
At noon or at eve with its mellow light?

Or wilt thou defer until time has shorn
Us of all but the gloom of coming night?
If then we meet—in a desert place,
Will a loving heart in anguish awaken;
And find naught left it but to retrace,
The path which love has then forsaken.

Comus.
Akron, Feb. 11, 1850.

For the Offering.

Thou Bid'st Me "Not to Curse Thee."

To M.

At times when I remember
Thou'st acted falsehood's part,
I wish to curse the tongue that said,
"I give thee all my heart."
And yet I cannot curse thee,
Though thou art false to me,
'Tis better far to say that I
Have e'er been true to thee.

And oft I dream in fondness,
That thou art still the same;
I hear thee call me as thou hast,
By an endearing name;
Then do I wake and listen,
To hear that voice again:—
But no: The rose has perish'd,
And thorns alone remain.

Thou bid'st me "not to curse thee":
Nor will I. Doubt me not;
I yet will truly love thee,
Although I am forgot.

My wish is for thy happiness,
No truth in love could be;
If I should ever fail to bless,
Or breathe a curse for thee.

And should I strive to curse thee,
My heart would interfere;
My lips refuse to speak unkind,
Of her who yet is dear.
Come, ask me when the hand of death,
Is soothing my distress;
If I can love thy false heart still,
And hear me answer *yes.*

Go pluck the blooming flower,
And crush it 'neath thy feet;
Its offering's are gentle and still,
Its latest breath is sweet.
Thus with the heart that loveth,
No hatred there doth live;
And other lips must curse thee,
For mine have none to give.

T.
Akron, Feb. 14, 1850.

For the Offering.

Prayer.

By Vesper.

Reader do you love to pray? Have you ever felt a holy calmness, a perfumed sweetness gently distilling in your heart as you have left the "altar of prayer?"[21] If you have never realized this you have not the gem that can turn keen anguish into joy, you have not the power to extract pleasure from pain.

Prayer is the atmosphere in which a christian breathes. Prayer strengthens the soul, gives it weight and energy, enlightens and beautifies it. Prayer

21. The first of many short quotations from the Bible or bible commentaries of the period.

softens the asperities of our nature, subdues anger, humbles pride, turns envy and hatred into purity and love. For while anger burns in our hearts we cannot commune with the being who giveth joy and peace.

Our prayers will meet clouds and winds; no incense will be blended with the offering, so seraph be delegated to bear to us refreshing draughts from the streams that water Paradise. In love we must pray.

Prayer sweetens life, it relieves a burdened soul, however coarse or homely the garb, however low in the world's estimation, however poor or sick, the praying soul is sure of one listening ear, one being in whose languid eye floats the tenderest love, one powerful arm that sustains and upholds in a loving embrace. How dark indeed is that mind, and how sad that heart which has never felt the sweet influence of prayer! The soul becomes calm and happy, when we bow and pour our supplication into the ear that hears our "softest sigh," though the words be uttered in bitterness, and the heart be writhing in deep and pungent sorrow, yet is the prayer borne far, far away to the pure and holy land which "no mortal hath seen," and a spotless dove brings to us on his "consecrated plume" rich odors which distill in our hearts like dews on flowers. Oh! who would not pray? The "prayer of faith" not only brings to our hearts, rich blessings, but it bringeth fresh mercies to those we love.

Who can tell the amount of good which one poor soul can accomplish by prayer? *Eternity alone can reveal it!*

We have many powerful incentives to urge us to the mercy seat; we find there the best of society, though apparently alone, yet in reality surrounded by a host, yes, I might say legions of white-robed seraphs, bending o'er us their brows of love; gazing upon us with eyes of "chastened fire," and tenderly and sweetly infusing into our souls their own peacefulness and purity. And here cometh the spirits who once inhabited tabernacles like ours, and I fancy *they* are not dilatory when they behold upon their Father's footstool, a loved one in the attitude of prayer; *here* too is the *Saviour*; regardless (I had almost said) of "Heaven's Hallelujahs" he watches with intense anxiety the worshipper, scans the depths of his heart, and if he findeth faith and love, he quickly sheds upon him the richest blessings, smiles away his fears, and gives unto him the "joys of his salvation." We have also great examples left us on record, of great and good men having been much in prayer. It is urged, by opposers of religion, that this ado about prayer is useless, as we can have grateful feelings, at all times, and "the Lord knoweth of what we have need before we ask."[22] So He does, and to feel a lively sense of gratitude to the giver of all good gifts, constitutes a portion of the christian's happiness; but the christian esteems it a great privilege to talk with God, to tell him his wants, and know that God will give whatsoever he needeth.

Oh! infidel, atheist, or prayerless souls of whatever name, you are welcome to your spectres of happiness, your visionary joys—welcome to your wealth, your honors: ah yes! welcome to ten thousand worlds like this with all

"Their lofty domes and brilliant ore,
Their Gems and crowns,"[23]

But give to me the altar of prayer, "well perfumed with the 'blood of Christ,'" with no "shelter from the storm, or shade from the heat,"[24] and my "peace would be as a river, and my joy unspeakeable."[25] Besides all this, we have the great example of our God incarnate; how often *He* retired from the busy turmoil of life, and continued "all night in prayer to God."[26] Consider, this, ye who lightly esteem prayer; here was a being without "spot or blemish," no sin had ever marred his pure soul, yet he felt the need of pouring out "strong cries and tears," and would wander alone by "moonlight's pale beams," and continue in earnest supplication till dawn of day. If a pure being was often at the mercy seat, and felt it necessary, how much more is it *our* duty, who are full of "wounds and putrefying sores;" how much more do *we* need to continue all night in prayer. *He* had no stains to wash away, but we are polluted from the "crown of our head to the sole of our feet." *He* had never offended a loving Father, in whose "bosom he had dwelt from all eternity," but *we* are constantly invoking God to unsheath his "sword of vengeance," and pour upon our guilty heads the "cup of wrath." The Saviour has left us an example, and bid us "walk in his footsteps," and let us be careful to follow him in this respect and "pray without ceasing."

---

22. Matthew 6:8.

23. Lines from the hymn beginning "The faithless world promiscuous flow." See Hymns, *Selected from Various Authors for the Use of the Evangelical Association*, 4th ed. (New Berlin: W. Tea, 1846), 442, Google Books, http://books.google.com/books?id=zP1LAAAAYAAJ.

24. Isaiah 25:4.

25. Isaiah 48:18.

26. Luke 6:12.

For the Offering.

A Tribute of Respect to the Memory of a Friend.

By Adelia.

How is the strong man bowed:—alas! how soon
    His manhood's glory, pride—his power and might,
His brightly rising sun clouded ere noon,
    By the thick gloom of death's long dreamless night.
How deeply veiled in mystery his ways,
    Who rides upon the wave and rules the storm!
What darkness clothes his manifold displays
    Of kindness, love and tender mercy shown.

His thoughts are not as ours; we look around,
    Upon the vast assembled crowd, a mingled throng,
And here and there behold one bowing down
    Beneath life's load of ills; their days prolonged
To four score years; their cup of sorrow full;
    Their burthened hearts with weight of grief oppressed,
Waiting and wishing that some prosperous gale
    Would waft them safely where the weary rest.

Others we see with thin and wasted form,
    With sorrow's mark upon their furrowed brow,
Who long have struggled with life's adverse storms.
    And felt that anguish such alone can know.
Who long to see the hour approaching near,
    When all their sufferings and their toils shall cease,
When they'll exchange a world of trouble here,
    For one above where all is joy and peace.

Death sees not thus:—he passes heedless by
    Earth's weary pilgrims wandering sad and lone,
And seeks with eager haste to bear away
    Its choicest treasures, its most cherished ones;

He sees the smiling babe;—with blighting breath,
He nips the tender bud, so fresh and fair;
With rude, relentless grasp, prostrate beneath
His withering tread, leaves it to perish there.

He sees the rose just opening into bloom,
Adorned with queen-like beauty on its parent stem,
Shedding around a soft and sweet perfume,
Amid the clustering group the richest gem:
Seeming too bright and fair to droop and die,
And yet he steals along with noiseless tread,
And joys to see this lovely flower decay;
And early numbered with the slumbering dead.

The Mother too, amid her little band,
Of happy hearts he views with jealous eye,
And from the loved embrace of Friends and home
Bears her away 'mid tears of agony.
The Father too; their hope, their guide and stay;
Bound to his home by fond endearing ties,
From all is rudely torn; forced to obey,
The hasty call, to yield a sacrifice.

And this is death! his ruthless sway,
Crushes the mountain oak and fragile flower,
The high and low alike are swept away,
And forced to own the heartless conqueror's power.
His coming now we deeply feel to mourn,
To kindly shed the sympathising tear,
With that loved circle, how bereaved and lone,
That widowed Mother's heart now sad and drear.

Weep not in anguish, though your light has flown,
And he you fondly loved returns no more;
Though desolation marks your cheerless home,
And sorrow's bitter cup is full and running o'er.
'Tis not in wrath He sends affliction down;

Or wounds the hearts of those He most approves:
Nor yet His power, in anger to make known;
'Tis but to try your faith, to prove your love.

Then bow submissive, kiss the chastening rod;
He gave and now for wise design removes.
"Be still; and know that I alone, am God;"
And you will richly all His kindness prove.
A few more days you still may struggle on,
Amid life's raging scenes of toil and care.
Ere you rejoin him in that glorious home,
Where no more sorrow's known, no parting there.

Lancaster, Ohio, Feb. 1850.[27]

Selected for the Offering.

Education.[28]

We utterly repudiate, as unworthy, not of freemen only, but of men, the narrow notion, that there is to be an education for the poor as such. Has God provided for the poor a coarser earth, a thinner air, a paler sky? Does not the glorious sun pour down his golden flood as cheerfully as upon the rich man's palace? Have not the cotter's children[29] as keen sense of all freshness, verdure, fragrance, melody and beauty of luxuriant nature, as the pale sons of kings? Or is it in the mind that God has stamped the imprint of a base birth, so that the poor man's child knows, with an unborn certainty that his lot is to crawl, not climb?

It is not so. God has not done it. Man cannot do it. Mind is immortal. Mind is imperial. It bears no mark of high or low—rich or poor. It heeds no bound of time or place, or rank of circumstances. It asks but freedom. It requires but light. It is heavenborn, and aspires to, heaven. Weakness does not enfeeble it. Poverty cannot repress it. Difficulties do but stimu-

27. See n. 6, p. 252.

28. This passage by Episcopal Bishop George Washington Doane (1799–1859) was widely reprinted in the 1830s and 1840s. Cumings probably selects it from the 1840 *Ladies' Garland*. See *The Ladies' Garland* 3, no. 5 (November 1839): 116, Google Books, http://books.google.com/books?id=msNBAAAAYAAJ.

29. A "cotter" (or cottager) is someone who lives on public land without owning property or paying rent; a squatter.

late its vigor. And the poor tallow chandler's son,[30] that sits up all night to read the book which an apprentice lends him, lest the master's eye should miss it in the morning, shall stand and treat with kings,[31] shall bind the lightning with a hempen cord, and bring it harmless from the skies. The common school is common, not as inferior, not as the school for the poor men's children, but as the light and air is common. It ought to be the best school, and in all good works the beginning is one half. Who does not know the value to a community of a plentiful supply of the pure element of water?—And infinitely more than this is the common school, for it is the fountain at which the mind drinks, and it is refreshed and strengthened for its career of usefulness and glory.—*Bishop Doane.*

For the Offering.

Lines Written by Miss A. P. on the Death of Her Mother.

Oh how can I relate my sorrow,
Since I have lost my dearest friends,
No happy day, nor coming morrow,
Shall bring them back to me again.

Stern death first robbed me of a brother!
A brother ever good and kind;
Oh! how can I my anguish smother!
Why was *I*, Oh! why left behind.

But two weeks past a sister followed,
Cut down by death in early bloom;
Oh may my tears, for her be hallowed
For her I loved! laid in the tomb.

Oh! yet there is a deeper sorrow,
My God, my hope, be thou my trust.
But one day past—and e'er the morrow
My mother slumbers in the dust!

30. A "tallow chandler" makes candles from the fat (tallow) of goats, deer, sheep, or oxen.

31. "To treat with" means to negotiate.

My Mother! Oh she's gone forever;
    I can behold her here no more!
How does the thought my heart-strings sever,
    And make it bleed at every pore!

Afflictions deep are sent upon us,
    But may I to Thy will submit,
Oh! may I never, never murmur,
    For what thou doest is surely right.

Oh sure there is a joyful morrow,
    When we shall meet them all again,
Where every grief and every sorrow
    Is hushed in joy that never ends.

Selected for the Offering.

The Days of Old.[32]

The days of old! the days of old!
    A magic spell is in the name;
It breathes upon the bosom cold,
    Where passion slumbers mild and tame;
And years of grief, and guilt, and shame,
    Pass slowly from the heart away,
As memory fans its dying flame,
    And Hope renews its fading ray.

The days of old! the days of old!
    How like a dream they glided by,
Ere desolating time had toll'd
    The knell of hopes that bloom to die!
On Love awhile our hearts rely—
    But that brief madness soon is o'er:
The fountain of our hearts grow dry,
    And though we live—we love no more!

32. The poem also appears without attribution in *The Ladies' Garland* 3, no. 10 (April 1840): 229, Google Books, http://books.google.com/books?id=msNBAAAAYAAJ.

The days of old! the days of old!
 Alas! they ne'er may dawn again;
Yet joys there are, and manifold,
 That wither'd Age can still retain—
In spite of want, and woe, and pain!
 Bright visions of eternal love;
When freed from earth's unhallow'd stain;
 The spirit seeks its home above.

Good Humor.—Is the clear blue sky of the soul, on which every star of talent will shine more clearly, and the sun of genius encounter no vapors in his passage. 'Tis the most exquisite beauty of a fine face; a redeeming grace in a homely one. It is like the green in the landscape, harmonizing with every color, mellowing the glories of the bright, and softening the hue of the dark; or like a flute in a full concert of instruments, a sound not at first discovered by the ear, yet filling up the breaks in the concord with its deep melody.[33]

Religion.—How many calamities has religion soothed? how many tears wiped away? how many hopes inspired, when there was not longer room for hope? how many doors of mercy thrown open to the guilty supports given to innocence? If religion was designed only for the consolation of the miserable, it was, of course, designed for the promotion of that of the human race. The beauties of nature bear witness to the existence of God, and the miseries of man confirm the truths of religion.[34]

Intellect.—When the intellect is employed on low objects, man becomes habitually degraded, and loses all taste for things that are not visible and tangible.[35]

33. At the end of the run of the *Offering*, Cumings learned to provide short pieces that printers could include if they fit nicely in the available space. This is a popular, anonymous selection used by a variety of periodicals for this same purpose. One example is *The New-York Mirror* 17, no. 16 (October 12, 1839): 128, Google Books, http://books.google.com/books?id=JMAiAQAAMAAJ.

34. Directly or indirectly, this quotation appears to have come from a work by French writer Jacques-Henri Bernardin de Saint-Pierre (1737–1814). See *St. Pierre's Studies of Nature*, trans. Henry Hunter (Philadelphia: Joseph J. Woodward, 1835), 118, Google Books, http://books.google.com/books?id=gXhTAAAAYAAJ.

35. This quotation was also used as column filler in *Waldie's Select Circulating Library* 2, no. 17 (October 22, 1839): 480, Google Books, http://books.google.com/books?id=koNaAAAAYAAJ.

For the Offering

Extract from Hap-Hazard Ideas.[36]

By Porcia.

By permission from Porcia, this takes the Editor's place for this Number.

All persons who thoroughly understand the English language, although they may differ in their opinion of the Grammars of the same and the different methods of teaching it, will agree as to the words that form a correct sentence. All such will experience a disagreeable, uneasy sensation when compelled to listen to expressions that have not even a *leaning* toward grammatical propriety. For instance—their politeness will be severely taxed when they hear a person say "I seen it" or "I have saw it"—"I done it" or "I have did it," "I had ought to have went"—"If I had went," "I shot the door," "boughton Coffee," "Riz Bread," "the Cornish of a house," "The Ribets of knives, &c, &c., &c." But such expressions are often heard from some who make great pretensions to knowledge and refinement; and many of them would be indignant at any one who should, even in a spirit of kindness, correct them, and we will let such go, blundering along in their *happy*, no *wretched* ignorance, imagining that none but the greatest writers can transcribe anything fit for them to read; no person they have ever *seen* can think such noble thoughts as swell their *own* bosoms, or express even their meager ideas in any thing but disgusting words.

Yes, let them go—there are enough in this world, who deem it worth their while to minister to their wants and help them to imagine themselves what they never were and never will be—Ladies or Gentlemen.

Anger.—Never be angry with a person, merely because his opinions are not your opinions; never be angry because you cannot persuade him to change his opinions; and, above all, never do him an injury, or hesitate about doing him a good, because his opinions and yours are different.[37]

36. "Extract" does not mean "selection" as "Porcia" was writing these "Hap-Hazard Ideas" for *The Offering*. This must have been a part of a longer work submitted by Porcia. Perhaps to spite the editor and the author of this piece, this paragraph was brutally mangled by the compositor(s) at *The Offering*'s job printer.

37. Another popular page-ender. Cumings probably clipped this from *The Ladies' Garland* 3, no. 5 (November 1839): 110, Google Books, http://books.google.com/books?id=msNBAAAAYAAJ.

Lily Lute, Adelia, Elizabeth and all other Contributors to the Offering, may be assured of our respectful gratitude.

C. Cumings.

THE
AKRON OFFERING.
April, 1850.

Selected for the Offering.

A Discourse,

Delivered by the Rev. W. Hamilton, before the Miller Township branch of the Knox Co., Bible Society.[1]

"But as it is written, Eye hath not seen, nor ear hath not heard, neither have entered into the heart of man, the things which God hath prepared for them that love him.

"But God hath revealed them unto us by his Spirit, for the Spirit searcheth all things yea, the deep things of God.

"For what man knoweth the things of a man, save the spirit of man which is in him? even so the things of God knoweth no man, but the Spirit of God."—1. Cor. chap. 11, 9, 10 and 11 verses.

The Apostle intends in this passage to assert the divine origin of religion, and the inspiration of those, through whom it was communicated to man. There are some who consider that reason, in itself, is sufficient to discover the existence and nature of God, and to teach men to yield him a reasonable service. There are others, who would, in regard to religious things, cast reason entirely away and depend wholly upon Inspiration. In

1. This Hamilton may be the W. Hamilton who appears in various Baptist publications of the 1840s and 1850s as a Irish missionary. With such a common name, however, is it difficult to know this with confidence. He appears to have been only visiting Miller township when he gave this speech. The original printing cannot be found. Miller township lies about 70 miles south and west of Akron, and had about 1000 residents in 1850. See N. N. Hill, *History of Knox County, Ohio* (Mt. Vernon: A. A. Graham, 1881), 512–29, Google Books, http://books.google.com/books?id=DBAtAAAAYAAJ.

the present discourse I would endeavor, avoiding both extremes, to show, in the first place, the insufficiency of mere human reason. 2d. The possibility of a revelation. 3d. The desirableness of such a revelation.

1st. We are first to show that reason is not in itself an unassisted by revelation, a sufficient guide for man. We understand by the term Reason, the intellectual and moral faculties with which man has been endowed. Reason in this sense may be viewed *in two aspects*—either as it was in the perfection of its exercise when man was an unfallen being—or as it appears now, when he has become degraded and defiled by sin. As instinct in the lower animals now acts uniformly and with unerring accuracy; so did reason in man before the fall. Yet even then he was not left without a superior guide. His Maker appeared to him by his counsel; and we have reason to believe that angels, the elder born immortals, were his companions and friends. In his present state man is an exile from Paradise, an alien from God. His reason is clouded and his moral sense deranged. When the question then is asked whether reason be sufficient for the guidance of man without the light of revelation, we must understand it as having regard to the present condition of man the present state of human reason.—We must therefore appeal, on this subject, to the records of experience. It is probable that, at no period were the great nations of antiquity wholly devoid of the influences of revelation. The primitive traditions regarding the creation of the word, the origin of man, the existence and attributes of a Supreme Being, shed light upon the philosophy of Egypt, Greece, and Rome; but still we can show that, in none of those heathen nations did reason, even with this assistance, attain to correct or influential ideas of God and divine things. We do not here refer to the barbarous and uncivilized nations of mankind, far remote from the fountains of revealed truth, and ask "what has reason done among *them*?" We turn to Greece, the land of philosophy, civilization, eloquence and song; to Rome, at once the pupil and the conquerer of that ancient land—and we ask—What did *their* philosophers and sages accomplish in regard to the great question respecting God, and his relations to man?

The first great principle of Religion is a belief in the existence of God. "He that cometh," &c., Heb. xl, 6. Some seem to doubt that this fundamental principle of Religion may be *discovered* by the light of reason, as there is certainly no doubt that it can be *proved* by reasonable argument and demonstration; but it is one thing to establish by argument a fact or principle which is known, and another thing altogether to discover one that is not yet ascertained. When Columbus returned to Spain, after having discovered the New World, there were some persons foolish enough to depreciate the merit of the discovery, and to say that it involved no great genius in the man, or difficulty in the achievement. He overheard their remarks, and lifting an egg from the table, at which they were sitting, he asked them whether any of them could make it stand on end. They tried by various methods and failed—when the illustrious adventurer took it himself, broke one end, set it erect, and said "yes! gentlemen, it is quite easy when you know *how*." So it may be said to our Natural Theologians,[2] who have ascended to the high elevations of moral science—"You have indeed erected a noble structure—a mighty strong-hold against the Atheist and Sceptic; but it was by the aid of Revelation you gained your post of power—the weapons of your warfare have been drawn from her armory—and it is only under *her* banner that your victories shall be won." The ancients, by the combined immemorial tradition and the knowledge of God manifested in his works, did indeed attain to unanswerable arguments for the existence of a Deity, but the truth made little impression upon their own minds, and had still less influence on the masses of men around them. The Deity was considered by philosophers more as the *soul of the world*, the animating principle of Nature, than as the intelligent moral Governor of the Universe; while the common people mistook every object of Nature for Him. The heavens, the earth, the sea, every mountain, stream and valley, were filled with imaginary gods—while even *vice* had its celestial patrons, and *crime* was attributed to the immortals. Parnassus was little better in morality than our State Penitentiary.[3] Thus it

2. In the mid-nineteenth century "natural theology" reconciled the advancing sciences with knowledge received through the "revelation" of the Bible. A fundamental work is *Natural Theology* (1802) by English theologian William Paley (1743–1805). This is the book that makes the famous argument that we know God exists when we study nature just as we can know a watchmaker exists when we study a watch. An early edition is *Natural Theology, or, Evidences of the Existence and Attributes of the Deity, Collected from the Appearances of Nature*, 6th ed. (London: R. Faulder, 1803), Google Books, http://books.google.com/books?id=rkf4I36W_DIC. An American edition of the 1840s is *Paley's Natural Theology*, ed. Alonzo Potter (New York: Harper and Brothers, 1842), Google Books, http://books.google.com/books?id=72ZRAAAAYAAJ. One prominent American of this school was geologist Edward Hitchcock (1793–1864). His *Elementary Geology* (1840) reconciles biblical history with the geologic record. For decades it was a standard textbook for American colleges. See *Elementary Geology*, 2nd ed. (New York: Dayton and Saxton, 1841), Google Books, http://books.google.com/books?id=CVgZAAAAYAAJ.

3. Mount Parnassus, the mythological home of the Muses, often figures in nineteenth-century poetry as the birthplace of poetry and learning. "O were I on Parnassus' hill," wrote Robert Burns, "That I might catch poetic skill, / To sing how dear I love thee." See *The Complete Poetical Works*, ed. James Currie (New York: Appleton and Company, 1844), 385, Google Books, http://books.google.com/books?id=nZkoAAAAMAAJ.

was in ancient Greece and Rome, whose gods were reckoned by thousands; thus it is now in India, whose learned and intellectual Brahmins are lost in the mazes of licentious polytheism, while the people bow down to idols, as hideous as they are obscene.[4]

But let us next inquire, what were the *moral truths* which reason elicited among the ancients? And what was their influence upon mankind? We freely admit that, in this respect, Socrates[5] and his great followers among the Greeks, and Cicero[6] among the Romans have left behind them admirable treatises of morality; but we must also assert in many leading principles, they were in error, and that the influence of their doctrines upon mankind, and even upon themselves, was very slight. Cicero asserted that *glory* was the proper end, and after which virtue sought; her only and her best reward. Zeno[7] maintained that all crimes are equal, and that a person who has injured us, should never be forgiven. Other philosophers maintained the vilest positions regarding licentiousness; while humanity was scorned, and *self* exalted and deified.—The state of public morals was such that the most valuable and polished literary works which have come down to us as the productions of Virgil & Horace,[8] for instance, give indubitable evidence that practices of the vilest nature were commonly followed without shame and without reproof.

I need only allude to the darkness that prevailed generally regarding the doctrine of a future rewards and punishments because such were the aboriginal traditions of their fathers; but philosophers who on these subjects seemed to have some light, groped uncertainly; and feebly after the truth. Cicero confesses that the arguments for immortality left him still in

4. American readers learned about religion in India mainly through Christian missionaries and travellers who wrote for Christian periodicals. Not all accounts were this unflattering. Readers interested in seeing India through the eyes of an 1850 American reader might start with *Continental India* (London: Thomas Ward, 1840), Google Books, http://books.google.com/books?id=ZoxCAAAAcAAJ, by British missionary and abolitionist James William Massie (1799–1869). Or *A History of Asia and Oceania* (Louisville: Morton and Griswold, 1850), Google Books, http://books.google.com/books?id=HY718SAkBNkC, by the beloved "Peter Parley," children's textbook writer Samuel Griswold Goodrich (1793–1860).

5. Greek philosopher of the fifth century BCE.

6. Roman statesman of the first century BCE.

7. Roman emperor of the fifth century CE. A Google Books search for this full sentence finds it in both the essay "Theology" in *The Popular Encyclopedia, or "Conversations Lexicon"* (Glasgow: Blackie & Son, 1841), 6:585, Google Books, http://books.google.com/books?id=XbErAAAAYAAJ, and John Dick, *Lectures on Theology* (Philadelphia: F. W. Greenough, 1840), 1:19, Google Books, http://books.google.com/books?id=o3grAAAAYAAJ.

8. Roman poets of the first century BCE.

doubt; and Socrates acknowledged the same hesitation and uncertainty just before his death. Well may it be said that *life and immortality* were brought to life by *the gospel.*

2d. Having thus endeavored briefly to show that reason unassisted by Revelation cannot evolve the great truths of Religion or render them operative and influential in the world, we proceed to consider whether it be possible for a revelation to be made to man.

Those who deny the possibility of a Revelation, refer to the dreams and delusions of enthusiasts, who may be fully satisfied of the truth and reality of the notions, they have foolishly adopted. We reply that such reference is entirely inapplicable; for the revelations in which we believe, were given to men who showed that they were neither fanatics nor enthusiasts—that they did not "follow cunningly devised fables;"[9] but that they spoke "the words of truth and soberness."[10] The man who will calmly read the lives of the apostles and study their writings, will find more good sense, more sublime morality, more heavenly mindedness and practical piety in a dozen pages, than in all the philosophy of Greece and Rome. Besides, we may well ask whether it was not possible for the Deity to infuse into the mind, whose faculties he had created, such ideas as he deemed necessary for the enlightenment of the world; and also to convince that mind of the absolute certainty that such revelation was from God. Can one man communicate ideas to another man; and shall it not be possible that God shall communicate the knowledge of his will to the creatures he has made? We are not now disputing with the Atheist—we are arguing with the men that admit the being of God, and that he is the author of our faculties as well as of our existence—and we ask whether He that created the soul cannot communicate to it the ideas he thinks fit.

And if it be possible for a man to receive a revelation and be convinced of its truth, is it not equally possible that he may, by miracles, convince others, that he has been commissioned to make a revelation of the will of God? I know that miracles have been cavilled at and objected to; but their evidence appeals to sense and reason and cannot reasonably be rejected. God has indeed established laws in nature; but the same almighty power can restrain or alter these laws when there is any important purpose thereby gained, and is it not an object of sufficient moment that his messengers may be received as duly accredited by him? It may be said, it has been said, that there is no

9. 2 Peter 1:16.

10. Acts 26:25.

necessary connection between truth and the exercise of miraculous powers. We reply that *He who gave the power, communicated it only for the special purpose of demonstrating the revelation; and He could restrain its exercise to the establishment and enforcement of the truth.* Simon Magus imagined that the power of working miracles might be communicated by the apostles irrespective of personal character or of the great end which those miracles had in view in the propagation and establishment of Christianity; but it was not by their own power or holiness, as Peter testified, that the miracles of the Apostles were performed; and surely if any one had lived in those days, and seen the sick restored to health, the blind receiving sight, and the dead raised from their graves, he ought not to have hesitated in admitting that those who did such things, were sent by God.[11] Jesus therefore appealed to the works that he performed, as well as to the doctrines that he taught, saying—"If I had not done among them the works which none other man did, they had not had sin; but now have they both seen and hated both me and my Father."[12] Thus do we argue from the nature of the human mind and from the nature of miracles that it is possible for a revelation to be given to man, and to be fully established by sufficient proof.

3d. That a revelation is desirable will appear at once from what we have already shown regarding the insufficiency of reason and the heathen world. If Revelation had done nothing but clear up and roll away the clouds of obscurity, in which all the great questions of Moral Philosophy were involved, it would have been an object worthy of the merciful interposition of God. Socrates and Plato longed for the true light; and they said that they hoped God would reveal it. But when we consider how little influence religion exercised upon the ancient world for good—and how inefficacious were the moral teachings of the ancient philosophers, we see how desirable it was, even in this respect, that a revelation should be given. Christ said that the least in the Kingdom of Heaven, that is, the least member in the Christian Church, was greater than John the Baptist, who was inferior to none of the ancient prophets; with equal propriety may we affirm that the least child in our Sabbath Schools has clearer notions of the real foundations of morality than the most eminent of the ancient philosophers. "Love your neighbor as yourself,"[13] is a simple precept, but it is one which was unknown to the ancients, and is entirely the product of Revelation. If man

11. The story of Simon the Sorcerer and Peter is told in Acts 8:9–24.

12. John 15:24.

13. "The golden rule." Mark 12:31.

was not for ever to remain in doubt and darkness; if society was ever to be regenerated by principles and motives of sufficient cogency and power; if the gloom of the grave was ever to be dispelled and the sorrows of human life to be alleviated—then was a revelation most desirable for man.

The ideas that we have now advanced seem to be similar to those, which were before the Apostle's mind, when he wrote the words of our text. It was not by human wisdom that the doctrine of the Trinity was advanced, that the way of salvation through a Redeemer, was exhibited, that the resurrection of the human body, and the blessedness of the Saints in Heaven were established.—"Eye hath not seen, ear hath not heard, nor have entered into the heart of man the things which God hath prepared for them that love him; but God hath revealed them to us by his spirit."[14] Those doctrines are not against reason but above it. They belong to a higher sphere. God hath made known to us the mystery of his will, according to his good pleasure, which he hath purposed within himself. Reason—human and corrupted reason, is not the judge nor the arbiter of faith—nor are her principles the rule for the regulation of our belief. Reason is like Hagar, the handmaid of religion—and subordinate to scripture—not like Sarah, the mistress of faith.[15] We do not, with the Romanists, reject the use of reason and common sense in matters of religion; nor do we with the Socinians, exalt her to be a Judge and a Ruler in matters revealed.[16] There are some doctrines which are spiritual in their character, but which may be represented by sensible emblems.—As far as they are spiritual or supernatural, reason cannot be a rule respecting them; but, as far as they are exhibited by visible symbols, they come under the cognizance of our judgment and our senses. Thus our Lord has declared that he will be with his people to the end of the world; but we know that his, being a true body, is now in Heaven; and therefore we understand his promise in a spiritual sense; and when the Romanists appeal to Christ's promise, and say that is fulfilled after a sensible manner in the sacrament of the supper; we separate the sensible from the spiritual and we allow reason to judge in her own sphere—while faith rejoices in the spiritual fulfillment. In like manner

14. 1 Corinthians 2:9–10.

15. In the Old Testament, Hagar is Abraham's concubine and Sarah is his wife. Sarah, who cannot bear a child, gives Hagar to Abraham so that he can father an heir. Hagar conceives. She then despises Sarah. Sarah deals hardly with her, and Hagar flees into the wilderness where an angel of the Lord commands her to return and submit to Sarah. See Genesis 16:1–15.

16. "Romanist" is a derogatory term for a Roman Catholic. Strictly defined, "Socinians" were sixteenth-century Christian followers of Italian theologian Faustus Socinus (1539–1604). In this case, it may be a derogatory term for Unitarians.

also, with regard to the miracles of our Lord the sensible and the spiritual—the rational and the supernatural, were evidently combined. Thomas had sensible testimony of the miracle of the resurrection till at last he embraced the glorious truth "the Lord hath risen indeed" which involved many comfortable and exhalted spiritual doctrines of supernatural revelation. Reason has manifold uses in connection with religion for illustration, inference, and argument—and true philosophy will always be found as an auxilliary to faith; but after all, we must still remember that it is by the spirit of God alone that the deep things—the mysteries of God are revealed savingly to man. Look at any ordinary congregation you will find in it men of equal powers of mind, of similar dispositions and moral characters. They are all apparently in the same circumstances. They hear the arguments of the preacher—they comprehend the general scope of his discourse—they seem equally attentive to his statements—yet some of them will be savingly impressed with the truth; while to others his words are as the lovely song of one that hath a pleasant voice and can play well on an instrument; for they hear his words but do them not. What then is the reason of the difference? There may be something in the present temperament and circumstances of the individuals that may predispose the one class and yet be wanting in the other—but this will not account for the entire result and issue of the matter. Ask the man whose after life will be found to be affected by the sermon—whose destiny for eternity seems to turn as it were upon that pivot—ask him what has caused the change—what has opened his eyes, and softened his heart—and renewed his nature—and he will tell you that no voice, nor argument nor eloquence of man has done it; but God has wrought in him effectually by his Holy Spirit.

And as it is in congregations of public assemblies so it is in the frequent lessons which God gives by his providence to the world. The event, which awakens a new interest in one man, is unobserved or unnoticed by another—and even with regard to the same person at different periods of his life the same things will differently affect him. A man may have spent a great part of his life in carelessness and indifference about God and the future destiny of his soul; yet a word spoken by a child, may call up ideas, that have long been forgotten—or the most trivial incident may awaken trains of association, that shall change the entire complexion and character of his future life. The day and hour of his conversation, and the means by which it has been effected, may be afterwards forgotten or unknown; but the man knows and feels that he is not what he once was in heart or mind.

And now my dear brethren let me close with a few words of application. To most of you I am still a stranger. I know not the character or the circumstances of most of those whom I address; but am I not warranted in saying that you have, each for himself, either received the truth, or up to this moment, rejected it? I have this day set before you the claims of revelation as an embassy from God thro' His Son and Holy Spirit. Let me exhort those who have embraced the faith of the Gospel, that they "*follow on to know the Lord*."[17] The same Spirit by which you have been enlightened, is still necessary to bring all things profitable to your remembrance, and to keep you faithful to your God. Grieve not the spirit away by your neglect of his admonitions or by the indulgence of feelings at variance with His. Remember Him in whom your strength lies and come to Him for continual supplies of grace and for guidance and direction in all our ways.

To those who have not yet professed religion, let me say—if you believe yourselves to be immortal and accountable beings, there is no subject that is more important for you immediately to examine, than the claims of the christian religion upon your attention and belief. Consider its high pretensions—it professes to be from God. If it be not true, it is one of the most abominable and impious systems of imposture that ever was presented to man—for it would be a forgery in the name of God in every page—but if it *be* true as innumerable witnesses have testified, then your eternal salvation depends upon your acceptance of its offered mercy. No other system has ever revealed the plan of reconciliation with God and atonement for sin—no other is enforced with such tremendous threatenings, and recommended with such attractive motives and encouraging hopes. Delay not then in yielding its message an attentive consideration. It is not necessary that you should visit colleges or universities in order to ascertain its truth. The bible is its own witness. Your conscience will bear testimony while you read; and the Spirit by which the sacred pages were dictated, will bring home their truths to your heart. I would recommend you to read Leslie on Deism, Watson and Nelson on Infidelity[18] and other books of a similar character. It

---

17. Hosea 6:3.

18. Irish clergyman Charles Leslie (1650–1722) published his *Short and Easy Method with the Deists* in 1694. An American edition of the 1840s is *A Short and Easy Method with the Deists* (New York: Henry M. Onderdonk, 1846), Google Books, http://books.google.com/books?id=xA1MAAAAYAAJ. Relevant publications of English theologian Richard Watson (1781–1833) might be "Watson's Reply to Gibbon" and "Watson's Reply to Paine," two editions published by the American Tract Society. They are included in volume 14 of their Evangelical Family Library, *Infidelity*

is well for you to learn that the opponents of christianity have been encountered and defeated on every field of controversy; and that every attempt to obscure the sun of our religion has only ended in greater effulgence of glory, when the little cloud has passed away. To a mind well trained and furnished, the writings of infidels seem pitiless and poor. I have read some of those in which Deists most delight, and I must say that their unfairness: their ignorance of the real question in dispute—and the inconclusiveness of their arguments, have greatly confirmed my own faith in religion. I have said within myself—are these the only weapons that minds of such power can bring against the Bible? Is this all the result of their mighty boastings and parade? Then surely it is because they have ventured to assail a cause, which is so strong in itself, that it can be attacked only to cover its assailants with defeat—on the contrary, many of those who have devoted themselves to the defence and illustration of the christian doctrine, have been men of the noblest powers, and they have never appeared more illustrious than they seem when contending in the cause of Christ.

Milton, Newton, Locke and Chalmers[19] are men, whose fame has resounded through the world; and they were all employed in the defence of revealed truth. Their works cannot be mentioned by any reasonable or well-informed man without respect. We read them with profit and delight—but, after all, the majestic simplicity of Jesus, the inspired eloquence of Paul, the tender pathos of John, and the heart-touching, soul-elevating strains of David, carry in themselves an inherent evidence of truth, that must ever be their surest recommendation to the soul. Come then, beloved, to these sacred pages—here you will find examples the most attractive—eloquence the most lofty,—tenderness and sentiment, the purest and most refined; but above all, you will discover what is nowhere else to be met with—*the way of peace and reconciliation to your God.*

(New York: American Tract Society, n.d. [c. 1837]), 181–438, Google Books, http://books.google.com/books?id=8VMXAAAAYAAJ. American surgeon David Nelson, M.D. (1793–1844) lived in Kentucky, Missouri, and Illinois. He was "a card-playing, fun-loving infidel" who got religion in 1823, turned evangelist, and authored *The Cause and Cure of Infidelity: With an Account of the Author's Conversion* (New York: John S. Taylor, 1837), Google Books, http://books.google.com/books?id=zyM3AAAAMAAJ. The source of this biographical information is Edwin Francis Hatfield, *The Poets of the Church* (New York: Anson D. F. Randolph, 1884), 460–62, Google Books, http://books.google.com/books?id=1X9Na4_B8TsC.

19. English poet John Milton (1608–74), English physicist Isaac Newton (1642–1727), English philosopher John Locke (1632–1704), and Scottish minister Thomas Chalmers (1780–1847).

For the Offering.

"Who Shall Win the Prize?"

The flowers together met one day,
In Flora's hall in richest array,
    The prize for beauty to win;
All anxiously sought their charms to display,
In hopes from the Judge, as he passed that way,
    A smile of applause to win.

The rose spoke first, seeming fully aware
Of her beautiful charms, so rich and rare,
    Though suffused with blushes all o'er;—
"What flower with me can for beauty compare?"
In the mead or vale, is there one so fair,
    One flattered or cherished more?"

A Lily, gracefully seated, close by her side,
All glowing with smiles of conscious pride,
    For a moment deigned no reply;
"I am not your boasting to deride,
That you have charms, won't be denied;
    But do you all others defy?"

"I speak not of my own bright, matchless glow;
But there is Miss Tulip, who is rising just now,
    Can many more beauties display:
Behold her gay leaves, what a brilliant hue,
How rich, how lovely, how varied too,
    How fit to reign Queen of the day."

At this, all the flowers indignantly came,
Each striving with warmth her right to maintain;
    And each of the prize fully sure.
The Jasmine and Jonquil well knew they should gain,
The blooming carnation with pride, thought the same,
    And scarce could such boasting endure.

To view the assemblage—"I'll take a peep in"—
Thought the violet raising her head just then,
    Not meaning to join the company,
And, shrinking behind them, sought to screen
Her humble form, 'mid leaves so green
    To see the beauties pass by.

As she thus reclined her modest head,
The Judge arose and with noiseless tread,
    A step or two advanced;
Each eye was turned as if to read
To whom the prize would be decreed
    As round the hall he glanced.

"To the Violet," said he, "I award the prize,"
"Who shrinks from the gaze of passing eyes
    So timidly and shy;
For sure there's no beauty so bright and fair,
So enchantingly beautiful and rare,
    So truly sweet as modesty."

Adelia.
Lancaster, Ohio.[20]

Selected for the Offering.

The Old Man's Address to His Staff.[21]

Yes, staff, we have brunted many a year together, but thou hast now the best of it. Old Time in wrecking my frame, and blanching my beauty, has been able but to polish thee, so I know that thou wilt remain uncrumbled when this form of mine is dust, but you will not desert me while I live; I know it: I am half grateful for the thought. Ha! love a senseless thing? Yes, I will, for thou art a tree around which many sweet memories cling: thou canst remind of the past, old Staff! Not a grief track marked my face or eye when I saw thee first, not a page of the true history of life had I perused.

20. See n. 6, p. 252.

21. Searches of American Periodicals, Google, and Google Books do not yield an earlier publication of this essay. It could be from an obscure Western magazine that is not included in these digital archives.

Ha! I never tottered then, I had no need of thee then; but the infant oak that I found in the forest, I decreed should never be a tree from mere boyish wantonness, and I cut you from the clump there on the hill side. That clump now! why the trees are lofty acorn-bearing oaks. Even the shoot that rose beside thy stump is nodding up yonder in the sunlight as though it would triumph over us. Staff, thou wouldst have been a tree too, I dare say a beautiful one, but for my little penknife. I would not let thee be a tree, I destroyed thee, and thou in return hast proved a faithful support.

O just so with so many mortals! True friends scorned and trampled upon;—minds that love us; hoping ones blasted by us; how often do they repay our wayward deed, and our murderous unkindness, with the sacred devotion of their last withered energies.—So it is with thee my oaken staff.

The first time you went abroad with me, how well I remember! well, I shall never forget aught of that time; I don't believe that death will kill the memory of it, when I die! You had been standing idle behind my father's door for some weeks, when one sunset time, I carefully arranged my attire, clasped the knee buckles of the olden time,[22] and took thee in my warm right hand, (what a poor shriveled fist now!) then tremblingly I hastened, and still half lingered,—on the path—O! it was in shade then:—it led to the cabin where Mary lived.

She became my solace—memory wait—I'll begin back:—Staff, you leaned against my knee that eve, but though I gazed on your wooden head, I saw only Mary's eyes, though I grasped you in my hand, I only wanted to press Mary's dear fingers—those fingers caressed my brow afterwards—hold again memory! too fast, too fast. Staff, you witnessed our marriage, and when my new wife hanging on my right arm, accompanied me home; ha! ha! never jealous, thou wast in my left hand for the first time. But memory is getting black. O Mary! my life's morning star! my life's sunshine, my life's night-gloom!

She was mine: she died.

Staff, did I lean on thee when I wept at her grave? memory is gone, and my brain whirls.

Well, Well, I cannot take my eyes off theme, staff, for I know that Mary's hand has often clasped thee, but as the vine tendril fades and vanishes from the tree it has encircled, so has vanished thy hand and thy life, Mary.

22. Breeches (pants with legs that end just below the knee) were often worn with buckles or strings to close the leg opening. In 1850 they were no longer worn in the cities. They were associated with the "olden" times—the late eighteenth and early nineteenth century—but they were still worn by some men when riding horses in the country.

Ha! I can smile yet. Did not a bright boy once ride astride thee, staff, and call you his horse? a stately man, a dutiful son, he lives yet, and loves his father, and laughs with his mother's eyes.

Thou hadst a rival once. I left thee at home and went away with thy rival—the sword. There are records of thy rival's doing—in Germantown, in Trenton, and Yorktown, where the Lily and the Stars met to greet the Goddess of Liberty.[23] That was a time when the soul seemed lifted above itself, when Heaven seemed bowed smilingly, cheeringly to earth, to our redeemed land.

I returned: change! change had marked every thing but my staff. I found thee in the closet among cobwebs, and my crippled leg had use for thee:—I feel pain in that leg now, and the hot blood of other days begins to throb my heart out of its clogged lethargy, no! no! it is not my blood that heats, it is the lingering flame that dwells in my spirit. I am thinking of Freedom's war, I am thinking of Washington. Ah! yes, but the thought of my country is uppermost. I could wish both my legs had been broken to have insured a lasting liberty, that which I toiled for. O! that my country as uncorrupted as thou art, staff, might remain when I am dust!

Well, well, again. Staff, we'll lie in one grave: it will be as well: am I childish? I can't help it. Our epitaph shall be,

Here lies
the
OLD MAN
and his
STAFF

For the Offering.

Thoughts on Visiting the Home of My Childhood.

Old Time, I see thou hast been here, 'mong rocks,
and hills and dales,
For oft thy impressed steps appear, where'er I
chance to roam;
And busy quite, hast thou been too, in the sequested vales
Of my beautiful, my lovely, my childhood's happy home.

23. Battles of the American Revolution (1775–83). The fleur-de-lis, a symbol of the French forces who fought with the Americans against the British, is a stylized lily.

While standing here upon the brow of this old pastured hill,
I see the lov'd familiar scenes, "successive rise to view;"[24]
There, in the bright and glowing mead,[25] appears the
winding rill,
And here below, across the way, those orchard trees I knew.

But all how changed! How sadly changed! once Grand-sires
home appears,
Where, in our young and thoughtless days, we all
were wont to throng,
To hear the gladsome stories told, of by-gone, olden years,
And all enjoy those pure delights, to childhood that belong.

Ah! then my young and gladdened heart knew naught
of life's decay,
For aught was bright and beauteous, with none of life's alloy;
And then no sadd'ning thoughts came o'er my childhood's
pleasant way,
To mar those merry, peaceful hours, so frought with
purest joy.

But those were only cheerful hours of life's young happy day,
And few, of those loved kindred ones, are here to greet
me now;
The lovely, gentle, outward forms, of some, have passed away,
And now the brightly silvered threads come mingling
o'er my brow.

Thus Old Time admonishes, that he's busy too with me,
And that all earthly outward forms are subject to decay;
" 'Tis ever thus:" and we by faith, "our Father's love may see,"
For we, from earth to the "spirit home," shall go far away.[26]

24. Phrase from "Dear Ones Far Away" by American poet and editor Park Benjamin (1809–64). The poem was often reprinted; one publication is *Western Literary Messenger* 7, no. 11 (October 24, 1846): 184, Google Books, http://books.google.com/books?id=7olMAAAAMAAJ.

25. Meadow.

26. These two lines quote "The Forest Trees," a poem signed "E. C. T." in *The Lowell Offering* 2 (September 1842): 191, Harvard University Library, http://pds.lib.harvard.edu/pds/viewtext/2669789?op=t&n=669.

Then let's renew the "inward man" with spiritual strength
each day,
While lone pilgrims journeying, "through earth's wilderness
we roam,"
And ever strive, the glorious, "gracious precepts, to obey,"[27]
Until the bright archangel's trump shall call us to our home.

W. B.
Windsor, Vt., Sept. 1848.[28]

Selected for the Offering.

Woman's Best Ornament.

By Rev. E. P. Rogers[29]

Let me urge upon my female readers, especially those who are in youth, the importance of taking loftier and better views of life than those taught by the vain world. It is a sad thing to see so many of the young and fair, whose life is almost blank—I will not say a blot—whose keen susceptibilities, whose noble powers, whose deep affections, whose precious time is lavished only upon dress and gayety, and fashionable visiting; who wear the white apparel of the butterfly, and are as light and graceful, and as useless too; whose conversation finds no higher or more improving subject than the idle gossip of the day, the last party, or the never failing topic—dress; whose reading is the miserable trash which is inundating every community, and enervating and

27. 2 Corinthians 4:16 describes renewing the "inward man," but these lines appear to allude to a single poem that may not be in the digital archives mentioned throughout these notes.

28. The Cumings and Fay families came to Ohio from Windsor, Vermont. See introduction, p. 9. Buried with them in Akron's Glendale Cemetery are a few "Barretts." A forty-two-year-old William Barrett from Vermont was counted by the 1850 Census in Brunswick, Ohio—about twenty miles north and west of Akron—working as a shoemaker and living with a large family. United States of America, Bureau of the Census, *Seventh Census of the United States, 1850*. NARA microfilm publication M432. (Washington, D.C.: National Archives and Records Administration, n.d.), roll M432_709, page 380A, Ancestry.com.

29. Ebenezer Platt Rogers (1817–81) preached in Augusta, Georgia in the late 1840s. This was a prospering town of about ten thousand people; cotton and tobacco were shipped out of Augusta by railroad and canal, and the merchants of Augusta did much business with residents of the now-densely settled upper country. Augusta had expensive, elegant public buildings, factories, and many churches and schools. See *The Rev. E. P. Rogers, D.D.* (Privately printed, 1882), 8, Google Books, http://books.google.com/books?id=vcA_AAAAYAAJ, and Thomas Baldwin and J. Thomas's *Gazetteer of the United States* (Philadelphia: Lippincott, Grambo, 1854), Google Books, http://books.google.com/books?id=_5s6AAAAcAAJ. This item is selected from *Godey's Lady's Book*. See (February 1850): 141–42, American Periodicals (126096313).

dissipating the minds of our youth; whose whole life seems to be an aimless, frivolous life; and who as they flit by us on their airy wings, provoke the inquiry: "For what were these pretty creatures made?"—I pray you take loftier views of life than these. While I would not draw you from the rational pleasures of society, nor bring one gloomy cloud upon your youthful sky, I still would plead for some serious hours, some industrious moments; some time apportioned to the culture of the mind, the enriching of the memory with stores of useful knowledge. I would plead that the capacities and aspirations of the immortal part receive some ministration, and that the moral faculties be cultivated and stimulated, and the generous impulses of the soul be expanded in labors for the best good of those around you. Be assured there is no beauty like that of goodness—there is no power like that of virtue; personal beauty may attract the admiration of the passing hour, but it is the richer beauty of moral worth, the loveliness of the soul, that commands the deepest reverence, and secures the most enduring affection. Even men who have no religion themselves, but who are men of judgement, and whose opinion is worth the most, respect and admire a lady most, who displays in her character the "beauty of holiness."[30]

If there is one sight more than any other, in this world of sin and sorrow, which combines all the elements of beauty, of nobleness, and of worth, it is that of a young and lovely female, whose youth and beauty, whose depth and richness of affection, and whose powerful influence on human hearts, are all consecrated to the cause of truth and holiness, laid as an humble offering at the Savior's feet! Such a being is, indeed, worthy of the reverence and admiration of every true and noble heart; and she will command it, even when the light of her beauty is quenched, and the flower of her loveliness is faded. But if there is a sad, heart-breaking sight on earth, it is that of one gifted with all the charms which nature lavished upon her daughters, prostituting them upon the altar of vanity or fashion, and starving the soul on the unmeaning flattery of a vain and hollow-hearted world; running a giddy round of gayety, frivolity, and dissipation; laying up in the future a cheerless and forsaken old age, and a miserable, remorseless eternity.

"Oh, what is woman? What her smile,
Her lips of love, her eyes of light?
What is she, if those lips revile
The lowly Jesus? Love may write
His name upon her marble brow,

30. 1 Chronicles 16:29, 2 Chronicles 20:21, Psalm 29:2, Psalm 96:9.

And linger in her curls of jet:
The light spring flowers may meekly bow
Before her tread; and yet—and yet
Without that meeker grace, she'll be
A lighter thing than vanity."[31]

For the Offering.

Hap-Hazard Ideas.

Perhaps all may think it strange to find any thoughts respecting so serious a subject as Religion, connected with the title under which I write; but nevertheless, if they are not deemed out of place by the Editor of the Offering, all its readers may have the pleasure of criticising and dissenting from them if they find sufficient cause and no one will be offended.

What is Religion? is a question that has often been suggested to my mind. Passing by what we have read, let us look at what we have all seen.

In every society, we occasionally see men or women whose every look, and word, and every movement seem to say that they consider themselves the favored of Heaven—peculiarly fitted by the Great Inventor above, to work out, without the possibility of failure, happiness *for themselves.* For the faults of their *fellow-beings* they have no mercy—Does any one ask what articles of faith are found in their creed? Calvinism[32] stands there in all its horror and why should not a stern, chilling shadow rest on all their souls, and cast its sickening gloom even beyond their own paths, diffusing a wide-spread wretchedness? How can they expect that they will not be deemed selfish, conceited and egotistical; or how can they blame others for feeling that the image of their God we reflected by their distorted imaginations, is a short-sighted, narrow minded being like themselves, exhibiting none, or

31. The closing stanza of "Misanthropic Hours" by American poet Nathaniel Parker Willis (1806–67). It was republished several times in the antebellum decades, often in religious magazines. The first printing appears to be *The New-York Mirror, and Ladies' Literary Gazette* 4, no. 7 (September 9, 1826): 56, Google Books, http://books.google.com/books?id=8_LVAAAAMAAJ.

32. The rigorous Protestantism founded by French theologian John Calvin (1509–64). Calvinism was fundamental to the religious practice of the Puritans and Pilgrims of early New England. In mid-nineteenth-century America, it was thought to characterize the Baptist, Congregational, Evangelical Lutheran, German Reformed, and Presbyterian churches—at least, according to the various church historians who contributed to *The History of All the Religious Denominations in the United States*, ed. Israel Daniel Rupp and John Winebrenner (Harrisburg: John Winebrenner, 1849), Google Books, http://books.google.com/books?id=4bQOAAAAIAAJ.

but few of the attributes of Divinity, that appear when they are seen through a more perfect medium where self-abasement and benevolence are allowed to combine with the rays that bear to the mental vision, the light of God's countenance? Does true Religion place on its votaries the shackles of an unconquerable fate? Does it wind them up in the small compass of one's own circle of life; "are we but as clay in the hands of the Potter"[33] in every sense of the word and must we give God glory for fashioning us for destruction or take peculiar unction to ourselves in thinking that we are destined for an eternity of bliss? I tell you nay!—sooner should we abjure the christian's creed altogether and under the banner of Infidelity, bring upon ourselves our own dark doom. But hark the votaries of another faith are singing of Free Grace[34] and here there should be no bigots, no selfish eagerness to dictate to others, the terms of Immortal Life. But alas! even here there are some who understand not the glorious liberty of the Gospel; but take it upon themselves to mark out the path of duty for intelligencies far superior to their own and seem to imagine that reproaches and denunciations screamed into the ears of all they meet, will be sufficient to convert a world to the calm and peaceful Religion of Jesus. It is Religion that warms the hearts of those inconsistent beings who can forget or disregard the decent courtesies of life, the claims of mind upon mind and all the inexpressibly delicate sensibilities of high minded, conscientious christians who are capable of understanding their duty as taught by the spirit of their Heavenly Father and are earnestly striving to be faithful in all that devolves upon them? No—this is the intolerance of ignorance and we will let them go with their disgusting frothy exhibitions of zeal without knowledge and for a moment, look upon the course of one fitted to be an example to his fellows and a way mark to Heaven for earth's weary pilgrims. His heart is warmed with the purest feelings of benevolence and he speaks deep, earnest words of faith, of hope, of love, of heavenly trust in the wisdom, power and mercy of God—he prays the prayer of faith; and his hearers are in spirit carried with him to the throne where sitteth their Redeemer and their Judge and yet we know as we look

33. Isaiah 64:8.

34. Universalists believed that all souls would go to heaven in the afterlife; in other words, they believed that God offered grace freely to all. In 1849 this was a controversial belief. Many Universalist hymns celebrate "free grace." For example, see "Ho! every one that thirsts, draw nigh," which includes the lines "Come to the living waters, come! / Gladly obey your Maker's call:— / Return, ye weary wand'rers, home, / And find his grace is free for all." George Rogers, *Universalist Hymn Book,* 2nd ed. (Cincinnati: R. P. Brooks, 1843), 340, Google Books, http://books.google.com/books?id=z3UWAAAAYAAJ.

upon him and mark his daily course, that it is no transient excitement that lights his eye; no evanescent devotion that so evidently bears him above the trials of life. Thought, like a mantle rests upon him; consideration for the feelings of others, marks every movement; he denounces their sins but all feel that he is the sinner's friend; and thus does he fulfill the law of Christ.

But here I see Infidelity lifting its deformed head to deny the truth of revealed religion as taught by Christ and his followers.—And what is it that Christians should hide their heads? It bids its *victims* feel that no God watches over them—that they must wander through the gloomy path of mental and moral darkness in this world, and when they die, be wrapped in the cold shades of annihilation; or of all things, it says,

> "All are but parts of one stupendous whole,
> Whose body nature is, and God the soul."[35]

Thus puffing up proud man with an idea that he is divine—that no sin was committed by the inhabitants of Eden and no atonement made by Christ. And of all the methods used by leaders in the Infidel ranks to disseminate their principles, Phrenology, Mesmerism and Clairvoyance[36] are the most disgusting. "Alas!" says one, "dare you trespass upon such ground as this and undertake to say ought against doctrines taught by such a host of superior intelligencies?" Yes, kind friends, even against the *really* bright array, in all humility, we shall undertake to speak what we honestly believe. Phrenology first demands a passing glance; but first let me say that, to a certain extent, I believe Phrenology to be true and that, rightly understood, it would do no harm; but when people are taught to place it among the sciences with all its unavoidable deductions; and to depend on the revealings of the cranium for testimony as to character, independently of actual deeds, we feel that it has a direct tendency to pervert justice; and when we see

35. Well-known lines from the poem "An Essay on Man" (1734–35) by English poet Alexander Pope (1688–1744). See *The Complete Poetical Works of Alexander Pope* (New York: A. Leavitt, 1848), 2:19, Google Books, http://books.google.com/books?id=LFkZAAAAYAAJ.

36. For phrenology, see n. 16, p. 87. "Mesmerism" was the controversial practice of "animal magnetism" (something like hypnotism) started by Viennese physician Franz Anton Mesmer (1734–1815). "All persons who desire to practise mesmerism for the cure of diseases, and to alleviate the sufferings of their fellow creatures" are invited to read Thomas Buckland's *Hand-book of Mesmerism*, 2nd ed. (London: Hippolyte Bailliere, 1850), Google Books, http://books.google.com/books?id=dTv1riToiMoC. Clairvoyance is the extra-sensory visual perception of distant objects. It was associated with mesmerism. T. H. Pasley explains the physiology of Mesmerism in *The Philosophy which shows the Physiology of Mesmerism, and Explains the Phenomenon of Clairvoyance* (London: Longman, Brown, Green, and Longmans, 1848), Google Books, http://books.google.com/books?id=mhUEAAAAQAAJ. Much was written on these subjects in the 1840s.

people trying to prove, to the still doubting ones, the truth of Phrenology by Mesmerism, we feel that it is strange that a deception so palpable can blind intelligent beings. A few years ago it was no uncommon thing to see Phrenological and Mesmeric Lecturers, after their lectures were closed and their subjects put into the magnetic sleep, touching different places on their heads, where they had been pleased to tell you certain faculties were located, and by the immediate action of that faculty, declare Phrenology *proved*, forgetting (it may be) that they had before told their hearers that their subjects would obey their (the mesmerisers') will; and not thinking that any one who supposed this to be the fact would imagine that had they placed their hand upon the foot or arm of the subject, or not touched them at all, the same effects might have been produced. And what says one has all this to do with Religion? Much dear friends very much—many were *honestly* duped into the belief that they had obtained a key to help them understand every thing that had before appeared beyond their comprehension. A *natural* cause could be assigned for every thing.—Christ was only a human being, his miracles only mesmerism—all were naturally religious—there was to be no general day of judgment and no one was accountable to God &c., &c., and yet all of this was not *quite enough*—did not give the Infidel *sufficient* power to overthrow the Christian's faith in the atonement made by Christ; and the widely disseminated idea of a judgment to come; and lo! it was discovered that some of the mesmerised subjects were *independant* of the minds of the Mesmerisers and could wander at will, seeing things invisible to others, gathering the history of the past, exhibiting the present; and unveiling the future. Soon they travelled into the world of spirits, bringing back the consoling assurance that all departed beings were securely and supremely happy in their eternal home. "Now," says the rejecter of the Bible, "is my day of triumph!—superstition *must now* yield its place to nature and reason; for, *proof* of our belief is now obtained and the victory *must* now be ours!" Not so fast, friends. Look at your position a little. You talk of superstition, and yet ask us to believe *many things* more strange than ought that taxes our credulity in the Bible. You say that your doctrines are *proved* and we say that we have investigated them to a considerable extent, with an ardent desire to *know the truth* and have failed to find any thing *like proof*; while we have found in *every* instance, more or less of what we believe to be *intended* deception, therefore we feel that your doctrines are *not proved* and until they are, we must feel that the glorious Gospel of the

Son of God is worthy to be received by us; and that by obeying its injunctions, we may hope for happiness here and hereafter.

Perhaps I have not proved what Religion is or is not; but I have thrown together a jumbled up mess of thoughts that I have not time to finish and must bid you a hasty adieu.

Porcia.[37]

Virtue may be misrepresented, persecuted—consigned to the grave; but the righteous wake not more assuredly to the reality of their hopes, than this to an immortal remembrance.[38]

For the Offering.

Lonely Musings on a Future State: OR, What Are the Joys of Heaven?

Oh! could we but go to the bright world above,
With all the heart's sympathy, tenderness, love,
That here, so much happiness, misery, make,
And miss the lov'd friends, with whom, counsel we take?
Would not the rich chords, all so sensitive, here,
Bear back to our spirits, a bitter pang there?
It can not be otherwise, love is not blest,
If its object, a moment, in sorrow must rest,
E'en the bright shores of Canaan[39] would sicken the view,
If we gain'd them alone, while our friends lov'd and true,
We were conscious, were qualing 'neath God's angry frown.
And no Lethean waters[40] their sorrows could drown.
It cannot be memory then, that will bless,
Else, all would partake of Heaven's pure peace,
Then follows the fact, our identity is gone,

37. For more of Porcia's thoughts, see pp. 97, 148, and 417.

38. Page filler clipped from *The Ladies' Garland* 3, no. 11 (May 1840): 260, Google Books, http://books.google.com/books?id=msNBAAAAYAAJ. Google Books locates four other such uses of the anonymous quotation in various periodicals.

39. Heaven; the afterlife, as described in the Old Testament.

40. In Greek mythology, Lethe is a river in Hades. When the dead drink from it, they forget their previous life.

And all must be spirits, unseen, or unknown,
Our happiness made by one sovereign thought,
The mercy of God our ransom has bought,
Or, if other thoughts or feelings there be,
We must learn Heaven's language their nature to see.
——Ah! cease, prying heart, God's justice to doubt,
And learn that "His ways are past finding out."[41]
I have tried to discern the true path-way to life,
And my spirit is pain'd by its own torturing strife.
Oh! give me thy grace, my Father above,
And write on my soul thine own perfect love,
With the trust, in thy mercy, thy goodness and power,
That will bless me in life, and in death's solemn hour,
And fit for the Future, whate'er shall be given,
As bliss for the souls that are garnered in Heaven.

Alma.[42]

For the Offering

Letters for the Offering.

My Dear Offering:—How I love the spring. The bright, the beautiful, the all glorious spring! All hail! thou fairest daughter of the season. Thou that bringeth the warm sunshine and lengthening days. That breaketh the icy fetters of cold winter and setteth the streams dancing again in their own glad melody. That bringeth sweets to the honey-bee and green pastures to the gentle kine. That openeth the swelling buds and bringeth refreshing dews to the tender flowers. That coverth the hillside with green herbage and leafeth the naked wild wood. With thee cometh the balmy winds and the choral of the wild songsters. The plowboy's song is again heard from the fields and the crow calls loud from the tree-tops, for the buried corn. The gardener sinks his spade into the mellow earth and stops to chat with the children as they hunt blue violets in the fence-corners—Ah! those blue violets—how the sight of them carries my mind back to the days of my early girlhood, when I was a happy log-cabin child, and the merry spring-time was to me almost a heaven. Yes how glad was I when came the sunny

41. Romans 11:33.

42. For more by "Alma," see pp. 47, 76, 78, 92, and 184.

days of spring, for then I could roam at will over meadow and woodland, pulling butter-cups and daisies; but most of all, I loved the modest violet:—and far away down the vale, would I follow the clear brook, for on its bank, grew they the most beautifully.

I had thus wandered one day, until cottage, fields and all home scenes, were far back in the distance; and when I stopped to rest found myself in a deep valley sheltered on each side by high hills, which I then thought were mountains. Tall trees grew high above me and threw their many long branches far out, almost hiding the blue sky and bright sun. I was still by the pretty brook, whose glowing banks had led me away, and my little check apron was so full of wild flowers, my tiny hand could scarce hold them in. I espied a path winding up the hillside and though tired, I began to follow it, for I know not why it is, but somehow I never saw a winding path but I longed to trace its windings.

In my ascents I passed a shelving rock, which projected out so far it almost overhung the streams, and after I had climbed to the hill and saw that the path led towards home, I returned to the rock and throwing myself upon its broad surface, spread out my flowers and began to tie them up in bunches. Then as I sat there, looking now at the petty blossoms and then down at the bubbling brook, hurrying on over the bright pebbles reflecting in its limpid waters the green hills and giant trees, and dropping the flowers, clapped my hands, exclaiming, "how beautiful! beautiful! everything is beautiful!" Then echo caught up the sound and I could hear it away over the hills, saying "beautiful! beautiful!"

In a few moments my storm of delight was over and a sweet calm stole over me, and there on that old mossgrown rock was woven the first day-dreams my fancy ever spun. Yes, I built there my first air castle, which like all others "came tottering down." It was very unlike the castles I built in after years, with "sweet shady walks for the Gods and their loves,"[43] for I knew not then of Cupid's barbed shafts and lover's sight—I was but a five year old buckeye girl, wild and green as my native forest, and had no knowledge of other love than that I felt for parents and brothers. Then 'twas but a simple childlike castle that I built, but I reared it high for I was ambitious even then.

---

43. These quotes allude to "From The Castle in the Air, to The Little Corner of the World," a poem by English political writer Thomas Paine (1737–1809). See *The Theological Works of Thomas Paine* (London: R. Carlile, 1824), 380–81, Google Books, http://books.google.com/books?id=57UUAAAAYAAJ.

I at first thought of my sick father at home, and I wondered if things so lovely to the sight and sweet to the smell as flowers were could not cure the sick.

Then said I, these would I carry to papa: and if one pretty bunch would cure him, how many I would have to cure others with. And often when I had given to each of my sick friends a bunch, I would go to the town where my good grandpa lives, and carry a bunch to all the sick people there; then how they would love me, and grandma would give me pretty patches to sew in my little quilt, and I could gather the sweet pinks that grew in her garden.

Then I will go away to that country where my mother used to live, and there I shall see my uncle and girl cousins, who will love me very much when they see what I can do with only flowers and mayhap will give me a new dress.

Well, after I cure all the sick there, I will travel to that beautiful country, that my father tells me of, where it is always spring and flowers are ever blooming; and when it is known that I can heal the sick, the people will gather about me and I will be a great person, and all the fine ladies will come and beg of me to stay with them, but I shall not, for I must sail to those countries far over the seas, that my father reads about; he says that Kings and Queens live there, and when they hear that I can make all the sick people well, the king will make a great party for me and the king's people will bow before me because I am so great—my name will be put in the books and I shall be a very great woman then; and when I came home I guess my brother, who thinks he is so very great and wont play with me because he is just a little the biggest, will be glad to get even a word from me. Here my dream was broken by a whizzing in the air above my head, and looking up, I saw a wounded bird fall from the tree, and the next moment my roguish brother bounded down the hill in search of it.

"O, Henry!" exclaimed I, "why did you kill the little bird?"

"Why, I wished to try my new bow," said he, "and only look! Lily, how pretty! Uncle Horace has come and he made it for me, and now you may have my old one, and if you were not such a very little girl might shoot with this sometimes."

"But I'll show you I can shoot, if I am *such a very little girl*," said I pettishly, and snatching the bow I fastened his best arrow in the tree top.

"There I'll pay you for that, madam Lily," said he, sweeping my pile of flowers into the stream.

I looked after them and saw the rapid current bearing off all that was left of my castle; then my heart was ready to burst and I began to cry. Henry's sympathies were easily enlisted and the sight of my tears touched a tender chord in his bosom, and with many expressions of regret and promises to gather more for me, he ran to a tree and brought out a basket he had hid there, saying only, "see what a beauty of a basket Uncle Horace made for you to put posies in—it is much prettier than my bow and we will pick it full of blue violets while we walk home."

"Yes and carry them all to Uncle Horace," said I, as we tripped lightly down the vale hand in hand, my heart lightened of all its sorrows.

O! would that my heart was as easily disburdened. But alas! the spring-time is past and I have felt the winter in my heart—such as I had not felt then, when in the spring of life the spring of the year was to me as one bright May-day.

For the Offering.

The Gilliflower.

Translated from the Italian.

By Alice Leland.[44]

A Gilliflower in beauty smiled, and 'mid
Its kindred plants, none led so happy life,
For Geva loved the gentle flower, and long
Had watched its growth with strictest care, and marked
Its loveliness expand, from early years.
When Spring came forth, with all her lovely train,
And Sol poured gently down his warming rays,
She bore it from her humble cot, and placed
It 'neath his healthful beams, and oft its leaves
Bedewed with water from the crystal fount:
And then at night in fear a storm would rise,

44. Searches of Google, American Periodicals, Google Books, and WorldCat discover no other publications from this period with the signature "Alice Leland," and the 1850 United States Federal Census, when searched through Ancestry.com, does not yield a good match for the name. This is disappointing but not surprising. The author could have moved on, married, or died before the Neenah census was taken in July 1850. She could have evaded the census-taker. And this could be a pen name.

And chilling winds might crush her tender plant,
Perchance destroy its life, she placed it back
Within the cot: The artless girl, oft that
Addressed her cherished one,—"my only love
Art thou, sweet plant, no other care I know,
Or hope, but thee, and ne'er will I forget
To love, and nourish thee, while life remains."
Alas! the artless one dreamed not, that soon
Her dearest flower would seek to free itself
From all her watchful care, and leave her lone.
Yet thus it was, when there, a stranger came,
A lady very beautiful, and decked
In silken garments, wrought with gold, while on
Her brow shone rarest gems. With stately step
She moved, and cast a hasty glance, o'er all.
The Gilliflower in wonder gazed on one,
Whose beauty far outshone meek Geva's charms;
And as she nearer came, some rarer flowers
He saw, that decked her breast, and envy, hate,
Are quick aroused. "Ah me!" he sighed, "mine is
A cruel fate; *I* too, have beauty's gift,—
Indeed, more lovely far am I, than those
The lady fair, hath chosen for her own,
And wherefore should I live in this lone place,
With none beside that *country girl*, to view
My charms unfold! My peerless beauty should
Adorn the palace of the rich, and cheer
The gay of heart. Nor was I formed to bloom
Unseen, and spend my days for one alone.
Oh! when, from this dread fate shall I be freed,
And leave these scenes so dull!—The lady heard
These words, low-breathed, and sighed, but feigned
To take no note of aught that passed, yet paused
To list the mourning strain. At length, she said,
"O! sigh not thus, thou lonely one,—I will
Not leave thee here, to pine in grief, and die;—
With joy I'll take thee to my heart, and thou

Shalt share my love." With glad surprise, he heard
These kindly words, and raised the drooping head.
Her first bouquet, was cast aside, and in
Its place the Gilliflower, in triumph smiled,
Nor grieved, that he was wrested from the spot
That gave such joy in early days, and scarce
Bestowed a passing thought on her, who had
So gently watched his days, with artless love.
But quick the time of boasting fled; for when
The leaves began to droop,—the petals fade,
He too, away was cast,—a worthless thing:—
A rose-bud newly culled, his place supplied.
And now, alone, upon the chill, damp ground,
Expiring lies, the once fair flower, and thus
He mourns:—"Ah wretched fate! is this the doom
Of one so late, all filled with hope, and joy,
Must I then end my wretched days alone,
Despised, and scorned? I see my folly past,
But all too late. My foolish *pride* has caused
This sudden fall, has wrought the direful change.
Would I had never sighed to leave the place
Which gave me birth, then would my Geva's hand
Have ever guarded me from ought of ill,—
Her gentle voice have soothed in time of fear.
Yet now, in solitude I die, my fate
Unwept by true, and faithful ones. My sighs
Unheard by mortal ear. Ah yes, I die."
'Tis thus in life, when those of humble lot
Above their proper sphere, aspire to rise,
And if perchance they gain a giddy height,—
Anon they fall neglected and despised.

Neenah, Wisconsin.[45]

45. Neenah is on the Neenah River at the foot of Lake Winnebago, southwest of Green Bay. About this time, the town had flouring mills and a sash and blind factory. See Thomas Baldwin and J. Thomas's *Gazetteer of the United States* (Philadelphia: Lippincott, Grambo, 1854), Google Books, http://books.google.com/books?id=_5s6AAAAcAAJ. As the crow flies, Neenah is more than 400 miles north and west of Akron. It is a long trip from Akron to Neenah. It is curious that *The Akron Offering* would have a contributor from such a distant place. Perhaps the author had recently migrated to Wisconsin (which became a state in 1849) from or through Akron.

Havn't the Change.

By Mrs. Mary Graham.[46]

It was house-cleaning time, and I had an old colored woman at work scrubbing an cleaning the paint.

"Polly is going," said one of my domestics, as the twilight began to fall.

"Very well. Tell her that I shall want her to-morrow."

"I think she would like to have her money for to-day's work," said the girl.

I took out my purse, and found that I had nothing in it less than a three-dollar bill.

"How much does she have a day?"

"Six shillings."

"I hav'nt the change this evening. Tell her that I'll pay her for both days to-morrow."

The girl left the room, and I thought no more of Polly for an hour. Tea time had come and passed, when one of my domestics who was rather communicative in her habits, said to me:

"I don't think old Polly liked your not paying her this evening."

"She must be very unreasonable, then," said I, without reflection. "I sent her word that I had no change. How did she expect that I could pay her?"

"Some people are queer, you know," remarked the girl who had made the communication, more for the pleasure of telling it than any thing else.

I kept thinking over what the girl had said, till other suggestions came into my mind.

"I wish I had sent and got a bill changed," said I, as the idea that Polly might be really in want of money intruded itself. "It would have been very little trouble."

This was the beginning of a new train of reflections, which did not make me very happy. To avoid a little trouble, I had sent the poor old woman away, after a hard day's work, without her money. That she stood in need of it, was evident from the fact that she had asked for it.

"How very thoughtless in me," said I, as I dwelt longer and longer on this subject.

46. "Mrs. Mary S. Graham" published about two dozen stories in the late 1840s. Most were "household sketches" and many appeared, like this one, in *The Ladies' Wreath*. A search of the 1850 U.S. Census yields well over one thousand matches for the name. OCLC's WorldCat catalog of North American research libraries suggests Graham's stories were not collected as a volume.

"What's the matter?" inquired my husband, seeing me look very serious.

"Nothing to be very much troubled at," I replied.

"Yet you are troubled."

"I am; and cannot help it. You will perhaps, smile at me, but small causes sometimes produce much pain. Old Polly has been at work all day, scrubbing and cleaning. When night came she asked for her wages, and I, instead of taking the trouble to get the money for her, sent her word that I hadn't the change.—There was nothing less than a three dollar bill in my purse. I didn't reflect that a poor old woman, who has to go out to daily work, must need her money as soon as it is earned. I'm very sorry I did not get the change."

My husband did not reply for some time. My words appeared to have made considerable impression on his mind.

"Do you know where Polly lives?" he inquired at length.

"No; but I will ask the girl." And immediately ringing the bell, I made inquiries as to where Polly lived; but no one in the house knew.

"It can't be helped now," said my husband in a tone of regret. "But I would be more thoughtful in the future. The poor always have need of their money. Their daily labor rarely does more than supply their daily wants. I can never forget a circumstance that occurred when I was a boy. My mother was left a widow when I was but nine years old—and she was poor. It was by the labor of her hands that she obtained shelter and food for herself and three little ones.

"Once (I remember the occurrence as if it had taken place yesterday,) we were out of money and food. At breakfast time our last morsel was eaten, and we went through the long day without a mouthful of bread. We all grew very hungry by night; but our mother encouraged us to be patient a little and a little while longer, until she finished the garment she was making, when she would take that and some other work home to a lady who would pay her for the work. Then, she said, we should have a nice supper. At last the work was finished, and I went with my mother to carry it home, for she was weak and sickly, and even a light burden fatigued her. The lady for whom she had made the garment was in very good circumstances, and had no want unmet that money could supply. When we came into her presence, she took the work, and after glancing at it carelessly, she said,

" 'It will do very well.'

"My mother lingered; perceiving which, the lady said rather rudely, 'You want your money, I suppose. How much does the work come to?'

" 'Two dollars,' replied my mother. The lady took out her purse; and after looking through a small parcel of bills, said, "I haven't the change this evening. Call over any time and you shall have it."

"And without giving my mother time more earnestly to urge her request, turned from us and left the room."

"I never shall forget the night that followed. My mother's feelings were sensitive and independent. She could not make known her want. An hour after her return home, she sat weeping with her children around her, when a neighbor came in, and learning our situation, supplied the present need."

This relation did not make me feel any more comfortable. Anxiously I awaited, on the next morning, the arrival of Polly. As soon as she came I sent for her, and, handing her the money she had earned the day before, said,

"I'm sorry I hadn't the change for you last night, Polly. I hope you didn't want it very badly."

Polly hesitated a little, looked downcast, and then replied.

"Well, ma'am, I did want it very much, or I wouldn't have asked for it. My poor daughter Hetty is sick, and I wanted to get her something nice to eat."

"I'm very sorry," said I, with sincere regret. "How is Hetty this morning?"

"She isn't so well, ma'am. And I feel very bad about her."

"Come up to me in half an hour, Polly," said I.

The old woman went down stairs. When she appeared again, according to my desire, I had a basket for her, in which were some wine, sugar, fruit, and various little matters that I thought her daughter would relish, and told her to go at once and take them to the sick girl. Her expressions of gratitude touched my feelings deeply. Never since have I omitted, under any pretence, to pay the poor their wages as soon as they were earned.—*Ladies' Wreath.*[47]

Selected for the Offering.

The Music of a Dream.[48]

By Ensis.

When cloudless is the sky of night
  Around a world at rest,

47. Selected from *The Ladies' Wreath: An Illustrated Annual*, ed. S. T. Martyn (New York: Martyn & Miller, 1850), 326–28, Google Books, http://books.google.com/books?id=RrYQAAAAYAAJ. For more about the promotion of sympathy for the poor in 1850s Akron, see introduction, pp. 4–5.

48. See n. 5, p. 387.

When dew-drops catch the lunar light
    And gild the flow'rets crest.

When Zephyr's voice is scarcely heard
    Low breathing in the grove,
And when no more the evening bird
    Pours forth her notes of love.

O! then's the hour when music sweet
    Seeks softer scenes than ours,
Where Fancy's peerless minstrels meet
    In Fancy's airy bowers.

My soul hath been at that sweet time
    Where sleep's faint visions rise,
And heard a softer sweeter chime
    Than when the zephyr signs.

Ah! mortal tongue can never tell
    Those symphonies which seem
Too high for harp or evening bell;
    The music of a dream.

The tremblings of the sweetest strain
    By mortal minstrels given,
Vibrate to rival these in vain,—
    The Dream-song touches Heaven!

When Mem'ry whispers of the years
    That mark'd life's opening stream,
Although it tells of childhood's tears,
    There's music in the Dream.

When well lov'd accents greet us then,
    And love is still the theme,
Wild rapture bids us court again
    The music of a Dream.

A "still small voice," a luring sound,
Cheers life's anfractuous stream,
'Tis hope:—her mystery profound
Breathes music in a Dream.

But ah! the phantom minstrel flies,
And dream charmed souls awake
To speak regret in *real* sighs
That his sweet strains should break.

'Tis thus with life—its terms of bliss
Are measured by a song,
The flitting form of Happiness
Ne'er tarries with us long.

The sweetest joys, the brightest hours
That on life's pathway gleam,
Die like the harp whence Fancy pours
The music of a Dream.

To Our Readers.

A year has passed away, gentle Reader, since the first number of the Offering was issued, and we might now dwell on the changes that, since that time, have occurred; or we might give our opinion of some, or all the topics of the day; but these have all been more or less treated of in the Offering, and a repetition here would be entirely out of place. We might refer to many of the articles in this volume as advocating what we believe to be right views and correct principles; but the work is before you, and we are willing you should all judge for yourselves of its real merit, without the possibility of being prejudiced, either for or against, by a knowledge of the real names of the writers of many of the articles.

Our own views of the propriety, necessity and practicability of such a work are not the least changed; but we have found that there must be more business done to meet its heavy expenses and make a fair profit, than one woman can accomplish and as we have not yet found a Lady who is at liberty to devote her time and strength as she pleases, that feels herself qualified to assist in the double task of editing, travelling to obtain subscribers, delivering books, collecting subscriptions, keeping accounts, &c. &c., or is willing to take upon herself so much toil and care and risk of pecuniary loss, we are compelled for the *present* to give it up.

It will be uncertain when the first No. of the second volume will be published—perhaps never—and here we must be permitted to say to all who have aided in this enterprise, by subscription, by contribution or by friendship in any form, that they have secured our lasting gratitude and we can not but hope that some little good has been accomplished by our united efforts; and trust that these efforts will, in some form, be continued, and that from this humble beginning, may arise a work that shall truly be a blessing to all.

There are articles from two or three new contributors in this No. and several have been received too late for insertion.

Thanks dear friends for your many favors. We shall not soon forget the pleasure we have experienced in the interchange of thoughts and feelings, as we have journeyed along together; and now, as we bid you farewell, we can not forbear expressing the desire that the richest blessings of our Father in Heaven, may ever be showered upon you all.

With grateful respect,
Your humble Servant,
C. Cumings.

Appendix
The Akron Offering and *Moore's Western Lady's Book*

In late June, a note appeared in Akron's newspaper, *The Summit Beacon*. The notice, which may have been purchased, directs local readers to look up the publisher of a new literary magazine from Cleveland who was evidently holding court, perhaps in the book store or in a hotel lobby.

> New Periodical.—The publisher of a new and very promising periodical just commenced at Cleveland, is in town, and will wait upon our citizens. The work is very handsomely got up, and is certainly cheap enough.[1]

A week later, the magazine was reviewed in the "Book Table" column:

> I HAVE COME, to elevate and expand the mind—to teach the Sciences, defend Religion and Morality and instil into the heart the love of Virtue and Truth. A Moore, Editor, Cleveland. $1 per annum. 32 pages.
>
> This is the nameless monthly hailing from Cleveland, to which we alluded last week. It comes unheralded. There are marks of haste in the preparation of a portion of the original matter, a few inexcusable errors in a literary work; but on the whole, we like the countenance of this new acquaintance, and trust that it will prove the medium through which shall be reflected the concentrated rays of Literature in Northern Ohio. Two engravings accompany each No.[2]

This once "nameless" magazine—which called itself *I Have Come*, part of a phrase that may have been printed on the front wrapper—would soon continue as *Moore's Western Lady's Book*. This was published alternately at

1. "New Periodical," *Summit Beacon* 11, no. 10 (June 27, 1849): 3.
2. "Our Book Table," *Summit Beacon* 11, no. 11 (July 4, 1849): 3.

Cleveland, Columbus, and Cincinnati, as A. and H. G. Moore relocated over the next decade, perhaps as a strategy for continually adding subscribers. William Henry Venable describes the periodical as one "of much vitality" and speculates, incorrectly, about its earliest numbers.[3] Frank Luther Mott describes *Moore's* as a magazine that avoided demise in the 1850s by "using steel plates freely." Mott also notes that after moving to Cincinnati, *Moore's* absorbed a "woman's rights paper," *The Genius of Liberty*, that had been published by E. A. Aldrich.[4]

Bound into my copy of *The Akron Offering* are the first two numbers (thirty-two pages each for July 1849 and August 1849) of *I Have Come*. The OCLC's WorldCat database reports no extant copies, and given Venable's failed search to find the earliest examples of *Moore's*, these have been very rare for some time. The first number includes an engraving of a lady with her dog ("Mrs. Adelia Hoyt") and an engraving of Cincinnati. The Library Company of Philadelphia has cataloged the same engraving as appearing in several other publications; Moore evidently purchased his copies from an engraving publisher in New England.[5] The second number includes an engraving of "The West" and a page of sheet music. In Moore's editorial "Chat with Subscribers" he boasts that he met "over twelve hundred" of his subscribers in person on his fundraising tour of the Western Reserve. He notes that he has nearly two thousand subscribers in total.[6] Notable authors from the first numbers include John B. Gough, John Milton, Phoebe Cary, Ned Buntline, Martin Tupper, Lydia Maria Child, and Lily Lute, the woman from Seville who contributed so much to *The Akron Offering*.

Moore, a married man, gushes over Lily Lute.

> Think so much of the following piece of poetry, that I have concluded to put it in the "Editor's Casket." *If* I was not a married man, and *if* Lily was not engaged, and *if* I was where she is, or *if* she was where I am, I think *we* might have quite a flirtation, *if* Lily was *willing*. Lily is just the right kind of

3. *Beginnings of Literary Culture in the Ohio Valley* (Cincinnati: Robert Clarke & Co., 1891), 83, Google Books, http://books.google.com/books?id=QhgUAAAAIAAJ.

4. *A History of American Magazines, 1850–1865* (Cambridge: Belknap Press of University of Harvard Press, 1938), 52–58, ACLS Humanities E-Book, http://hdl.handle.net/2027/heb.00678. Wendy Jean Katz discusses this incarnation of *Moore's* in her *Regionalism and Reform: Art and Class Formation in Antebellum Cincinnati* (Columbus: Ohio State University, 2002).

5. See "Hoyt, Adelia, 1802–1843?" The Library Company of Philadelphia Digital Collections. http://lcpdams.librarycompany.org:8881/R/?func=dbin-jump-full&object_id=64116&local_base=GEN01.

6. *I Have Come* 1, no. 2 (August 1849): 56.

> a girl for a wife. Hear her; she speaks volumes in her own favor, in the following excuse for her poetry. I have the promise of more.

It is not hard to see why Moore's new paper would try the patience of Calista Cumings. The Akron paper reviews Moore's first efforts with the suggestion that his new magazine would outshine Akron's own *Offering* with "concentrated rays of Literature." And Moore's public wooing of Lily Lute, one of *The Akron Offering*'s most conspicuous contributors, only completes a mutual admiration society founded by Lute herself. Here is the contribution that so inspires Moore:

> The lines I send you were written on a jump between the kitchen and the pen, so that they are full of blunders; besides, my muse is nearly drowned in dish-water, buttermilk, and starch. But if they will not do to publish, they will kindle fire as well as any paper.
>
> I HAVE COME.
>
> By Lily Lute.
> A July morning, sunny and fair,
> An old man sat in his easy chair;
> And the tedious hours of summer-day,
> With his pipe and book he whiled away.
> His brow grew smooth, and his eye grew bright;
> And anon, he smiled, then laughed outright,
> So pleased was he with the book, I ween—
> That book, reader, was a magazine.
> I read it through, and I found 'twas "*sum*:"
> And its pretty name is "*I Have Come*."
>
> A sturdy youth, with an ample brow,
> Had left to rest his team and plow,
> And thought to spend the noon's dull hour,
> By lounging in his garden bower.
> But there on the old table lay
> A pretty book and sweet boquet;—
> The fair young flowers were soon thrown by,
> For, ah! the book had caught his eye.
> Unlike the books he'd read whilom,
> Its pretty name was "*I Have Come*."

The noon at length in profit spent,
He blessed the hand such blessing sent;
And well he knew the gentle hand,
That such a treat for him had planned.
And while he blessed, in shame he thought,
That such a book he might have bought—
Had he but dared to spend his pence
For what would neither build a fence,
Nor make a plow, nor raise a barn,
Nor shear his sheep, nor spin his yarn;
Nor would his tea and coffee buy—
As if to work, eat, drink and die,
Was all man had in life to do.
Alas! how many have that view.

Evening had come; matron and maid
Had for a time their labor staid,
And now were busy pouring o'er
A book well filled with useful lore;
The dame seemed half to lose her care—
The maiden smiled a smile more fair—
The sire drew near, well pleased to see
The book had pleased his family;
And joyed to think 'twould cheer his home.
That book, reader, was *"I Have Come."*[7]

Finally, in the section of "Literary Notices" that concludes the second number, Moore promises to notice other publications as he receives them in exchange. This was a common practice at the time: editors of periodicals exchanged copies through the mail, for various reasons. Moore praises a number of periodicals that would not obviously compete with his magazine. He admires *The Spirit of the Lakes and Boatman's Magazine*, noting that two of its three editors have just died from the cholera. He mentions *The Western Reformer* of Milton, Indiana, to express his "warmest thanks" for the "kind notice" it made of *I Have Come*. And he reviews Cumings' work, which she has evidently sent to him:

> *The Akron Offering*. Miss C. Cumings has commenced publishing an "Offering" in Akron, that purports to contain "Tales, Essays, and Poetry."

7. *I Have Come* 1, no. 2 (August 1849): 63.

> It has too many "Tales" to give general satisfaction. I am always opposed to light reading. Much of the matter, however, is very well written. Thirty-two pages,—price, $1.[8]

Thus Cumings' uncharacteristically passionate outrage over the comments of the "*gallant*" Mr. Moore (241).

For what it's worth, Moore was not a favorite with other Ohio editors. In a review of *Moore's* that appeared in an 1854 number of Columbus's *The Ohio Cultivator*, the editors (M. B. Bateham and S. D. Harris) chide their friend William T. Coggeshall for publishing in *Moore's*. "We cannot say much for the matter of the No. before us," they write. Moore is described as shifty and changeable—he "has been *turning up* in various guises for the last few years between Cleveland and Cincinnati." And his magazine is described as parasitic: "We have a settled conviction that this meteoric publisher, and several others of the same cast, have done more to damage respectable Magazine publishing in Ohio, than their after lives can ever remedy." Referring to Moore's purchase of a Cincinnati woman's rights paper, the editorial concludes, "We are sorry to see that Mrs. Aldrich has sunk the '*Genius of Liberty*' in this concern."[9]

Cumings labored under a number of disadvantages with *The Akron Offering*. While it's doubtful that the start of *Moore's* played a significant role in her decision to end her periodical after one full volume, it was certainly discouraging. Lute may have felt badly about the way Moore paraded her enthusiasm shortly before slandering Cumings' magazine. Regardless, Lute redoubled her support of *The Akron Offering* by visiting Akron, calling on the Cumings family, and writing an amusing description of her travels. See pp. 307–12.

8. *I Have Come* 1, no. 2 (August 1849): 64.

9. *Ohio Cultivator* 10, no. 6 (March 15, 1854): 89, Google Books, http://books.google.com/books?id=8xVOAAAAYAAJ.

Index

A

B

M

N

O

P

R

S

T

U

V